...e event of this day—The...
...t of the United States...
...ummoned of the votes in...
...son, 84. for John Quincy Adams of Massachusetts
...d 37 for Henry Clay of Kentucky. In all 261.
...ning and counting the votes in joint meeting of
...s immediately proceeded to the vote by ballot
...hn Quincy Adams received the votes of 13,
...ford of 4. States. The election was thus complete
...der H. Everett gave me the first notice, both of
...s, as announced in the joint meeting; and of
...a few minutes afterwards—Mr. Bolton and Mr.
...W. Crowninshield, calling on his return from
...od the reports. Congratulations from several of
...d from J. Brent, G. Ironside, W. Slade, and
...nd family were cordial and affecting; and I
...us King of New-York, written in the Senate
...ames Strong M.H.R. from New-York came with
...stacles to the election of Ambrose Spencer, as
...g. He asked if my friends considered Spencer
...considered him as favouring the election of Gen
...r pledged at least, if elected, not to come with
...said I did not—He said Spencer was an honest
...ithful to it. after dinner the Russian Minister

John Quincy Adams in 1840
by Edward Marchant
Adams National Historical Park

Library of America, a nonprofit organization,
champions our nation's cultural heritage
by publishing America's greatest writing in
authoritative new editions and providing resources
for readers to explore this rich, living legacy.

JOHN QUINCY ADAMS
DIARIES 1821–1848

John Quincy Adams

DIARIES
II: 1821–1848

David Waldstreicher, *editor*

THE LIBRARY OF AMERICA

John Quincy Adams:
Diaries
is published with support from

THE BODMAN FOUNDATION

and

SIDNEY AND RUTH LAPIDUS

Contents

Preface

"A Diary is the Time Piece of Life, and will never fail of keeping Time, or of getting out of order with it. A Diary if honestly kept is one of the best preservatives of Morals. A man who commits to paper from day to day the employment of his time, the places he frequents, the persons with whom he converses, the actions with which he is occupied, will have a perpetual guard over himself. His Record is a second Conscience."

> John Quincy Adams to George Washington Adams,
> November 28, 1827

JOHN QUINCY ADAMS's diary is one of the most extraordinary works in American literature. Begun in 1779, when Adams was twelve, it was maintained more or less faithfully until his death almost seventy years later, and extends over fifty manuscript volumes and more than fourteen thousand closely written pages, including an unbroken string of daily observance spanning more than twenty-six years. Its entries, which range from five hundred to five thousand words or more, record the events of Adams's public and private lives, including detailed accounts, sometimes verbatim transcripts, of cabinet meetings, diplomatic interviews, congressional debates, dinner conversations, and social calls; incisive character sketches of presidents and princes; painful confessions of anxiety about his own shortcomings, and about the welfare of his family; reflections on sermons he heard and books he read; experiments in verse and translation; theater reviews; and scientific and natural observations. The devotion with which Adams maintained his diary, even when the press of events made doing so burdensome, suggests that it served a number of essential purposes for him, as a confessional, an aide-mémoir, and a proving ground for his thoughts on everything from public policy to philosophy.

This Library of America volume, the second of a two-volume set, presents a selection of diary entries from March 1821, the beginning of the second term of President James Monroe, under whom Adams served as secretary of state, to February

20, 1848, just three days before Adams's death, when he made his final entry, a brief poem written for a youthful admirer. Daily entries, when possible, are presented in full. In some, certain passages, especially such recurring features of the diary as meteorological observations, records of social visits received and returned, and accounts of bills paid and due, have been cut for space and to avoid repetition. Resulting breaks within an entry, or at the end of an entry followed by the next day's entry, are indicated with the ≈ symbol. All other breaks are indicated with a small centered rule line. An asterisk at the beginning of an entry indicates that it was recorded by an amanuensis. The Note on the Texts in this volume offers more information on the history of the diaries and on the textual policy followed in this edition.

———

A NOTE ON IDENTIFICATION: Adams's diary records his interactions with or reflections on a very large cast of characters. Where these individuals are referred to by surname, identification is provided in the Index. Where they are designated only by their first names, or where additional explanation is warranted, they are identified in the Notes.

CHAPTER VIII ❦ 1821–1825

Secretary of State

[March 1821]

4. VII. Sunday — And the Commencement of the second term of the Administration of James Monroe, fifth President of the United States. But the Administration of the Official Oath, which the Constitution prescribes that he shall take *before* he enter on the Execution of his Office, being postponed till to-morrow this day was a sort of interregnum, during which there was no person qualified to Act as President; an event of no importance now, but which might be far otherwise under supposable circumstances. I attended Church at the Treasury building, where a very small Society of Presbyterians now meet, who are building a Church — There were two officiating Clergymen; Mr. Campbell the Chaplain of the late House of Representatives, and a Mr. Van Coop — Campbell is a man of talents and eloquence, but has some disagreeable peculiarities of manner — T. Cook and Dr. Thornton called at my house after Church. I spent the Evening at home writing.

5. V:15. Second inauguration of James Monroe as President of the United States — The arrangements were made at the Hall of the House of Representatives, by the Marshal of the District, in concert with the Clerk, and by consent of the late Speaker of the House. There were Seats reserved for the Ladies of the Heads of Departments and others, for the members of the Diplomatic Corps, and members of Congress. The President had requested the Heads of Departments to assemble at his House and accompany him to the Capitol. The Marshal had recommended that the Ladies should go early to secure their admission into the Hall, and their Seats. Mrs. Adams with Mary Hellen went first to the Capitol, and sent back the Carriage for me — Madame de Neuville went in company with her. A quarter before twelve, I went to the President's House, and the other members of the Administration immediately afterwards came there — The Marshal and one of his Deputies

I

was there, but no assemblage of People. The President attired in a full suit of black broad cloth, of somewhat antiquated fashion, with shoe and knee buckles rode in a plain Carriage with four horses, and a single coloured footman — The Secretaries of State, the Treasury, War and the Navy, followed, each in a Carriage and pair — There was no escort nor any concourse of people on the way — But on alighting at the Capitol, a great crowd of people were assembled, and the avenues to the Hall of the House were so choaked up with persons pressing for admittance, that it was with the utmost difficulty that the President made his way through them into the House — Mr. Canning and Mr. Antrobus in full Court dress Uniforms were in the midst of this Crowd unable to obtain admission — We got in at last after several minutes of severe pressure. There was not a soldier present, nor a constable distinguishable by any badge of Office — The President took a seat on a Platform just before the Speaker's Chair — The Chief Justice was seated at his right hand, the other judges of the Supreme Court, in Chairs fronting him; the President of the Senate and late Speaker of the House at his left hand. The Heads of Department side-long at the right and the Foreign Ministers in the Seats of the Members at the left — The House and Galleries were as thronged as possible — There was much disorder of loud talking, and agitation in the Gallery; not altogether ceasing even while the President was reading his Address; which he did immediately after taking the Oath — At this Ceremony the Chief-Justice merely held the book, the President repeating the Oath in the words prescribed by the Constitution. The address was delivered in a suitably grave, and rather low tone of voice — After it was finished several persons came up to the President and shook hands with him by way of congratulation — At his departure from the House, there was a cheering shout from the people in the Galleries, and the Music of the Marine Band played both at his entrance and departure — I returned home with my family; and immediately afterwards went to the President's House, where there was a numerous Circle for congratulation — I then passed a couple of hours at my Office; and in the Evening attended a Ball at Brown's Hotel. The President and his family were there, but retired before supper — We came home immediately after, and finished a fatiguing and bustling day about Midnight.

———

9. VI. ≈ Mr. Clay called at the Office — He is pressing upon the President, his claim for a half outfit for the Negotiation of the commercial Convention of 3 July 1815 with Great-Britain. I told him I thought it could not be allowed, without a special appropriation for it by Congress, to which he said he did not know that he should have any objection. But he wants the money now. Clay is one of the Commissioners for taking my Answers to interrogatories in the case of Levett Harris against W. D. Lewis. I agreed if I could have them ready in time to call at the Capitol, where he is in attendance on the Supreme Court, and be sworn to them, Monday or Tuesday. I had some conversation with him on political topics, and on his own present retirement from public life. I asked him if it would be consistent with his views, in case there should within two or three years be a vacancy in any of the Missions abroad, to accept an appointment to it — He said he was obliged to me for the question, but it would not — The state of his private affairs, and his duty to his family had dictated to him the determination of a temporary retirement from the public Service. But by a liberal arrangement with him, the Bank of the United States had engaged him as their standing Counsel in the States of Kentucky and Ohio. He expected that in the course of three or four years this would relieve him from all the engagements in which he had been involved and enable him to return to the Public Service — In that case he should prefer over all others the Station from which he had just retired, a Seat in the House of Representatives, because that would be the place where he could hope to render the most useful service, to the Country. But he said he considered the situation of our Public Affairs now, as very critical and dangerous to the Administration — Mr. Monroe had just been re-elected with apparent unanimity; but he had not the slightest influence in Congress — His Career was considered as closed — There was nothing further to be expected by him or from him. Looking at Congress, they were a collection of *materials*, and how much good, and how much evil might be done with them, accordingly as they

should be well or ill directed. But henceforth there was and would not be a man in the United States possessing less *personal* influence over them than the President — I saw Mr. Clay's drift in these remarks which was to magnify his own importance, and to propitiate me, in favour of his outfit claim — His total forbearance of attack upon me, either by himself or his underlings in the late Session of Congress, and his advance through Mr. Brush, I attribute to the same cause. I told him the President must rely as he had done upon the public sentiment and upright intention to support him, and with these his Administration must get along as well as it could — He said he regretted that his views had differed from those of the Administration in relation to South-American Affairs — He hoped however that this difference would now be shortly over. But he was concerned to see indications of unfriendly dispositions towards the South-Americans, in our naval Officers, who were sent to the Pacific, and he was apprehensive they would get into some quarrel there which might alienate the minds of the People in the two Countries from each other. — I said the Instructions to the naval Officers were as positive and pointed as words could make them, to avoid everything of that kind. I hoped no such event would occur, as we could have no possible motive for quarreling with the South-Americans — I also regretted the difference between his views and those of the Administration, upon South-American Affairs. That the final issue of their present struggle would be their entire Independence of Spain I had never doubted. That it was our true policy and our duty to take no part in the contest I was equally clear. The principle of neutrality to *all* foreign Wars, was in my opinion fundamental to the continuance of our Liberties and of our Union. So far as they were contending for Independence I wished well to their cause; but I had seen and yet see no prospect that they would establish free or liberal Institutions of Government. They are not likely to promote the Spirit either of Freedom or of Order by their example. They have not the first Elements of good or of free Government. Arbitrary Power, Military and Ecclesiastical was stamped upon their education, upon their habits and upon all their Institutions. Civil dissension was infused into all their seminal principles; War and mutual destruction was in every member of their organization; moral, political and physical — I had little expectation of any beneficial result to this Country, from any future connection with them, political or commercial — We should derive no improvement to our own Institutions by any communion with theirs — Nor was there any appearance of a disposition in them to take any political lesson from us. As to the commercial connection I agreed with him that little weight should be allowed to arguments of mere pecuniary interest; but there was no basis for much traffic between us. They want none of our productions, and we could afford to purchase very few of theirs. — Of these opinions, both his and mine, *Time* must be the test; but I would candidly acknowledge, nothing had hitherto occurred to weaken in my mind the view which I had taken of this subject from the first — He did not pursue the discussion. Clay is an eloquent man with very popular manners, and great political management. He is like almost all the eminent men of this Country only half educated — His school has been the world, and in that he is a proficient. His morals, public and private, are loose, but he has all the virtues indispensable to a popular man. As he is the first very distinguished man that the Western Country has presented as a Statesman to the Union, they are proportionably proud of him, and being a native of Virginia, he has all the benefit of that Clannish preference which Virginia has always given to her Sons. Clay's temper is impetuous and his Ambition impatient — He has long since marked me as the principal rival in his way, and has taken no more pains to disguise his hostility, than was necessary for decorum, and to avoid shocking the public opinion — His future fortune and mine are in wiser hands than ours; I have never even defensively repelled his attacks. Clay has large and liberal views of public Affairs, and that sort of generosity which attaches individuals to his person. As President of the Union his Administration would be a perpetual succession of intrigue and management with the Legislature — It would also be sectional in its Spirit, and sacrifice all other interests to those of the Western Country, and the Slaveholders. But his principles relative to internal improvements would produce results honourable and useful to the Nation. We spent this Evening at Mr. William Lee's.

———

20. V. ≈ Here closes the sixth Volume of the Journal, which I
have kept, without the intermission of a day, since the first of
January 1795. Had I spent upon any work of Science or Literature, the time employed upon this Diary, it might perhaps
have been permanently useful to my Children and my Country
— I have devoted too much time to it — My physical powers
sink under it. On the day with which I close, it was in arrear
from the preceding 6th of November, and I have only brought
up that arrear on the 14th day of July. I had hoped to keep this
as a minute and circumstancial record of my share in the Affairs of
my Country, while I continue a member of its administration
— I must renounce this hope, and content myself with a mere
abridgment of memoranda in future — In Summer, I can barely
keep pace with the current of Events. In Winter, during the
Sessions of Congress, one indispensable occupation succeeds
another, which absorb the morning hours, and leave me none
for the daily narrative of yesterdays.

———

25. VI. I went with Dr. Thornton this Morning to the Quaker
Meeting. There were from forty to fifty men present, and
about as many females. We sat nearly two hours in perfect
silence — No moving of the Spirit, and I seldom in the course
of my life passed two hours more wearily. Perhaps from not
having been enured to this mode of public worship, I found
myself quite unable to reduce my mind to that musing meditation which forms the essence of this form of devotion — It was
rambling from this world to the next, and from the next back
to this, chance-directed, and curious to know what was really
passing in the minds of those around me. I asked Doctor
Thornton after we came out what he had been thinking of
while we had been there — He said he did not know; he had
been much inclined to sleep. Solitude and Silence are natural
allies, and social Silence may be properly allied with social
labour — But social meditation is an incongruity — I felt on
coming from this Meeting as if I had wasted precious time —
Passed the remainder of the day at home, assiduously writing.
Mrs. Adams spent the Evening at W. S. Smith's — He is yet
confined to his chamber.

———

[September 1821]

30. V:15. I had a sleepless Night — Cares for the welfare and future prospects of my children; mortification at the discovery how much they have wasted of their time at Cambridge, and concern for the health of George, agitated my mind so much that through the Night I could not close my eyes — I had hoped that at least one of my Sons would have been ambitious to excel — I find them all three, coming to manhood, with indolent minds — Flinching from study whenever they can, and if not content to hold the 30th and forty-fifth rank in their class, incapable of the exertion necessary for raising them higher. It is bitter disappointment. The blast of mediocrity, is the lightest of the evils, which such characters portend — My reflections on my pillow were occupied in the enquiry what was the path of my own duty upon this state of things; and I concluded, after expressing my sentiments to John and Charles, to direct them to pass their next winter vacation, here at Quincy, with my father. For which I this day asked his permission and obtained his ready consent — I shall take George with me to Washington, and have him under my own eye — He is not without ambition, and has lost his time more by a social disposition, than actual neglect — Upon the others I can operate only indirectly.

———

[October 1821]

15. VI. At the Office, the day was nearly occupied, by visits from Bresson one of the Secretaries of the French Legation, who brought me three Notes from the Baron Hyde de Neuville; from Baron Stackelberg the Swedish Charge d'Affaires, and from Mr. Calhoun. ≈ Mr. Calhoun came to mention the determination of the President, upon some question relating to the Barracks at St. Augustine — He also spoke of the altercations between Gen'l Jackson, and Col'l Callava, and Judge Fromentin, about which he is much concerned. He thinks that the President ought to come immediately to the City, and determine upon the course to be pursued by the Administration, in these cases — I concur in that opinion — Calhoun fears that a wrong direction may be given to public sentiments, on these transactions by the Spirit of faction, and the crude precipitancy

of newspaper Commentaries — Calhoun is a man of fair and candid mind; of honourable principles: of clear and quick understanding: of cool self-possession; of enlarged philosophical views, and of ardent patriotism — He is above all sectional, and factious prejudices, more than any other Statesman of this Union, with whom I have ever acted. He is more sensitive to the transient manifestations of momentary public opinion, more afraid of the first impressions of the public opinion than I am — In all cases of controvertible conduct in public men; when the conclusion upon the whole subject is more favourable than its first aspect, the more hastily and the more virulently they are in the first instance attacked, the more strong and effectual is the final recoil in their favour. In such cases I think the true policy is to let the hostile portion of the public Journals extravagate to their hearts content — Let them waste their strength, and emit all their venom, upon misapplications of Law, and perversions of fact; and when the victory is upon the balance, seize and turn their batteries against themselves. ≈

16. V:45. First day of the Washington City Races, and Dr. Thornton's horse Rattler, lost the race, to his great disappointment. I was not there ≈ A young man by the name of Cooper, of Georgia, whose father lost a number of Slaves by capture from the British during the late war came to enquire into the State of the Negotiation upon the Subject. I told him that upon Mr. Middleton's arrival in Russia the Emperor had been absent, and very lately returned. We had as yet received no information that the subject of the arbitration had been brought before him; but I was assured Mr. Middleton would not delay it. He asked upon what principle indemnity would be made if the decision should be in our favour — I said we had hardly reached that question yet. We should obtain all that we could — He said that indemnity for the mere value of the Slaves carried away, and only interest upon that value at the rate of six per Cent a year would be no adequate compensation for the loss. The increase of the Slave, and the improvement of the plantation by his labour ought to be paid for. I told him I thought it would be difficult to ascertain; he said not at all. I said it was like a merchant's claiming for indemnity, the profits of a voyage which he might have made; but he did not see the

analogy. I asked him how he could say that any given slave would not have died, within a week after he had been carried away — He said he could not; but allowance might be made for that — I advised that his father should have his whole argument set forth in its utmost extent and forwarded to this Department, where all the use that could, would be made of it — He took leave giving me thanks for my attendance to the business.

———

20. V:30. Walk with George over the Tyber by the Bridge near the old Theatre; and returned by the new Bridge from 14th Street, which has been built this Season, and opened while I was absent — There were received this morning from the President a number of bundles of papers, forwarded by him from Oakhill; some of them public papers to be deposited at the Department; others which he had directed to be sent to his house — Among them was a Letter from Spencer Roane, the Virginian Chief-Justice, enclosing to him his lucubrations in the Richmond Enquirer, against the Supreme Court of the United States — George Hay told me last Summer that Roane was the author of the pieces signed Algernon Sidney, against the Supreme Court, and that they had been excited by the words "we command you" in the Mandamus, in the case of Cohens vs Virginia — Roane in his Letter to the President glorifies himself as a very virtuous patriot, and holds himself out as a sort of Jefferson or Madison — All this is "close ambition varnished o'er with zeal." Jefferson and Madison did attain power by organizing and heading a system of attack upon the Washington Administration, chiefly under the banners of State rights and State Sovereignty — They argued and scolded against all implied powers, and pretended that the Government of the Union had no powers but such as were expressly delegated by the Constitution — They succeeded. Mr. Jefferson was elected President of the United States, and the first thing he did was to purchase Louisiana, an assumption of implied power, greater in itself and more comprehensive in its consequences, than all the assumptions of implied powers, in the twelve years of the Washington and Adams administrations put together. Through the sixteen years of the Jefferson and Madison Administrations not the least regard was paid to the

doctrines of rejecting implied powers, upon which those Gentlemen had vaulted into the seat of Government, with the single exception that Mr. Madison negatived a Bill for applying public money to the public internal improvement of the Country. But the same Mr. Madison signed a Bill for incorporating a Bank of the United States, against which he and all the Virginian party had stubbornly contended as Unconstitutional, because *express* power was not given to the Congress to incorporate Banks. The Virginian opposition to implied powers therefore is a convenient weapon, to be taken up or laid aside as it suits the purposes of State turbulence and ambition; and as Virginia has no direct Candidate to offer for the next Presidential Election, her aspiring demagogues, are casting about them to place her again at the head of a formal opposition to the administration of the Union, that she may thus again obtain by conquest the administration itself. On the former occasion this attempt was greatly favoured by circumstances — It was favoured by its novelty — Favoured by the bad management of its adversaries. It has most of the same advantages now. They still possess in a superior degree the art of political management — They will be favoured by circumstances; and if not by novelty, yet by the success of the former example. The tactics of the former war are again resorted to, and Roane comes forth as the champion of Virginia — There was also among the papers a copy of the President's answer to this Letter; declining a positive answer upon the special point of Roane's assault; but giving countenance to it, by referring to his own resistance against the right of the general Government to make internal improvements.

———

[November 1821]

8. V. ≈ There was a Cabinet Meeting at the President's at Noon; when the case of La Jeune Eugénie was again reconsidered. ≈ At this meeting, it was also concluded, that the Note from Mr. Gallatin to Baron Pasquier of 28 June last, on the case of the Apollon, should not be sent ≈ The most extraordinary part of Gallatin's conduct is that after a long argument to the French Government, upon grounds entirely new, and different from those we had taken here, he gives us distinctly to understand that he considers all these grounds,

ours and his own as not worth a straw — I asked Calhoun to-day, what he thought it could mean. He said perhaps it was the pride of opinion — I think it lies deeper — Gallatin is a man of first rate talents, conscious and vain of them; and mortified in his ambition; checked as it has been, after attaining the last step to the summit — timid in great perils; tortuous in his paths; born in Europe; disguising and yet betraying a supercilious prejudice of European superiority of intellect, and holding principles pliable to circumstances, occasionally mistaking the left, for the right handed wisdom.

———

15. IV:45. Cabinet Meeting at the President's. ≈ I delivered to Mr. Wirt, the papers from Mr. Canning, relating to the Newfoundland fishing vessel piracy: for his opinion upon three points — 1. Whether we can deliver up the British subject, charged with British Statute piracy? — 2. Whether we can try our own Citizens, charged as accessories to the same crime? 3. Whether we can restore to the owners, the vessel, which is under seizure for a breach of our revenue Laws? On the first point Mr. Canning alledges an obligation by the Laws of Nations, to deliver up atrocious criminals. ≈

16. V. Mrs. Adams was unwell, and kept her chamber. George was also complaining of a headache. I received this morning a Note from Mr. Wirt the Attorney-General, requesting the loan of Books, upon the Laws of Nations; to make up his opinion upon this demand for the Newfoundland Pirates. I sent him such books as I had. ≈ I received this Evening a Note from Mr. Canning, with enclosures; being copies of applications from the Governors of New-York, and of Vermont, to the Governor of Canada, requesting him to deliver up, two fugitives, one from the State of New-York, charged with forgery; and the other from Vermont, with murder. The Governor General of Canada Earl of Dalhousie answers and delivers up both the men. ≈

17. IV:30. Mrs. Adams continues unwell; confined to her chamber, and this morning was again bled. I went at noon with George to Brown's Hotel, and saw the models of the Capitol, and of the Baltimore Exchange. Mr. Shaler called this morning at my Office, and spent the Evening with me at my

house. E. Wyer was also at the Office — I took to Mr. Wirt the Attorney General the Note I had received last Evening from Mr. Canning, and a Volume of Burlamaqui containing precisely the same passage relating to the delivery of fugitive criminals as that in Vattel — both these writers, as well as Grotius do in very explicit terms assert the moral obligation of Nations, to deliver up fugitives guilty of heinous crimes. Mr. Wirt had the English translation of Grotius with a part of Barbeyrac's Notes, and I had sent him the French Edition of Barbeyrac; which we compared together; but Wirt did not seem to be satisfied with the authorities — He wanted a Latin Grotius; but finally came to the denial of the President's authority to deliver up. I told him that was the ground I had alledged to Mr. Canning, though I was not entirely satisfied that there was a want of authority — It was made by the Constitution the Duty of the President to take care that the Laws be faithfully executed, by which may be understood the Laws of Nations as well as the Laws of Congress. Now if it were clearly and unquestionably the Law of Nations that fugitives charged with heinous crimes should be delivered up, it would be the duty of the President to take care that that Law should be faithfully executed as well as others — and he could not be bound by the duty without possessing the authority necessary for its discharge — He said that doctrine was too bold for him: he was too much of a Virginian for that. I told him that Virginian Constitutional scruples were accommodating things. Whenever the exercise of a power did not happen to suit them, they would allow of nothing but powers expressly written; but when it did, they had no aversion to implied powers — Where was there in the Constitution a Power to purchase Louisiana? — He said there was a power to make Treaties — Ay! a Treaty to abolish the Constitution of the United States? — "Oh! No! No!" — But the Louisiana purchase was in substance a dissolution, and recomposition of the whole Union — It made a Union totally different from that for which the Constitution had been formed — It gives despotic powers over the territories purchased — It naturalizes foreign Nations in a mass. It makes French and Spanish Laws a part of the Laws of the Union — It introduces whole systems of Legislation, abhorrent to the Spirit and character of our Institutions; and all this done by an Administration which came in, blowing a Trumpet against implied powers. After this, to nibble at a Bank, a Road, a Canal, the mere mint and cummin of the Law, was but glorious inconsistency — He said the People had sanctioned it — How the People? — By their Representatives in Congress; they were the People — Oh! said I, *that doctrine is too bold for ME.* But as to this power of the President to take care that the Laws of Nations be faithfully executed, without waiting for an act of Congress; it had been exercised by President Washington, by seizing and restoring vessels illegally captured at the commencement of the Wars of the French Revolution, before any Act of Congress upon the subject; and it was now exercised continually by the admission duty free of baggage and Articles imported by foreign Ministers — All this seemed to make little impression upon Mr. Wirt, and I asked him whether he thought the Governors of the States had the power to deliver up fugitive criminals — He thought they had — I said it was no more delegated to them than to the President; and they no more than he possessed any other than delegated powers — They were certainly not specially charged to take care that the Laws of Nations should be faithfully executed in their respective States, nor had they any power to arrest or detain any individual otherwise than conformably to the Laws of the Land. Wirt mentioned the Treaty of 1794, by which it was stipulated that persons charged with *murder* and *forgery* should be delivered up, from which he drew two inferences — first that it proved the sense of both parties that without the Treaty, there would be no obligation to deliver up criminals of any description; and secondly that even in making the Stipulation, the specification of those two crimes, was equivalent to an agreement that they would deliver up no others — I objected to both these conclusions; at least in their entire Latitude. I said that Stipulations in Treaties were often only in affirmance of principles which would without them be binding, and that the specification might only be of the two crimes for which the refuge would be most likely to be sought, and would be reciprocally most dangerous to bordering Countries. We both agreed that it was a subject deserving the attention of Congress.

———

24. IV:45. Rain, Hail and Storm — Call at the President's —
He fixed Monday next at one O'Clock, to see Mr. Canning
and receive from him, the Letter from the King of Great-Britain,
announcing the death of the Queen — I remarked to the
President that in the language of Mr. Canning's Note, there
was something of the pretension which he had advanced last
Summer — He desired me to take the President's pleasure,
only with respect to the time, when he would receive the Letter; as if the manner of receiving it was not to be optional — I
said I did not think it worth while to notice this now; but it
would be advisable to bear it in mind, and not suffer the pretension to take root, by acquiescence in it — The President
said he should take care to keep the mode of receiving these
Letters, always subordinate to his convenience.

———

[January 1822]
2. VI:30. I took over to the President a translation of the Spanish Minister Anduaga's Letter of 27 Dec'r to me, and a copy of
my answer — Mr. Thompson the Secretary of the Navy came
in immediately afterwards. There was some conversation relating to the capture by Lieutenant Stockton in the Alligator, of a
Portuguese vessel, which fired upon him, mistaking him for a
South-American privateer. Stockton has sent her into Boston
— The President read a Letter which he had written to General Jackson, accepting his resignation as Governor of Florida
— It was expressed in warm, though general terms of regard,
and Mr. Thompson objected that it would import the President's approbation of General Jackson's late transactions in
Florida — This led to some discussion of them, in which Mr.
Thompson admitted that he had a very imperfect knowledge
of all the Circumstances, not having seen a great portion of the
papers; but upon the facts as far as he was acquainted with
them his opinion was unfavourable to Jackson. The President
asked him to read all the papers, which he promised to do. The
President asked me, if I thought the expressions in the Letter
were too strong? I said they were such, that after receiving the
Letter, General Jackson, would naturally not expect that the
President would at any future period express public disapprobation of any thing done by him as Governor of Florida — But
in my opinion there was not one word too much. General

Jackson I thought had done nothing, with the exception of the papers seized at St. Augustine, but what he had a right to do. It was indeed impossible for me to scan the actions of General Jackson, as I might those of an indifferent person — General Jackson had rendered such services to this Nation, that it was impossible for me to contemplate his character or conduct without veneration.

———

[April 1822]

29. V:15. Col'l Trumbull came this Morning to enquire where his third picture was to be hung, and who was to give him a receipt for it. I referred him to the President. ≈ Mr. Jonathan Russell came, for the Letter of the President to the Emperor of China, and mine to the Vice-roy of Canton. He said he liked my substitute for the draft of the President's Letter, much better than the draft itself. Dropping this subject I told Mr. Russell that I thought the Letter he had left at the Department to be communicated to the House of Representatives in answer to Dr. Floyd's Resolution was a very extraordinary paper; and his conduct in the whole transaction relating to it, as equally extraordinary — He knew I had been at Paris, and that he was in habits of daily, and professedly friendly intercourse with me when the original Letter was written. That he should have written it, without notice to his colleagues whose conduct it so severely arraigned was strange. That he should now have furnished a paper as the duplicate of that Letter, but materially differing from it, was still more so — He said that I would remember when on the 25th of December 1814 — I had made the draft of the joint Letter of the Mission to the Secretary of State, mentioning that *we* had offered to the British Plenipotentiaries the Article, confirmative of the fisheries to us, and of the Mississippi Navigation to the British, Mr. Clay had desired, that an alteration should be made, saying that *a majority* of us determined to make this offer. This was Mr. Clay's desire, and not his; but when the joint Letter was so written, as he had voted in the minority on the question, he thought it necessary to justify his conduct to the Government, and therefore had written the Letter from Paris — That when he came to this Country in 1816, there had been a paragraph in the Boston Centinel, charging him with having been willing to sacrifice

the fisheries at Ghent. That Mr. Floyd had moved his Resolution calling for the Ghent papers, without consulting him; but as upon the first call of Mr. Floyd, his, Russell's separate Letter of 25 December 1814 had been reported it became necessary for his justification that the Letter containing his reasons, as promised in that Letter should also appear. He had written to his daughter at Mendon, for his own original draft of the letter; she had found and sent it to him all but the two last sheets — There was therefore some variation between the original and the duplicate of his Letter; and he had inserted some passages to defend himself with those who feel a particular interest in the fisheries. But there was no alteration of *facts*. I told him he was mistaken — There was an alteration of fact in the form of the most aggravated of all his charges against the Majority of the Mission, that of a wilful, direct, and positive violation of Instructions. This was not in the original Letter; but on the contrary; there was an express acquittal of the violation of Instructions. But the charge was in the duplicate, in language as strong as he could make it. — He said the acquittal in the original and the charge in the duplicate referred to different Instructions ≈ But I could shew him that it was impossible he should have thought at Ghent that we had violated the passage cited in his *duplicate*, of the Instruction of 15 April 1813 because before the proposal was made, we had received the subsequent Instruction of 19 October 1814 which released us entirely from the restriction of that passage, and authorised us expressly to conclude a Treaty upon the Basis of the Status ante Bellum — I then shewed him on the Book of Records of the Department the Letter from Mr. Monroe to the Mission of 19 October 1814, which was received on the 24th of November of that year; and also another Letter of 6 October 1814 containing the same authority, but which I told him had not been received by the Mission — I further told him that President Madison, by a Message to Congress of 9 Oct'r 1814 had communicated to Congress, so much of our Instructions, as would shew the terms upon which we were authorised to make Peace; the Instructions of 15 April 1813 were included in that communication; but the passage cited in the duplicate in proof of violated instructions, was omitted, as having been subsequently cancelled. During the whole of this exposition, Russell's countenance gave the usual indications of detected imposture; alternately flushing and turning pale. He said he had no recollection of the receipt of this Letter of 19 October 1814 — and asked if I thought the Status ante Bellum, included necessarily the right of the British to navigate the Mississippi — I said that was a matter upon which he was at Liberty to make his argument; but when, with the authority to conclude on the Basis of the Status ante Bellum, was connected the omission from the Instructions communicated to Congress of the paragraph cited by him as having been violated; when copies of these Instructions, thus communicated were transmitted to us, as shewing the terms on which we were authorised to conclude, it was impossible for me to doubt that the passage now cited by him, had been cancelled — At all events it had been so considered at Ghent, for this Instruction of 19 October had not only been received, but was actually produced in the course of the discussions of the Mission. He said if I recollected that there could be no question but it was so. But he said he could assure me he had not acted in this case in concert with my enemies, and had never written or published a word against me in the newspapers. He had acted from no motive of hostility to me — I then said to him, Mr. Russell, I wish not to enquire into your motives. — Henceforth, as a Public man, if upon any occasion whatever I can serve either you or your Constituents, it will afford me as much pleasure as if nothing had ever occurred between us; but of private and individual intercourse, the less there is between us from this time forward, the more agreeable it will be to me — He only replied "I wish you well" — and left me.

———

[May 1822]

9. V. Commodore Rogers called this morning at my house, and informed me that the experiment of cradling the frigate Potowmack, would be resumed this morning at eleven O'Clock, and invited me to attend — I went first to my Office, where D. P. Cook, member from Illinois, called and took leave — He was proceeding on his way homeward. — He told me that he had heard that during the latter part of the Session of Congress, Governor Edwards the Senator from Illinois, had ranged himself among the partizans of Mr. Calhoun, for the

succession to the Presidency. He said he had spoken to Mr. Edwards about it; he had denied the fact, but Cook intimated that he nevertheless believed it to be true — But he said that as to the vote of the State, Mr. Edwards well knew it would not be for Mr. Calhoun; nor for any Southern man. Cook last Summer, married Edwards's daughter. Until this Session of Congress, Edwards has constantly held himself out to me, as peculiarly and earnestly my friend — He has this Session sought no occasion of conversing with me, and I have no doubt has chained himself to the Car of Calhoun. As the time of that Election approaches it becomes daily more apparent, that the Election will be a contest between two factions in Congress, which is now an open market for the purchase of votes. The two Houses of Congress are the Pretorian Guards, who will in substance if not in form set up the Empire at Auction. It has been nearly so once before. Were it consistent with my principles to work for my own advancement any otherwise than by public service, it is now too late for me to commence bidding for the Presidency — Neither have I any faculty at driving such bargains — I told Cook that I thought it impossible the present Executive Administration should hold together through another Session of Congress — It is now nothing but a system of mining and countermining between Crawford and Calhoun; to blow up each other; and a continual underhanded working of both jointly against me, which has been the more effective, because I have neither creature nor champion in either house of Congress. At this game, Crawford is a much superior artist to Calhoun, whose hurried Ambition will probably ruin himself and secure the triumph of Crawford — Such is the present prospect.

———

[July 1822]
8. VI:30. A multitude of visitors, both at my house, and at the Office — Two persons by the name of Smith, and a Mr. Perkins — Dr. Thornton — Mr. Rice and Dr. Sewall, about the loan to the Columbian College — Edward Wyer, with news, never to be depended upon. In the Evening Mr. Calhoun, and afterwards General Scott, with Mr. Dick, the District judge of the United States in Louisiana. They came while Mr. Calhoun was with me and interrupted our Conversation. The relations in which I now stand with Calhoun are delicate and difficult. At

the last Session of Congress he suffered a few members of Congress with an Irishman named Rogers, Editor of a newspaper at Easton Pennsylvania, at their head to set him up as a Candidate for the succession to the Presidency — From that moment the caballing in Congress, in the State Legislatures, in the Newspapers, and among the people against me has been multiplied tenfold — The Franklin Gazette of Philadelphia, under the direction of R. Bache, G. M. Dallas, J. Sergeant, and Ingham, in concert with Rogers, opened immediately upon me, and has kept up ever since an insidious fire against me — Calhoun's partizans have countenanced it, and have been as busy as those of Mr. Crawford in their efforts to degrade me in the public opinion. Meanwhile Calhoun has always professed to be a friend and admirer of mine, and to persons whom he knew to be my friends has said that he did not mean to be a Candidate against a Northern Man; & that he himself was decidedly for a Northern President. There was a time during the last Session of Congress when so large a proportion of members was enlisted for Calhoun, that they had it in contemplation to hold a Caucus formally to declare him a Candidate. But this prospect of success roused all Crawford's and Clay's partizans against him — The administration of his Department was scrutinized with severity sharpened by personal animosity and factious malice — Some abuses were discovered, and exposed with aggravations — Cavils were made against measures of that Department in the Execution of the laws, and brought the President in collision with both houses of Congress — Crawford's newspapers commenced, and have kept up a course of the most violent abuse and ribaldry against him, and his projected nomination for the Presidency has met with scarcely any countenance throughout the Union — The principal effect of it has been to bring out Crawford's strength, and thus to promote the interest of the very man whom he professes alone to oppose. Calhoun now feels his weakness but is not cured of his ambition. My personal intercourse with him now is necessarily an intercourse of civility and not of confidence. The President returned this Evening from Loudoun.

———

II. V. ≈ Five years have this day past since Dr. Tillary by way of felicitation upon my birth day, congratulated me upon being between fifty and sixty — I have now turned the half-way corner — They have been five memorable years of my life, and certainly the five most laborious of the whole — They have also been crowned with blessings for which I am grateful to the giver of all good. They have had their trials of many kinds, among which the severest was the decease of my ever dear and lamented mother. I am now in the midst of another and far different trial — A trial for my character, before my Country. It is but one of many which are preparing for me, and through which I must pass as it shall please Heaven — The caballing against me is so extensive, and so many leading men in every part of the Union are engaged in it, that the prospect before me is not hopeful. This particular plot will in a great measure, though not entirely fail — Russell will be disappointed, and will have the public voice against him; but Clay for whom Russell has performed the part of the Jackall, will so far gain his point, that it will form a theme for prejudice in the Western and Southern Country against me. I have now the advantage of Russell entirely in my hands. But the management of my cause, requires discretion and firmness, both in an eminent degree. My cause is the cause of truth, of honesty, and of my Country. There is hardly a bad passion in the human heart, but is arrayed against me. But in controversies of this kind, success depends much upon the manner in which it is conducted. I have my own errors to dread more than the power of the adversary. A single false step would ruin me; I need advice very much; but have no one to advise me. I finished yesterday the draught of a rejoinder to Russell's publication in the Boston Statesman of 27 June — But it replies only to his false statements of the manner in which his Letters were brought before the House of Representatives; and is already so long that it will with difficulty be crowded into one newspaper. I have so much more to say upon the subject, that it will at least fill another newspaper; and I am apprehensive the public will grow weary of the subject, before it can be fully laid open to them. I began this morning the draught of the sequel to my rejoinder.

———

31. V:30. Potowmack Bath with George — The day passed without interruption at the Office. I dined with George at Mr. Frye's. George Johnson was there — After dinner, Mrs. Frye

having retired to the parlour, I left the table and joined her; when being alone with me she enquired if I had ever spoken with disapprobation of her marriage with Frye. I was surprized at the question, and assured her that I had not — She had been told that I had; and in terms which would have been as unbecoming in me, as mortifying to her — I immediately named to Mrs. Frye the person who had told her this, which she did not deny; but said she could not tell me who it was — I assured her it was utterly false — That far from disapproving her Marriage, I had been much gratified when informed of it. Having always respected the character of Mr. Frye, and having a regard for him which has increased the more I have known him — There is the venom of vipers in such tongues as these. This has been rankling for years in the mind of Mrs. Frye; and in all probability in that of her Husband. There was not the shadow of a foundation for it — But it was said to gratify some momentary malice, and a natural propensity to mischief-making — Walk home.

Day. Rise between 5 and 6. Breakfast about 9. Write till between 1 and 2, attend at the Office till 5 or 6, dine, and thence spend the Evening, walking, or sitting at a window or at the Street door, without Candles — Occupation, either of reading or writing, I find impracticable, for the heat and the bugs. Occasionally I attend the Theatre — I have been however deeply engaged the whole Month in my controversy with Jonathan Russell. I received on the first day of the Month his publication in the Boston Statesman of 27 June, and replied to it in part by a paper in the National Intelligencer of the 17th. I then promised another, but in taking up and discussing thoroughly the topics of his Letter of 11 February 1815 from Paris, I have found it necessary to write three papers, each of them too long for publication in one Newspaper — I have this day finished the first draught of the last of those papers — But the arrangement is yet to be completed, and some additions and some retrenchments are to be made — But in the present Stage of the controversy the public Sentiment is almost universal against Russell; and very strongly expressed — A Volume more in the Newspapers would weaken instead of strengthening that impression — It would look like mangling a fallen enemy. I have no such inclination, and have no wish to exult over him. But the doctrines of his Letter must be put down. I think of

publishing a pamphlet — The writing of these papers has so totally absorbed all my morning hours, that my Diary has been
running the whole Month in arrears.

———

[August 1822]
10. V:30. Mr. Richard Bland Lee called this morning at my
house with a Mr. Dennyman, from Virginia, who is a solicitor
for employment — A woman by the name of Bridget Smith
came to apply for a pardon for her brother, the man who is in
prison at Boston, for Slave-trading — Miss Smith operated
with the usual female weapon, a shower of tears. It seldom fails
to disconcert my philosophy, especially when I see the Spring is
from the social affections — Here it was a brother — necessary
for the comfort and subsistence of a mother — I promised to
do my best to obtain his release, though in his own person he
has very little claim to mercy, or even to compassion.

———

[September 1822]
9. V:30. Mr. Homans the chief Clerk of the Navy Department
came this morning with a Mr. Trask from Gloucester Massachusetts, who is here to solicit, the appointment of Collector
at that Port. I advised him to apply at the Treasury Department, under which all the revenue Officers are appointed. Mr.
Calhoun likewise called, and a Mr. Magruder — Also Mr.
M'Kenney, the Editor of the Washington Republican, who
wished to borrow a file of the New-York National Advocate,
from the Month of May till this time. He afterwards wrote me
a note, repeating the request, and asking also the loan of a
Report made by Mr. Crawford in January 1817. I had not the
latter, but sent him a file of the Advocate. The establishment
and progress of this Newspaper, forms an epocha in the History of Mr. Monroe's Administration. Mr. Crawford's party
was organized before the close of Mr. Madison's. He was a
Caucus Candidate in 1816 against Mr. Monroe, and had then
the address ostensibly to decline opposing Mr. Monroe, seeming to sacrifice his own pretensions in his favour, so as to secure
a seat in the administration under him, during which he has
been incessantly engaged in preparing the way to succeed him.
Among the most powerful of his agents have been the Editors
of the leading Newspapers; — The National Intelligencer is

secured to him by the belief of the Editors that he will be the successful candidate, and by their dependence upon the printing of Congress. The Richmond Enquirer, because he is a Virginian, and a Slave-holder — The National Advocate of New-York, through Van Buren — the Boston Statesman, and Portland Argus, through William King — the Democratic Press of Philadelphia, because I transferred the printing of the Laws, from that paper to the Franklin Gazette, and several other presses in various parts of the Union, upon principles alike selfish and sordid. Most of these papers have signals by which they understand one another; and the signal at Washington is given by the City Gazette, which has been resecured since Irvine ceased to be its joint Editor, and which from time to time gives notice of the newspapers which are successively induced to join in the train. All this has been going on successfully for some Months past, with little counteraction of any kind, till the Establishment of the Washington Republican. That paper began by a succession of seven numbers addressed to the People of the United States, in which the course of Mr. Crawford's management is very distinctly laid open, and its character vigorously exposed. It has already manifestly disordered the composure of Mr. Crawford's Editorial Phalanx — The Intelligencer has ventured a slight skirmish in his favour — The Advocate, the Boston Statesman, and the Richmond Enquirer, have attacked M'Kenney with personalities, and menaces; the City Gazette has said nothing of him till this day — On Saturday, Elliot acknowledged the receipt of an anonymous communication, styled Instructions to Office Hunters, and refused to print it without having the name of the author — This day it appeared under the title of Extracts from Instructions to political beginners; headed by the words Help! Help! Help! and then reprinting as "From the Washington Republican of the 7th inst't Edited by Calhoun and M'Kenney," a notice in that paper calling for payment of subscriptions — The Instructions profess to be after the manner of Dean Swift, but they are imitations only of his vulgarity and venom without any of his wit. They are infamously scurrilous and abusive, not only upon Mr. Calhoun, but upon his Mother in Law — This is Mr. Crawford's mode of defensive warfare.

———

12. V:30. Morning bath in the Potowmack with George — This is the last week of the Season, that I shall be able to enjoy for this mode of exercise, against which there are here very strong and I believe very unjust prejudices — I swam this morning a full half hour, without touching ground. The two great advantages of the swimming bath are cleanliness and muscular exercise, without being heated — I have never suffered any inconvenience from it, but have always found it conducive to my health. Edward Wyer came, and renewed with great earnestness, the promise he had made me on the 2^d of this month, to see me again on or before the 15th. He told me this day that a person not friendly to me, had told him that he had examined with the strictest Scrutiny my accounts at the Treasury, with the expectation of finding in them something against me; but he had been disappointed. They were perfectly correct, and he was very sorry for it. I asked him who it was, but he declined telling me. I have long believed that this was one of the machines intended to be used against me for electioneering purposes, and that Mr. Crawford has had it among the ways and means of his Presidential Canvas — The person who made this confession to Wyer, I have no doubt was one of Crawford's subalterns; probably a Treasury Clerk; and Wyer, after telling it to me, to shew how much secret information he could give, was afraid to tell me the name of the person; least he should make enemies to himself — This is one of many incidents shewing the system of *Espionage*, which Crawford keeps on foot over his Colleagues; and the means, which he is willing to use to depress them. My Accounts were kept five years unsettled upon a cavil without foundation in Law or Justice — I was all but entrapped last winter, into a Report to Congress which would have given a handle against me; which was prepared at the Treasury, and of which it was with the utmost difficulty that I obtained the rectification; and now I have it in proof that there is a person having access to all the Treasury documents, mousing for errors in my accounts upon which to raise a popular clamour against me. Wyer said he would ask the person's consent to tell me his name; but that is a mere evasion. At the Office the heat of the weather again kept me almost idle. Evening at the Play. Cooper's last appearance and benefit. Virginius and the Highland Reel. I sat in the Pit. The house

was overflowing and the heat suffocating. The Tragedy, is a contrast to Bertram. The Plot well adapted to the Roman History. The characters well drawn with perhaps too much imitation of Shakespeare's Coriolanus and Julius Caesar. The language nervous and unaffected, and the Sentiments, properly Roman — The worst part of the Play is the Catastrophe, by which Virginius strangles the ex-Decemvir Claudius, in the prison, with his own hands, which is revolting. The whole fifth act seems to be superfluous. The Highland Reel is an amusing Comic Opera, which I had seen once before, this Season.

———

14. V:30. ≈ The Newspaper war between the Presses of Mr. Crawford and Mr. Calhoun waxes warm. This day, the City Gazette, has three Columns of brevier type, of the foulest abuse upon M'Kenney and upon Mr. Calhoun personally — first in a long Editorial Article; and then, in copious Extracts from the National Advocate and Boston Statesman — The exposure already made, and the developement further threatened by the Washington Republican, of Crawford's practices, and those of his partizans, has thrown them into a paroxysm of rage; and their only attempt to meet these charges hitherto, has been by personal invective and menace. The Republican replies this Evening with firmness and moderation to the National Advocate and Boston Statesman; and reviews his own progress hitherto. — If this Press is not soon put down, Mr. Crawford has an ordeal to pass through before he reaches the Presidency, which will test his merit and pretensions as well as the character of the Nation — As yet not much notice is taken of the Washington Republican, and its disclosures, excepting by the fury of Crawford's Presses — His party is so strong; and they have such a ruffian-like manner, of bearing down opposition, that impartial and disinterested persons are intimidated; brow-beating, is among the choicest expedients of his partizans. The progress of this conflict will be a very curious subject of observation; and its result important to the History of the Union.

———

27. V:45. Rain Storm. Received a Note from the President, calling the Meeting of the Members of the Administration, at one O'Clock. At the Office I found a despatch from R. Rush,

with the information that on the 12th of August, the Marquis of Londonderry, the British Secretary of State for foreign Affairs, committed suicide by cutting his throat with a small penknife — "With a bare Bodkin." His mind was like the cable that drew up the frigate at the Navy-Yard, upon the inclined plane — stretched till it snapped. Attended at the President's at one O'Clock — Mr. Calhoun only was there, Mr. Wirt being unwell, and not able to attend. — The proposition of Mr. Sanchez, as disclosed in Mr. Duponceau's Letter to General Mason was discussed — There was also a second Letter, explanatory of the first and more strictly confidential. The question was discussed what was to be done. Mr. Calhoun has a most ardent desire that the Island of Cuba should become a part of the United States, and says that Mr. Jefferson has the same — There are two dangers, to be averted by that event. One that the Island should fall into the hands of Great-Britain; the other that it should be revolutionized by the Negroes — Calhoun says Mr. Jefferson told him two years ago, that we ought at the first possible opportunity to take Cuba, though at the cost of a War with England; but as we are not now prepared for this, and as our great object must be to gain time, he thought we should answer this overture, by dissuading them from their present purpose, and urging them to adhere at present to their connection with Spain — I thought it advisable to take a different course — To give them no advice whatever — To say that the Executive of the United States is not competent to promise them admission as a State into the Union; and that if it were, the proposal is of a nature which our relations of amity with Spain would not permit us to countenance. Mr. Calhoun suggested, that it would be proper for the President to make it a subject of a confidential communication to Congress, at their next Session; and he objected that if much stress should be laid upon our relations with Spain as forbidding our acceptance of the proposal, it might be considered as indirect instigation to the declaration of Independence, inasmuch as that would release us from the obligation of considering it as involving any of the rights of Spain. I replied that there would be no possibility of proceeding in the business by confidential Communication to Congress — First because there has not been one Message, with closed doors, during the present Administration; nor I believe since the Peace — The very notice of a secret Session would rouse an insatiate curiosity throughout the Nation to know, what could be its object. And secondly the proposal was of a nature which would not admit of secresy; the power of Congress itself to act upon it was questionable — It involved external War and internal revolution, in its essential and inevitable consequences — It would neither be possible nor proper that such business should be transacted by secret Sessions of Congress. The whole affair would be divulged in a week — perhaps in a day. All Europe, as well as America would have notice of it, and the very communication of the proposal to Congress as a subject for their deliberations by the President, might be taken by Spain as hostility to her, and give warning to Great-Britain, to take an immediate and determined stand against it. As to taking Cuba at the cost of a War with Great-Britain, it would be well to enquire before undertaking such a War, how it would be likely to terminate; and for the present, and for a long time to come, I held it for certain that a War with Great-Britain for Cuba, would result in her possession of that Island, and not ours. In the present relative situation of our maritime forces, we could not maintain a War against Great-Britain for Cuba. Nor did I think that a plain distinct answer that our relations with Spain forbid our encouragement of a proposal to annex one of her Colonies to our own Union could be construed into an instigation to revolt. It was a reference to a plain principle of moral duty expressly applicable to the case; suitable to be acted upon as a motive, and honourable to the good faith of the Nation. I would give them at the same time to understand that the Government of the United States entertain the most friendly sentiments towards the inhabitants of Cuba; and are fully aware of the common interests which point to a most intimate connection between them and the United States — But to advise them to cling to their connection with Spain, would expose them to be transferred to Great-Britain by Spain, of which there is double danger, first by the present revolutionary Government of Spain to purchase support against the holy Alliance; and secondly by Ferdinand, to purchase the aid of Great-Britain to consummate a counter-revolution in his favour. Now by advising the People of Cuba to adhere to Spain, we expose them to both these dangers; and if the transfer should be made; they would charge the result upon us, and a heavy responsibility for the consequence would bear upon us, for such ill-judged interposition — Mr. Calhoun said he inclined to think there would be no immediate danger of a transfer of the Island to Great-Britain. The President directed an adjourned meeting for to morrow.

—

30. VI. ≈ I attended the Cabinet-Meeting at the President's — Mr. Calhoun and Mr. Wirt were there. The Letters from Duponceau to General Mason, and the proposals of Mr. Sanchez were again discussed. The proposition is that the People of Cuba should immediately declare themselves Independent of Spain without any co-operation of the United States, and then ask admission to this Confederation as one of the States of the Union. By his first Letter, Duponceau had understood the offer to be that they should come in as Louisiana had been received — To be governed first as a territory, and afterwards admitted, as one or more States. The second Letter rectifies this error. They ask admission at once; as one State, with full interior Sovereignty of its own. I doubted the authority not only of the Executive, but of Congress to perform this — Mr. Calhoun thought the case of Louisiana had settled the Constitutional question. But a transaction which should make an Island separated from this Continent by the Ocean, at once a member of the Union, with a Representation in both Houses of Congress, would certainly be an act of more transcendent power, than a mere purchase of territory contiguous to our own. I observed also that we had not sufficient foundation for presenting the proposal to Congress in any shape. We had nothing but Mr. Sanchez's word, that he had authority from anyone. We knew not from whom his authority came, nor how it had been given him — We knew not how far the project had been matured, nor what were its prospects of success. More information upon all this would be necessary before we could take a step of any kind in an affair of deeper importance and greater magnitude than had occurred since the Establishment of our Independence. It was concluded that the answer to Mr. Sanchez must be negative, as to giving any encouragement to the Revolutionary movement; but Mr. Calhoun still

thought we should dissuade them from it. I observed that whatever answer we should give must be one, which we must be prepared to see divulged — We must not expect it will be kept secret; whatever General Mason writes to Duponceau, he will make known, to Sanchez, and Sanchez to his Constituents whoever they may be — It is said that the project has been long in agitation, and is even much discussed publicly at the Havanna. The controul of the secret, will not be in our power, and even if it should be faithfully kept, we must answer as if it would not. There was a proposal, that General Mason should separately answer each of Duponceau's Letters — one for communication to Sanchez, as our answer, and the other as suggestions to be made to him through Duponceau, as from General Mason himself. I thought this would make no difference; so far as secresy was the object whatever should go from the Government, would be known to go from the Government, however enveloped in forms — Mr. Wirt made a short draft, of what he thought might be given to General Mason for an answer to Duponceau, which after some discussion the President said he would keep, and prepare a draft from it, to be considered to-morrow. I took an Evening walk, and then played Chess with Smith.

Day — Distribution of time as the preceding Months; but morning baths have ceased since the 17th and since the 21st I have resumed this Diary, the arrears of which I have retrieved to the first of August, this day commenced. Since the 21st also the Theatre has been closed, and as the Evenings lengthen and grow cool, I am enabled to employ a part of them in reading or writing. But more frequently at Chess.

[October 1822]
1. V:30. A Sleepless Night. The cause of which I could not assign to myself: but it was with a dispersion of Spirits which disabled me from turning to account the time thus cast upon me; towards the dawn only I fixed my mind upon a train of thought suited to the occasion, and rose just after day-light — Received a Note from the President, desiring the members of the Administration to meet at his house at 11 O'Clock — Mr. Calhoun and Mr. Wirt were there. The President had prepared answers for General Mason to return to both Mr.

Duponceau's Letters — The substance of them was that he was sure the Government as well as People of the United States entertained the most friendly Sentiments; towards the People of Cuba, and felt the most lively interest in their welfare; but that their relations with Spain, did not admit of their forming any engagements in the present state of things; such as were implied in the proposals of Mr. Sanchez; and that the Executive Government would not in any event be competent to form them, without the concurrence of Congress. The more secret Letter suggested as General Mason's own idea, that it would be well for Mr. Sanchez to give information more explicit and precise of the authority by which he acted; whence it came — who were the persons concerned in the project — how far it was matured, and what means and resources they had for accomplishing their purpose — I suggested the expediency, that General Mason should furnish copies, both of Mr. Duponceau's Letters and of the answers — to which the President said he would attend — Mr. Wirt gave a written opinion in the case of the Danish Slave, which was that the President had the power to deliver him up. I asked him where he found the grant of the Power in the Constitution. He said it was in the general instruction to take care that the Laws should be faithfully executed. I said that in his opinion that the President could *not* deliver up a Pirate, he did not admit that doctrine — where did he find it now? He said, laughing, that he took it from me. But his opinion as to the mode in which the delivery is to be effected was altogether nugatory — It presumes that the President might order the Marshal to take the man and deliver him over to the Danish Minister without ceremony; but he recommends that the Governor of New-York should be written to, and invited, to deliver up the man — I said that I should ask to be excused from writing either the order to the Marshal, or the Letter to the Governor of New-York; for I was convinced that in the first case if the Marshal should obey the order, the man would be taken out of his custody by Habeas Corpus, and very probably he himself be prosecuted in a State Court for False Imprisonment, by the manumission Society; and in the second we should have an answer from the Governor of New-York, not only refusing to deliver up the man but subjoining a commentary upon the demand, which would be any thing other than palatable. Mr. Wirt said that this subject was quite as much political as legal; and he wished the President would take other opinions as well as his — The truth is that between his Virginian aversion to constructive powers, his Virginian devotion to State-Rights, and his Virginian *autocracy* against Slaves, his two opinions form the most absurd jumble of self-contradictions that could be imagined — If the President has not power to deliver up a Pirate, he cannot possibly have power to deliver up a Slave — Mr. Calhoun agreed entirely with Mr. Wirt as to the power of the President, in the case of fugitive Slaves; but felt more the difficulty of carrying it into execution. Calhoun has no petty scruples about constructive Powers, and State-Rights — His opinions are at least consistent — I have no doubt that by the Constitution the President has the Power; but perhaps a Law of Congress may be necessary, providing the process, by which the power should be exercised. Despotism itself would be startled at Wirt's opinion that the Marshal under a bare order from the President, through the Secretary of State, should have power to seize a man, without judge or jury, pack him on board ship, and send him out of the Country, like a bag of cotton. An invitation to the Governor of New-York to do the same thing is not less absurd. The President said he would take time to reflect upon the subject, before coming to his determination. He left the City for his Seat in Albemarle County, immediately after the Meeting.

———

7. V:15. ≈ Received a Letter from George M. Dallas of Philadelphia, enclosing a copy of the Oration, which I delivered, on the 17th of July 1787 at Commencement, upon taking my degree of bachelor of Arts. He says he found it among some of his late father's papers, but does not know how it came there — Nor do I: but it is the copy which at the request of the late Dr. Belknap, I furnished him, for publication, in a Monthly Magazine, then published at Philadelphia; and it was printed in the number for the Month of September 1787. I little thought of ever seeing the manuscript again — but the delivery of that Oration was one of the most memorable Events of my life — The incidents attending it were of a nature to make and leave a deep impression upon my mind. The appointment to deliver it was itself a high distinction — Yet it was but the second

honour of the Class; and he who took the first, the preferred rival, sunk at the age of 35, to be forgotten — I reperused this production now with humiliation; to think how proud of it I was then, and how much I must blush for it now.

———

[November 1822]

7. VI:30. The day after I dismissed John B. Colvin from the Department of State, I saw his hand in the Washington City Gazette. He has since commenced a series of numbers under the Editorial part of that paper, headed the Presidential Question; each of two or three Columns — Five numbers have appeared, written in Colvin's best manner, professing to give a delineation of my character, and scanning my pretensions to the Presidency. They present me in caricature, and touch upon every thing true, and everything false that can be made to resemble truth, which could degrade me in the popular opinion. They are written with just so much regard to truth, as to seize on single facts, to which a suspicious colouring may be given, from which a whole tale of falsehood is fabricated and asserted as fact to exhibit me as a base and despicable character. Between three and four years ago, Colvin attempted to fawn himself into my favour, by eulogising me in newspapers — He published a characteristic Portrait of me, so highly charged, that, on being informed it was written by him, I requested him to abstain from any such publications having any personal reference to me whatever — That if he inclined to political newspaper discussion, and would defend and vindicate any measures of the administration which might be assailed, his labours would be acceptable, but that I wanted no personal panegyrist — He continued to cringe however, and to work windingly for my good graces, but besides the warning of his old treachery to Robert Smith, the more I saw of him, the more reason I had for distrusting him; and I never placed any confidence in him. He had shrewdness enough after a year or two of ineffectual parasitical courtship, to discover his failure, and among my present characteristics enumerates, a lurking and distrustful suspicion in the eye — He would occasionally endeavour indirectly to get sight of the secret diplomatic documents, but they were kept out of his reach — His absences from the Office, and neglect of his duties, in the mean time

kept increasing with his habits of intemperance till they could no longer be tolerated. I had long been aware that it must ultimately come to this; and have been gradually breaking his hold from the Office till he could be dismissed without inconvenience. I knew that from that moment he would become the bitterest of my revilers; and of the whole tribe he is the only one, who can be instigated to injure me, by revenge — A comparison between his Portrait of 1819 and his Caricature now, would be curious, as marking the depraved ingenuity of unprincipled intellect. The five numbers on the Presidential Question, teem with falsehoods. I wrote this morning, and sent to Gales and Seaton, a short paper containing a direct contradiction of two among the basest of those falsehoods — I did this in deference to feelings in my family more sensitive to such Slanders than my own. No man in America has made his way through showers of ribaldry and invective of this character, more frequent and various than I have breasted — A new storm of them has in the last eighteen months burst upon me; and will rage, until every indication of a party holding my name up as a Candidate for the Presidency, shall have vanished.

—

9. VI. My short Note to Gales and Seaton, exposing two of the many falsehoods in Colvin's abusive papers on the Presidential question, was published this Morning in the National Intelligencer, as a Communication, and a reply appeared in the Washington Gazette of this Evening re-asserting them, adding a number more of falsehoods, and redoubling scurrilous invectives ≈ Reading further in Walpole's Memoires, or secret History of the British Administrations from 1750 to 1760, I find in them many things that remind me of the present state of things here. The public History of all Countries, and all ages, is but a sort of mask, richly coloured — The interior working of the machinery must be foul. There is as much mining and countermining for power, as many fluctuations of friendship and enmity, as many attractions and repulsions, bargains and oppositions, narrated in these Memoires as might be told of our own times. Walpole witnessed it all as a sharer in the sport, and now tells it to the world as a Satirist — And shall not I too, have a tale to tell?

—

30. VI:15. Mr. John W. Taylor, member of Congress from the Saratoga district, State of New-York called on me this morning, and had a long conversation with me. He has been re-elected to the next Congress, in opposition to what they call in that State a regular nomination — In the National Advocate, it has been stated that he would be a Candidate for the Office of Clerk of the House of Representatives; he assured me that he had not at the time had a thought of it, but asked my advice whether he should offer himself as a candidate or not — He said he inclined himself against it. He thought it would be a descent from his present Station; but several members had asked him if he would be a candidate; and had promised him their votes and support if he should be — Even several of his colleagues who had last year opposed his election as Speaker — I told him I thought it was the least they could do for him by way of reparation for what they had done — I thought with him that the situation of Clerk of the House, though very respectable would carry less Consideration than that of a member, especially of his long standing; but it was more profitable and more permanent. With regard to his personal views, I thought he could take counsel only from himself — If he concluded to be a candidate he would have my best wishes, and any services that it might be in my power to bestow — Upon public considerations, I should prefer to have him remain a member of the House, believing that he would be more useful there, and that his sphere of action would be much larger than in the Clerk's Office. He entered very fully into particulars with regard to his own situation, prospects and purposes — Said Mr. Clay was coming to the next Congress, with the intention of making the Speaker's chair, a step for his own promotion to the Presidency — As on the very probable contingency, that the election would fall to the House of Representatives, his influence in the House, and the Esprit de Corps in favour of their own Speaker would operate strongly upon the members in his favour — But he said he had lately seen Mr. Shaw, formerly a member of Congress from Berkshire Massachusetts, and a very particular friend of Mr. Clay with whom he is in correspondence, who told him that he believed there had been some understanding between Mr. Clay and me, or between our friends, who would move in concert

— He said he did not wish to draw from me any thing that I might wish not to disclose, but his own views at present might in some sort be influenced by the knowledge of the facts — I told him that I had no motive for concealment or hesitation with him — There was no understanding or concert between Mr. Clay and me, on this subject; and never had been — When Mr. Clay left Congress two years ago we parted upon friendly terms, and although Mr. Clay's political course as a member of the House had not been remarkably friendly to me, I had never been unfriendly to him — As to the next Presidential election I had no concert or understanding with any one. He said he had been for some time convinced that there would be but one candidate from the North; for although the Vice-President was coming to take the Chair of the Senate; and proclaimed his health restored he would not be restored as a Candidate. Now on the score of qualifications and services, if the South in the present case, could not be induced to vote for the Northern Candidate, he considered that their acquiescence in the choice of such a Candidate would be postponed indefinitely — There was no reason to believe it would *ever* be obtained: because there was no reason for expecting that the claims of the North, would ever stand upon more unequivocal ground — But at the last Session of Congress there were numbers of the Northern men, and particularly Holmes of Maine, who professed a very high opinion of the Northern Candidate, but always insisting that there was no chance in his favour — No possibility of his being elected — He had heard during the recess of Congress frequent Conversations to the same effect; and had constantly maintained the opposite opinion. I observed that he had never before spoken to me in a manner so explicit on this subject — That I had not known what his opinions concerning it were, but that intimations had been given to me, that they were favourable to Mr. Crawford; which I had not credited — He said that his own wishes were in favour of a Northern Candidate — Should it ultimately appear that the chance of election in his favour is desperate, he should perhaps incline to favour that of Mr. Crawford — He had been two years ago in favour of the reduction of the army; as he understood Mr. Crawford to have been. He knew not what my opinion had been, but had heard it was opposed to the reduction. But Mr. Calhoun had been unjust and he would say ungrateful to him in that transaction; for it was through his means, that Mr. Calhoun's plan for the reduction had finally been adopted in preference to that of the Committee of the House — I said that as to the reduction of the army, I had taken no part whatever in relation to it — I had inclined against it, because the Head of the Department immediately concerned in it had disapproved it — And as a member of the Administration, I had been governed by two general principles — One to support to the best of my power the Administration, and the other not to intermeddle with the Departments, at the head of which other persons were placed. I believed Mr. Calhoun was now sensible he had been misadvised in preventing the election of Taylor as Speaker, but it was the prejudice raised by the Missouri Slave question that had been the cause of it. Taylor repeated to me the circumstances of his having been promised as he understood it the Office of Judge of the Northern District of New-York, and its having been given to Skinner; a subject upon which he is sore.

———

[January 1823]

12. VII. Heard Mr. M'Ilvaine at the Capitol, from Job 11:7–8. "Canst thou by searching find out God? Canst thou find out the Almighty unto perfection? — It is as high as heaven; what canst thou do? deeper than hell; what canst thou know?" Easy declamation upon the incomprehensibility of the divine Nature — After Church I called at Claxton's and saw General Cocke ≈ I next went to Dowson's, and saw Mr. Macon — In making the appointments to these South American Missions the President wishes to distribute them, to Citizens of the different parts of the Union. He wishes particularly to take some distinguished notice of North Carolina; it happens that the weight of talents in that State is with the federalists; so that the politics counteract the geography — Among the persons recommended to the President was John Lewis Taylor, now Chief Justice of the State, and the President had requested me to call upon Mr. Macon, and make enquiries concerning him. Last Evening I received a Note from the President, saying it would be proper in these enquiries to ascertain if Mr. Taylor is of the republican party. I made therefore that enquiry among the

others — Mr. Macon spoke of Mr. Taylor, as of a man of accomplished manners: but said nothing of any more elevated qualifications, and as to his politics, he had understood him to be among the warmest federalists in the State — But he added that politics had never been so hostile between the parties in North-Carolina, as in either of its neighbouring States of South Carolina or of Virginia, and that Mr. Taylor had been elected to the Office of Chief Justice of the State by a Legislature of different politics from his own — On returning home I found a Note from the President requesting me to call at his house this day, to confer with him on the proposed nominations of Ministers. I went to him immediately; and found him very anxious to make the nominations. I reported to him what Mr. Macon had said of Mr. Taylor, upon which he said it would not do to nominate him — He added that it had been a great object of his administration to conciliate the people of this Union; towards one another; and to mitigate the asperities of party Spirit. But in effecting this, he was obliged to consider how far he could yield to his own dispositions, without losing the Confidence of his own party — He would go as far as the public Sentiment would support him; but to overstep that boundary would be to defeat his own object — He had concluded to nominate Hugh Nelson of Virginia to Spain, and Richard C. Anderson of Kentucky to Colombia — and C. A. Rodney to Buenos-Ayres. For Mexico and Chili, he was yet undetermined. I mentioned to him General Jackson for Mexico, and John Holmes of Maine for Chili — He received favourably the name of Jackson, but doubted whether he would accept, and made some question whether his quickness and violence of temper might not in the opinion of a great part of the Nation make the expediency of his appointment questionable — I said that although the language of General Jackson was sometimes too impassioned and violent, his conduct had always appeared to me calm and deliberate. Acting under responsibility, I did not apprehend he would do any thing to the injury of his Country; and even if he should commit any indiscretion, he would bear the penalty of it himself, for the Nation would not support him in it. — There was another difficulty which I thought more serious — He had been unanimously nominated by the members of the Legislature of

Tennessee as a Candidate for the Presidential election. To send
him on a Mission abroad, would be attributed by some perhaps
to a wish, to get him out of the way — The President said
there was something in that — As to Holmes, he said his conduct in the Senate had not been friendly to the Administration;
of which I was well aware — As I was that his dispositions were
far otherwise than friendly to me — But I considered him as
perhaps the ablest man, in the delegations from New-England,
and highly qualified for the public Service. I believed also that
he would faithfully discharge the duties of any public service
abroad — The President took further time to consider of the
subject.

———

[June 1823]

19. V:15. Swam in the Potowmack a full hour; Antoine was
with me. I follow this practice for exercise, for health, for
cleanliness and for pleasure. I have found it invariably conducive to health, and never experienced from it the slightest inconvenience. Dr. Huntt and all my friends think I am now
indulging it to excess — I never before this day swam an hour
at once; and I must now limit my fancies for this habit, which
is not without danger — The art of swimming ought in my
opinion to be taught as a regular branch of education. There
was a Cabinet Meeting at the President's at One O'Clock.
Messrs. Crawford, Calhoun and Thompson present — Mr.
Wirt absent — My project of a Convention for the suppression
of the Slave-trade; answer to Mr. Canning, and Instruction to
R. Rush were first considered. Mr. Crawford and Mr. Calhoun
started objections on various grounds — Crawford to the argument in the Letter to Canning against the right of Search,
which he said was completely given up in the project of Convention, and therefore the Argument might be represented by
the British as a mere Declamation, against a practice which the
project essentially conceded — This objection had weight, and
I had been fully aware of it in drawing up the papers — But
two objects were to be aimed at in the papers. One fully to
justify the repugnance which we have heretofore manifested
against the right of search as practised by Great-Britain in War;
the other to carry into effect the Resolution of the House
of Representatives, recommending negotiation to obtain the

recognition of the Slave-trade, to be Piracy by the Law of Nations — To Piracy by the Law of Nations, Search is incident of course, since wherever there is a right to *capture* there must be a right to search. The end desired by the Resolution of the House of Representatives cannot be obtained without conceding the right so far of search, and all that is left us is to keep it still inflexibly within the Class of belligerent rights, as exercised only against Pirates, the enemies of all mankind. It was therefore that in my project of Convention, the first Article assumes as a fact that both parties have declared the Slave-trade, Piracy, and my Instructions to Mr. Rush are not to offer it, but after an Act of Parliament, declaring the Slave-trade to be Piracy. Mr. Calhoun's objection was to the admission of the right of capture by foreign officers at-all; as weakening us upon the general objection to conceding the right of search. Mr. Thompson, did not think the right of search conceded in the project at-all — The search for Pirates had, he said absolutely nothing in common with the search of neutral vessels — Much discussion which I cannot record. Mr. Calhoun thought we should at once say we will never concede the right of Search for Slaves, unless Britain will renounce search for her Seamen in our vessels in War. I said I was willing to make one the Condition of the other — It was finally understood by the President that the project much as drafted should be proposed, provided the British make the offence Capital, by act of Parliament; and not be communicated in detail to the British Government without that. Crawford hinted at an additional guard, that lists of the vessels authorised to capture the Slave-traders should be mutually furnished. But it would be very inconvenient to us, as Instructions of capture are issued to all our Cruizers — The project is to go, but the Letter to Mr. Canning is to be modified. Upon the subject of the average value of the Slaves carried away, and to be paid for, it was determined that we have not the necessary information, and that it must be left to be fixed by the Commissioners or otherwise according to the Convention. After the other members of the administration had withdrawn, I requested of the President to mark the passages of the Draft to Mr. Canning, which he would have omitted — for which purpose he kept the papers. George dined at Mr. Petry's — Melting heat. Mr. Frye here this Evening, returned from

Bladensburg; where he has left Mrs. Frye, with Mrs. Adams
— Verses.

———

[July 1823]
8. VI. Swam with Antoine in the Potowmack — to the Bridge
— One hour in the water. While we were swimming there
sprung up a fresh breeze, which made a surf and much increased the difficulty of swimming — especially against it and
the current — This is one of the varieties of instruction for the
school. It sometimes occurs to me that this exercise and
amusement as I am now indulging myself in it is with the
constant risk of life. Perhaps that is the reason, why so few
persons ever learn to swim — And perhaps it should now teach
me discretion ≈ The Count de Menou, came to enquire where
were the Quirpon Islands: I shewed him upon Mitchell's map
— We had much conversation upon the subject of the french
claim to exclusive fishery from them to Cape Ray — He said
he had received further Instructions from the Viscount de
Chateaubriand, on this affair; but there were still two previous
instructions which he had not received. He saw it was an affair
of great delicacy; and he did not see how they and we could
enjoy a concurrent right of fishery on the same coast — I told
him, the whole affair was a question between France and Great-
Britain, with which we had but a secondary concern —
Great Britain was bound to maintain her own jurisdiction.
And if she had conceded to us a right which she had already
granted as an exclusive possession to France, she must indemnify us for it. The Count spoke also upon the subject of the
maritime questions, arisen from the War between France and
Spain; upon which he said he should write to me. We examined
the State-papers, and found Mr. Jefferson's answer to Genet of
24 July 1793, and the reference to it in Mr. Pickering's Instructions to Mess'rs Marshall, Pinkney and Gerry. It was as I had
stated yesterday to Mr. Wirt — Mr. Jefferson's assertion of the
principle that enemy's property is liable to capture and condemnation in the vessel of a friend is not absolute — His words
are, I believe it cannot be doubted.

———

11. VI. And I commence upon my 57th year. Swam with Antoine
an hour in the Potowmack — We started for the Bridge,

but after swimming about half an hour, I perceived by reference to a house upon the shore, beyond which we were to pass, that we had ascended very little above where we had left our clothes, and that the current of the tide was insensibly carrying us into the middle of the river — We continued struggling against the tide about twenty minutes longer, without apparently gaining a foot upon the tide — I then turned back and in fifteen minutes landed at the rock where I had left my Clothes, upon which in the interval, the tide had so much encroached, that it began to wet them and in another half hour would have soaked them through, or floated them away. We had been an hour and five minutes in the water, without touching ground, and before turning back I began to find myself weary — At my house B. O. Tyler came about the books he had for sale, and an engraved portrait of my father — George Johnson a cousin of Mrs. Adams's came to request me to purchase Mills in this neighbourhood which have belonged to him, and upon which he says he has spent near sixty thousand dollars; but which he has conveyed in trust, for a debt to the Bank of Columbia. The debt, is 20000 dollars; and they are willing to receive payment of it by yearly instalments in five years — But to set the Mills at Work, from ten to twelve thousand dollars more are necessary as capital, to purchase wheat, and pay the charges of the establishment — G. Johnson can raise no part of this money, and unless he can make some other arrangement with the Bank before next Thursday, they will rent out the Mills as their property and turn him adrift upon the world — He urged me to buy the Mills for 20000 dollars — to furnish from 10 to 12000 dollars to set and keep them constantly at work — To put them under his management for such portion of the profits as I shall think proper; and reserve to him the right of repurchasing half the Estate on his paying ten thousand dollars — I have taken time for consideration of this proposal, to the acceptance of which many motives, all just and virtuous, urge me; but which I cannot accept but at great hazard, and with deep stakes to myself and my family — I promised to answer definitively before next Thursday ≈ After dinner I rode out with Mrs. Adams, Johnson Hellen and George, to the Columbian Mills, on Rock Creek. They are in rather a neglected condition, but appear to be a valuable property — The heat of the weather continues unabated.

12. VI. ≈ George Johnson was here about the sale of the Mills, and gave me further information concerning them — This affair involves the comfort of my future life, and that of all my family — My personal independence, and a system of projected occupation for the remnant of my life, after my retirement from the public Service. That event is approaching, and now so near at hand, that it is time seriously to provide for it — Less than two years will terminate my political career, and leave me to the support of my private resources — Is not this a gracious offer by Providence of the means of devoting the time which may yet be allotted upon Earth, to useful and respectable purposes? Such is the hope I have conceive[d] — But it is yet beclouded with doubts, and beset with perils — It must be, at all Events, in a great degree a leap in the dark — But man must trust — Of my motives I am sure — G. Johnson is to bring me further papers on Monday.

———

14. VI. George Johnson came and brought an original deed of the land which I have agreed to purchase on the terms proposed by him, to which I suggested some slight modifications.

———

17. V:30. George Johnson came this Morning and requested me to make in writing a proposition to the President and Directors of the Bank of Columbia, for the payment of his debt, and the purchase by me of the Mills. I went to the Branch Bank and made my proposal to the Cashier R. Smith. He said he would write immediately to the Bank at Philadelphia and had no doubt my offers would be accepted, as they were preferable to any others proposed by the Bank of Columbia — I gave my written proposal to G. Johnson to take with him to the Bank of Columbia — Mr. Brent called about the Correspondence of the old Congress about to be published. At the Office Baron Tuyll came, and enquired if he might inform his Government that Instructions would be forwarded by Mr. Hughes to Mr. Middleton, for negotiating on the North-west Coast question. I said he might. He then manifested a desire to know, as much as I was disposed to tell him, as to the

purport of those Instructions — I told him as much as I thought prudent, as he observed that it was personally somewhat important to him to be so far confided in here, as to know the general purport of what we intended to propose — I told him specially that we should contest the right of Russia, to *any* territorial Establishment on this Continent; and that we should assume distinctly the principle that the American Continents are no longer subjects for *any* new European Colonial Establishments. We had a conversation of an hour or more, at the close of which he said that although there would be difficulties in the Negotiation, he did not foresee that they would be insurmountable ≈

18. V:30. Heavy Showers of Rain the whole day — This Affair of the Mills now absorbs too much of my time — I have been preparing a draft of Articles of Agreement with George Johnson to be executed after the purchase shall be completed — This morning I examined all the Deeds received yesterday, and find some links in the chain of evidence wanting.

———

28. V:30. ≈ I called at the President's with the Draft of Instructions to R. Rush, to accompany the project of a Convention to regulate neutral, and Belligerent rights in time of War. The President had suggested a single alteration, in the Draft of a Convention which I had sent him on Saturday — Mr. Calhoun came in while I was relating to the President the draft of the Instruction; and after I had finished, started several doubts as to the propriety of proposing this project at-all. He was confident it would not be accepted by Great-Britain; and I have no expectation that it will, at this time — But my object is to propose it to Russia, and France, and to all the maritime Powers of Europe, as well as to Great-Britain. We discussed for some time its expediency; I appealed to the primitive policy of this Country as exemplified in the first Treaty with Prussia. I said the Seed was then first sown; and had born a single plant, which the fury of the revolutionary tempest had since swept away. I thought the present a moment eminently auspicious for sowing the same seed a second time; and although I had no hope it would now take root in England, I had the most cheering confidence that it would ultimately bear a harvest of

happiness to mankind and of glory to this Union — Mr. Calhoun still suggested doubts, but no positive objections, and the President directed me to send the draft of the Articles round to the members of the administration, and to call a Meeting of them for to-morrow at one. I was not surprized at Mr. Calhoun's doubts — My plan involves nothing less than a Revolution in the Laws of War — A great amelioration in the condition of man — Is it the dream of a visionary? or is it the great and practicable conception of a benefactor of mankind? I believe it the latter, and I believe this to be precisely the time for proposing it to the world — Should it even fail, it will be honourable to have proposed it — Founded on Justice, Humanity and Benevolence, it can in no Event bear bitter fruits.

—

30. V:30. ≈ Mr. George Johnson called at my house this Evening. He has received the Deed from his father, executed, and said Mr. Dunlop would come with him to-morrow and execute his — But the business does not proceed so smoothly as he had expected — He finds that more considerable repairs must be made than he had supposed would be necessary, and that they will scarcely be able to go to work in less than ten days — His assistant has not yet arrived; nor can he find the key of the warehouse at Georgetown. These are circumstances of no encouraging tendency, but I have laid my account for many such. My Son George who is recovering, asked two days since my consent for him to engage himself to Mary Hellen — I asked him this Evening for how long he expected the engagement to continue — He said no limited time; perhaps five or six years, till his prospects would warrant his marrying — I gave my consent on a certain condition to which he fully assented. Mrs. Adams went this Evening to Mrs. Frye's — Her child is in a very dangerous state of health. I passed the Evening at home with George, yet confined to his chamber.

31. V:15. ≈ *Day.* For the distribution of the time, like the last Month, with the exception of the sittings to King the Painter — The important labour of the Month has been the preparation of Instructions to R. Rush and to H. Middleton upon the North-west Coast question, and upon the project of a Convention for the regulation of neutral and Belligerent rights.

These are both important transactions, and the latter especially one which will warrant the special invocation of wisdom from above — When I think, if it possibly could succeed, what a real and solid blessing it would be to the human race, I can scarcely guard myself from a Spirit of enthusiasm, which it becomes me to distrust. I feel that I could die for it, with joy, and that if my last Moments could be cheered with the consciousness of having contributed to it, I could go before the throne of omnipotence with a plea for mercy, and with a consciousness of not having lived in vain for the world of mankind. It has been for more than thirty years my prayer to God, that this might be my lot upon Earth — To render signal service to my Country and to my Species — For the specific object, the end and the means I have relied alike upon the goodness of God — What they were or would be I knew not. For "it is not in Man that walketh to direct his steps." I have rendered services to my Country, but not such as could satisfy my own ambition. But this offers the specific object which I have desired — And why should not the hearts of the Rulers of mankind, be turned to approve and establish it? I have opened my Soul to the hope, though with trembling — In the course of this month also I have made a disposal of a large portion of my private property which may have great influence upon the remainder of my days — This too cannot prosper, but with the blessing of Heaven which I implore — In the preparation for my retirement to private life, the main object of my pursuit is a state of mind over which I may preserve entire controul.

———

[August 1823]

9. IV. ≈ At the President's — He received me in his bedchamber, which he was advised not to leave this day — He recommended to me to strike out from the Instruction to Mr. Middleton, upon the neutral and belligerent right project, all the reference to the Holy Alliance: because that Treaty being considered in this Country as a mere hypocritical fraud, any reference to it whatever, would have a turn given to it of odious misconstruction here, against myself. I said my reference to the Holy Alliance was merely an *Argumentum ad Hominem* — It was a call upon the Emperor of Russia, for an Act unequivocally corresponding with the Sentiment that he had

proclaimed — A direct appeal to his Conscience to support by Deeds his Professions, and I had been so far from expressing approbation of his Acts, or those of the Holy Alliance, that I had distinctly alluded to them as liable to censure and warned him of the danger to him that the judgment of posterity would contrast them with his Declaration in the Treaty — The President said he had remarked this guard, but still thought it would be best to omit the reference to the Holy Alliance altogether — I accordingly struck it out, and thereby gave up, what I considered the main Spring of the argument to the Emperor — I relied upon its operation, incomparably more than upon any thing else — The President is often afraid of the skittishness of mere popular prejudices, and I am always disposed to brave them — I have much more confidence in the calm and deliberate judgment of the People than he has — I have no doubt that the Newspaper Scavengers, and Scape-gibbets, whose republicanism runs in filthy streams from the Press, would have attempted to exhibit this reference to the Holy Alliance in a false and odious point of view, but I would have trusted to the good sense of the people to see through their sophistry and their motives — They would have seen in it what was intended — A powerful engine of persuasion; applied to the heart of him whom it was all important to persuade — A bold and direct address to his intimate conscience; and a warning voice to check and controul his acts bearing hard upon the Liberties of Nations. — In this case as in all others for which Mr. Monroe as the Head of his Administration is responsible, I submit my own judgment to his. The only case in which I insisted upon my own, was in the controversy with Jonathan Russell — because in that all the responsibility rested upon me.

———

25. V:30. Morning walk with George — We breakfasted at Walpole, and left Fuller's about 8 O'Clock. At Dedham, while the Carriages stopped I went to the Registry of Deeds, and took two Deeds which I had left there to be recorded in October 1819. We parted at Dedham from our fellow travellers who were going in to Boston — Missed our way, and went to Roxbury Street before turning off to Quincy. Just at one, we arrived at my father's house; and I was deeply affected at meeting him — Within the two last years, since I had seen him, his

eye-sight has grown dim; and his limbs stiff and feeble. He is bowed with age, and scarcely can walk across a room without assistance.

—

[November 1823]
7. V:30. Rainy day. Cabinet Meeting at the President's from half-past one till four. Mr. Calhoun Secretary of War, and Mr. Southard Secretary of the Navy present — The subject for consideration was the confidential proposals of the British Secretary of State George Canning to R. Rush, and the correspondence between them, relating to the projects of the holy alliance upon South-America. There was much conversation, without coming to any definitive point. The object of Canning appears to have been to obtain some public pledge from the Government of the United States, ostensibly against the forcible interference of the Holy Alliance between Spain and South-America; but really or especially against the acquisition to the United States themselves of any part of the Spanish American Possessions — Mr. Calhoun inclined to giving a discretionary power to Mr. Rush to join in a declaration against the interference of the Holy allies, if necessary even if it should pledge us not to take Cuba, or the Province of Texas — Because the Power of G.B. being greater than ours to *seize* upon them, we should get the advantage of obtaining from her the same declaration we should make ourselves — I thought the cases not parallel — We have no intention of seizing either Texas or Cuba — But the inhabitants of either or both may exercise their primitive rights, and solicit an Union with us — They will certainly do no such thing to G. Britain. By joining with her therefore in her proposed declaration; we give her a substantial, and perhaps inconvenient pledge against ourselves, and really obtain nothing in return — Without entering now into the enquiry of the expediency of our annexing Texas or Cuba to our Union, we should at least keep ourselves free to act as emergencies may arise, and not tie ourselves down to any principle which might immediately afterwards be brought to bear against ourselves. Mr. Southard inclined much to the same opinion — The President was averse to any course which should have the appearance of taking a position subordinate to that of Great Britain, and suggested the idea of

sending a special Minister to *protest* against the interposition of
the Holy Alliance — I observed that it was a question for separate consideration whether we ought in any event if invited, to
attend at a Congress of the allies on this subject — Mr. Calhoun
thought we ought in no case to attend. The President referring
to Instructions given before the Congress at Aix-la-Chapelle,
declaring that we would if invited, attend no meeting relative
to South America, of which less than its entire Independence
should be the object, intimated that a similar limitation might
be assumed now. I remarked that we had then not recognized
the South-American Independence ourselves — We would
have been willing to recognize it in concert with the European
allies, and therefore would have readily attended, if invited, a
meeting of which that should have been the object. We could
not now have the same motive — We *have* recognized them.
We are very sure there will be now no Meeting of the Allies
with that object — There would therefore be no use or propriety in resorting to the same limitation — Our refusal to attend
should be explicit and unqualified — To this the President
readily assented — I remarked that the communications recently received from the Russian Minister Baron Tuyll afforded
as I thought a very suitable and convenient opportunity for us
to take our stand against the Holy Alliance, and at the same
time to decline the overture of Great-Britain — It would be
more candid as well as more dignified to avow our principles
explicitly to Russia and France, than to come in as a Cock-boat
in the wake of the British man of War — This idea was acquiesced in on all sides, and my draft for an answer to Baron
Tuyll's Note announcing the Emperor's determination to refuse receiving any Minister from the South-American Governments, was read — Mr. Calhoun objected to two words as
sarcastic — The word *Christian*, annexed to Independent
Nations, and the words *of Peace*, added to the word Minister. I
told him laughing that all the point of my Note was in those
two words, as my object was to put the Emperor in the wrong
in the face of the world as much as possible — The President
proposed one or two other alterations, but after examination
did not insist upon them — But it was thought the best
method of making the profession of our principles would be in
answering that part of Baron Tuyll's communication to me

which was verbal — The intimation of the Emperor's hope that we should continue to observe neutrality, in the contest between Spain and South-America — It was proposed that I should in my written answer to the Baron's written Note, introduce a commentary upon the verbal part of his conferences — The discussion continued till four O'Clock when Mr. Calhoun had an engagement and the Meeting broke up without coming to any conclusion. ≈ Evening at home, writing in part this day's Journal.

———

13. VI. Morning occupied in making a draught of minutes, for the Message of the President, upon subjects under the direction of the Department of State ≈ I took to the President's my draught of minutes and copies of the Instructions to R. Rush, despatched last Summer. I read and left my draught with him — I find him yet altogether unsettled in his own mind, as to the answer to be given to Mr. Canning's proposals — And alarmed far beyond any thing that I could have conceived possible, with the fear that the Holy Alliance are about to restore immediately all South-America to Spain. Calhoun stimulates the panic, and the news that Cadiz has surrendered to the French, has so affected the President that he appeared entirely to despair of the cause of South-America — He will recover from this in a few days, but I never saw more indecision in him — We discussed the proposals of Canning, and I told him if he would decide either to accept or to decline them I would draught a despatch conformable to either decision for his consideration — He said we would talk further about it to-morrow.

———

21. VII. George Johnson was here this morning — His business drags heavily on, and gives me too much reason to fear will terminate in disappointment — The fluctuations of the market render it always precarious — The water fails, as he says, unaccountably — obstacles of various kinds occur — Yet I will not despair, while there is a prospect for hope ≈ I had received a Note from the President, requesting me to attend a meeting of the members of the Administration at one — The meeting lasted till five — I took with me the draft of my despatch to R. Rush in answer to Canning's proposals, with

the President's projected Amendments, and my proposal of
amendment upon amendment — We had a very long discussion upon one phrase, which seemed to me to require none
at-all. The Sentiment expressed was that although we should
throw no impediment in the way of an arrangement between
Spain and her Ex-Colonies by *amicable Negotiation*, we should
claim to be treated by the South-Americans upon the footing
of equal favour with the most favoured Nation — The President had proposed a modifying amendment, which seemed to
admit that we should not object to an arrangement by which
special favours or even a restoration of authority might be
conceded to Spain — To this I strenuously objected, as did
Mr. Calhoun — The President ultimately acceded to the substance of the phrase as I had in the first instance made the
draft; but finally required that the phraseology of it should be
varied — Almost all the other amendments proposed by the
President were opposed, principally by Mr. Calhoun, who
most explicitly preferred my last substituted paragraph, to the
President's projected amendment — The President did not
insist upon any of his amendments, which were not admitted
by general consent; and the final paper though considerably
varied from my original draft, will be conformable to my own
views — The Supplementary Instruction, I had not finished;
but read the part that I had prepared — I mentioned also my
wish to prepare a paper to be delivered confidentially to Baron
Tuyll; and the substance of which I would in the first instance,
express to him in a verbal conference. — It would refer to the
verbal communications recently made by him, and to the Sentiments and Dispositions manifested in the Extract of a despatch
relating to Spanish Affairs, which he lately put into my hands
— My purpose would be in a moderate and conciliatory manner, but with a firm and determined Spirit, to declare our dissent from the principles avowed in those communications — To
assert those upon which our own Government is founded; and
while disclaiming all intention of attempting to propagate
them by force, and all interference with the political affairs of
Europe, to declare our expectation and hope that the European Powers will equally abstain from the attempt to spread
their principles in the American Hemisphere, or to subjugate
by force any part of these Continents to their will — The

President approved of this idea; and then taking up the sketches, that he had prepared for his Message read them to us — Its introduction was in a tone of deep solemnity; and of high alarm — intimating that this country is menaced by imminent and formidable dangers; such as would probably soon call for their most vigorous energies, and the closest union — It then proceeded to speak of the foreign Affairs, chiefly according to the sketch I had given him some days since, but with occasional variations — It then alluded to the recent Events in Spain and Portugal, speaking in terms of the most pointed reprobation, of the late invasion of Spain by France, and of the principles upon which it was undertaken by the open avowal of the king of France — It also contained a broad acknowledgment of the Greeks as an Independent Nation, and a recommendation to Congress to make an appropriation for sending a Minister to them — Of all this Mr. Calhoun declared his approbation — I expressed as freely my wish that the President would reconsider the whole subject, before he should determine to take that course. I said the tone of the Introduction I apprehended would take the Nation by surprize, and greatly alarm them. It would come upon them like a clap of thunder — There had never been in the History of this Nation a period of so deep calm and tranquility as we now enjoyed. We never were upon the whole in a state of peace so profound and secure with all foreign Nations as at this time — This Message would be a summons to arms — To arms against all Europe; and for objects of policy exclusively European, Greece and Spain — It would be as new too in our policy as it would be surprizing — For more than thirty years, Europe had been in convulsions; every Nation almost of which it is composed alternately invading and invaded — Empires, Kingdoms, Principalities, had been overthrown, Revolutionised and counter-revolutionised; and we had looked on, safe in our distance beyond an intervening Ocean, and avowing a total forbearance to interfere in any of the combinations of European Politics. This Message would at once buckle on the harness, and throw down the gauntlet to all Europe — It would have the air of open defiance to all Europe, and I should not be surprized if the first answer to it from Spain, and France, and even Russia, should be to break off their diplomatic intercourse

with us — I did not expect that the quiet which we had enjoyed for six or seven years would last much longer — The aspect of things was portentous; but if we must come to an issue
with Europe, let us keep it off as long as possible — Let us use
all possible means to carry the opinion of the Nation with us;
and the opinion of the world — Calhoun said that he thought
there was not the tranquility that I spoke of: that there was
great anxiety in the thinking part of the Nation — That there
was a general expectation the Holy Alliance would employ
force against South-America; and that it would be proper that
the President should sound the alarm to the Nation. A time
was approaching when all its energies would be needed, and
the public mind ought to be prepared for it — The President
told us confidentially that G. W. Erving had written, praying
that it might be kept secret, because whatever any person
wrote there was reported back against him; but that whatever
might be reported here, we might set it down for certain that
France and the allies, would support Spain in the attempt to
recover her Colonies by force — I observed to the President
that I put very little reliance on any thing written by G.W.
Erving — It might or might not eventuate as he said — But he
knew nothing about the matter, more than was known to the
world; and had views of his own in whatever he wrote — Mr.
Southard said little; but inclined towards my view of the subject — The President finally said that he would draw up two
sketches for consideration, conformable to the two different
aspects of the subject — The President and Mr. Calhoun, intimated the idea that there was a material difference in the Wars
and Revolutions which since the year 1789 to this time have
been raging in Europe; and this last invasion of Spain by
France. That this was a more direct attack upon the popular
principle — And that although no former Message, ever cen-
sured those overthrows and conquests before, yet it might be
very proper to censure this now — The question however is
deferred — Eve at home, writing.

—

27. VI:30. Mr. D. Brent brought me this morning a Note from
the President, with the draft of my observations on the communications recently received from the Russian Minister; advising the omission, of all the paragraphs to which objection had

been made at the Cabinet Meetings; and requesting me to see the Baron de Tuyll immediately. — I directed a copy to be made of the paper omitting all the passages marked by the President for omission, and desired Mr. Brent, to write a Note in my name to the Baron requesting him to call at the Office of the Department at three O'Clock — In the meantime, I went to the President's, and took the draft of my Statement of what has passed between me and the Baron since the 16th of October — I told the President that I had directed the copy to be made out, of the Observations, conformably to his direction — That I cheerfully gave up all the passages marked for omission, excepting one; and that was the second paragraph of the paper, containing the exposition of our principles — That paragraph was in my own estimation, the heart of the paper — All the rest was only a series of deductions from it — The paper received from Baron Tuyll, and to which the Observations were intended for an answer, was professedly an exposition of Principles — I had thought it should be met directly by an exposition of ours. This was done, in three lines, in the paragraph in the question — The first paragraph of my paper stated the fact that the Government of the United States was Republican. The second; what the fundamental principles of this Government were — referring them all, to *Liberty* — *Independence* — *Peace* — These were the principles, from which all the remainder of the paper were drawn — Without them the rest was a fabric without a foundation. The positions taken in the paragraph were true — I could not possibly believe they would give offence to any one — I was sure they would not to the Emperor Alexander, unless he had determined to invade South-America; and if he had, this paper which was to be our protest against it, could not too distinctly set forth the *principles* of our opposition to his design — The object of the paragraph was to set those principles in the broadest and boldest relief — To compress into one sentence, the foundation upon which the mind and heart at once could repose, for our justification of the stand we are taking against the Holy Alliance, in the face of our Country and of Mankind — I had much confidence in the effect of that paragraph; first as persuasion to the Emperor Alexander, and if that failed as our manifesto to the world — I added by way of apology for the solicitude that I felt on this subject, that I considered this as the most important paper that ever went from my hands.

———

[December 1823]

2. VI:30. ≈ In the Evening I called again upon Mr. Clay; and afterwards upon Mr. Gaillard to inform them of the arrangements made for the funeral of Mr. Greuhm — They said it was probable the two Houses would adjourn over the day; without public assignment of the reason — But Clay said he did not know but there might be a debate in the House upon it. He entered also into conversation upon the Message, which he said seemed to be the work of several hands — And that the War and Navy Departments made a magnificent figure in it; as well as the Post-Office — I said there was an account of a full treasury; and much concerning foreign Affairs, which was within the business of the Department of State — He said yes, and the part relating to foreign affairs, was he thought the best part of the Message — He thought the Government had weakened itself and the tone of the Country, by withholding so long the acknowledgment of the South-American Independence, and he believed even a War for it against all Europe, including even England, would be advantageous to us — I told him I believed a War for South-American Independence might be inevitable, and under certain circumstances might be expedient, but that I viewed War in a very different light from him — as necessarily placing high interests of different portions of the Union in conflict with each other, and thereby imminently endangering the Union itself — Not a successful War, he said — But a successful War to be sure created a military influence, and power, which he considered as the greatest danger of War — He said he had thoughts of offering a Resolution, to declare this Country an Asylum for all fugitives from oppression; and to connect with it a proposal for modifying the naturalization Law, to make it more easily attainable — The foreigners in New-York, are petitioning Congress to that effect, and Clay will turn his liberality towards them to account. It was near eleven in the Evening when I got home.

———

[January 1824]

8. VII. Mr. Bradley of Vermont called this morning and introduced Col'l Watson of this City. I called at the President's, and while I was there Mr. Calhoun came with a deputation of five Cherokee Indians — This is the most civilized of all the tribes of North-American Indians. They have abandoned altogether the life of Hunters, and betaken themselves to tillage — These men were dressed entirely according to our manner — Two of them spoke English, with good pronunciation, and one with grammatical accuracy — This was a young man of 23 who has passed three or four years at a missionary School in Connecticut — He interpreted for his father, who made a speech to the President in the figurative Style of Savage Oratory; with frequent recurrence to the idea of the Great Spirit above — They gave us some account of their present Institutions, which are incipient. ≈ This being the Anniversary of the Victory at New-Orleans, we gave an Evening party or Ball to Gen'l Jackson, at which about one thousand persons attended — General Jackson came about eight O'Clock, and retired after supper — The dancing continued till near one in the Morning. The crowd was great and the House could scarcely contain the company — But it all went off in good order, and without accident — The President this Morning excused himself from attending, as I had expected he would — He said that when Mr. Crawford went into Virginia last Summer, he the President had pointedly avoided meeting him — even when he was sick at Governor Barbour's. And at the present moment, if he should depart from his rule of not visiting at private houses, it might be thought he was countenancing one of the Candidates for the next Presidency, while he had so cautiously abstained from giving even seeming countenance to another.

———

30. VII. The day was absorbed by visitors and applications for the vacant office in the Department of State. Col'l R. M. Johnson, Mr. R. King and Mr. Fuller had long Conversations with me concerning the movements of the parties here for the Presidential Succession — Johnson says that Calhoun proposed to him an arrangement by which I should be supported as President, General Jackson as Vice-President; Clay to be

Secretary of State and he himself Secretary of the Treasury —
Not as a bargain or Coalition; but by the common understanding of our mutual friends. I made no remark upon this;
but it discloses the forlorn hope of Calhoun; which is to secure
a step of advancement to himself, and the total exclusion of
Crawford, even from his present Office at the Head of the
Treasury — Johnson said that Governor Barbour, Senator
from Virginia, after a Conversation with him, in which he had
insisted, and Barbour agreed that upon an Election in the
House, should it come there, the vote would be at least two
thirds for me against Crawford, said he had thoughts of giving
in his adhesion to me; which Johnson advised him by all means
to do. Mr. King spoke of the state of Affairs in New-York —
His own views are in some respects biassed by his situation —
He has been heretofore himself a Candidate for the Presidency
— He had at one time during the present Administration
hopes of being the next in Succession — There is a spice of
disappointment in all his opinions — and his grounds of preference now are too much sectional — There is something peculiar in the state of his mind; for it is transparent in his conduct
and discourse that although strenuous for the Northern Man,
he would in the event of his failure, not be without consolation
— King is one of the wisest, and best men among us. But his
own ambition was inflamed by splendid success in early life;
followed by vicissitudes of popular favour, and hopes deferred
till he has arrived nearly at the close of his public career — He
has one Session of Congress to sit in Senate, but talks even
now of resigning. Fuller mentioned the meetings which have
been held and are holding to ascertain the number of the
Members of Congress who deem it inexpedient at this time to
make a Caucus nomination for the next Presidency.

—

[February 1824]
4. VII. ≈ S.D. Ingham called again, and I had a full and explicit conversation with him respecting G.M. Dallas; and generally respecting the treatment of me by Mr. Calhoun and his
friends. The professions of friendship, and the acts of insidious
hostility — The requisitions upon me to dismiss the Democratic Press, and appoint the Franklin Gazette to publish the
Laws in Philadelphia; the vindictive malice of Binns which they

thereby excited against me; the flaunting declaration in the Franklin Gazette, immediately afterwards, that they were under no obligation to me for the appointment — The decided part taken against me by that paper in the controversy with Jonathan Russell, and its frequent ill disguised attacks upon me since — The Courtship of the New-England federalists for Mr. Calhoun. The toast to the Memory of Fisher Ames at the Edgefield dinner to M'Duffie — The newspapers set up in Massachusetts, to support Mr. Calhoun — The smuggled paragraphs, asserting that my friends in New-England, had abandoned me for him, and the panegyric of the Washington Republican upon the Boston Galaxy, a paper for years advertised for Sale to the highest bidder of the Presidential candidates, and which has at last opened a battery of scurrilous abuse upon me, and in avowed support of Mr. Calhoun. I mentioned all these things to him in frankness; but told him they had not the slightest effect upon my opinion with regard to the appointment of Mr. Dallas. He wished to apologize for Norvell, the Editor of the Franklin Gazette, who he said entertained the highest respect for me — And whose appointment had been urged not from any hostility to me — The papers published against me, in the controversy with Russell, he Ingham had disapproved — and had written to Norvell to refuse them; but it happened that before receiving his Letter, Norvell had promised to publish the first, and then could not reject the others — The main foundation of the opposition of the Franklin Gazette and of the Republicans in Pennsylvania, to me, was owing to their seeing that I was supported by Walsh. I told him that Mr. Walsh's support of me had not been solicited by me. It was voluntary and spontaneous; and had been by no means uniform — In the Russell controversy he had been at first against me; and upon other occasions had not been sparing of censure upon me — The friends of Mr. Calhoun had no doubt the right to set him up as a Candidate for the Presidency, and if they chose to promote as the head of an administration, a man whose elevation must of itself operate as a proscription from the Executive of the Nation, of *all* the other men who were distinguished before the Nation, they surely might; but the error seemed to be in supposing that this might be done, without any manifestation of enmity towards them. My complaint was, not that attempts were made to tear my reputation to pieces for the benefit of Mr. Calhoun; but that they were preceded and accompanied by professions of great respect and esteem, and with the expression of earnest desires for harmony and good understanding. He said that it had not been considered that mere age was the decisive qualification for the Presidency. I said certainly not — But ours was practically more a Government of personal consideration and influence, than of written Articles — There was in the Genius of our Institutions a graduated subordination among the persons by whom the Government was administered. Reputation was the basis of our Elections; and the emblem of its organization was a pyramid at the point of which was the Chief, under whom men of high Consideration though not equal to his naturally found their places — Among the sources of this Consideration, Age and Experience had their share; and unless superseded by very transcendent merit, a decisive share — This had never yet been otherwise under our present Constitution. Not a single instance had occurred of a person older than the President of the United States accepting Office as a Head of Department under him — This was not the result of any written Law, but it arose from the natural operation of our system. What the effect of such a departure from it, as the Election of Mr. Calhoun might be, I could not undertake to say; but this I would say; and had said to those of my friends who had spoken to me on the subject; that if the harmony of the Country could be promoted, by setting me altogether aside, I would cheerfully acquiesce in that disposition; and never would be the occasion or the supporter of factious opposition to any Administration whatsoever. Mr. Ingham professed to be satisfied with this exposition of my views and feelings; but as I gave him no reason to expect I could be reconciled to the appointment of Dallas to Mexico, he was doubtless not satisfied with the result of the Meeting — At the Office, Mr. Hicks came and I gave him a Letter to J. S. Wilcocks our Consul at Mexico — I attended in the Evening the Drawing Room at the President's. Mrs. Adams being not very well, did not go. The Assembly was less numerous than at the last. The Judges of the Supreme Court were there. On returning home I found J.W. Taylor at my house, and had a long Conversation with him — He told me that Jesse B. Thomas a Senator from Illinois, had strongly urged upon him the expediency of my acquiescing in the nomination as Vice-President, with Mr. Crawford for the Presidency. He said that Mr. Crawford would certainly be elected. And he spoke of certain members of Congress, as ultimately to vote for him, who appear to be far otherwise disposed at this time. That it was however very desirable that he should carry with him the strength which he would derive from the co-operation of my friends. That from the state of Mr. Crawford's health it was highly probable the duties of the Presidency would devolve upon the Vice-President which had made it necessary to select with peculiar anxiety a person qualified for the contingency which was to be anticipated. That a compliance with the views of Mr. Crawford's friends on this occasion would be rendering them a service, which would recommend me to their future favour and would doubtless secure my election hereafter to the Presidency. Taylor said he had answered, that admitting even the certainty that Mr. Crawford should be elected, that was no sufficient reason, for the acquiescence of my friends in the proposed arrangement. If the election should be carried against them, they will at least have followed their own sense of what was right and fit — They could not place me in subordination to Mr. Crawford without inverting the natural order of things, and placing the North in a position of inferiority to the South — Should they be so placed by the Constitutional voice of the People, they must undoubtedly submit; but they could not consent to be so placed by their own act — Taylor said Thomas had asked him to see him again after thinking on the subject. I said he might tell him then if he thought fit, that he had seen me; and I had told him that I was so satisfied of the inexpediency of a Congressional caucus nomination at this time that I should decline accepting it, were it even for the Presidency — He said he thought it would be better that without referring to me, or to my determination, he should simply state the perseverance of my friends, in the sentiments he had already expressed as being theirs.

———

[March 1824]

12. VII. ≈ Received a Note from the President, requesting the attendance of Mr. Calhoun, Mr. Southard and me at his

house, at ten O'Clock this Morning. We met there accordingly
— The first subject of consultation was a Letter from M'Lane
Chairman of the Committee of Ways and Means to Mr. Crawford, enquiring, whether in consequence of the decease of the
fourth Auditor, any Appropriation for the Salary of that Officer
would be necessary ≈ The next subject submitted for consideration by the President was more important — By a compact
made between the U. States, and the State of Georgia in 1802,
the United States stipulated to extinguish as soon as should be
practicable peaceably and upon reasonable terms the Indian
titles to lands within the State of Georgia. And since that time
many Treaties have been made and many Millions of miles
purchased in fulfilment of the Article — The State of Georgia
continually pressing to obtain more. At last the Cherokees
have come to the determination that they will on no consideration part with any more of their Lands, and their delegation
now here have most explicitly so declared; in answer to a Letter
from the Secretary of War, strongly urging upon them the necessity of a further cession. The answer of the Cherokees was
communicated to the Georgia delegation here; and they have
addressed to the President a Letter of remarks upon the correspondence between the Secretary of War and the Cherokees,
which the President said was an insult. It is in terms of the most
acrimonious reproach against the Government of the United
States, whom it charges almost in terms, with fraud and hypocrisy, while it broadly insinuates, that the obstinacy of the
Cherokees, is instigated by the Secretary of War himself —
Calhoun remarked that it was in the hand-writing of Cobb,
but it was signed by the two Senators Elliott and Ware, and by
all the members of the house from the State, excepting Tattnall who is not here. The question was how it should be
treated — The conclusion was that the President should send
a Message to Congress, with the Correspondence, and an exposition of what has been done by the Government of the
United States in fulfilment of the compact — Calhoun thought
that the message should communicate, but take no notice
of the Letter of the Georgia delegation — I said as the charges of
the Letter could not be overlooked, it was scarcely possible to
avoid a direct allusion to it; and I thought it indispensable,
that it should in substance be fully answered. The President

said it should be answered, and in the tone of defiance best suited to it. Southard said Georgia would find very little support in Congress to such a paper as that. The President said he had never received such a paper — I said it was an issue tendered between Georgia and the Government of the United States — Calhoun dwelt upon its incorrectness with regard to the facts, and I observed it was a peremptory demand to do by force, and upon most unreasonable terms, that which had been stipulated only to be done peaceably, and upon reasonable terms — It was asked what could have kindled this raging fever for Indian Lands — Calhoun thought it was the State system of disposing of them by Lottery — A system which he said was immoral and corrupt. Instigating insatiable cupidity, for Lands; and alternately seized by the conflicting parties as Engines for the advancement of one upon the ruin of the other. I suspected this bursting forth of Georgia upon the Government of the United States was ominous of other Events. We were kept till past 3 at the Presidents.

———

29. VI:45. ≈ Received a Note from the President calling a Cabinet Meeting at one, which I attended. Calhoun, Southard, and Wirt were there — Southard said he had been told that Mr. Crawford had sent the President a Message to inform him that his health was now sufficiently restored to attend Administration Meetings, if he should call him to them — The President said Mr. Crawford might have said this to Dr. Everett, but he had heard nothing of it. There were now two subjects for consultation — The re-nomination of Bates, as Collector at Bristol, Rhode-Island, and the Message on the compact with Georgia, and the Cherokee titles. ≈ On the Georgia compact and Indian Land rights, the President read a new draft of a Message, different from that of the last Meeting — In this, he very distinctly declared his opinion that the Indians cannot with Justice be removed from their Lands within the State of Georgia by force — But after setting forth all that has been done by the Government of the Union, in fulfilment of the compact; the positive refusal of the Cherokees, to cede any more of their lands upon any terms whatever, and the impossibility of devising any other means short of force to prevail upon them to go, there was a new and rather elaborate

argument introduced, of the absolute necessity that the Indians should remove, West of the Mississippi. And after concluding that nothing further could be done by the Executive, there were distinct intimations that something should be done by Congress. I objected that this gave an appearance of incongruity to the message. For it was an issue between the National Executive and the Georgia Delegation; and after taking completely from under them the ground upon which they themselves stood, it gave them new ground to stand upon. It gave them the means of peremptorily claiming something further, and immediately from Congress. And if that was intended, I insisted, that the Executive ought to have some practicable project matured, and requiring nothing but the sanction of Congress to carry it into effect — The President said that no such project was prepared, nor had he any particular measure in view — Five or six years since about one-third part of the Cherokee Nation were prevailed upon to surrender their Lands and remove beyond the Mississippi, and there is now in the City, a deputation from them also, complaining that they are as much disturbed and crowded upon by the whites, as they were before their removal — I asked if it could be supposed that the deputation from the old Georgia Cherokees now here, were ignorant of this, or that they would be encouraged to abandon their old establishments for promises of a new one such as their tribesmen had found West of the Mississippi — Calhoun and Southard, inclined to support my remarks. Mr. Wirt proposed the omission of certain passages directly recommending to Congress to decide upon some measure to be taken. But I thought the proposal of a measure necessarily followed from the purport of the argument, which I thought it would be best to omit altogether. The President said he would consider of it further.

———

31. VI:45. ≈ I attended alone the Drawing-room at the President's — Thinner than usual. Conversations with W. Plumer, Crowninshield, J. W. Taylor, and Burton — All accounts from Albany unfavourable to the Crawford interest, but otherwise uncertain and contradictory — Taylor's Letter from Stewart, holds up Clay as predominant — His conversations with Moore a Calhounite transferred to Jackson — Calhoun's game now is to

unite Jackson's supporters and mine upon *him* for Vice-President — Look out for Breakers!

Day. Rise at 7. Write or read papers till 9–10. Breakfast — Receive visitors, and interruptedly read or write till 1–2. At the Office Daily Mail — Current business, Call at the President's, visitors, reading and writing till 5–6. Home to dine — Evening abroad, with company at home, or at the Theatre till 11–12. about once a week at home, writing — I have received in the course of this Month two hundred and thirty five visitors, which is an average of about eight a day. A half an hour to each visitor occupies four hours a day, but that is short of the average. The interruption to business thus incessantly repeated is distressing; but unavoidable.

> Lord of all Mercy! grant thy aid!
> My Soul, for thy behest prepare,
> Of bliss or bane, the varied shade
> With humble fortitude to bear.
> Submissive to thy Sovereign Will
> And led by thy unerring hand —
> Be mine, thy purpose to fulfill;
> And thine, to bless my native Land!

———

[April 1824]

22. VII. ≈ T. Fuller, member from Massachusetts called late in the Evening — He asked if I had seen a piece in the New-York Patriot, signed Mercury — I had — It asserts that while my friends are boasting of my purity and exemption from intrigue, and pretending that I rejected with indignation; a proposal from Mr. Crawford's friends to support him for the Vice-Presidency, I had been guilty of the same corruption. For that Fuller more than a year since had stated that I had authorised him to offer the Vice-Presidency to Mr. Clay — Fuller was excessively incensed at this paltry electioneering squib, and said he would compel the publisher of the Patriot to give up the author of it, or would prosecute him for a libel. He said it was not only false, but there never had been any thing which could give rise to it — That I had never said one word to him about supporting Clay for the Vice-Presidency — nor he to

any human being. I advised him to be cool. To cause to be published an explicit contradiction of the falsehood; and if upon demand, the author would not avow himself, that would be enough; but that political prosecutions for any thing published in the Newspapers against a public man were in this Country desperate remedies. The juries always favoured the slanderer — Fuller said this was a charge of *corruption*. That I said, if he prosecuted would be explained away — It would be said to have been used only with reference to my supposed fastidious purity. It would be said the fact charged, if true was no Evidence of Corruption. That if I had authorised him to propose to Mr. Clay's friends to support him for the Vice-Presidency, there would have been no corruption in it, and that therefore there was no libel in the charge although the matter stated as fact was not true. I further said, that although I never had authorized any man to make such a proposal to Clay, yet friends of mine, and friends of Clay too had often suggested it to me as desirable; nor is there any thing in it, unconstitutional, illegal or dishonourable. The friends of every one of the Candidates have sought to gain strength for their favourite by Coalition with the friends of others, and to deny very indignantly an imputation of that which is not wrong in itself, is giving the adversary the advantage of fastening upon you a consciousness of wrong where there is none — Fuller seemed still to think he could get the author or publisher of the piece indicted; but I suppose he will not attempt it.

———

[May 1824]

8. VII. ≈ Mr. M'Lean the Postmaster General called — He wrote me some days since a Letter, asking my opinion upon the subject of internal improvement; and a copy of the Resolution offered by me to the Senate on the 23ᵈ of February 1807 — I answered his Letter, and he now came to ask my leave to send a copy of my answer to his brother in the State of Ohio. I told him I had no objection, but wished him only not to suffer it to get into the newspapers — As that would look too much like advertising my opinions — He said he would take care of that — His brother is one of the names on the proposed electoral ticket for Ohio; and writes that he is sanguine of success — We know so little of that in futurity which is best for

ourselves, that whether I ought to *wish* for success, is among the greatest uncertainties of the Election. Were it possible to look with philosophical indifference to the Event, that is the temper of mind to which I should aspire — But who can hold a fire brand in his hand, by thinking of the frosty Caucasus — To suffer without feeling, is not in human nature, and when I consider that to me alone of all the Candidates before the Nation, failure of success, would be equivalent to a vote of censure by the Nation upon my past service, I cannot dissemble to myself, that I have more at stake upon the result than any other individual in the Union — Yet a man qualified for the elective Chief Magistracy of ten Millions of People, should be a man, proof alike to prosperous and to adverse fortune. If I am able to bear success, I must be tempered to endure defeat — He who is equal to the task of serving a Nation as her chief-ruler, must possess resources of a power to serve her even against her own will — This is the principle that I would impress indelibly upon my own mind; and for the practical realization of which in its proper result, I look to wisdom and strength from above.

———

10. VII. Dr. Thornton called upon me this morning to say that he had prepared a Book to be deposited in the Congress Library at the Capitol; to contain the subscriptions of all persons in the Service of the United States at Washington, for the Greeks — His project was that every individual would subscribe one day's pay — He had requested the subscription of the President, who told him he would consult the members of his Administration upon the propriety of his subscribing — The Doctor hoped I should advise him to it — The Secretaries of War and the Navy had said they would subscribe, if the President and I did — Lord Eldon the English Chancellor had subscribed a hundred Pounds Sterling, and even the Quakers in England, had subscribed upwards of 7000 pounds — The Greeks were in great want of it, and deep distress — There was a tremendous force of Turks, going against them, but the Bashaw of Egypt had declared himself independent of the Sultan, and there was no doubt that by the diversion he would make the cause of the Greeks would be triumphant. I told him he ought to have a subscription book number two, for the Bashaw of Egypt — at which he laughed, and said yes, it would

be very proper — But to answer seriously his question I told him I should not subscribe for the Greeks, nor advise the President to subscribe. We had objects of distress to relieve, at home, more than sufficient to absorb all my capacities of contribution; and a subscription for the Greeks, would in my view of things be a breach of neutrality, and therefore improper. The Doctor said he was very sorry to find in me instead of an assistant as he had expected an opponent, and urged all the arguments of the crusading Spirit, applicable to the case, but I was inflexible. While he was flourishing for the Greeks and their cause, Mr. Benton, Senator from Missouri came in, and introduced the Revd. Salmon Giddings of St. Louis, who had a subscription Book for building a Presbyterian Church at that place — I subscribed for that instead of the Greeks.

———

14. VII. Mr. R. King called this Morning on me, and said he was apprehensive it would be absolutely necessary for the Senate to annex in some form a limitation to the Slave-trade Convention now before them — He was much averse to it himself, and thought it very absurd — But there was no reasoning with fear — The members from some of the Southern States, had taken a panic, at the late Speeches in the British Parliament, looking to the abolition of Slavery, and were exceedingly adverse to forming any concert with the British Government whatever, in reference to the subject of Slavery — The question was whether the limitation should be for a term of years; or that the Convention may at any time be annulled, on either side, by giving a notice of days or Months — I said of the two evils, the limitation for a term of years would be the least — But either would be highly pernicious — That it would defeat the joint attempt to influence other Nations to make the Slave-trade piracy — For how absurd that we should try to prevail upon all other Nations, to declare it piracy, when they might retort upon us that we have shrunk from our own obligations, and made it a piracy for a term of years, reserving ourselves the right of repealing our own Law — I said also that *any* limitation would be peculiarly ungracious from us, the whole project being our own, and adopted at our instance by Great-Britain — of all which Mr. King himself is fully sensible.

———

19. VII. Col'l Dwight, a member of the House from Massachusetts, called to make a morning visit. Mr. Mower of New-York was here, as I inferred from his conversation to renew, in behalf of De Witt Clinton, the attempt to obtain for General Jackson, the electoral vote of New-York for the Presidency — He told me that he had seen Mr. Clinton, and a particular and intimate friend of his (Ambrose Spencer) who thoroughly approved of all the arrangements of Mower here — and were decidedly of opinion that there was, *in the Legislature*, no chance for any person against Mr. Crawford but me — Mr. Clinton was however doubtful, whether by the purchase of Young, of Peter B. Porter, and with them of Clay's party, Mr. Crawford would not ultimately prevail in the Legislature — But Mr. Crary and Solomon Van Renssalaer were confident that Crawford could under no circumstances whatever obtain the vote of New-York — But Governor Yates had determined to call the Legislature together and recommend to them the passage of an Act, giving the choice of Electors to the People. The Proclamation was already prepared, and would issue immediately after the adjournment of Congress — It would instantly kill two men, William H. Crawford and Henry Clay — and if the election went before the people, no man could stand in competition with General Jackson. The 8th of January, and the Battle of New-Orleans was a thing that every man would understand, and Mr. Clinton had told him that General Jackson, would beat him, Clinton himself, before the People of New-York by 33⅓ per cent. Mower added that the Editor of the Columbian Observer, Jackson's paper at Philadelphia, had mentioned to him that my father's Administration, and federalism would be objections against me. He said he supposed I knew this — I said I had heard of it. ≈

20. VI:30. Mr. M'Kean, a member of the House of Representatives from Pennsylvania came to take leave, and introduced to me an acquaintance of his, a Mr. Eldridge, from the State of New-York — Mr. Plumer was here, and we had long conversation upon political topics generally — He shewed me a Letter, from General Cocke of Tennessee to him, not signed, enquiring, concerning conversations at the boarding house at which they both lodged in 1821 — concerning my opinions the

year before upon the restriction of Slavery in Missouri. Cocke
intimates that he had understood Plumer to have said, I was in
favour of the restriction — And Plumer said he had a Letter
from Hill, the Editor of the New-Hampshire Patriot now a
thorough Crawfordite, saying he had formerly understood
Plumer to have told him that I was in favour of the restriction,
and now it was published that I had been against it. Plumer
said he very indistinctly recollected, both the conversations to
which Cocke referred, and any thing that had passed between
him and me on the subject — The object of Cocke, was to get
an electioneering weapon against me for the Southern Country, and that of Hill to get one against me for the North, and
also one against Plumer himself. — Plumer said Barton, one of
the Missouri Senators told him that Cocke had been all this
Session at him to get a certificate from him, about those Conversations; but that Barton, considering the whole controversy
as past and gone by, had refused to give him. Plummer said he
had written to judge Archer, who had also been present at the
boarding house conversations to enquire of his recollections
concerning them; and he asked me for mine, of what my opinions had been — I told him that the only conversation I recollected to have had with him on the first Missouri question,
that of the Restriction was on the 23^d of February 1820 and I
read to him the account of it given at the time, in my diary of
that date. He said he particularly recollected the distinction I
had drawn between a restriction upon Illinois, and one upon
Missouri, and wished me to give him a copy of the extract
from my Diary which I promised — Both Houses of Congress
have agreed to adjourn this day week; and Plumer still thinks
the investigating Committee will report in favour of Crawford
upon Edwards's charges, avoiding all research into the attack
of Crawford upon him ≈ Walter Forward, member of the
House, from Pittsburgh Pennsylvania, came, he said, by the
advice of some of my friends, to ask me, what were my opinions upon the subject of the Tariff, and the protection of
manufactures — He said it was a subject of great interest
among his Constituents, and he knew he should be enquired of
by many of them concerning my opinions with reference to it
— I told him I had no desire either to obtrude, or to withhold
them — I was glad the Tariff bill had passed, though I had no

other knowledge of its details, than had been elicited in the debate; and had formed no decisive opinion upon them — I hope its operation would be satisfactory to those whose interests it was particularly adapted to promote without being oppressive upon the agricultural, and commercial interests as had been apprehended — I was cautioned to distrust Forward, by my Pittsburg Correspondents two years ago — He attended the Caucus last February and voted there for Crawford — Since then, my correspondents themselves have come out; held a public meeting, and nominated Crawford; and now Forward comes and asks me these questions — for what? — n'importe. ≈ I received a note from the President expressing great solicitude for the fate of the Convention before the Senate — I went over to his house, and he said he would send a Message to the Senate concerning it. I advised him to send with it a copy of the last note concerning it received from Mr. Addington which he said he would; and he asked me to draw up and send him this Evening such observations as I might think proper to introduce into the Message — On returning to the Office, finding all the Clerks gone, I sent for Mr. Ironside, who came and made out a copy of Mr. Addington's Note — Wyer was at the Office — On leaving it, I met Mr. Mills a Senator from Massachusetts, and asked him how the Convention stood in Senate — He said he thought it would be rejected; which he greatly regretted. I told him the President would send in a Message upon it to-morrow — Mills said, he wished to Heaven he would; for nothing else would save it.

———

23. VII. Mr. George Hay, called this Morning, to enquire from the President concerning the decision of the Senate upon the Convention, the substance of which I told him; mentioning the modifications and exceptions which Col'l Taylor had spoken of, as having been adopted. Mr. Hay seeing this Book on my Table, and observing that he had seen it almost always on my table enquired jestingly whether it was Bishop Burnet's History of his own Times — I said perhaps it might be. At least I believed it to contain the most complete materials for the History of Mr. Monroe's Administration extant — And I added that I proposed to devote the leisure of my life hereafter to that design — But the Conditions of my undertaking it

were Life, Health, and Leisure — And upon the form I had
not yet seriously reflected — He said it was a pity that Mr.
Monroe had not kept a Diary — a very brief one in comparison
with mine would have sufficed — But he now remembers
nothing as to time and circumstance — Mr. Hay spoke as
he always does with extreme bitterness of Mr. Jefferson, whom
he declares to be one of the most insincere men in the world. He
reminded me of a Letter written by Mr. Jefferson to Mr. Monroe in 1818–19 upon my controversial papers with Spain and
relating to the Seminole War. They were in a style even of extravagant encomium — Precisely at the same time, Hay says,
Ritchie of Richmond told him that Mr. Jefferson had spoken
of the same papers in terms of severe reprobation, to a Gentleman from whom he had it — Hay said he told Ritchie that that
Gentleman *lied* — but he knew better — the Gentleman was
Edward Coles, and he had told the truth. But Mr. Jefferson!
— His enmity to Mr. Monroe was inveterate, though disguised,
and he was at the bottom of all the opposition to Mr. Monroe
in Virginia. ≈

24. VI:45. ≈ Hayden of New-York, and M'Duffie of South
Carolina, members of the house, came to take leave. M'Duffie,
having reference to the Presidential Election said he was returning to Carolina, and as there might be in the Legislature
of that State a contested support of Mr. Crawford and of me,
he should be glad, if I had no objection to stating them, to
know my sentiments upon the Tariff policy. I told them freely
— That it was one of those subjects, in which great opposing
interests were to be conciliated by a Spirit of mutual accommodation and concession — I was satisfied with the Tariff-bill
as it has passed, because it appeared to me to have been elabo-
rated precisely to that point. I thought I had seen in it an admirable illustration of the practical operation of our National
Government. The two parties had contested every inch of the
ground between them with great ardour and ability; and the
details of the bill had finally brought them to questions decided by the casting vote of the presiding Officer in each house;
and an adjustment by conference between the two houses —
With the result it was reasonable to expect that both parties
would be satisfied. M'Duffie appeared to be well satisfied with

it himself, and he said that the final vote upon it in the house gave a majority of fifty votes in its favour — I told him that there was another subject, upon which my opinions had been greatly misrepresented in the Southern Country, with a view to excite local prejudices against me. It was upon the Slave question generally and the Missouri Restriction particularly — My opinion had been against the proposed restriction in Missouri, as contravening both the Constitution, and the Louisiana Treaty. This was the first Missouri question — The second was upon an Article introduced into the Constitution of the State of Missouri, which I thought contrary to the Constitution of the United States. I then stated explicitly what my opinions had been upon both questions, and noticed the artifice of the misrepresentation which from my opposition to the Article in the Missouri Constitution inferred my having favoured the restriction. I added that the Article of the Missouri Constitution required the Legislature of that State to do precisely what the Legislature of his own State of South-Carolina, had since done — and which Judge William Johnson, a native and Citizen of the State itself had pronounced to be contrary to the Constitution of the United States — M'Duffie said he had no doubt it was so; and was very glad I had given him this explanation.

———

26. VII. ≈ I called upon Col'l Taylor, the Senator from Virginia, and mentioned to him the paragraph in the National Intelligencer of this Morning, stating that by a Rule of the Senate, no Extracts from their executive Journal could be taken; and that the removal of the injunction of Secresy was only with respect to the facts, and not to the documents — Taylor said it must be a trick to evade the publication; but that was not the intention of the Senate, and he would see to have it rectified — Col'l Taylor told me he should leave the City to return home to-morrow. He spoke therefore freely upon the Presidential Election — The Legislature of Virginia he said had been *managed* into a declaration in support of Mr. Crawford, as the Caucus Candidate; and the State would support him if he continued on the list of Candidates — But he was again ill — rumours were afloat that he had suffered a paralytic affection of the tongue, and since Sunday had been quite or

nearly speechless — It was doubtful whether he would recover; at least so as to be sustainable for a Presidential Candidate — The State of Virginia would be compelled to look elsewhere, and he felt perfectly sure that neither Mr. Clay nor General Jackson could obtain the vote of the State — The Richmond Junto would attempt to bring up Clay; but they could not succeed, and if the choice should come to the House of Representatives I might take it for a certainty that the vote of the Virginia delegation would be neither for Jackson nor Clay — He thought every thing depended upon the State of New-York, and he had not a doubt that Virginia would declare for me, if New-York should do so. That event however is now less probable than it was three Months since — I told Col'l Taylor what I knew of the state of the question, in every part of the Union: Prospects every where — Nothing to be relied upon any where.

———

[July 1824]

31. V. We had intended to make a party this day, to the great Falls of the Potowmac; but the arrival of the President last Evening in the City; and the great heat of the day induced a postponement of it ≈ At eleven O'Clock I went with Mr. Everett to the Presidents; who half an hour afterwards received the deputations of Indians, who have recently arrived in the City — They are of six tribes, among the most savage of the desert — part of them all but naked — They were Saukeys or Sturgeois, Musqukeys or Foxes, Piankashaws or Mianicas, Pah-a-ges or Ioways, the people seen in a fog — Menomine or Wild Oats, Chippeways, and Nacatas or Sioux's, the amicable people — They speak five different languages, and the discourse between the President and them was rendered by as many interpreters — For the Sauks and Foxes there was a double interpretation, first into French, and thence into English — The President made a very short speech of welcome to them, which was answered with like brevity, by a principal chief of each tribe — There were among them three Squaws and one female child five or six years old — In the speeches of the chiefs there was much gravity, and painful earnestness — They were mostly painted red; but one chief had his whole face coloured with yellow Ochre — Mrs. Southard and Mrs. Wirt, with their daughters,

Old Mrs. Calhoun, were there as Spectators, and many others. C. W. King the Painter among the rest ≈

Day. I rise between five and six; and when the tide serves swim between one and two hours in the Potowmack — Breakfast about nine, then write or meditate, or receive visitors till one or two. Attend at my Office till six; then home to dine — Take an evening walk of half an hour, and from ten to eleven retire to bed — There are eight or ten Newspapers of extensive circulation published in various parts of the Union, acting in close concert with each other, and pouring forth continual streams of Slander upon my character and reputation, public and private — No falsehood is too broad, and no insinuation too base for them; and a great portion of their calumnies, are of a nature, that no person could shew or even assert their falsehood but myself — As the Presidential Election approaches, numerous Correspondents from every quarter, write me Letters professing good will, or enquiring of my opinions, from men, most of them entirely unknown to me; I answer very few; and perhaps ought to answer none of them — Particular friends write to me, by way of consultation, and of anxiety; and they can seldom be answered with entire Freedom. The result is a great waste of time, and of mental occupation upon subjects personal to myself, to the necessary neglect of public business, and detriment to the public service — I have no reason to hope to be released from this state of trial for many months to come — To pass through it with a pure heart, and a firm Spirit, is my duty and my prayer.

———

[August 1824]

12. V:30. Morning undisturbed — Letter from P. U. S. Wyer and Watkins at the Office — Ride after dinner with Mrs. Adams. Walk with G. Hay, who afterwards passed an hour with me — He told me that the President had lately received an anonymous Letter, in a disguised hand and affecting false spelling; but undoubtedly from an able hand; advising him to dismiss all the members of his Administration, except Mr. Crawford — Calhoun because he is presumptuous, and extravagant — Southard; to go and keep School in New-Jersey — Wirt, because he is treacherous, and no real friend to Mr. Monroe; and me, because I despise his abilities — Hay said he did not consider Mr. Crawford as a member of the

Administration at all — and he persists in thinking his state of health desperate — This is prejudice —

—

28. V:30. Swam alone; to the Bridge and back, in an hour and 25 minutes, against a strong tide, much the same as yesterday. — This is the tenth day in succession, of my Potowmack Baths, with the morning tides — Five days before the New-Moon; the day of the New Moon, and four days after. It was probably my last bath in the Potowmack, at least if I should go next week upon my Eastern tour — For on my return the bathing Season will be past, and I shall probably never pass another Summer in this City.

—

31. VI. ≈ *Day*. The distribution of my time differs not from that of the last Month. The bitterness and violence of Presidential electioneering increases as the time advances. The uncertainty of the event continues as great as ever. It seems as if every liar and calumniator in the Country was at work day and night to destroy my character — It does not surprize me; because I have seen the same species of ribaldry year after year heaped upon my father, and for a long time upon Washington — But it is impossible to be wholly insensible to this process while it is in operation — It distracts my attention from public business, and consumes precious time — I have finally concluded to take a Month of Holiday to visit my father, and dismiss Care.

—

[September 1824]
3. VII. Mrs. Adams concluded to go with me to Quincy: and we took the Stage for Brunswick at ten this morning, distance 28 miles. We arrived at Brunswick at 3 in the afternoon. Steam-boat *Legislature*. Followed immediately by the Thistle, of the opposition line — There was a great crowd of Passengers, and the deck was covered with barrels and baskets of peaches; going to the New-York market. Among the passengers were several who recognized me; and the market-man, insisted upon my accepting two or three of his peaches as a brother yankee. He told me his name was Barrett. That he came from Vermont, and his father had been of Boston. Mr. Dufief the author of the Grammar and Dictionary, likewise recognized, and spoke to me. There was a race between the two boats; and

in the narrowest parts of the Raritan river, for about half an hour the bow of the Thistle, was within ten feet of our Stern, both going at a rate of at least ten miles an hour. As soon as there was width of passage for both Boats, the Thistle passed us and reached New-York before us a few minutes. We landed about 7 in the Evening, and came to the City Hotel — From the competition between the two lines, the fare between Philadelphia and New-York is reduced to 2 dollars and the passage from Brunswick to N.Y. to 12½ cents.

———

6. VII. ≈ At about eleven we took a Hack, and came out with George to my father's House at Quincy. I found my Son Charles here; it being vacation time at Cambridge. Mr. Degrand came out in the Evening. The infirmities of age have much increased upon my father since I was here last year — His sight is so dim that he can neither write nor read — He cannot walk without aid; and his hearing is partially affected. His memory yet remains strong; his judgment sound; and his interest in conversation considerable.

———

8. VI. ≈ The remainder of this day I passed in Conversations with my father. He bears his condition with fortitude; but is sensible to all its helplessness. His mind is still vigorous; but cannot dwell long upon any one subject. Articles of news, and of political speculation in the Newspapers are read to him; on which he remarks with sound discernment. He receives some Letters, and dictates answers to them — In general the most remarkable circumstance of his present state, is the total prostration of his physical powers, leaving his mental faculties scarcely impaired at-all.

———

20. VI:15. George went to Boston in the Stage. Mrs. Adams was very unwell, and confined to her chamber — I walked in the burying-yard and viewed, the Granite tombstones, erected over the graves of my ancestors, by my father — Henry Adams, the first of the family who came from England — Joseph Adams Senior, and Abigail Baxter his wife. Joseph Adams junior and Hannah Bass, his second wife — John Adams, senior my father's father, and Susanna Boylston his wife — Four Generations; of whom very little more is known than is

recorded upon these Stones. There are three succeeding Generations of us, now living. — Pass another century, and we shall all be mouldering in the same dust, or resolved into the same elements — Who then of our posterity shall visit this yard? — And what shall he read engraved upon the Stones? — This is known only to the Creator of all — The record may be longer — May it be of as blameless lives.

———

24. VI:15. Visit from Col'l Trumbull. This day we took our departure, to return to Washington — I took leave of my father, with a heavy and foreboding heart. Told him I should see him again next year. Came with Mrs. Adams in to Boston to Mr. Cruft's — My visit to my father has only been of 18 days, during three-fourths of which I have been called away; spending only the Nights at his house, and parts of the Morning. Mr. Webster called upon me at Mr. Cruft's. I had a long Conversation with him; chiefly on political subjects. ≈ On the fifth of next Month, my Son George, is to be admitted as an Attorney at the Court of Common Pleas. He has been for the last year reading Law with Mr. Webster, who this day, made a friendly proposal to him, which may hereafter be of service to George — But for the ensuing Winter, George proposes to go in to the Office of Mr. Cook, an Attorney, in considerable practice; and with a view to acquiring the forms of practice — I leave him with an anxious feeling for his welfare and success in life.

———

[October 1824]
1. V:30. ≈ At 2 O'Clock we embarked, Elizabeth C. Adams and I, in the Steamboat, and at seven in the Evening, arrived at Philadelphia. On board the boat I met, my old School-mate Jesse Deane — he was the person who had yesterday accosted me from the wharf at New-York, with Mr. Mumford; and whom I did not then recognize — He was now accompanied by his daughter Mrs. Alden, and her husband — The last time I had seen Mr. Deane was in August 1785 at Hartford, which is also now his residence. We had a long conversation in the Boat, and told over to each other the tales of our Childhood, in the Boston Frigate, and at the Schools of Le Coeur and Pechigni. ≈

2. VI. Called this Morning before breakfast again upon Gen'l La Fayette; he had not risen; but a few minutes after sent me

word he was rising and wished to see me — I went immediately, and found him in his bedchamber, dressing — In his breakfast chamber, I met also his Son, George Washington, and his Secretary Mr. Le Vasseur ≈ I told General La Fayette, that I should call on him to-morrow Morning, and introduce to him, my old School-mate Jesse Deane.

———

5. VII. Morning visit from Major Jackson — Mr. John Vaughan called upon me, and I went with him to the Academy of the fine arts. Mr. Hopkinson the President, delivered Diploma's to General La Fayette and his Son, as honorary members — I met there Mrs. Meredith, and part of her family. Thence went with Mr. Vaughan to the Athenaeum — and thence to the State House. General La Fayette was received in the Hall of Independence — so called from being that where the Congress of the Confederation used to meet, and whence the Declaration of Independance issued — Its interior has however since been entirely altered — From the Hall, General La Fayette went upon the Steps of the South-front door of the State house, where the Children of the Schools, passed in review before him. 2250 girls, and 1800 boys, chiefly from seven to fourteen years of age — There were several Addresses — numerous emblematic and mottoed banners — one Song — And a speech in French by General Cadwalader's son; a lad of about fourteen — Some of the teachers came up the steps and shook hands with the General; and many of the children, especially of the girls, succeeded, though against the previously announced regulation, and in spite of much opposition, in obtaining the same favour. This procession took up nearly three hours during which the General declined being seated, or covered, even with an Umbrella.

———

7. VI:30. The Night was fine, and we rose this Morning in sight of North-Point. We had barely time to Breakfast; when four Steam-Boats, crowded with Passengers came down from the City to meet, and escort the General — There was great shouting and cheering at the Meeting; and we proceeded up the river with the four Boats, two in front and two in rear of ours and at equal distances — We landed in barges at Fort M'Henry — The barge in which the General went, and in

which I accompanied him was rowed by six Captains of Merchant vessels — At the Fort the General was received by Col'l Hindman the Commandant in handsome military Style. Col'l Jones, General Macomb and Major Vandeventer were present — The Tent used by General Washington during the revolutionary War, borrowed from Mr. Custis of Arlington was spread there, and beneath it the General was met by Governor Stevens of Maryland who addressed him in a respectable Speech, which he answered with his customary felicity — Mr. Charles Carroll of Carrollton, one of the three surviving signers of the Declaration of Independence, Col'l John E. Howard, one of the highly distinguished Officers of the Revolutionary War, and several other veterans of the same class were there; all deeply affected by the Scene, which was purely pathetic.

———

[November 1824]
Wednesday 10 November — Cabinet Meeting — Present W. H. Crawford, J. C. Calhoun, Sam'l L. Southard and J. Q. Adams — Subject of Consideration the Slave-trade Convention with G. B. I read the despatches N. 11 and 12 of the separate series from R. Rush — and my drafts of a public, and of a Secret and confidential despatch to him — Also a note from Mr. Addington, the British Chargé d'Affaires, announcing his receipt of a full Power to conclude a new Convention, with the single addition of the words "of America" to that sanctioned by the Senate — The opinion was unanimous against acceding to the proposal for concluding a new Convention; at least for the present ≈ Mr. Crawford told twice over the Story of President Washington's having at an early period of his Administration gone to the Senate, with a project of a Treaty to be negotiated, and been present at their deliberations upon it — They debated it, and proposed Alterations, so that when Washington left the Senate chamber, he said he would be damned if he ever went there again. And ever since that time, Treaties have been negotiated by the Executive, *before* submitting them to the consideration of the Senate — The President said he had come in to the Senate about eighteen months after the first organization of the present Government; and then heard that something like this had occurred ≈ This was the first Cabinet Meeting at which Mr. Crawford had attended since last April. His articulation is yet

much affected, and his eye-sight impaired. But his understanding remains, except with some deficiencies of memory, and ignorance of very notorious facts — probably because he was many months unable to read with his own eyes.

———

[December 1824]

15. VI:30. ≈ A. H. Everett called; and we attended the first Commencement of the Columbian College at Dr. Laurie's Church. ≈ The exercises closed before two O'Clock — I was invited to dine at Dr. Stoughton's house at the College at four. In the interval I attended at the Office — Gen'l Brown was there, and gave me to read a part of a Letter from Ambrose Spencer, late Chief Justice of New-York, who thinks he will be elected Senator from the State of New-York with little opposition. Brown spoke in strong terms of Calhoun's duplicity to him; and repeated his wishes that there might be a good understanding between De Witt Clinton and me, and he intimated a desire that Mr. Clinton might be a member of the next Administration. I told him again that with regard to the motives which he urged, the only person to be convinced was Mr. Clinton himself. That as to the formation of an Administration, I had never thought the probability of my election sufficient to warrant me in thinking about it, at-all — If the case should occur, it must be considered with reference to a system, comprizing all the great public interests. I could not say how I should form my Administration if I should have one to form; but Mr. Clinton already knew my opinion of his Talents and Services — It was for him to determine how far it might be for his interest to maintain towards me the attitude of a competitor, or otherwise — Wyer came also to the Office, and told me that he had it from good authority; that Mr. Clay was much disposed to support me, if he could at the same time be useful to himself — and Wyer wished much to bring Mr. R. W. Meade and me to a good Understanding — I had not time to listen to him — Mr. A. H. Everett went with me to the dinner at Dr. Staughton's — Gen'l La Fayette, Mr. Clay, James Barbour and R. M. Johnson, Mr. Calhoun and Gen'l Dearborn were there. The President declined going — I had conversation at dinner with Mr. Clay.

———

17. V:15. Rain Storm, the whole day. At the Office, Visits from
W. Kelly, Senator from Alabama — Letcher, member of H.R.
from Kentucky; and G. B. English — Letcher came ostensibly,
with a claim of an assistant to the Marshal of Kentucky, for
additional compensation for his service in taking the Census of
1820. But his apparent main object was to talk about the Presidential Election. The account was yesterday received of the
choice of Electors in Louisiana, by the Legislature; from which
it is rendered almost certain that three of the votes have been
for General Jackson; probably four; and perhaps all five — but
certainly none for Mr. Clay — This leaves Mr. Crawford with
41 and Mr. Clay with 37 electoral votes; Mr. Crawford therefore will, and Mr. Clay will not be one of the three persons
from whom the House of Representatives, voting by States,
will be called to choose a President. Mr. Letcher is an intimate
friend of Mr. Clay's, and lodges at the same house with him.
He expects that after the result is known that Mr. Clay cannot
be voted for in the house, there will be meetings of the People
in the several Counties, instructing their members to vote for
Jackson; and perhaps that similar Instructions will be sent on
by their Legislature — These he supposes will be gotten up, by
what they call the *Relief* party, in the politics of the State; and
by men like Rowan, Barry and Bibb, secondary leaders of the
State, not daring to oppose Clay openly on account of his own
popularity in the State, but seizing upon the first opportunity
afforded them indirectly to put him down — Letcher is evidently alarmed at this; and in the midst of strong professions
of independence, and of indifference about retaining his Seat,
is plainly not prepared to act definitively in opposition to the
will of his Constituents — He intimated that the Relief party
were in fact hostile to Mr. Clay — That of the Kentucky delegation here, a large portion were warmly attached to him
— That lately speaking of what might ensue here, he had expressed the wish to go in harmony with his friends; which
Letcher said he interpreted as a wish that his friends would go
in harmony with him. Col'l R. M. Johnson Letcher thinks is
warmly of the Relief party; and as to the Presidency determined
to be at all Events on the strongest side — I observed to
Letcher that Col'l R. M. had candidly told me so himself —
Letcher wished to know what my Sentiments towards Clay

were; and I told him without disguise that I harboured no hostility against him — that whatever of difference there had been between us, had arisen altogether from him and not from me — I adverted to Jonathan Russell's attack upon me, which I said I believed Mr. Clay had been privy to, and countenanced — But having completely repelled that attack, I felt no animosity against any person concerned in it — Letcher said Clay's friends thought he had been wrong in his Letter against me, concerning that affair — It was written in a moment of excitement — He was sure Clay felt now no hostility to me. He had spoken respectfully of me, and was a man of sincerity — Of the 14 Electors of Kentucky, seven voted for Calhoun as Vice-President; and this vote I thought, and Letcher fully concurred in the opinion was more hostile to Clay, than any vote for Jackson as President could be — It held up Calhoun as a future competitor against Clay, and thereby postponed all his prospects indefinitely. The drift of all Letcher's discourse was much the same as Wyer had told me; that Clay would willingly support me, if he could thereby serve himself, and the substance of his *meaning* was that if Clay's friends could *know*, that he would have a prominent share in the Administration, that might induce them to vote for me, even in the face of Instructions — But Letcher did not profess to have any authority from Clay for what he said, and he made no definite propositions. He spoke of his interview with me as altogether confidential; and in my answers to him I spoke in mere general terms.

——

22. VIII. An Irishman by the name of Garry applied to me for employment as a teacher of the Greek and Latin languages: he brought only one paper as a recommendation; and that quite equivocal. A Mr. Welles who gives Lectures upon Eloquence came with a subscription paper, and desired my attendance at one of his Lectures this Evening. Visits from Mr. Vance of Ohio, Mr. Lawrence of New-York — Mr. Newton of Virginia with a Captain Drummond and from Mr. James Barbour Senator from that State — with whom I had a confidential conversation of more than two hours upon the prospects of the Presidential Election — He spoke at first of papers relating to the Piracies, which I had sent him as Chairman of the

Committee of Foreign Relations of the Senate, and for copies of which there is now a Call by Resolution of that body. He soon however introduced the other topic, and freely stated to me his own impressions, and what he believed to be those of a majority of the Virginia Delegation in the House of Representatives — Their first choice had been Mr. Crawford. The Electors of the State had voted for him, and a majority of the People of the State were favourable to him. The representation of the State in the House would vote at first for him; and adhere to him, as long as they could hope for success; but if they should find that impracticable, their next preference would be for me — He had no doubt this was the feeling of the people of the State — That I was much more popular there than General Jackson, or even than Mr. Clay, though he was one of their own natives. He said he thought it would be Treason to the Constitution, to hold out and prevent an election by the House until the fourth of March, so as to give the actual Presidency to the Vice-President. He asked if I thought my friends in the house would not, if they must make a choice, prefer Mr. Crawford to General Jackson — I said I believed they would not make an option, but would adhere to me, until they should obtain a majority of States, or that one should be made against them — He said something about a moral majority of votes in New-York for Mr. Crawford; but he did not press much this argument, nor did I think it deserved waste of time in refuting it — He spoke of my Letter, jointly with Mr. Calhoun, Mr. M'Lean and Mr. Wirt, relative to the 5th of July dinner, as having produced an impression against me, very strong in Virginia; by its appearance as if I had joined in a combination, against Mr. Crawford. I gave him the same explanation of that Event as I had already given to A. Dickins: assuring him that I had on that occasion not acted in hostility to Mr. Crawford; but to avoid being made to partake in a public insult to Mr. Edwards. I said that if it was to do over again, I thought I should do the same. I had been placed in a difficult situation, and if I had erred, it had been an error of judgment, and not of intention hostile to Mr. Crawford. He then passing to matters of greater importance enquired of my Sentiments concerning the Tariff and Internal Improvements; which I gave him with perfect Candour — I said that the ultimate principle of my system with reference to the great interests of the Country was *conciliation* and not *collision* — I was satisfied with the Tariff as now established, and should if any change in it should be desired incline rather to reduce than to increase it — There was in my opinion no Constitutional question involved in the discussion — The revenue was abundant, and the protection to manufactures adequate to their fair claims for support — and if the Tariff should be found to bear hard upon the agricultural and commercial interests, I should incline to an alleviation of it in their favour — As to internal improvements, my opinions had been published in most of the newspapers, in extracts of Letters from me, and had no doubt been seen by him — Since the Act of Congress establishing the Cumberland Road, there had been no Constitutional question worth disputing about, involved in the discussion. It was certainly a great power to be exercised by Congress, and perhaps liable to great abuses. So were all the other great powers of Congress, and the controul over it was in the organization of the Government, the elective franchise, the State authorities, and the good sense and firmness of the people — Upon these subjects we had much discourse, and he left me with the impression that the interview had been entirely satisfactory to him. ≈

23. V:15. Call on T. Newton — Sat to Sully for my picture; at King's house. At one O'Clock I presented the Baron de Mareuil to the President, and he delivered his Credential Letter from Charles the 10th the new King of France — He also introduced the Count de Ganay, and Mr. Sontag to the President. He made a short speech, of which he gave me a copy, requesting the substance of the President's answer, also in writing. At the Office, W. Lee came and introduced D. Strobel our Consul at Bordeaux. R. P. Letcher had a long conversation with me, upon the subject which he had broached the other day — We had company to dinner; Tracy remained the Evening with me. Mrs. Adams and the girls, were at a party at Col'l Bomford's — Charles arrived. The object of Letcher appeared to me to be, to convince me of the importance of obtaining an Election in the House of Representatives, at the first ballot; and that it would be obtainable; by securing the votes of the States of Kentucky, Ohio, Indiana, Illinois, Missouri,

and Louisiana — I told him candidly that however desirable this might be, it would be utterly impracticable; and that I had no expectation of receiving the vote of his own State of Kentucky — He seemed anxious to convince me that I *might* receive it, and enumerated the whole delegation, stating how each of them was now disposed — a majority of them being *uncommitted.* — I consider Letcher as moving for Mr. Clay; and this anxiety of a friend of Clay's that I should obtain the election at the first ballot in the house is among the whimsical results of political combination at this time. "Incedo super ignes" — Our company to dinner were Mess'rs Clay and Calhoun, Senators Knight and Van Buren; members of H.R. Burleigh, Fuller, Letcher, Livingston, M'Lane, Morgan, Swan, Tomlinson, Tracy, Tucker of Virginia, and Udree; Mr. Babcock, Russell Freeman, M'Call, and Trumbull. Mess'rs Brown and Elliott, Senators, and Hemphill, Hooks, Owen, and Tattnall had been invited, but did not come — Tracy's conversation with me was confidential — He thinks the vote of New-York in the house very doubtful. Counts upon 7 for Jackson, and 14 in the first instance for Crawford.

———

[January 1825]
1. VI:30. Saturday. ≈ At Noon I went with my Sons John and Charles to the President's drawing room, which was much crowded. Mrs. Adams being quite unwell did not go, nor Elizabeth Adams, who was also unwell; nor Mary Hellen — At the Drawing-room, I presented to the President with Mr. Rebello, the Brazilian Chargé d'Affaires, Mr. Oliveira, Secretary of Legation, whom he had yesterday introduced to me, at the Department of State. Robert P. Letcher a member of the House of Representatives from Kentucky, asked me if I should go to the Department after the Drawing-room. I said I should. He said he would call there, and did. He told me he had received from home many Letters lately and several this morning. That the members of the Kentucky Legislature would in their private capacities and not by Legislative Act, recommend to the members from the State in the House, to vote for General Jackson as President, and popular meetings to pass similar Resolutions had been and would be got up — But I might rely upon it they would have no effect. The vote of Kentucky in the

House was fixed and unalterable. He spoke of the difference between Mr. Clay and me, as giving concern to some of the members of the delegation, and intimated a wish that I should have some conversation with Mr. Clay, upon the subject. I told him I would very readily, and whenever it might suit the convenience of Mr. Clay. I merely read the despatches and Letters that came by the mail, and signed a few official papers at the Office. Mr. T. B. Johnson, Mr. and Mrs. Frye, and Mr. and Mrs. W. S. Smith, dined with my family at my House — I attended the dinner given by the members of both Houses of Congress to General La Fayette, at Williamson's Hotel. It was attended also by the President. About 150 members of the two houses were present; and about thirty Officers of the Government, Civil and Military. There were sixteen regular toasts; after which the President, General La Fayette, and most of the invited guests retired to the rooms of Col'l Hayne and Mr. Livingston; where they took coffee with Mrs. Hayne, Mrs. Livingston, Mrs. Ticknor and Miss Gardner. I came home about 9 in the Evening, and our family party soon after retired. A Storm of rain, afterwards turning to Snow, continued through the day. The President's Administration was toasted, to which he answered by a short address of thanks — General La Fayette answered also very briefly the toast to himself — Mr. Clay made a speech about Bolivar and the cause of South-America, and seemed very desirous of eliciting speeches from me and Mr. Calhoun — He told me that he should be glad to have with me soon, some confidential conversation upon public affairs; I said I should be happy to have it whenever it might suit his convenience. At the beginning of this year, there is in my prospects and anticipations a solemnity, and moment, never before experienced; and to which unaided nature is inadequate.

———

9. VI:30. Note from H. Clay. Heard Little, from Ecclesiastes 7:23. — "I said, I will be wise; but it was far from me." And in the afternoon, at Mr. Baker's, a Son of Dr. Mason, formerly of New-York, from Hebrews 11:1. "Now faith is the substance of things hoped for, the evidence of things not seen." This discourse was not ineloquent, but the learning and morality, and instructiveness of Mr. Little's Sermon was more satisfactory to me — In the interval between the two services, I visited J. W.

Taylor and A. H. Tracy. They are speculating upon the approaching event still without conclusive materials for judgment. I received a Letter from James Tallmadge, now Lieutenant Governor of New-York; at Albany. Mr. Clay came at 6 and spent the Evening with me, in a long Conversation explanatory of the past, and prospective of the future — He said that the time was drawing near, when the choice must be made in the House of Representatives, of a President, from the three Candidates presented by the electoral Colleges. That he had been much urged and solicited with regard to the part in that transaction that he should take, and had not been five minutes landed at his lodgings, before he had been applied to, by a friend of Mr. Crawford's, in a manner so gross that it had disgusted him — That some of my friends also, disclaiming indeed to have any authority from me, had repeatedly applied to him directly or indirectly, urging considerations personal to himself as motives to his course — He had thought it best to reserve for some time his determination to himself. First, to give a decent time for his own funeral solemnities as a Candidate; and secondly to prepare and predispose all his friends to a state of neutrality between the three Candidates who would be before the House, so that they might be free ultimately to take that course which might be most conducive to the Public Interest — The time had now come, at which he might be explicit in his communication with me, and he had for that purpose asked this confidential interview — He wished me as far as I might think proper to satisfy him with regard to some principles of great public importance, but without any personal considerations for himself — In the question to come before the House, between General Jackson, Mr. Crawford and myself, he had no hesitation in saying that his preference would be for me.

———

15. VII. Visitors at my house; ≈ Horatio Seymour S. U. S. from Vermont in great concern about the Instructions, from the Kentucky House of Representatives to the members of that Delegation here, to vote for General Jackson as President. He is alarmed for its probable effect on the votes of all the Western States — I advised him to see and converse with Mr. Clay — Col'l R. M. Johnson S. U. S. from Kentucky; who told me there was an Article in the Lexington Reporter, stating that it

was said the Instructions had been given by the advice of one of the Senators of the State at Washington — And as it was known Talbot took no part in the election, the imputation was upon him, Johnson — But he solemnly protested that he had not written any such Letter, and intimated that the Instructions were given in consequence of Mr. Clay's own partizans having taken so much pains to make me unpopular in the State, for which he believed they were now very sorry. Johnson professed neutrality between Gen'l Jackson and me; and said he should be well satisfied if either of us should be elected.

———

17. VI. W. C. Bradley M.H.R. from Vermont was here, and afterwards W. Plumer j'r of New-Hampshire, much concerned about these Instructions from the Legislature of Kentucky. Bradley said he had seen Clay this morning, who told him the Resolutions would confirm the majority of the delegation, in their determination to vote otherwise. But who spoke of the Event of the Election as exceedingly uncertain — Of Missouri and Illinois particularly, the votes of both the States being in single persons. Bradley said he had urged Clay to see me, but Clay had told him it was altogether unnecessary, that his course was fixed, and he should consider the elevation of the Hero, as the greatest calamity, which could befall the Country.

———

19. V. ≈ D. Webster and J. Reed were at the Office; and conversed upon the topic which absorbs all others. Webster said there were persons who pretended to know how a member would vote, by the manner in which he put on or took off his hat — Wyer told me that there had arisen a coolness between the President, and Mr. Rufus King — occasioned by the publication of the President's Letter to Gen'l Jackson, which charged some of the leading federalists with monarchical designs. That Mr. King had not called to take leave of the President at the close of the last Session of Congress, as he had been wont to do; and had not visited him, or been invited to dine with him this Session. Wyer spoke also of Garnett, who is again very ill — T. Fuller came just before I was leaving the office. I told him I had seen Mr. Clay, and found his impressions respecting the Western Delegations such as mine.

———

21. V:30. Morning visits from R. P. Letcher of Kentucky, J. Scott of Missouri, J. Reed of Massachusetts, I. M'Kim of Maryland, and W. R. Bradley of Vermont, Members H.R. and from B. O. Tayloe and P. Force. Letcher brought me a Letter from G. Robertson formerly a member of the House, now in the Kentucky Legislature; and he told me that Scott would call upon me this morning; and he mentioned the proceedings in the Kentucky Delegation, after they received what they call their Instructions. Scott came and gave me the list of the Printers whom he wished to have appointed for printing the Laws in Missouri — They were the same that had been appointed last year. Scott explained to me his causes of complaint against me, which consisted only in my having appointed several years since one Newspaper to print the Laws in Missouri, which was politically opposed to him. He appeared to be satisfied with the assurances that I gave him, that I had not in that or any other instance acted with intentions unfriendly to him; he spoke of the application to the President for the removal of his brother as a judge in the Territory of Arkansas, for having killed in a duel his Colleague on the bench — I told him there was such an application, which had been made, as long since as last Summer. But as the President had not acted upon it hitherto, I thought he would not. Scott then proceeded to speak of the approaching Election, and said that he had made up his mind to vote with the other Western Delegations — but intimated that he should incur great opposition for it in his own State. He spoke of himself as being devoted entirely to Mr. Clay, and of his hope that he would be a member of the next Administration. I told him that he would not expect me to enter upon details with regard to the formation of an Administration, but that if I should be elected by the suffrages of the West, I should naturally look to the West for much of the support that I should need. He parted from me apparently satisfied. Reed came to speak about Webster, Louis M'Lean, and the federalists. His own disposition is favourable to me; but Webster is specially apprehensive that the federalists will be excluded from Office by me — I told Reed that I should exclude no person for political opinions, or for personal opposition to me. That my great object would be to break up the

remnant of old party distinctions, and bring the whole people together in sentiment as much as possible.

———

25. VI. George Sullivan was here, and conversed with me on the subject of the Massachusetts claim, which he has within a few days been desirous of bringing forward *now*. But he has had intimations from friends of mine, that at this time it might excite heats and affect the prospects of the Election — I have uniformly advised him to bring forward the claim at the time most advantageous for its success, whatever might be its effects upon the election: but I recommended to him to advise with the members, best acquainted with the temper of the house, whether the claim itself, would now have so fair a chance of success, as after the election. There is at this moment a very high state of excitement in the house, Mr. Clay, and the majority of the Ohio and Kentucky Delegations having yesterday unequivocally avowed their determination to vote for me — This immediately produced an approximation of the Calhoun, Crawford, and Jackson partizans; and will effectually knit the Coalition of the South with Pennsylvania. W. Plumer j'r and A. H. Tracy were here; and both spoke of this incident, as having produced a great sensation in the house. It appears that Gen'l Jackson has not visited Mr. Crawford, but that the La-dies, have interchanged visits and that Mr. Samuel Swartwout of New-Jersey, has mediated a peace between the General and the Secretary of the Treasury — Plumer had yesterday a con-versation with L. M'Lane of Delaware, who told him they would overthrow the Capitol, sooner than he would vote for Jackson, but who professed an intention almost as decided, not to vote for me. The impression almost universal made yesterday was that the Election was settled in my favour; but the result of the Counter-movement, will be the real crisis, and I have little doubt that will be decisive the other way. My situa-tion will be difficult and trying beyond my powers of expression — May but my strength be proportioned to my trial.

———

27. VI:30. ≈ While Plumer was with me I received a Note from H. Clay proposing to call on me this Evening at six. I asked Plumer who was going immediately to the House to say to

Mr. Clay that I had company to dine with me this Evening, but would see him at any other time that would suit his convenience, at my house or at his lodgings — D. Brent called also at my house. At the Office E. J. Lee came to request my aid to obtain a Midshipman's warrant for Samuel Phillips Lee, a Son of Francis Lightfoot Lee and Grandson of Richard Henry Lee. General Brown came and told me that he had had a long and grave conversation this morning with Mr. Calhoun, who with the most solemn asseverations had declared himself neutral between General Jackson and me; and that his personal wish was for my election. This contrasts singularly with the conduct of all his electioneering partizans. Letcher called and mentioned Mr. Clay's wish to see me this Evening. I told him of my engagement, but promised to be at home to receive him to-morrow Evening. ≈ Mr. Rufus King, S. U. S. from New-York, came and had a long conversation with me, upon the present state and aspects of things. They are flattering for the immediate issue, but the fearful condition of them is that success would open to a far severer trial than defeat.

———

29. VII. ≈ I dined with Mr. George Sullivan. The party consisted of Mr. Clay the Speaker, Mr. Salazar the Colombian Minister, J. S. Johnston S. U. S. and E. Livingston M. H. R. from Louisiana. T. Newton, W. Archer, and J. Taliaferro Members from Virginia. James Hamilton M. H. R. from South-Carolina, A. H. Everett, and Miss Stockton who is residing with Mrs. Sullivan. The party, though variously selected, was exceedingly good-humoured and jovial, and it was past nine in the Evening when we broke up — On my return home, Mr. Clay came in and sat with me a couple of hours, discussing all the prospects and probabilities of the Presidential election. He spoke to me with the utmost freedom of men and things — Intimated doubts and prepossessions concerning individual friends of mine, to all which I listened with due consideration. He was anxious for the conciliation of Webster and Louis M'Lane, and expressed some jealousy as from Webster, of the persons by whom he supposed me to be surrounded — I told him the source of Webster's anxieties, and my own earnest desire to conciliate him. The manner in which my overtures had been received by him, and my own high opinion of his talents and

capacities for service. He spoke of Jabez D. Hammond as being here to promote the views of Governor Clinton of New-York, though he said Hammond was his friend also — and he was very desirous of learning whatever might come to my knowledge in the course of the ensuing week, and which it may be interesting for him to know — His own situation is difficult and critical. He is attacked with fury in the Newspapers for having come out for me, and threats of violence have been largely thrown out, by the partizans of General Jackson; particularly those of the Calhoun interest. Richard M. Johnson told me at the Drawing-room, last Wednesday, that it had been seriously proposed to him in the event of the failure of Jackson's election, to erect his standard; and I received this morning an anonymous Letter from Philadelphia, threatening organized opposition, and civil war, if Jackson is not chosen ≈ This blustering has an air of desperation — But we must meet it.

——

[February 1825]

7. VI. The City swarms with strangers, and the succession of visitors this morning was so numerous, that the names of several of them escaped my recollection. ≈ Mr. Warfield came upon the notice given him as I had yesterday requested, by Mr. Webster — He said that he had not expressed his determination for whom he should vote in the House on Wednesday — His friends Mr. Charles Carroll of Carrollton, and Mr. Taney of Baltimore had urged him to vote for General Jackson, under an impression that if I should be elected, the administration would be conducted on the principle of proscribing the federal party — I said I regretted much that Mr. Carroll, for whose character I entertained a profound veneration, and Mr. Taney, of whose talents I had heard high encomium, should harbour such opinions of me. I could assure him, that I never would be at the head of any administration of proscription to any party — political or geographical. I had differed from the federal party on many important occasions, but I had always done justice to the talents and services of the individuals composing it; and to their merits as members of this Union — I had been discarded by the federal party, upon differences of principle, and I had not separated from one party to make myself the slave of another — I referred in

proof of my adherence to principle against party, to various acts of my public life, and Mr. Warfield declared himself perfectly satisfied with my exposition of my Sentiments. ≈

8. VII. Among the morning visitors of this day, between thirty and forty in number, ≈ Bradley, Seymour and Fuller came to give me advices, respecting the prospects of Election; but from continual interruptions could not freely converse with me. Force told me several incidents which occurred yesterday, indicating the approximation to the inevitable coalition between the Calhoun, Jackson, and Crawford forces ≈ This Evening Mrs. Adams's Tuesday party was more fully attended than ever before. There were 16 Senators 67 members of the House, and at least 400 Citizens and Strangers.

9. VI. May the blessing of God rest upon the event of this day — The second Wednesday in February; when the Election of a President of the United States for the term of four years from the 4th of March next was consummated. Of the votes in the electoral Colleges there were 99 for Andrew Jackson of Tennessee, 84 for John Quincy Adams of Massachusetts, 41 for William Harris Crawford of Georgia, and 37 for Henry Clay of Kentucky. In all 261. This result having been announced on opening and counting the votes in joint meeting of the two Houses, the House of Representatives immediately proceeded to the vote by ballot from the three highest Candidates, when John Quincy Adams received the votes of 13, Andrew Jackson of 7 and William H. Crawford of 4 States. The election was thus completed, very unexpectedly by a single ballot — Alexander H. Everett gave me the first notice, both of the issue of the votes of the electoral colleges, as announced in the joint meeting; and of the final vote as declared. Wyer followed him a few minutes afterwards — Mr. Bolton and Mr. Thomas the Naval Architect succeeded; and B. W. Crowninshield, calling on his return from the House to his lodgings at my house confirmed the reports — Congratulations from several of the Officers of the Department of State ensued — from D. Brent, G. Ironside, W. Slade, and Josias W. King — Those of my wife, children, and family were cordial, and affecting, and I received an affectionate note from Mr. Rufus King of New-York, written

in the Senate chamber after the event. On my return home James Strong, M.H.R. from New-York came with some solicitude of enquiry concerning the obstacles to the election of Ambrose Spencer, as Senator from that State in the place of Mr. King. He asked if my friends considered Spencer as hostile to me. I said I believed they had considered him as favouring the election of Gen'l Jackson. He asked if I did not consider Spencer pledged at least, if elected, not to come with purposes of hostility to the Administration — I said I did not — He said Spencer was an honest man; and if he gave such a pledge would be faithful to it. After dinner the Russian Minister Baron Tuyll called to congratulate me on the issue of the Election. I attended with Mrs. Adams, the Drawing Room at the President's — It was crowded to overflowing. General Jackson was there, and we shook hands. He was altogether placid and courteous — I received numerous friendly salutations. D. Webster asked me when I could receive the Committee of the House to announce to me my Election. I appointed to-morrow Noon, at my own house. The Committee consist of Webster, Vance of Ohio, and Archer of Virginia. I asked S. L. Southard the Secretary of the Navy to call on me to-morrow morning at ten O'Clock. Mr. Daniel Brent had called on me this morning, and said that Mr. John Lee M. H. R. from Maryland had told him that he should at the first ballot, be obliged to vote for Jackson; but if the election should not be completed this day he would come and see me to-morrow Morning — He was disposed to give me his vote, but wished some explanation from me of certain passages of my Oration delivered on the 4th of July 1821 which had been offensive to the Roman Catholics. I said I would very readily see and converse on this subject with Mr. Lee; regretting that any thing I had ever said in public should have hurt the religious feelings of any person. Dr. Watkins came likewise and expressed much confidence in the issue that took place. But urging me, if it should be otherwise, and I should attend the Drawing room this Evening, to carry a firm and confident countenance with me, and remarking that a bold outside was often a herald to success — There was fortunately no occasion for this little artifice. I enclosed Mr. R. King's Note with a Letter of three lines to my father, asking for his blessing and prayers on the event of this day; the most important day of my life, and

which I would close as it began with supplications to the father
of mercies, that its consequences may redound to his glory, and
to the welfare of my Country. After I returned from the Drawing Room, a Band of Musicians came and serenaded me at my
house — It was past midnight when I retired.

10. VI:30. ≈ Mr. Southard called as I had requested at ten — I
invited him to remain at the Head of the Navy Department; to
which he consented. I told him that I should offer the Department of State to Mr. Clay; and should invite Mr. Crawford, to
remain in the Department of the Treasury — I read to him the
answer which I had written for the notification which I expected. He suggested a very judicious objection to one passage
of it which I altered. At Noon Daniel Webster of Massachusetts, Joseph Vance of Ohio, and William S. Archer of Virginia
came as a Committee of the House of Representatives and
announced to me that in the recent Election of a President of
the United States, no person having received a majority of all
the votes of the Electors appointed, and the choice having
consequently devolved upon the House of Representatives;
that House proceeding in the manner prescribed in the Constitution, did yesterday choose me to be President of the United
States, for four years, commencing on the 4th day of March
next — I observed to the Committee that the only preceding
occasion since the Establishment of the Constitution of the
United States, upon which a similar notification had been
made from the House of Representatives, was at the Election
of Mr. Jefferson, who had returned to the Committee, a written Answer. I had thought it would be proper to follow this
example, and I read and delivered to Mr. Webster the answer
that I had prepared — The Committee informed me that they
had already notified the President of this Election — The
Committee reported my answer to the House where it was
read ≈ This Evening I wrote to Mr. Crawford, inviting him to
remain at the Head of the Treasury. Attended with Mrs.
Adams the Military Ball, at Carusi's Rooms — The President,
Gen'l La Fayette, and Mr. Calhoun were there.

11. V:15. Visitors — S. L. Southard. Arthur Livermore M. H. R.
from New-Hampshire, anxious that Mr. Crawford should have

the offer of remaining in the Treasury. Lowrie, had mentioned it to him — H. Niles of Baltimore. Joseph Wheaton. P. Force. D. P. Cook. G. Sullivan a conversation with whom yesterday, had been interrupted, and was now resumed — He said he would tell me what the Calhounites said — That if Mr. Clay should be appointed Secretary of State a determined opposition to the Administration would be organized from the outset — That the opposition would use the name of General Jackson as its head — That the Administration would be supported only by the New-England States. New-York being doubtful — The West much divided, and strongly favouring Jackson as a Western Man — Virginia already in opposition; and all the South decidedly adverse — The Calhounites had also told him what Administration would satisfy them — namely Joel R. Poinsett, Secretary of State — Langdon Cheves, Secretary of the Treasury — John M'Lean, now Postmaster General Secretary of War, and Southard, of the Navy — I asked Sullivan with whom he had held these Conversations — He said with Calhoun himself and with Poinsett. I told Sullivan that I would some day call on him to testify to these facts in a Court of Justice — He said surely not. I insisted that I would, and told him that he would find it necessary under this threatened opposition of Mr. Calhoun, between him and me. That I had no doubt Mr. Calhoun in holding this language to him, intended it should come to me, and that its object was to intimidate me, and deter me from the nomination of Mr. Clay — That I had heard the same intimations from him through other channels, and in all probability at some future day some occasion would arise of necessity for proving the facts judicially, in which case I should certainly call upon him — He said he should certainly then refuse to answer — I said his refusal to answer would be as good for me, as the answer itself. He then said surely I would not call upon him to betray a private and confidential conversation which he had only told me to make me acquainted with all that he knew, interesting to me at this moment. That in telling it he had already violated the confidence of Mr. Calhoun, who far from intending that it should be reported to me, had strictly enjoined it upon him to say nothing of it to any one. I said this altered the case; and he might consider my declared intention of calling on him to testify publicly to these facts as withdrawn. I nevertheless believed Mr. Calhoun had intended he should report to me his threats of opposition in the event of Mr. Clay's appointment, and believed that if he would ask Calhoun's permission to communicate the substance of it to me he would give it — This conversation, connected with Ingham's, and M'Duffie's electioneering siege upon D. P. Cook, Richard M. Johnson's disclosures to me, at the drawing-room, and Benton's screw upon Scott; with Poinsett's recommendation to the President of Benton as Minister to Mexico, unfolds the system of opposition as formed by Mr. Calhoun — It is to bring in General Jackson as the next President under the auspices of Calhoun — To this end, the Administration must be rendered unpopular and odious; whatever its acts and measures may be, and Mr. Calhoun avows himself prepared to perform this part — I am at least forewarned — It is not in man that walketh to direct his steps.

———

[March 1825]

3. VI. This day closed the Second Session of the Eighteenth Congress, and the Administration of James Monroe, as President of the United States — I had passed a sleepless Night, occasioned by the unceasing excitement of many past days; the pressure of business in the Department of State, always heavy at the close of a Session of Congress, now redoubled at the close of my own Service of eight years in the Office of Secretary; the bustle of preparation for the new Condition upon which I was to enter — The multitudes of visitors, upon great varieties of business, or for curiosity — The anxieties of an approximating crisis; and above all the failing and threatening state of my wife's health. ≈ Mr. Clay was here in the Evening. Mrs. Adams very unwell all day, was seized with a violent fever this Evening; and was bled — Near Midnight I received from the Office of the National Intelligencer, a proof copy of my Address, which I corrected and returned.

CHAPTER IX ❧ 1825-1829

President

[March 1825]

4. V. Mrs. Adams was very ill, the whole Night, and before day this morning, had a long and alarming fainting fit, succeeded by violent fever — I sent and had Dr. Huntt called up to attend her. After two successive sleepless Nights, I entered upon this day with a supplication to Heaven, first for my Country; secondly for myself, and for those connected with my good name and fortunes, that the last results of its events may be auspicious and blessed — About half past eleven O'Clock, I left my house, with an escort of several companies of militia, and a cavalcade of Citizens; accompanied in my Carriage by Samuel L. Southard Secretary of the Navy, and William Wirt, Attorney General, and followed by James Monroe, late President of the United States, in his own Carriage. We proceeded to the Capitol, and to the Senate Chamber. The Senate were in Session, and John C. Calhoun presiding in the Chair, having been previously sworn in to Office, as Vice-President of the United States and President of the Senate — The Senate adjourned, and from the Senate chamber, accompanied by the members of that body; and by the Judges of the Supreme Court, I repaired to the Hall of the House of Representatives, and after delivering from the Speakers Chair my inaugural Address to a crowded auditory, I pronounced from a Volume of the Laws, held up to me by John Marshall, Chief Justice of the United States, the Oath faithfully to execute the Office of President of the United States, and to the best of my ability, to preserve, protect and defend the Constitution of the United States. After exchanging salutations with the late President, and many other persons present, I retired from the Hall; passed in review the military companies drawn up in front of the Capitol, and returned to my house with the same procession which accompanied me from it. I found at my house a crowd of visitors which continued about two hours, and received their felicitations — Before the throng had subsided I went myself

97

to the President's House, and joined with the multitude of
visitors to Mr. Monroe there — I then returned home to dine;
and in the Evening attended the Ball which was also crowded,
at Carusi's Hall. Immediately after supper, about Midnight I
withdrew and came home. Mrs. DeWint and Johnson Hellen
had already come home, both unwell. Mrs. Adams, extremely
ill as she was had received the company in the Drawing-room
before dinner, but was not able to attend the Ball — The
weather was cloudy all the morning, and the Evening rainy —
I closed the day as it had begun with thanksgiving to God for
all his mercies and favours past, and with prayers for the continuance of them to my Country and to myself and mine.

5. VII. ≈ An Administration was to be formed. Soon after
Noon, James Lloyd, and Nathanael Macon, came as a Committee from the Senate to notify me, that they were in Session,
ready to receive any Communication from me; to which I answered that I should make them a Communication, at an early
hour this day — On the Evening of the 3^{d} I had at about nine
O'Clock received a Note from Mr. Monroe, informing me
that he had shortly before received a Letter from Mr. Crawford, resigning the Office of Secretary of the Treasury. I now
sent by Daniel Brent, Chief Clerk of the Department of State,
a Message to the Senate, nominating

Henry Clay of Kentucky	to be	Secretary of State
Richard Rush of Pennsylvania		Secretary of the Treasury
James Barbour of Virginia		Secretary for the Department of War
Alexander Hill Everett of Massachusetts		Envoy Ext'y and Min'r Plen'y to Spain
Christopher Hughes of Maryland		Charge d'Affaires to the Netherlands
Thomas Ludwell Lee Brent of Virginia		Charge d'Affaires to Portugal
John M. Forbes of Massachusetts		Chargé d'Affaires at Buenos-Ayres
William Miller of North-Carolina		Chargé d'Affaires to Guatemala

Condy Raquet of	Charge d'Affaires to
Pennsylvania	Brazil — and
Lieut't Colonel Roger	Adjutant General of
Jones	the Army

I sent at the same time four other messages with nominations.

1. Officers of the Customs, whose Commissions are about
   expiring —   renominated
2. Registers of the Land Offices and
   Receivers of Public Monies   d'o
3. Navy Agents   d'o
4. Governor, and Legislative Council of Florida — Certain
   Consuls, and others

Most of the renominations had been already made by Mr. Monroe; but as the Commissions of the incumbents would not expire within the term of his administration, the Senate had declined acting upon them — Efforts had been made by some of the Senators to obtain different nominations, and to introduce a principle of change, or rotation in office, at the expiration of these Commissions. Which would make the Government a perpetual, and unintermitting scramble for Office. — A more pernicious expedient could scarcely have been devised. ≈ I did not this day send nominations for the Missions to Great-Britain, or to Mexico; nor of a Chargé d'Affaires to Sweden. The first I leave open some days, at the earnest request of some of Mr. Clinton's friends, for the possible chance that he may reconsider his determination. I wait for the decision of the Senate upon the nomination of C. Hughes, to vacate his place at Stockholm; and I concluded after much deliberation to offer to Joel Roberts Poinsett of South-Carolina, the nomination of Minister to Mexico. I accordingly sent for him this morning, and made him the offer — It had been made to him by Mr. Monroe, early during the late Session of Congress, and declined upon Considerations, most of which do not now apply. He made however now two objections. One that upon his vacating his Seat in Congress, a very troublesome and unprincipled man, would probably be chosen in his place. The other that he had recommended to Mr. Monroe another person for the mission to Mexico — I knew who this person was. it was Thomas H. Benton a Senator from Missouri, who from being a furious personal and political enemy of Gen'l Jackson, became about the time of this recommendation, a partizan not less ardent in his favour — I now told Poinsett, that with regard to the consequences of his vacating his Seat in Congress, I could form no judgment, having little knowledge of the state of Politics at Charleston, and no acquaintance with the person who might be his Successor; but that if he should decline, I should not offer the mission to the person whom he had recommended to Mr. Monroe — He asked time for consideration; and promised to give me a definitive answer to-morrow ≈ After returning home I called upon Mr. Rufus King at his lodgings at Williamson's — His term of Service as a Senator expired on the 3^d and he had declined a re-election, intending to retire from the Public Service — He leaves the City to-morrow Morning to return home — I told him of the nominations I had made; and that I had omitted that for the mission to England, at the earnest desire of some of Mr. Clinton's friends. But I said the reason assigned by Mr. Clinton for declining the appointment was in my opinion one which he could not *reconsider*, nor had I any expectation that he would. I therefore asked Mr. King, if *he* would accept that mission? His first and immediate impulse was to decline it — He said that his determination to retire from the public service had been made up, and that this proposal was utterly unexpected to him. Of this I was aware; but I urged upon him a variety of considerations to induce his acceptance of it — The general importance of the Mission, in my estimation not inferior to that of any one of the Departments — The special importance to the States of New-York and of Maine, of certain interests in Negotiation with Great-Britain — His peculiar qualifications for the conduct of those Negotiations. His duty to the Country; not to refuse Services so important, and for which perhaps no other individual would be so well suited — The Satisfaction which the appointment and his acceptance of it would give to the federal party throughout the Union — The tendency that it would have to heal our divisions, and harmonize the feelings of the People — The opportunity which he would afford me of promoting this reconciliation of parties, and at the same time of proving by my example the sincerity of the Sentiments avowed in my address — I dwelt with earnestness upon all these motives, and apparently not without effect — He admitted the force of them and finally promised fully to consider of the proposal before giving me a definitive answer. On returning home, I found B. W. Crowninshield who came to take leave. Going to-morrow. Long conversation with him.

6. VII. I sent this morning for A. H. Everett and informed him that I had nominated him to the Senate as Minister to Spain. Heard Mr. Little from Deuteronomy 16.20 "That which is altogether just shalt thou follow, that then mayest live, and inherit the Land which the Lord thy God giveth thee" — And in the afternoon at Mr. Baker's, Mr. Post, from Proverbs 23.26 "My Son, give me thine heart." — After the morning Service, I called upon Mr. Clay at his lodgings, where he is confined by indisposition. Mr. Storrs of New-York was with him, but soon withdrew. I mentioned to Mr. Clay the nominations sent to the Senate yesterday; my proposal of the Mexican Mission to Mr. Poinsett; and my Conversation last Evening with Mr. King — Mr. Clay was well satisfied, that Mr. King should go to England; but wished that Gen'l W. H. Harrison, of Ohio should receive the appointment to Mexico. Harrison has just now taken his Seat as a Senator from the State of Ohio; but is himself exceedingly anxious to obtain the appointment to Mexico, and solicits recommendations for it, of which he has succeeded in obtaining many. Mr. Clay had however no particular objection to Mr. Poinsett. He spoke of the threatened opposition to the Administration, and thought it would not be formidable. He did not expect more than three or four votes against the confirmation by the Senate of his nomination as Secretary of State — But Mr. King told me last Evening that Mr. Van Buren had assured him the nomination would be opposed though he Van Buren would not join in it. Clay spoke of a Letter from General Jackson to Samuel Swartwout, just published and which I had not seen. ≈ Mr. Poinsett called and accepted the Mission to Mexico.

———

[April 1825]
30. V:30. ≈ *Day*. Since my removal to the Presidential Mansion, I rise about five — Read two Chapters of Scott's Bible and

Commentary, and the corresponding commentary of Hewlett
— Then the morning Newspapers, and public papers from the
several Departments — Write seldom, and not enough —
Breakfast; an hour from nine to ten — Then have a succession
of visitors, upon business, in search of place, Solicitors for donations, or for mere curiosity, from eleven, till between 4 and
5 O'Clock — The Heads of Departments of course occupy
much of this time. Between four and six I take a walk of three
or four Miles. Dine from about half past five till seven, and
from dark till about eleven, I generally pass the Evening in my
chamber, signing Land-grants or Blank Patents; in the interval
of which for the last ten days, I have brought up three Months
of Arrears in my Diary-Index — About eleven I retire to bed.
My Evenings are not so free from interruption as I had hoped
and expected they would be; nor have I the prospect of meth-
odising the distribution of my time to my own Satisfaction.
There is much to correct, and reform, and the precept of Dili-
gence is always timely.

———

[May 1825]
13. IV:45. ≈ Mr. Clay took leave, and departs to-morrow upon
his tour home; to fetch his family — He asked me how long I
would give him permission of absence; I told him at his own
discretion; being sure that he would not lengthen it without
necessity; and understanding of course that in case of any
sudden emergency requiring his presence here, we could give
him timely notice of it. He said he expected to return with his
family about the middle of July — He had sent me a Letter to
him from W. Brent, member of the House from Louisiana,
strongly urging the removal of Sterret the Naval Officer at
New-Orleans, as a noisy and clamorous reviler of the administration, who was concerned in a project of some worthless
persons like himself to insult Brent, when he passed through
New-Orleans at the Theatre, for his vote at the Election —
which project however failed. And Brent's Letter says that a
vast majority of the people of Louisiana, are entirely satisfied
with the election — Mr. Clay also urged the removal of Sterret,
and observed that with regard to the conduct of persons holding Offices at the pleasure of the President, the course of the
administration should be to avoid on the one hand political

persecution; and on the other an appearance of pusillanimity. That so long as the election was pending, every man was free to indulge his preference for any of the Candidates, but after it was decided no officer depending upon the will of the President for his place, should be permitted to hold a conduct in open and continual disparagement of the Administration and its head — I said these principles were undoubtedly correct; but there was some difficulty and great delicacy in the application of them to individuals. If the charge could be specifically brought home to Sterret of having concerted or countenanced a purpose of public insult to a member of Congress for the honest and independent discharge of his duty, I would not hesitate to remove such a black guard as unworthy of holding any public trust, whatever — But Mr. Brent only mentions this as a design of Sterret's, never carried into execution — And as a design it could scarcely be susceptible of proof. Should I remove Sterret by a mere executive fiat — he would consider himself injured and immediately demand the cause of his removal. To answer merely that it was the pleasure of the President, would be harsh and odious, inconsistent with the principle upon which I have commenced the Administration, of removing no person from Office, but for cause, and would lead to the inference that I was ashamed to assign the real cause — That real cause, an *intention* never carried into act, would scarcely justify the removal of a man from office in the public opinion — It would be thought to indicate an irritable, hasty, and vindictive temper; and give rise to newspaper discussions of which all the disadvantage would fall upon the Administration — Besides, should I remove this man for this cause, it must be upon some fixed principle, which would apply to others as well as to him. And where was it possible to draw the line? Of the custom house officers throughout the union, four-fifths, in all probability, were opposed to my election — They were now all in my power, and I had been urged very earnestly and from various quarters to sweep away my opponents, and provide with their places for my friends — I can justify the refusal to adopt this policy, only by the steadiness and consistency of my adhesion to my own — If I depart from this in one instance, I shall be called upon by my friends to do the same in many: an invidious and inquisitorial scrutiny into the personal dispositions of public officers, will creep through the whole union, and the most selfish and sordid passions will be kindled into activity to distort the conduct and misrepresent the feelings of men, whose places may become the prize of Slander upon them. Mr. Clay did not press the subject any farther.

———

15. V:15. Mackintosh, Chilly; Mackintosh, Col'l; Tallazan, Jim; Tallazan, Ben. These four Creek Indians called on me this morning before breakfast, with a Letter from Gov'r Troup of Georgia, and a talk sent by him to certain other Creek Chiefs — The Letter which is in a style similar to that which the same personage used with Mr. Monroe, announced to me the murder of the Chief called General Mackintosh, which was confirmed by Chilly who narrowly escaped himself with his life. It was on Saturday the 30th of last month — that a party of about 400 surrounded, and set fire to his house; and killed him, and another chief his next door neighbour. Troup charges Crowell the Agent with having instigated this massacre, and vows revenge, with a Spirit as ferocious as ever inspired any Creek Indian — I told Chilly that I was deeply distressed at these melancholy tidings, and would do all that would be in my power for him: advising him to call upon the Secretary at War to-morrow — I stopped myself at his house as I was going to Church, and he being gone out, left the papers with word that I would call again after Church ≈ I again called at Governor Barbour's house, and found him at home; deeply affected at the intelligence from Georgia; thinking Governor Troup a madman, and very apprehensive of opposition — I desired him to confer with these Indians to-morrow Morning; ascertain what they wished to have done; what disposable force may be directed to the threatened part of Georgia; and what answer should be given to Gov'r Troup. ≈

16. V. ≈ Governour Barbour came in ≈ He had seen Chilly Mackintosh, and the other Creek Chiefs. They charge Crowell the Agent with having refused the Mackintosh party rations at the Council Meeting, and insinuate that he instigated the other chiefs to the murder of Mackintosh. I desired Mr. Barbour to bring them to some specific charge against Crowell, which he might be called to answer — He proposes to send a trusty special sub-agent, to carry an answer to the Governor of

Georgia, who threatens on the part of that State, immediate acts of violence for retaliation or protection — to inform the Governor of Georgia, that the United States never have interposed, and cannot interpose in transactions of internal feuds in an Indian tribe — that the messenger go to the upper Creeks, and inform them of the horror with which we have received the information of these outrages: to warn them against further violence; advise them to return to their homes, and give them permission to send a deputation here next winter as they have requested — I approved of these measures, but am persuaded they will be insufficient; and apprehend this massacre is only the signal for a ferocious Indian War, bursting upon us like a thunderbolt. I requested the Secretary of War to ascertain and let me know, what military force we could bring to bear immediately upon the menaced borders of Georgia ≈

17. V:15. ≈ Governor Barbour had further Letters from Governor Troup of Georgia; with enclosures leading to the expectation that within three days from the time when they were written a hostile incursion of Creek Indians into Georgia, was thought inevitable. Barbour had prepared an answer to Troup's first Letter, which has now become unsuitable. Chilly Mackintosh has made written specific charges against the Agent Crowell, and presents various claims for protection and indemnity — Referring to the 8th Article of the Treaty of Indian Springs, which contains a promise of protection, very insidiously introduced and the purport of which was certainly not considered by the Senate when they advised to the ratification of the Treaty — I directed that Crowell should be suspended from the Agency, and called to answer to the Charges of Governor Troup and of Mackintosh — In the mean time that a special temporary agent should be appointed — That General Brown should be consulted and General Gaines ordered to repair to the neighbourhood of the Creek Territory and to wait there for Instructions. No report yet from Crowell — The instant we begin to move, the want of money is felt; the means of the Executive are so limited; and the aspect of War is so menacing, that I know not how we shall avoid the necessity of calling Congress together in the midst of Summer.

———

20. V. Governour Barbour read to me his definitive Letter to the Governor of Georgia and his instruction to Gaines — He was to despatch Major Andrews this day. The powers to Gaines are contingent upon the continuance of outrage by the Indians. Should they have dispersed he is to assemble them in council, and urge upon them the necessity of carrying the Treaty of Indian Springs into Execution. And an explicit warning is given to the Governor of Georgia, to postpone the surveying of the Territory, a design to do which prematurely proclaimed by the Governor of Georgia, as his motive for calling a Session of the Legislature, and with the sanction of Mackintosh to the measure ostentatiously displayed, was in all probability the cause of the bloody proscription of that chief. I begin to indulge the hope that a war may yet be avoided ≈ Mr. Hay has been several days in the City — He spoke with much concern of the disturbances among the Indians and in Georgia, and strongly expressed the opinion that the Treaty of Indian Springs ought not to have been ratified — It ought never to have been made; but nothing could have arrested the progress of this iniquity, after the Selection of two Georgians, as Commissioners for negotiating the Treaty — They concluded the Treaty directly in the face of their Instructions; but when the Treaty came here, the President could not withhold it from the Senate; and when before the Senate no one would take the invidious task of exposing its injustice — The Senate sanctioned its ratification without giving it an examination, and I had no practicable alternative but to ratify it accordingly — The Clark party in Georgia already make it a matter of public reproach against me. Mr. Hay's concern is more sympathetic.

———

24. IV. ≈ Mr. Cassedy and his Son, are travellers, who left their home to visit some of the cities of the union, for their amusement, and came to see me to gratify their curiosity. ≈ Mr. Barbour had a private Letter from J. S. Skinner, corresponding Secretary of the Maryland agricultural Society, mentioning that in March the Society had invited me and him, and the other heads of Departments, to attend the next annual Cattle Show, and exhibition of household manufactures at a tavern, four miles out of Baltimore. That answers had been received

from all, but from him and me; at which the Society were a little hurt. That they were to meet next Saturday at his house, at which time our answers might be received; and there was an argument on the President's attendance, to give countenance and encouragement to Agriculture — The Exhibition is to be the first and second of June — The best exhibitions on the first; and the distribution of the Premiums which they wish the President to make is on the second — Mr. Barbour had not received his invitation. I had received mine, and had delayed answering under some hesitation whether to go or not. I now concluded for various reasons not to go. From Skinner's Letter to Barbour it is apparent, that the Society wish to make the President of the United States a part of their Exhibition — To gratify this wish, I must give four days of my time; no trifle of expense, and set a precedent for being claimed as an article of exhibition at all the Cattle-shows throughout the Union — From Cattle-shows to other public Meetings for purposes of utility, or exposures of public Sentiment the transition is natural and easy. Invitations to them would multiply from week to week, and every compliance would breed the necessity for numerous excuses and apologies — Finally this is no part of my duties; and some duty must be neglected to attend to it — Seest thou a man diligent *in his* business? — I answered Mr. Skinner, declining the invitation.

———

30. IV:15. ≈ The Commissioner of the Public buildings Elgar, brought a new design for the Tympanum of the Capitol, drawn by Persico from the Ideas which had been suggested when Col'l Bomford and C. B. King were here — I made some remarks upon this design, and he proposed to me to ask Mr. Persico, and Mr. Bulfinch to call upon me to-morrow to converse with me on the subject; to which I agreed.

31. IV:15. Bulfinch and Persico came at one O'Clock, and we discussed the new design; which was a personification of U.S. standing on a throne leaning upon the Roman fasces surmounted with the cap of Liberty with Justice at her right hand, blindfolded, holding the suspended balance, and in the other hand an open scroll; and Hercules at her left, seated on a

corner of the throne, embracing the fasces, and emblematical of Strength — To which were added, separately drawn, and to fill up the space, Plenty seated with her Cornucopia, in one Corner, and Peace, a flying Angel extending a garland of Victory towards America with one hand and bearing a palm in the other. These two last figures I advised should be discarded — as well as the Roman Fasces, and the Cap of Liberty. The Hercules had also too much of the heathen mythology for my taste, and I proposed to substitute in his place a figure of Hope with an Anchor, a scriptural Image, indicating that this Hope, relies upon a Supreme disposer of Events — Which Hope we have as an Anchor to the Soul, sure and steadfast — Instead of the fasces, I proposed a Pedestal, with 4 July 1776 inscribed on its base; and 4 March 1789 on its upper Cornice. The whole design then would represent the American Union, founded on the Declaration of Independence, and consummated by the organization of the general Government under the federal Constitution, supported by Justice in the past, and relying upon Hope in Providence for the future. Persico objected that all the figures of the group would be females, and thought there should be at least one male figure. However he is to make a drawing of the Design and we shall examine it ≈ Mr. Barbour, the Secretary of War, came with a Letter from J. Crowell the Agent with the Creek Indians; who is convinced that they will commit no act of violence or hostility unless instigated by further violence from Governor Troup of Georgia. Mr. Barbour had received also another insulting Letter from Governor Troup which he thought it best to leave unanswered.

———

[June 1825]
8. V. ≈ After dinner I heard Dr. Caldwell's Lecture upon the organ of amativeness, which I thought more indelicate than philosophical — The weather was intensely warm, and I had no temptation to learn more either of phrenology or of Craniology.

———

13. III:30. I attempted to cross the river with Antoine in a small canoe; with a view to swim across it to come back — He took a boat in which we had crossed it last Summer without

accident — The boat was at the shore near Van Ness's Poplars but in crossing the Tiber to the point, my Son John who was with us thought the boat dangerous, and instead of going with us went and undressed at the rock, to swim and meet us midway of the river as we should be returning — I thought the boat safe enough; or rather persisted carelessly in going without due attention to its condition — Gave my watch to my Son. Made a bundle of my coat and waistcoat, to take in the boat with me. Put off my shoes, and was paddled by Antoine, who had stripped himself entirely naked — Before we had got half across the river the boat had leaked itself half full, and then we found there was nothing on board to scoop up the water and throw it over. Just at that critical moment a fresh breeze from the Northwest blew down the river as from the nose of a bellows. In five minutes time it made a little tempest, and set the boat to dancing till the river came in at the sides. I jumped over-board, and Antoine did the same; and lost hold of the boat, which filled with water and drifted away — We were as near as possible to the middle of the river, and swam to the opposite shore. Antoine who was naked reached it with little difficulty — I had much more, and while struggling for life, and gasping for breath had ample leisure to reflect upon my own discretion — My principal difficulty was in the loose Sleeves of my shirt, which filled with water, and hung like two 56 lb weights upon my arms — I had also my hat, which I soon gave however to Antoine — After reaching the shore I took off my shirt and pantaloons, wrung them out, and gave them to Antoine to go and look out for our clothes, or for a person to send to the house for others, and for the Carriage to come and fetch me — Soon after he had gone, my Son John joined me having swum wholly across the river expecting to meet us returning with the boat. Antoine crossed the bridge; sent a man to my house for the Carriage, made some search for the drifted boat and bundles, and found his own hat with his shirt and bracers in it, and one of my shoes. He also brought over the bridge my Son's Cloathes, with my watch and umbrella, which I had left with him. While Antoine was gone, John and I were wading and swimming up and down on the other shore, or sitting naked basking on the bank, at the Margin of the river. — John walked over the bridge home. The Carriage

came and took me and Antoine home, half dressed. I lost an
old Summer coat, white waistcoat, two napkins, two white
handkerchiefs, and one shoe. Antoine lost his watch, jacket,
waistcoat, pantaloons and shoes — The boat was also lost —
By the mercy of God our lives were spared; and no injury befell
our persons. We reached home about a quarter before nine,
having been out nearly five hours. I had been about three
hours in the water, but suffered no inconvenience from it —
This incident gave me a humiliating lesson, and solemn warning not to trifle with danger — The reasons upon which I
justify to myself my daily swimming in the river did not apply
to this adventure. It is neither necessary for my health, nor
even for pleasure that I should swim across the river, and having once swum across it, I could not even want it as an experiment of practicability — Among my motives for swimming
that of shewing what I can do, must be discarded as spurious,
and I must strictly confine myself to the purposes of health,
exercise, and salutary labour.

                              —

[July 1825]
22. IV. I walked as usual to my ordinary bathing place, and
came to the rock where I leave my clothes a few minutes before
sunrise — I found several persons there, besides three or four
who were bathing; and at the shore under the tree a boat with
four men in it, and a drag net. There was a large two-mast boat
in the channel opposite the rock, at anchor; and a man on the
shore who requested those in the two-mast boat, to raise their
anchor, and drop thirty or forty-yards down the stream, as
they were in the way of the boat with the drag net which was
going in search of a dead body. I enquired if any one had been
drowned, and the man told me it was old Mr. Shoemaker, a
clerk in the Post-Office; a man upwards of 60 years of age, who
last evening between 5 and 6 O'Clock, went in to bathe with
four other persons — That he was drowned in full sight of
them, and without a suspicion by them that he was even in any
danger. They had observed him struggling in the water, but as
he was an excellent swimmer had supposed he was merely
diving; until after coming out they found he was missing —
They then commenced an ineffectual search for him which was
continued late into the Night — The man said to me that he

had never seen a more distressed person than Mrs. Shoemaker last Evening — While the two mast boat was dropping down the stream and the other boat was preparing to go out with the drag, I stripped and went in to the river; I had been not more than ten minutes swimming when the drag boat started, and they were not five minutes from the shore when the body floated, immediately opposite the rock; less than one hundred yards from the shore, at the very edge of the channel and where there could not be seven foot deep of water — I returned immediately to the shore and dressed — a rope was tied round one of the arms; and the boat remained at the spot, till a blanket had been sent for, which was spread under the tree; the boat then returned to the shore drawing the body through the water, and it was lifted from the water and brought and laid upon the blanket and covered up. The only part of the body which had the appearance of stiffness was the arms, both of which were raised at the shoulder joints and crooked towards each other at the elbows, as if they had been fixed by a spasm at the very moment when they were to expand to keep the head above water — There was a dark flush of settled blood over the face, like one excessively heated, and a few drops of thin blood and water issued from one ear — There was nothing terrible or offensive in the sight; but I returned home musing in sympathy with the distressed Lady; and enquiring uncertainly whether I ought to renounce altogether my practice of swimming in the river — My conclusion was that I ought not — deeming it in this climate indispensable to my health — so that whatever danger there may be in the exercise, and that there is much danger, this incident offers melancholy and cumulative proof — there would be yet greater danger in abstaining from it, or in substituting any other effective exercise in its place — We are and always must be in the hands of God, and to him are indebted for every breath we draw.

———

29. V. As a substitute for my morning bath, I took a walk immediately after rising of nearly an hour and a half, which was more fatiguing than my usual walk and swim of double that time. The weather has become cooler, but without restoring energy of action ≈ Van Zandt — publisher of the life of Paul

Jones. He had left yesterday a copy of it handsomely bound for me; and also two volumes of Laws and documents relating to the New-York Canals, printed by order of the Legislature of the State — There is a volume of plates and maps to follow, and the publisher wishes to dispose of copies of the work — The morning slipped away while I was reading Jones's Life, which brought to my mind many pleasing and mournful recollections of my boyhood and youth. I told Van Zandt some anecdotes concerning Jones, from my own memory.

———

[August 1825]
28. V:15. Sun rose 5:28 behind chimney Gen'l Brown's house. ≈
With Gen'l La Fayette. Heard Little 1 Timothy 4:7.
The General thought his Sermon Ultra-Unitarian.
Read Johnson's Sermon 18 upon Fraud.
Conversation with Gen'l La Fayette after Breakfast. I take every opportunity to dissuade him from having any participation in revolutionary projects in France — He says he will go quietly to La Grange — That he is 68 years old, and must leave revolutions to younger men — But there is fire beneath the cinders. ≈

29. V:15. ≈ Major Van de Venter brought a Letter of 15 August from Governor Troup of Georgia, to the Secretary of War, full as usual of "Guns, Drums, Trumpets, Blunderbuss and Thunder" — but declaring that he will not make the threatened survey of the Creek Indian Lands.

———

[October 1825]
27. VI. — Walk to Georgetown. 1 hour — Mark 11:12. In the Steamboat Frenchtown I had observed a large circle round the moon, and expected foul weather within 48 hours — It came in a heavy gale and copious showers all this day, and Evening — Yet my time was absorbed from Breakfast till dinner, with the visitors. The Secretaries all conversing upon public affairs and bringing me multitudes of papers which I had no time to assort; and still less to dispose of in a satisfactory manner. Mr. Clay is in deep affliction, having lost two daughters in the course of a Month — The last was married at New-Orleans, and he has received within a few days the account of her death

— His own health is so infirm that he told me he feared he should be obliged to resign his Office — But said he would try to retain it through the Winter, and declared himself entirely satisfied with my conduct towards him, and with the course of the Administration hitherto.

———

[November 1825]

21. IV:30. ≈ Barbour James — S. W. who took back his papers relating to Indian concerns — particularly the draft of his Report, urging the necessity of incorporating the Indians within our own system. He mentioned having had a conversation with Mr. Gaillard; a Senator from South-Carolina, who wished that something conciliatory to the South might be said in the Message to calm their inquietudes concerning their Slaves — He wished something to sustain the friends of the Administration against the overwhelming influence of the Calhoun party, which they had been unable to resist, and by which they were oppressed — I said I should be glad to do any thing in my power to gratify Mr. Gaillard; but the Legislature of South-Carolina itself had put it out of my power to say any thing soothing to the South on that subject — by persisting in a Law, which a Judge of the Supreme Court of the U.S. himself a native and inhabitant of South-Carolina had declared to be in direct violation of the Constitution of the United States — which the Attorney General of the United States had declared to infringe the rights of foreign Nations; against which the British Government had repeatedly remonstrated, and upon which we had promised them that the cause of complaint should be removed — a promise, which the obstinate adherence of the Government of South-Carolina to their Law had disenabled us from fulfilling. The Governor of South-Carolina, had not even answered the Letter from the Department of State, transmitting to him the complaint of the British Government against this Law — In this state of things, for me to say any thing gratifying to the feelings of the South-Carolinians on this subject, would be to abandon the ground taken by the Administration of Mr. Monroe, and disable us from taking hereafter measures concerning the Law, which we may be compelled to take — To be silent is not to interfere with any State rights, and not to interfere renounces no right of

ourselves or others. ≈ I had intended to convoke the members of the Administration to-morrow for the first reading of the Message. But Mr. Clay being yet unwell, I postponed it till the next day.

—

23. V:30. ≈ Cabinet Meeting — Wirt, Attorney General absent. ≈ I read the first draft of the Message which took me about an hour and a half — There was some conversation as to the mode of discussing its topics. It was observed that Remarks of a general nature might occupy this day; and at the next Meeting, Friday at one O'Clock, it should be read again by Paragraphs. Governor Barbour objected to the whole concluding recommendations on the subject of internal improvements — and Mr. Clay thought there was much force in his remarks. The consideration of this however was postponed — but Mr. Clay objected to a sentiment expressed relating to the claims of our Citizens upon France, and several other European Governments. After stating that the justice of the claims on France was undenied and undeniable; and that reparation for them had long been sought in vain, I stated that the United States would be fully justified in resorting to their own force for redress — But that force instead of obtaining redress was more adapted to aggravate than to repair such wrongs; and that our policy would be to persevere in urging the claims until Justice for them shall be obtained, but explicitly without resorting to force, or committing any hostility. Mr. Clay insisted that this would be equivalent to a total abandonment of the claims — He was for recommending the issuing of Letters of Marque and Reprizals; which he insisted would not be war; or at least for intimating to Congress that that measure would hereafter be advisable, if France should continue to disregard the Representations of our Minister — To this measure or any thing like it Governor Barbour was quite averse — He thought Reprizals, even special Reprizals would be War; or certainly lead to War — That these claims, though considerable, were of long standing — That nobody in this Country had the remotest idea of going to War for them — That excepting among the claimants there was not much excitement concerning them; and that to talk of going to War for them would excite more surprize than approbation — He said that he as chairman of the Committee

of Foreign Relations of the Senate had proposed in a Report to use expressions far short of this which were yet deemed too strong — and he deeply deprecated War — Mr. Clay proposed three alternatives — To recommend reprizals immediately. To recommend them prospectively and contingent — And to say nothing about them. He would like the first the best, but either better than my abandonment of the claims, as he thought it would be generally considered to be. Mr. Rush inclined to Mr. Clay — Mr. Southard expressed no opinion at the Meeting; but after it, on my enquiry said he thought the recommendation against the use of force should be omitted.

—

25. V:15. ≈ Cabinet Meeting from one till near five — I read over again by Paragraphs the Draft of a Message, except the concluding paragraphs respecting internal improvements — Numerous alterations, and several omissions were proposed; chiefly by Mr. Clay and Governor Barbour. The suggestion that we ought in no event to resort to force, to obtain indemnity for claims upon France, was struck out; but the substitute I had prepared was thought to savour too much of a recommendation of reprisals — I am to find a middle term between the two — An intimation that the rank of our naval commanders ought to be raised is to be struck out on the confident belief that it would be unavailing, expressed by Mr. Clay — Mr. Southard being however of a different opinion — And a paragraph relating to the Greek Insurrection, of which I had myself the strongest doubts, is also to be expunged — These changes are in no wise material, and abridge the Message very little; but Governor Barbour expressed the wish that the whole of the concluding part, respecting internal improvements, should be suppressed — Mr. Clay coincided in this opinion partially — Was for discarding the University, and perhaps some other objects; but for retaining great part of the other things proposed. Mr. Clay was for recommending nothing, which from its unpopularity would be unlikely to succeed — Governor Barbour nothing so popular that it may be carried without recommendation — Clay good humouredly remarked this alternate stripping off from my draft; and I told them I was like the man with his two wives — one plucking out his black hairs and the other the white till none were left. However we

adjourned till two O'Clock to-morrow, to discuss the question thoroughly. ≈

26. V:30. ≈ Calhoun, J. C. Vice-President, called to visit me — conversed upon some topics of interest, and others indifferent — Generally of the prosperous state of the Country.

Barbour S. W. with O-poth-le-Yoholo, Mad Wolf, Yoholo Micco, Emothla-Yoholo, Menewee, alias Ke-lis-he-ne-haw, Corsa-Tuftenugge, Nah-estue Hopoie, Charles Cornalls, Oc-chi-efisice, Ledagi, Mistepi, John Ridge and David Kern — Cherokees — This was the deputation of Creek Indians who now came merely to take their Great Father, as the President is usually called by the hand — After shaking hands with them all; and when they were all seated; I told the Interpreter to say to them, that I was glad to see them; and happy to meet them all in good health; safe here after their long Journey — I had heard some of them had met with an accident on the way, and had taken hurt; I hoped not seriously. The interpreter explained this — and Opothle Yoholo the Speaker of the Nation, and first Chief on the deputation answered for them all — Said some of them had met an accident by the overset-ting in the Stage, and had been hurt — But they were now well; and another part of the deputation were coming on. — I said I was glad they were coming, hoped they would arrive soon, and that we should all meet in friendship. — He said they were glad to be here, as things had happened which had frightened them, and they hoped that now all would be well again — I said that was my desire — I had also heard of things that displeased me much; but I expected that they would arrange matters with the Secretary of War to the satis-faction of all. After refreshments had been carried round, the Secretary of War, enquired if there was any thing further that they wished to say — Opothle-Yoholo answered not for the present, nor until the other part of the deputation shall arrive — They all shook hands with me again and took leave — They are almost all good-looking men — Dressing, not as the Cher-okees entirely in our Costume; but somewhat fantastically — But their countenances, and especially that of Opothle-Yoholo was remarkable by a dark and settled gloom.

The adjourned Cabinet Meeting, followed immediately after the departure of the Indians — The first question was upon the whole of the concluding division of the Message, as projected — Mr. Rush desired that the whole of it might be read again — I read it. Governor Barbour then withdrew his objection to it as a whole; but he and Mr. Clay persisted in objections to many detached parts of it — Mr. Clay wished to have the recommendations of a National University; and of a new Executive Department struck out — almost everything relating to the Patent Office; and the final enumeration of all the purposes of internal improvements for which I asserted that Congress have powers — I agreed to give up, all that relates to the Patent Office; and upon discussion, most of the particular objections were abandoned. The University Mr. Clay said was entirely hopeless — and he thought there was something in the Constitutional objection to it — For it did not rest upon the same principle as internal improvements, or the bank — I concurred entirely in the opinion, that no projects absolutely impracticable ought to be recommended — but I would look to a practicability of a longer range than a single Session of Congress — General Washington had recommended the Military Academy more than ten years before it was obtained — The plant may come late though the seed should be sown early. And I had not recommended a University — I had only referred to Washington's recommendations, and observed they had not been carried into effect. — The new Executive Department, Mr. Clay said was of most urgent necessity. No one knew it better than he — Yet he was sure there would not be twenty votes for it in the house — He did not believe there would be five. I said it was not very material to me whether I should present these views in the first or the last Message I should send to Congress — They would not suit any other — but in one of them I should feel it my indispensable duty to suggest them — There is this consideration for offering them now. That of the future I can never be sure — I may be not destined to send another Message — Mr. Rush very earnestly urged the communication, at this time — And Clay said he was anxious that almost the whole of what I had written should go — He himself was fully convinced that Congress had the powers — but he had no doubt that if they did not exercise them, there would be a dissolution of the Union, by the Mountains. The result of all was that Barbour very reluctantly withdrew his objection to the whole topic. That Clay approved of the general principles, but scrupled great part of the details. Rush approved nearly the whole; and Southard said scarcely any thing — Thus situated the perilous experiment must be made. Let me make it with full deliberation and be prepared for the consequences.

———

28. V:30. Walk to the Capitol Square.

W. Elliot's Son came to ask some questions concerning his almanach for the next year.

Johnson, George, desires some appointment for subsistence. I asked him to account for the monies he received from me more than two years since, which he promised he would; but cannot — It being all wasted in the payment of his own debts. Wirt — Attorney General, here. Has been several weeks at Baltimore, and goes to-morrow again to Annapolis. — He desired to see my Message. I read to him the concluding part respecting internal improvements which he thought excessively bold — He said there was not a line in it that he did not approve — But it would give strong hold to the party in Virginia, who represent me as grasping for power — He had been travelling about in Virginia, last Summer. He had found the Administration was gaining strength and friends there — But this subject was a great source of clamour there — Patrick Henry's prophesy would be said to have come to pass — That we wanted a great, magnificent Government — It was a noble spirited thing, but he dreaded its effects upon my popularity in Virginia — The reference to the Voyages of Discovery, and Scientific researches in Monarchies, would be cried down as a partiality for Monarchies, and the project of a Voyage in search of the Northwest passage, would be brought as Evidence that I am a convert to Captain Symmes — He held an argument of two or three hours to this effect — Mr. Rush came in the while, and discussed the subject with him — Rush is as earnest for it as Wirt is against it. I concluded to make some alterations in that part of the draft; and if it were fitting to be intimidated should abandon the whole of it.

———

[December 1825]

7. V:30. ≈ Cabinet Meeting at one — Present Mr. Clay S. S., Mr. Rush S. T., Mr. Barbour S. W. and Mr. Southard S. N. The question for discussion was upon the answer to be given to the deputation of Creek Indians — Governor Barbour read their Letter and the draft of his answer. General Gaines had been authorised to propose to them a cession of all their Lands in the State of Georgia — His Journal states that this was his proposal. But they now say that they understood the Proposal to be the Chatahouchy for the boundary — And Crowell the Agent sustains them in the allegation — But Gaines had no authority either to propose, or to accede to this — And Mr. Clay thought this the principal difficulty of the case — Mr. Clay said Mr. Webster and Mr. Everett had been at his house, and Mr. Webster had urged above all things not to let the Georgia question go before Congress. And Mr. Clay said his great apprehension was that if it went before Congress they would do nothing — and he shewed the various motives by which different members would be actuated to do nothing. I asked him if this would not release the Executive from the obligation to do any thing also — We ask of Congress to annul the Treaty, or to furnish means to compel the execution of it by the Indians — Congress do nothing — We consider the Treaty as binding, but the Indians refuse to comply, and remain on the Lands after September 1826 — We have no means to compel their compliance, and therefore can do nothing till Congress meet again — After much discussion it was concluded that the Secretary of War should answer the Letter of the Indians, declining to treat except on the basis of the cession of all the Lands in Georgia, and should call upon General Gaines to explain the difference between his views of the proposals last made by him to the Indians, and their Understanding of it — The meeting adjourned about four O'Clock.

———

14. VI. ≈ Mr. Bailey spoke of several Resolutions which he has offered in the House of Representatives, concerning Roads

and Canals, and an Amendment of the Constitution — He
said he had not shewn me those Resolutions before he offered
them, on account of the imputations upon him heretofore,
arising from his former relations to me in the Department of
State — I told him that the discussion of his Resolutions might
be useful, but I must in candour say that my opinions did not
concur with them, I thought the power of making Roads and
Canals, given by the Constitution; and thus an Amendment
asking the grant of that which was already granted; equally
impracticable and useless — Vandeventer came for some papers relating to the Creek and Georgia controversy. Dickins
brought me as I had requested a list of the Members of the
Columbian Institute; and had some conversation with me relating to the Address to be delivered by Dr. Watkins to the
Society on the 7th of January next — He spoke also of his own
situation; his wish for a more lucrative place than that which he
now has at the Treasury; and of his disappointment in the recent election of Walter Lowry, as Secretary of the Senate.
Dickins said he had been not only disappointed but deceived
by many of Mr. Crawford's friends who had encouraged him
to expect their votes for that Office; and yet he could not account for the election of Lowry unless several of General
Jackson's friends had joined in voting for him. He then enlarged upon the services he had rendered especially during the
last two years in the Treasury — intimating that he had really
performed all the duties of the Secretary — And he added that
he supposed I knew that he had been the medium of communication between the Treasury Department, and the President,
after all personal communication between Mr. Monroe and
Mr. Crawford had ceased — This fact had not before been
known to me; and I told Dickins so — He said that a few
weeks before the close of the Administration, some words used
by Mr. Monroe to Mr. Crawford had induced the latter to abstain thenceforward from coming to this house, or ever seeing
Mr. Monroe again — When Mr. Southard came in, I asked him
if this fact had been known to him — He said yes — That one
day last Winter, on coming here on business, he found Mr. Monroe walking to and fro across the room in great agitation — That
he told him Crawford had just left him — He had come to
him concerning the nomination of certain Officers of the

Customs, in Northern Ports — That Crawford recommended the nomination of several persons against whom Mr. Monroe expressed several objections — that Mr. Crawford, at last rose, in much irritation, gathered the papers together, and said, petulantly, well — if you will not appoint the persons well-qualified for the places, tell me whom you will appoint; that I may get rid of their importunities. Mr. Monroe replied with great warmth; saying that he considered Crawford's language as extremely improper, and unsuitable to the relations between them; when Crawford turning to him, raised his Cane, as in the attitude to strike, and said "you damned infernal old Scoundrel" — Mr. Monroe seized the tongs at the fire-place for self-defence; applied a retaliatory epithet to Crawford and told him he would immediately ring for servants himself and turn him out of the house, upon which Crawford beginning to recover himself said he did not intend and had not intended to insult him; and left the house. They never met, afterwards — Mr. Southard does not recollect the precise day upon which this happened. I told him that if I had known it at the time, I should not have invited Mr. Crawford to remain in the Treasury Department — It resembles the Scene between Bolingbroke and Oxford in the last days of Queen Anne.

We had this Evening the first drawing room for the Season, which was fully attended, and continued from 7 to half past ten.

———

22. V:30. ≈ From one O'Clock till near five was the Cabinet Meeting upon the Affairs with the Creek Indians and Georgia — The letter from the Creek Delegation, finally refusing the cession of all their lands within the State of Georgia was read. Much desultory conversation was had upon the course to be pursued — Governour Barbour said Forsyth of Georgia had told him yesterday, that he had infinitely rather that we should take a cession to the Chatahoochy, than that the Treaty should be sent to Congress; although as Representatives of Georgia they must protest against any thing short of the late Treaty — Governor Barbour recurred to his plan for incorporating the Indians within the States of the Union — ceasing to make Treaties with them at-all; but considering them as altogether subject to our Laws — I asked him if he did not think there

would be made question of the Constitutional Power of Congress to change so essentially the character of our Relations with the Indian tribes — He said he had no doubt there would; but that it would soon be unavoidably necessary to come to such a System — Mr. Clay said he thought it would be impracticable — That it was impossible to civilize Indians — That there never was a full blooded Indian who took to civilization — It was not in their nature. He believed they were destined to extinction — and although he would never use or countenance inhumanity towards them, he did not think them as a race, worth preserving. He considered them as essentially inferior to the Anglo-saxon race, which were now taking their place on this Continent. They were not an improvable breed; and their disappearance from the human family will be no great loss to the world. In point of fact they were rapidly disappearing, and he did not believe that in fifty years from this time there would be any of them left — Governor Barbour was somewhat shocked at these opinions, for which I fear there is too much foundation. But the question was what should now be done. The observation suggested yesterday by Mr. Forsyth gave the idea that the Secretary of War should write to the Georgia delegation, stating to them the refusal of the Creeks to cede their whole lands in Georgia, and their offer to cede to the Chatahoochy, and enquiring whether this would be acceptable to Georgia. It was supposed that the Georgia delegation would send an insulting and violent refusal for answer; but this at least will take from them hereafter the power of reproaching us for not obtaining the cession to the Chatahoochy, when it was in our power, with the pretence that Mr. Forsyth had distinctly though verbally given us to understand that it would be acceptable to Georgia — A treacherous reference to things said, or pretended to have been said in private Conversations has been much resorted to by the Georgians in this controversy. It was concluded that Governor Barbour should write this Letter. ≈

23. VI:30. Broad day-light. Walk to Georgetown — Fahrenheit 16. The library chamber at the Capitol was on fire at about one O'Clock this Morning — It was somewhat damaged and some books were destroyed by fire and some by water — The whole

building had a narrow escape. ≈ The Secretary of War Barbour, brought the draft of his Letter to the Georgia delegation, which with one slight alteration he approved. But he said that Mr. Cobb the Senator from Georgia had been with him this Morning in a state of very high excitement, and had threatened that unless we should concede this point, Georgia would necessarily be driven to support General Jackson — And Barbour said, if Mr. Clay's ideas yesterday were correct, and the Indians were going to inevitable destruction, what need was there for us to quarrel with our friends, for their sakes, and why should we not yield to Georgia at once. I said I had considered Mr. Clay's observations yesterday as expressing an opinion of results founded upon the operation of general causes; but not as an object to which we ought purposely to contribute — That we ought not to yield to Georgia, because we could not do so without gross injustice. And that as to Georgia's being driven to support General Jackson, I felt little concern or care for that. I had no more confidence in one party there than in the other.

———

31. V:30. ≈ *Day* and *Year*. The life that I lead is more regular than it has perhaps been at any other period of my life — It is established by custom that the President of the United States goes not abroad into any private companies, and to this usage I conform — I am therefore compelled to take my exercise, if at-all in the morning before Breakfast — I rise usually between five and six; that is at this time of the year from an hour and a half to two hours before the Sun — I walk by the light of Moon or Stars, or none, about four Miles, usually returning home in time to see the Sun rise, from the Eastern chamber of the house. I then make my fire, and read three chapters of the Bible, with Scott's and Hewlett's Commentaries. — Read papers till 9. Breakfast; and from ten, till five P.M. receive a succession of Visitors; sometimes without intermission — Very seldom with an interval of half an hour — Never such as to enable me to undertake any business requiring attention — From five, to half past six we dine; after which I pass about four hours in my chamber alone — Writing in this Diary, or reading papers upon some public business — excepting when occasionally interrupted by a visitor — Between eleven and

twelve I retire to bed; to rise again **♀ ☽ ⛢ ♆ ♃** at 5 or 6 the next Morning.

The year has been the most momentous of those that have passed over my head — Inasmuch as it has witnessed my elevation at the age of 58 to the Chief Magistracy of my Country — To the summit of laudable or at least blameless worldly ambition — Not however in a manner satisfactory to pride, or to just desire — Not by the unequivocal suffrages of a majority of the People — With perhaps two thirds of the whole people adverse to the actual result. Nearly one year of this service has already past, with little change of the public opinions, or feelings. Without disaster to the Country; with an unusual degree of prosperity public and private.

—

[January 1826]

2. VI. ≈ The usual Visitation of the New-Year's day, was made at this house from Noon till three O'Clock, and the crowd of company was said to have been greater than ever had been known before — amounting from two to three thousand persons. The greater portion of the members of both Houses of Congress were here; and formed only a small part of the company — The British and Mexican Ministers came, and the Brazilian Charge d'Affaires; but neither the Russian nor French Ministers, nor any persons of their Legations — They had applied last week to Mr. Clay, the Secretary of State, suggesting their old objection to coming with the crowd, and proposed to come in State, another day; say to-morrow, which I explicitly declined; being unwilling to make two days of ceremony instead of one; and still more so to yield to their pretensions, which I think quite unreasonable. I desired Mr. Clay to inform them, that if they were desirous of avoiding a crowd they might do so by coming before half past twelve, or about three. The Chevalier Huygens the Minister from the Netherlands came; after three, and left Cards, but did not come in ≈ I was until dinner time much fatigued with the ceremony of the morning. The Band of Musick of the Marine Corps, enlivened the day while the company were here; and left something of depression after they were gone.

—

[February 1826]

7. V:15. Rain and fog. Dr. Watkins spoke of the transformation recently undergone by the Newspaper called the Washington City Gazette — It has been sold by its Publisher Jonathan Elliot, and Watkins says purchased by John H. Eaton, Senator from Tennessee — Its name is changed to that of "United States Telegraph" and its first number was published last week — The Prospectus avows a determined opposition to the present Administration, and from a sample of bad English peculiar to Calhoun, I have no doubt is from his hand. Watkins asked me if I thought any notice should be taken of this Declaration of War. I said no. ≈ Mess'rs Rush, Barbour, Southard and Wirt were here in Cabinet Meeting upon Mr. Barbour's Letter to the Chairman of the Committee on Indian Affairs of the House of Representatives — The Letter was read and variously commented upon by the other Members of the Administration. Mr. Clay was absent, confined to his house by a relapse of the Influenza — Mr. Barbour's plan is differently modified, from that which he had at first prepared — He has given up the idea of incorporating the Indians into the several States where they reside — He has now substituted that of forming them all into a great territorial Government West of the Mississippi — There are many very excellent observations in the paper; which is full of benevolence and humanity — I fear there is no practicable plan by which they can be organized into one civilised or half-civilised Government — Mr. Rush, Mr. Southard, and Mr. Wirt, all expressed their doubts of the practicability of Governor Barbour's plan; but they had nothing more effective to propose; and I approved it from the same motive.

———

16. V:30. Mr. Lowrie brought me this morning the two Resolutions of the Senate adopted in Executive Session — The first declares that the question of the expediency of the Panama Mission, ought to be debated in Senate with open doors, unless the publication of the documents to which it would be necessary to refer in debate would prejudice existing Negotiations — The Second is a respectful request to the President of the United States, to inform the Senate whether such objection exists to the publication of all or of any part of those documents,

and if so to specify to what part it applies? — These Resolutions are the fruit of the ingenuity of Martin van Buren, and bear the impress of his character. The Resolution to debate an Executive nomination with open doors is without example; and the 36th Rule of the Senate is explicit and unqualified, that all documents communicated in confidence by the President to the Senate shall be kept secret by the members — The request to me to specify the particular documents the publication of which would affect existing negotiations was delicate and ensnaring. The limitation was not of papers the publication of which might be injurious; but merely of such as would affect existing negotiations; and this being necessarily a matter of opinion, if I should specify passages in the documents as of such a character, any Senator might make it a question for discussion in the Senate, and they might finally publish the whole under the colour of entertaining an opinion different from mine upon the probable effect of the publication — Besides, should the precedent once be established of opening the doors of the Senate in the midst of a debate upon Executive business, there could be no prospect of ever keeping them shut again. I answered the Resolutions of the Senate, by a Message stating that all the communications I had made to the Senate on this Subject had been confidential, and that believing it important for the Public Interest that the Confidence between the Executive and the Senate should continue unimpaired, I should leave to themselves the determination of a question, upon the motives for which, not being informed of them, I was not competent to decide.

—

[July 1826]
1. IV:15. Saturday. Sun rose beclouded. Swam alone ½ an hour. ≈ Gov'r Barbour proposes that on the 4th inst't after the usual ceremonies at the Capitol he should address the Audience and invite an immediate subscription for the benefit of Mr. Jefferson — Says he proposes to give 100 dollars himself — Mr. Rush came in while we [were] speaking of it — I doubted the expediency of the measure, and its success; and thought it would be more likely to succeed, if a meeting should be called and a subscription raised as elsewhere. Gov'r Barbour says the late rains have done immense and irreparable damage to his Estate

— His loss many thousands ≈ After dinner I rode with John round by S. H. Smith's and the College; and collected in the woods, twigs of seven different varieties of Oaks, which after returning I compared with the Plates in Michaux's first Volume — one or two of them seem different from any of those described by him — We found also the Shell-bark Hickory. Mary Hellen was confined by illness to her chamber.

2. IV. Sun rose 4:36 — By my Chronometer (French) 4:41. ≈ Heard at Hawley's R. Darneille an Address to promote the Civilization of the Indians. The preacher said he was going to settle with his family in the Arkansas Territory, and devote the remainder of his Life to the cause. He solicited contributions; but the collection was for the colonization Society. Baker, from 1 Peter 3:15: "But sanctify the Lord God in your hearts; and be ready always to give an answer to every man that asketh you a reason of the hope that is in you with meekness and fear" — Before he had got through, a thunder shower was coming up, and he dismissed the auditory with a blessing ≈

3. IV:30. Sun rose 4:36 — French 4:41–40. Swam from Rock ½ an hour. Mr. Darneille brought a subscription paper for a discourse to be published by him, containing his plan for civilizing the Indians. His plan embraces a farm and a school; and his object is to civilize the Indians by securing to them Settlement on the soil. I asked him if he had communicated his plan to the Secretary of War. He said he had, and that he had a Letter from Mr. Hamilton the Clerk in the Department charged during Mr. M'Kenney's absence with Indian Affairs, to the Governor of Arkansas requesting his assistance to promote his contemplated establishment. I told him that his object was laudable; but the means were not approved by the white people settled in Arkansas, their very earnest object being the removal of the Indians from their neighbourhood. I advised him to see the Secretary of War again and make known to him his whole plan ≈ Beverley Randolph Marshal of the Arrangements for the celebration of to-morrow brought me a note from Gen'l Walter Smith, with notice that the volunteer Corps of the Brigade under his command, would if agreeable pay me a passing salute at my door at 9 O'Clock to-morrow

Morning. I desired Major Randolph to return verbally my thanks to Gen'l Smith for the compliment. Dr. Watkins called to say that he and Mr. Asbury Dickins two members of the Committee of Arrangements would attend me to the Capitol to-morrow. He also shewed me the answers from the surviving signers of the Declaration of Independence, and Ex-Presidents, declining the invitations to attend the celebration here — Mr. Jefferson's is in his freest Style — My fathers is signed with his own hand — Mr. Carroll's apparently written with his own hand; as are Mr. Madison's and Mr. Monroe's ≈ Rush doubted much the expediency of Governor Barbour's projected address to-morrow, but as it was announced in the papers this morning, it is best to carry it through.

4. IV:30. Independence Jubile — Sun rose beclouded. Light Showers. ≈ Arriving at the door of the Capitol I was there met by Mr. Anderson the Comptroller, with whom we entered the Hall of the House of Representatives.
The Revd. Mr. Ryland made an Introductory Prayer
Joseph Anderson the Comptroller, read the Declaration of Independence.
Walter Jones delivered an Oration commemorative of the 50th Anniversary.
The Revd. Mr. Post Chaplain H.R.U.S. made a concluding prayer.
After which Governor Barbour delivered an Address to the Citizens assembled, soliciting subscriptions for the relief of Mr. Jefferson — Mr. Rush also upon the floor of the House made a short address to the same purpose. Not more than four or five subscribers were obtained, and notice was given by Governor Barbour, that others would have the opportunity to subscribe afterwards. The procession, with the exception of the military companies, returned to the President's House, where we received visitors till about 3 O'Clock, when I withdrew to my Cabinet. The company was far less numerous than the last year — Miss Pleasonton dined with us — and we celebrated my Son John's twenty-third birth-day. There were fire-works in the Evening ≈ Jones's Oration was ingenious, and far wide from the commonplaces of the day — But he had written it in loose fragments without much connection, and had not

committed it to memory — So he read from his notes, and commented upon them extemporaneously, which made a desultory composition full of interesting matter, but producing little effect as a whole. Governor Barbour's Address was the overflowing of a generous, benevolent, and patriotic heart respectable even in its inefficiency — Mr. Rush spoke also very impressively, and with correct elocution — I received a Letter from Mr. Gallatin, who is not satisfied with his Instructions — He sailed on the first of this Month from New-York, on his Mission to Great-Britain.

———

VI. III:45. Sun rose 4:38. Walk to the Race-ground. Governor Barbour brought information of the decease of Mr. Jefferson at Monticello, on the 4th inst't at 10 minutes past one in the afternoon. A strange, and very striking coincidence. It became a question, whether the event should not be noticed by some act of the Administration. Several measures suggested themselves and were taken for further Consideration. The Precedent in the case of General Washington's decease was adverted to and examined — But the Congress were then in Session, and excepting the orders for military honours, all was done at the recommendation and by Resolutions of that body — We now concluded that general orders to the army and navy would be proper and indispensable, and would reflect till to-morrow on the expediency of issuing a proclamation to the People — Gen'l Barbour will prepare the order to the army, and Mr. Rush in the absence of Mr. Southard that to the Navy. And I prepared this evening the draft of a Proclamation, but after writing it became convinced in my own mind that no such paper should issue ≈

7. IV:15. ≈ There was a meeting of the members of the Administration; Mr. Southard having returned from his visit in Virginia. It was upon full consideration that there should be no proclamation, upon the occasion of the decease of Mr. Jefferson, but I mentioned my opinion that it should be noticed in the next annual Message to Congress which was approved — General Orders from the War and Navy Departments, for the exhibition of funeral honours to the deceased were deemed proper ≈ Henry Lee called and told me that he had been last week to Monticello, to consult some papers relating to the

revolutionary War, in Mr. Jefferson's possession, and of which he had promised Mr. Lee the perusal — He was there last week on Thursday, when Mr. Jefferson was though ill, yet able to converse with him on the subject, and hoped to be able to examine the papers with him in a few days. But from that time Mr. Jefferson grew worse, and on Sunday Lee gave up all expectation of seeing the papers, and left Monticello and Charlottesville and returned ≈

8. IV:5. Sun rose 4:35 — Swam 45 minutes from the Boat. The mail this morning brought me three Letters — One dated the 3ᵈ from my brother Charles's daughter, Mrs. Susan B. Clarke, informing me that my father's end was approaching — that she wrote me, because my brother was absent in Boston — That Dr. Holbrook who was attending as his Physician thought he would probably not survive two days, and certainly not more than a fortnight — The second was from my brother written on the morning of the fourth, announcing that in the opinion of those who surrounded my father's couch, he was rapidly sinking — That they were sending an Express for my Son George, in Boston, who might perhaps arrive in time to receive his last breath — The third was from my brother's wife to her daughter Elizabeth, to the same purport, and written in much distress. I immediately took the determination to proceed as speedily as possible to Quincy, and the remainder of the day was occupied in making preparations for my departure to-morrow Morning. Mr. Southard, Mr. Rush, and Mr. Barbour were here separately in the course of the day, and together in the Evening; as was Mr. Brent of the Department of State ≈ The further proceedings of funeral honours to Mr. Jefferson, I left altogether to be settled by the Heads of the Departments. Mrs. Frye and Mrs. W. S. Smith were with us this Evening, and I was up in anxiety and apprehension till near Midnight. The suddenness of the notice of my father's danger was quite unexpected. Some weeks since my brother had written to me that he was declining, though not so as to occasion immediate alarm, and my intention had been to visit him, about the beginning of the next Month. I had flattered myself that he would survive this Summer, and even other years.

9. IV. — Sun rose 4:39 — Washington — Baltimore — French-town. At 5 this morning I left Washington, with my Son John, in my own Carriage with four horses — Yesterday had been one of the hottest days of the Summer, and there was every prospect that this day would be not less so. A light easterly breeze however came up as the Sun rose, and continued through the day — The heat of the Sun was however intense — My Servant William Pote was sent with our trunks of heavy baggage in the Stage — We stopp'd half an hour between seven and eight at Ross's tavern; and reached Merrill's at Wa-terloo, where we breakfasted, before eleven — Mr. Merrill told me that he had come this morning out from Baltimore, and was informed there that my father died on the fourth of this Month, about five O'Clock in the afternoon. From the Letters which I had yesterday received, this event was so much ex-pected by me, that it had no sudden and violent effect on my feelings — My father had nearly closed the ninety-first year of his life. A life illustrious in the Annals of his Country, and of the World — He had served to great and useful purpose his Nation, his Age, and his God — He is gone, and may the blessing of Almighty Grace have attended him to his Account — I say not, may my last End be like his! it were presumptuous — The time, the manner, the coincidence with the decease of Jefferson, are visible and palpable marks of divine favour, for which I would humble myself in grateful and silent adoration before the Ruler of the Universe — For myself all that I dare to ask is that I may live the remnant of my days in a manner worthy of him from whom I came, and at the appointed hour of my maker die as my father has died; in peace with God and man, sped to the regions of futurity with the blessings of my fellow men.

———

12. V. ≈ Dined at Fuller's at Waltham, and at ½ past 9 in the Evening alighted at Hamilton's Exchange Hotel, at Boston — Four days from Washington — The weather all the time fine; but the heat intense — Fahrenheit's Thermometer this day at 96. Immediately after arriving, I sent for my Son George to Dr. Welsh's — He was then out, and after waiting for him till past eleven I retired to bed — He came in shortly after, and was with me till near one in the morning. He informed me of

the circumstances of my father's last moments; and of those attending the funeral — George himself was on the 4ᵗʰ at Boston, expecting to attend with his company at the celebration of the day; an Express was sent for him, and he came out about noon — My father recognized him, looked upon him, and made an effort to speak; but without success — George was with him at the moment when he expired, a few minutes before six in the Evening — Mr. Quincy who on the 4ᵗʰ delivered an Oration at Boston came out the next Morning — The arrangements for the funeral were made with his concurrence — It took place on Friday the 7ᵗʰ. There was a great concourse of people from this and the neighbouring Towns — Mr. Whitney delivered a Sermon, from 1 Chron. 29:28 "He died in a good old age, full of days and honor." About two thousand persons took a last look, at his lifeless face; and all that was mortal of John Adams was deposited in the Tomb.

13. IV:30. Boston. Quincy. — Night of intense heat. ≈ After breakfast, I came out with my two sons, George and John to Quincy — I found at my fathers House, my brother with his family ≈ Every thing about the house is the same. I was not fully sensible of the change till I entered his bed chamber, the place where I had last taken leave of him; and where I had most sat with him at my two last yearly visits to him at this place — That moment was inexpressibly painful, and struck me as if it had been an arrow to the heart. My father and my mother have departed. The charm which has always made this house to me an abode of enchantment is dissolved; and yet my attachment to it, and to the whole region round is stronger than I ever felt it before — I feel it is time for me to begin to set my house in order, and to prepare for the Church-yard myself — Other duties in the meantime devolve upon me from this recent event, the full extent of which I pray that I may know — As I do for the holy Spirit of grace to discharge them.

14. IV. ≈ The company occupied most of the day — My reflections upon my own situation and duties engrossed the remainder, so that I found barely time for writing to my wife. My father by his Will has given me the option of taking this House, and about 93 Acres of Land round it, upon securing the

payment of ten thousand dollars with interest in three years from the time of his decease. After making this bequest he made a donation to the town of part of the Lands; detaching eight Acres on the road, of the grounds opposite to the house, but leaving the condition unaltered. It is repugnant to my feelings, to abandon this place where for near forty years he has resided, and where I have passed many of the happiest days of my life — I shall within two or three years if indulged with life and health need a place of retirement — Where else should I go. This will be a safe and pleasant retreat where I may pursue literary occupations, as long and as much as I can take pleasure in them. I cannot sufficiently anticipate my own dispositions to know, whether the Country will for the whole remnant of my days fill up my time and attention so much as to sustain the interest of existence — From an active and much agitated life, to pass suddenly and forever to a condition of total retirement, and almost of Solitude, is a trial to which I cannot look without some concern, and with far more for my immediate family connections than for myself. Perhaps I shall find that in the Winter Season, the excitement of a City will prove to be a necessary of Life — But even in that case the Country will be not less indispensable as a Residence for the Summer — By taking this place I avoid the necessity of building a house which would be a heavy aggravation of expence — It is also no small object to me to secure to my brother and his family the means of remaining here, at least until he can look round him to find a residence more suitable to him — This he probably could not do before the ensuing Spring. Mr. Gimbrede, is an Engraver and Instructor of drawing at West-Point — He wishes to engrave a Design, embracing Portraits of my father, and of Mr. Jefferson, in one picture; to which I gave him strong encouragement. He asked permission to copy for engraving, the Portrait of my father last painted by Stuart, for me, which is at Mr. Cruft's — and I consented.

—

16. V. — Sun rose beclouded — Cleared off warm. Heard Mr. Whitney from 1 Corinthians 15:19 "If in this life only we have hope in Christ, we are of all men most miserable" — A discourse somewhat occasioned, upon the decease of my father — But he preached a Sermon at the funeral — I have at no

time felt more deeply affected by that Event, than on entering the Meeting House, and taking in his pew the Seat which he used to occupy — Having directly before me, the pew at the left of the pulpit which was his father's, and where the earliest devotions of my childhood were performed — The memory of my father and mother; of their tender and affectionate care, of the times of peril in which we then lived, and of the hopes and fears which left their impressions on my mind came over me, till involuntary tears started from my eyes — I looked around the house, with enquiring thoughts — where were those whom I was then wont to meet in this house — The aged of that time; the Pastor by whom I had been baptized, the deacons who sat before the communion table, have all long since departed — Those then in the Meridian of life have all followed them — Five or six persons then children like my self, under the period of youth were all that I could discern, with grey hairs and furrowed cheeks; two or three of them with families of a succeeding generation around them. The house was not crowded, but well filled — though with almost another race of men and women — It was a comforting reflection that they had the external marks of a Condition much improved upon that of the former age.

——

21. IV:15. ≈ Dr. Holbrook, who as a physician attended my father, gave me some particulars of his last days. He retained his faculties till life itself failed. On Saturday the first of this Month he had rode down to Mr. Quincy's, and after his return dined below. on Sunday he was much distressed by his cough, but neither then, nor on Monday kept his bed — My brother that day went to Boston — Mrs. S. B. Clarke, my brother Charles's daughter on Monday asked my father, whether she should write to me — He said at first "no — why trouble my Son" — but after a momentary pause, said "yes; write to him" — She wrote accordingly — In the Night of Monday, he suffered much — On Tuesday Morning, an express was sent for my Son George, who was at Boston attending on the celebration of the day — He came out immediately; was here between Noon and One — He was recognized by my father, who made an effort to speak to him, but without success — George received his expiring breath between five and six in the

afternoon — He had in the morning been removed from one bed to another and then back. Mrs. Clarke said to him that it was the 4th of July, the 50th Anniversary of Independence — He answered — "It is a great day. It is a good day." — About one afternoon he said "Thomas Jefferson survives," but the last word was indistinctly and imperfectly uttered. He spoke no more — He had sent as a toast to the celebration at Quincy, "Independence forever." — Dr. Holbrook said his death was the mere cessation of the functions of nature by old age — without disease.

———

26. III:45. ≈ Mrs. Cushing, widow of the late Judge Cushing came to spend some days here. A Mr. Hammatt, her nephew and his daughter came with her; but proceeded to Boston; to return and take her on Friday or Saturday — I called at Peter Turner's, but he was gone to Boston — The morning was very warm; but just after dinner there was a thunder shower, followed by steady rain till late in the evening; which confined us all to the house — Mrs. Cushing entertained us with many anecdotes of antient days, from the time of my fathers Law studies with Mr. Putnam at Worcester, down to the decease of her husband in 1811 — Among the rest she says that, on the day when my father argued his first Cause in the Superior Court, some of the judges were afterwards enquiring at dinner, who he was — and Governor Hutchinson, then chief Justice, said, that whoever should live to see it, would find in him a great man. She also told of the last meeting of the Judges of the Superior Court under the king's Government in 1774 — to which her husband had then just been appointed in the place of his father, when at the dinners given to the judges by Sheriff Greenleaf and others she heard much political conversation, and Mrs. Putnam said that 500 redcoats would set all the minute men throughout the Colony a-scampering — We took yesterday morning three different sets of insects from the Lime trees on the bark, all of which have this day undergone changes — The eggs have hatched. A small bug has cast off his cowl, and seven caterpillars, each about an inch long, lying apparently torpid, side by side, upon one leaf have cast off an outer skin with a brush of dark hair, and come out with a white brushed coat.

———

31. IV:15. ≈ I read to the family Mr. Edward Everett's Oration delivered at Cambridge on the 4th of this Month. It is like all his writings full of thought, of argument, and of Eloquence — intermixed with a little humorous levity, and a few paradoxical fancies — There is at this Time in this Commonwealth a practical School of popular Oratory, of which I believe myself to be the principal founder, by my own Orations and Lectures, and which with the blessing of him who reigns, will redound to the honour and advantage of this Nation, and to the benefit of Mankind.

———

[August 1826]
2. IV:30. Wrote a Letter to my wife, to be sent by Dr. Huntt ≈ At 11 I went again to the Senate Chamber in the State House; where the Governor and Lieutenant Governor Thomas L. Winthrop, were with the Mayor, and authorities of the City were assembled, and when we went in procession to Faneuil Hall, and heard an Eulogy upon John Adams and Thomas Jefferson by Mr. Daniel Webster — The prayers were performed by Charles Lowell — There was a funeral symphony, Anthem and Dirge — The Streets from the State House to the Hall were thronged with a greater concourse of People than I ever witnessed in Boston — The Hall itself was crowded to the utmost of its capacity. Mr. Webster was about two hours and a half in delivering his discourse, during which attention held the whole Assembly mute. He returned with us to the Hotel, and thence to his own home ≈ I have received high, though melancholy gratification from these performances, but found myself much too overcome with fatigue.

———

13. V. Rain. Heard Mr. Bowes Whitney of Hingham, this morning from Proverbs 15:3 "The eyes of the Lord are in every place, beholding the evil and the good" and in the afternoon from Proverbs 30:8, 9, "Remove far from me vanity and lies; give me neither poverty nor riches; feed me with food convenient for me: — Lest I be full, and deny thee, and say, Who is the Lord? or lest I be poor, and steal, and take the name of my God in vain." It rained almost without interruption, the whole day. There were at Meeting, less than forty persons in the morning, without a female or a singer — In the

afternoon about fifty — one woman, and singers enough to make discord. I invited Mr. Whitney home to dine with us, and took him to Mr. Peter Whitney's when the afternoon services were closed — John went to Mr. Quincy's, and obtained his signature to several papers relating to the Execution of my father's Will — Mr. Bowes Whitney, is an intelligent man and a sensible preacher, but has not much conversation. He told me however some anecdotes, and among the rest one — of my father's Cousin Zabdiel Adams, Minister of Lunenburg, who at the time when my father was President, complained to Mr. Whitney's Father, that he himself, had not made the Law his profession instead of preaching — For, said he, why should not I have been President of the United States as well as my Cousin John? — The Law might have carried Mr. Zabdiel Adams to Congress — perhaps to the Senate of the United States; for he was a man of good Talents; and in this Country the Law, is the natural profession of men, aspiring to political distinction. But in the notices which I have collected from the Town records, from the few papers [of] the preceding ages which have come to my hands, from Mather's Magnalia, and Hutchinson's History, and lastly from the Catalogue of Harvard College, I cannot overlook the difference of Fortune in Life, between those of my kindred, who were educated at Cambridge, and those deprived of that advantage — My father's uncle Joseph was graduated at Harvard, and became an eminent Minister, at Newington, New-Hampshire. If my Grandfather himself had received the same education, he would have been distinguished, either as a Clergyman or as a Lawyer.

> But knowledge to his eyes, her ample page
> Rich with the spoils of Time, did ne'er unroll —

and the summit of his political elevation, was the Office of a Selectman of Braintree.

———

26. V. ≈ Mrs. Willard my next visitant is the keeper of a female Seminary of Education at Troy in New-York — About a week since I received a Letter from her, urging the expediency that Congress should patronize an institution for female education, with a small pamphlet published by her, recommending the

same subject to the Legislature of New-York — Mrs. Willard is a sensible and spirited woman, and I told her that her purpose of improving female education, had my approbation and hearty good wishes; and with regard to any assistance from Congress I was sorry she must expect nothing more — Congress I was convinced would now do nothing — They will do nothing for the education of boys, excepting to make Soldiers; they will not endow an University — I hoped this disposition would change; but while it continues, any application to Congress for female education must be fruitless — Mrs. Willard thanked me for the frankness with which I had spoken, which she said she preferred to the delusive flattery with which her sex were usually treated, and after some intelligent discourse on female education, took leave.

———

[September 1826]
8. III:30. Rose and lighted my lamp, the first time this Season. I wrote a Letter to the Supervisors of the Temple & School fund, established in Town, by my father, expressing to them my wishes with regard to the erection of a modest monument to his Memory ≈ I spoke to Mr. Whitney upon the subject of building the Temple; and he mentioned again the expediency of having in it an Apartment, to receive the Library, given by my father to the Town — which I approved — I informed Mr. Whitney also of my wish to join in Communion with the Church of which he is the Pastor. I ought to have joined it thirty years ago and more; but the tumult of the world, false shame, a distrust of my own worthiness to partake of the communion, and a residence elsewhere and continually changing made me defer it to a more convenient opportunity — But my fathers for nearly two Centuries have been members of this Church — My purpose is if my life should be spared till the end of my term of Public Service, to return and be gathered to my fathers here. It is right that I should make a public profession of my faith and hope as a Christian; and no time can be better for it than now immediately after the Death of my father and before my retirement from the public service, and the worldly cares of life. Mr. Whitney told me the next Communion day would be the first Sunday, which is the first day of next Month — That it was usual for the Minister to announce

the intention of the communicant on the preceding Sunday, and that before administering the first communion he called upon the communicant, for a profession of faith in Christianity very short, and in general terms — He did this conforming to antient usage, but he had exceedingly abridged the profession of faith, from that used formerly by his Predecessor Mr. Wibird; and his own inclination was that it should hereafter be omitted altogether. ≈

9. V:15. Boston ≈ I received a Letter from De Witt Clinton, Governor of New-York with enclosures complaining of an Advertisement in the National Intelligencer, for the Sale of a coloured Man, whom they claim as a Freeman, and a Citizen of New-York. I enclosed all the papers to Mr. Clay at Washington, with a request that he would act upon them, as the laws would warrant.

———

13. V:30. ≈ Elizabeth Robson the female Quaker preacher, with two other women and two men, came upon their Morning visit — Wistar and one of the women are from Philadelphia — The other woman came from England with Elizabeth, and Bassett is of Lynn. They are returning from a tour to Nantucket, and Elizabeth is now going to Montreal and Quebec. After the usual Salutations, Elizabeth sat some time with her hand covering her face as in deep meditation, and then addressed me in a formal religious exhortation of about a quarter of an hour concerning the cares and duties of the Ruler of a Nation, but particularly upon the condition of the poor, oppressed coloured people in this Country. after finishing her Address, and a short pause, she rose from the Sofa, turned and kneeled before it, and made a short prayer to God in my behalf — A short time after she had finished, the woman from Philadelphia made also a formal brief address; but in general terms and without reference to the Slaves — My wife and my brother with his family were present. We heard them with respectful attention, and when they rose to withdraw, I thanked them for their exhortations and their prayers — observing that in the public trust with which I am charged, I had great need of the prayers of all worthy persons; and as to what Elizabeth had said concerning the condition of the poor coloured people in

this Country, I should lay it seriously to heart and should act
with a view to promote the glory of God, and the best interests
of this great people. They then took leave.

———

30. V:30. Boston ≈ I went to dine with Mr. Nathanael Amory
at Watertown, but missed the way, and did not reach his house
till five O'Clock, when I found him and his company at the
Dessert. Mrs. Amory and Miss Elwyn were at the table. J.
Welles, T. H. Perkins, Charles and B. Joy, J. Callender, W.
Sullivan, I. P. Davis, and some others were there — the remnants of an old Saturday's club, of which I was an associate
from 1791 to 1794 — We sat recounting the tales of other
times till about nine in the Evening, after which I returned
with William to Quincy; about 18 Miles — I reached home as
the Clock struck 11.

Day. The month like the two preceding ones has been
chiefly devoted to the Settlement of my father's Estate. As the
Sun rises later my hour of rising has dallied correspondingly,
and I have passed several days in Boston, though not altogether
idle — I have prepared in great measure for myself a place of
retirement from March 1829, for the remainder of my days,
and when that day comes, if indulged with health and peace, I
trust it will find me ready and willing to renounce the vain
pomp and tumult of the world, and finish my life with an employment of Time, worthy of that which has engaged my
youth and mature years.

———

[October 1826]
21. IV:30. Rain almost without intermission the whole day. It
confined me to the house, but did not interrupt the stream of
visitors, the reception of whom forms the occupation of four
fifths of my time, and renders long continued attention to any
subject of business, public or private, utterly impracticable ≈
Mr. Clay spoke of the Negotiations with Great-Britain, which
are in ill, and threatening Condition — I had read the recent
despatches from Mr. Gallatin. The British Government have
assumed the new ground of refusing to negotiate upon the
subject of the Colonial Trade — They have also made a proposal to compromise the Slave indemnity question, by giving

£250,000 Sterling, which I desired Mr. Clay to authorise Mr. Gallatin to accept, after using all reasonable efforts to obtain more — I firmly believe we shall in no other way ultimately obtain any thing.

———

28. V:30. ≈ I desired Mr. Clay to make a minute of the Subjects which would require notice in the annual message to Congress, connected with the Department of State — He spoke of the strong representations by which I have been urged to remove the principal Custom-house Officers at Philadelphia and at Charleston, S.C — They are no doubt hostile to the Administration, and the Collectors use all the influence of their Offices, against us by the appointment of subordinate officers of the same stamp, against us. They alledge therefore that the friends of the Administration have to contend not only against their enemies but against the Administration itself, which leaves its power in the hands of its own enemies, to be wielded against its friends — There is no doubt some justice in these allegations, but no positive act of hostility is proved against the Collectors — Steele at Philadelphia, from the state of his health has for more than a year been unable to perform his duty — Swift the surveyor at New-York is under indictment for a conspiracy to cheat, and the jury were discharged, as not being able to agree upon their verdict — eight of them being for conviction and four for acquittal. I think it best to wait some time longer, before making any removals, and I see yet no reason sufficient to justify a departure from the principle with which I entered upon the Administration, of removing no public Officer, for merely preferring another Candidate for the Presidency — I finished this day the reading of the proceedings of the Court-Martial upon Lieutenant Constantine Smith of the Marine Corps, and was not satisfied with them. I passed too much of the day in reading, and not enough in writing. Much of the Evening wasted — Mrs. Adams again very unwell, and confined to her chamber.

———

30. V:15. Circum capitoline walk. — Sun rose 6:48. ≈ This is my fathers birth day and the Sonnet here enclosed is the meditation of my Morning's walk. I record it thus that it may

be legible only to myself, or to a reader who will take the
trouble to pick it out of the short-hand — If it were better
poetry I would have written it at full length ≈

> Day of my fathers birth. I hail thee yet
> What though his body moulders in the grave
> Yet shall not Death the immortal soul enslave
> The Sun is not extinct — his orb has set.
> And where on Earth's wide ball shall man be met
> While time shall run, but from thy spirit brave
> Shall learn to grasp the boon his maker gave
> And spurn the terror of a tyrants threat.
> Who but shall learn that Freedom is the prize
> Man still is bound to rescue or maintain
> That Natures God commands the Slave to rise
> And on the oppressor's head to break his chain
> Roll, years of promise, rapidly roll round
> Till not a Slave shall on this earth be found.

——

[November 1826]

10. VI:15 — Round Capitol Square in one hour. Sun rose at 7:
while I was out. I made a race round the Capitol Square by
way of experiment to ascertain in how short a time I could
perform it and was exactly one hour by the Clock on my Mantle piece. Dr. Lane came for my decision upon his claim; it appeared by the Report of the Secretary of the Navy, that the
Negroes for the maintenance of whom he claimed, at the rate
of 40 cents a day per head, for two years were actually not in
his custody one month — many of them not ten days. Mr.
Southard had made out an account for the actual time
amounting to 420 dollars — I told Lane, I doubted whether I
should direct the payment even of that — I said that the presentation of such a claim, was a transaction, the character of
which I knew of no honest word to designate — The Court
had decreed that the Negroes should be placed in the custody
of three persons, authorised to employ them in work to pay
for their cloathing and subsistence, and upon *condition* that
they should cause no expence to any person — they were so
delivered: received and kept upon that condition; and this man
charges 32000 dollars for keeping them two years, that is as

long as he had the office of Marshal not having had them in his charge after the order of the Court a single day — He said that Armstrong, the present Marshal had been paid by my express direction, for the same charge, after he came into office, and that the Marshals of Georgia and Mississippi had been paid, for keeping the same negroes. The payment of Armstrong's charge was by my order upon a Report of the Secretary of the Navy — But Armstrong had them actually in his charge; by an order of the Court, which authorised him to employ them at moderate work to pay for their maintenance. Armstrong was allowed something additional, which the order of Court did not prohibit; though if I had known of this order of the Court, I should not have sanctioned the additional payment. That to Morel the Marshal of Georgia was made by direction of Mr. Monroe, much to my dissatisfaction, though it being business of the Navy department, I took little part in the affair — Of the payment to the Marshal of Mississippi I knew nothing.

———

22. IV:45. Round Capitol Square. 1 hour 5 minutes — Sun rose 7:12. Mrs. Weedon was a solicitor for Charity — She said she had rent to pay; and if she could not obtain money to pay it this day, her Landlord threatened to *distrain* upon her furniture — Of such visitors I have many.

———

27. VI. Round Capitol Square — 1 hour 3 minutes — Sun rose 7:16. Col'l Trumbull came to inform me that three of his great Pictures, painted for Congress were now placed in the Rotunda at the Capitol, and the other would be in its place to-morrow Morning — He asked me when it would be convenient to me to go and see them, and I appointed to-morrow at Noon. He said they were exceedingly well placed, and he thought when I should see them, I should be of the opinion they were not so badly painted as some people had pretended. ≈ In the Evening I had a visit from Mr. D. P. Cook, Representative from Illinois. He has been much out of health, and has lost his Election to the next Congress. Among the causes of his failure is said to have been his resistance to projects for altering the system of the Land Laws, and for distributing all the Lands in the Western Country, among the people there, for

little or nothing — Benton has been the first broacher of this system, and he relies upon it to support his popularity in the Western Country — He made a proposal in the Senate last Winter for this graduation, of the prices of public Lands; and supported it by a speech, the whole drift of which was to excite and encourage hopes among the Western people, that they can extort the Lands from the Government, for nothing. He printed an Edition of this speech in a pamphlet, and Cook says he scattered copies of it all over the Country, as he went home; and now as he is returning to Congress — Cook says that the minds of the people upon this subject are all debauched; that they say they must have the lands for nothing, and that the debt they owe for those they have bought, must be spunged — He adds that Benton made himself amazingly popular by the Resolution he offered for graduating, and reducing the price of the Lands, though his popularity has been somewhat shaken, by a powerful exposure of him in the newspapers in the course of the Summer. I have no doubt however that he will be re-elected. Cook himself has prepared three Resolutions, much to the same purport; but I think under bidding even upon Benton — Cook is too late to save himself, but the best days of our Land sales are past — We shall have trouble from that quarter.

28. V:45. Round Capitol Square 1 hour 15 minutes — Sun rose 7:17. ≈ At Noon I rode up to the Capitol, and met Col'l Trumbull in the Rotunda — His four pictures are placed and in such a favourable light, that they appear far better than they had ever done before. There are four other spaces to be filled with pictures of the same size, for which the Col'l is very desirous of being employed. He had therefore placed under them, his small pictures of the Deaths of Warren & Montgomery, and two others from sketches, one of the Death of Mercer at Princeton, and the fourth another Battle, and with them he had brought two small pictures, for churches, religious subjects which he said he had painted this present year, and had taken here with him to shew that he was not too old to paint yet. A French workman in Sculpture engaged upon a Bas-relief of Penn's Treaty, came and asked me to go up on his scaffolding and view his work which I did — But all the Bas-reliefs in the

Rotunda are execrably bad. I went up likewise within the scaffolding to the Pediment, where Persico was at work. One of his three figures is nearly finished, and I think the design when completed will be good. ≈

29. V:30. Round Capitol Square. 1 hour 15 minutes. Sun rose 7:17. Cabinet Meeting — At which I read the first draft of the annual message to Congress; upon which not much of observation was made — Mr. Wirt said he did not see what there was for the Richmond Enquirer to take hold of. The Richmond Enquirer will find or make enough. But there are several supplementary paragraphs yet to be added — I gave the draft to Governor Barbour, and it was agreed that the members of the Administration should meet at the War Department tomorrow Morning, where they will examine the message among themselves; minute such passages as they may deem objectionable, and then come and discuss them with me. I have consented to this mode of scrutinizing the message, because I wish to have the benefit of every objection that can be made, by every member of the administration — But it has never been practised heretofore, and I am not sure that it will be safe precedent to follow — In England where the Speech or Message is delivered by a person under no responsibility, it must be made by those who are responsible for its contents — But here, where he who delivers it is alone responsible; and those who advise have no responsibility at all, there may be some danger, in placing the composition of it, so much under the controul of the Cabinet members, by giving it up to a discussion entirely among themselves.

——

[December 1826]

7. V:30. ≈ I wrote very little this Evening, and my Diary now runs again in arrear day after day, till I shall lose irretrievably the Chain of Events, and then comes another Chasm in the record of my life. The Succession of visitors from my breakfasting to my dining hour, with their variety of objects and purposes is inexpressibly distressing — And now that members of Congress come and absorb my evening hours, it induces a physical impossibility that I should keep up with the stream of time in my record. An hours walk before daylight is

my only exercise for the day. Then to dress and breakfast I
have scarce an hour. Then five and twenty visitors or more,
from ten of the morning till five in the afternoon, leave me not
a moment of leisure for reflection, or for writing — By the
time evening approaches my strength and Spirits are both
exhausted — Such has been the course of this day. Such will be
that of how many more?

———

12. VI. ≈ T. Jefferson Randolph is the grand-son of the deceased Ex-President, and had brought me last Spring a Letter
of introduction from him. I asked him what had been the
success of the Lottery granted by the Legislature of Virginia
last Winter for the sale of his Grand-father's Estate: He said it
had totally failed; but that the Contractors for the Lottery,
Yates and M'Intire, thought it might succeed, if by an Act of
Congress it could be connected, with a City Corporation
Lottery — I asked him if there were any constitutional difficulties in the way of such an arrangement. He said yes — That the
Virginia delegation, had it now before them for consideration.
He knew not how they would decide upon it. I told him I
should be happy to give him any assistance in my power and
consistent with my duty.

———

16. IV:30. ≈ John A. King late Secretary to the Legation to
Great Britain arrived; bringing with him a Convention concluded on the 13th of last Month by Mr. Gallatin, with the
British Plenipotentiaries Huskisson and Addington, by which
if it please God, the long controversy respecting Slaves carried
away from this Country in violation of the first stipulation of
the Treaty of Ghent, will be closed, by a payment on the part
of Great-Britain of a sum a little exceeding twelve hundred
thousand dollars to be distributed by the American Government among the claimants. I receive this intelligence with the
most fervent gratitude and joy. Mr. Clay came to speak of the
arrangements to be made for sending the Treaty to the Senate;
for which to avoid delay, many original papers must be sent.
J. A. King dined and spent the Evening with me, and gave me
information as far as he was informed of the general state of affairs in Europe. Mr. Gallatin is determined to return next May.

———

21. V. ≈ Mr. Clay spoke of the ensuing presidential Election, and intimated that some of his friends, Eastern and Western had expressed a wish that he should be supported as the Candidate for the Vice-Presidency. He said he thought the Selection ought to be made exclusively with reference to its influence upon the issue of the Election of President — That for himself he had no wish either to be a Candidate for the Vice-Presidency, or to withhold himself from it, if it should be thought useful to the cause that he should be run for that office — I told him that I had hitherto heard very little said upon the subject — That if the failure of his health should render the duties of the Department of State too oppressive for his continuance in it, I should be satisfied, if he should be transferred to the Vice Presidency; but otherwise, I should think it more advantageous both for the public and personally for him that he should continue in the far more arduous and important office of Secretary of State; which in the event of his retiring from it, I should find it extremely difficult to fill. I said it was not my intention to compliment him, but I must say it would be no easy matter to supply his place in that Department. He said he was entirely satisfied with it. That without complimenting me, he would say that he had found every facility in transacting business under me; and he should be equally well pleased to continue in the Department of State, or to pass to the Vice-Presidency, according as the general cause of the Administration might be promoted by either event — He said he had sometime in the course of the last Summer mentioned to Governor Barbour, his own disposition that the friends of the Administration might unite in supporting him (Barbour) for the next Vice-Presidency — and that he should be satisfied with that arrangement, but he believed it would be expedient to come to some definitive understanding concerning it.

—

[February 1827]

3. V:45. ≈ Southard, S.L. — Letter from Gen'l Jackson — Not that heretofore threatened, but another, brought by General Houston — The Letter asks explanations of matters alledged to have been spoken last Summer by Mr. Southard at a dinner Table at Mr. Welfords at Petersburg in Virginia — The

General affects to consider this conversation as in the nature of charges against him by a member of the Government.

———

5. V:45. ≈ Southard said Houston asked him on Saturday Night, to deliver his answer to General Jackson's Letter to him — *open* — and not to send it through the Post-Office — I suggested to Mr. Southard the propriety of his answering the Letter by a cool denial of the imputations upon General Jackson, which imported a departure on his part from public duty; without indicating any sensibility to the violation of the confidence of social intercourse, or to the tale-bearing misrepresentations which had called forth the General's Letter — and without noticing the insidious allegation of the General, imputing to the *Government* of the United States, the Sentiments expressed on a casual topic of conversation at a dinner table — I observed if Jackson should be content with the denial of all imputation upon his character, the controversy would cease there with Southard's answer; but if Jackson intended to make a public quarrel of it, these outrages of decency and delicacy on his part, might be discussed more usefully to the public, than with him.

———

25. V:30. ≈ I wrote to my Son George and was engaged till near Midnight, in tracing through the second Volume of U.S. Laws, the Journals of the old Congress, and the Speeches of President Washington, the History of our Relations with the Indian Tribes since the Revolution — and the origin of the Army, with its progressive increase — This examination like many others leads me deeper and deeper in research till I am compelled to stay my enquiries for want of Time to pursue them. In the controversy with Georgia, the powers of the General Government, and those of the Government of Georgia, are in conflict, and it is indispensable to know the whole History of our Indian relations of Peace and War, to understand the ground upon which we stand — It was debateable ground far more under the Confederation than now, but Georgia and some other States are disposed to revert to the State Claims under the Confederation.

———

[March 1827]

15. VI. Columbian College — Sun rose beclouded — Varied my morning walk, from the Capitol Square to the College Hill — the distance being the same — Mr. Anderson the Comptroller called this morning, to converse with me upon the Circular Instruction to the Collectors to be sent with the Proclamation. He spoke also of other subjects; and particularly of the bitter and rancorous spirit of the Opposition — It has produced during the late Session of Congress four or five Challenges to duels, all of which however happily all ended in smoke — and at a public dinner given last week to John Randolph of Roanoke, a toast was given, directly instigating assassination. Mr. Anderson remarked to me, that General Jackson was deeply indebted to me for his character before the Nation, and thought I had been ill requited for kindness and service to him.

———

18. V:15. — Cloudy — Rain — Storm. There came on this morning a heavy storm of rain, which detained me from attendance at Church — I finished a long Letter to A. Gallatin. I write few private Letters, and those under irksome restraints — I can never be sure of writing a line, that will not some day be published by friend or foe — Nor can I write a sentence susceptible of an odious misconstruction, but it will be seized upon and bandied about like a watchword for hatred and derision — This condition of things gives Style the Cramp — I wrote also the weekly Letter to my Son — These at least will escape the torture of the Press.

———

[April 1827]

2. IV:15. Mr. Southard called twice in the course of the Morning, first to mention letters received from Commodore Hull in the Pacific, and from Rodgers at Malta, in December; and afterwards to read to me a reply from General Jackson, to the answer Southard had sent him to the Letter which Jackson had written to him about the dinner Conversation last Summer at Fredericksburg. The reply is in two or three sheets of paper; written in a coarse and insulting Style, somewhat verbose, and with passion partly suppressed; alledging that he had received

the statement of Mr. Southard's remarks from Dr. Wallace and a Mr. Johnson, in writing — these were two of the guests at table — He complains that Mr. Southard's answer is argumentative, instead of plain matter of fact; which he had expected; and then it enter into large historical details to shew that he received no proper supplies from the War Department for the defence of New-Orleans, but saved that City by obtaining pistol flints from Barataria. He finishes the Letter by announcing it as a close of the Correspondence.

——

9. V. Round Capitol Square. Rain. In my morning walk round the Capitol Square, I noticed the putting forth of the leaves of some of the trees — It is already late in the Season for such observations. They should have been commenced in February; with the shooting of the willow — I have marked the order in which the trees falling under my observation, put out their leaves — The variety in their manner of vegetating is so remarkable, that I am humiliated by the heedlessness with which I have suffered this process, to pass at least fifty times before my eyes, without bestowing a thought upon it.

——

13. V:30. Just at Sunrise — Walk to the bathing rock. I have already been tempted by the prevailing warm weather to bathe in the Potowmack, but have been deterred by the Catarrh, still hanging upon me, and by the warnings of physicians, whose doctrines are not in harmony with my experience — I took however for this morning's walk, the direction to the River, and visited the rock whence I most frequently go into the River — It is yet adapted to the purpose; but all trace of the old Sycamore tree which was near it, and blew down the winter before last, is gone. There is yet one standing a little below; but it is undermined with every high tide; and must be soon over-thrown. The borders of the river are strewed with dead herring and shads and the waters are not so high as usual at this Season.

——

24. V:15. ≈ I am inclining to resume my enquiries, relating to the production and growth of fruit and forest trees. Since I first entered upon them last Summer, a few Books treating of the Subject, have been procured for the Department of State,

from London and Paris — I have Loudon's Encyclopaedia of gardening, fourth Edition 1826 an Octavo Volume of 1240 pages — And his Encyclopaedia of Agriculture, 1825: a similar volume of 1224 pages — And I have this day borrowed from the Department, Treatises of Du Hamel Du Monceau, upon the cultivation of Trees and the uses and treatment of Wood, which have been procured at my request — I find upon consulting them, that there are two others wanted to complete his entire work upon the forests — Looking into these Books I find a wide field opened before me, which I cannot expect that the remnant of life allotted to me, will afford me time to explore: and at present the time that I can bestow upon it is so very little, and cut up with such incessant interruptions, that I fear the result of my pursuit will plunge me into inextricable confusion of mind, without contributing to any useful end — I brought home yesterday from the Race-ground, a twig covered with white blossoms, which upon examination I found to be the Dogwood — Cornus Florida. I had seen it in blossom about a week at the Capitol garden without knowing it — I found the description and Print of it in Michaux's North American Sylva Vol. I, p. 265 and in Bigelow's Medical Botany Vol. 2, p. 73 — And another Dogwood in Bigelow Vol. I, p. 93 — This morning also, with Antoine I planted four Rows of large Pennsylvania Walnuts — 9 Quincy Walnuts and 8 Hazelnuts in one Row and three Peters Chesnuts, with the rest of the Row in Apple seeds in a different part of the Garden, from that where I planted last November. That bed is now covering itself with weeds; but there was not a symptom of any of my nuts having vegetated — Upon digging however, Antoine found one of the Pennsylvania Walnuts had put forth a shoot which will probably show itself above ground in June — which gives me hopes that others will appear also — The time that I can snatch for this fantastical humour is now the only hour

> Not wanting power to mitigate and swage
> With solemn touches troubled thoughts and chase
> Anguish, and doubt, and fear, and sorrow, and pain —

26. V. ≈ Doctor Watkins had a paper containing a printed list of persons in many, of the States of the Union, named as my

friends, and with whom correspondence is invited. It was dated Washington City 5 March 1827 but he received it Post-marked at Cincinnati, and he thought it an indiscreet publication. He also shewed me a Letter from J. Binns at Philadelphia, with a printed Circular — The Letter complains that the Administration does not support its friends, and intimates that sacrifices of time and of money must be made — I have observed the tendency of our electioneering to venality; and shall not encourage it — There is much money expended by the adversaries to the Administration, and it runs chiefly in the channels of the Press — They work by Slander to vitiate the public opinion, and pay for defamation to receive their reward in votes.

—

[May 1827]
6. V. ≈ I heard Mr. Campbell at Mr. Baker's. His text was from Revelation 2:16 "Repent, or else I will come unto thee quickly." Mr. Campbell, dwelt largely and earnestly upon the universal depravity of mankind — It is matter of curious speculation to me, how men of good understanding and reasoning faculties can be drilled into the sincere belief of these absurdities — The Scripture says that the heart is deceitful above all things and desperately wicked — this is certainly true; and is a profound observation upon the human character. But the language is figurative — by the *heart*, is meant in this passage the selfish passions of man — But there is also in man a Spirit, and the inspiration of the almighty giveth him understanding — It is the duty of man to discover the vicious propensities, and deceits of his heart to controul them — This with the grace of God, a large portion of the human race in Christian Lands to a considerable extent do accomplish. It seems therefore to be worse than useless for preachers to declare that mankind are universally depraved. It takes from honest integrity all its honours — it degrades men in their own estimation — Mr. Campbell read a hymn, which declared that *we* were more base and brutish than the beasts — a spiritual Song of Isaac Watts' — what is the meaning of this? If Watts had said this on a week day to any one of his parishioners, would he not have knocked him down? And how can that be taught as a solemn truth of

religion, applicable to all mankind, which if said at any other time to any one individual would be punishable as Slander.

———

10. V:15. ≈ I spoke to Mr. Southard of my desire to obtain information of the natural history and cultivation of foreign plants, fruits and forest trees, of special usefulness, with a view to introduce the cultivation of them into this Country: and suggested the expediency of a circular Letter of Instruction to the Captains of our Public Ships who visit distant parts of the world, to lend their assistance in co-operation with the Consuls to effect that object — He said he would be thinking of it; and would converse with Mr. Rush concerning it.

———

12. IV:50. ≈ Mr. Van Buren paid me a morning visit; he is on his return from a tour through Virginia, North- and South-Carolina, and Georgia, with C. C. Cambreleng, since the close of the Session of Congress. They are generally understood to have been electioneering, and Van Buren is now the great electioneering manager for General Jackson as he was before the last Election for Mr. Crawford. He is now acting over the part in the affairs of the Union, which Aaron Burr performed in 1799 and 1800 and there is much resemblance of character, manners and even person between the two men — Van Buren however has improved as much in the art of electioneering upon Burr, as the State of New-York has grown in relative strength and importance in the Union. Van Buren has now every prospect of success in his present movements, and he will avoid the rock upon which Burr afterwards split. His discourse with me this day was upon the late Mr. Rufus King, his History and Character, and upon Mr. Monroe and his Affairs — Also upon the Petersburg Horse-races which he has been attending — He proceeds on his journey homeward to-morrow, and on Mr. Rush's coming in took leave.

———

[June 1827]
8. III:30. ≈ Mr. Clay was here this Evening — He proposes to leave the City on Sunday for a visit to Kentucky, intending to return here by the first of August — I found myself unable to write, the greater part of this day — My health and Spirits

droop, and the attempt to sustain them, by exciting an anxious interest in Botany, the natural History of Trees, and the purpose of naturalizing exotics, is almost desperate. The design is fascinating, but the practical execution is beset with difficulties — one of them is the consumption of time in search of knowledge on the subject — I seek it blindfold, and now with an anxiety which causes sleepless Nights — I began last Summer with Michaux's North-American Sylva, and formed some little acquaintance with the Oaks, but learnt little or nothing of the best manner of cultivating them — This Summer I have more books — But with them the objects of enquiry, and investigation spread — I believe ten Summers, of unrelaxing attention will be necessary to accomplish any thing useful for posterity, and after all it may terminate in disappointment — This night I change my bedchamber, in the hope of obtaining less unquiet sleep, and more repose.

———

[July 1827]
9. IV. ≈ Judge Cranch called here this Evening, and gave me three Letters from me to him, written at Newbury-Port dated 14 October and 8 December 1787 and 16–February 1788 containing my objections to the Constitution of the United States, which was then before the people for consideration — Also a Letter from my father to him, of 10 March 1823 — and one of James Lloyd of 10 February 1825 — The fortieth year is revolving since my own Letters were written; and now their best use is to teach me a lesson of humility, and of forbearance — I was so sincere, so earnest, so vehement in my opinions, and time has so crumbled them to dust, that I can now see them only as monumental errors — Yet the Spirit was such as even now I have no reason to disclaim — A Spirit of Patriotism of Order and of Benevolence. In the last of the Letters, is an allusion to my own state of mind at the time, more affecting than all my political Speculations.

———

31. IV:15. Shower and Tub Bath. Baltimore — All the morning till noon was employed with the interruptions of visitors, in concluding business of the several Departments, and disposing of papers public and private. Many were yet left without arrangement, and in disorder — About an hour before I left the City Major Nourse came with several despatches from Gover-

nor Cass of the Michigan Territory, announcing hostilities by the Winebago Indians, and much alarm. I hesitated whether I should not postpone my Journey; but I had some weeks since directed a re-occupation of the Post at Prairie du Chien — Governor Cass appeared by his Letters to have taken all the measures of precaution required by the emergency; and the Secretary of War, having notified his intention to be here to-morrow or the next day, I desired Major Nourse to call his special attention to the subject on his return, and left to his discretion such further measures as he may deem advisable — Nourse afterwards wrote me a note, stating that since he saw me he had received information that a detachment of Troops had been ordered from St. Louis to Prairie du Chien. Mr. Southard called twice — the second time to mention that he had information of the arrival of Commodore Rodgers with the line of Battle ship North-Carolina, at Norfolk — He had expected she would arrive at New-York, and would probably be there, at the time of my arrival at that City; in which event he had urged me, and I had promised to visit the ship, which he thinks the finest Ship in the world — Mr. Rush, Mr. Anderson and Mr. Graham called merely to take leave. — At Noon I left the City of Washington, with my Son Charles, in my own Carriage, and four horses. Michael Anthony Giusta, my Butler and Steward who has lived with me since June 1814 had preceded us in the Stage, at ten O'Clock, with our heavy baggage. My own purpose is to pass the two Months ensuing in retirement at Quincy, with my brother and his family; and if it may be to recover my flagging health, and prepare myself for the trials of the next winter. My Son Charles after having since he was graduated at Harvard University passed two years in pursuit of his Law Studies with me, goes to Boston, to follow them up in the concluding year before his admission to the Bar, in Mr. Webster's Office. ≈ I dined at Merrill's, and after a parting glass of wine with the members of the Committee, proceeded to Baltimore, and alighted at Barnum's Hotel between 8 and 9.

———

[August 1827]

11. V:30. ≈ Immediately after dinner, Mr. Quincy called, and I rode with him in his Carriage to the Railway. We found Col'l T. H. Perkins at the Stone House which the Company built

there the last Autumn — We walked with him to the Quarry, were overtaken by a thunder Shower and took shelter under the shed where the Stone-cutters were at work upon the Blocks for the Bunker Hill Monument. The Railway has been about nine Months in full and successful operation, but it appears to me that there has already some impression been made on the iron tire of the way, and still more on the pine-wood rail beneath it. Col'l Perkins and Mr. Quincy think not, but the Colonel has made an experiment for a small space of substituting, a granite rail in the place of the Pine-wood — This will be more durable, but may occasion the more rapid wearing out of the iron. The question still to be solved is the result of this undertaking with reference to profit. Col'l Perkins has great means, ardent public Spirit, and pertinacious enterprize — It is generally thought that the greater part if not the whole of the expense of the work is sustained by him; and that he is liberal even to profusion in expense upon it. — It has already been of great advantage to the town of Quincy, and promises to be of still more — But the danger that the Railway may prove a bill of expense to its owners casts a shade over the whole enterprize, and rather increases than diminishes. Col'l Perkins is now about commencing to build a large Hotel near the Railway — The blocks of Granite at the shed near the Quarry, are some of the most beautiful building Stones I ever saw — There is danger of accidents on the way; and Col'l Perkins himself has once been thrown from his horse over it, and fell at least 20 feet, but without much hurt, it being on soft ground. After the Shower, Mr. Quincy took me home, where I found my Son George, and Mr. John Winthrop, with whom he had come out from Boston — Mr. Winthrop returned to the City — Mr. Webster and his brother had been here, while I was gone.

———

13. IV:15. ≈ I paid an evening visit to Mr. Marston, and on my return home, found Letters from R. Rush, Nath'l Frye jr and B. O. Tyler. The last was from Harrisburg, Pennsylvania, dated the 7th inst't and announced the very sudden decease there, on the Evening of the 6th, of Mr. Robert Little, the Minister of the Unitarian Church at Washington. He died after an illness of little more than 24 hours, of an inflammation of the brain;

after having preached morning and Evening at Harrisburg, on Sunday the 5th the day before his death — This is an event deeply to be lamented by his Congregation, of whom I was one. I had constantly attended on his ministration for the last seven years; though I had never formally joined his Society — I did not subscribe to many of his doctrines; particularly not to the fundamental one, of his unitarian creed — I believe in One God, but his nature is incomprehensible to me, and of the question between the Unitarians and Trinitarians, I have no precise belief, because no definite Understanding. But Mr. Little's moral discourses were always good, and sometimes admirable. I listened to them with pleasure and profit; and shall miss them if I live to return to Washington. His place will not easily be supplied.

———

20. V:10. Mr. Cary is from Bridgwater and came to renew a solicitation for the appointment of his Son in Law Dunham as keeper of a Light house now building in the State of Maine. I was not sure whether the place was yet open or had been filled a few days before I left Washington. Cary asked me if I remembered a Company of Militia, who about the time of the Battle of Lexington in 1775 came down from Bridgwater, and passed the Night at my father's house and barn at the foot of Penn's Hill; and in the midst of whom, my father placed me, then a boy between seven and eight years, and I went through the manual exercise of the musket, by word of command from one of them. I told him I remembered it as distinctly as if it had been last week. He said he was one of that company.

———

[October 1827]

23. V. ≈ Mr. Clay spoke to me again of the Instructions to be prepared for Mr. Gallatin relating to the North-eastern frontier. He spoke also, under some excitement, of the political course of conduct pursued by Mr. M'lean the Postmaster-General; whom he believes to be bitterly though insidiously hostile to the Administration. Mr. M'lean has greatly improved the condition of the Post-Office Department since he has been at its head; and is perhaps the most efficient Officer that has ever been in that place — But it is a place of more patronage, and personal influence, than those of all the other Heads of

Departments put together. In the exercise of this influence, Mr. M'lean has so managed as to conciliate to himself all the opposition party, while every other member of the administration has been the object of the most violent and outrageous abuse — Many of the friends of the administration believe that Mr. M'lean has secured to himself this exemption from persecution, by a system of duplicity in his conduct; and by favouring so far as has been in his power, the views of the opposition — I have been slow to believe this; and while he himself has repeatedly protested his firm and faithful attachment to the administration, no decisive act of his has been detected, necessarily importing his insincerity. Mr. Clay mentioned some cases in the present distribution, and modification of his Contracts, which have an unfavourable aspect; but nothing of which it appears to me that notice can be taken — His friendship is suspicious — His war is in disguise.

———

25. V:15. Georgetown Walk. I walked this morning before Breakfast to Georgetown, and returning stopped at Mr. Rush's house — He has been several days confined there, unwell, of which I was informed only by the National Intelligencer of yesterday Morning. The Servant who came to the door told me that he was not up; but so much recovered that he intended to go this day to the Treasury — He afterwards came to see me, but without transacting business — Mrs. Johnson is a young woman of pleasing personal appearance, and education, who came to solicit an appointment of Clerk in any of the Departments for her husband — She gave me a full account of their domestic establishment, and their urgent wants; a mother, two Sisters, an infirm brother to support — all without means — She repeatedly expressed the hope and belief that I was accessible; and assured me of the everlasting gratitude, of the whole family, if I would give an Office to her husband — It is among the heaviest burdens of my place to hear this cry of distress, almost every day of the year — often several times in a day, and scarcely ever to have it in my power to administer the desired relief — There is no pleader of this cause so eloquent as a young and handsome woman; and none who ought to be more firmly resisted — I told Mrs. Johnson that the Law gave

the appointment of Clerk's in each Department, to the Head of the Department itself, and that any interposition on my part, unless desired by them, was unusual and perhaps improper. I advised that her husband should apply personally to the heads of Departments, and furnish testimonials of good character, and fitness for the Office he wished to obtain, and if the Head of Department should consult me upon the appointment, I would say in favour of her husband what I could with propriety — Mr. M'lean the Postmaster General said it was the first day since my return that he had been able to call upon me — That for the last fortnight he had been every day at his Office from early in the morning till Night — Having even his dinner sent him there from his house. He has now nearly got through his business with the contractors and says the new contracts will afford very great additional facilities, both to the transportation of the mail and for travellers. I desired him to furnish me at his convenience the usual annual Report, for the preparation of the message to Congress. Charles Pinkney was here a few minutes — Dr. Watkins called, with a Letter from A. H. Tracy the former member of Congress from the Western part of the State of New-York; enquiring with great solicitude, whether I am, and also whether General Jackson is a Freemason. He says that it is circulated there with indefatigable assiduity that I am, and that he is not a Mason — That the object of these Reports is to influence the elections; and that they do more powerfully operate upon it there than all other electioneering topics put together. About fifteen Months since a man by the name of William Morgan, published or attempted to publish at Batavia a Book professing to divulge the Secrets of Free Masonry — He was shortly afterwards kidnapped carried away — murdered, and thrown into lake Ontario, where his body has within a few days been found — No positive proof of his death had been till now produced; but as there has been ample evidence of a conspiracy among the freemasons, which succeeded in carrying him away, and had the purpose of destroying him, the consequence has been a universal excitement and popular fermentation in that vicinity which has extended throughout New-York, and has at length brought a mass of obloquy upon the Institution of Masonry itself — I told Watkins he might answer Tracy that I am not, and never was a Freemason — but whether General Jackson is or not I do not know.

———

[December 1827]
1. VI:15. Sun rose 7:18. Walk to the Capitol. The names in the margin arranged in alphabetical order are those of members of Congress, who called in the course of this day and Evening, 37 members of the House and three Senators — They occupied so large a portion of the time, that little was left me for writing, and none for attention to other business — Of these visitors about one third are moderate opposition men, whose votes will always be against the administration; but who are yet willing to be upon terms of social intercourse with me. At the first Session of the last Congress there was only one Senator, and not more than three members of the House, who declined coming to the house — Every one, without exception was invited — The besotted violence of John Randolph at that Session excluded him thenceforward from all right to personal civility from me. Half a dozen other frequenters of gin lane and beer alley, after dinner Speech-makers, in the House, put themselves into the same position, and two or three Slanderers, drunk with faction, though not with Alcohol, must be added to the gang — Besides those, whom I have disdained to notice, there were at both the Sessions of the last Congress a number of members of both Houses, bitter as wormwood in their opposition, indulging themselves, in the warmth of debate in personal reflections as ungenerous as they were unjust, who yet came to the drawing Rooms, and when invited, to the dinners; always ready to introduce their friends to the President; to partake of his hospitality; and to recommend candidates for every vacant appointment. The highest Class of opposition, consisted of men, whose personal deportment was always courteous and respectful — who abstained from all insulting personalities both in their public Speeches, and their private conversations, but applied all their faculties to opposition of measures — Of these there are very few — Mr. Drayton of South-Carolina who called this day was one of them. They are more formidable enemies than the foul-mouthed Scavengers of the party — But some of them under the courtesies of

life conceal a rancour of heart as corrosive as the rabid foam of Randolph.

———

13. IV:30. ≈ Mr. Clay told me he would shew me the draft of a publication which he proposed to make, in further refutation of the charges of bargaining and corruption, which General Jackson, and some of his partizans, have trumped up against him and me. They have already been amply refuted — But Voltaire observes in a Letter to Thiriot, "je vois que les Calomnies s'accréditent toujours," and the remark is specially applicable in this Country to the affairs of Politics and Politicians. In the excitement of contested elections and of party Spirit, Judgment becomes the Slave of the Will — Men of Intelligence, Talents, and even of integrity upon other occasions surrender themselves up to their Passions — Believe every thing, with, without, or even against Evidence, according as it suits their own wishes.

———

17. IV:30. ≈ Mr. Pearce of Rhode-Island came with Mr. O'Brien and Mr. Butman, members of the House from Maine — They spoke of the North-eastern Boundary question, and of Governor Enoch Lincoln's Rhodomontades about the State's maintaining her own rights by War; and refusing to be bound by the Stipulations of the Treaty; which I thought a very awkward imitation of Governor Troup of Georgia — The difference was that Troup knew he could bluster, and talk big with safety — He well knew that the only adverse party to him was the Creek Indians, and that he would certainly obtain his end against them — and probably the sooner, the more insolent and insulting his language and conduct should be towards the Government of the United States. But the adverse party to Governor Lincoln's pretensions was Great-Britain — The Treaty that he was for trampling under foot, was of unquestioned obligation upon the Union; and if Governor Lincoln should, as he had threatened at his Militia Reviews, to go to War against it, he must like Don Quixot, sally forth alone, for neither the Union nor the people of his own State would sustain him. O'Brien said he had heard that Governor Lincoln of Massachusetts disapproved of his brother's impetuosity and wrong-headedness — which I well knew. Mr. Pearce's father,

died last week. Mr. Clay called, and took the draft of his Address to the Public — I advised him to change entirely the concluding paragraph; which presented the idea, of his retiring from public life, and being sacrificed as a victim to calumny — He asked if my objection was that it had an appearance of despondency. I said yes — but that was not all — I thought it highly probable that the base and profligate combination against him and me, would succeed in their main object of bringing in General Jackson at the next Presidential Election — And that one of their principal means of success will be this infamous Slander, which he had already more than once branded with falsehood and upon which he would again stamp the lie, by this address and its Appendix. The conspiracy would nevertheless in all probability succeed — When suspicion, has been kindled into popular delusion, truth, and reason, and justice spoke as to the ears of an Adder — the sacrifice must be consummated, before they can be heard — General Jackson will therefore be elected. But it is impossible that his Administration should give satisfaction to the people of this Union. He is incompetent both by his ignorance, and by the fury of his Passions — He will be surrounded and governed by incompetent men, whose ascendancy over him will be secured by their servility, and who will bring to the Government of the Nation, nothing but their talent for intrigue. Discordant in the materials of their composition — rancorously hostile to each other, and all more skilled to pack the cards than to play the game, there will be no principle of cohesion among them, they will crumble to pieces, and the Administration will go to wrack and ruin. Then too will come the recoil of Public Opinion in favour of Mr. Clay, and it will be irresistible. If human nature has not changed its character, Kentuckey and the Union will then do Justice to him and to his Slanderers — In the Event of General Jackson's election, *he* would of course, retire (he said he should resign, and not give the General the opportunity to remove him.) He would return to his home in Kentuckey and there wait the course of Events — But I thought it would be better not to allude to it, in this publication, and particularly not to countenance the idea of his intending it, as a final retirement — He said this reaction of public opinion he thought very probable, but that it would be so long in coming that it might go beyond his term of active life — I said it might be very sudden and rapid — And reminded him of the instantaneous effect in favour of De Witt Clinton, of the removal of him by the Legislature as a Canal Commissioner — I concluded however by remarking that I had only made this suggestion relating to the closing paragraph of his Address, and he said it had already occurred to him, that it might be liable to such an objection.

———

[January 1828]
22. V:45. ≈ Mr. Tracy, member from New-York, and Dr. Watkins, called together. Mr. Tracy's object was to ask of me a renewed declaration that I was not a freemason — I had already told him that I was not: and he made many apologies for repeating the question, but said that in the Western part of New-York this was now the only test of Elections, and he read me a part of a Letter from one of his friends; who wrote him that altho' a positive denial had been published that I was a Mason, the assertion that I was had been republished with promises to produce extracts from the Books of the Lodge to which I belonged. This is a sample of electioneering falsehoods. I had received this morning two Letters full of anxiety for the effect which the belief of my Masonry would have against me; and one of them intreating me to give a denial of it under my own hand — I told Tracy that if I should deny it, I should not be surprized if they were to produce a forged extract from some imaginary lodge to counteract my denial. Such are the morals of electioneering. I signed an order for the discharge of Henry Colson, in prison at Alexandria for petty Larceny. Sent Message to Congress N. 5 with the Communications from the Governor of Georgia, concerning their boundary with Florida — And Message N. 16 to the Senate with the Creek Indian Treaty.

23. V:30. ≈ Mr. Lincoln came with Mr. M'Coy, a Baptist Missionary among the Indians, with whom I had some conversation upon the subject of that unfortunate race of hunters who are themselves hunted by us like a Partridge upon the Mountains. Mr. M'Coy wishes the Government of the United States to assume the Protection of them, and assign to them a

territory where they may remain unmolested — I observed that the Secretary of War had proposed a plan for the Government of them at the last Session of Congress, which had not been acted upon — I observed that our engagements with the Indians, and those among ourselves in relation to their Lands were inconsistent with each other. We had thus contracted with the State of Georgia to extinguish the Indian Title to all the Lands within the State of Georgia, and at the same time stipulated with the Creeks and Cherokees that they should hold their Lands for ever — We have talked of benevolence and humanity, and preached them into civilization; but none of this benevolence is felt where the right of the Indian comes in collision with the interest of the white man — The Cherokees in Georgia have now been making a written Constitution; but this imperium in imperio is impracticable; and in the instances of the New-York Indians removed to Green Bay, and of the Cherokees removed to the Territory of Arkansas, we have scarcely given them time to build their wigwams before we are called upon by our own people to drive them out again. My own opinion is that the most benevolent course towards them, would be to give them the rights and subject them to the duties of citizens as a part of our own people. But even this the People of the States within which they are situated will not permit.

———

29. V:45. ≈ Mr. Biddle, the President of the U.S. Bank, called with his brother Richard from Pittsburg — There had been a question between them, whether the quotation video meliora proboque; deteriora sequor was from Horace or Ovid — I had pronounced it from Horace, and so had the President of the Bank, and Mr. Everett. They had now ascertained that it is in the Metamorphoses Book 7, lines 20 and 21, a Speech of Medea.

30. IV:45. ≈ Mr. Everett called to make enquiry concerning an infamous calumny upon me contained in a note to an electioneering life of General Jackson, published by Isaac Hill, Editor of a Newspaper in New-Hampshire — It is that while in Russia, I attempted to make use of a beautiful girl to seduce the passions of the Emperor Alexander, and sway him to political

purposes — This is a new form of Slander — one of the thousand malicious lies which outvenom all the worms of Nile, and are circulated in every part of the Country, in newspapers and pamphlets. I told Mr. Everett the incident upon which this tale was raised. That when we went to Russia, a very beautiful girl, a native of Boston named Martha Godfrey went with us, as Chambermaid to my wife and nurse to our Son Charles then a child two years old. Soon after our arrival at St. Petersburg Martha wrote a Letter perhaps to her mother, relating Stories that she had heard there of the Emperor's amours and gallantries. This Letter having been sent to the Post-Office, was according to the custom there opened, and sent as a curiosity to the Emperor, who was diverted with it and shewed it to the Empress — They both felt a curiosity to see the girl, who had written this Letter; and some of the Ladies of the Court who had visited Mrs. Adams, having seen Charles, with his Nurse, had spoken to the Empress of both in such manner as still further to excite her curiosity. The Empress had a Sister then living with her, the Princess Amelia of Baden — She expressed a wish to see Charles, and he was sent one morning to her Apartment in the Palace — Martha his Nurse went with him, and while they were in the Princess's Apartment, the Emperor and Empress both went there, and passed perhaps ten minutes in talking to the child, and at the same time they had an opportunity of seeing the Nurse, whose Letter had afforded them some amusement — It is from this trivial incident, that this base imputation has been trumped up — There never was any other foundation for it — Martha Godfrey was a girl of irreproachable conduct — She returned to the United States with Mrs. Smith; married a very respectable musical instrument maker in Boston, and died there within the last three or four years.

———

[February 1828]
1. V:30. ≈ Mr. Edward Ingersoll called, and spoke of the Memoir of my father written by him, and published in the biography of the Signers of the Declaration of Independence. I told him of my design to write Memoirs of the Life of my father; and perhaps a History of the United States from the formation of the present Constitution of the United States — But I said if I

did I should probably leave the work to be published after my decease.

———

8. V. ≈ Mr. Rush brought me some papers from Alabama — a Message from the Governor (Murphy) to the Legislature of the State, and a Remonstrance from the Legislature, addressed to Congress against an Instruction from the Treasury Department to the Receivers of Public Monies, at the Land Offices, dated last August, directing them to receive in payment for lands, only Specie, Bills of the Bank of the United States or its branches, or Bills of Specie paying Banks of the State. The remonstrance of the Legislature is in language little short of frantic — A blustering, bullying Style which many of the State Governors and Governments adopt towards the General Administration, as if they considered insolence as their only means of demonstrating their Sovereignty. Mr. Rush proposed some modification of the Instructions to remove any possible inconvenience to the purchasers; He is himself of a temper so mild, and a Deportment so courteous, that the bitter invective, slanderous imputations, and reproachful malignity of this Alabama manifesto was quite distressing to him — I shewed him a Letter from a man in prison at New-York for some debt to the United States, addressed to me, which I had just received, written in much the same insulting Style; and I told him I prized them both at about the same value.

———

17. VI:30. ≈ Returning home from the Capitol I met Mr. Edwards of the Treasury Department, who stopped and asked me, if I had heard the news — I said "none" — He informed me that the Northern Mail had brought the account of the sudden Death of De Witt Clinton; Governor of New-York. Mr. Sergeant soon afterwards called upon me, and sat with me in Conversation, about an hour — This was one of the distinguished and ambitious Statesmen of this Union — He was one of the first Post-revolutionary great men of the age, but his mind was of secondary size, deluded by success and flattery into the self-conceit that he was of the first magnitude — He came forward at a very early age with a brilliant reputation, sustained by all the weight and influence of his Uncle George Clinton, then transcendent in New-York — was of the Council

of Appointment that broke down, and drove into retirement John Jay, and in 1802 was elected to the Senate of the United States. He there sat only one Session, and in October 1803 resigned his Office for that of Mayor of the City of New-York, then extremely lucrative, but as far beneath that of a Senator of the United States in dignity, as surpassing it in profit — This step of political bathos marked in characters indelible the measure of De Witt Clinton's mind — From the Senator of a Sovereign State in the most select Council of the Union he shrunk into the police officer of a single City, and busied his mind with the regulation of go-carts and the punishment of Shop-lifters. He never afterwards got beyond the bounds of the State of New-York, as a public man, though in 1812 he made a desperate plunge at the Presidency of the United States; purchasing the support of the federal party, by a sudden, and even indecent desertion of his own — more literally purchasing influence in various parts of the Union by hired Agents, venal presses, and even stipended itinerant preachers — to the utter ruin it is said, of his private fortune — alieni appetens, sui profusus. He thus became a formidable competitor, and received 89 electoral votes, Mr. Madison receiving 128. Mr. Clinton has since gone through at least four vicissitudes of political fortune in his own State, and was now reduced to the last Stake of declaring himself a partizan of General Jackson, to rivalize with Mr. Calhoun for the Vice-Presidency — The New-York Legislative Caucus therefore in nominating Jackson forbore to make any nomination of Vice-President, and Clinton was feeding his hopes of the China-Jordan, when arrested by the tamer of all Ambition, and consigned to the Sepulchre and the worm — I hear in his fate the voice of the same teacher — Be ye also ready — Lord, teach us so to number our days that we may apply our hearts unto wisdom.

23. V:30. ≈ Mr. Rush was here, with Letters from W. Astor, President of the American Fur Company, urging the re-establishment of a Revenue Cutter on Lake Superior — There has been one there heretofore, but of late none — Mr. Astor complains of smuggling carried on with Canada, which after having been suppressed by the former Cutter, is again reviving by the disuse of such a guard — A Letter from Mr. Stuart the Collector at

Michillimackinac but now here, countenances the application
of Mr. Astor. I thought the request should be complied with.
Mr. Rush also shewed me a confidential private Letter to him,
from Robert Mitchell, Collector at Pensacola, mentioning that
a friend of his, there had spent some weeks last Summer in
South-Carolina, and had frequently seen Mr. Calhoun, with
whom he had formerly been intimate as a Schoolmate — That
he was in the habit of speaking in the most disrespectful and
unbecoming manner of the whole Administration — Said that
all the Departments were in a state of the greatest disorder;
and that if *he* was at the head of the Treasury Department, he
would effect the same reform in its organization, as he had
done in the Department of War — The truth is that of the
reforms in the War Department made while he was at its
head, the most important was the reduction of the army from
ten thousand to six thousand men, utterly against his will,
against all the influence that he could exercise, and to his entire
disapprobation — And all the other changes of organization,
were upon plans furnished by Generals Brown and Scott, and
carried through Congress chiefly by the Agency of John Williams of Tennessee. Mr. Calhoun had no more share of mind
in them, than I have in the Acts of Congress to which I affix
my signature of approbation — Calhoun is a man of considerable talent, and burning ambition, stimulated to frenzy by
success, flattery, and premature advancement. Governed by no
steady principle; but sagacious to seize upon every prevailing
popular breeze to swell his own sails — Showering favours with
lavish hand to make partizans; without discernment in the
choice of his instruments, and the dupe and tool of every knave
cunning enough to drop the oil of fools in his ear — My Son
John dined at Governor Barbour's — Holzey, the black boy
belonging to Johnson Hellen, and who has been several years
with us, died about five O'Clock this afternoon. He has been
sinking several months in a consumption.

———

25. IV:30. Monday ≈ My second Son John Adams was married
to Mary Catherine Hellen, by the Reverend William Hawley,
Rector of St. John's Church in this City — The persons present
as witnesses, were besides my wife and myself, Abigail Smith
Adams, Judge William Cranch and his daughter Elizabeth,

Edward Everett, Mr. and Mrs. Frye, and their Son Thomas, Johnson and Thomas J. Hellen, Dr. Henry Huntt, Columbus and Frances Munroe, Matilda Pleasonton, George and Sophia Ramsay, Tench Ringgold, Mary C. Roberdeau, Mr. and Mrs. W. S. Smith, Dr. Watkins and his Son William — The Servants of the family were likewise all present — After the ceremony we had a supper, and the company retired about midnight. May the blessing of God Almighty rest upon this Union!

———

28. V:15. Thursday. My wife was almost the whole of this day, extremely and alarmingly ill, and I was, as more than once has happened in the course of my life, distracted with a multitude of company, and at the same time in the deepest distress for her. — The agony of mind, which at such times I endure is indescribable — The suffering that must be suppressed, the cheerfulness that must be assumed, the indifference or gaiety which surround me, the various calls of sympathy with those whom business or pleasure brings in society with me, form altogether a sort of convulsive state of existence, which sometimes seems as if it would burst every ligament of self-controul.

———

[March 1828]
4. VI. Tuesday. — Sun rose 6:20. This day commencing the last year of my public Service was clear and cold. ≈ Mr. Clay was here, and I returned to him the Letters he had left with me for my perusal. He asked my opinion with regard to the publication of his Letter to Blair, which I thought might be expedient, though it is precisely one of those Letters, the production of which is so justly and severely reprobated in the divine Philippic of Cicero. It is dated the 8th of January 1825 the day before his interview with me at my house, when he declared to me his determination to vote for me at the approaching election — and seven days after Letcher had explicitly informed me that such would be the vote of the majority of the Kentucky Delegation — The Letter is written as he says with too much levity — The criticism to which it is liable is that its object was to impress his friend with an elevated idea of his own importance. He represents the *friends*, of all three of the Candidates then before the house, as courting him with great anxiety, and he represents mine as addressing him with tears in their eyes.

This was meant by him only as a joke upon my infirmity of a watery eye; but malignity will give it a construction, as if intended to insinuate that in these overtures of my friends I myself participated. If this was his suspicion, he will be abundantly punished by that which will befall himself by the publication of the Letter — It is indeed insinuation of suspicion, perhaps not unnatural in the situation which he then held: but utterly without foundation. No friend of mine had ever been authorized by me to avow the slightest wish that he should vote for me; but his friend Letcher had seven days before explicitly told me that the majority of the Kentucky Delegation were irrevocably determined to vote for me. The tendency of the Letter will not be to remove the unjust suspicions, which malice and political profligacy have cast upon him, but it will give them no confirmative proof, and the suppression of the Letter, would pass for proof with all those disposed so to receive it — The publication of the Letter will be the best because the frankest course; but it will prove nothing except the treachery of the friend to whom it was written. The divulging of private and confidential Letters is one of the worst features of electioneering practices among us — Though often tempted and provoked to it, I have constantly refrained from it.

———

7. IV. Friday ≈ Stephen Fitch a man having the appearance and manners of a quaker, came and told me that he had come hither with Red Jacket, and two others of the New-York Seneca and Oneida Indians: to complain of wrongs, in regard to the purchase of their Lands. That he himself had been extremely anxious to see me; and although he had been advised not to come, and told that I should probably not receive him, he had yet determined to make the experiment, and Red Jacket was equally desirous to see his father the President. I told him that I had been glad to see him, and would with equal pleasure [see Red Jacket] — But that any complaint or representation that they had to make with regard to the Lands must be to the Department of War — I had this day sent to the Senate Message N. 23 with all the papers addressed directly to me, relating to these complaints of the New-York Indians — I sent them in answer to a Resolution of the Senate, requesting all the papers, relating to the Treaty, made by Governor Cass and T. L.

M'Kenney, at the Butte des Morts, last Summer, with the Winnebago and Menominie Indians, which is now before the Senate — The direct access to the President, in all their transactions with this Government and especially in the representation of all their grievances, they take greatly to heart; and with much more reason than the white hunters — that is office hunters — This access I have never denied to any one of any colour; and in my opinion of the duties of a Chief-Magistrate of the United States it ought never to be denied — The place-hunters are not pleasant visitors or correspondents and they consume an enormous disproportion of time — To this personal importunity the President ought not to be subjected; but it is perhaps not possible to relieve him from it; without secluding the man from the intercourse of the people more than comports with the nature of our Institutions. ≈

8. IV:45. ≈ Mr. Bailey of Massachusetts came and passed a couple of hours with me this Evening: His object was to make a proposition, in the first instance not very distinctly disclosed, but which I chose immediately to understand, and to meet in a manner altogether explicit. He ultimately informed me that it had been suggested to him by Mr. Webster. He said that the Election of Governor, and of the Legislature of Kentucky would take place next August — That the great and decisive struggle of the parties would be at that election, which would decide the fate of the subsequent election of electors of President and Vice-President, in November. These Electors, by a recent act of the Legislature, are to be chosen by a general ticket throughout the State — Immense exertions are making by the opposition party to carry this Election of august — They spend much money, and there is an indispensable necessity of counteracting them in the same manner. Now Mr. Bailey's question to me was whether I had a sum from five to ten thousand dollars, that I was disposed to give, without enquiring how it would be disposed of, but which would be employed, to secure the Election of General Metcalfe as Governor of Kentucky next August — I answered that there was a sentiment, expressed first by the late Mr. Lowndes, much repeated since, by General Jackson and his friends, though not practiced upon by them, but hitherto invariably observed by

me; that the Presidency of the United States was an office neither to be sought nor declined — To pay money for securing it
directly or indirectly, was in my opinion incorrect in principle
— This was my first and decisive reason, for declining such a
contribution — A second reason was that I could not even
command a sum of five thousand dollars without involving
myself in debt for it — And a third was that if I once departed
from the principle, and gave money, there was no rule either
of expediency or of morality, which would enable me to limit
the amount of expenditure which I ought to incur. I could
certainly appropriate half a million of dollars to the same object
without transcending any Law, and with as much propriety as
I could devote 5000 to the election of a Governor of Kentucky
— Mr. Bailey seemed surprized to hear that I could not raise
five thousand dollars without borrowing — and said Mr. Webster had told him, I had a large sum, fifty or sixty thousand
dollars lying dead, in a Bank at Boston — I told Mr. Bailey
candidly the state of my Affairs — That the expenses of my
family, and the support of my three Sons now absorb very
nearly the whole of my public Salary — That all my real Estate
in Quincy and Boston is mortgaged for the payment of my
debts. That the income of my whole private Estate, is less than
6000 dollars a year, and that I am paying at least 2000 of that
for interest upon my debt. Finally that upon going out of Office in one year from this time, destitute of all means of acquiring property, it will only be by the sacrifice of that which I now
possess that I shall be able to support my family — I note as a
remarkable incident this proposition to me to contribute five
or ten thousand dollars to carry the election of a Governor and
Legislature of Kentucky — The mode of expenditure is by the
circulation of newspapers, pamphlets and hand-bills — It is
practiced by all parties, and its tendency is to render elections
altogether venal. The coincidence of Mr. Clark's proposal that
I should write a pamphlet in answer to Ingham's Slanders
about my Accounts, with Mr. Clay's opinion that Mr. Webster
if he insists upon it should be appointed to the Mission to
Great-Britain, and with Mr. Webster's proposal that I should
sport five or ten thousand dollars upon the election of a Governor of Kentucky, is perhaps all accidental; but in the opera-

tions of parties objects of great dissimilarity to each other are often connected by imperceptible links together.

9. VI. Sunday — I heard Elizabeth Robson preach at the Capitol, in the Hall of the House of Representatives — Her text was Ephesians 5:1. "Be ye therefore followers of God, as dear Children. 2. And walk in Love, as Christ also hath loved us, and hath given himself for us, an offering and a sacrifice to God for a sweet smelling favour." She repeated these words without announcing in what book of Scripture they were, but said they had occurred to her reflections while she was sitting there — This implies that she had waited for the out-pourings of the Spirit for the extemporaneous suggestion of a text — That she had taken no thought of what she should say. Yet she discoursed without interval or hesitation for about an hour upon those words — This power of unpremeditated speech is neither very rare nor very valuable; but is of great use to those who possess it — In Elizabeth Robson it consists in the faculty of stringing together a succession of passages from Scripture, principally from Paul's Epistles, which she has committed to memory, and through which her discourse runs like a line of pack thread through a row of pearls. Her manner is earnest and affectionate, and the tone of her voice falls into cantation — Her eloquence and Genius are not of so high an order as those of Harriet Livermore, but she more cautiously avoids giving offence to her hearers. When she had finished her Sermon and sat down, a great part of the auditory thought she had finished, and were going away. One of her male companions however gave notice that the services were not concluded, and asked indulgence for a short and quiet pause after which she kneeled and made a very fervent prayer, and then her friend signified that the meeting might separate.

———

17. V. Monday ≈ Mr. Baker the Minister came to inform me of his intended removal to Savannah, and to make proposals for the arrangement of his concerns with me, to which I readily agreed. He read me part of a Letter to him from Mr. Marks the Senator from Pennsylvania, making enquiries concerning my subscriptions to pious and charitable Institutions; of which

I told him I had little to say. He made also some enquiries concerning my religious opinions, and particularly concerning my ideas of the Trinity — I spoke to him as freely as I did with the General of the Jesuits at St. Petersburg. Told him in substance what I had written to my Son George — That I was not either a Trinitarian or a Unitarian. That I believed the Nature of Jesus Christ was superhuman — but whether he was God, or only the first of created beings was not clearly revealed to me in the Scriptures — He lent me a small printed pamphlet, by a Mr. Lewis Tappan of Boston, who has lately been converted, from Unitarianism to Orthodoxy; and who is now desirous of making proselytes to his new faith — Mr. Baker was in extasies at this pamphlet, which he thought full of the milk of kindness, and altogether lovely; but which I thought illiberal and even libellous — Mr. Webster paid an evening visit to me, and also to the Ladies. He spoke of the result of the recent election in New-Hampshire, as more flattering than the event will probably warrant. Yet there is reason to hope it has been more favourable than I had expected. In Elections promising first accounts are almost invariably dashed with final disappointment.

———

20. V:45. ≈ Governor Barbour called respecting the appointment of a professor of Philosophy at West-Point. The present Professor, Mansfield asks a furlough till the first of September and that resignation may then take effect. Governor Barbour brought also with him an original Letter dated October 1812, from General Jackson to George W. Campbell, then a Senator from Tennessee, demanding the removal of Silas Dinsmoor, then an Indian Agent, because he had stopped a Negro trader who was passing through the Indian Country; he not having a Passport — Jackson was so highly incensed at this that he wrote to G. W. Campbell, requiring him to call upon the Secretary of War, and give him warning that if Dinsmoor should not be immediately removed, the people of West-Tennessee would burn him up in his agency — This Letter and several others relating to the same subject have lately been found at the War Department in the searches for the correspondence concerning the execution of the Tennessee Militia men at Mobile. Another motive too has spurred the search for some

of his original Letters — In the Legislature of Louisiana last Spring, some of his partizans got up a Resolution, inviting him to attend in person the anniversary celebration of the 8th of January at New-Orleans — He caught eagerly at this bait, and went with a numerous train of attendants, from Nashville to New-Orleans in the dead of Winter, to exhibit himself in pompous pageantry. His reception was equivocal; with a laborious effort of magnificence, and mortifying indications of ill-will and disgust among the people. Deputations were sent from various other States, from Meetings of his devotees to meet him at the celebration, and five or six Addresses of fulsome adulation were delivered to him; to which he returned answers of cold and high wrought rhetorician eloquence — These Answers were all written by Harry Lee, who has become an inmate in his family, and attended him to New-Orleans — As they were in an ambitious and Court-dress Style, some of his impudent Jackalls fell into extasies in the Newspapers at his eloquence and fine literary composition; and they were boldly claiming for him the reputation of an elegant writer — But the General in one of his raving fits, had sent one of his Nashville white-washing Committee's pamphlets on his matrimonial adventures, to Peter Force, Editor of the National Journal, and had written with his own hand, though without signing his name, on the title page, about four lines insulting to Force, and grossly insolent to the Administration. Coarse, vulgar and false in its invective, it was couched in language worthy of Antient Pistol, and set all grammar and spelling alike at defiance — When the Panegyrics upon the composition of the answers to the New-Orleans addresses began to thicken, and the peal of parasitical applause to swell, Force published literatim the manuscript note sent him with the Nashville Committee Report, and in a very short commentary marked the contrast between the wording of the Note, and the tawdry-elegance of the Answers to the addresses — On the day of Force's publication, White the Senator and Polk a member of the House from Tennessee, called at his Office, and asked to see the pamphlet with the note — It was shewn them, and to the enquiry whether they recognised the hand-writing of the Note they answered with equivocation and evasion. The Liars of the Newspapers were more bold; they denied that the manuscript note was written by Jackson, and treated as infamous calumny the assertion that it was — This has stimulated to the discovery of more of Jackson's autograph Letters, and among the rest is this one to G. W. Campbell — It is still more ferocious than barbarous in Style and composition. It has got wind among the friends of the Administration, and some of them are struggling to get it into Light. It is evidently from the same hand as the Note on the pamphlet sent to Force ≈ General Macomb called and spoke of the appointment of a Professor of Philosophy at West Point, and earnestly recommended Lieutenant Courtnay. The General for the first time spoke to me of the political topics of the time, and avowed his own partiality for the present Administration — He has hitherto so far as I have known maintained an exemplary neutrality. ≈

21. V:15. Friday. Mr. Baker, the Presbyterian Minister, came, with his Son, a boy seven or eight years of age — to take leave of me previous to his departure for Savannah, to settle the interest of his two Notes to me, and to give me earnest and affectionate advice for the salvation of my Soul — He exhorted me particularly to believe in the Doctrine of the atonement, which is to sound Presbyterians just what transubstantiation is to the Roman Catholics — I returned him Mr. Lewis Tappan's Letter, with thanks; but without giving him my opinion of it: Mr. Baker in his zeal means well; and with these Clergymen who have the passion for making conversions, it is an act of kindness to indulge them with the belief that they have the best of the argument.

———

[April 1828]

15. IV:45. ≈ Governor Barbour brought me from General Macomb a copy of the Letter of the Secretary of War, Calhoun, written to him at the reduction of the army in 1821 — and a Letter of General Jesup, now written at Macomb's request, and stating the circumstances under which Macomb, accepted the office of Chief Engineer with a reduction of his rank — I had already sent Message N. 26 to the Senate with nominations, and among them Macomb's name for the appointment of Major-General. I sent at the same time Message N. 8 to the House of Representatives, with a Report from the Secretary of

War and documents in answer to a call for the charges made against the Agent to the Creek Indians Crowell since 1 January 1826. In carrying these Messages, my Son John, after having delivered that to the House, was passing through the Rotunda, with that to the Senate, when he was personally assaulted and struck on the face by Russell Jarvis, one of the Printers to the Senate. He returned the blow, and an affray between them was arrested by the interference of persons who were accidentally there. The origin of this outrage was that Jarvis came to the last Drawing-Room, and my son, indignant at seeing here a man who lives by the detail of daily Slander upon me, said to Mr. Stetson, that if Jarvis had the feelings of a gentleman, he would not shew himself here — This was on the 2^d of the Month. On the 8th Jarvis wrote a note to John stating that he had learned that while he was here on Wednesday before, he had spoken of him disrespectfully. He sent this note by a man named M'lean, who he said would receive any explanations — John repeated to M'lean, what he had said, declined giving any written answer and said he would hold no correspondence with Jarvis — This day Jarvis followed him out from the House of Representatives, came up to him from behind, accosted him by name, asked him if he had given him his final answer, and upon John's answering that he had, struck him on the face, and retreated back so that John could only strike at him in return, before they were separated. The whole Scene was witnessed by William Emmons of Boston, by Clement Dorsey a member of the House from Maryland; with another person from Prince George's County and by Col'l Gardner of the Post-Office — who said that Jarvis was right. ≈ Mr. Everett called here in the Evening, and spoke of the Assassin's attack upon my Son at the Capitol while he was in the discharge of a public duty. I had heard nothing of it before. Mr. Everett related the circumstances as he had heard them, and enquired whether I should propose to make any communication to Congress concerning it. I said I should not immediately — The transaction occurred immediately under the notice of both Houses of Congress, and within the walls of their own building — It seemed to me it was rather their affair than mine to act upon it, and I should prefer that they would act upon it, setting aside every consideration personal either to me or to my Son — Under this Congress, it is doubtful whether any remedy for such brutalities, will be found, short of being provided with arms for self-defence.

———

[May 1828]

15. IV:45. ≈ Abdal-Rahman is a Moor, otherwise called Prince or Ibrahim, who has been forty years a Slave in this Country. He wrote two or three years since a Letter to the Emperor of Morocco in Arabic in consequence of which the Emperor expressed to our Consul a wish that this man might be emancipated and sent home. His owner, residing at Natchez, Mississippi, offered to emancipate him, on condition, that he should be sent home by the Government of the United States; which we accordingly determined to do. He has now come on from Natchez with his wife, and met Mr. Clay at Baltimore. He came in while Mr. Southard was with me, and we had some consultation how and where he should be despatched to his home, which he says is Tombuctoo — He says he has left at Natchez five Sons and eight grand-children, one of them only four days old when he came away; all in Slavery, and he wishes that they might all be emancipated, and be sent with or to him — He says he is 66 years of age, and assumes to have been the lawful Prince of his Country.

———

20. IV:45. ≈ General Metcalfe, member of the House from Kentucky and Mr. Merwin from Connecticut were here. Metcalfe to take leave — He goes for home to-morrow. He is the Administration Candidate for Governor of the State, and according to the usage of that part of the Country must before the election travel round the State, and offer himself to the people, and solicit their votes. The election is to be held next August, and his competitor has already made his canvassing tour. Metcalfe is nevertheless sanguine in his expectation of success.

———

31. IV. ≈ Day. I rise generally before five; frequently before four. Write from one to two hours in this Diary. Ride about 12 Miles in two hours, on horseback, with my Son John — Return home about nine. Breakfast, and from that time till Dinner between five and six afternoon, am occupied incessantly with visitors, business, and reading Letters, despatches

and newspapers — Spend an hour sometimes before and sometimes after dinner in the Garden and Nursery — An hour of drowsiness on a Sopha, and two hours of writing in the Evening. Retire usually between 11 and Midnight. My riding on horseback is a dangerous and desperate resort for the recovery of my health.

———

[June 1828]

2. V:30. Monday. ≈ Mr. Monroe called here about one O'Clock with Mr. Southard, and about an hour afterwards I went with Mrs. Adams and visited him and Mrs. Monroe, at Marshal Ringgold's; we found there Mr. M'lean the Postmaster General, and Mr. G. Graham the Commissioner of the Land Office, who had been out with the Marshal to meet Mr. Monroe, but missed him — Col'l Roberdeau was also there. Mr. Monroe declined the invitation to dine and lodge with us. He looks very little altered since I last saw him in August 1825. Mrs. Monroe is much out of health and reduced ≈

3. V. Thunder gust in the Night. Rain — No ride — The loss of the morning ride even for a day, impairs its efficacy for the restoration of my health, and the heavy thunder gust of the Night was followed, by a day so sultry that my excursion from the house was confined to an after dinner visit to the nursery — I there counted ninety-seven Spanish Cork Oaks; but found nothing further. I observe only that a few of every kind of tree that had come up are perishing, the causes of which are various — the heat of the Sun withers some — others suffer prostration from rain — Insects above ground devour the leaves — vermin beneath nip the stalks — The infancy of plants seems to be as delicate as that of animals — I have however now so many varieties and so many of each kind that I can bear the loss of a portion of them; and have now little more to expect for the remainder of the Season — I make two remarks — One that the self-planted seeds, thrive the most vigorously — The other that the plants which I most cherish are the most apt to disappoint me and die.

———

10. IV:30. ≈ From Breakfast, I was called by Judge Thruston, who in his peculiar way came to scold because his Son had not

been appointed a Lieutenant in the Marine Corps, and to supplicate some appointment for him, to save him from desperation. The judge met Mr. Southard in the Antichamber and was scarcely civil to him. I have now been so long acquainted with judge Thruston, and have witnessed so many of his sensitive paroxysms that they produce little impression upon me. — I told the judge that I could do no more for his son than was compatible with my duties to others, and if the occasion should occur I should readily do that — The judge is partially insane, and knows and avows it; but retains intelligence enough to make his insanity a plea to his title to compassion.

———

16. IV:30. ≈ Mr. Clay called, being about to leave the City upon his Summer excursion. He had sent me his draft of General Instructions to Governor Barbour as Minister to Great-Britain, which I approved. He left with me a copy of a pamphlet just published by him, supplementary to the former one, in defence of his own character against the charges of General Jackson ≈ Mr. Wirt the Attorney General spent an hour with me. Spoke of the unlucky controversy that has arisen between the Chesapeake and Ohio Canal, and the Baltimore Rail-road Companies, which must terminate in a Law-suit. He intimated that the Rail-road Company had applied to him for his professional services, and asked if this would interfere with his official duty as Attorney General — I said I thought it would — the United States being interested in the Stock of the Canal company by their subscription of one Million of Dollars — After dinner I visited the Nursery, where I found 120 Cork Oak trees up in 26 out of 30 rows that were planted. They are still coming up.

———

19. IV:30. ≈ The wife of Willis Anderson came again, to petition for his pardon — All importunities are trials of temper. The importunities of women are double trials — I had refused this woman three times, and she had now nothing new to alledge — I now desired her not to come to me again — She hinted, that her husband did not wish to be discharged from prison himself, and that it would be no relaxation of his punishment to turn him over to her. It reminded me of the old Song about Orpheus and Eurydice — Major Gibbon, the Collector at Richmond, made a transient visit, returning home-

ward from a Northern excursion — Mr. Clay came with General Peter B. Porter, the newly appointed Secretary of War, who arrived this morning — The General had written to me that he would defer his final answer, with regard to his acceptance of the appointment till his arrival here — He now mentioned that there was only one scruple which had occasioned hesitation in his mind. There is a question pending with respect to the amount, of his compensation, as Commissioner under the 6th and 7th Articles of the Treaty of Ghent — The Treaty iself; an agreement made at the Exchange of the Ratifications and two Acts of Congress, passed at different times have bearings upon the question; and his accounts as Commissioner are yet unsettled. I said that as he would have no agency in the settlement of his account, the questions upon it could not be affected by his acceptance of the Office of Secretary of War, and Mr. Clay was of the same opinion.

———

22. IV:15. Sunday — Sun rose 4:42. Heard at the Unitarian Church this morning, Mr. Burnap, from Romans 14:7 "For none of us liveth to himself, and no man dieth to himself." A Dissertation, upon the importance to the character and conduct of every individual, of his influence upon the destinies of others — The most remarkable part of the Sermon was a contrasted parallel between the Characters and historical fortunes of Buonaparte, and of Washington; of the former of whom he spoke in terms of unqualified severity and of the latter with equal panegyric. Buonaparte should have said when dying "Oh! what a wounded name I leave behind" — Mr. Burnap said his influence over the fortunes of others was greater than that of any man that ever lived — and that he turned it all to bad purpose — Neither of these assertions was correct. When Buonaparte was at the pinnacle of his power in the summer of 1810 I told poor Six d'Oterleek, then Minister of Louis Buonaparte at St. Petersburg, that Napoleon knew nothing but how to win Battles; and that after all standing by itself it was but a precarious kind of knowledge — Six then all but worshipped him; but he told me that Napoleon, had conceived the opinion that he was possessed of supernatural power. That he was more than a human being; and that this phantasy had taken possession of all his family. Six believed that he would

finish by establishing a Western Empire, embracing the whole Continent of Europe, and that he would claim to be the prophet of God, and enact over again the Tragedy of Mahomet. He also believed that he would succeed in carrying that plan into effect — Bonaparte was a man of great genius for military combinations and operations — whose head was turned by success — who had magnificent imaginations, and some generous purposes; but was under no controul of moral principle. Very shortly after my conversation with Six, here referred to Napoleon drove his brother Louis from the throne of Holland, which he annexed to the French Empire — Six d'Oterbeck was recalled, and not long afterwards drowned in one of the Canals of Amsterdam — Napoleon and his preternatural power have crumbled into dust; and now he becomes the Moral of a Sermon against selfishness.

———

[July 1828]

3. IV:45. ≈ Mr. Rush called for a few minutes but was going to attend the adjourned Meeting of the Stockholders of the Chesapeake and Ohio Canal Company. The Arrangements for the ceremony of breaking ground to-morrow are published in the newspaper of this morning, and also a notice that in consequence of my attendance at that ceremony there will be no reception of visitors at the President's House ≈ Mr. Brent was here; and I spoke with him of the applications of the two Priests Harold and Ryan, for the interposition of this Government, with that of the Pope to obtain the revocation of an order from his Holiness to them, to repair forthwith from Philadelphia to Cincinnati in the State of Ohio. I desired Mr. Brent to make a draft of such a Letter to the Cardinal Secretary of State, as would answer the views of Mr. Harold and Mr. Ryan, and at the same time not be offensive to the papal Government — and I charged him with this duty the more readily, because being himself a Roman Catholic, a Letter known to be written by him would probably [be] more acceptable, and more likely to be useful to those in whose behalf it was requested, than if written by a protestant. Mr. Brent brought me also a Letter from Mr. Rodney, the Consul at the Havana, but now at Wilmington, Delaware, denying totally the truth of the charges against him of the anonymous Letter,

a copy of which had been sent to him. Mr. Southard called shortly before dinner — I had some conversation with him upon judge Brackenridge's letter respecting the cultivation of the Live Oak. I also read to him the Address which I propose to deliver to-morrow, on breaking the ground of the Chesapeake and Ohio Canal — Mr. Mercer called this Evening, and mentioned to me the definitive arrangements for the ceremony — The company to assemble between 7 and 8 to-morrow Morning at Tilley's Union Hotel, in Georgetown. To walk in procession to the Steam-boats — then ascend the river to the first bridge and thence in Canal Boats to the spot where the work is to commence — Where he will present to me a spade; addressing me with a few sentences, occupying not more than five minutes — I told him that as at this time, I must expect that whatever I might say would be severely criticised, and misrepresented, I had thought proper to write what I should say, so that at least I might be responsible for nothing else. That deeming the work to be commenced of great importance to the Country and to future ages I thought it suitable to the occasion to give to the ceremony somewhat of a religious character, and I read to him the address as I proposed to deliver it — He approved of it altogether, though he thought the last paragraph, expressing good wishes for the success of the Baltimore Rail-road which is also to be commenced to-morrow, would not meet with sympathy from my hearers, as they believed that to be a rival project: but it was nevertheless entirely proper for me to speak thus and the religious cast of my address was conformable to his own Sentiments. He would adapt the few words that he should say on presenting me the Spade to the purport of my own discourse.

4. IV:15. Friday. Independence day. Chesapeake and Ohio Canal commenced — John 25 — Between seven and eight this morning I went with my Son John to the Union Hotel at Georgetown, where were assembling the President and Directors of the Chesapeake and Ohio Canal Company; the Mayors and Committees of the Corporations of Washington, Georgetown and Alexandria — The Heads of Departments, foreign Ministers and a few other invited persons. About eight O'Clock a procession was formed preceded by a band of music to

the wharf where we embarked in the Steam-boat Surprize; followed by two others we proceeded to the entrance of the Potowmack Canal, and up that in Canal boats to its head: near which, just within the bounds of the State of Maryland, was the spot selected for breaking the ground — The President of the Chesapeake and Ohio Canal Company with a very short Address delivered to me the Spade, with which I broke the ground: addressing the surrounding auditory, consisting perhaps of two thousand persons — It happened that at the first stroke of the Spade, it met immediately under the surface a large stump of a tree; after repeating the stroke three or four times without making any impression, I threw off my coat, and resuming the Spade, raised a shovel full of the Earth, at which a general shout burst forth from the surrounding multitude, and I completed my Address, which occupied about fifteen minutes. The President and Directors of the Canal, the Mayors and Committees of the three Corporations; the Heads of Departments, members of Congress, and others followed, and shovelled up a wheelbarrow-full of the Earth — Mr. Gales the Mayor of Washington read also a short Address, and was answered extemporaneously by Andrew Stewart, the Director of the Company from Pennsylvania. After a short repose under a tent on the banks of the Canal, we returned by the Canal boats to the landing and thence in the Steamboat, where as we redescended the Potowmack, the company partook of a light Collation upon the deck — I was asked for a Toast and gave the Chesapeake and Ohio Canal. Perseverance. — Mr. Mercer and Mr. Rush also gave toasts — About half past two I was landed at Davidson's wharf where my Carriage was waiting; and after taking Mr. Rush home I returned to mine. The Marshals of the day escorted me home on horseback; came in and took a glass of wine, and took leave with my thanks for their attentions. A young man named Dorset from Maryland, was the only other visitor — Dr. Huntt and Thomas J. Hellen dined with us. The day was uncommonly cool for the Season, with a fresh breeze, and towards Evening there was a gentle Shower — The exertion of speaking in the open air made me hoarse, and with the anxiety more oppressive than it should have been to get well through the day, exhausted, and fatigued me so that I was disqualified for thought or action the remainder of the day — As has happened to me whenever I have had a part to perform in the presence of multitudes, I got through awkwardly, but without gross and palpable failure. The incident that chiefly relieved me was the obstacle of the stump, which met and resisted the Spade, and my casting off my coat to overcome the resistance — It struck the eye and fancy of the Spectators, more than all the flowers of Rhetoric in my Speech, and diverted their attention from the stammering and hesitation of a deficient memory — Mr. Vaughan, Chevalier Bangeman Huygens, Barons Krudener and Stackelberg, and several other members of the Corps Diplomatique were present, and thought it perhaps a strange part for a President of the United States to perform. Governor Kent of Maryland was there as one of the Directors of the Company; and compared the ceremony to that said to be annually observed in China. I wrote a short Letter this Evening to Charles.

———

7. IV:15. Monday — Sun rose 4:45. Boat-Bath. Garden. Presbyterian Church election of Pastor. Took the morning bath from the Boat in the river, and the day was absorbed, by a succession almost uninterrupted of visitors from the breakfast to the dining hour — First from Mr. Mercer, next from a man who said his name, was Arnold: that he belonged to the County of Middlesex, Massachusetts — that he had been travelling, and found himself here without money; he would be much obliged to me for a loan, to bear his expenses in returning home, which I declined — Col'l Thomas followed; going shortly for New-York, and his suttling expedition to Bangor, Maine — He spoke very favourably of the new Treasurer Mr. Clark; and mentioned to me some new indications of the political treachery of the Post-master General M'lean — Of this I can no longer entertain a doubt — He has been all along a supple tool of the Vice-President, Calhoun; but plays his game with so much cunning and duplicity, that I can fix upon no positive act that would justify the removal of him.

———

25. IV:30. ≈ General Porter had an insolent Letter from Duff Green one of the Editors of the Telegraph, demanding inspection and copies of Documents in the War Department, for the defence of General Jackson against charges contained in

publications of C. S. Todd and T. H. Shelby, republished from Kentucky papers in the National Journal of Yesterday. This demand was made in minatory language, and with a lying charge of partiality in the late Secretary of War, in cases of similar demands made upon him — General Porter expressed a doubt whether he should answer this Letter at-all — but shewed me a draft of an answer, which he had written — It declared a readiness to furnish inspection or copies of any documents to persons having any right to claim them; but declined granting them in this instance on account of the reflections in Green's Letter upon Governor Barbour, with some argument to justify this course. I thought it would be better after the first sentence to say that the tenour of Green's Letter was such as forbade the compliance with his request, and the holding [of] any further communication with him — Mr. Passet is a Frenchman, who keeps an upholsterer's shop here; but who on the 4th of July sent me a card announcing himself as having been a high Officer in the army of Napoleon — and this day he came and in a *style ampoulé*, offered me a present of a gold breast pin, which he said he had received from his sister — now in France. I declined his present. Antoine says he has fallen into habits of intemperance.

—

[August 1828]
5. IV:30. Tuesday — Ride from Rossburg to Baltimore. There had been too much baggage packed behind our light Carriage; and we left two of our Trunks to be sent on by one of the Stages to Baltimore — Edward Wyer passed through Rossburg in a Hack from Washington in the Night — We left Rossburg at five A.M. and arrived at Merrill's tavern at Waterloo 15 miles, at 8. There breakfasted — rested our horses till half past eleven — and then rode to Baltimore and at 15 minutes past two, alighted at Barnum's tavern — The morning was cloudy with a succession of light drizzling Showers, by which being on horseback I was not a little annoyed. And having been so long disused to this exercise, the ride of 27 Miles this day, following that of 9 last Evening was very fatiguing. I found myself also somewhat sore from excoration — We dined immediately after our arrival at Baltimore; and from four in the afternoon till near eleven at Night, had a continual stream of visitors,

almost all Strangers, but who came to shake hands with the President — In the Evening there was a Jackson-party popular meeting, in the Square adjoining to Barnum's house, at which a young man named M'Mahon, a member of the State Legislature, harangued the multitude for about three hours upon the unpardonable sins of the Administration, and the transcendant virtues of Andrew Jackson — He was still speaking when I retired to bed, and I heard his voice like the beating of a mill-clapper, but nothing that he said. The meeting dispersed about eleven at Night. There was a similar Meeting of the friends of the Administration a few Nights since; and there are Ward Meetings or Committee Meetings of both parties, every day of the week. It is so in every part of the Union. A Stranger would think that the People of the United States have no other occupation than electioneering.

6. IV:15. Wednesday. — From Baltimore to Philadelphia — After a very good Night's rest I embarked at 5 this Morning in the Steam-boat United States. ≈ At seven in the Evening we arrived at Philadelphia — There was a large concourse of People assembled on the wharf who gave three cheers at my landing, and a multitude of whom followed me as I walked from the wharf to Head's Mansion-House in South third Street. They shouted continually as I went along, and crowded round me so that I had barely room to pass along. With their Shouts occasionally two or three voices among them cried Huzza for Jackson — The throng chiefly of boys came into the yard, and remained there, still shouting after I entered the House; till in a few minutes I went out upon the Porch, and said "Fellow Citizens, I thank you for this kind and friendly reception, and wish you all good Night" — upon which they immediately dispersed.

———

[December 1828]

1. V. Monday — 20 Congress. 2 Session — Senator from Kentucky — quite shocked at the virulence of Newspaper Slanders agt. the Administration — Allen thinks I have suffered, for not turning my enemies out of office; particularly the Post-master General. Committee of both Houses of Congress, notified me that they had formed Quorums and were ready to receive any

Communication from me. Answered that I should make one at
12 to-morrow. Mr. Rush read me the draft of his annual report
on the finances — Very pleasing — corrected the message by
the revised figures of this Report — Sanford says Van Buren
is not coming. He is elected Governor by a minority, in New-
York. Condict spoke of Southard's coming as Senator from
New-Jersey. Fears they will make him a non-resident, as they did
Bailey. Asked if Southard could not withdraw and return to
New-Jersey. I thought it unnecessary. ≈ Collated the two Copies
of my Message for the two Houses of Congress — My Son
John's wife was taken in labour this day — Dr. Worthington at-
tends her. Mrs. Nowland is her Nurse.

———

3. V. Wednesday. Ride. College Hill and Capitol. A continual
stream of visitors, members of Congress and a few others
from Breakfast till near four P.M. when I took my ride of an
hour and a half on horseback. Most of the members of Congress who came were friends, and they had but one topic of
conversation; the loss of this day's election. I have only to
submit to it with resignation — and to ask that I, and those
who are dear to me, may be sustained under it — The Sun of
my political life sets in the deepest gloom. But that of my
Country shines unclouded — Mr. Crowell the Agent to the
Creek Indians came to ask for the Argument of Walter Jones
that he had left with me, claiming for the Indians the balance
of a sum, stipulated by Treaty of 1821 and reserved for indemnity to Citizens of Georgia — I had given it to the Attorney
General Wirt, for his opinion — The Legislature and delegation of Georgia claim the same balance for Citizens of that
State — Nalls came to solicit an appointment of Lieutenant in
the Marine Corps — I visited this Evening my Grand-daughter
— Received this Morning a Letter from the late President
Monroe. I was myself engaged on the draft of an answer to the
Boston federalists.

———

9. V. Tuesday. ≈ Mr. Bailey spent the Evening with me — He
enquired if I would accept a Seat in the Senate, from Massachusetts if it should be offered me — I answered that the first
objection would be that I would on no consideration displace
any other man — He said he believed Mr. Silsbee was very

averse to coming again to the Senate, and would be glad to decline, if I would accept — I said there were other objections, my intention being to go into the deepest retirement, and withdraw from all connection with public Affairs. He said Dr. Condict of New-Jersey, had expressed to him the hope that I should not thus withdraw.

———

11. IV:30. Thursday ≈ Miner asked me if I had determined definitively to withdraw from all public Service after the expiration of my present term — I told him that my intention was absolute and total retirement — But my principle would be what it had been through life — I should seek no public employment in any form, directly or indirectly — It was not for me to foresee whether my Services would ever be desired by my fellow Citizens again. If they should call for them, while I have life and health, I shall not hold myself at Liberty to decline repairing to any Station which they may assign to me; except for reasonable cause — But I desired him to receive this in Confidence, as a candid answer to his question; for I wish not even to give a hint to the public that I am yet eligible to their Service.

———

31. V:45. ≈ Mr. Clay spoke to me with great concern of the prospects of the Country — The threats of disunion from the South, and the graspings after all the Public Lands, which are disclosing themselves in the Western States — He spoke of a long Message from Ninian Edwards, Governor of Illinois to the Legislature of that State — who he said wished to take the lead from T. H. Benton, Senator from Missouri, who commenced this inroad upon the Public Lands — I told Mr. Clay, that it would be impossible for me to divest myself of a deep interest in whatever should affect the welfare of the Country — But that after the third of March, I should consider my public life as closed; and take from that time as little part in public concerns as possible — I shall have enough to do to defend and vindicate my own reputation, from the double persecution under which I have fallen ≈

[January 1829]
1. IV:30. Thursday — New-Year — Drawing Room — The year begins in gloom — My wife had a sleepless and painful

Night — The dawn was overcast; and as I began to write my shaded lamp went out, self-extinguished; it was only for lack of Oil; and the notice of so trivial an incident may serve but to mark the present temper of my mind — But in every situation in which mortal man can be placed there is a line of conduct before him, which it is his duty to pursue; and the Season of Adversity, though depriving him of the means which in prosperity he may possess of doing good to his fellow men, is perhaps not less adapted to the exercise of virtues equally conducive to the dignity of human Nature. But in good or in evil fortune "It is not in Man that walketh to direct his steps." — Let him look to the fountain of all Good — let him consult the Oracles of God — I began the year with prayer — and then turning to my Bible read the first Psalm — It affirms that the righteous man is, and promises that he shall be blessed — This is comfort and Consolation — and points in general terms to the path of duty — May the light of this Lamp never forsake me!

———

11. V:45. Sunday. ≈ In the afternoon at St. John's Church Mr. Hawley read the abridged evening Service for the first Sunday after the Epiphany, and Mr. Johns preached from 2 Kings 20–1 the latter part of the verse — "Thus saith the Lord, Set thine house in order; for thou shalt die, and not live." May I without superstition consider this as a third warning? And if so, may I pray to be spared to set my House in order, till after I shall be released from the burthen of my public duties? The Sermon of Mr. Johns was deeply impressive, and closed with a solemn address to every individual of his Hearers which I ought to lay to heart — May it not be lost upon me! Mr. Bailey and Col'l Dwight of Massachusetts and Mr. R. Sprague of Maine, dined with me, and we had much convivial conversation after dinner — I was over-talkative, and in a flow of Spirits contrasted with the solemnity of feeling inspired by the exercises of the day.

———

19. VI. Monday. Mr. Fendall called upon me this Morning and mentioned his design of publishing a History of the present Administration. He read to me a Prospectus which he had prepared of the work, but said that upon further reflection he inclined to adopt a different plan, less marked with the character of a partisan, which I approved — I observed to him that

impartiality was the Law of History, and that as the correctness of the popular voice at the recent election, was to be tested by time and experience, it would not be wise or just to assume before hand that it was all error and delusion — We had much desultory Conversation upon the manner in which the History should be written, and I mentioned to him the projects floating in my own mind of writing Memoirs of my fathers life and my own, perhaps even a History of the United States, from the formation of their Confederacy. I told him also that his Cousin Richard Henry Lee had informed me that *he* had the intention of writing a History of the present Administration, and he spoke of a Mr. Rogers of New-York, who had expressed a similar design ≈

20. V:45. Tuesday. Dr. Wallace called upon me, and we had a long conversation upon fire and Water, Rain and Snow; but especially upon Water, which he said was composed of three of the most combustible elements in Nature — Oxygen, Hydrogen and Electricity — He referred all to the glory of God — and I read to him the first verse of the 19th Psalm. Mr. Force brought back the part of my manuscript upon the Brevet, which I had given him, and shewed me the pamphlet sent him by General Jackson, with the passionate and illiterate writing of his own upon a blank page of it ≈

21. VI:45. Wednesday. ≈ Mr. Crowninshield called to say that his Son Benjamin had been taken dangerously ill with a fever at Salem, and he feared he should be obliged to go home. He spoke to me, of the Deportment that I should hold towards my Successor, which I told him would depend upon his towards me — I should treat him with respect to his Station, but should make no advance to conciliation with him, as I had never wronged him; but much the reverse — but he had slandered me.

———

31. VI:45. Saturday. Snow the whole day. ≈ *Day.* My rising hour has ranged from IV to VII:15. The average being about V:30 and the changes regulated by the time of my retirement to bed which has varied from X:30 to 1 A.M., which happened only once — The day of the last Drawing-room. My usual time of retirement is XI:30. Giving six hours to the bed — On

rising I light my lamp, by the remnant of fire in the Bed-
chamber — dress and repair to my Cabinet, where I make my
fire and sit down to writing till between nine and ten — After
Breakfast I read the morning National Intelligencer and Journal; and from X A.M. to IV P.M. receive visitors, transact business with the Heads of Departments, and send Messages to
one or both Houses of Congress — My riding on horseback
has been interrupted almost the whole Month by the weather,
and the Snow and Ice — from four I walk an hour and a quarter till half past five — Dine, and pass one or two hours in the
bed-chamber or Nursery. Then write again in my Cabinet till
the time for repose — This routine has now become so habitual to me, that it forms part of the comfort of my existence,
and I look forward with great solicitude to the time when it
must be totally changed, I never go abroad unless to visit a sick
friend. But a large dinner party once a week, a Drawing room
once a fortnight, occasional company of one two or three to
dine with us in the family, and the daily visitors, eight or ten,
sometimes twelve or fifteen keep me in constant intercourse
with the world; and furnish constant employment the oppres-
siveness of which is much relieved by its variety. This is a happy
condition of life, which within five weeks more must close —
The prosperous condition of the Country takes from the load
of public care, all its pain, and almost all its weariness. My wife
was exceedingly ill the first days of the Month, but has been in
better health and Spirits, for the greater part of it — Mr. and
Mrs. W. S. Smith, Thomas B. and Abigail S. Adams and
Thomas J. Hellen have been with us all the Month — My Son
John's wife has kept her chamber till the last three or four days
— Her daughter is close on two Months Old, and is a fine
thriving healthy child. With deep gratitude for the enjoyments
yet indulged, let me not despair of the mercy with which they
are to be withdrawn, and above all prepared to meet the
change of fortune, about to befall me — "As ever in my task
masters eye."

———

[February 1829]
21. VI:15. Saturday — Walk round the Square The Seneca Indian Chief Red Jacket, called upon me, with his interpreter
Henry Johnson to take leave of me, and to ask some assistance

for him to return home, for which I referred him to the Secretary of War — He has been exhibiting himself for sometime past upon Theatres in several of our Cities for Money — He carries with him a small silver mounted emblematic tomahawk. He told me that he came to take leave of me for that he and I were of the last Age and should soon be called for by the Great Spirit. I answered him that was true; and I hoped it would be to a better world than this.

———

28. VI. Saturday. ≈ *Day* — Much the same as last month. With the exception of two or three light Colds, my health has been better than for several preceding years. I have recovered much of my bodily strength, and only find the difficulty of writing increase upon me. This is a source of deep concern to me, as all the usefulness and all the promise of comfort before me, for my remnant of life will consist in the faculty of writing — But I must take the dispensations of Providence as they come — Thankful to Heaven for the good — Resigned and submissive to the severe. The month has been remarkable as the last of my public service, and the preceding pages will shew that the business of my office crowds upon me, with accumulation as it draws near to its end — Three days more and I shall be restored to private life and left to an old age of retirement, though certainly not of repose. I go into it with a combination of parties, and of public men, against my character and reputation such as I believe never before was exhibited against any man since this Union existed — Posterity will scarcely believe it — but so it is — that this combination against me has been formed, and is now exulting in triumph over me, for the devotion of my life, and of all the faculties of my Soul, to the Union — and to the Improvement, Physical, Moral and Intellectual of my Country. The North assails me for my fidelity to the Union — the South, for my ardent aspirations of improvement — Yet bate I not a jot of heart and hope — Passion, Prejudice, Envy and Jealousy will pass — The Cause of Union and of Improvement will remain; and I have duties to it and to my Country yet to discharge — On the eleventh of this Month, Andrew Jackson of Tennessee was declared to be elected President and John C. Calhoun Vice President of the United States for four years from the fourth of March next. On the

same day, the President elect, arrived in this City, and took lodgings at Gadsby's Hotel. A self-constituted Central Committee, of persons pretending to be his exclusive friends and partizans, with John P. Van Ness at their head; undertook to usher him into the City; to order the firing of guns, and manifestations of public rejoicing in his honour; and to assume the Office of Masters of Ceremonies to introduce to him all his visitors. They continued to exercise these functions till the public disgust became audible — They even published a regulation of the ceremony of his inauguration, and proclaimed Col'l Towson the Paymaster General, and one of their own number, Marshal for arranging the procession to the Capitol. This however has since been given up — The President elect, a few days since sent for Col'l Towson, and requested him to resign his Office of Marshal for the central Committee, which he did, and the Marshal of the District of Columbia, is to have the ordering of the Commission as has been customary heretofore. Mrs. Jackson having died in December, the General has signified his wish to avoid all displays of festivity or rejoicing, and all magnificent parade. He has not thought proper to hold any personal communication with me since his arrival. I sent him word by Marshal Ringgold, that I should remove with my family from the House so that he may if he thinks proper receive his visits of congratulation here on the 4th of March. He desired Ringgold to thank me for this information — Spoke uncertainly, whether he would come into the House on the 4th or not; but said if it would be in any manner inconvenient to my family to remove he wished us not to hurry ourselves at-all, but to stay in the house as long as should suit our convenience, were it even a Month — He has with him his nephew Andrew Jackson Donelson with his wife, a Miss Easten, an adopted Son, named Jackson, and perhaps some others. His avoidance of me has been noticed in the newspapers. The Telegraph Newspaper has assigned for the reason of this incivility, that he knows I have been personally concerned in the publications against his wife, in the National Journal — This is not true — I have not been privy to any publication in any newspaper, against either himself or his wife — Within a few days another reason has been assigned. Mr. David Hoffman of Baltimore, urged me to attend the inauguration, and said, in that event he was informed it was General Jackson's intention to pay me a visit — His reason for not having done it before having been, the chance there might have been of his meeting Mr. Clay with me. Mr. Ringgold says Mr. M'lean the Postmaster-General told him that he had conversed with the General, upon his abstaining from visiting me, and that the General had told him he came here with the intention of calling upon me, but had been dissuaded from it by his friends — Mrs. Adams went out to Meridian Hill on Thursday; and my Son's wife and Abigail Adams this day. As I shall be constantly occupied with public business until and including the third of March I shall not be able to leave this House until the Evening of that day. The removal of my Effects, and the preparation of the House for the reception of another family, have so much absorbed the time that it has been, and will be impossible till after the third to take the inventory of the furniture belonging to the house, and to be delivered over. As the General had sent a courteous Message desiring us not to hurry our removal and had expressed himself very doubtful whether he should come in, I sent word to him by Mr. Ringgold that it might take two or three days beyond the third before the inventory could be taken; he sent for answer that he wished not to put us to the slightest inconvenience, but that Mr. Calhoun had suggested that there might be danger of the excessive crowds breaking down the rooms at Gadsby's House, and the General had concluded if it would be perfectly convenient to us to receive his company at the President's House after the Inauguration on Wednesday next. — I have therefore concluded at all Events to leave the House on Tuesday. Michael Antony Giusta the man whom I engaged in my Service at Amsterdam in June 1814 and who has lived with me ever since; and his wife have both been engaged by the General to remain in the house and in the same capacity which they now hold — This Separation from Domestics who have so long lived in the family is among the painful incidents of the present time.

———

[March 1829]
3. V:30. Tuesday. Meridian Hill. Close of the 20th Congress, and of my public life — General Porter brought me the papers relating to a claim of Captain Campbell's company of Ohio

Volunteers in the year 1812; I wrote a decision that they should be allowed pay for 12 Months, at the foot of Mr. Whittlesey's Letter. Mr. Johnston the Indian Agent came for a decision upon the sale of an Indian reservation but I was compelled to decline it — He said he should be removed, for there were at least four here after his place. Mr. Clay brought me his resignation of the Office of Secretary of State, on which I wrote my acceptance, and he took it to be deposited at the Department of State. Mr. Graham called to take leave. Daniel Parker with a great budget of Papers, to explain to me his claims and convince me of the error of my opinion, given to P. Hagner — But I referred him to my Successor. ≈ About Noon I rode with my Son John, and T. B. Adams j'r to the Capitol, and sent to both Houses of Congress, Message N. 8 with the Panama Instructions — I signed 15 bills, and between 2 and 3 O'Clock, a joint Committee S. Smith and Burnett of the Senate, Ward and Bates of Massachusetts, announced to me that the Houses were ready to adjourn — I told them I had no further communication to make to the Houses, and wished to every individual member health and happiness. I walked back to the President's House, concluded the contract with Persico, consulted the members of the Administration, whether I should attend the inauguration to-morrow — all were against it except Mr. Rush — About nine in the Evening I left the President's House, and with my Son John, and T. B. Adams j'r came out and joined my family at Meridian Hill — Dined, received and accepted the Resignations, of R. Rush, P. B. Porter, S. L. Southard and W. Wirt.

CHAPTER X ❧ 1829–1831

Retirement

[March 1829]

4. VI. Wednesday. This day, Andrew Jackson of Tennessee was inaugurated as President of the United States. I had caused a notification to be published in the National Intelligencer and Journal, requesting the Citizens of the District, and others, my friends who might be disposed to visit me according to the usage heretofore, to dispense with that formality. Very few therefore came out. Mr. Williams of North-Carolina, and Mr. Bartlett of New-Hampshire came with Mr. Gales, who brought the Inaugural Address of the President — It is short, written with some elegance; and remarkable chiefly for a significant threat of Reform. ≈ The day was warm and Spring-like; and I rode on my horse, with Watkins into the City, and thence through F Street to the Rockville Turnpike, and over that till I came to the turn of the Road by which I returned over College Hill, back to the House. Near the Post-Office, I was overtaken by a man named Dulaney, who first enquired whether I could inform him how he could see John Quincy Adams, and when I gave him my name, told me his, and that he came from Waterford, in Virginia, and was charged to ask of me a return of papers sent to me last Summer, and relating to the Post-Office at that place. He came with me to my House, and I gave him the papers which he took away — I resumed drowsily this Evening the writing of my reply to the Appeal of the Confederates — Wrote two short Letters, and received two from my Sons George and Charles. I can yet scarcely realize my Situation. Hitherto I have prayed for direction from above, in concerns of my Country, and of mankind. I need it not less, and pray for it with equal fervor now, for those of myself, my family, and of all whose dependence is upon me — From Indolence and despondency, and indiscretion may I specially be preserved.

5. VI. Thursday — rain. Storm. Confined to the House the whole day, by a steady rain, attended in the afternoon and

Evening by a heavy gale. Dr. Reynolds came out this morning
with Lieut. Slidell of the Navy, to lament with me the loss in
the Senate of the Bill for the Scientific expedition to the South
Seas. Reynolds said he had been assured that at the next Session of Congress the project would be resumed, and even
recommended by the President — The opposition to it has
been altogether factious. The Bill passed the House of Representatives by a large majority; and almost without opposition. It
was defeated in the Senate by Robert Y. Hayne of South-
Carolina, Chairman of the Naval Committee and Littleton W.
Tazewell of Virginia, both men of some talents, but whose
sense of Justice, of Patriotism and of truth is swallowed up by
the passions of party, combining in both with overbearing arrogance, rancorous tempers, and in Tazewell with a never
dying personal hatred of me, because I once told him at my
own table, upon his pertinaciously insisting that Tokay and
Rhenish wine were much alike in taste, that I did not believe
he had ever drank a drop of Tokay in his life. He had provoked
this retort, by saying a few minutes before that he had never
known a Unitarian, who did not believe in the Sea Serpent —
As however it was at my own table, I made him some months
afterwards through Dr. Watkins an apology for the rudeness
of my Speech, which he accepted — But the shaft was sped,
barbed with truth, and it will rankle in his side till his dying
hour. Mr. Vaughan the British Minister also paid me a visit
this morning. I occupied the day and Evening in writing upon
my reply to the appeal of the Confederates. My time is now
all leisure; like an instantaneous flat calm in the midst of a
Hurricane — I cannot yet settle my mind to a regular course
of future employment — My Son John's Child was suddenly
taken with a fainting fit, which alarms us — I read part of the
second Philippic.

———

12. V. Thursday. Mr. Clay came out this morning and took
leave of us — He goes with his family by the way of Baltimore
to-morrow. Last Saturday, his friends and those of the late
Administration gave him a dinner, at which he made a Speech.
He told me some time since that he had received invitations at
several places on his way to Lexington, to Public Dinners, and
should attend them; and that he intended freely to express his

opinions — I mentioned to him the Letter from Rahwey New-Jersey and the answer I had given to it — He expressed himself much gratified with what I told him, I had said in it of him — and told me he had written a very short answer to the Letter which he had received. He manifested some sensibility at parting, and expressed a wish occasionally to hear from me. ≈

13. V:30. Friday — Ride. Call on R. Rush. The day was uninterrupted by visitors, and from an oppressive burden of business, I find myself transferred to a Season of total leisure; though with private concerns which ought already to occupy me with constant employment, but upon which I cannot yet prevail upon myself to engage — I have yet numerous Letters to answer, and my reply to the Boston confederates seems lengthening as I go. Before dinner I rode round by the Race-ground, and Capitol Hill into the City. In the Pennsylvania Avenue, I passed by Mr. Clay, in his carriage; on his way to Baltimore; and a last salutation passed between us — I stopped at Mr. Southard's house. His nephew told me, that he was this day a little better, but still confined with fever to his bed, and not able to see me. I then called upon Mr. Rush who told me that he had this day received the answer of Alexander Baring, to the enquiries addressed to him the last Autumn concerning the negotiation of a loan for the Corporation of the City, and the Chesapeake and Ohio Canal Company. The answer is rather encouraging, and the Corporation of the City have it in contemplation to employ Mr. Rush himself to go to England as an Agent to negotiate this loan — He says that C. F. Mercer the President of the Canal Company told him that he was afraid from something that had fallen from General Jackson, that his disposition was adverse to the Canal; which if true will not promote his popularity here. — His appointments continue to contrast with his Speech to the Tennessee Legislature two years since — He then said that if Members of Congress continued to receive appointments to Office, corruption would be the order of the day — He has already appointed nearly as many members of Congress, as I did in four years — The last are John Chandler Ex-Senator from Maine, appointed Collector at Portland; and Thomas P. Moore, member of the House from Kentucky, Minister Plenipotentiary to the

Republic of Colombia, in the place of W. H. Harrison, superseded. An appointment carrying with it, the useless waste of a
fresh outfit, Harrison having been appointed only last Spring;
and having scarcely yet reached the place of his destination.
Moore's character and talents are inferior to those of Harrison.
His integrity is problematical, and his only public service the
servility of his prostitution to the cause of Jackson's election,
and the baseness of his Slanders upon me — Abigail S. Adams
went to Mrs. Gales's in the City.

14. V:30. Saturday. ≈ My horse was hurt last Night in the Stable; so that this day I walked before dinner to Mr. Southard's
— Found him again convalescent. He told me some anecdotes
of the manner in which the new Administration is commencing its operations, and which portend no good. To feed the
cormorant appetite for place, and to reward the prostitution of
canvassing defamers are the only principles yet discernible in
the conduct of the President; and indecision and instability are
already strongly marked in his movements. He dropped from
my naval nominations Stockton and M'Keever for Masters
Commandant — then at the remonstrance of M'Keever sent
them in by themselves — The Senate rejected them; and this
morning he sent them in again.

———

17. V:45. Tuesday. Rain. Rain all the morning. Towards Evening it cleared off Cold, and with a fresh Gale. A little Snow. I
began reading the third Philippic of Cicero; and consulted in
Plutarch the lives of Cicero, of Antony and of Brutus, for the
cotemporary facts — Looked likewise into Shakespear's Antony and Cleopatra — There is something strange, and which
would now be thought very affected in the language of Shakespear, whose most common thoughts are expressed in uncommon words ≈

18. VI. Wednesday — A cold and blustering day. Mr. Fendall
came out and brought back the part of my manuscript that I
had lent him. He made a few judicious remarks, particularly
advising me to leave out passages unnecessary to the controversy, and tending to multiply antagonists. This I told him was
excellent advice, and I would avail myself of it — But how far

must this be carried — The disunion project of 1804 cannot be fully exposed without developing the causes of dissatisfaction with Mr. Jefferson's administration by which it was instigated — most of these were well founded. I felt them deeply myself; and now on reviewing them, I think of them as I did in 1804. Shall I tell them — If I do there is another Hornet's Nest that I shall disturb, and more controversy to be foreseen — If I leave it even for publication after my death, my children will be made to feel the resentments that it will kindle — They are feeling now the effects of those which have been stirred — Selfish motives admonish me to silence — On the other hand a great moral lesson to my Country may be taught by exposing the errors both of those federalists who conspired against the integrity of the Union, and of Mr. Jefferson himself, and of his Administration — My present course is to write with the boldness of truth — I shall prune by the Counsels of Prudence.

———

26. V:30. Thursday. — Ride to Capitol Hill. Mr. Persico came and took a sitting of three hours, but during the greater part of which time I was reading the first Volume of Pelham, or the Adventures of a Gentleman. The most prolific School of Literature at present is novel-writing. The marvelous of character and manners is substituted in the place of the marvellous in narrative — Pelham the Gentleman, is a compound of dandy, Statesman and Philosopher — Epicurean, Coxcomb, Duelist, Courtier, Patriot, Satirist, Demagogue and political Vicar of Bray — Who begins by presenting his father and mother as odious and ridiculous characters and speaks of his own vices, and what he means to pass off for good deeds with equal indifference — The book is nevertheless interesting and abounds with keen observations, and ingenious reflections.

———

31. V:15. Tuesday. Commodore and Mrs. Rodgers called to pay us a Morning visit, but Mrs. Adams was gone into the City when they were here — The morning was clear Summer Sunshine, but the weather clouded up towards Evening — I rode my horse from three to five, and was musing as I rode upon the construction of half a dozen Elegiac Stanza's to versify a Similitude upon Corinthian Brass — I accomplished it in part;

and very much to my dissatisfaction — It is with poetry as with Chess and Billiards — There is a certain degree of attainment, which labour and practice will reach, and beyond which no vigils and no vows will go — So the motto for my Stanzas shall be

Non licat cuivis adire Corinthum. ≈

[April 1829]
Meridian Hill. Washington. Latitude 38:55:38. Longitude West from Greenwich 76:56:59.

Wednesday 1. April 1829. V:15. My Diary will henceforth be a record of thoughts rather than of facts — This day was a day of Showers — and in the Evening there was a long, Heavy Storm of Thunder, Lightening, Rain and Hail. Mr. Persico was here all the morning, and took a final sitting for the mould of my Bust in clay. I walked an hour before dinner — and passed the remainder of the day and Evening with my family, or in my study reading and writing. I was suffering with a rhumatic head-ache, which dulled my faculties, and prevented me from finishing my Letter to Governor Barbour; and also from making much progress in my Reply to the Appeal of the Boston confederates — I read two or three Chapters of Pelham, among which that containing the Character of Christopher Clutterbuck, the twin brother as the author acknowledges of Dominie Sampson; but he has given Christopher a Shrew and Slattern for a wife, and has degraded the Classical Studies by representing them as destructive of health and of life, and as leading to no more useful result, than a voluminous Dissertation upon the Greek participle; with a self-conceit of the writer, as if it placed him on a level with Newton. Now that the tendency of Classical Studies, may be to absorb too large a portion of the mind, in the contemplation of language, may be true — but it is not necessary — The most important and laborious duty of a Protestant divine is the composition of Sermons; the weekly Instruction in Religion and Morality, of which he is the dispenser to his flock — To qualify him for the performance of this duty, Classical learning is no useless lumber — It is no unprofitable study to him; that which enables him to read the Scriptures in their original Languages — which acquaints him with the writings of the fathers — which makes him familiar with the Philosophers, the Poets, the Historians, the Orators of Greece and Rome — If the teacher of Religion, can use the knowledge of the language in which Christ spoke, and his apostles wrote to no better purpose than to compose a Dissertation upon the Greek participle; if the teacher of morals, can draw no available funds from the language of Pythagoras and Plato: if the Christian Orator can draw no shaft from the quivers of Aristotle and Quintilian, or of Demosthenes and Cicero; the fault is surely not in his studies — If his Lamp affords no light, it is not for lack of Oil, but because he hides it under a bushel. — I began also to read the eleventh Philippic of Cicero.

———

4. V:15. Saturday. Mr. Van Buren, the new Secretary of State, paid me a morning visit with Mr. Hamilton — Of the new Administration he is the only person who has shewn me this mark of common civility — General Jackson had received from me attentions of more than a common character, besides obligations of a much higher order, which at the time when they were rendered he had expressly acknowledged, and declared he would remember. All the members of his Administration have been with me upon terms of friendly acquaintance, and have repeatedly shared the hospitalities of my house — I never was indebted for a cup of cold water to any one of them; nor have I ever given to any one of them the slightest cause of Offence — They have all gradually withdrawn from all social intercourse with me — from the old impulse odisse quem laeseris. They hate the man they have wrong'd — Ingham is among the basest of my Slanderers — Branch and Berrien have been among the meanest of my persecutors in the Senate — Among them all there is not a man capable of a generous or liberal Sentiment towards an Adversary, excepting Eaton, and he is a man of indecently licentious life — They have made themselves my Adversaries, solely for their own advancement, and have forfeited the characters of Gentlemen, to indulge the bitterness of their self-stirred gall. Van-Buren, by far the ablest man of them all, but wasting most of his ability upon mere personal intrigues, retains the forms of civility; and pursues enemity, as if he thought it might be one day his interest to seek friendship. His principles are all subordinate to his ambition,

and he will always be of that doctrine upon which he shall see his way clear to rise — Our conversation was about the weather and the climate, and upon the negotiation with the Porte, which from a late paragraph in an English newspaper, I fear is broken off.

———

6. V:15. Monday — Mr. Persico came and cast the mould of the bust. He told me that he would come again in two or three days — Mr. Fendall came out and I gave him five sheets of my Reply to the Appeal — I had a long conversation with him upon his projected history of my Administration; and upon my political Life — He has asked me repeatedly to furnish him some Notes for a preliminary political view of parties from the formation of our confederacy, which I have promised to give him; but which I have not yet had time to prepare. But he said he thought of making that the last Chapter, which he should write, which I told him I thought would be his best plan. He has not yet been dismissed from the Department of State, but expects it from day to day. He remarked upon the singularity of my fortune and history that I was perhaps the only man who had risen to the highest Office in the Union, by a course of action, independent of all parties.

———

16. V:15. Thursday. Dr. Huntt came out this morning, and vaccinated my Son's infant daughter. He sat and talked with me perhaps an hour with me, upon the only subject which now furnishes materials for conversation at Washington; which is the removals and new Appointments to Office — They are effected a few at a time, and in such manner as to keep up a constant agitation and alarm among the Office-holders — Multitudes of applicants are kept in suspense, and now and then one goes off gratified. The appointments almost without exception are conferred upon the vilest purveyors of Slander during the late electioneering campaign, and an excessive disproportion of places are given to Editors of the foulest presses — Very few reputable appointments have been made and those confined to persons who were indispensably necessary to the Office, such as Asbury Dickins to the place of Chief Clerk in the Treasury Department.

———

18. V:15. Saturday. ≈ The newspapers announce this morning the appointment of Louis M'Lane of Delaware, as Envoy Extraordinary and Minister-Plenipotentiary to Great-Britain in the place of James Barbour removed — This is the most painful incident to me which has occurred since the change of the Administration; and it proves the utter heartlessness of Van-Buren — He, and M'Lane and Governor Barbour were all partizans of Crawford in 1825. M'Lane voted for him in the house, and thereby gave him the State of Delaware — M'Lane is utterly incompetent to the Mission to London; and if he does not disgrace the Country, will effect nothing for her interest. His only merit is the sale of himself and his Crawford Stock to Jackson — But he will give him and Van-Buren trouble — No Administration can make bad appointments abroad with impunity.

19. V:15. Easter — Anniversary of Lexington Battle. Warm day. Trees all blossoming or putting out their leaves. I walked to the Presbyterian Church, and heard a Stranger preach from John 1:29 "Behold the lamb of God, which taketh away the sin of the world." It is painful to me to hear a Calvinist preach upon this text; and to witness the solemn and fervent sincerity with which they pour out absurdity and nonsense — The mind of man delights in Truth in the abstract, and is perpetually seeking falsehood in the concrete. Warned of the imperfection of my own reason, I distrust its conclusions as I do those of others, and when I consider what man is, whence he comes and where he goes physically, I wonder only at the degree in which he does possess the power of linking together cause and effect — That he should form the conception of God, of eternity, of a future State; of mind, independent of matter; and I cannot account for the Passion which I most intensely feel, for continued existence hereafter — The preacher told us to-day that it was all owing to curiosity, which he said was innate in man — and he illustrated it by reminding his hearers how anxious they were to see General La Fayette, when he was in this Country. He further said that if there was a great Military Commander who had saved his Country in War (General Jackson was present) or if there was a Great Man in another line, who had rendered services as a Statesman (God forgive

me for my thoughts when he said this) there was a universal
curiosity to see them — but how he got from this to his text I
scarcely remember — he did however get there.

———

27. V. Monday ≈ Elliott Cressen called upon me again. He has
been these three or four Months in Virginia, and is now on his
way returning to Philadelphia — He asked me again to write
something in his Album, which I promised to do. I had not
had Time when he sent it to me before, in January. He is of the
Society of Friends and spoke much of the Colonization Society: of the success of which he has a very favourable opinion
— with which in this respect mine does not agree. He has a
profound horror of the condition of the Slaves in our Southern
States — There is I believe in this respect some misapprehen-
sion and much prejudice — There are no doubt cases of
extreme oppression and cruelty, and the impunity for them is
complete; but I believe them to be very rare, and that the
general treatment of Slaves is mild and moderate — Elliott
spoke of some things relating to the present state of public
affairs, with great severity, and especially of some Scandals in
great circulation ≈ I rode to the Navy Yard, and composed part
of the Fable of the Wolf and the Dog. Abigail S. Adams came
home, and Elizabeth Cranch came to spend the week with her
— My wife, my Sons wife and child are all ill — and I am sick
at Heart.

———

[May 1829]
1. V. Friday. ≈ Dr. Huntt was here and spoke of the universal
Consternation of all the Office-holders at Washington, upon
the dismissions which have taken place within the last two
days. A large portion of the population of Washington, are
dependent for bread upon these Offices; and it is a proscription
of which no one knows upon whom it will fall next — Every
one is in breathless expectation — trembling at heart and
afraid to speak ≈ I rode this day to the Navy Yard, and Eastern
Branch, the weather being pleasant and rather cool. I got
through with the Fable of Simonides; but very imperfectly,
much to my dissatisfaction, and taking in not half the ideas of
La Fontaine. In the Evening however I got through with
Horace's Ode to Grosphus, as well as I believe I am capable of

performing — In this and the Ode of Horace to Licinius I have succeeded so well, that if I could be equally fortunate every day it would afford me a useful and creditable occupation for my leisure — But there is a secret of composition which I cannot discover — The reason why I find the extreme difference in the facility of writing, one day over another — And the great difficulty is the standard beyond which I cannot rise; which however golden for the condition of life, is but a Saturnian age of lead for poetry. I wrote this Evening part of a Letter to Mr. Clay, in answer to two from him.

2. V:30. Saturday. Mr. Frye came out this day about 1 O'Clock and asked me if I had received my Letters by the Mail. I had not. He asked if I had heard any thing of my Son George — No. He said he had seen a short paragraph in the Baltimore American of this morning; that George had been lost from the Steamboat Benjamin Franklin, between Providence and New-York, on Thursday Morning before daylight — Judge Cranch came out about half an hour after and confirmed the fact — brought with him three Letters which came by the Mail — one from Charles King — one from George Sullivan; and one from Davis and Brooks, who took charge of the trunk and effects of my unhappy Son. God be merciful to him and to his wretched Parents — The Condition of his Mother, from the time I informed her of the Event is not to be described — John and Mary are in deep affliction — Judge Cranch returned soon to the City and sent out Dr. Huntt, who stayed till the Evening. But there was no medicine for this wound. Mr. Frye remained here about two hours, and left Mrs. Frye here to pass the Night.

3. VII. Sunday. Judge Cranch, Mr. Frye and Dr. Huntt called again successively to day and from them and from two New-York newspapers which Mr. Frye brought with him I gleaned some further particulars of that fatal Event, the loss of my Dear, Dear Son George — I see the causes of it distinctly — The motion of the Stage and Steamboat in twenty-four hours had produced a fever, with a rushing of the blood to the brain — He had complained of it in the Evening: said he wished the motion would be great enough to produce Sea-sickness; and spoke of stopping a day at New-York to be

bled. He had been pleasant and cheerful in conversation with several of the passengers in the afternoon; but got up in the Night, and spoke to two or three persons in a manner indicating a wandering mind — And thus walking on the upper deck of the boat; alone and in the dark; it pleased the disposer of all Events, to take him to himself — Blessed God! forgive the repining of mortal flesh, at this dispensation of thy will! forgive the wanderings of my own mind under its excruciating torture! have compassion upon the partner of my Soul; and bear her up with thine everlasting arm. — Deep have been her afflictions heretofore — But this! oh this! Stay thy hand God of Mercy — Let her not say — My God! My God! why hast thou forsaken me? — Teach her and me; to bear thy holy will; and to bless thy name ≈ Last Sunday at Church, Dr. Laurie read the 14th Chapter of Job, with an impressiveness of manner which struck me exceedingly. How much more deeply is it brought home to me now — It was proper that some one of the family should go to New-York, to receive possession of my poor Sons effects, and to ascertain if it might be possible to recover his remains — I was desirous of going myself, and had so determined, but at the earnest recommendation of Mr. Frye consented to let my Son John go in my place, remaining myself here, with my dear and most afflicted wife. John wrote to my nephew W. S. Smith, to ask him to go with him, and received an answer that he would.

4. VI. Monday. ≈ This was a day of deep and dreadful affliction to the partner of my life, whose state of health is itself alarming. by the still flowing mercies of God, our reason has not deserted us, but imaginations wild and unsustained by reason came over us both — I walked this afternoon, round the square at the back of the College, and in the deepest anguish of my Soul, saw a rainbow suddenly spread before me. It touched my heart by no superstitious fancy, but by an association of ideas, as an admonition to trust in the goodness and mercy of God.

5. VI. Tuesday. ≈ I walked alone; two hours before dinner; to the Rockville Road thence to the Turnpike, and back by the way of the College — In this walk I meditated a prayer to God:

believing that the severe dispensations of his providence are intented for wise and good purposes, imploring him that his purpose in this may be known and felt by us, and that it may bear the fruits of blessedness upon us and upon our conduct — This is the temper of mind into which I believe I ought to be brought by this Event, and for which the grace of God is yet necessary to controul the depravity of my nature — I long to cast off the world; and would henceforth commune only with God, and with my own family. — The Law of my members wars with the Law of my heart. I was not able effectually to accomplish my prayer, and must meditate over it again — Oh! my unhappy Son! what a Paradise of earthly enjoyment I had figured to my self as awaiting thee and me — It is withered for ever. But let not murmuring or repining pass from my lips.

———

7. V:30. Thursday. ≈ My mind still wanders; and spent itself again in composing a prayer — I believe that Special Providences enter into the general purposes of the Creator, and trust it was in his designs to chastise me in the immature and lamentable fate of my Son. This thought I have reduced to writing and to Rhyme; and with it I have joined an admonition of duty to the blessings yet left me, and for whom this sudden judgment strikes me with involuntary terror; and I have added an ejaculation of Soul, for the suffering victim himself— There is a pressure upon my heart and upon my Spirits, inexpressible and which I never knew before. — As it subsides, it gives way to dejection and despondency, equally unknown to my feelings before. I endeavour to return to the occupations which interested me before this calamity; but hitherto without success — All the prospects for the remnant of my life, in which I had delighted are broken up — and I have nothing left to rely on but the Mercy of God.

———

13. V:15. Wednesday. I received this morning a Letter from my Son John at New-York, dated on Monday and declaring that he had concluded to stay one day longer there. I finished the first draught of my reply to the appeal of the Boston confederates. It has occupied me three Months, and I feel a satisfaction that it is written and may remain behind me for my justification. But the events of the present time, and above all my

domestic calamities warn me against the publication of it for
the present: and probably it might be advantageously abridged
by one half. ≈ My dear wife was quite unwell again this Evening. I have invited Mrs. W. S. Smith to go with us to Quincy:
and I consented at Abigail S. Adams's request that she should
go home with Mr. and Mrs. Bigelow.

14. V:15. Thursday. ≈ I began this morning some remarks upon
parties in the United States — Rode my ten mile round, and
on my return, found my Son John returned from New-York,
without tidings of his brother's remains — Every measure has
been taken however to recover them, if so be the Will of God.

———

26. V. Tuesday. Morning ride on horseback to Georgetown, and
ride after dinner with my Son John into the City. Dr. Huntt was
here after breakfast — My observations upon parties in the
United States now absorbs all my time, and have swollen to a
much greater extent than I had intended — I must break off
writing further on them now or postpone my return to Quincy,
and I fear if I do break off that I may never resume them —
They lead me over much of the same ground that I have already
traversed in the Reply to the Appeal — These compositions
upon the past, abstract me from contemplations of the future,
and alone preserve me from despondency, which I cannot controul. I had foreseen evil enough — All that I had foreseen has
come, and it is nothing — Nothing to that stroke which I did
not foresee, and which has unman'd me.

———

[June 1829]
8. V:15. Monday. Rode the ten mile round before Breakfast —
Met Mr. Van-Buren riding also his horse, and we stop'd and
exchanged salutations — Van Buren is now Secretary of State.
He is the manager by whom the present Administration has
been brought into power. He has played over again the game
of Aaron Burr in 1800 with the addition of political inconsistency, in transferring his Allegiance from Crawford to Jackson
— He sold the State of New-York to them both — His first
bargain failed, by the turn of the choice of Electors in the
Legislature. The second was barely accomplished by the system of party management established in that State, and Van

Buren is now enjoying his reward — His pale and haggard looks shew that it is already a reward of mortification — If it should prove as there is every probability that it will, a reward of treachery, it will be but his desert — Divine retribution is often accomplished by the perfidy of man — Nec lex est justior ulla. I was again occupied the whole day in the arrangement and assortment of papers, and preparing for departure — Yet I shall leave them in great disorder.

———

18. IV:15. Thursday. Walpole to Quincy — Home. I rose with the Sun, and at a Quarter past six we left Fuller's. Stop'd at the Post-Office five miles from his house, and left the Letter for my wife to be taken by the Mail from Boston to Washington. At a quarter past eight we came to Pride's at Dedham, where we breakfasted, and at half-past eleven alighted at my paternal Mansion in Quincy; which if it please God, is to be my home for the short remnant of my days — My brother and his family had left in April — It was now uninhabited, and with scarcely any furniture in it. I determined however to take up my abode in it from this day. ≈ My situation here now strongly reminds me of that in which my father first came into the same House in June 1788 — I enter it with a feeling of deep solemnity at the responsibilities devolving upon me and at the prospects before me.

———

[July 1829]
11. IV. Saturday. — My birth day. 62. I enter this day upon my grand climacteric, with a consciousness that the actions of my life, have not in gratitude to God, or in services to my fellow creatures been such as they ought to have been. I have no right to hope or expect so well of the future than I can think of the past. My life for the public is closed and it only remains for me to use my endeavours to make the remainder of it useful to my family and my neighbours if possible. To this I am directing my purposes, for which I find a great deficiency of energy. I pray that it may be supplied me from abroad.

———

[August 1829]
4. IV:15. Tuesday. There was a copious Thunder Shower this morning, and a light rain continued through great part of the

day — Charles went to Boston and returned this Evening, and I was without interruption of Visitors. I commenced my daily occupation in the Library, and wrote there till dinner time ≈ I removed to the Library a part of my father's papers, and propose commencing to-morrow, the arrangement of them. The work that I undertake must be pursued with steadiness and perseverance, and in its progress will require the exercise of other qualities — Prudence, Moderation, Justice, and an entire controul over my own feelings — Nor can it succeed without indefatigable Industry — These qualities, with continued health can be dispensed only from above, and all will be of little avail, unless my mind can be tempered to its subject; its vision cleared of obscurity — its weakness fortified with power, that the object of my affection and reverence may be known to future ages as he was; and that the narrative of his life, like his life itself may contribute to the welfare and improvement of mankind.

5. IV:15. Wednesday. ≈ I began upon the collection of minutes and memoranda preparatory to the biographical Memoir of my father. I propose to devote henceforth three hours a day to that portion of my business — My brother reminded me that it is this day twenty years since I embarked at Charlestown, for Russia — I embark this day upon a more perilous, perhaps a more difficult expedition.

6. IV:15. Thursday. Proposing to write one page every day of the preparatory matter of my intended work, I began by collecting some of the Books which I possess relating to the first Settlement of New-England. Looking successively into them, matters of curiosity presented themselves, which absorbed the morning so that I was barely able to write my second page before dinner — The Volume, which I accidentally purchased at Berlin, contains three pamphlets, each somewhat rare, and all, relating to this subject — Thomas Morton's Book, purports to be printed at Amsterdam in 1637. It is in three Books — The first giving some account of the Indian natives — The second a description of the Country, and the third is a disguised and mystified narrative of his own adventures with the Colonists. But it is told in a conceited and figurative Style, with intersper-

sion of poetry, or rather of rhymes and Satirical fictitious names applied to the principal persons of the Plymouth and Massachusetts Colonies — This Book is to be further examined, and compared with the other cotemporary publications, and with Winthrop's Journal. I also looked into Mather's Magnalia, and read his Lives of the three Thomas Shepherds, the first of whom married the daughter of William Tinge, and was my ancestor — Their daughter having married Daniel Quincy, the father of John Quincy my great grandfather; whose name I bear — Mather mentions several publications of the first and second Thomas Shepherd, probably not recoverable — He gives also an abstract of Instructions given by the second Thomas Shepherd to the third, upon his entering College, and says that he had received similar instructions from his father — They have much of the religious enthusiasm of the age; but are otherwise admirable — The quotation of Proverbs 14:23 is particularly impressive, and should be printed on the Memory of every man throughout life — After dinner, and the nap I read a few Letters of Madame du Deffand, and part of a book lately sent me by Mr. G. W. Erving upon the antiquity and perfection of the Basque Language — I worked towards Sunset an hour with the Spade — Charles brought me out Letters from my wife, my Son John, and Dr. Waterhouse.

———

[September 1829]

3. IV:45. Thursday. ≈ Charles took leave of the paternal mansion this Morning and went into Boston — At ½ past four this afternoon, I rode with T. B. Adams jun'r to Boston — stopp'd at Cary the Stone-Cutters, who not being at his work-yard, I left with his partner Dickinson, the Monumental inscription — Left a Note from Louisa Foster to her Sister Mary, at her father's house; and called to leave a parcel for Charles at his House; we then went over Craigie's Bridge to Mr. Peter C. Brooks's at Medford, where my Son Charles was married by the Rev'd Caleb Stetson, the Minister of the Parish, to Abigail Brown Brooks, youngest daughter of Peter Chardon Brooks, and of Anne, daughter of Nathanial Gorham of Charlestown. They were married according to the Congregational form of worship ≈ After the Ceremony there was a joyous supper — Charles and his bride went into Boston, to their own House,

and the rest of the company went to their several homes; excepting Lieutenant T. B. Adams and myself, who by invitation of Mr. and Mrs. Brooks remained to pass the Night at Medford — Mrs. Brooks is in declining health, and only by great exertion was able to attend the festive solemnity — May the blessing of God rest upon this marriage and upon the parties to it.

———

24. V. Thursday. There was a training day for a Regiment of Militia, upon the fields behind my House, at the foot of Penn's Hill; but I had no inclination to behold it. I worked with the Spade upwards of an hour before dinner, wrote to my Son John, and towards Evening took an hour's walk. ≈ In the Evening I read several of Madame du Deffand's Letters. It belongs probably to the effect of age upon the taste and judgment that these Letters are more interesting to me than any novel — They are records of realities. In youth it was directly the reverse — Fairy Tales; the Arabian Nights, fictitious Adventures of every kind delighted me — And the more there was in them of invention; the more pleasing they were. My imagination pictured them all as realities, and I dreamed of enchantments as if there was a world in which they existed — At ten years of age I read Shakspears Tempest, As you like it, Merry wives of Windsor, Much Ado about Nothing, and King Lear — The humours of Falstaff scarcely affected me at all. Bardolph and Pistol and Nym were personages quite unintelligible to me; and the lesson of Sir Hugh Evans to the boy William was too serious an affair. But the incantations of Prospero, the Loves of Ferdinand and Miranda, the more than etherial sprightly loveliness of Ariel, and the worse than beastly grossness of Caliban, made for me a world of Revels and lap'd me in Elysium. With these books in a closet of my mother's bed chamber there was also a small Edition in two Volumes of Milton's Paradise Lost, which I believe I attempted ten times to read and never could get through half a book. I might as well have attempted to read Homer before I had learnt the Greek Alphabet — I was mortified even to the shedding of solitary tears, that I could not even conceive what it was that my father and mother admired so much in that book, and yet I was ashamed to ask them an explanation. I smoked tobacco and read Milton, at the same time and from the same motive,

to find out what was the recondite charm in them which gave my father so much pleasure — After making myself four or five times sick with smoking I mastered that accomplishment, and acquired a habit, which thirty years afterwards, I had much more difficulty in breaking off — But I did not master Milton. I was nearly thirty when I first read the Paradise Lost with delight and astonishment — But of late years I have lost the relish for fiction — I see nothing with sympathy but men, women and children of flesh and blood — Madame du Deffand's Suppers, afford me savoury food, and I was charmed this Evening with her picture of the Lucan family sending a Piano to her apartments — the father making his daughters play and sing an hour or two — Lady Stormont joining in the concert — The Piano and children being then sent home and leaving a party to sup. The visit of Dr. Franklin and Silas Deane, with Mr. Le Roy, is also very amusing; and her remark that all the company, were in favour of the Americans, excepting herself and Mr. de Guignes who were for the Court, is more interesting to me than ten Volumes of Waverly's. Can Philosophy tell me why this is so?

———

[December 1829]

30. IV. Wednesday. Morning visit from Dr. Sewall, who as usual spoke to me about judge Cony and his visit to me last Summer. I returned several visits; leaving Cards. Met Count Menou the Chargé d'Affaires from France at the door of Baron Stackelberg the Charge d'Affaires from Sweden — A new Minister by the name of Roux de Rochelle, is coming out from France — The only person whom I found at home was Mrs. Rush; and while I was there General Mason came in — They have just received Letters from Mr. Rush, at London of 24 Nov'r announcing his success in obtaining a loan of one Million of Dollars for the Chesapeake and Ohio Canal Company, at Amsterdam. He had failed to obtain it in England — And he writes to Mrs. Rush that he proposes to embark on his return to this Country the 16th of this Month — General Mason mentioned Letters received from his Son John, who has been Secretary of Legation to Mr. Poinsett in Mexico — The Mexican Government finally demanded the recall of Poinsett which was immediately granted, and Col'l Antony Butler was sent as

Chargé d'Affaires to take his place. Mrs. Rush spoke about the paragraph in the President's Message against the Bank, and about Mrs. Eaton, wife of the Secretary of War, now the centre of much political intrigue and controversy — Mrs. Eaton is the daughter of a man named O'Neal who some years since kept a Tavern and failed so that his house was sold to pay his debts. Mrs. Eaton was wife to a purser in the Navy named Timberlake, who being on service in the Mediterranean Squadron, his wife lived at her father's, where Mr. Eaton and General Jackson when a Senator were lodgers. When O'Neal's house was sold it was purchased by Mr. Eaton — About a year and a half since Timberlake died, and very shortly after Eaton married his widow — Her reputation was not in good odour; and last Spring when Eaton was appointed Secretary of War, a grave question arose among the dignitaries high and low of the Administration, whether Mrs. Eaton was to associate with their wives — This question has occasioned a schism in the party some of whom have more and some less of moral scruple, the Vice-President's wife Mrs. Calhoun, being of the virtuous, and having then declared that rather than endure the contamination of Mrs. Eaton's company she would not come to Washington this Winter, and accordingly she remains in the untainted atmosphere of South Carolina. I told Mrs. Rush that this struggle was likely to terminate in a party division of Caps and Hats. Settled my tax-bill with W. W. Billing.

31. V. Thursday. ≈ At the close of the year the only Sentiment that I feel to be proper is of humble gratitude to God, for the blessings with which it has been favoured — Its chastisements have been most afflictive; but I have experienced Mercy with Judgment — The loss of Power and of popular favour I could have endured with fortitude, and relief from the Slavery of Public Office was more than a compensation for all the privations, incident to the loss of place — Its vanities I despised, and its flatteries never gave me a moment of enjoyment. But my beloved Son! Mysterious Heaven! let me bow in submission to thy Will — Let me no longer yield to a desponding or distrustful Spirit — Grant me Fortitude — Patience — Perseverance; and active Energy — And let thy Will be done.

———

[January 1830]

3. IV:30. Sunday. Heard the morning service at the Unitarian Church. Mr. Lincoln preached from Matthew 16:26 — "what shall a man give in exchange for his Soul?" a very sensible discourse, much injured by very defective elocution and some incorrect pronunciation. Mr. Lincoln afterwards administered the communion of which I partook ≈ In the Evening I heard Mr. Campbell at the Presbyterian Church, from Acts 8:1, "And Saul was consenting unto his death." A Lecture upon the character of St. Paul before his conversion — I was not very well; much fatigued; and not duly attentive to the preacher. After returning home, I found myself, utterly unable to read or write, owing to a heaviness and lassitude, which grows upon me with age, and which I attempted in vain to overcome. William Lee came about nine in the Evening, and spent two hours with me — He arrived last Evening from New-York, and told me he saw Mr. Gallatin the evening before last at Baltimore — He says Gallatin spoke to him slightingly of the President and members of the Administration — commented upon the President's obstinacy and ignorance; and said if Jefferson had treated him, as Jackson treats all the members of his Cabinet, he would immediately have resigned his Office.

———

5. III:45. Tuesday. ≈ I paid a visit to Baron Krudener and spent an hour with him, in conversation upon Russia and Turkey. He had over his mantle piece a Portrait of the Emperor Nicholas, which he said was an excellent likeness, and in which he has apparently eleven or twelve years more upon his head than when I last saw him in England. I told him that I expected and hoped great things from him for the benefit of mankind. I hoped he would expel the Turks from Russia, and at least make great advances towards the extinction of the Mahometan imposture — I regretted that he had now stopped short of Constantinople; but as the Emperor had yet the prospect of a long reign before him it would be impossible for him to remain long at Peace with the Turks ≈ While we were at dinner Mr. Gerry came in, and in great agitation told us that the President had yesterday sent to the Senate a nomination of General M'Neill as Surveyor of the Port of Boston in his place — And that when he went to him this day, and reminded him

of his promise; he flew into a passion, denied that he had made him any promise, and ordered him out of his house, for his impertinence in circulating a report that he had. General Hayne the Senator from South-Carolina was present and advised Gerry to take this answer as conclusive. Gerry went to Ingham who at first refused to see him, and when he did receive him sullenly refused to give him any reason, but that Offices were not hereditary. Gerry supported from the emoluments of his Office his mother, and four unmarried sisters. His father was a Signer of the Declaration of Independence and died Vice-President of the United States. His distress was great and affected me deeply.

———

[February 1830]
6. IV:30. Saturday. ≈ All the members of Congress, are full of rumours respecting the volcanic state of the Administration — A busy-body Presbyterian Clergyman of Philadelphia named Ezra Styles Ely, is the principal mischief maker in the affairs of Mr. and Mrs. Eaton. He has been called here for the third time to pacify internal commotions. He was here several days, but went away without accomplishing any thing. The President had determined to remove Branch, the Secretary of the Navy; but H. L. White the Senator from Tennessee, and it is said Edward Livingston went in deputation to the President and informed him that if Mr. Branch should be dismissed, the Senators from North-Carolina would join the opposition, and all the dubious nominations now before the Senate would be rejected. He was also given to understand that Ingham is Secretary of the Treasury and Berrien, the Attorney General would resign. He concluded therefore to retain Mr. Branch, and became a Mediator between him and Eaton to bring them to speaking terms together. Such is their present state — Ingham, Branch, Berrien, Towson have given large Evening parties to which Mrs. Eaton is not invited — On the other hand the President makes her doubly conspicuous by an overdisplay of notice — At the last drawing-room the Night before last she had a crowd gathered round her, and was made the public gaze — But Mrs. Donelson, wife to the President's private Secretary, and who lives at the President's House; held no conversation with her. The Administration party is split up into a blue and a

green faction, upon this point of morals; but the explosion has hitherto been deferred. Calhoun heads the Moral Party — Van Buren that of the frail sisterhood; and he is notoriously engaged in canvassing for the Presidency by paying his Court to Mrs. Eaton — He uses personal influence with the wives of his partizans to prevail upon them to countenance this woman by visiting her — There is a story current here which whether true or false is significant of the general estimate of Van Buren's character. It is that he asked for a private conversation with Mrs. Donelson, and for three quarters of an hour urged her with pathetic eloquence to visit Mrs. Eaton — That she defended as well as she could her own course, but being no match for him at sophisticating, she at last said — Mr. Van Buren, I have always been taught that "Honesty is the best Policy" — Upon which he immediately started up; took his hat and departed — Mrs. Eaton is as much a character as Van Buren — Dr. Sim and his wife are among her enemies — They live next door to her; and in a house leased by her husband. About a fortnight since Mrs. Donelson was visiting Mrs. Sim, and Mrs. Eaton saw the carriage standing before the door — The next day Dr. Sim received notice from Eaton, to quit forthwith the house, though his lease will not expire till next December — The story goes that a day or two afterwards, Mrs. Eaton telling her milliner; a Mrs. Williams, of the notice given to Dr. Sim to quit, said "if it had not been for that d—d old granny, nothing of all this would have happened" — Whether she spoke these or the like words on that occasion or not, is uncertain, but it is her Style of conversation — and there are many speeches of the same kind, reported about the Country; as genuine examples of her ordinary discourse — John's told me that when she went to Philadelphia first, last Summer, she went to the same boarding house where he was lodging. That his landlady asked him if he was acquainted with Mrs. Eaton, to which he answered that he was not, and did not wish to be — The second time she went to Philadelphia, though Mrs. Barry the Postmaster General's wife was with her, the same Landlady declined receiving her.

———

11. IV:30. Thursday. In my walk this morning, I met Chief Justice Marshall, near the head of the avenue, and he turned

and walked down with me to its termination opposite the yard of the Treasury building. I asked him who, since the decease of the late Judge Washington, was the owner of President Washington's papers. He said he did not know but that they were now in the possession of Mr. Sparkes who was to publish his Letters, and some of the Letters to him — I asked the judge if there ever had been an adjudication in England, of the *property* of Epistolary Correspondence — He knew of none. I mentioned the opinion or statement in a later number of the North American Review, that the property is in the writer of the Letter, to whom or to whose Representatives it ought to be returned after the decease of the receiver — He said he had formed no deliberate opinion upon the question, but that his first crude impression was that the property was in the receiver, a property qualified by the confidence of the writer — I mentioned to him the extraordinary character of the recent publication of Mr. Jefferson's papers; which have given rise to a scene as extraordinary in the Senate of the United States — Jefferson makes a minute 13 February 1801 that Edward Livingston told him, Bayard had offered Sam. Smith the Office of Secretary of War, if he would vote for Burr, which W. C. Nicholas had confirmed. Mr. Jefferson's Executor now publishes this minute — Hayne last week to gratify the malignity of his nature, reads from a volume of Jefferson's works, his tale of my having told him that certain federalists in New-England, during the War plotted a dismemberment of the Union during the late War. No answer was made to this: but Clayton a Senator from Delaware, read this minute about Bayard; and called upon Sam Smith and Edward Livingston to say whether it was true. Smith declared in the most explicit manner that neither Bayard nor any other man ever made any such proposal to him. Edward Livingston said he had tasked his memory to the utmost, and had been unable to recollect any thing about it — Benton bristled up, and blustered about attempts to impeach the veracity of Mr. Jefferson. Clayton answered that his object was not to impeach the veracity of Mr. Jefferson, but to vindicate the character of Mr. Bayard, and that he had attained his object — That Mr. Benton had chosen to fall into a furious passion about it, which to him Clayton was a matter of great Indifference — I said the most extraordinary part of this minute of Jefferson's was — that it was the direct reverse of the real fact: as Mr. Bayard had told me what passed at that interview between him and Smith — The Judge said he had also told it to him. He added that he himself had been here, a witness of that Scene — altogether indifferent upon which of the two men the choice of the house would fall, and that by comparing what he then saw, with what afterwards came to pass, there were certain conclusions which it was very difficult to resist — but he did not say what they were. I suppose he meant that Livingston, who was then making his own bargain for his vote; told Jefferson this tale of Bayard's offers to Smith, to make Jefferson out-bid Burr for Livingston's own vote — Livingston was accordingly appointed District Attorney at New-York; and in due time went off with a hundred thousand dollars of the public money, to Louisiana: the judgment for which has never been paid till within the last six Months.

———

15. IV:45. Monday. Mr. Bell, the Senator from New-Hampshire called on me with a subscription paper for a new Edition of Belknap's History with Notes, by Mr. Farmer, of Concord, to which I readily put down my name — Mr. Bell spoke of the nominations to Offices now before the Senate, and said that in the whole forty years since the Government of the United States has existed it would be impossible to collect a number of infamous and degraded characters in the list of Officers of the United States, equal to that in the list of nominations now before the Senate. He had hoped that the whole tribe of Editors of Newspapers would be rejected; for he thought it the most dangerous precedent that could be established; and if now sanctioned by the Senate, he despaired of its ever being controuled hereafter — Possibly Isaac Hill might be rejected; he feared no other of the Printers would be. Henry Lee he believed would be rejected. The evidence of his infamy, in transactions of private Life was accessible, and would if necessary be produced. But I very strongly doubt whether any one of the nominations will be rejected. He said that with regard to the arbitrary removals from Office; there was not an entire agreement between the opponents of the present Administration themselves as to the Constitutional principle — He inclined to the opinion that the concurrence of the Senate to the

removal may be inferred as necessary, because it is necessary for an appointment. But some were of opinion that the president had only the power of suspending an Officer, and if the person whom he nominated as Successor should be rejected by the Senate, then the previous incumbent still continued in Office — I said that the Discretionary power of the President to remove was settled by Law, and by the uniform practice of forty years. I thought it correctly settled; but if the discretion was palpably abused, I thought it impeachable misdemeanor — In questioning however this abuse of power, I thought it would be unsafe and certainly unsuccessful to advance any new principle. He said there would be a call this day, for the detected correspondence between Timberlake and Eaton, as bearing upon the nomination of Amos Kendall. I told him I thought it doubtful whether the really significant Letters would be sent if called for. Mr. Bell told me that he was almost discouraged as to the permanency of our Institutions; witnessing as he does the profligacy with which the Government is administered; and the tendency of all corruption, from bad to worse — My own hopes are better — I have seen this Country once go through a political convulsion, nearly as profligate as the present, and recover from it to pure and quiet elections — I hope that it may do so again. Every present symptom indeed is gloomy and discouraging — every thing looks to decay and not to improvement. Every thing has an aspect of pulling down, and not of building up.

———

19. IV:15. Friday — Sun rose 6:36. The days are rapidly lengthening, and I have now to go out before half past five to return from my walk before Sun rise. I saw its first beam this morning from the Eastern window. Mr. Foot and Mr. Clayton, Senators from Connecticut and Delaware, paid me a morning visit followed by Mr. White Delegate from Florida, and the newly appointed Marshal of that Territory — The debate in the Senate upon Foot's Resolution concerning the Public Lands, continues, and has elicited a number of able and animated Speeches. Benton and Hayne, by a joint and concerted attack upon the Eastern portion of the Union, proposed to break down the Union of the Eastern and Western Sections, and of restoring the old joint operation of the West and the South

against New-England. Benton's object is personal advancement, and plunder — Hayne's personal advancement by the
triumph of South-Carolina over the Tariff and Internal Improvement, and Calhoun's succession to the Presidency. The
assault was so vehement and rancorous, and desperate, that it
roused the Spirit of the East, and Webster, and Sprague have
made eloquent Speeches in its defence — Holmes finished a
powerful Speech this day. Barton has replied to the personalities of Benton, by personalities, cutting because founded in
truth — There is another question now in sharp discussion
upon the nominations before the Senate in the place of persons removed. — Mr. Clayton asked my opinion upon the
construction of the words in the Constitution authorizing the
President to fill vacancies happening during the recess of the
Senate — I gave him my opinion, and also mentioned my experience of the practice under the Government, almost coeval
with its existence. Mr. Clayton seemed to think that the President could not remove an Officer without the concurrence of
the Senate ≈ Mr. Mercer after dinner spoke with great severity
and indignation of Mr. Jefferson and of the recent publication
of his works. He said he had no opinion of Mr. Jefferson's
principles since he saw a copy of the Correspondence between
him and Col'l Walker, certified as authentic by Chief Justice
Marshall, and another person — I asked him if Jefferson Randolph had published *that* Correspondence, as part of his
Grandfather's works. He laughed and said no.

———

23. V:15. Tuesday — Shrove Tuesday. There was frost again last
night and this morning; but the river is open, and the winter is
essentially broken up. I had no morning visitors, but in the
Evening Miss James and Miss Danforth came to solicit a contribution for the infant School; and brought me a Letter of
Solicitation from the Revd. Joshua N. Danforth — They said
they had collected nearly contributions enough for the erection of their buildings; and when that should be completed
they hoped they should not need to beg any longer — A man
by the name of Stewart brought me a Razor Strap superior as
he said to all others, which he left with me to try — My reading and writing tries me by peine forte et dure — In the Bible
I am upon the prophet Isaiah — Sublime beyond all written

composition, in some particular passages — obscure, unintelligible almost throughout. A collection of rhapsodies, without apparent connection with one another — wild and wonderful — and of which it seems the more I read, the less I understand — The National Intelligencer had this day half a recent speech of Mr. Webster, which has been much celebrated, in reply to a violent invective against him of R. Y. Hayne — It fills almost two sides of the paper, and the other half is to come on Thursday. It is defensive of himself, and of New-England, but carries the war effectively into the enemy's Territory — It is a remarkable instance of readiness in debate — a reply of at least four hours to a Speech, of equal length — It demolishes the whole fabrick of Hayne's speech so that it leaves scarcely the wreck to be seen — There was also in the National Journal a third part of a speech of Barton, Senator from Missouri in the same debate; as severe upon Benton his Colleague as Webster's upon Hayne. This debate is a symptom of the Times. Personalities, malignities and hatreds seem to take the place of all enlarged discussions of public concerns.

———

[March 1830]
27. V. Saturday. ≈ Mr. Bell the Senator from New Hampshire passed two hours with me. He was enquiring who had been the former Comptrollers of the Treasury — He entertains a feeble hope that some of the most profligate publishers of scurrilous newspapers now in nomination before the Senate for offices will be rejected: but he will be disappointed ≈ The movements upon these nominations pending in the Senate, are intimately connected with a controversy between the Telegraph, Calhoun's newspaper here, and the New-York Courier, Van Buren's paper, upon the question whether Jackson is or is not a Candidate for re-election as President. The Courier insisting that he is; and the Telegraph declaring it premature to ask the question. Mr. Van Buren has got the Start of Calhoun in the merit of convincing General Jackson that the Salvation of the Country depends upon his re-election. This establishes the ascendency of Van Buren in the Cabinet, and reduces Calhoun to the alternative of joining in the shout of hurra for Jackson's re-election; or of being counted in opposition. Tun' contra Caesaris nutum?

———

[April 1830]

3. V. Saturday. Morning visit from Dr. Croghan, from Kentucky, a brother of Mrs. Jessup who is our Neighbour. ≈ Mrs. Dickenson, and Mrs. B. O. Tayloe paid visits to the Ladies. — My leisure is again oppressive, and I am not well advised how to employ it.

4. V. Sunday. Heard Mr. Campbell, this morning from Matthew 13:17 "If ye know these things, happy are ye if ye do them," and in the Evening from Matthew 13:3–8 "And he spake many things unto them in parables, saying, Behold, a sower went forth to sow &c" — the parable of the Sower — The doctrine drawn from this parable by Mr. Campbell, was rather harsh. It is the general character of Presbyterian preaching to terrify rather than to allure — This does not altogether suit my temper. Believing in the goodness and Mercy of the Creator, I disbelieve those who represent him as existing only to hurl thunder — Nothing but Thunder. Nor do I think the moral character improved by tempering the mind to action under the perpetual terror of the scourge — incredulus Odi — The system is much easier for a preacher than that of operating either by argument or persuasion, and its tendency is to stiffen the influence of the preacher into Authority. The Negro Slave dreads the Overseer who holds the whip, more than the Master in whose name it is brandished. I listen with pleasure to expositions of the goodness and mercy of God, and delight in the 136th Psalm. Exhortations to righteousness and truth, brotherly kindness and charity, have more prevailment over me, than unceasing denunciations of vengeance and punishment — There are however denominations of Christians who hold different opinions, and insist upon being doomed weekly, by their Pastors to the infernal Regions, and such are perhaps the Major part of Mr. Campbell's Auditors.

———

6. V. Tuesday. ≈ Mr. Bell and Mr. Burnet, Senators from New-Hampshire and Ohio paid me a morning visit — They said Mr. White, Senator from Tennessee, was making a Speech in support of a Bill, which he has reported from a Committee, for exporting the Southern Indians to the Territory West of Arkansas. Mr. White, they said, usually made his speeches three times over. He had been speaking about three quarters of an

hour, and was about commencing his first repetition, when they thought they might indulge themselves with a walk, and return without losing any thing. These gentlemen think that the Editorial nominations now before the Senate, that is the writers and publishers of scurrilous newspapers electioneering Skunks, of whom there are about fifty appointed to Office, and perhaps twenty of them now in nomination before the Senate, will be rejected. But they will all or nearly all pass — one or two may fail. General Jackson rules by his personal popularity, which his partizans in the Senate dare not encounter, by opposing any thing that he does, and while that popularity shall last, his majorities in both houses of Congress will stand by him for good or evil. It has totally broken down in the Senate, both the Esprit de Corps, and the combination against the Executive, which from the last Session of Mr. Jefferson's Administration, had presided in many of their deliberations, and governed many of their decisions. And indeed it produced so many pernicious consequences, that I sincerely believe the subserviency of these days less mischievous — In the moral Government of the world one vice is oftener punished by another, than either is reformed by virtue — A servile Senate is contemptible — A factious one is more dangerous.

———

15. V. Thursday. As I was walking out, I met Mr. Sparks who was coming to see me; and walked with him round the Capitol Hill — He said he had just returned from a visit to Pittsburg, where he had been to inspect the spot of Braddock's defeat in 1755 which he had done much to his satisfaction. There was no person left there, who had any recollection of the Event, but there were many traditions, from which he had collected valuable information. I asked him when he expected to publish his Correspondence of Washington. He thought there would be a Volume out before the end of this year — I asked him how many volumes he supposed would complete the work — he said ten or twelve. I observed that the English Quarterly Review advised him to retrench the publication, and give but little — advice quite natural for Englishmen, who the less they heard about Washington, and the American Revolution the better pleased they were.

———

[May 1830]

13. V:45. Thursday. I was unable this morning to put on my own Clothes, but was indebted for it to the assistance of my wife — I can moralize upon this event as well as younger and more disinterested philosophers — It is one admonition more to set my house in order. May they not all be lost. Mr. Poinsett our late Minister to Mexico, called to visit me. He has been at Philadelphia and Baltimore where they have given him public dinners; where Speeches were made and toasts given. He told me he was going immediately home to South-Carolina; even at this Season of the year; to see if he could by good advice calm the excitement which he does not share — He spoke of a toast recently given by the Governor of the State — The right to fight — and said it was unfortunate that the most violent man they had was to be their next Governor — James Hamilton. South-Carolina has been potioned and philtered and back scourged, like an old lecher into a frenzy of excitement, and has now a prospect of coming into physical collision with the Government of the Union — As the Government is now administered, there is every prospect that her bullies will succeed, to the sacrifice of the interest of all the rest of the Union; as the bullies of Georgia have succeeded in the project of extirpating the Indians, by the sacrifice of the public faith of the Union and of all our Treaties with them ≈ The day was passed not in absolute idleness; but in reading occasionally interrupted by sharp pangs, and by writing without satisfaction — I read an Article in the American Quarterly Review of September last, upon Shakespear, and some pages of Beloe's Herodotus.

14. IV:45. Friday. — Sun rose 4:54. The occasional severe pains of the last two days subsided, leaving some soreness, and incapacity of bodily labour — I renewed, but abridged my Morning walk, and rode with my Son John to the Mills after dinner. I found them at work, grinding wheat at the large Mill and Indian Corn at the small one. The demand for Corn meal, and for what they call Rye-chop continues, and the prospect of profitable business for the year remains fair — The experience of the last years, forbids sanguine hope; but my anxieties for the future condition of my family have no other reliance upon Earth — Mr. Jefferson died at 84 amidst the most abject

supplications for eleemosinary contributions for bread to his children — Mr. Monroe's groans of famishing distress are incessant, and ring throughout this continent — My father screened the poverty of his last years by a severity of domestic frugality, which neither Jefferson, nor Monroe, nor I had energy of mind to practice. My experience of the last 15 Months leaves me nothing to expect but a rapid consumption of what property I have, to defray the cost of my own sustenance, and that of my children — If the industrious and prudent employment of these Mills, will give me no relief, the close of my animal life, will to all appearance be as needy, and as comfortless as that of Mr. Jefferson — Yet will I not despair — Mr. Fendall called and asked me again for that manuscript dissertation upon parties which I had written and which yet remains unfinished. I told him I would look for it. There is doubt in my mind whether Fendall will ever write the History of the late Administration which was advertised — I am yet upon the Orations of Cicero against Verves, and the more thoroughly I know this admirable Orator, the higher my estimate of him rises. The practice which I have now adopted of allowing one hour every day to classical reading has been to me a source of so much enjoyment that I hope to persevere in it as long as life and health will permit — One year will just carry me completely through Cicero — The collection of the Regent's Classics will occupy about four, if Providence has destined to me so long a date — and if my own heart and mind can derive little or no improvement from this tardy study, perhaps it may enable me to give useful hints to my Sons.

———

22. IV:45. Saturday. ≈ I rode with John after dinner to the Mills — two wheels again grinding corn — The week not so brisk as several that preceded. After returning home, I called and spent an hour of the Evening with Mr. Rush — Mrs. Rush and part of the family were gone to the theatre — Three of their children have had the measles — Two others have them now. This has delayed the removal of the family from the City. He has determined to remove to York, and expects to go in the course of the next Month. He told me some particulars of the late Jefferson birth day dinner lately got up by Benton and Calhoun, to proclaim anti-tariff and nullification doctrine

under the shelter of Jefferson's name. The ostensible purpose was to honour Jefferson's birth-day; by an assemblage of Members of Congress, dining together upon Republican principles — The real object was to trick the Pennsylvania Members into the drinking of anti-tariff and nullification toasts. Eight members of the Pennsylvania delegation; Jefferson Republicans dyed in the Wool, agreed to go — The company were assembled — The President was there by invitation. George R. Leiper one of the Pennsylvania members, told Miller, his colleague one of the toast-making Committee, that he should like to see the toasts before drinking them. Miller brought him the list of toasts, and read them till he came to the 13th when Leiper told him he had enough — he need not read any more — He then collected the whole eight together and told them he should not sit down at the table where those toasts were to be drank; and they all agreed to withdraw together, which they accordingly did. The obnoxious toasts were drank — But President Jackson being called upon for his toast; gave "The Union — it must be preserved." — Aio te, AEacida, Romanos vincere posse — and from that day the two sides of the faction have been each claiming the Presidential toast to itself. The Union must be preserved says South-Carolina, by repealing the Tariff — The Union must be preserved says Pennsylvania, by sustaining the Tariff to the muzzle of the gun — Since the dinner Leiper has published a Letter from Mr. Jefferson to his father, charging opposition to domestic manufactures upon the anglo-federalists. In conversing with Mr. Rush upon the prospects of the Country, we agreed that the Indians are already sacrificed — That the Public Lands will be given away — That domestic Industry and internal Improvement will be strangled — and when the public debt will be paid off and the Bank Charter expired, there will be no great interest left upon which the action of the general Government will operate. The future must be consigned to the sweet little Cherub that sits up aloft.

———

[June 1830]

1. V. Tuesday — From New-Brunswick to New-York — Steam-Boat President ≈ At New-York we came to the Washington Hotel newly fitted up and kept by Hamilton, who

heretofore kept the Exchange Hotel in Boston — We only stopp'd to dine; and found that John Kirke, with the Horses and Carriage was at the City Hotel. At Hamilton's I received several visitors; Oliver Wolcott, a man whose condition somewhat resembles my own — Having survived the age of active life, he has no fixed abode; but resides chiefly with his Children. He is nearly or quite four-score years of age; and until about three years past was Governor of Connecticut — They then quietly dropp'd him and elected Gideon Tomlinson in his place — Mr. Wolcott appears to retain possession of his faculties, and was much disposed to conversation upon the prevailing politics of the time. But we were very soon interrupted, against my inclination, for I should have been glad to listen long to Mr. Wolcott: He views the prospects of the Union, with great sagacity and with hopes more sanguine than mine. He thinks the continuance of the Union will depend upon the heavy population of Pennsylvania; and that its gravitation will preserve the Union — He holds the South-Carolina turbulence, rather too much in contempt — The domineering Spirit, naturally springs from the institution of Slavery; and when as in South-Carolina, the Slaves are more numerous than their masters; the domineering Spirit, is wrought up to its highest pitch of intenseness. The South-Carolinians are attempting to govern the Union as they govern their Slaves, and there are too many indications that abetted as they are by all the Slave-driving interest of the Union, the free portion of the population will cower before them, and truckle to their insolence. This is my apprehension. Mr. Wolcott considers their bullying only according to its own character, and supposes it will be harmless because it is impotent.

—

6. V. Sunday. ≈ General Dearborn and Mr. De Grand took tea here. Dearborn, who was removed from the Office of Collector at Boston, is now a member of the Senate from the County of Norfolk in the State Legislature. They are now in Session, but will adjourn to-morrow or the next day — The first Session of the 21st Congress was closed last Monday. Of the four Bills of internal improvement, which passed both houses of Congress on Saturday the President approved only one; and with that he sent a Message announcing that he signed it with

the Understanding that it should receive a particular Construction. As it was an Appropriation for a road, the construction of the Law, will depend entirely upon himself, but this explanatory Message, qualifying the signature of the President to an Act of Congress, is unexampled in this Country, and contrary to the Spirit of the Constitution — a Usurpation of the judiciary power, and susceptible of great abuse as a precedent — The Appropriation for the Road from Washington to Frederick he returned to the Senate with his objections, and the subsequent vote upon it there was 22 for and 16 against it. His negative thus controuls decided majorities in both houses of Congress — He defeated the appropriation for the continuation of the Cumberland Road, and the Bill authorizing the erection of several new Light-house, and directing many new surveys, in a different manner. When the joint Committee of the two Houses went to inform him that they were ready to adjourn, and to enquire if he had any further communication to make to them; he said he had nothing further, except that he retained those two Bills for further consideration. The provision of the Constitution is that a Bill presented to him shall become a Law, without his signature, if not returned by him within ten days, Sundays excepted; unless the Congress by their adjournment *prevent* its return. His remark to the Committee doubtless was to give warning that Congress by their adjournment would prevent his returning those Bills — These are remarkable Events as bringing into operation Constitutional principles — The Presidential veto has hitherto been exercised with great reserve. Not more than four or five Acts of Congress have been thus arrested by six Presidents and in forty years — He has rejected four in three days. The overseer ascendancy is complete.

———

25. IV:15. Friday. Mr. Bailey was here with Mr. Martin, who is the Postmaster at Milton; but who came as Chairman of a Committee of Arrangements from a Company of Citizens of Quincy and Milton, who propose on Monday the 5ᵗʰ of July to celebrate the Anniversary of Independence at the new Railway Church. ≈ I apprehended the state of my health would not admit of my attendance. I observed that I would send him a written answer if it was desired; but that I wished to avoid all public meetings — He said my verbal answer

would be sufficient — Abigail S. Adams came with Mr. and
Mrs. Davis, and Mrs. Derby and Mrs. Minot came together
— Davis said that Mr. Webster had yesterday received a Letter
from Mr. Clay, who approved of the omission to nominate
him at the close of the recent Session of Congress, and who
represented the state of public opinion in the West as entirely
satisfactory. I thought the state of public opinion would be
collected from the result of the elections which will commence the next Month in Louisiana, and then follow successively in the other Western States till the Winter — Nothing is
more delusive than anticipations of the event of elections, and
expectations of great changes in popular suffrages are almost
always disappointed — I suppose that the sacrifice of the Indians, and of the interest of internal improvement and domestic
Industry, will strengthen rather than weaken the popularity of
the present Administration. I have cherished the principle and
the system of internal improvement under a conviction that it
was for this Nation the only path to increasing comforts and
well being, to honour, to glory, and finally to the general improvement of the condition of mankind — This system has
had its fluctuations from the time of the Establishment of the
present Constitution of the United States — During the Administration of Mr. Monroe, it was constantly acquiring
strength in Congress and in the public opinion — It was then
favoured by Calhoun and Lowndes, both of whom had hopes
of rising upon it, and with them the State of South-Carolina
was devoted to it — The combination in Congress, became
by their means so strong, that it overpowered the resistance of
Mr. Monroe, and produced the Act of Congress of April 1824
— The Slave-holders of the South have since discovered that
it will operate against their interests — Calhoun has turned
his back upon it; and Jackson, who to promote his election
and obtain Western votes truckled to it for a time, has now
taken his decided stand against it — My devotion to it has
sharpened all the fangs of envy and malice against it, and
multitudes oppose it, only because its success would contribute to my reputation. The cause will no doubt survive me;
and if the union is destined to continue, will no doubt ultimately triumph — At present it is desperate.

—

[August 1830]

14. III:30. Saturday. ≈ It is, says Cicero, 1st Tusculan, Section 14 — "It is a tacit judgment of Nature herself, and the greatest argument in favour of the immortality of Souls, that all men take a deep interest in that which will happen after death" — He plants trees says Statius in his Synephebi, for the benefit of another century: for what purpose, if the next century were something to him? The diligent husbandman then shall plant trees, upon which his own eyes shall never see a berry? and shall not a great man plant laws, institutions, a Commonwealth? — I have had my share in planting Laws and Institutions, according to the measure of my ability and opportunities — I would willingly have had more — My leisure is now imposed upon me by the will of higher powers, to which I cheerfully submit, and I plant trees for the benefit of the next age, and of which my own eyes will never behold a berry. To raise forest trees requires the concurrence of two Generations, and even of my lately planted Nuts seeds and Stones, I may never taste the fruit — Sero arbores quae alteri seculo prosint — Bright Northern Light this Evening.

[September 1830]

18. V:30. Saturday. ≈ I was called into the house to Mr. John B. Davis, who came to make inquiries concerning the character of Mr. Connell. Mr. Davis has an interest in a claim upon the French Government, of those which Connell is endeavouring to obtain from the claimants an authority to the Government of the United States to settle by compromise. I told Mr. Davis that with regard to the expediency of giving the authority for the Settlement, I had nothing to say; but I could give unqualified testimony to the character of Mr. Connell, both for capacity and integrity — While Davis was here, Mr. Richardson came; and Davis said he had seen in the newspaper that he declined a re-election to the next Congress. He said it was a determination long since taken by him. That he thought it due to the people of his Congregation at Hingham; who had been exceedingly reluctant at his going even to the present Congress; and he said he came purposely to inquire of me, if I would serve, if elected as member for the District. I said I had observed in a paper, the Editor of which, without any cause known to me, had invariably

been hostile to me, a nomination to that effect, about ten days since — From whom the nomination came I knew not; but had believed it made, in no friendly Spirit towards me. I had not supposed it serious; or that any person had a thought of holding me up for that election — Mr. Richardson said that if I would serve he believed the election could be carried; by a large majority — as the Old Colony Memorial and the Hingham Gazette, the only Newspapers printed in the District, and another paper published in the adjoining District, and taken by some of his constituents, would support the nomination — but if I should decline, it was not probable that the District would unite upon any other person, and there would be no election. He then said he thought that the service in the House of Representatives of an Ex-President of the United States, instead of degrading the individual, would elevate the Representative Character — I said I had in that respect no scruple whatever — No person could be degraded by serving the people as a Representative in Congress — Nor in my opinion would an Ex-President of the United States be degraded by serving as a Selectman of his town, if elected thereto by the People — But age and infirmity had their privileges and their disqualifications. I had not the slightest desire to be elected to Congress — and could not consent to be a candidate for Election — I knew not how the Election would turn; and if chosen it might depend upon Circumstances whether I should deem it my duty to serve or to decline — The state of my health — the degree of opposition to the choice, the character of the candidate in opposition might each or all contribute to my determination. Mr. Richardson said this was sufficient and he would go to work. He desired Mr. Davis to consider as secret and confidential what had passed here, which he promised. After dinner I rode with Mrs. Adams to the Milliner's at Weymouth. Saw there Matthew Pratt, an old man who formerly lived several years on my father's place at the foot of Penn's Hill — Gathered a few Acorns from a White Oak Tree on the summit of Penn's Hill — which I propose to plant, and call Cap white Oak. Evening so cold that I could not write.

———

22. III:45. Wednesday. ≈ Deacon Spear came and informed me that he had seen Mr. Humphreys, who if the weather should be

fair will come to resurvey the Penn's Valley farm next Monday. The Deacon spoke of the Election for the House of Representatives to come on the first Monday in November; and asked me if I considered myself an Inhabitant of Quincy. I said certainly — If not an inhabitant of Quincy, I was an inhabitant no where. He said that was all he wished to know: but he nevertheless did give some further hints, that there were persons very desirous of electing me to Congress; and others equally anxious to prevent it. He said the Jackson men would do every thing to defeat the choice, and that they included all the most violent men of both the parties; federal and democratic — He said there would be a District Convention soon to fix upon the person to be chosen — That he had formerly attended these Meetings; but it was rather hard for Quincy to have to send so far — I asked how it happened that Quincy had been cast into the Plymouth District for Elections to Congress. He said he attributed it to Mr. Thomas Greenleaf who was in the Council when the thing was done; and the object of it was to make Plymouth a certainly federal district but now, what with antimasonics and Jackson men, parties were all broken up, and no one could tell what any man was.

———

[November 1830]
6. IV. Saturday. At the mount Wollaston farm, I planted with Chesnuts, Shagbarks and Acorns, the fourth side of the border round my projected Orchard, in five rows; which occupied Salmon Farrar, Alpheus Spear, his Son Charles Adams Spear, and me, great part of the morning. ≈ I came home to dinner, and returned to lay out the ground for the Orchard ≈ The Newspaper of this Evening brought the last returns of the Congressional Election for the District of Plymouth. Twenty-two Towns gave 2565 votes, of which 1817 were for John Quincy Adams, 373 for Arad Thompson (Jacksonite), 279 for William Baylies (federal,) and 96 scattering votes — The authentic returns will perhaps make some slight difference in the number of votes, but can make none in the result — I am a member elect of the twenty-second Congress.

7. V:30. Sunday. My Son Charles came out from Boston, dined with us, and returned this Evening. I heard Mr. Whitney in the

forenoon from John 3:20 "For every one that doeth evil hateth the light, neither cometh to the light, lest his deeds should be reproved" — and in the afternoon from 1 Timothy 1:17 "Now unto the king, eternal, immortal, invisible, the only wise God, be honour and glory for ever and ever, amen." These were both old Sermons — Spent the Evening in writing; and reflecting upon this new incident which has drifted me back again amidst the Breakers of the Political Ocean — It is also a novelty in the history of the Country; and as a precedent may have no unimportant bearing upon future Events — By the Constitution of the United States, the President is re-eligible as long as he lives — Washington, Jefferson and Madison, voluntarily retired after one re-election — and Jefferson no doubt intended to make the example a practical exposition of Constitutional principle — It was followed by Mr. Monroe; perhaps with not much cordiality; and will be continued as long as a Presidential Term of eight years shall wear out the popularity of the person holding the Office. One of the consequences of this has been and will be that Ex President's will survive many years the termination of their Offices — That as individuals they will take a part in public affairs, and that they will sometimes solicit, and sometimes be elected to subordinate Offices — All the preceding President's have held Offices of a public nature, after the expiration of their Presidential Service — None however as a member of either house of Congress; and there are many who think it now a derogatory descent — This is a mere prejudice; and had I alledged my former Station as a Reason for rejecting the suffrages of the People, assigning me a Seat in the House of Representatives, I should not merely have been chargeable with Arrogance, but should have exposed myself to ridicule. So far as concerns myself I consider this new Call to the public Service as a misfortune; inasmuch as it takes from me the last hope of an old age of quiet and leisure. I am still to be buffeted with political rancour and personal malignity; with more than equal chances of losing the favour even of those who now think they honour themselves by their suffrages more than me. My return to public life in a subordinate Station is disagreeable to my family and disapproved by some of my friends; though no one of them has expressed that disapprobation to me — For the discharge of the duties of this particular Station I never was eminently qualified; possessing no talent for extemporaneous public speaking; and at this time being in the decline of my faculties both of mind and body. This event therefore gives me deep concern and anxious forebodings. Yet can I not withhold my grateful acknowledgment to the disposer of human Events, and to the People of my native region for this unexpected testimonial of their continued confidence, after all the combinations of personal rivals, and political competitors to shake it. — "The heart knoweth its own bitterness; and a Stranger, intermeddleth not with its joys" — No one knows, and few conceive the agony of mind that I have suffered from the time that I was made by circumstances, and not by my volition a candidate for the Presidency till I was dismissed from that Station by the failure of my Re-election. They were feelings to be suppressed, and they were suppressed — no human being has ever heard me complain — Domestic Calamity far heavier than any political disappointment or disaster can possibly be, overtook me immediately after my fall from power, and the moment of my distress was seized, by an old antagonist, to indulge a hatred overflowing with the concentrated rancour of forty years; and who could not resist the pleasure of giving me what he thought the finishing blow, at the moment when he saw me down — It seemed as if I was deserted by all mankind, and precisely at that time the American Academy of Arts and Sciences, a Literary and Scientific Institution of my native State which for a Series of years during my prosperity had annually elected me their President when it was impossible for me to attend their Meetings, thought proper to substitute another President in my place — In the French Opera of Richard Coeur de Lion, the minstrel Blondel, sings under the walls of his prison a song beginning

> "Oh! Richard! Oh! mon Roi —
> L'univers t'abandonne."

when I first heard this Song, forty-five years ago, at one of the first Representations of that delightful play, it made an indelible impression upon my memory, without imagining that I should ever feel its force so much closer home — In the year 1829 scarce a day passed that did not bring it to my thoughts

— In the course of last Winter a vacancy occurred in the Board of Overseers of Harvard University — Absent, I was very unexpectedly elected to fill that vacancy. I attributed this to the personal friendship and influence of President Quincy — But this call upon me by the People of the District in which I reside, to represent them in Congress, has been spontaneous; and although counteracted by a double opposition; federalist and Jacksonite, I have received nearly three votes in four, throughout the district. My Election as President of the United States was not half so gratifying to my inmost Soul — No election or appointment conferred upon me ever gave me so much pleasure — I say this to record my Sentiments — but no Stranger intermeddleth with my Joys, and the dearest of my friends have no sympathy with my Sensations.

———

[January 1831]

4. VII. Tuesday. Warm and Sultry Southwest wind. Walk round the Capitol Square; Mrs. Adams called upon Mrs. Frye; but was quite unwell. The Resolutions of the Legislature of Georgia setting at defiance the Supreme Court of the United States, are published and approved in the Telegraph, the Administration Newspaper at this place. By extending the Laws of Georgia over the Country and People of the Cherokees, the Constitution, Laws and Treaties of the United States were quoad hoc set aside. They were chaff before the wind. In pursuance of these Laws of Georgia, a Cherokee Indian is prosecuted for the murder of another Indian before a State Court of Georgia, tried by a Jury of white men and sentenced to death. He applies to the Chief Justice of the Supreme Court of the United States, who issues an injunction to the Governor and Executive Officers of Georgia upon the appeal to the Laws and Treaties of the United States. The Governor of Georgia refuses obedience to this injunction, and the Legislature pass Resolutions that they will not appear to answer before the Supreme Court of the United States — The Constitution, the Laws and Treaties, of the United States are prostrate in the State of Georgia. Is there any remedy for this state of things? — None. Because the Executive of the United States is in league with the State of Georgia. He will not take care that the Laws be faithfully executed. A majority of both Houses of Congress

sustain him in this neglect and violation of his duty — There is no harmony in the Government of the Union. The arm refuses its Office — The whole head is sick, and the whole heart faint. This example of the State of Georgia, will be imitated by other States, and with regard to other National Interests. Perhaps the Tariff — Still more probably the Public Lands. As the Executive and Legislative now fail to sustain the Judiciary, it is not improbable that occasions may arise in which the judiciary will fail in turn to sustain them. The Union is in the most imminent danger of dissolution from the old inherent vice of Confederacies, Anarchy in the Members. To this end, one third of the People is perverted — one third Slumbers — and the rest wring their hands, with unavailing Lamentations, in the foresight of evil which they cannot avert — The Ship is about to founder. A Merciful Providence can save.

———

10. V:30. Monday. Snow all Night — This morning the ground was covered, and it continued to Snow at intervals till noon — In the evening there was rain — I took my usual walk before dinner, and for the rest of the day wrote little and read much — My Diary Index was nearly four months in arrear; besides the old one of nine years. A few days will redeem the last. There is nothing that brings home to me the rapid lapse of time so effectively as the constant accumulation of these arrears — I answered Mr. Monroe's Letter, and made some observations upon the present State of Europe — Perhaps the most important point of view in which we should consider it is the influence which it will exercise over this Country. Its first effect will be, or rather has been to strengthen the principle of democracy over all Europe and America, and it will proportionably diminish the securities of property. In England the Reform in Parliament cannot be effected without intrenching upon very extensive rights of property. The reduction of taxes will necessarily require at least a partial spunging of the National debt. It is scarcely possible to foresee the extent to which this will stagger the rights of property and shatter the confidence of credit. The abolition of tithes must overthrow the established Church, and dissolve the connection between Church and State, and shake the pillars of the Christian Religion. That it will only shake its pillars I hope and believe — If the gates of

Hell shall not prevail against it, neither will the Revolutions of
Empires, nor the Convulsions of the People. In France the
Alliance between political reform and religious infidelity is
closer than in England. It is every where formidable — The fall
of the Church in England will exclude the Bishops from the
House of Peers, and the Hereditary rights of the temporal
peerage will not much longer withstand the consuming blaze
of public opinion. A hereditary crown, has no support in popular sentiment, and none in reason, but as forming part of one
system with an hereditary Peerage. All are equally obnoxious
to democracy — The abolition of Slavery, will pass like a pestilence over all the British Colonies in the West-Indies; it may
prove an Earthquake upon this Continent. The present English Ministry are nearly as much pledged to it, as to the Reform in Parliament — They will flinch from it, and forfeit their
pledge, but they will probably not last long; a more democratic
ministry will succeed, and reform will not, cannot stop short,
till it makes an effective attempt for the abolition of Slavery
— This is perhaps the only part of the doctrine of European
democracy which will find no favour here. It may aggravate
the condition of the Slaves in our Southern States; but the result of the Missouri Question, and the attitude of Parties, has
silenced all the declaimers for the abolition of Slavery in the
Union. This State of things however is not to continue forever.
It is possible that the danger of the abolition doctrine, when
brought home to the Southern States, may teach them the
value of the Union; the only thing that can maintain their
system of Slavery. However this may be, I apprehend that the
inevitable predominance of democracy which is impending
over Europe, will not end without producing bitter fruits in
our own Country.

11. V. Tuesday. Resumed my walk before Breakfast and kept
house the rest of the day — Mr. and Mrs. Tayloe introduced
Mr. Stevenson of Albany. I answered a Letter some time since
received from Gen'l Peter B. Porter, and read the debate in
the British House of Commons upon the Civil List — part of
the third Canto of Childe Harold, and about 50 pages of the
first Volume of Jefferson's Memoirs — He states that he began
his autobiography on the 6th of January 1821 in the 77th year

of his age — He says little of his lineage; tracing his paternal ancestry only to his grandfather, and to a tradition that the family came from the neighbourhood of Snowdon in Wales. His mother was a Randolph, a family claiming to be very illustrious both in England and Scotland — pretensions which he prudently declines to investigate — The account of his childhood and youth is short and not boastful — but there are no confessions. He tells nothing but what redounds to his own credit. He is like the French Lady who told her Sister, she did not know how it happened, mais il n'y a que moi au monde qui a *toujours* raison — Jefferson by his own narrative is always in the right. This is not uncommon to writers of their own Lives — Dr. Franklin was more candid. Mr. Jefferson names the teachers from whom he learnt Greek, Latin and French, and speaks gratefully of William Small — a Scotchman, professor of Mathematics at William and Mary College, who became attached to him, and probably fixed the destinies of his life. It is rather intimated, than expressly told that Small initiated him in the mysteries of free-thinking and irreligion which *did* fix the destinies of his life — Loose morals necessarily followed — If not an absolute atheist, he had no belief in a future existence. All his ideas of obligation or retribution were bounded by the present life. His duties to his neighbour were under no stronger guarantee than the Laws of the Land, and the opinions of the world. The tendency of this condition upon a mind of great compass and powerful resources is to produce insincerity and duplicity which were his besetting sins through life. He says nothing of his adventure with Mrs. Walker, nor of the correspondence to which it gave rise — but it is extant, though it forms no part of this Edition of his works. Small returned to Europe, about the time that Jefferson left the College, in 1762, after introducing him as a student at Law to George Wythe, and to the acquaintance and table of Governor Fauquier, the ablest man who had ever filled that Office. His friendship with Wythe continued through life. In 1769 he was chosen a member of the house of delegates, and so continued until the Revolution — He began by an effort to obtain a permission for the emancipation of Slaves, which failed, and he claims the invention of Committees of Correspondence between the Colonies in 1773. With the Revolution commenced the important Series of his Labours, in Congress and in the Legislature of Virginia — He was foremost among those who pressed forward to the Separation from Great-Britain, and the most active and energetic of those who after that event, laboured to adapt the Legislation of the State, to its new Republican Character — By one Act he converted all Entailments into Fee-simple Estates; by another he abolished the Law of Primogeniture — by a third for the Establishment of Religious Liberty, he cut off the Establishment of the Epis-copal Church, and by a fourth he partially introduced Juries into the Chancery Court, though Pendleton defeated this by an amendment, making the call of a Jury, contingent upon the option of either party to the suit — I propose to continue these notes as I proceed in reading the book.

12. VI. Wednesday. The Sky cleared off in the Night, and this was a day of bright Sunshine, with a North-wester, and grow-ing colder from Morn to Night. I took my walk before break-fast, and passed the remainder of the day without interruption at home. There is no condition of existence which affords me here and in the winter Season so much enjoyment, with an occasional visitor now and then for variety of conversation. My only discontent is with myself for my own misapplication of Time — I wrote this day a Letter to William Hobby at Boston, in answer to two received from him; read a remainder of the third Canto of Childe Harold, and a few pages in the first Volume of Jefferson — I finished the Memoir of his life, which terminates on the 21st of March 1790 when he arrived at New-York to take upon him the Office of Secretary of State. There it ends, and there as a work of much interest to the present and future ages it should have begun — It is much to be regretted that he did not tell his own Story from that time until his retirement from the Office of President of the United States in 1809. It was then that all the good and all the evil parts of his character were brought into action — His ardent Passion for Liberty and the Rights of Man — His Patriotism — the depth and compass of his understanding — the extent and variety of his knowledge, and the enviable faculty of apply-ing it to his own purposes. The perpetual watchfulness of public opinion, and the pliability of principle and temper with

which he accommodated to it his own designs and opinions, all these were in ceaseless operation during those twenty years — and with them were combined a rare mixture of infidel philosophy, and Epicurean Morals — Of burning Ambition, and of Stoical self-controul — of deep duplicity and of generous sensibility, between which two qualities and a treacherous and inventive Memory, his conduct towards his rivals and opponents appears one tissue of inconsistency. His treatment of Washington, of Knox, of my father, of Hamilton, of Bayard, who made him President of the United States, and lastly of me, is marked with features of perfidy, worthy of Tiberius Caesar, or Louis the 11th of France — This double-dealing character was often imputed to him during his life time, and was sometimes exposed — His Letter to Mazzei, and the agonizing efforts which he afterwards made to explain it away. His most insidious attacks upon my father, with his never ceasing professions of respect and affection for his person and character, and his Letter to Giles concerning me, in which there is scarcely a single word of truth indicate a memory so pandering to the will that in deceiving others he seems to have begun by deceiving himself — The doubly posthumous attack upon James A. Bayard, admits not even of that extenuation. After bargaining through Samuel Smith for the vote of Bayard in 1801 and obtaining it by the pledge which he authorised Smith to give, he first violates his pledge, then solemnly denies that he had given it — attempts to pervert the transaction into a charge against Bayard of tampering with Smith in behalf of Burr five years afterwards, when Bayard and Smith had given depositions upon Oath to the facts. Jefferson makes a private memorandum, charging Bayard's statement with falsehood, and affirming that it is contradicted by Smith, when in fact Smith's deposition confirms that of Bayard completely. This Memorandum he carefully files in his Porte Folio, and eleven years after the death of Bayard leaves it to be published by his own Executor after his own death — In the discord of human nature could a baser string be sounded?

———

14. V:30. Friday. ≈ I received a Letter from John C. Calhoun; now Vice President of the United States, relating to his present controversy with President Jackson and William H. Crawford.

He questions me concerning the Letter of General Jackson to Mr. Monroe, which Crawford alledges to have been produced at the Cabinet Meetings on the Seminole War; and asks for copies if I think proper to give them of Crawford's Letter to me which I received last Summer, and of my answer — I answered Mr. Calhoun's Letter immediately; rigorously confining myself to the direct object of his enquiries — This is a new bursting out of the old and rancorous feud between Crawford and Calhoun, both parties to which, after suspending their animosities, and combining together to effect my ruin, are appealing to me for testimony to sustain themselves; each against the other. This is one of the occasions upon which I shall eminently need the direction of a higher power to guide me in every step of my conduct — I see my duty to discard all consideration of their treatment of me — to adhere in every thing that I shall say or write to the truth — To assert nothing positively of which I am not absolutely certain — To deny nothing, upon which there remains a scruple of doubt upon my Memory. To conceal nothing which it may be lawful to divulge, and which may promote truth and justice between the parties. With these principles, I see further the necessity for Caution and Prudence in the course I shall take — The bitter enmity of all three of the parties, Jackson, Calhoun and Crawford against me, an enmity the more virulent, because kindled by their own ingratitude and injustice to me. The interest which every one of them and all their partizans have in keeping up that load of obloquy, and public odium which their foul calumnies have brought down upon me; and the disfavour in which I stand before a majority of the People, excited against me by their artifices. Their demerits to me are proportioned to the obligations to me — Jackson's the greatest — Crawford's the next — Calhoun's the least of positive obligation, but darkened by his double-faced setting himself up as a Candidate for the Presidency against me in 1821, his prevarications between Jackson and me in 1824 and his icy-hearted dereliction, of all the decencies of social intercourse with me, solely from the terror of Jackson, since the 4th of March 1829 — I walk between burning ploughshares — Let me be mindful where I place my foot.

———

17. V:30. Monday. ≈ I met in my walk an Indian Chief who recognized me, and with a look of old acquaintance offered me his hand which I took and shook heartily. We could not speak to each other, and I did not distinctly remember his person; but believe it was one of the Cherokees who were here with Ross and Ridge during Mr. Monroe's administration. I met also Mr. Hutchinson our Consul at Lisbon, whom I did not recognize until he told me his name — nor did I immediately recollect that he had called upon me last Summer at Quincy — In philosophising upon the decay of my own memory, I remark, that my recollection of persons whom I have but casually seen and of their names is most imperfect. This I attribute to the great multitudes of persons whom I have seen, and who have been introduced to me but with whom I have had no relation of intimate acquaintance. There is always something mortifying to the pride of a man who remembers another, not to be recognized by him — But there are bounds to the retention of the human memory, and the nomenclature of the antient Romans was a useful Officer. ≈ There is in the Memoir of Mr. Jefferson's Life a copy of the Declaration of Independence as finally adopted by Congress — with marginal Notes, Italics in brackets; and of the final declaratory paragraph a concurrent column, shewing the paper as reported by the Committee — these he gives because he says the Sentiments of men are known, not only by what they receive, but by what they reject. There is also at the close of the fourth Volume, a fac simile of his original draught with the alterations proposed by my father and Doctor Franklin — There were in the paper reported by the Committee, a good many erasures and considerable alterations from the draught — They appear to me to have been all, improvements upon it. The draft was declamatory, argumentative, and overloaded with crudities — A great deal too much of these was left in the Report of the Committee — Too much even in the final Declaration — which is nevertheless one of the best composed State Papers that I ever saw — The Declaration was a novelty in the annals of the world — It was founded upon the principles of Natural Right. It was an Apology to the world for the revolt of thirteen Colonies united into one confederacy, separating themselves from the Nation of which they had formed a part, and announcing

themselves as a new Nation to the world — The reason assigned for this Declaration, is respect for the opinions of mankind — the cause alledged is the tyranny of the king, supported by the People of Great-Britain — The acts of tyranny are specified — The fact of previous petitions disregarded is alledged; the concurrence of the British People with the king affirmed, and the necessity for the Separation, is conclusively deduced from these facts — There was struck out by Congress from the Report of the Committee 1. A frantic paragraph against the Slave trade and negro Slavery — 2. A paragraph affirming that the Colonists in constituting their forms of Government had adopted one common king with Great-Britain, but that submission to their Parliament was no part of the Colonial Constitution, nor ever in idea 3. A paragraph quite declamatory against the British people — For re-electing members of Parliament opposed to the Colonial Cause, and for permitting their chief magistrate to send over not only soldiers of our common blood, but Scotch and foreign mercenaries to invade and destroy us. 4. About half the final declaratory paragraph. These two last alterations appear by the fac-simile to have been proposed by Dr. Franklin in the Committee, and are there enclosed in brackets, with a marginal entry of the words "a different phraseology inserted". The Solemn and Sublime appeal to Heaven, at the beginning and close of the declaratory paragraph was added in Congress, and not "cooked up" by the Committee. The parts struck out by Congress, sound to my ears like effusions of frenzy — The paragraph against Slavery indiscreet beyond measure, and not a little unjust. Mr. Jefferson says that in the ground which he took that the British Parliament never had any authority over the Colonies, any more than the Danes and Saxons of his own age had over the People of England, he never could get any one to agree with him but Mr. Wythe — It was too absurd. In truth the question of right as between Parliament and the Colonies, was one of those upon which it is much easier to say who was wrong, than who was right — The pretension that they had the right to bind the Colonies, in all cases whatever, and that which denied them the right to bind in any case whatever, were the two extremes, equally unfounded — and yet it is extremely difficult to draw the line where the authority of Parliament commenced, and where it closed. Lord Chatham's line was taxation — Burke's was usage, precedent, and wise discretion — My father's is in the Resolutions of the First Congress — There is a very remarkable passage in page 39 and 40 of the Memoir, shewing that although Jefferson was not inclined in his last days to avow his perseverance in his opinions upon Negro-Slavery, he was willing to let them loose after his death — the motive for which appears to be to secure to himself posthumous fame as a prophet.

18. V. Tuesday. ≈ I received a Letter from R. Walsh re-urging me to write upon the late Colonial trade arrangement with Great-Britain; and a note from W. B. Hodgson; with some proof sheets of the next Volume of the Transactions of the American Philosophical Society at Philadelphia, containing his Speculations upon the Berber Language. I answered a Letter received last August from R. H. Lee — and had time left to read only a few pages of the Correspondence of Jefferson — His continuance in Congress after the adoption of the Declaration of Independence was short — In October 1776 he was elected by his County a member of the Legislature of Virginia; where he took his Seat, after resigning that in Congress — From that time till June 1779 he continued a member of the Legislature, and was then elected the Governor of the Commonwealth — In the interval he was occupied with the revisal of the Legislation of the State. Even before the Declaration of Independence, the Organization of the State Government had been altered by the Legislature itself; from the Royal Charter Government, to what they called a Constitution, but which was never submitted to the People — By this anomaly the State of Virginia has been governed to this day. They have now however a more formal Constitution prepared by a Convention about a year since, and adopted by the People, but not yet in operation — In the revision of the old System of Laws Mr. Jefferson took an active and leading part. He presented Bills for the establishment of Courts of Justice — for converting tenancies in tail into fee simple — for prohibiting the importation of Negro Slaves — for abolishing the establishment of the Episcopal Church; and for asserting the natural right of expatriation, and prescribing the mode of exercising it. He also

proposed and carried through a Bill for a general revision of the whole Code of Laws, by which the Colony had been governed; and he was appointed with four others to execute the work. One of the Committee soon resigned, and one died. The three others divided the work between them — Jefferson had the Common Law and statutes till 4 James 1 — when the Virginia Legislature was first established — Wythe the British Statutes from that time to *the present day* (1776) and Pendleton the Virginia Laws — Now if Mr. Jefferson's pretension that the British Parliament had *never* possessed the right of enacting Laws for Virginia had been well founded, what would Mr. Wythe have had to do — Every British Statute affecting Virginia from 1607 to 1776 was a flagrant usurpation, which by the Declaration of Independence alone would have been swept away. This thought however never occurred to the Committee — The first question they settled was not to abolish the whole existing system of Laws and prepare a new and complete Institute, but to preserve the general system and only modify it to the present order of things — Pendleton was for the former, and Lee, Jefferson, with Mason and Wythe for the latter — Mr. Jefferson and Pendleton on this occasion both changed sides — Pendleton assuming the character of the bold innovator, and Jefferson that of the special pleader and defender of antient things — He gives the reasons of his own opinion; but not those of Mr. Pendleton. But there were far other reasons than those assigned by Mr. Jefferson for not reconstructing the edifice of Legislation in Virginia de novo; which he felt and understood, though he has had the Prudence not to disclose them — 1. Mr. Jefferson was not a Legislator — His Genius was *de*structive, but not *con*structive — He could demolish, deface, and cast down — He could not build up or preserve — 2. The principle of setting aside the whole code of their Legislation, would of itself have emancipated all their Slaves — In renovating their Code they must have restored Slavery after having abolished it — They must have assumed to themselves all the Odium of establishing it as a positive Institution directly in the face of all the principles they had proclaimed — They must have abandoned their Laws privileging lands from responsibility for debts — and they must have enlarged their elective franchise, confined as it was almost exclusively to freeholders — For all this Mr. Jefferson was not prepared. It was easier to abolish the Law of primogeniture, the establishment of the Episcopal Church — Capital Punishments, except for Treason and Murder; and the Professorships of Divinity and the Oriental Languages in William and Mary College — All this was accordingly done — But the Lands of the Planters retained their exemption from liability for the debts of their owners — The freeholders retained their exclusive right of voting at Elections, and the bill on the subject of Slaves was a mere digest of the existing laws respecting them, without any intimation of a plan for a future and general emancipation. This was however agreed upon by the Committee, to be proposed by way of amendment, on the passage of the Bill — But it was found that the public mind would not bear the proposition. The amendment was never offered, and Mr. Jefferson contents himself with a posthumous prophecy that it must soon come or that worse will follow — With regard to the criminal Law the Committee substituted for some capital punishments the Lex Talionis, which on further reflection Mr. Jefferson justly disapproves — and he attempted to introduce Juries into the Chancery Court, which Pendleton defeated by an Amendment making it optional with either of the parties. The Committee after near three years, had accomplished their labour of revision of all the Laws in 126 bills making a printed folio of 90 pages only. These bills were brought forward piece-meal in the Legislature until 1785 when most of them by the exertions of Mr. Madison were adopted.

———

20. V. Thursday. Morning visitors engrossed the morning. Elliot Cresson is here as a delegate from the Pennsylvania Colonization Society — The general Society have last Evening had their annual Meeting which I received from the Managers a written invitation to attend. Cresson who is of the Society of Friends is a member, and ardent Supporter of the Colonization Society, which I never have been — believing their principal objects impracticable, and entertaining great doubts of the usefulness of their measures which have been successful. I therefore did not attend their meeting, and had in like manner abstained from attending that of the last year. I told Cresson candidly what had been and were my impressions on the

subject. I said that I did not believe it would diminish the number of Slaves in the United States by a single individual — And that so far as it did effect the emigration of free People of Colour it was rather a public injury than a public benefit — This Society however [is] yearly increasing in numbers and in power; and my opinions found no sympathy in those of Mr. Cresson. ≈

21. V. Friday. Snow. On my morning's walk ≈ A person near Brown's tavern, accosted and walked on with me a few minutes. Said his name was Hall, a native of Virginia, and now an Inhabitant of Kentucky. His motive for introducing himself to me was curiosity, because I had been "our President." Leslie Combs whom I had seen at New-York called, and told me he was going this evening or to-morrow on his return to Kentucky — He spoke of some public controversy with General Jackson, which I had forgotten; and he told me two anecdotes which whether verities or inventions are characteristic — one that Jackson upon his last Summer's tour to Tennessee was earnestly urged by a clergyman to stand a Candidate for re-election; upon which he said — well, if my fellow-citizens insist upon my serving them another term, I hope they will give me a Vice-President in whom I can have some confidence — The other, that Calhoun, within a very few days has said that if Jackson had followed *his* Advice the Administration would have been approved by the People — But as it was, it had lost all its popularity.

———

25. IV:30. Tuesday. ≈ read a few Stanzas of Childe Harold, and further in the Correspondence of Jefferson, till the Letter of 28 May 1781 to General Washington, announcing his long declared resolution of retiring from the oppression of his Office as Governor of Virginia, to private Life — He says he shall relinquish it to abler hands: and from that time there is a gap in the Correspondence of nearly 3 years, the next Letter being again to General Washington, and dated at Annapolis 16 April 1784 — A note of the Editor says that during the interval he preserved only Memoranda of the contents of the Letters written by him. It is very evident that this period of his life brought to him no pleasing recollections. He withdrew from his Office at the

very agonizing moment of his Country's struggle. He thought a Military Governor would be at that Time more useful to the State — Why was he not himself a Military Governor. He was ex officio Commander in Chief of the Armies of the State — What was Joseph Warren? What was Nathaniel Greene? what was Benjamin Lincoln? what was Henry Knox? It is the necessary nature of civil Wars to make Military Men out of Lawyers and Farmers, Physicians and Booksellers, aye, and out of Ministers of the word of God. The condition of Virginia at the moment when he abandoned the helm of State was such as should have created Soldiers under the ribs of death — His correspondence for a year before is languid and desponding. He complains of the discovery of extensive disaffection; speaks with terror of the enemy's successes, and broadly intimates that the minds of the People may be led to acquiescence under those events which they see no human power prepared to ward off — And this is the Moment which Mr. Jefferson selects to retire from the responsible Office of Governor of the State — And within four Months from that day Cornwallis surrenders his Arms and his Army at Yorktown — Not a line of congratulation upon this great and sudden turn of the tide of success is found in his Correspondence. Not one word about it in the Memoir of his Life — This Silence is expressive — Where was he from June 1781 to the close of the War — No mortal man can tell, from the Memoir or the Correspondence. In that very June 1781 at the moment when he resigned his Office as Governor of Virginia, he was appointed one of the Ministers for negotiating Peace with Great-Britain, then (he says) expected to be effected through the mediation of the Empress of Russia. He declined this appointment, he says for the same reasons, for which he had declined in 1776, and what were they? take his words — Such was the state of my family that I could not leave it, nor could I expose it to the dangers of the Sea, and of capture by the British ships then covering the Ocean. I saw too, that the laboring oar was really at home, where much was to be done, of the most permanent interest, in new modelling our Governments, and much to defend our farms and fire sides from the desolations of an invading enemy, pressing on our Country, in every point — The first of these reasons are mere private considerations — He could not leave his family, and

would not expose his family to capture by British Ships — John
Adams three times exposed himself and two boys to capture by
British Ships during the war. He left his wife, daughter and
one infant Son to the protection of his Country — John Jay's
wife and children went with him — Dr. Franklin went safe in
1776 as Jefferson would have gone if he had been with him
— Henry Laurens was taken and sent to the Tower; and
harshly treated; but his Son was not even imprisoned, and was
allowed to visit him; and so might it have been with Mr. Jefferson, if he had gone, with or without his family and been taken.
There are dangers which a high-souled man, engaged in a sacred cause must encounter, and not flinch from — To assign
them as reasons for declining the Post of Honour savours
more of the Sybarite than of the Spartan — They remind one
of the certain Lord, neat, trimly dressed, who but for those vile
guns would himself have been a Soldier — As to the other
reason of staying at home, to defend our farms and fire-sides,
it certainly did not apply to Mr. Jefferson either in 1776 when
there was neither active nor threatened invasion of Virginia,
nor in June 1781 when Mr. Jefferson had slunk from that very
defence into the inactive safety of a private citizen — Perhaps
Mr. Jefferson was sufficiently punished for his dereliction of
the cause, by the humiliating necessity under which he has
been of drawing a veil over this portion of his Life — Pends
toi, brave Crillon, wrote Henry of Navarre to one of his Heroic followers — nous avons vaincu, et tu n'y etois pas. Mr.
Jefferson's doctrine, that in times of public danger a professional Soldier is preferable for the head of the Nation to an
eminent Statesman is anti-republican. Deliberate valour is a
quality as necessary to a Statesman as to a Warrior — and if it
was not an attribute of Mr. Jefferson, it is but so much de-
tracted from the greatness of his character. His successor
General Nelson, certainly did nothing which he might not
have done in his place — and how much more illustrious
would his name have been, if his Portrait could have appeared
in Trumbull's picture of the Surrender of Cornwallis, as conspicuous, as in that of the Declaration of Independence.

———

27. V:30. Thursday ≈ Consumed much of the Morning in reviewing my Diary from October 1817 to January 1819 upon

the Negotiation with Spain, the Transactions at Amelia Island, and of the Seminole War in Florida — Recurred also to my file of Letters from Mr. Monroe while I was Secretary of State and to my Letter-Books — My Diary now absorbs much time — In the Evening I read a few pages of Jefferson's Correspondence — The Memoir gives a short account of the composition and publication of his Notes on Virginia — Which originated in the practice of committing to writing on loose and disconnected sheets, any information of his Country, which might be of use to him, in any Station, public or private — An excellent habit which cannot be too earnestly recommended to every young man. It had been however pursued by Mr. Jefferson without premeditated method, till it formed a bundle of loose papers, without order, and difficult of recurrence, when he had occasion for any particular one — The best of all systems for this purpose is to combine and carry on together a Diary, and a Common Place Book upon the plan of Locke's — These should be upon paper of one size and stitched in Quires of six or eight Sheets each, to be bound in Volumes as the matter sufficiently accumulates. In 1781 Mr. de Marbois of the French Legation, having been instructed by his Government to obtain statistical accounts of the several States of the Union, addressed to Jefferson a number of Queries relative to the State of Virginia. This gave him an occasion, to embody the substance of his materials, which he did in the order of Mr. Marbois Queries, so as to answer his wish, and to arrange them for the writer's own use. Friends to whom they were communicated, wished for copies — which, their Volume rendering it too laborious by hand — He proposed to get a few copies printed — This in America, he found would have been too costly an undertaking — At Paris, discovering that it could be done, for a fourth of what he had been asked at home, he had 200 copies printed which he distributed among his friends in Europe and America. A bad French Translation but partly corrected by him was published in Paris; and a London Bookseller, on seeing the French Translation, requested his permission to reprint the original, which he granted. This he says is the true History of that publication — and it added very greatly to his reputation — The work is still somewhat defective in its arrangement, but contains much valuable matter

— There is added to the work at its close, a draught of what he thought would be a suitable Constitution for Virginia, but no part of which was I believe ever adopted. In his correspondence at the time when he first printed the Book he appears to have been under some alarm, lest the freedom and severity of his remarks upon Slavery, and upon the Constitution of Virginia then existing would occasion irritation and retard the reformation which he wished to promote — Mr. Jefferson's love of Liberty was sincere and ardent, not confined to himself like that of most of his fellow Slave-holders. He was above that execrable sophistry of the South-Carolina nullifiers which would make of Slavery the corner stone to the temple of Liberty — He saw the gross inconsistency between the principles of the Declaration of Independence and the fact of Negro Slavery; and he could not, or would not prostitute the faculties of his mind to the vindication of that Slavery which from his Soul he abhorred — Mr. Jefferson had not the Spirit of Martyrdom — He would have introduced a flaming denunciation of Slavery into the Declaration of Independence; but the discretion of his Colleagues struck it out. He did insert a most eloquent and impassioned argument against it in his Notes upon Virginia, but on that very account the book was published almost against his will. He projected a plan of general emancipation in his revision of the Virginian Laws, but finally presented a plan leaving Slavery precisely where it was — And in his Memoir he leaves a posthumous warning to the Planters, that they must, at no distant day emancipate their Slaves, or that worse will follow; but he withheld the publication of this prophecy till he should himself be in the grave.

———

31. VI:30. Monday ≈ *Day.* The hours of rising and of retiring to rest, of breakfast and dinner, are as at the close of the last Month — I frequent no Society, and with the exception of my daily walks, we are confined within the walls of our house as if it were a ship at Sea — I spend about six hours of the day in writing Diary — Arrears of Index — and Letters — I have given up entirely my Classical reading; and almost all other; excepting the daily Newspapers, and interruptedly a few pages of Jefferson's writings — My reflections upon these, as I proceed, I now introduce into this Journal, and it swells the record of almost every

day — I enjoy a degree of tranquility such as I never before experienced; interrupted only that by my own as yet insuperable indolence it is a time of *fainéantise*, and by the consciousness that it must be speedily changed for a return to all the cares, mortifications and perplexities of ungracious public life — The Month has been of winter unusually severe; but my own condition is one of unparalleled comfort and enjoyment.

—

[February 1831]

2. V. Wednesday. ≈ Elliott Cresson paid me a Morning visit: just from President Jackson, who had been treating him roughly — Elliott is a member, and Delegate of the Colonization Society, who wish to have a public vessel stationed to Cruize on the Coast of Liberia, to protect our Commerce with that flourishing Settlement, and look out for Slavers. But the Colonization Society is out of favour with Jackson, as it always has been with me — Cresson says that his language was almost abusive — That he charged me with having squandered the public money upon this establishment without Law — That he said there were not 300 colonists at the place. That almost all who went out there, died of Pestilence, and that every word that Mr. Kendall had said was true — Cresson was in amazement at his ignorance — The public expenditures with which Jackson reproached me, were made under a construction of an Act of Congress passed during Mr. Monroe's Administration; sanctioned by him, by the Secretary of the Navy, Smith Thompson, and by W. H. Crawford, Secretary of the Treasury, a member and Vice-President of the Colonization Society — The language of the act was ambiguous, and the construction given to it was against my opinion. At the ensuing Session of Congress, however, Mr. Monroe gave notice to that body by a message of his construction of the Act, that they might controul it if they thought proper — They never did controul it, and the expenditures under it continued during my administration because I did not feel myself at Liberty to reverse the decision of Mr. Monroe; and two or three eminent lawyers his Secretaries, tacitly supported by Congress itself.

—

13. VII. Sunday. Fahrenheit, 14 — Sun rose 6:44. Mrs. Adams was very ill all Night: and extremely so in the course of this

day. Sent for Dr. Huntt — who bled her — There were symptoms of the direction of the Erisypelas to the brain — She was somewhat relieved in the Evening. ≈ I called at Gadsby's Hotel, and had a long conversation with Mr. Wirt, who now lodges there — I had sent him an invitation to dine with us this day, which he declined. ≈ Wirt spoke to me also in deep concern and alarm, at the state of Chief Justice Marshall's health — He is 75 years of age; and has until lately enjoyed fine health — exercised great bodily activity, and sustained an immense mass of bodily labour. His mind remains unimpaired but his body is breaking down. He has been 30 years Chief Justice of the Supreme Court, and has done more to establish the Constitution of the United States on sound Construction than any other man living — The terror is that if he should be now withdrawn, some shallow-pated wild-cat like Philip P. Barbour, fit for nothing but to tear the Union to rags and tatters would be appointed in his place — Mr. Wirt's anticipations are gloomy, and I see no reasonable prospect of improvement. On returning home, I found the young Quaker to whom Gales and Seaton had given a Letter of introduction Lindley and another by the name of Benjamin Lundy, Editor of a weekly paper, called the Genius of Universal emancipation — It was first published in Tennessee, afterwards in Baltimore, and now comes out in this City — Its object is to promote the abolition of Slavery; of which Lundy freely expressed his confidence and hopes.

———

23. V:30. Wednesday. ≈ I have been till this day much occupied in redeeming the arrears of this Diary, which is now completed — The inflammation of my eye has subsided, but the oppression upon my lungs continues — I composed one Stanza, of the paraphrase of the 149th Psalm, a task which is not very difficult. Perhaps I could thus paraphrase the whole Book of Psalms — but to what good purpose? The spinning out of Rhymes is but laborious idleness. I began this morning a Poem of another character, the conception of which is amusing but requiring more continuity of purpose, more poetical imagination, and more command of language and power of harmony than belongs to me.

———

[March 1831]

2. V:15. Wednesday — Sun rose 6:24. Fahrenheit 30. The Spring is advancing and the first time for the Season, I had no fire made in my writing chamber — Very little in the adjoining bed-chamber. Walking round the Capitol Square, I met Judge Cranch — Morning visit from Mr. Williams of North-Carolina, who introduced to me his friend from Tennessee — Also from Dr. Kent the former Governor of Maryland and Member of Congress, and afterwards from Mr. Calhoun the Vice-President — This is the first time that he has called upon me since the last Administration closed. He said something about political Considerations as he had done in one of his Letters to which I made no reply then or now. Explanation can do nothing. I meet Mr. Calhoun's advances to a renewal of the intercourse of common civility, because I cannot reject them. But I once had confidence in the qualities of his heart — It is not totally destroyed, but so impaired that it can never be fully restored. Mr. Calhoun's Friendships and Enmities are regulated exclusively by his interests — His opinions are the sport of every popular blast, and his career as a Statesman has been marked by a Series of the most flagrant inconsistencies.

——

8. V:30. Tuesday — Sun rose 6:16. Fahrenheit 30. It is a doctrine of the medical faculty that bodily exercise to be salutary, should be taken with a vacant mind, and such is the precept of Mr. Jefferson. By the instruction of Buchan I have during the greater part of my life, followed this rule, and it has saved me from the composition of mechans vers douze fois, douze cens and ten times more — At certain Seasons however the propensity becomes too strong for me. I walk and muse, and pour forth premeditated verse, which it takes me six or nine months to lay by, and then resume to find it good for nothing — It never appears so to me, when I compose it — In a few instances I have suffered the publication of my effusions, and I am accredited, as one of the smallest Poets of my Country — Very short fugitive pieces and translations are the only rhymes I have ever committed to the press. One short poem; the lines to Mrs. Hellen on the death of her two children — and one translation, the 13th Satire of Juvenal have been favourably noticed. One Satirical song, overlooked when first published

was dragged into light twenty years afterwards, for political effect against me because it laughed at the party lama Jefferson. All the rest of my published poetry has passed from the press into the waters of Lethé — One of these rhyming fits is now upon me — brought on by the inflammation of my eye, which debarred me from reading and writing, and threw me back upon my own scanty resources — I write every morning one Stanza of paraphrase from the Bible; and in my morning walk from two to three Stanzas of a Tale which I have undertaken, far beyond my depth, and which I shall obviously never get through — But so totally does it absorb my attention while engaged upon it, that in my morning walk round the capitol square, I go out and return almost without consciousness of the passage of Time — the melancholy madness of Poetry without the inspiration — I cooked up this morning one Stanza before rising from bed — Then after reading three Chapters of Isaiah — one Stanza, of paraphrase from the 3^d Chapter of Proverbs — Then in my walk three Stanzas more of the Tale and this Evening after dinner, severely threatened with an inflammation of my left eye, and therefore daring neither to read nor write, took up an Ode of Horace, exquisitely beautiful, from which more than twenty-five years ago I had wrung three Stanzas, and then given up the rest in despair — They were three of the best Stanzas I ever wrote — to which I now added two of the worst — The thoughts of Horace, are as unmalleable as Platina.

———

10. VI. Thursday — Sun rose 6:13. Fahrenheit 30. In my morning walk I met Mr. Peter Hagner, and we walk'd together till we parted at the market — He told me he had ten children and had never lost one. And that he always made it a practice, to prevent their getting their feet wet, and to make them wear flannels. I lost one or two Stanza's of Dermot, by my walk with Mr. Hagner, and should therefore get something by way of composition — As I proceed with Dermot, the subject opens upon me, and I feel distressingly my wants. I supposed I could make out of it a Tale of about 50 Stanza's — I now think I cannot get through with it in less than one hundred. My Style is the mock heroic; but it wants vivacity, humour, poetical invention and a large command of Language. — I want besides,

a knowledge of Ireland, physical moral and political — A knowledge of the manners, usages, prevailing opinions, modes of life, social habits and dress of the twelfth century. I want a faculty of inventing and delineating character, of naturalizing familiar dialogue and of spicing my treat with keen and cutting Satire. I want the faculty of picturesque description: of penetrating into the inmost recesses of human Nature — of moralizing in harmonious verse — of passing from grave to gay, from lively to severe — of touching the cords of sympathy with the tender and sublime — and to consecrate the whole by a perpetual tendency to a pure and elevated morality — I do not believe there is in human history a happier subject for a mock-heroic Poem than the Conquest of Ireland by Henry the second — But where are the legendary fables of Ireland for machinery — where the art of painting the intrigues of Dermot at the Court of Henry; where the art of describing Battles, and Sieges, the desolation of the Country during the progress of the Conquest, the destruction of Fernes, the Capitol of Leinster; the interior of the monastery where Dermot concealed himself upon his return after his expulsion — All this a true Poet might paint with touches of the terribly sublime — If I had undertaken it forty years ago I might have made something of it now — At present, I might as well undertake to paint a Scene of the Deluge upon Canvas; or to compose the music of an Opera — or to execute the Pediment of the Capitol which I designed. Mr. John W. Taylor was here, and took leave of me — Going in a day or two for home. I had a long conversation with him upon the aspects of political affairs, and upon the prostitution of principle as well as the hostility to me, manifested by the party now holding up Mr. Clay as the Candidate for the next Presidential Election — I gave him instances and proofs, some of which were already known to him; others he had not heard of before.

———

12. V. Saturday. Morning walk omitted. Proportional deduction from the progress of Dermot. After breakfast I walked to the Capitol, and heard J. Sergeant for about three hours before the Supreme Court, upon the Injunction prayed by the Cherokee Nation of Indians against the State of Georgia, the Legislature of which has passed a Law, extending the Jurisdiction of

the State over them and their Lands. The question is upon the Jurisdiction of the Court — The Governor of Georgia was summoned to appear, but refused; and the Legislature passed Resolutions denying the right of the Court to issue the Summons, and declaring their *regret* that Chief Justice Marshall had issued it — Sergeant and Wirt are now arguing the question of Jurisdiction, without any Counsel to oppose them — but the weight of the State will be too heavy for them — The old vice of Confederacies is pressing upon us, anarchy in the members. Whenever a State does set itself in defiance against the Laws or power of the Union, they are prostrated — This is what the States having Indian Tribes within their limits are now doing with impunity, and all the powers of the General Government for protection of the Indians, or the execution of the Treaties with them are nullified — Mr. Sergeant's argument made it necessary for him to maintain that the Cherokee Nation are a Foreign State, and this is the very point upon which the judgment of the Court may be against him. — The argument was cold and dry, resting upon Constructions of passages in the Constitution, and precedents of authorities — There were however several Ladies among the auditory who sat and heard him with exemplary Patience.

———

[April 1831]
16. IV:30. Saturday — Rain. I finished this Morning the fair Copy of my Poem of Dermot MacMorrogh, and have now the measure of my own Poetical Power — Beyond this I shall never attain, and now it is an important question whether I should throw this, and almost all the other verses I have ever written into the fire — Hitherto I have confined myself to Translations, and fugitive pieces of a very few Lines or Stanza's; a small portion of which have been published in Newspapers and Magazines. I have now completed a historical Tale, of upwards of two thousand lines; the subject of my own Selection — The moral clear and palpable — the characters and incidents strictly historical — The Story complete and entire — It has amused and occupied two Months of my life, and leaves me now like a pleasant dream, to dull and distressing realities — To a sense of wasted Time and to the humiliation of enterprize, ashamed of performance — Yet at the same

Time with an insatiate thirst for undertaking again higher and better things. ≈

17. V. Sunday. A beautiful Spring-like day. I attended the morning-Service, at the Presbyterian Church, and heard Mr. Smith, from Proverbs 3.31 "Envy thou not the oppressor, and choose none of his ways." Mr. Smith's creed may, and I suppose must be Calvinistic. But that is not the character of his Mind — This discourse was chiefly upon the force of example; and his treatment of his subject was original — There is nothing of Common-Place about him — His Sermon was a short and sensible moral Treatise; argumentative and earnest — without a word upon election, reprobation, atonement or Trinity — and asserting the Liberty of Religious opinions, and the adherence exclusively to the Scriptures as a rule of faith, in which the practice of all the Protestant Churches, but especially the Presbyterians is widely variant from their theories — All Creeds are bundles of absurdities; and it is their absurdity alone, which causes the practice of tying men's minds down to them — Rational Conclusions of mind rest upon their own foundations, and need no buttress to support them — And whenever a Man repeats a formulary of his belief, it must be taken as an act not of his judgment, but of his Will.

———

20. IV:30. Wednesday. The Globe Newspaper of this Morning contains a Letter from Martin Van Buren Secretary of State to the President, dated the 11th of this Month, tendering the Resignation of his Office, and assigning at some length his reasons for this step — And the answer of the President dated the 12th accepting his Resignation — The Globe further states that the Secretary of War, John H. Eaton, tendered his resignation, on the 7th which was accepted, and that Samuel D. Ingham, Secretary of the Treasury, and John Branch resigned yesterday — from which it infers that there will be a new organization of the Cabinet — The Telegraph of this Evening says that Ingham and Branch resigned at the request of the President. Wyer and Mr. Frye called here this morning; and afterwards M'lean, who told me, what had been hinted to me before by Wyer and also indirectly through Mr. Frye; that Duff Green wished to converse with me — I told Mr. M'lean,

that I was perfectly willing to converse with Mr. Green, when he should please. That I intended to leave the City and return to my Residence at Quincy — and should go to-morrow but I should probably be here again, early the next Autumn — I found Mr. M'lean's objects were to ascertain, whether Mr. Clay would certainly be nominated for the Presidency at the proposed National Republican Meeting at Baltimore next December. I told him I had no doubt he would, though I knew nothing about it — Also whether I should be nominated at the Anti-Masonic Convention next September — I told him I had no communications with the Anti-Masons, and knew nothing of their intentions. — He said that if Mr. Clay should be nominated Mr. Calhoun would not be a Candidate; but if he should not be, Mr. Calhoun would be a Candidate, with Mr. Ingham as Vice President and that Mr. Clay's Western friends were very favourably disposed to Mr. Calhoun, if they should find the prospects of Mr. Clay desperate. He spoke of Duff Green, as being an obstinate and indiscreet man often needing advice and not always disposed to take it.

———

25. V. Monday. ≈ Mrs. Adams with the family left Philadelphia, at one O'Clock, to go this Evening to lodge at Trenton — and thence proceed to-morrow to Brunswick, where I am to overtake them. I called at the U.S. Bank to see Mr. Biddle, but he had been called out — I dined with him — Mrs. Biddle was present, and Dr. Chapman, Robert Walsh, and Richard Peters — There is scarcely any other topic of Conversation than the recent breaking up of the President's Cabinet at Washington. His Correspondence with each of the Ex-Secretaries on this occasion has been given one by one: each day one. Those of the Secretaries of State, and of War were published before I left the City — That with Ingham on Friday, and that with Branch on Saturday. The Letters to the two last were apparently written by Jackson himself, and they afford matter for much amusement. Ingham and Branch were not inclined to resign: and he was not willing to pass for having requested them to resign — He puts it upon the ground that his Cabinet proper was a Unit which had come together in great harmony — and as two individuals of the Unit had voluntarily withdrawn, he thought it necessary to reorganize the whole

Cabinet — There was a Caricature published here on Saturday upon this incident, called the Rats leaving a falling house — Four Sleek rats, with faces of recognizable likeness to the four Secretaries are scampering away upon the floor. Jackson is struggling to sustain himself in a Chair that is breaking under him; and his right foot is pressing upon Van-Buren's tail, as if to detain him — An Altar of Reform is falling over, with an imp having the head of an Ass, the body of a monkey, and the wings of a bat, armed with a broom — The room is hung round with Papers on each of which is inscribed Resignation: and the Presidents spitting box and broken tobacco pipe are on the floor. Two thousand copies of this Print have been sold in Philadelphia this day. Ten thousand Copies were struck off; and will all be disposed of within a fortnight — This is an indication of the estimation in which Jackson and his Administration are held. Not a human being of any party regrets the loss of the Services of any of the Secretaries withdrawn.

———

27. V:30. Wednesday — Steam-boat President — Long-Island Sound. We took passage on board the Steam-boat President, Captain Bunker for Providence. She was to depart at five in the afternoon, but our Carriage and horses, were embarked at Noon, when the tide was low, and the deck of the vessel on a level with the wharf. I paid a visit to the Ex-President Monroe at the house of his Son in Law Samuel L. Gouverneur — He was confined to his chamber, and extremely feeble and emaciated — Congress passed at their last Session an Act, making a further allowance to him for his claims of thirty thousand dollars which have been paid him. He has advertised for Sale his Estate in Loudoun County Virginia, and proposes to go there in a few weeks; but it is doubtful whether he will ever be able to leave his chamber. Mr. Monroe is a very remarkable instance of a man whose life has been a continued Series of the most extraordinary good fortune; who has never met with any known disaster, has gone through a splendid Career of public service — Has received more pecuniary reward from the public than any other man since the existence of the Nation; and is now dying at the age of seventy-two in wretchedness and beggary. I sat with him perhaps half an hour. He spoke of the commotions now disturbing Europe, and of

the recent Quasi-Revolution at Washington; but his voice was so feeble, that he seemed exhausted by the exertion of speaking. I did not protract my visit; and took leave of him in all probability for the last Time.

———

[June 1831]

7. IV. Tuesday ≈ I am writing a third discourse upon the Declaration of Independence — to be delivered on the next fourth of July, to the Inhabitants of Quincy, if they should hold the proposed celebration; and if not, for use hereafter — To avoid repetitions of what I have said before upon the same Subject, is one of the difficulties of my present task. As I proceed, I perceive the effect of age upon the Style of composition. I know not that the influence of age upon Style has ever been observed by critics — Yet it must be discernible — Voltaire wrote his Œdipe at 18 — his Agathocle at 80. Compare them together.

8. IV. Wednesday. Mrs. Adams and Charles's wife went in to Boston; dined at Mr. Frothingham's and returned here after dinner. Charles came back to dine. I wrote all the Morning with much dissatisfaction — I cannot suppress my thoughts, and find myself constantly treading upon embers — A craven scruple, a thought which has ever three parts coward, then comes in and mutters of consequences. Shall I speak my thoughts, or shall the fear of man deter me? I was bolder in youth than now. I had then consequences only to myself to dread — Others are now made responsible for my words and deeds — I wrote this morning what I must blot out, and I shall be ashamed of myself for doing so.

———

19. IV:40. Sunday. ≈ The intervals of the day were occupied with the revisal of my discourse for the 4th of July — Why is it that I feel more anxiety and more apprehension of failure on this occasion than I ever did in youth, when success was important to my standing in the world, and to the hopes of a long anticipated futurity upon Earth? Success or failure is now of little consequence to me, who have and can have but a few days to live — I fear the exhibition of faculties in decay — I fear a severity of judgment of the hearers, and yet more of after readers — I experienced this on my second 4th of July Oration

delivered at Washington ten years since at the Meridian of my Life — I shall now assail Passions and Prejudices as earnestly as then, deeming it now as I deemed it then my duty — but I cannot now flatter myself that what I shall say will be received even with so much indulgence — I intended to have been short; but I have written more than the length of any Oration heretofore delivered by me, my subject spreads upon me as I proceed, and I find myself unwilling to abridge — The Style of my first draught is so plain, dry, and unadorned that it would lull the auditory to Sleep — In revising, I am endeavouring to put what Doctor Waterhouse used to call the plums in the pudding; but they are few and more relishing to myself than they will be to others. I copied and enlarged industriously this day.

———

26. V. Sunday. Heard Mr. Whitney in the Morning from John 18:38 "Pilate saith unto him, What is truth." And in the afternoon, from Job 14:14. "If a man die, shall he live again?" In both these discourses, Mr. Whitney gave some of his own peculiar opinions, and in that of the afternoon inveighed vehemently against Fanny Wright an English female Atheist who has been delivering Lectures in the principal cities of the United States, against Slavery, Marriage and Christianity. She has every where gained numerous Proselytes, and there is a party scattered all over the Country, who call themselves the working man's Party; but who are generally called by others Fanny Wright's Party — Fanny makes no pretension to believe in a future State; nor even in the existence of a God; but she has an inveterate aversion to Slavery of all kinds. To African Slavery — Matrimonial Slavery — Religious Slavery — She declaims against them all, and never wants an Auditory — There is a Religious Sect rapidly growing in this part of the Country denominated Universalists who approach very nearly to the doctrines of Fanny, but they profess to be Christians — They suppose the Soul and body to perish together, but that the Soul at the judgment day will revive or be created afresh, to enjoy eternal happiness — And particularly that there will be no future State of punishment — This is a compound of Atheism, and Superstition well suited to the inconsistencies and absurdities incident to the reasoning faculties of man; and the Sect is spreading marvellously. They have had preachers here,

for these two years, and have taken from Mr. Whitney, about one third of his Parishioners. They have now the project of building a Church, though with Slender means to incur the expence, and still less for supporting a Pastor — Mr. Whitney himself inclines to believe the ultimate Salvation and happiness of all mankind — but he believes a state of retribution, and that vice and crimes here will be punished hereafter. — The question of Pilate; and the question of Job furnish therefore objects of interesting enquiry to Mr. Whitney — My brother was here this Evening — I visited my garden and Nursery — The Seedlings of my last Summer and Autumn Plantations, have totally ceased coming up — Certainly not one in ten have appeared, and of these it is doubtful whether one in ten will live — I have however Oaks, Chesnuts, Shagbarks, Pignuts, Apples, Pears, Peaches, Plums, Apricots, Strangers, Honey Locusts and two or three unknown, upon whose destinies I fear I shall watch till I see them all die — I read over again my discourse prepared for the fourth of July and marked about one third of it to be struck out.

———

29. IV:30. Wednesday. ≈ Thomas and Daniel Greenleaf were here in the Evening; and spoke of the arrangements for the 4th of July — They shewed me a List of Toasts which they had prepared; and upon which they asked for any observations which I might be disposed to make and requested me also to add to them any other toasts which I might chuse to propose — I remarked upon one of their Toasts, and requested them to omit one, in honour of myself; observing that I disliked the practice of toasting a man to his face — They said the usage of toasting the Orator of the day was so universal that it could not well be omitted. I then requested that the toast might be postponed until after I shall have withdrawn from the Hall — They said it was proposed, that the procession should go from the Town-Hall, first to Mr. Whitney's — Then round by Mr. Potter's, to take them up, and then come to my house — I thought this procession would be too long — I urged that the Toasts should avoid as much as possible all controversial Sentiment; and therefore that a compliment to the harmony of my Administration, which they had introduced into the Toasts should be omitted, as containing an indirect reproof of the

present Times — I said I should in my own discourse which I feared would be an hour long carefully avoid all offensive allusion to the present Administration; the main scope of it being an argument against the South-Carolinian doctrine of nullification — It was probable from present appearances, that the Successors to the last Administration would do justice to themselves; and I felt no inclination to assist them in the performance of the Task — I propose to confer with these gentlemen again, before the day, which I am expecting, with an anxiety and dejection of Spirit, almost incredible to myself, and of which I am ashamed ≈ I read before dinner a few pages of my father's Journals, and towards Evening a few pages of Loudon's Encyclopaedia of gardening — Live and learn says the Adage — but at my time of life is it possible to learn any thing? — They say Cato, learnt Greek after he was sixty — I doubt if he learnt it well.

———

[July 1831]
3. IV:30. Sunday. ≈ I was occupied much of the day in writing a closing paragraph for my Discourse — At this late hour I absolutely sickened at that which I had written — It was gloomy, inauspicious, and affectedly rather than affectingly full of myself — The new paragraph, totally changed its character: gave to the future an aspect of hope and gladness instead of despondency — urged to generous and energetic action, and to calm reliance on a superintending Providence — leaving a slight allusion to my own age and proximity to my end, at the close; but merely to give additional Solemnity to the dying Sentiment of my father, and linking the perpetuity of Union with that of Independence pointing all at the same time to the future Prospects of my Auditory — As it is, my judgment pronounces the Peroration good — As it was till this very day, it was execrably bad, and I was utterly unaware of it — My self-criticism, was disarmed by the pathos of a close, in the last words of my father, and I had not remarked the awkwardness of manner in which I had brought it forth — How severe a Censor, it behooves me to be upon myself.

4. IV. Monday — Sun rose 4:29. Independence Day ≈ My Discourse occupied an hour and twenty-five minutes in the

delivery, and I omitted, about one third of what I had written — It was well received — frequently interrupted by applause, and closed with Plaudits long continued — The procession then moved to the Town Hall, where was a dinner of about one hundred and twenty persons, Mr. Thomas Greenleaf presided — The dinner was too long; and after six or seven of the Toasts, had been given, alternating with Symphonies and Songs, I rose and said — Friends, Neighbours, and Fellow Townsmen — "I will now with your permission, take my leave of you, for the present; and before parting from you, wish to add a few, a very few more last words, to the many, which you have already heard this day, from me, with so much indulgence — They are, first to thank you heartily for that Indulgence; and then to propose a Toast in honour of the primitive Mother of New England — May I add, the primitive Mother of those principles which have made this day, a day of Glory and of Joy — The Plymouth Colony.

To that Colony, our native Town, did not originally belong — But I see around me more than one, of those who number among their Sires, the fortunate youth, from the Mayflower, who first alighted upon the Rock — The Legislature of this Commonwealth have seen fit to link you in political Association with the District of Plymouth, and to that Association I am indebted for the honour of having been selected as their and your Representative in the Councils of the Union — an honour the more preciously prized by me, as a spontaneous and unexpected testimonial of confidence from that, which above all other Lands I am entitled to call *my own, my native Land* — Upon this day, I cannot forget Plymouth and her History — I cannot forget the Mayflower, and the social compact of her Pilgrims — I propose to you the following Toast — The Root, struck from the Seed of the Mayflower, and the Plant ascending from it — Salutary — Fruitful — Perennial — It shall rise to Heaven, and Over-spread the Earth." This was received with three times three, and I left the Hall and walked home. There was a fresh breeze of air all day; but the Sun was blazing and the Thermometer above 90 — I never experienced atmospherical heat more intensely than from the Time, when I left my house in the morning till my return to it after dinner — In delivering the Discourse, I began a pitch too high, and, before I had got through the first page strained my voice till it broke — I thought I should be totally disabled from proceeding, but by lowering the pitch gradually found relief and spoke much more easily towards the close, than at the beginning.

———

7. IV:30. Thursday. Received this Morning a Letter from Samuel L. Gouverneur, of the 4th and one from George Sullivan of the 5th at New-York announcing the decease at 3 O'Clock in the afternoon of the 4th of the Ex-President of the United States James Monroe; a man whose life has been marked with vicissitudes as great, as have befallen any Citizen of the United States since the beginning of our National Existence. An Officer of the Revolutionary Army, wounded at Princeton in December 1776 — a Member of the Confederation Congress — Then of the Senate of the United States — Minister to France under Washington's Administration. next, Governor of Virginia. Then Minister to France, Great-Britain and Spain — Governor of Virginia again — Secretary of State — Secretary of War, and eight years President of the United States; elected for the second Term by a vote of the Electors unanimous save one, his life for the last six years has been one of abject penury and distress, and they have brought him to a premature grave, though in the seventy-third year of his age. His administration happening precisely at the moment of the breaking up of old party divisions, was the period of the greatest tranquility which has ever been enjoyed by this Country — It was a time of great prosperity, and his personal popularity was unrival'd — Yet no one regretted the termination of his Administration, and less of popular veneration followed him into retirement than had accompanied all his Predecessors — His last days have been much afflicted, contrasting deeply with that triumphal procession which he made through the Union in the years 1817 and 1819.

———

13. IV:40. Wednesday. ≈ Mr. Seaver the Town Schoolmaster, and Secretary to the Committee of Arrangements for the celebration of the 4th sent for the copy of my Oration, which he was to take to the Printer at Boston — I sent it accordingly; a copy of the whole discourse, as I had written it — to which I added a copy of my version of the 149th Psalm, sung by the

Choir, immediately before I spoke — Thus goes into the world my third Independence day Rhapsody, to be like the second lacerated, and cut to pieces by the Critics, after having been received with the warmest approbation by the auditory.

———

19. IV:15. Tuesday. Began the version of the third Psalm — Charles and his wife left us — He went as usual this morning to Boston, and did not return — His wife went after dinner. Mine took her in the Carriage into town, and came back alone this Evening — They have been here two Months, from the 18th of May, and have made our residence here very cheerful. But she is expecting to be confined shortly, and they both prefer that this Event should take place in Boston — It is probably a full month distant, but I have forborne to utter a word of interference with their inclinations, in a matter so immediately concerning themselves. If there is a lesson necessary for my peace of mind in this world, it is to form no strong attachment to any person or thing that it contains; and if I have a weakness growing upon me above all others it is that of attaching myself inordinately both to persons and things — To persons from whom I must part — To things which bring me nothing but disappointment — The remnant of my days so far as my physical and intellectual powers will hold out, ought to be devoted to reading and writing, to honour the memory of my father and mother — I suffer numberless things day after day to divert me from them; and whatever I undertake turns to bitter dust and ashes.

———

31. IV:30. Sunday ≈ *Day*. I had not even completed the revisal of my fourth of July Oration for the press, when the application came from the corporation of Boston, to deliver an Eulogy upon Mr. Monroe, which I had scarcely the right, and could not have the inclination to decline — But it has from that time oppressed me with reading and writing almost night and day, in the heart of a Summer damp and sultry beyond example — And I have been not less oppressed with anxiety than with labour — The Oration succeeded far beyond expectation and has been hitherto spared very generally by malignant criticism — Non nobis domine sed nomini tuo sit gloria — It touched upon popular topics, and presented them under new views

— This I cannot again do, nor can I do Justice to the subject without coming in collision with Passions and Resentments which will not sleep — There is a combination of parties against me including almost the whole population of the Country, and of which my former supporters are the most inveterate — The Clay Masons, and so called National Republicans — This Eulogy will furnish them an occasion to assail me — I now employ the day from morning dawn till dark in reading and writing, and all other business runs in arrear.

———

[August 1831]

25. III:30. Thursday — Boston Eulogy on James Monroe at Old South Church. ≈ The house was crowded to suffocation; the heat excessive — crowds of People at the Church door, wrangling and fighting to get in — Trucks, Waggons and Carriages rolling over the pavement in the Streets adjoining the Church, all the Time I was speaking; and as the Sun went down it grew so dark that it was becoming impossible for me to read my Manuscript. I was forced to read so rapidly that my articulation became indistinct, and my voice and my eyes affected both by the State of the Atmosphere, were constantly threatening to fail me — My situation was distressing but I pushed on — I shortened the discourse much more than I had intended, and finally overleaped ten or twelve pages at once. They lighted at last the two lamps at the sides of the Pulpit, and I got through in an hour and a half, omitting more than half of what I had written — There was constant attention in the auditory — occasional applause in one or two instances long continued and repeated.

———

30. IV. Tuesday. Lieut't Adams was here, and Mrs. Adams went again upon a fishing party at the Creek — I wrote a short Letter to S. L. Gouverneur at New-York, returning to him the Papers which he had sent me some weeks since; which were 1. A Letter from John Rhea of Tennessee to James Monroe, dated in June last (a copy) [2.] copy of a Letter from Mr. Gouverneur, to W. Wirt, asking his advice, whether this Letter should be shewn to Mr. Monroe; who was then drawing fast to his end — Two original Letters from Mr. Wirt, in answer, urging very earnestly that the Letter of Rhea should be shewn

to Mr. Monroe — Copy of a declaration of Mr. Monroe attested by two witnesses; and solemnly denying the Truth of Rhea's Statement — I have retained copies of Rhea's Letter, and of Mr. Monroe's declaration contradicting it — There is a depth of depravity in this Transaction, at which the heart sickens — A total disregard to Truth, is chargeable upon so many men of the very highest standing, in this age and Country as well as in all others; that in the estimation of the world, it seems scarcely to carry with it an imputation — But the working up of a circumstantial fabrication, by practising upon the driveling dotage of a political parasite is beyond the comprehension of an honest mind. Jackson's excessive anxiety to rest the justification of his invasion of Florida, upon a secret, collusive and unconstitutional correspondence with Mr. Monroe, can be explained, only by an effort to quiet the stings of his conscience for the baseness of his ingratitude to me. Writhing under the consciousness of the return which he has made to me; for saving him from public indignation, and defending him triumphantly against the vengeance of Britain and Spain, the Impeachment of Congress, the disavowal of Mr. Monroe, and the Court-Martial of Calhoun and Crawford, he struggles to bring his cause before the world and before posterity upon another basis — This basis is itself as rotten as his own heart. It is that his conquest of Florida, was undertaken and accomplished, not as I had successfully contended for him, upon principles, warranted by the Laws of Nations, and consistent with the Constitution of the United States, but by a secret fraudulent concert between him and Mr. Monroe in direct violation of the Constitution, and of all its conservative principles — To establish this he resorts to his own unprincipled Letter, which I never saw, to the recreant desperation of Crawford, and to the ravenous imbecillity of John Rhea — he has succeeded with them both — both have made themselves by impudent, unblushing falsehoods Panders to his unnatural Passions, and to glut his revenge upon me, for benefits such as he never received from any other man he has been labouring not only to blast the good name of Mr. Monroe, but to cover with infamy his own — His moral perceptions are so confused, and decomposed by his convulsive Passions, that in his eagerness to throw off his obligations to me, and to ruin the reputation of Mr. Monroe, he blinds himself entirely to the inevitable recoil upon himself. It is fortunate that Mr. Monroe lived and retained his faculties, to make a solemn and authentic declaration of the total falsehood of John Rhea's abominable statement.

———

[September 1831]

5. V. Monday. — Sun rose 5:35. Louisa Smith spent the day here with Mrs. Cushing — Price Greenleaf came after dinner, and examined the Apple and pear stocks which he had budded; and loosened the ligaments of some of them. He thought most of the buds had taken, and three or four [of] them had already put out shoots — I wrote to my Son John, and also a Letter to John C. Calhoun, to be enclosed with copies of my last fourth of July Oration, and of my Eulogy. Mr. Calhoun was a member of Mr. Monroe's Administration, and during its early part pursued a course from which I anticipated that he would prove an ornament and a blessing to his Country — I have been deeply disappointed in him, and now expect nothing from him but evil. His personal relations with me have been marked on his part with selfish and cold blooded heartlessness — Yet in his controversies of last winter, I sustained him as far as truth would warrant against the profligate falsehoods of Crawford — Since the publication of my 4th of July Oration, he has published what he calls his views of nullification, but has not been explicit in his exposition of them. I propose by sending him my two discourses to give him an opportunity if he pleases to discuss with me the question upon which we so essentially differ. I walked towards Evening to my brother's, and found him yet very dangerously ill — though apparently a little better than yesterday — After my return I read my fourth of July Oration to Mrs. Cushing, and the Ladies.

———

8. IV:30. Thursday. Finished yesterday the version of the 18th Psalm, and began this morning upon the 20th having already versified the 19th. This work comes on slowly but steadily — It exemplifies to me, what I have often had occasion in life to remark — The power of perseverance. A power which like the other faculties of the mind strengthens itself by exercise — It is

a virtue of the first order, and connected with the moral principle of undertaking none but honest ends, and with sagacity
to select useful ones is the certain indication of a great and
good man — My own perseverance has been and is very
imperfect — My purposes have been honest; so far as a mortal
may bear testimony to his honesty before God — Honest, allowing for the involuntary self-deception of the heart — My
judgment in selecting objects for persevering action, exceedingly defective, and that has been the great drawback to my
success in life — and by success I do not mean my own individual prosperity; for that with great vicissitudes has been far
beyond my deserts — but I mean the success of usefulness to
my fellow Creatures — I have wasted my perseverance upon
trifling objects — the result of which could have no operation
on the happiness of mankind — One of the best objects of
practical perseverance with which a young man should begin
life, and pursue to its end, is the keeping of a diary — This I
began at twelve years of age — but I have failed of perseverance in keeping it, at least twenty times, and often for long and
most important intervals — Few men however, have in this
point had perseverance equal to mine; and they were assuredly
useful men — But I have filled my journals with trash, and
with every whimsey that passed across my mind — This has
been an idle waste of time, and a multiplication of books to no
end and without end — I greatly doubt the usefulness of this
end upon which I am now engaged; a metrical version of the
Psalms — But I have ventured upon it, and persevere in it.

———

[November 1831]
9. V:30. Wednesday. ≈ I called upon Nicholas Biddle at the
U.S. Bank; and received two dividends of my bank Stock, by
an order upon the branch Bank at Washington. I left with Mr.
Biddle my Certificate of Stock to be sold, and the proceeds to
be remitted according to such directions as I may give. I told
him that as I might be called to take a part in public measures
concerning the bank and was favourable to it, I wished to divest myself of all personal interest in [it] — I indorsed my
name in blank on the certificate.

CHAPTER XI ❧ 1831–1835

Twenty-Second and Twenty-Third Congresses

[November 1831]

13. VI:30. Sunday — From Baltimore to Washington. ≈ I return to Washington with less tranquility of mind than at the last and the preceding Winter — That before me is of an aspect to which I look with an aching heart. — One experiment which I have made upon this Journey has been successful as far as it could succeed — I mean that of employing my time — I have lost none — Since I left Quincy, I have composed 23 Stanzas of versions of the Psalms — all bad — but as good as I could make them.

———

18. V:45. Friday. Began the version of the 39th Psalm — one of those with which I have found the greatest difficulty and of which I have been obliged finally to put up with a complete failure — There are some of which the versification comes to me almost as easily as prose — Some which I labour painfully for hours, and give up in despair; substituting a mutilated fragment for the whole Psalm — and some, upon which after ranging through many varieties of expression altogether dissatisfactory, I finally alight upon a turn which pleases my fancy — There is an agitation of mind in this habit of composition resembling the intense interest of a gamester in the fluctuations of his fortune; and not unfrequently I am quite delighted with my success in producing a Stanza, which upon reperusal a week after sickens me as flat, stale and unprofitable. — I walked round the Capitol this morning — There was a double attack upon me this morning in the National Journal, which I take for the Clay Declaration of War — It has been preceded by clandestine hostilities enough. — I am still engaged in answering the Circular from the Committee on the question of imprisonment for debt: my opinions are not all favourable to their views, and it might be more prudent for me to give a short and unmeaning answer to them; evading in substance their question — but it is not in my nature — My life has been

spent in stemming currents of popular opinions and until lately, with occasional and great success — But the runs of luck in life, are as at whist — The tide in the Affairs of men when it has once begun to ebb, will go down. This free and bold expression of my opinion which I disdain to withhold will hasten my downward course, and nothing can redeem it — Let me fulfil my destiny; and so far as may be possible sustain my character.

———

21. VI:45. Monday. ≈ Finished my Letter on Imprisonment for debt — in which without opposing the project of those who are pressing for the total abolition of it, I have endeavoured to impress them with the necessity of providing some other substitute for the security which it gives to credit. In this light it has not been viewed by those gentlemen — They consider nothing but the popularity of relieving prisoners from jail — I shall surely get no thanks from any one, for pointing to the consequences of their innovations upon the security of property, and upon fidelity to contracts, as well as upon Credit. — There was a great change of weather this Evening, from a month, fair and mild, to a very heavy peal of Thunder, and Snow — The child is most distressingly ill.

22. IV:45. Tuesday. Finished the version of the 40th Psalm and began the 41st — The ground was this morning covered with Snow, and the gale through the Night was tempestuous — The union of heavy thunder and sharp lightening with Snow, was a coalition of elements almost as strange as that which terrified Horace into devotion — namque Diespiter, Igni corusco nubila dividens Plerumque, per purum tonantes. Egit equos volucremque currum. Ode 1.34. I walked round the Capitol Hill before dinner — Wrote to my Son Charles and read the remainder of Edward Everett's Address to the New York Institute, and some pages of Opinions upon Masonry — This Institution of Free-Masonry is one of the phenomena in the History of mankind — That it is a most pernicious institution I am profoundly convinced — and how it has arisen and grown, and spread over the world, and drawn into its vortex so many wise and good and great men is scarcely credible — There is however a charm in secret, and in exclusive association

— In principle it is unjust, but in power it is great. Here is Secresy — there is the enjoyment of exclusive privilege — Then come Mystery — terrifying Ceremonies; horrid oaths and penalties; sprung upon the initiated by surprise — All mingled up with benevolence and Charity — with pretensions to antiquity coeval with the Creation — continual prayers and lessons from the Bible, mingled up with impostures about Solomon, Hiram king of Tyre, Hiram Abiff. John the Baptist and John the Evangelist — as absurd and senseless as they are false — Religion — Charity — pure benevolence and morals, mingled up with superstitious rites, and ferocious cruelty, form in their combination Institutions the most powerful and the most pernicious that have ever afflicted mankind — They account for the prevalence of the Mahometan Religion — They governed the crusading ages — They are in great part the foundation of the Monastic Institutions; and especially of the Jesuits — I believe Free-Masonry to be an Institution less than two Centuries of Age, but it has undoubtedly borrowed much from others of higher antiquity — and probably something from the Eleusinian Mysteries.

—

[December 1831]
5. V:45. Monday. — Fahrenheit 13 — Sun rose 7:17. The first Session of the Twenty-second Congress of the United States commenced — Half an hour before Noon I attended in the Hall of the House of Representatives, and took the Seat N. 203. At Noon the Members were called to order, by Matthew St. Clair Clarke, the Clerk of the House in the last Congress. — The members were called alphabetically by States, and two hundred answered to their names — one or two more afterwards came in — The Clerk sent round the ballot-boxes to collect the votes for Speaker, and when the boxes were returned to his Table, asked Mess'rs Bates of Maine, Crawford of Pennsylvania and M'Coy of Virginia to act as Tellers — There were only 195 votes returned, of which 98 were necessary to a choice. Andrew Stevenson of Virginia had 98 votes, and was declared to be chosen — Elutheros Cooke a member from Ohio, brought up his vote to the Table after the other votes had been given in — The Tellers refused to receive it. His vote was for Joel B. Sutherland of Philadelphia, the principal

competitor of Mr. Stevenson; who had 54 votes — If Cooke's
vote had been received Stevenson would not have been chosen
at that ballot, and probably not at-all — There were votes for
John W. Taylor 18; Wickliffe 15; and some others would have
rallied after two or three ballots upon Sutherland; the two
Candidates are both men of principle according to their interest, and there is not the worth of a wisp of straw between their
value — Phineas L. Tracy told me that he, and his Anti-Masonic
friends had agreed to vote for John W. Taylor and I voted for
him. I was pleased that there was not a second ballot; for I was
unwilling to be brought to the test whether I would under any
circumstances vote either for Stevenson or Sutherland. He
seemed disposed to contest the election, and said he had
known yesterday that Stevenson would have 98 votes, and that
he could not get one more — The Speaker was conducted to
the Chair by Mr. Newton the veteran of the house, who
administered to him the Oath to support the Constitution of
the United States. He administered the same oath to all the
members — calling them up by States — those of the largest
States in two or three divisions. Mr. Jesse Speight a member
from North Carolina, then moved the appointment of Matthew St. Clair Clarke as Clerk to the House by Resolution
which he took from the Journal of the House at the first Session of the last Congress — in this form Mr. Speaker, I move
the following Resolution — Then without reading it he took it
to the Clerk's table where it was read, and upon the question
being put it passed without opposition. The Speaker had made
his acknowledgments to the House from the Chair in a short
Speech, prepared for the occasion, but not well adapted to
the circumstances of his election. Resolutions of notice to the
Senate, and for a joint Committee to notify the President were
adopted — Resolutions also passed for furnishing the members
with newspapers equivalent to three daily; and for the appointment of two chaplains to interchange weekly; and the house
adjourned before two O'Clock — There were two districts of
Massachusetts unrepresented; seven trials in each of them to
hold the election having failed to obtain for any one person a
majority of all the votes returned — I suggested to Mr. Everett
the propriety of a Letter from the delegation to Governor
Lincoln, requesting him to recommend to the Legislature a

revision of the Law, to secure a full representation to the State at the opening of every Congress — Everett said if I would draw up such a Letter, he would sign it.

———

11. VI. Sunday. I am closing the task of bringing up the arrears of this diary, which had been for upwards of four months running up, and which it has taken me, one of close application to retrieve. Mr. Heuberger is the German Swiss, who some time since came here with Mr. Hassler — He called again this morning, and brought with him two small boxes of antient medals coins and gems, and two sheets of paper with lists of the whole collection which he wishes to sell — He has eighteen hundred of them and supposes they would be well adapted to the Museum of any College or University, as undoubtedly they would — but this worthy Gentleman has mistaken the taste of the Country to which he has brought these Treasures. Democracy has no forefathers — It looks to no posterity — It is swallowed up in the present, and thinks of nothing but itself — This is the vice of Democracy, and it is incurable — Democracy has no monuments — It strikes no Medals — It bears the head of no man upon a Coin — Its very essence is Iconoclastic. This is the Reason why Congress have never been able to erect a Monument to Washington — There is therefore no prospect for Mr. Heuberger to dispose of his jewels here. ≈

12. VI. Monday. — Sun rose 7:20. Fahrenheit 24 growing colder. Attended the House of Representatives. The appointment of the standing Committees was announced and I am Chairman of the Committee of Manufactures, a station of high responsibility, and perhaps of labour more burdensome than any other in the house — Far from the line of occupation in which all my life has been passed, and for which I feel myself not to be well qualified — I know not even enough of it to form an estimate of its difficulties. I only know that it is not the place suited to my acquirements and capacities such as they are. Yet as little as I esteem the Speaker I have no fault to find with him for the Appointment. The Petitions were called for, by States, commencing with Maine and proceeding Southward. I presented fifteen Petitions signed numerously by

Citizens of Pennsylvania, praying for the abolition of Slavery and the Slave-trade in the District of Columbia — I moved that they should be referred to the Committee on the District of Columbia — The practice is for the member presenting the Petition to move that the reading of it be dispensed with, and that it be referred to the appropriate or to a select Committee — but I moved that one of the Petitions presented by me should be read; they being all of the same tenor, and very short. It was accordingly read — I made a very few remarks chiefly to declare that I should not support that part of the Petition which prayed for the abolition of Slavery in the District of Columbia. It is so long since I was in the habit of speaking to a popular Assembly — the Assemblies in which I had ever spoken extemporaneously have been comparatively speaking so little popular; and I am so little qualified by nature for an extemporaneous Orator, that I was at this time not a little agitated by the sound of my own voice — I was not more than five minutes upon my feet; but I was listened to with great attention, and when I sat down it seemed to myself as if I had performed an achievement — So small and trivial are the things which often hang like burdens upon the Soul — I am grateful that this one has been removed — After the petitions were gone through the Resolutions to be offered were called for — Again by States; after which Mr. Wayne of Georgia moved that the House should resolve itself into a Committee of the whole upon the State of the Union. The Speaker requested General Adair to take the Chair — Mr. Wayne then offered a Series of Resolutions distributing the President's Messages into paragraphs, and referring each subject to a distinct Committee most of them were adopted as proposed; but the one to be referred to the Committee of Ways and Means made no mention of the Bank of the United States — George M'Duffie Chairman of that Committee moved as an Amendment to the Resolution, the words "so much as relates to the Bank of the United States" upon which a debate between those two members followed, in which Wayne pointedly referred to the contradictory opinions respecting the rechartering of the Bank of the United States, contained in the President's Message, and in the Annual Report of the Secretary of the Treasury upon the finances. M'Duffie's amendment prevailed by a large majority — Charles A. Wickliffe moved an additional Resolution to refer the subject of internal improvement to a select Committee — Wayne said he had left it out, because there was nothing about internal improvement in the Message — and there had already been appointed a Committee on Internal Improvement, on a Resolution offered by C. F. Mercer of Virginia — Wickliffe's Resolution was adopted in Committee of the whole, but in the house, was laid upon the table — The House adjourned about half past two. I spoke to the Clerk for the papers of sundry petitioners for pensions and for clearing a river; concerning which I had received Letters from Mr. Joseph Richardson my Predecessor as Representative of the District and from S. A. Turner — He said I should have them to-morrow Morning — I walked with John W. Taylor to his lodgings; but his dinner immediately came in and I promised to call upon him again. He said there had been a call of a meeting of National Republicans at Prentiss's last Thursday; that five persons had attended, that he had received an invitation but was confined to his bed and could not attend — That the Anti-Masonic Members were not invited — Mrs. Frye dined with us.

13. V:30. Tuesday. ≈ I had asked Mr. Everett to consent to exchange places with me on the Committees — To take my place as Chairman of the Committee of Manufactures, and to give me that of second upon the Committee of foreign Relations, where he was placed; to which he readily agreed if the Speaker would consent which he said he did not believe he would — After the adjournment I went into the Speaker's chamber, and proposed to him to authorize the exchange, but he said he had no power to make the alteration — That the appointment of Committees being once made was the act of the House, and he had no authority to change the arrangement in any manner. I referred him to an arrangement which had been made a few years since when John Randolph, was made Chairman of the Committee of Ways and Means, and George M'Duffie the second, and after a few days Mr. Randolph was at his own request excused, and M'Duffie acted as Chairman of the Committee during the remainder of the Session — He said it was the Act of the House upon a Letter from Mr. Randolph himself

and was granted with great reluctance — He then expatiated upon his discharge of his duties as Speaker — upon the general expectation of the Nation — Upon importance of that place above all others, particularly at this time — I told him that so far as concerned myself I was satisfied — I had no complaint to make; and he had discharged his duty as Speaker — but I had two reasons for wishing to be excused — one that I did not feel myself competent for the Station which he had assigned to me — the other that the state of my health was not fitted to the burden which it imposed upon me — He repeated that he had no power over the arrangement of the Committees after the Appointments were made. That the house alone could excuse me, and if they should, another distinguished Citizen from the East would be appointed, but not Mr. Everett — The humiliation of asking to be excused by the house I cannot yet endure, and I shall submit to my fate.

———

26. V:30. Monday. Snow. Mrs. Adams has watched the two last Nights with her sick grandchild Mary Louisa, severely afflicted with the Scarlet fever. I finished the version of the 57th and began that of the 58th Psalm — This employs on the average about two hours every morning, and is delightful occupation when I fancy myself successful — that is about one Psalm in five — The rest is teizing and bitter disappointment as especially it was this morning. I had a succession of visitors all this morning ≈ Mr. Clay asked me how I felt upon turning boy again to go into the House of Representatives — I told him that hitherto I had found the labour light enough, but the house had not yet got to business — He repeated several times that I should find my situation extremely laborious and that I knew right well before — Labour I shall not refuse so long as my hand — my eyes and my brain do not desert me — but what shall I do for that which I cannot give? — Mr. Clay spoke of the reduction of the Tariff, and said there were other points to be considered, besides the taking off of the duties — One was changing the mode of Valuation which he deemed highly important — Another was shortening the credits of importations, and introducing a system of cash payments as for the Public Lands — A third was the expediency of increasing the duties upon some of the protected Articles, so as to make them

nearly prohibitory — To increase the duties for the express purpose of diminishing the revenue, was an idea well deserving of meditation, and which had not occurred to me — I asked whether in the gracious operation of remitting taxes, there would not be a mixture of harshness in extending the protective system; and a danger of increasing the discontents of the Southern States, already bitterly complaining of the unequal operation of the duties — He said the discontents were almost all, if not entirely imaginary or factitious, and in almost all the Southern States had in a great measure subsided. Here is one great error of Mr. Clay.

———

28. V. Wednesday. Snow. ≈ In the Evening at seven I attended the meeting at Everett's — Appleton, Bates, Clay, Condict, J. Davis, Dearborn, Ellsworth, Evans, Huntington, J. S. Johnston, H. Niles, Pendleton, Stewart, J. W. Taylor, Vinton, and two others were there — Chilton Allan the Representative from Mr. Clay's District in Kentucky, and J. M. M'Kinnan, a member of the House from Pennsylvania. Niles was there at the request of some of the members of the Committee who reported to the Meeting — Mr. Clay was chairman of the Committee; and the Report was the draught of a Bill to be presented forthwith to the Senate for the immediate and total repeal of all the duties upon tea, coffee, spices, indigo, and many other Articles, almost the whole duty upon wines, and effecting a diminution of revenue for the coming year 1832 of upwards of seven millions of dollars — This is Mr. Clay's Scheme, which he has already attempted in the Senate, as General Dearborn attempted it in the house — It is now to be attempted in this form. Mr. Clay laid down the Law of his system — He said the Policy of our adversaries was obvious — to break down the American System, by accumulation of the revenue — Ours therefore should be specially adapted to counteract it, by reducing immediately the Revenue, to the amount of seven or eight Millions this very coming year. He would hardly wait for the first of January to take off the duties — And he would adhere to the protective system, even to the extent of increasing the duties on some of the protected Articles — Mr. Clay's manner with many courtesies of personal politeness, was exceedingly peremptory and dogmatical ≈

Clay's motive is obvious. He sees that next November at the choice of Presidential Electors, the great and irresistible Jackson electioneering cry, will be the extinction of the debt — By the instant repeal of all these duties, he wants to withdraw seven or eight Millions from the Treasury, and make it impossible to extinguish it by the 3ᵈ of March 1833 — It is an electioneering movement, and this was the secret of these Meetings; as well as of the desperate effort, to take the whole business of the reduction of the Tariff into his own hands. — When I remarked that the Bill would meet with opposition from many who might favour all its provisions, but would be governed in their votes by political and party Considerations, he said the subject should be treated without reference to any political considerations, and that he regretted there were any political considerations connected with himself.

—

[January 1832]
1. V:30. Sunday.

> O God, unto my prayer attend
>   O, lead me to the Rock on high
> For I, from Earth's remotest end
>   With heart oerwhelm'd to thee will cry.
> Thou art my Shelter, thou my Tower
>   My Soul to reach thy Temple Springs
> Trusts to the refuge of thy Power
>   Safe in the covert of thy wings   Psalm 61, v. 1–4.

Began the day by reading the 4ᵗʰ and two succeeding Chapters of Deuteronomy; and then made the version of the 61ˢᵗ Psalm, of which the above Stanza contains the first four verses or one-half — Deeming it eminently suited to the time and Circumstances I place it at the head of my Diary for the commencing year, and believe that the Trust in God which it imports is my sole reliance for this world and the next ≈ I began yesterday the rough draft of a Report to be laid before the Committee of Manufactures.

2. VI. Monday. Began the version of the 62ᵈ Psalm. The Presidential Mansion was open this day at Noon, and some of its overflowings came over the Square — From Noon till three there was a succession of visitors — Foreign Legations, Mem-

bers of Congress — Citizens, Shawanese Indians and Quakers — Officers of the Army and Navy, and some Strangers. Among the company was Mr. Smith the Register of the Treasury, and Major Lewis the Second Auditor of the Treasury whom I did not know. In a casual conversation with them, I adverted to the remark of Gibbon, that the courage of a Soldier is the cheapest quality in human Nature — By the looks of some persons present, I saw it was thought I had a special meaning in what I said, when in truth it was a mere thoughtless indiscretion.

———

5. VI. Thursday. Finished the version of the 63^d and began that of the 64th Psalm. I walked to the Capitol and attended the Committee on Manufactures at eleven this Morning. Dr. Condict, Mr. Findlay, Mr. Dayan, and John S. Barbour were present. Henry Horn and J. T. H. Worthington absent. They had met at ten, misnotified by the boy — though I had given him a written notification to shew them; appointing the hour to meet at 11. I read to them the answer of the Secretary of the Treasury to the Letter I had written him asking for information — and I proposed to them the question whether the remission of duties should be postponed till after the extinguishment of the National debt — and whether the whole debt should be paid off before the 3^d of March 1833 — I found opinions not at all matured or concurring on this subject — The opinion of Mr. Condict and Mr. Findlay was rather in favour of a considerable remission of duties immediately, Mr. Barbour's more decisively so, and Mr. Dayan wishing to proceed to a reduction of the Tariff without reference to that question — I read a Letter from Mr. J. B. Brown, which had been put into my hands yesterday by Mr. Davis. The Committee agreed to meet again next Monday Morning at eleven. Then adjourned and I entered the house just as the Speaker took the Chair. Sundry Resolutions were offered and Bills reported and read — The rule itself limiting the debates upon Resolutions to one hour was modified — The Bill for adjusting the claim of the State of South-Carolina was taken up, on the motion of Mr. M'Coy to refer the Bill, and the Report of the Committee of Military Affairs, to the Committee of Claims. Mr. M'Coy was not in the house, and I made a short speech in favour of the reference to

the Committee of Claims, which brought up M'Duffie, Speight, Everett, Burges, Reed, J. Davis and Drayton against me — Lewis Williams alone supported me; and the motion for reference was rejected by a large majority. The question then came upon the Bill, but it was near four O'Clock, and the house adjourned — What shall I do upon the lesson of this day? The Committee on Manufactures do not agree with my principles with regard to the payment of the debt — a speech of ten minutes brings down upon me a swarm from all quarters of the house, among whom three members from my own State — What is it? as I was coming home I overtook Stevenson the Speaker, who told me I was unquestionably right upon the principle, and that twenty members had told him they would have voted with me, but that it would have seemed like casting an imputation upon the military Committee — Shall I not take warning from these Symptoms of universal opposition? — Shall I not feel that my prudence and my escape from utter ruin depends upon my abstaining from taking part in all debatable questions; and is this compatible with the duties of my Station? —

———

10. V:30. Tuesday. Mr. Lewis is a Member of the Society of Friends and has taken much part for the last twenty years in the measures leading to the abolition of Slavery. He came to have some conversation with me upon the subject of Slavery in the District of Columbia — I asked him if he had seen the remarks that I made on presenting the Petitions from Pennsylvania — He said he had. But wished to know my Sentiments upon Slavery — I told him I thought they did not materially differ from his own. I abhorred Slavery; did not suffer it in my family, and felt proud of belonging to the only State in the Union, which at the very first census of population in 1790 had returned in the column of Slaves — none — that in presenting the petitions I had expressed the wish that the subject might not be discussed in the house — Because I believed discussion would lead to ill-will — to heart-burnings, to mutual hatred, where the first of wants was harmony, and without accomplishing any thing else. I asked him what he should think of the Inhabitants of the District of Columbia, if they should petition the Legislature of Pennsylvania to enact a Law, to compel all

the Citizens of that State to bear arms in defence of their Country? He said he should think they were meddling with what did not concern them. I said the people of the District of Columbia, might say the same of Citizens of Pennsylvania, petitioning for the abolition of Slavery, not in that State itself but in the District of Columbia. He said there were many persons of that opinion and he had been very desirous of distinctly knowing what my Sentiments upon the subject were.

———

28. VII. Saturday. ≈ We had a company of Gentlemen to dine: among whom the two Agents of the French Government de Beaumont and Tocqueville, who have been round to New-Orleans and through the Western Country, since I met them at Mr. Biddle's in Philadelphia — I had a long conversation with Beaumont after dinner — He had many inquiries respecting the political and Literary Institutions of this Country. He complained of not having been able to obtain all the information he had desired on these Subjects; but spoke with great Satisfaction of what he had seen and heard at Boston.

———

31. V:15. Tuesday. Began the version of the 73^d Psalm. Mr. Johnston of Louisiana called upon me this morning with his Colleague in the Senate newly elected, Mr. Waggaman, who apologized for not having called upon me before — They found me reading the Speeches still publishing, upon the nomination to the Senate of Martin Van-Buren as Minister to Great-Britain. Hayne and Miller from South-Carolina, Poindexter of Mississippi, and Moore of Alabama, by uniting with them accomplished their object, with the casting vote of the Vice-President — Mr. Johnston asked me if I knew any thing of a Treaty negotiated by G. W. Erving in Spain, by which the Rio del Norte was to be the boundary between the United States and Mexico — I said there certainly never had been such a Treaty. He said the President had assured them that there was, and that the proof of it was in the Department of State — I said I had no doubt this was one of G. W. Erving's lies, as there was not a greater liar upon Earth — That I was perswaded that the only colour for it that could be produced would be a Letter from him, written after the conclusion of the Treaty with Onis, in which detailing some interview that

he had with the Spanish Minister Pizarro he had said something from which Erving pretended to infer that they would
give up the boundary to the Rio Bravo — Johnston said there
was a Treaty with Mexico now before the Senate, which confirmed the boundary of the Treaty with Spain. That the people
of Louisiana did not wish for the Province of Texas; but that
the President believed in this Treaty of Erving's. — I said I
knew the President had been labouring very hard to get this
Province of Texas. That he would not get it by Treaty with
Mexico; but I believed the increasing Settlements in Texas
were all from this Country and that the inhabitants would
prefer to belong to the United States rather than to Mexico;
and it might perhaps be taken, as Florida was taken in 1812 —
But there would be one difficulty in it; as slavery had been
abolished in that Country. Johnston said that was only by a
Military decree, which the people there had resisted. — It was
only such a decree as Bolivar had issued in Colombia — I
walked to the Capitol. In the House, Mr. Jenifer's Resolution
was taken up, and with an amendment of Mr. Archer was referred to the same Committee appointed upon the Memorial
presented yesterday by Dr. Condict — There was the same
agitation which never fails to arise upon the approach to any
topic connected with Slavery.

———

[February 1832]
20. V. Monday. Finished the version of the 78th Psalm — One
of the longest and most difficult in the whole collection — But
what is [the] difficulty? Whether I ought to pray for life and
health to complete this task, or for grace and self-knowledge
to abandon it, and commit to the flames what I have done, I
do not know. There is a level of poetical power which a man
may attain, and which he cannot transcend — It differs in different men; and mine is very low — I have known it these fifty
years, for so long have I written verses, and yet I persevere. I
have published very little, and the success of that little has been
in no wise flattering — My prose writings published have fared
not much better — Why should I longer weary the world with
verse or prose? — This was a heavily rainy, gloomy day — I
rode to the Capitol — Being Monday, the States were successively called for presentation of Petitions, a most tedious oper-

ation in the practice, though to a reflecting mind a very striking exemplification of the magnificent grandeur of this Nation, and of the sublime principles upon which our Government is founded — The forms and proceedings of the House — this calling over of States for Petitions — the Colossal emblem of the Union over the Speaker's chair — the Historic Muse at the Clock, the echoing pillars of the Hall, the tripping Mercuries who bear the Resolutions and Amendments between the Members and the Chair — the calls of ayes and noes with the different intonations of the answers from the different voices — the gobbling manner of the Clerk in reading over the names — The tone of the Speaker in announcing the vote, and the varied shades of pleasure and pain in the countenances of the members on hearing it would form a fine subject for a descriptive poem.

———

22. VI. Wednesday. Centennial Birth-day of Washington. The Solemnities intended for this day at this place lost all their interest for me by the refusal of John A. Washington to permit the remains of George Washington to be transferred to be entombed under the Capitol. A refusal, to which I believe he was not competent, and into the real operative motives to which I wish not to enquire. I did wish that this Resolution might have been carried into execution. But this wish was connected with an imagination, that this federative Union was to last for ages. I now disbelieve its duration for twenty years, and doubt its continuance for five — It is falling into the sear and yellow leaf. For this among other reasons I determined that my celebration of this day, should only be by sharing in its devotions. I attended the performance of divine Service at the Capitol where a very ordinary prayer was made by Mr. Post the Chaplain to the House of Representatives and a singular though not ineloquent Sermon was delivered by Mr. Durbin, Chaplain to the Senate — His text was from Revelations 4:11 "Thou art worthy O Lord, to receive glory and honour and power: for thou hast created all things, and for thy pleasure they are, and were created." — The discourse was not written; nor was it composed to be preserved — It was extemporaneous and yet well suited to the occasion. It exalted the character of Washington perhaps too much — There were

close approaches to the expression of a belief, that there was something supernatural in his existence. There seemed little wanting to bring out a theory that he was a second Saviour of mankind — That he had a charmed Life, and was protected by a special Providence was explicitly avowed as a belief. The religious character of Washington was dwelt on with great emphasis. The House was well filled, but not crowded — The 148th and 100th Psalms were sung, without instrumental music, and a hymn at the close — The Vice-President, and Speaker of the House of Representatives were there, and the Judges of the Supreme Court; but neither the President of the United States nor any member of his Cabinet.

———

[March 1832]
1. VI. Thursday ≈ The apportionment Bill was taken up in the Senate where Mr. Webster made an eloquent Speech — I fear to no purpose — If reason or argument could effect any thing at this Time, I should hope that a great and inveterate defect in the apportionment Laws, might be remedied — But the conviction is pressed upon me more and more from day to day of my utter inability to render any valuable service to the Country — I would not prematurely despair of the Republic — but my forebodings are dark; and the worst of them is in contemplating the precipice before us — yawning at our feet, from the very pinnacle of prosperity to which we have been raised, and on which we stand.

2. V. Friday. ≈ Col'l Richard M. Johnson asked me to walk with him, and said he wished to speak with me of the state of the personal Relations between the President, Jackson and me — That he, Johnson, wished the relations of friendly personal intercourse between us to be restored — And that he thought the first advances to it should be made by him — He had also spoken of it, to Mr. Cass, the Secretary of War, who agreed with him on this point — I said that the personal intercourse between General Jackson and me had been suspended by himself, without informing me of the reason why — I had never known his reason — I had seen at the time in the Telegraph, an anonymous statement, that it was because *he knew*, that I had caused or countenanced abusive charges against

Mrs. Jackson in the Newspapers — The fact was not so — I never had caused or countenanced directly or indirectly any such publication. But General Jackson had never asked of me the question, and I did not deem it necessary to notice anonymous charges in the Telegraph. Col'l Johnson said he had always been sure it was so — That General Jackson had come here with dispositions entirely friendly to me, and intending to call upon me — That his mind had been poisoned here by scoundrel Office-seekers. That he was a warm tempered passionate man, and had been led to believe that I was the cause of those publications against his wife. But that he Johnson knew, that the President's feelings were now as friendly to me as they had ever been. He had told him that at the time of the debate in the House of Representatives on the Seminole War questions, he had received more assistance from me in drawing up the minority Report of the Military Committee than from all the world beside — He did not now speak by authority of General Jackson, but he knew that his disposition towards me was friendly, and had no doubt if a friendly advance from him would be accepted by me that he would make it — I said I had no desire that the interruption of social intercourse between us should continue, and was disposed to receive any friendly advance from General Jackson with kindness. He asked if I would accept an invitation to dine with him — I said no — That was an act of mere ordinary courtesy, usually paid to every Member of Congress, which I could not consider as an advance towards reconciliation — He asked if I would accept an invitation to a small and select party of friends — I said that would be liable to the same objection — It would pass for mere civility to a member of Congress, and set to the account of my present situation — He then asked what I should myself think proper — I said it was not for me to prescribe — I could only say that I was willing to receive in a spirit of conciliation any advance which in that Spirit, General Jackson might make — With this, the Colonel was satisfied and we parted — But it has placed me again in a situation of the delicacy of which it is my duty to be profoundly sensible ≈

3. VI. Saturday ≈ I received from Col'l Richard M. Johnson a Note without date or signature, which I copy for curiosity

— "Gen'l Jackson expressed great Satisfaction that I had the conversation with you which I detailed to him and expressed a wish that I should assure you of his personal regard & friendship & was anxious to have a social and friendly intercourse restored between you — There I left it and have satisfied my own mind. I shall communicate to Gov'r Cass the same and there it rests with me, having done what my heart suggested — The President expresses himself as perfectly satisfyed now that you never did countenance the publications to which I alluded & entertains for you the highest opinion as a man of honour &c. — Please destroy this when you read it." So far so good — The President is now perfectly satisfied that I never countenanced the Newspaper publications against his wife — and wishes the relations of social intercourse to be restored between us — Col'l Johnson is to tell this to Governor Cass and there leaves it. And what is now my duty to myself and to the Country? To seek Governor Cass? — no. — But to return to Col'l Johnson his paper instead of destroying it — letting him know that I have a copy of it — To thank him for the conciliatory part he has taken in this affair, and to assure him of my gratification that the President is satisfied I countenanced no newspaper publications against his wife. A restoration of friendly, social, and personal intercourse between President Jackson and me, at this time would attract much public notice, and could not fail to expose me to obloquy — The old federal party, now devoted to Mr. Clay have already more than once tried their hands at slandering me — They have drawn the sword and brandished it over my head — If I set my foot in the President's house, they will throw away the scabbard. I must therefore walk with extreme circumspection; even that will not protect me from their malignity — Some thing is due to myself — and the path is narrow to avoid on the one hand the charge of an implacable temper, and on the other of eagerness to propitiate the dispenser of power ≈

4. VI. Sunday. ≈ I received by the Mail several Letters, and with one of them a Memorial signed by several thousand persons upon the existing relations between the United States and the Cherokee Tribe of Indians, and the imprisonment of the Missionaries. The Memorial was the result of a very numerous

Meeting at New-York, and a Letter from a Committee of the Signers requested me to present and support it — Blunt wrote to me some days since, and mentioned that this Memorial would be sent to me, and I had intended to answer him, declining to present it — But his Letter had escaped from my memory, and remained unanswered — I now concluded, though after much hesitation, to present it to-morrow Morning, well assured that it will be of no avail, but willing to perform to the utmost of my power, my duty.

5. V. Monday. Rainy Morning — I rode to the Capitol, stopping at the Post-Office, to deliver a bundle of Speeches and documents, which I forward to the members of the Massachusetts Legislature from the County of Plymouth and others, among whom some of my friends. At the House it was the day for calling Petitions, and at the call of Massachusetts I presented the Memorial from New-York, concerning the Cherokees and the missionaries imprisoned in Georgia — it was read at my request, and I moved that it should be printed and referred to a Select Committee. This immediately gave rise to a debate which consumed the day — Speight moved its reference to the Committee on Indian Affairs — Bell, Chairman of that Committee, made one of those Speeches, common in the house, when a subject comes upon them unexpectedly, arguing against the reception of the memorial but closing with a repetition of Speight's Motion — The Georgia members were variously affected — Clayton raved, and said that before the decree of the Supreme Court should be carried into Execution, Georgia should be made a wilderness. — Thompson of Georgia finally moved that the Memorial be laid on the table — The question was taken by yeas and nays — 91 for 92 against laying on the table — The vote was first thought to be carried for Stewart of Pennsylvania had voted in the affirmative by mistake — He corrected it before the decision was announced — Wayne then attempted to move a postponement of consideration for a fortnight — Drayton actually moved a postponement. John Davis moved a reference to the Committee of the whole on the State of the Union — Everett had proposed this to me, and said it was an understanding between the parties that the subject should be discussed in Committee of the whole on the Union. This was

personally satisfactory to me, but did not discharge my duty to the Memorialists — Stewart moved the previous Question; but withdrew it at my request to give me the opportunity to give my reasons for not assenting to Davis's proposition — Beardsley of New-York followed with an argument that the Memorial should be laid on the Table — He said he thought I should have moved that myself. Cambreleng noticed that the Memorial, though from New-York, was not presented by any of the Representatives from that City. I said I had reason to believe, that it was from no disrespect to the members from New-York, that the memorial had been sent to me; but from a belief that it would be an un-pleasing task to them. It was no pleasing one to me. I had wished to decline it — But after examining the contents of the Memorial, had deemed it my duty to present it — The House were now in possession of it, and would dispose of it as they thought best — Stewart renewed his call for the previous ques-tion, which was seconded and taken — Wickliffe moved that the vote should be taken upon the simple question of commitment — I asked for the yeas and nays and they were taken. The Com-mitment was carried 96 to 93 — And then it was referred to the Committee of the Whole on the State of the Union without a division — This decision is precisely what I wished; though having moved for a select Committee, I did not feel at Liberty to assent to it — In Committee of the whole on the state of the Union, I may leave it to the management of other hands — and may take any part or no part in the debate as I may think proper.

———

11. V:30. Sunday ≈ I read attentively after Church the opinion of the Supreme Court of the United States, delivered by Chief Jus-tice Marshall in the case of Worcester the Missionary against the State of Georgia — It pronounces the Law of Georgia, under which Mr. Worcester is imprisoned in the Penitentiary, Unconsti-tutional, null and void — There is no doubt that the execution of this Sentence will be resisted, and defeated by the Government of Georgia — A cas[e] of collision between the Judicial authority of the Union, and the Authority of the State is now brought to an issue. The immediate Power is in the hand of the State — The Executive of the Union, is leagued with the State Authority; and the two Houses of Congress are about as equally as possible di-vided in the case — It is clear that the Constitution and Law of

the Union, and its judicial authority will be prostrated, before the despotic power of the State; and I would it were possible for me to anticipate the course to be taken, and the measure proper to be proposed, when the information shall come back — Convinced that I can effect nothing, my own course will be to withhold myself from all action concerning it.

14. VI:30. Wednesday. At the Committee on Manufactures at ten — Condict, Dayan, Worthington, Horn present, Findlay and John S. Barbour absent. My draft of a Bill was discussed without drawing near to any conclusion — Mr. Horn read a letter to him from a manufacturer expressing a strong aversion to repealing the minimum system of imposts — The majority of the Committee are equally averse to it, and I told them I would report just such a Bill as they should direct. But I assured them that I became from day to day more firmly convinced that this system of minimums must ultimately be abandoned, or that there would be an insurrection in the South — The main argument for sustaining the minimums in the Letter to Horn was that Congress would not directly levy so high duties as are levied by this winding process. We are to meet again to-morrow, and I told the members of the Committee I should wish to meet every morning until we shall have come to some determination upon my draught of a Bill ≈ At half past eight the house adjourned, and it was past nine when I got home — The family had just dined.

15. V:15. Thursday. ≈ Before the adjournment I asked to be excused from further service upon the Committee on Manufactures — but it was late; and at the request of Col'l Richard M. Johnson, and of other members, I waved the motion for the present, giving notice of my intention to renew it to-morrow Morning. In the Evening a Mr. Lane of Ohio brought me a note of introduction from Mr. Webster, and sat in conversation with me about an hour — It was the President's Birth-day — and the last Drawing-room for the Season, was held at the President's House.

16. V:45. Friday. ≈ In the House I renewed my request to be excused from further service on the Committee on Manufactures,

for reasons which I briefly stated. Much to my surprize it excited considerable debate — to abridge which, and particularly
at the request of Mr. Wayne of Georgia, I withdrew the motion
for the present, reserving to myself the right of renewing it ≈
Mr. Radcliff was here two hours of the Evening, discussing his
projected Railroad over the Isthmus of Panama. I received
Letters from Mr. Marston of Quincy and my brother's daughter Elizabeth and my wife had one from his, indicating his approaching dissolution.

17. V. Saturday. I attended this Morning at ten, the Bank-
investigation Committee ≈ While the House was in Session,
my Son John sent me a Letter from Charles received by the
mail informing me of the death of my dear and amiable brother
Thomas Boylston Adams, last Monday the 12th of March 1832
in his sixtieth year, which he would have completed on the 15th
of September next — I had engaged to dine this day with Mr.
Clay, but sent him an apology; and made one verbally to Mr.
Pendleton, who had invited me to dine with him next Tuesday
— The house adjourned soon after two O'Clock. I called and
saw Mr. Webster at his lodgings, and enquired of him the state
of the apportionment Bill — He said his Amendment had
failed by a vote of 24 to 23, Mr. Clay being absent, and probably to avoid voting against the Amendment, as if present he
would have done. He said Frelinghuysen and Tomlinson had
also voted against us; and now Chambers and Naudain were
called away by sickness in their families. Mr. Webster's dinner
was brought in, and I left him; telling him I would see him
again on Monday to have some Conversation with him on the
Tariff— Evening Snow Storm. I wrote to my brother's widow,
and to my Son Charles.

———

[December 1832]
2. V. Sunday. ≈ I answered the Letter yesterday received from
W. L. Stone, and one received this morning from Melvin Lord
at Boston. He says that his Edition of the Poem of Dermot is
all gone — That he has no copies left. — This has relieved me
from much anxiety — The puck of Critics are just opening
upon it; and if they now destroy it de fond en comble they
cannot injure the publisher. — My Shoulders must bear — I

comfort myself with the reflection that Jeffrey in the Edinburgh Review pronounced Byron a Poetaster, and Byron in his English Bards and Scotch Reviewers deals out the same measure to Walter Scott — I remember too that Byron was dissuaded by a friend from publishing his Childe Harold, and Scott from finishing his Waverley. A Poem is at best but a Lottery ticket and if I get a prize barely to repay me the price of my ticket, I must put up with it for good luck — Snow.

3. V:30. Monday. The Second Session of the Twenty-second Congress commenced. I walked to the Capitol. Andrew Stevenson Speaker of the House of Representatives took the Chair, precisely at Noon. Upon the call of the Roll by States 169 members answered to their names. Resolution passed, moved by J. W. Taylor, that a Message be sent to the Senate informing them that the House was organized and ready to proceed to business. Message from the Senate, that they were organized, and had chosen Hugh Lawson White of Tennessee their President — C. F. Mercer offered a Resolution that the members of the House would wear crape one month for Philip Doddridge. Ward moved the Resolution that the Members should be furnished with Newspapers — and Speight the joint Resolution for a Committee of both Houses to inform the President that they were ready to receive any Communication from him — Adjourned about half past one. The Salutations between the Members, were apparently good humoured and cordial. Walked home part of the way with Mr. Coke of Virginia, who appears highly excited upon the Tariff and Nullification. Thomas L. Thruston was here this Evening and introduced another Mr. Thruston — Mrs. Adams is recovering from her severe illness, but Louisa is yet very unwell — I answered a Letter from Theodore D. Weld, about exercise for Students.

4. V:30. Tuesday. I called this morning to see Mr. Brooks, but he was not at his lodgings. Mr. Josiah S. Johnston was there, and Captain Gordon of the Navy came in as a Visitor — Mr. Everett rode with me to the Capitol. In the House of Representatives the President's Message was received and read — It recommends a total change in the Policy of the Union, with

reference to the Bank, Manufactures, Internal Improvement and the Public Lands. It goes to dissolve the Union, into its original Elements, and is in substance a complete surrender to the nullifiers of South-Carolina — On motion of Speight of North-Carolina the Message was referred to the Committee of the whole House on the State of the Union, and ten thousand copies to be printed for the use of the Members of the House — Adjourned just after one — I went into the Library; and looked over some passages of Cary's Translation of Dante. Mr. Everett returned to his lodgings with me — I engaged him and Mr. Brooks to dine with us on Thursday next — I answered a Letter from James E. Hanslett a Student at the University of North-Carolina; who has written to me to enquire what I would advise him to read.

5. VI:30. Wednesday. Mr. Bell, Senator from New-Hampshire, paid me a Morning visit. The House of Representatives barely met and adjourned. The Senate did the same — The Message of the President gives great dissatisfaction to all those with whom I converse, and will be received with rapture by his partizans — He has cast away all the neutrality which he had heretofore maintained upon the conflicting interests and opinions of the different Sections of the Country, and surrenders the whole Union to the nullifiers of the South, and the Land-Robbers of the West. I confess this is neither more nor less than I expected, and no more than I predicted nearly two years since, in a Letter I think to Peter B. Porter. This Message already puts my temper and my discretion upon a trial equally severe — Dissimulation I cannot practice — Passion can do nothing but mischief. I walk between burning Ploughshares and have no support upon Earth, with a fearful foreboding that every effort I could make for the good of my Country would recoil in evil upon myself and my family.

———

10. V. Monday. ≈ In the House the standing Committees were announced — The Speaker has again appointed me Chairman of the Committee of Manufactures, but instead of Mr. Dayan of New-York has substituted Hoffman as a member, a change very inauspicious to the interest of Manufactures — Speight of N. Carolina moved the parceling out of the President's

Message to the Committees — The subject of the Bank concerns to a select Committee — the Committee of the whole on the State of the Union reported the other Resolutions to the House. That concerning the Bank was postponed; the motions of Amendment to be printed. Mr. Tomlinson sent for me to my Seat, and introduced to me Mr. Nicholls the preacher at St. John's Church yesterday, and assistant to the Bishop of Virginia at Richmond — The House adjourned at 3 P.M. and walking home with J. W. Taylor, we met Major Hamilton who gave him and he to me, the President's Proclamation to and against the South-Carolina nullifiers.

———

23. V:30. Sunday. I attended public worship this morning at the Capitol, to hear Mr. Hammett, the Chaplain of the House of Representatives — a Wesleyan Methodist — I had been much pleased and edified by his Prayers, before the Sittings of the House; and his discourse this day was not ineloquent — From John 18:36 "Jesus answered, my kingdom is not of this world: if my kingdom were of this world, then would my servants fight" — The House was crowded, and the preachers doctrine, against the Alliance of Church and State exceedingly popular — So popular, that it is dangerous in this Country to avow a different opinion — This was more of a stump electioneering Speech than of a Sermon — A compound of good principles, and of crudities. Full of Christian benevolence and meekness, yet bitterly censuring the Roman Catholic Church, tho' his fellow Chaplain at this very Session is a Roman Catholic Priest; and reviling the Church of England though assenting without qualification to the purity of her Creed — Upon the Alliance of Church and State, there is much to be said on both sides — It has produced enormous Evils — But whether any Religion can be maintained without it, is yet to be seen — The question is between Atheism and Superstition, between spiritual Anarchy and spiritual Servitude — Truth makes little progress when only one side of a question can obtain a hearing ≈

24. IV:30. Monday. The Committee of Manufactures having adjourned to ten O'Clock this morning, I attended at their chamber, in the Capitol — Mr. Hoffman was there and told me, that Dr. Condict had been with him; and they had agreed

to adjourn the Meeting till Friday Morning, Horn and Worth-
ington being absent, that is having gone home to enjoy
Christmas Holidays. Gen'l Findlay came soon after into the
Committee Room, and with him and Hoffman, I had a general
Conversation of upwards of two Hours. Mr. Hoffman is a New-
Yorker, of Dutch descent — A Lawyer, of the Democratic
Republican party, of the Albany Regency, and now a Van
Buren man. They are *now*, tenacious of State-rights, and polit-
ically leagued with the Anti-Tariff policy of the South — But as
Jackson men, they must be anti-nullifiers, and to these two
incoherent elements, subserviency to the Slave-holding policy;
and the personal animosities of President Jackson against
Vice-President Calhoun, may be traced the glaring inconsis-
tencies of principle, between the Message of this year and the
Proclamation. I told Hoffman that the real question now
convulsing this Union, was whether a population spread over
an immense territory, consisting of one great division, all
Freemen, and another of Masters and Slaves, could exist permanently together as members of one Community or not —
That to go a step further back, the question at issue was
Slavery. — He said he was of that opinion; and that if it should
come directly to a point nine-tenths, if not ninety-nine-
hundredths of his Constituents would take side against Slavery
— He said too that if this question with South-Carolina
should come to a struggle of force, and the nullifiers should
be overpowered, the whole population of the State would
emigrate to Mexico; but Findlay asked what they would do
with their Slaves — Slavery being abolished in Mexico, and all
the South American States except Brazil.

———

[January 1833]
4. IV:15. Friday. ≈ John C. Calhoun took this Morning his Seat
as a Senator from South-Carolina, having resigned his Office
as Vice-President of the United States — W. C. Rives had also
taken his Seat as a Senator from Virginia — I spoke with Mr.
Calhoun, and Mr. Clay — and with Mrs. White of Florida,
who invited me to a party at her House next Monday Evening
— When I returned to the House they were just about ad-
journing. Mr. Everett asked me to attend a Meeting of the
Massachusetts Delegation at his lodgings this Evening which I

did. The two Senators D. Webster and N. Silsbee, and the
members of the House Bates, Briggs, Choate, Dearborn, Everett, Grennell, Hodges, Kendall, Nelson and Reed were
present. Appleton and Davis absent. The object was a consultation upon the course to be pursued with regard to the
Tariff-Bill, reported by the Committee of Ways and Means —
The opinion was unanimous that its passage should be opposed; but no hope could be entertained by any one that the
passage of it in the House could be prevented — There were
some feeble hopes expressed that it might be defeated in the
Senate. — It was remarked that the protective system would
be abandoned by the Kentucky Delegation — Everett asked
me, if I thought Mr. Clay would be again a Candidate for the
Presidency — I said no doubt, if he could, with any prospect
of success — of which there was at present none.

———

9. V. Wednesday. ≈ Mr. Hoffman came up to me and we had
an hour's conversation upon the proposed Tariff-Bill. He professes to be a radical, and has all the contracted prejudices of
that political Sect. He has considerable Talent and some power
of Eloquence; but his whole system of Government is comprized in the maxim of leaving money in the Pockets of the
People. This is always the high road to popularity, and it is always travelled by those who have not resolution, intelligence
and energy to attempt the exploration of any other. Yet it appears to me that Hoffman is now somewhat distrustful of it
himself, and would take another road if he dared.

———

[February 1833]
13. V. Wednesday. ≈ At one O'Clock, the Senate came in —
Hugh Lawson White President pro Tempore of the Senate,
presided. The Electoral votes for President and Vice President
of the United States, were opened, counted, and announced
— Of 288 votes, Andrew Jackson had 219 for President —
Henry Clay 49. John Floyd 11. William Wirt 7. For Vice-
President, Martin Van Buren 189. John Sergeant 49 William
Wilkins 30. Amos Ellmaker 7. Wirt and Ellmaker were the
Antimasonic vote of Vermont. Floyd and Lee the nullification,
Anti-Tariff vote of South-Carolina. Clay and Sergeant the Ma-
sonic National Republican vote — and the 30 Jackson votes of

Pennsylvania, were given for Wilkins as Vice-President, instead of Van-Buren. Andrew Jackson was then proclaimed to be elected as President, and Martin Van-Buren as Vice-President of the United States for four years from the 4th of March next; the Senate withdrew, and the House shortly after 3 O'Clock adjourned. I had some conversation with John Davis, who disapproves the compromise between Clay and Calhoun; and said Clay had step'd over the Potowmack.

———

16. V:15. Saturday. Dr. Huntt bled Mrs. Adams this morning — In the House, several Appropriation Bills were passed in Committee of the whole, and reported to the House. Two or three private Bills occupied half an hour. There was a Call of the House, and three or four motions, successively to adjourn — No signs of the Tariff-bill. Drayton not in the House — Absent by reason of sickness — About two O'Clock the House adjourned. It was impossible to keep a Quorum in the House. I went to the Senate-chamber, which was so crowded that it was a full quarter of an hour before I could get in — Mr. Webster was speaking in answer to Mr. Calhoun, upon what is called the enforcing bill — His argument was to prove, that the Government of the United States was a Government of the People, and not a compact between States. It is both — and all Constitutional Government is a compact. He spoke till 3 when the Senate took a recess till 5 — Mr. Webster is a very handsome Speaker, but he overlaboured a point as plain as day; and he hung his cause upon a broken hinge, in maintaining that a Government was not a compact.

———

26. V:30. Tuesday. ≈ In the House, the Clay Tariff-Bill was passed by Previous Question 119 to 85. I desired to ask a question with regard to the construction of the first Section of the Bill, but was not permitted. The Revenue Collection Bill, otherwise called the Force Bill, or as the nullifiers call it the Bloody Bill was then taken up and a very disorderly struggle to put it off continued till four O'Clock, when the House took a recess until six.

———

[March 1833]
4. VIII. Monday. My health is wretched, and I know not all my disease. I consulted Dr. Huntt this morning and [he]

prescribed a blister on my arm. I have now an inflammation coming in the eye — Andrew Jackson was this day inaugurated for a second term of four years as President of the United States; and Martin van-Buren was sworn into Office as Vice-President. Mr. John Sergeant called here. He had attended the ceremony at the Capitol. The inaugural Speech was brief, and full of smooth professions. Sergeant himself was the Candidate for the Vice-Presidency of the National Republican Opposition. Henry Clay was their Candidate for the Presidency. They mustered 49 electoral votes, with the help of Massachusetts federalism. Had Mr. Clay been unshackled with Freemasonry, or manfully renounced it they would in all probability have carried the Election ≈

5. VII:30. Tuesday ≈ Haworth the Astrologer was here again and shewed me his Manuscript-Books of horoscopes — His calculations of Eclipses, Conjunctions and oppositions of Planets, and ascendant signs of the Zodiac. He says there will be trouble in South-Carolina, because there will be a total Eclipse of the Sun there in 1834. An argument as rational as nullification. I wished to know what his *theory* of Astrology was; but I find it will take too much time to study it. I wanted to compare it with Phrenology. ≈ We had a family party and others to dine with us.

6. VIII. Wednesday. The inflammation of my eye was disqualifying, and disheartening. Edward Everett was here; going to-morrow for home — He spoke to me of a purpose concerning which his brother had written to him — to unite the National Republicans and the Anti-Masons of Massachusetts upon me as a Candidate for the Office of Governor the next year, Mr. Lincoln having declined. Hallett has written to me on the same subject — I told Everett that I should much prefer to come again to the House of Representatives — That I was unwilling to involve myself in the Fracasseries of State Politics; and that I believed the Masonic National Republicans too much exasperated against me for my Anti-masonry to unite with the Anti-masons in supporting me — That if it could effect the union of those parties, I might consent to serve for a single year, though I had firmly resolved that I never would

accept that Office, having been all my life, with the exception
of a single year in the Senate of Massachusetts, in the Public
Service of the whole Union. ≈

7. VII. Thursday. ≈ Mr. Calhoun's Speech of 15 February upon
the enforcement bill, is published in the Telegraph. It contains
his system of nullification. His learning is shallow — His mind,
argumentative, and his assumption of principle, destitute of
discernment. His insanity begins with his principles; from
which his deductions are ingeniously drawn.

———

12. V. Tuesday. The analysis of the Law from Sinai, occupied
this morning with the Diary of yesterday till Breakfast — The
Report of the Minority of the Committee of Manufactures,
was published in the National Intelligencer of this day, 17
Columns — Visit from Mr. David Hoffman of Baltimore. He
is going to Europe, and had written to me, asking Letters of
introduction — I apologised to him for having delayed to answer him, and told him that I had not an acquaintance in Europe left to whom I could give him a Letter. He asked me for
a pamphlet copy of the Minority Report, which I promised
him. ≈ Then went to the office of the National Intelligencer,
and received from Mr. Gales the Manuscript of the Report. He
sent me forty copies of the Newspaper containing it, part of
which I distributed to some of my friends, despatching them
by this Evenings mail — This document is an appeal to the
People, I fear a vain and fruitless one, against the system of
Government promulg[at]ed in the last annual presidential
Message, leading to the dissolution of the Union.

———

[April 1833]
8. IV:30. Monday. ≈ Mr. Gales gave me several Boston Newspapers of Thursday last, containing Returns of the Congressional Elections — Choate, Everett, and Davis, certainly re-elected
— Bates, Grennell and Briggs doubtless — W. Baylies elected
in Bristol — Dearborn fails in Norfolk and Middlesex. F. C.
Gray in Boston — Cushing in North-Essex — Reed in Barn-
stable is chosen almost without opposition; and in twenty
of 24 Towns, constituting the 12th District, more than three

fourths of the votes are for me — This disposition of the People, is a subject to me of the most ardent gratitude to Heaven.

—

12. V. Friday. — From Baltimore to Philadelphia. Embarked in the Steamer George Washington, Captain Trippe the younger — On my way from the Tavern, Mr. Niles overtook me, and went with me to the Boat. — He has promised to republish my Minority Report in his Register. I asked him to print it from the Congressional document, for the sake of the quotation from Cicero in the Note, which he said he would. I promised to send him one of the documents from Philadelphia.

—

[May 1833]

10. V. Friday. ≈ The Newspapers contain accounts of a personal assault by the late Lieutenant Randolph of the navy, upon President Jackson, on board a Steamboat at Alexandria — He simply tweaked him by the nose, and went away — Jackson was much disposed to chastise him with his cane — but Randolph got away without even being arrested by the President's retinue. A bench warrant from the Circuit Court, and a Justice's warrant were issued against Randolph, but he got out of their reach, and out of the district into Virginia, before they could be served — A President of the United States pulled by the nose, is a new incident in the History of this Country; and as he himself has countenanced personal violence against members of Congress, he will not meet with much sympathy. The law provides no special penalty for this offence, the judicial proof of which would be a hundred times severer punishment upon the sufferer than upon the culprit. Randolph may run a risk of being mobbed, and certainly would be so, in a place where the President should be very popular — He is not so now, in the district of Columbia.

—

[June 1833]

7. IV:15. Friday. The first seedling Apple-tree that I had observed on my return here, just out of the ground was on the 22ᵈ of April. It had grown slowly but constantly since, and had put out five or six leaves — Last evening after my return from Boston I saw it, perfectly sound. This morning I found it

broken off, leaving one lobe of the seed leaves, and one leaf over it — This may have been the work of a bug, or perhaps of a caterpillar. It would not be imaginable, to any person free from hobby-horses, or fanciful attachments, how much mortification such an incident occasions — St. Evremond, after removing into the Country, returned to a City life, because he found himself in despair for the loss of a pigeon — His conclusion was that rural life induced exorbitant attachments to insignificant objects — My experience is conformable to this — My natural propensity was to raise trees, fruit and forest, from the seed. I had it in early youth, but the course of my life deprived me of the means of pursuing the bent of my inclination. One Shellbark walnut tree in my garden, the nut of which I planted 8 October 1804, and one Mazzard Cherry tree in the grounds north of The Stone of which I planted about the same time, are the only remains of my experiments of so ancient a date — Had my life been spent in the Country, and my experiments commenced, while I was at College — I should now have a large fruit-garden; flourishing Orchards of native fruit, and very valuable Forests — Instead of which, I have a Nursery of about half an acre of ground; half full of seedlings from five years, to five days old; bearing for the first time perhaps twenty peaches, and a few blossoms of Apricots and Cherries, and hundreds of seedlings of the present year, perishing from day to day, before my eyes.

———

17. III:45. Monday. Anniversary of the Battle of Bunker's Hill, and the burning of Charlestown; one of the first Events of which I have a personal recollection — Fifty eight years have since then elapsed — About one person in ten, then living yet exist — I was reminded of this anniversary, upon hearing with the rising Sun, a salute of 13 guns from Fort Independence; but passed the day in profound tranquility contrasting, with the deep and awful agitation of that day in 1775 — I am reading and making petty annotations upon the Book of Leviticus — Strolling about my Garden and Nursery; hoeing and plucking up weeds, a never ceasing occupation — The perpetual re-appearance of weeds is an admonition to me of my own faults, and should be a warning how it is necessary to treat them — And I looked over my seedling plants, my buds and

grafts as they grow — every day presenting some new aspect of observation ≈

18. IV. Tuesday. Called from my Nursery and Garden by a visit from Mr. Quincy, President of Harvard University — I asked him when it was proposed to appoint a professor of Natural History — He said the fund bequeathed by Dr. Fisher had not been received, two of the Doctor's relatives being authorised by his Will to retain the use of the fund, for one year after his decease. I mentioned to him the desire of Dr. Waterhouse to obtain this appointment, of which he said he had not been informed — He was apprehensive that Dr. Waterhouse would be thought too old — I suppose him to be about 76. Mr. Quincy thought Mr. Nuttall, the Curator of the Botanic Garden, must necessarily be the person chosen; but said Dr. Harris now the Librarian had also been mentioned — Mr. Nuttall is now in Europe, and Mr. Quincy had been longer without hearing from him than he thought proper — He told me also that as President Jackson is about visiting Boston, the Corporation of the University had thought it necessary to invite him to visit the Colleges — that he Mr. Quincy should address him in a Latin Discourse; and confer upon him the degree of Doctor of Laws — And he intimated that I should receive an invitation to be present at these ceremonies. I said that the personal Relations in which President Jackson had chosen to place himself with me were such that I could hold no intercourse of a friendly character with him — I could therefore not accept an invitation to attend upon this occasion — And independent of that, as myself an affectionate child of our alma Mater, I would not be present to witness her disgrace in conferring her highest Literary honours upon a barbarian, who could not write a sentence of Grammar, and hardly could spell his own name. Mr. Quincy said he was sensible how utterly unworthy of Literary honours Jackson was; but the Corporation thought it was necessary to follow the precedent, and treat him precisely as Mr. Monroe his Predecessor had been treated — As the People of the United States had seen fit to make him their President, the Corporation thought the honours which they conferred upon him were compliments due to the Station, by whomsoever it was occupied. Mr. Quincy said

it was thought also that the omission to shew the same respect to President Jackson, which had been shewn to Mr. Monroe, would be imputed to party Spirit, which they were anxious to avoid — I was not satisfied with these reasons, but it is college ratiocination and College Sentiment — Time serving and Sycophancy are qualities of all learned and Scientific Institutions — More than 50 years since the College gave this degree of Doctor of Laws to a Frenchman by the name of Valnais, about as fit for it as Andrew Jackson — Valnais was the first French Consul at Boston, and the People were so tickled with the glory of having a Consul to reside among them, that Dr. Cooper prevailed upon the then Corporation to make him a Doctor of Laws. I had some good humoured discussion with Mr. Quincy upon this occurrence, but adhered to my determination to stay at home.

———

22. IV:10. Saturday. ≈ There was much cannonading this afternoon, at the Presidents reviewing of the Military companies in Boston. The distant Report of them gave me a double relish for the solitary tranquility of my own occupations — No period of life has ever yielded me so much quiet contentment, as that which I enjoy with my family in health about me, totally uninterrupted by visitors, and cultivating in such health as I have, my Seedling plants and trees; labouring bodily from three to four hours a day, upon horticultural experiments, all hitherto fruitless, but some few of them beginning to promise fruit — Alteri Seculo is the motto of all my plantations; but I am yet sensible and conscious that this life of pleasure is not a life of profit.

———

24. IV. Monday — St. John's day. ≈ This day is one of those anniversaries which bring to my mind placid recollections. It is that of my arrival at Ghent — There is in the remembrance of the large half year which I passed in that City a charm, belonging to no other period of my life. — The Scenery through which I had passed from the painful day when I left my wife and Son Charles at St. Petersburg — the deep anxiety and almost despondency with which I looked forward to the prospect of failure in the object of the mission; the kindness and courtesy which I experienced from the Inhabitants of Ghent

during the whole term of our residence there — the comfort and tranquility, and friendly hospitality which marked the mode of existence of the People, the trying struggles and collisions, with the British Commissioners, and with my own colleagues which I underwent; the success beyond my most sanguine expectations which closed the Negotiation, and the subsequent signal discomfiture of a dark conspiracy there concerted against my character and good name have endeared that period of my life to my memory beyond any other — I arrived at Ghent, in company with Jonathan Russell, who then wore the mask of friendship — He is gone to his account, and was sufficiently punished in this world for his perfidy — And Bayard is gone; and in the most recent reports from England, I see announced the death of Lord Gambier, the first of the British Plenipotentiaries — Nineteen years have passed away since we met — I have since then endured great vicissitudes, deep distresses, and insidious prosperities — a merciful and protecting Providence has led me through them all. The Transactions at Ghent were the most fortunate occurrences of my life.

25. IV:20. Tuesday. A cold Northeasterly storm with rain almost without interruption the whole day. I was confined to my chamber with two or three intermissions, in which a sprinkling compelled me to return to the house. I despatched a number of public documents of which I receive several by every day's Mail. The President, must hasten back to Washington, or he will be glorified into his grave — They fagged him by their reception on Friday, and their presentations and addresses on Saturday that he failed going to Brattle-Street Church with Governor Lincoln on Sunday Morning; but made out to go with Lieut't Governor Armstrong to the old South Church in the afternoon — Monday Morning there were to be two exhibitions; one putting the Constitution Frigate in the new Dry Dock at the Navy-yard, Charlestown — the other was an Address delivered to him on Bunker's Hill by Edward Everett; and in the afternoon, he was to receive his scientific honours at Harvard University — He was sick in bed the whole day, under the care of Dr. Warren — This day, the weather alone would keep him in his lodgings at the Tremont-house; but he is

convalescent. The Constitution went into dry dock without him — The Bunker's Hill and Harvard University decorations are postponed.

26. IV:45. Wednesday. Charles went to Boston and returned to dine. The morning and evening were clear, with sprinkling showers in the middle of the day — The President went this day to Cambridge, and received the honorary degree of Doctor of Laws — Mr. Quincy delivered an Address to him in English, and a member of the Senior Class an Oration in Latin — From thence the President returned to Charlestown, where Mr. Edward Everett delivered the Address to him on Bunker's Hill, after which he proceeded to Salem. ≈

27. IV. Thursday. The Sun rose and set perfectly clear; but there were heavy Showers before noon. I was working in my Nursery, till Doctor Waterhouse came and dined with us — The Doctor is now near fourscore years of age, and his Constitution seems to be breaking up. He told me that he had never felt the effects of old age so much, as within the last six Months, and that this would probably be the last visit he should pay me. He found it troublesome to go so far from home, and must soon shut himself up and keep house — He was however present yesterday at the ceremony of conferring the Degree of Doctor of Laws upon President Jackson, and was much captivated by the ease and gracefulness of his manners. He shook hands with him twice, and told him he had heard of him many years ago; and was very glad to take him by the hand now — But he says Jackson is so excessively debilitated that he should not be surprized if he should never reach Washington again — I believe much of his debility is politic — part his own policy to suit his returns of civility to his own convenience, and pleasure, and part the policy of his physicians, pour se faire valoir — He is one of our tribes of great men, who turn disease to commodity, like John Randolph, who for forty years, were always dying — Jackson ever since he became a mark of public attention has been doing the same thing — He is so ravenous of notoriety, that he craves the sympathy for sickness as a portion of his glory — He is now alternately, giving out his chronic diarrhea, and making Warren bleed him for a Pleurisy,

and posting to Cambridge for a doctorate of Laws, mounting the monument of Bunkers Hill to hear a fulsome address and receive two Cannon Balls from Edward Everett, and riding Post to Lynn, Marblehead and Salem, receiving Collations, deputations and addresses at them all, in one and the same day — four fifths of his Sickness is trickery, and the other fifth mere fatigue — He will drag himself along in this way — disconcerting all the costly arrangements for his reception — disappointing three fourths of the People, male and female, who are agonizing to see him, and boast all their lives of having shaken hands with him, and finally crawl back to Washington, perhaps shut himself up one or two days, and then come forth in the Globe, never in better health and Spirits and determined to live these twenty years — Dr. Waterhouse discussed the propriety of the University's conferring upon him a Doctorate of Laws — I said a Doctorate for which an Apology was necessary, was a cheap honour, and that I thought it a Sycophantic compliment. The Doctor said it was thus truly characterised.

———

[August 1833]

5. V. Monday. Another painful day, with a gathering eruption upon my right hand. It suspends most of my labours of the hand in the garden and nursery and of the head in my chamber. Mrs. Adams sent for Dr. Woodward, to whom I gave a history of my complaints, of my Constitution and almost of my life. He prescribed sundry remedies, some of which I shall perhaps try; but with a strong conviction that my only effectual remedies are Patience and Resignation; and above all preparation for my last change — If this idea presents itself too often in these pages, it is because it is not often enough in my mind; and never with any good practical result — My present infirmity serves me only as an apology for wasting my time in idleness — I have for the last ten days devoted about an hour every day to teaching my Grand daughter, John's Child Louisa to read the Alphabet — She seems to make no progress, though not deficient in intelligence — I find here too that the qualities perhaps the most indispensable to a Schoolmaster are Patience and Perseverance — After repetitions almost numberless of pointing out the same Letter or the same Syllable to a child, it forgets them; and it seems as if the more pains you

take the more the memory of the child recalcitrates against the admission of the idea into the mind, which you would plant there — I sometimes find myself to believe it wilful obstinacy in the child — but in the teacher this is more to blame than the child for its inaptitude to learn — The belief that the child is obstinate excites anger in the teacher, and anger is impatient to punish. — The teacher is then the party that needs punishment — Soothing, coaxing, flattering, a little, very little shaming is needed by the child. Imperturbable equanimity, untiring Patience, unweariable Perseverance are the wants of the Instructor — What trials of temper for the teaching of one child — When I feel much exasperated at my Scholar's dulness of apprehension, my best resource is to tax myself with learning the Hebrew Alphabet, which I have been endeavouring to do, some forty odd years, and have not yet accomplished — The thickest skull upon which Instruction ever left its labour never resisted its impression more than mine has done to exclude it, and as the association of ideas is sometimes odd in its operations, Louisa's difficulties in learning the English Alphabet have put me for the twentieth, perhaps the thirtieth time upon surmounting those of the Hebrews. I make my own indocility the apology for hers.

———

[September 1833]

12. VI. Thursday. ≈ Immediately after dinner Pliny Merrick, Henry Gassett and Seth Whitmarsh, a Committee from the State Anti-masonic Convention which met yesterday at Boston came out and Mr. Merrick presented to me three Resolutions of the Convention, the last of which was a unanimous nomination of me to be Governor of the Commonwealth for the ensuing year. I had done every thing in my power to prevent this, which is an exceedingly unwelcome movement to me: but it was placed upon grounds which left me no honourable option of declining. So I concluded on reflection I promised the Committee to have my answer transmitted to them by ten O'Clock, to-morrow morning, and they took their leave. I sent my answer by Charles who returned this Evening to Boston. I accept the nomination, which casts me again upon the stormy ocean of political electioneering, when I hoped and believed I was snug in the Port. If there be a fatality that

pursues me, there is a Power above by whom it is guided — I cannot speak my forebodings but 𝒽 𝓃 ↘ 𝓎 𝓋 𝓏

———

28. IV:45. Saturday ≈ Mr. Clark, the late Clerk of the House of Representatives of the United States, and Mr. Force of Washington City, came and dined with us. I had met them in the Street in Boston on Thursday, and invited them — They are travelling in this part of the Country to procure documents for a compilation relating to the History of our Revolutionary War. They made some enquiries concerning the nomination of General Washington as Commander in Chief of the American Armies, and I read to them the passage on that subject in my father's manuscript biography, written by himself in 1802. This is one of the numerous incidents of our revolutionary history deemed so unimportant at the time when they happened, that no record of them public or private was made, and about which curiosity grows more intense from day to day — They become subjects of controversy, in which conjecture takes the place of evidence, and sometimes remain ultimately unsettled or become Articles of faith in conflicting political creeds — My Son Charles also came and dined with us. There is much agitation in the Public mind, about an order from President Jackson to withdraw the deposits of Public Monies from the Bank of the United States, and to place them in sundry State Banks — and about a paper read by him to the members of his Cabinet on the 18th of this month, followed by the dismission of William J. Duane, and the appointment of Roger B. Taney as Secretary of the Treasury — Upon all which I take time for reflection.

———

[October 1833]
10. IV:15. Thursday ≈ Mr. Bailey was here this forenoon. He wished for a minute of the principal public measures of Mr. Monroe's administration, in which I had the chief Agency; and also of the leading measures of my own administration as President of the United States — But in preparing such minutes I have an invincible repugnancy to taking any part whatever — I cannot reconcile myself to writing for the promotion of my own election — not even by the refutation of the basest calumnies. In all my election contests therefore, my character is at the mercy of every

Slanderer; and Slander is so effective a weapon in all our elections, that the Candidates for the highest Offices, use it without scruple against each other. It never was more atrociously used than it is at this moment against me — Mr. Bailey mentioned that the State Committee of the Anti-Masons had it in contemplation, and were very desirous of nominating John Welles, as their Candidate for the Office of Lieutenant Governor, which I fully approved, though very sure that he will not accept the nomination. Mr. Bailey has hopes that there will be a choice of Governor by the People, or at least that the largest vote will be for me. But I know by experience too well the power of Party Spirit upon the People, and the concentrated malignity of three great parties in the Commonwealth personally against me — There is no instance in the History of this State of a party nomination controuled by the votes of the People — Party triumphs over party; but the People are all enrolled in one party or another — The People can act only by the machinery of party.

———

13. V. Sunday ≈ I heard my Granddaughter read twice, and in the evening wade through 30 pages of Professor Dew's Review of the Debate, on the project for Slave emancipation. It is a monument of the intellectual perversion produced by the existence of Slavery in a free community — To the mind of Mr. Dew Slavery is the source of all Virtue in the heart of the Master — His argument against the practicability, of abolishing Slavery by means of Colonization, appears to me conclusive; nor do I believe that emancipation is the object of the Colonization Society, though it may be the day-dream of some of its members. Mr. Dew's argument that the danger of Insurrection among the Slaves diminished in proportion as their relative numbers increase over those of the white masters is an ingenious paradox in which I have no faith.

14. V. Monday. ≈ I read further in Professor Dew's review of the Slavery debate in the Legislature of Virginia. This pamphlet deserves grave meditation, and has in it the seeds of much profitable Instruction. Slavery is in all probability the wedge which will ultimately split up this Union. It is the source of all the disaffection to it, in both parts of the Country — A disaffection deeply pervading Mr. Dew's pamphlet. With my

multifarious occupations my Correspondence and Diary are running again into arrears, and the biography of my father is totally suspended — The Summer is irretrievably gone.

17. IV:30. Thursday. ≈ I spent half an hour in the garden, which at this Season, ceases altogether to be inviting — I am copying the Stanza's on the Astrology of the Zodiac for a revised Edition of Dermot MacMorrogh. I received a Letter from Lord, with one to him from Mr. Pierpont, who objects to the term Bard as applied to Cicero. Now that word was of all others the one, which I could not possibly consent to strike out, and Mr. Pierpont's Letter was otherwise not very encouraging to the publication of the Proem — I shewed it to my wife who objected to two of the Stanzas — precisely those which Lord thought the best of the whole — I immediately determined not to publish the Proem now. I merely altered one Stanza, supplied that which was in the first and second Edition left in blank, and wrote to Lord to direct the Contractor at Cincinnati to print from the second Edition, with these two alterations. I feel easier after this determination — Scarcely any man in this Country who has figured in public life, has ever ventured into the field of general Literature — none successfully — I have attempted it, in the Letters from Silesia, in the Lectures upon Rhetoric and Oratory; in occasional fugitive pieces in verse — original and translated, and finally in this Poem of Dermot MacMorrogh which is original, and at once a work of History, Imagination and Poetry — It has come to a third Edition, and will now be forgotten; as will be all my other writings in prose and verse — Like the rest of American Poetry, it resembles the juice of American grapes. It has not in ripening, the property of acquiring alcohol enough to keep it in preservation — I have pushed my experiment on the public temper far enough — In the Evening I read to the Ladies in an Edinburgh Review of 1823 the Article upon the memoirs of Lord Waldegrave, and of Lord Orford, relating to the Court History of the latter part of the reign of George the second — I took up again the fourth Book of Manilius and wasted some time upon it — I deeply regret that I have but a fortnight left before I am to depart for Washington.

21. IV:30. Monday ≈ I began and wrote three pages of a Letter to Governor Lincoln, in reply to his Letter of nine pages to me — The more I reflect upon that Letter the more unfair, bitter and rancorous it appears to me — He imputes to my Anti-masonic publications the falling off of his Supporters, and the consequent necessity to him of declining a Re-election — I believe him to be mistaken — My Letters have given strength to the argument of the Anti Masonic Cause, but they have roused and stimulated all the energies of all my personal Adversaries, against the Cause espoused by me — All personal opposition to me redounds to the benefit of Masonry — This will be the only cement to keep the National Republican party together — They would now go to pieces but for the rallying point of opposition to me — It is two years since I published the Letters on the Masonic controversy, with which I began, and one since the publication of those upon the Entered Apprentice's Oath — In that time the numbers of the Anti Masonic party do not appear to have increased in this Commonwealth at all — They have apparently diminished, in New-York and Pennsylvania — They are wavering in Rhode-Island, and although they have atchieved a signal triumph in Vermont their power is precarious, and a more complete union between the two political parties, would yet prostrate anti masonry — This controversy seems destined to destroy the comforts and tranquility of my last days, and to bring my life to close in hopeless conflict with the world.

22. IV:15. Tuesday ≈ Mr. Clay came out from Boston this Morning and paid me a visit, with Mess'rs Lawrence, Gorham, and Appleton — Mr. Clay arrived in Boston yesterday — He is making a tour, and since he reached the Atlantic border, has been received at Baltimore — Philadelphia — New-York — Providence and Boston, with great demonstrations of respect — This fashion of peddling for popularity by travelling round the Country; gathering crowds together, hawking for public dinners, and spouting empty Speeches, is growing into high fashion. It was formerly confined to the Presidents, but De Witt Clinton made some unsuccessful experiments of it. Mr. Clay has mounted that hobby often, and rides him very hard.

———

[November 1833]

8. V. Friday. — From New-York to Philadelphia. Blessed! ever Blessed be the name of God! that I am alive, and have escaped unhurt from the most dreadful Catastrophe, that ever my eyes beheld — We arrived at New-York, at half past six this Morning — I took leave of Mr. Harrod, his daughter, my niece Elizabeth, and Mr. Gourgas — took a Hack with Mr. Potter, and crossed from the East to the North River; put my baggage into the Steam-boat Independence Captain Douglas, and walked to the City Hotel. I found that my wife and family proceeded thence last Monday on their way to Washington — There was a card of invitation, to attend a public dinner to be given to Commodore Chauncey to-morrow, to which I wrote a declining answer. I then returned to the Steam boat, which left the wharf at eight and landed the Passengers at Amboy about twenty minutes past ten. The boat was crowded almost to suffocation; and people of every land and language seemed congregated in it — Among the rest a whole tribe of Wild Irish, whose language I now for the first time heard spoken. The only persons of the passengers whom I knew, were David B. Ogden of New-York, and Dr. M'Dowell, whom Dr. Condict introduced to me last winter at Washington, and who was then a Professor at Princeton College; but has since left it, and has removed to Philadelphia — There were upwards of 200 passengers in the Rail-road Cars — There were two Locomotive Engines, A and B, each drawing an Accommodation Car, a sort of moving Stage, in a Square, with open railing — A Platform, and a row of benches holding forty or fifty persons — then four or five Cars, in the form of large Stage Coaches, each in three Compartments with doors of entrance on both sides, and two opposite benches on each of which sat four passengers — Each train was closed with a high quadrangular open railed baggage waggon, in which the baggage of all the passengers in the train was heaped up — the whole covered with an Oil Cloth — I was in Car B N. I. and of course in the second train — Of the first ten miles, two were run in four minutes, marked by a watch of a Mr. De Yong in the same Car and division with me — They stopped, oiled the Wheels and proceeded — We had gone about five Miles further, and had traversed one mile in one minute and 36 Seconds, when the front left wheel of the

Car in which I was, having taken fire and burnt for several minutes, slip'd off the rail — The pressure on the right side of the Car then meeting resistance, raised it with both wheels from the rail, and it was oversetting, on the left side; but the same pressure on the Car immediately behind, raised its left side from the rail, till it actually overset, to the right, and in oversetting brought back the Car in which I was to stand on its four wheels, and saved from injury all the Passengers in it — The train was stopp'd I suppose within five seconds of the time when our wheel slip'd off the Rail; but it was then going at the rate of 60 feet in a second. and was dragg'd nearly two hundred feet before it could stop. Of sixteen persons in two of the three compartments of the Car that overset, one only escaped unhurt — A Dr. Cuyler — One side of the Car was stoved in and almost demolished. One man, John C. Stedman of Raleigh, North Carolina, was so dreadfully mangled, that he died within ten Minutes. Another named I believe Welles, of Pennsylvania can probably not survive the day. Captain Vanderbilt had his leg broken, as had Mr. West; Minister of the Episcopal Church at Newport Rhode-Island. Mrs. Bartlett wife of Lieutenant Bartlett of the U.S. Corps of Engineers, and her Sister dangerously hurt — her child, about three years old, is not expected to live. Mr. and Mrs. Charless of St. Louis, Missouri, severely cut and bruised; a Mr. Dreyfuss of Philadelphia, cut in the head, and sprained in the back and six other persons, among whom are Doctor M'Dowell, and a young Lady with him gashed in the head and otherwise wounded — The Scene of sufferance was excruciating. Men, women, and a child, scattered along the road, bleeding, mangled, groaning, writhing in torture and dying, was a trial of feeling, to which I had never before been called — and when the thought came over me that a few seconds more of pressure on the Car in which I was would in all probability have laid me a prostrate Corpse, like him who was before my eyes, or a cripple for life — and, more insupportable still; — what if my wife and grandchild had been in the Car behind me! Merciful God! how can the infirmity of my Nature express or feel the Gratitude that should swell in my bosom, that this torture, a thousand-fold worse than death, has been spared me — At my request a Coroner's inquest was called upon the deceased

— The other dying man, was left at Hightstown, 3 miles beyond where the disaster happened, and after a detention of nearly three hours, the train was resumed, and leaving the two broken cars behind, the rest proceeded to Bordentown 35 miles from Amboy. The Coroner's inquest held by a magistrate of the County had been sworn, and I had given my testimony before we left the fatal spot — Several of the wounded were left at Hightstown — The rest were transported on Cushions from the Cars over the Rail-way to Bordentown; and thence with us in the Steam boat New Philadelphia, to Philadelphia — On reaching the wharf, the Rev'd Mr. Brackenridge came on board, and told me he had heard I had been seriously injured, by the Accident on the Railway — Apprehensive that such rumours might circulate and reach my family, I wrote on board the Steam-boat, to my wife at Washington and to my Son Charles at Boston, and despatched the Letters to the Post-Office at Philadelphia. We landed at Chesnut Street wharf between six and seven in the Evening, and I took lodgings with Mr. Potter at the United States Hotel — I resolved to proceed on my Journey to-morrow morning, but called and spent an hour of the Evening at Mr. John Sergeant's.

———

26. V:30. Tuesday. ≈ This evening I was with a lamp in my hand reading a prosy Article in the Telegraph, when it lulled me to a doze, and my lamp set fire to the Newspaper which it took some expense of breath to extinguish — I made several efforts to write, but was obliged to give it up. I had a morning visit from Dr. Sewall; and before dinner walked to the Capitol — There I met Chilton Allen of Kentucky, and Mr. Foster of Georgia, and Mr. Potts of Pennsylvania — On coming out, I met in the Avenue Heman Allen of Vermont; and afterwards Col'l David Crockett of Tennessee. I did not recognize him, till he came up and accosted me — and named himself. I congratulated him upon his return here; and he said yes — It had cost him two years to convince the People of his District that he was the fittest man to represent them, that he had just been to Mr. Gales, and requested him to announce his arrival, and inform the Public that he had taken for lodgings two rooms on the first floor of a boarding House, where he expected to pass the Winter, and to have for a fellow lodger Major Jack

Downing — The only person in whom he had any confidence for information of what the Government was doing — This Major Jack Downing is the fictitious signature of a writer in some of the Newspapers, assuming the character of a shrewd, trickish, half-educated Yankee Major of Militia, writes Letters from the President's House, as entirely in his confidence, and telling all the petty intrigues of the cabinets and favourites by whom he is surrounded — After dinner Mr. Edward Everett called, and we had some conversation upon the state of Politics in Massachusetts — I found he was anxious to convince me that if the House of Representatives should elect Morton and me as the two Candidates from whom the Senate are to choose a Governor, the Senate would choose Morton — I told him I supposed they would, and should be much obliged to them if they should — I saw his object was to prevail upon me to decline in favour of Davis; but I was not disposed to let him know what my intentions are — He and his brother Alexander are both reeds shaken with the wind — I spent part of this Evening in assorting pamphlets.

——

[December 1833]

14. V. Saturday. It began to Snow early this morning, and continued through the whole day and Evening — increasing to a violent Snow-Storm — I received a Letter from my Son Charles, and answered a long one, from Benjamin F. Hallett, which was delivered to me yesterday by D. J. Pearce; both these Letters shew the delicate and very difficult position in which I am placed, as the Anti Masonic Candidate for the Office of Governor of the Commonwealth — There is great danger of displeasing all parties; and this is the position in which I have been ever since I returned to public life by accepting a Seat in Congress — I have now three fourths of the People of Massachusetts against me — By alienating from me the Anti masons, I shall become obnoxious to the whole, and my public life will terminate by the alienation from me of all mankind — It cannot be of much consequence, for I have but little time to live; and for that remnant of days retirement would be more suitable than the turmoil and collisions of public Service — It is scarcely possible for me to abstract myself from the great questions which agitate the Country, but it

is the experience of all ages, that the People grow weary of old men — I cannot flatter myself that I shall escape the common Law of our Nature — There is an ill-fortune that pursues in old age, especially men whom Fortune has much favoured in Youth — I have been of that Class, and must now pay the penalty of Good luck in my early years, and even till I became President of the United States — From that day is dated my decline, and every exertion made by me to arrest the course of the descent, has recoiled upon me — It is vain to struggle against the Will of Providence, and I must meet my Fate with what resignation I can — Above all it behooves me not to flatter myself that I can during my life, recover the good will of my Countrymen that I have lost — I have answered Hallett's Letter, adhering to the determination I had taken, of withdrawing from the canvas for Governor in the House of Representatives of Massachusetts.

———

22. V. Sunday. ≈ I despatched a Letter for my Son Charles, enclosing one to the Speaker of the House of Representatives of the Commonwealth of Massachusetts, withdrawing my name from the Canvas of Candidates to be sent from the House to the Senate for the election of a Governor — I have determined upon taking this step, against the earnest inclination and advice of the party by which I was nominated, and at the risk of making myself as unpopular with them, as I am with the two other parties in Massachusetts. To be forsaken by all mankind, seems to be the destiny that awaits my last days — In such cases a man can be sustained only by an overruling consciousness of rectitude — To withstand multitudes is the only unerring test of decisive character — Yet it requires wisdom as well as virtue — Stubborn adherence to a principle, is wise, only so far as the principle is important, and as the adherence to it may be productive of practical good — The useful end of stubborn adherence to Anti-masonry is yet problematical — Men of excellent moral principle, and of powerful intellect utterly disapprove of political Anti masonry — I have staked my reputation, character and fortune upon it — The wisdom of my course must be determined by the Event — It is yet upon trial.

———

24. IV:15. Tuesday. Finished my Letter to Charles, and received one from him and one from B. F. Hallett; exceedingly urgent upon points on which it is impossible for me to yield — They serve to shew the difficulty of my situation, and how much more difficult it would have been had the nomination of me succeeded and had I been elected Governor of the State under it — They would have attempted to controul me, in every act of my Administration, and insisted upon the regulation of all the affairs of the State with a view to sustain the party.

———

[January 1834]

2. VI:15. Thursday. Walking to the Capitol this morning, I overtook Mr. John Davis, and as he was to dine with me, told him I should be glad to have some conversation with him, this Evening, upon matters of public interest, to which he agreed — At the House there was a skirmishing debate on the question whether J. Davis's Resolution with the Memorial of Noah Fletcher should or should not be taken up for consideration — The memorial had been received the thirtieth day of the Session — There is a rule of the house that after the first 30 days Petitions and Memorials shall be received only on the first day of the House's sitting every week — But the rule applies only to the reception, and not to the consideration of them. By another Rule of the House Resolutions must lie over one day, and that Rule was enforced, in this case — Davis's Resolution thus passing over the 30ᵗʰ day, the Speaker now decided that it could not be called up before Monday, the day fixed for receiving Petitions — This was one of Stevenson's arbitrary extensions of a Rule, for the mere wantonness of party Spirit. It was contested by several members, and Lewis Williams appealed from it, but afterwards withdrew his appeal, well knowing that it was useless to appeal to a majority, from a decision made to favour a majority — The Speaker's immediate object was to give Polk the floor, to finish his Speech in answer to M'Duffie upon the motion to instruct the Committee of Ways and Means to report a joint Resolution for depositing the revenues to be hereafter collected in the Bank of the United States. Accordingly Polk took the floor, nearly half an hour before the usual time for proceeding to the orders of the day — He spoke nearly three hours, and his speech is said to have

given entire satisfaction to his party — It consisted of a repetition of all the matter which has been gathering for years against the Bank, sufficiently methodised, and delivered with fluency — But the galleries were empty, and there was scarcely a quorum in the house — Polk is the leader of the Administration in the House, and is just qualified for an eminent County-Court lawyer — par negotiis nec supra — He has no wit — no literature; no point of argument — no gracefulness of delivery — no elegance of language — no philosophy — no pathos — no felicitous impromptus — nothing that can constitute an Orator, but confidence, fluency, and labour — When he finished several members rose and addressed the Speaker — among them, Mr. Moore a new member from Virginia, said to be a man of talents — and H. Binney, who moved that the House should adjourn, and has of course the floor for Monday. We had all the Massachusetts delegation in both Houses to dine with us — I invited them all together, for the sake of promoting good-fellowship among them; but as they do by no means harmonize in political Sentiments I was apprehensive the party would be stiff, and cold — but it was quite otherwise — I avoided all conversation that could lead to unpleasant collisions and we talked about Egyptian Hieroglyphics and Militia Laws, and Rufus King — When the rest of the company went away, John Davis remained, and I had a long conversation with him upon the state of Affairs in Massachusetts. — I told him that I had sent a Letter to the Speaker of the House of Representatives of the State, withdrawing my name from the election in the House, and that I had done it, with a sincere wish that he might be chosen the Governor. I told him also that there had been approaches between the Anti masonic and the Jackson parties to combine with a view to exclude him from the election — That I had been urged to concur in this movement, which I had positively refused to do. That its object had been to unite the members of the two parties in the House, to elect judge Morton and me in the House, with the understanding that Mr. Morton should be chosen by the Senate — That this was all done under an impression that he, Davis, was so inveterately hostile to the Anti-masonic cause; that they could expect no favour from him; an opinion in which I had not concurred — That I was myself in favour of his election, and believed I was rendering a service to the public by apprising him of the course which affairs appeared to be taking, and believing it would depend upon the policy which he should pursue, whether the Anti masons should be reunited to the Antient National Republican party, or whether they should go entirely over to Jacksonism — That I was very solicitous to accomplish this reunion believing it indispensable to restore to us the influence in the general affairs of the union which by our internal divisions we had lost; and which would be worse than lost, if the People of the State should be delivered over to Jacksonism.

———

[February 1834]
6. IV:15. Thursday. ≈ George Chambers of Pennsylvania, made a very earnest Speech against Chilton's Resolution for extending the Pension system — The hour expired and he had not finished. Pinckney of South-Carolina moved to suspend the rule that Chambers might conclude, but the House refused. The deposit question then came up, and Bailey Peyton finished his Speech to the honour and Glory of Andrew Jackson against M'Duffie's Speech — He was followed by Henry A. Wise, a new and young member from Virginia who made a very keen, satirical Speech, in favour of the restoration of the deposits and of a National Bank, and against all those who are of the same opinions — He is coming forward as a successor of John Randolph; with his tartness, his bitterness, his malignity and his inconsistencies — Wise finished at about half past three when T. T. Bouldin obtained the floor and moved an adjournment. Immediately came a call for the yeas and nays, which explained M'Kinley's notice of yesterday — but the Majority are not yet screwed up to stop the debate. The adjournment was carried by a vote of 113 to 103.

———

11. IV:15. Tuesday. At the House, among the Reports from standing Committees was one made by Mr. Polk Chairman of the Committee of Ways and Means, with a Bill for the payment of the Pensioners — Ordered that ten thousand copies of the report and Documents be printed. ≈ The motion for reference of the Secretary of the Treasury's Report on the removal of the deposits to the Committee of Ways and Means;

with the Instructions moved by M'Duffie, and the Amendment proposed by S. Jones of Georgia came up. T. T. Bouldin of Virginia had the floor, from last Thursday, and a long and impressive Speech was expected from him — He rose and said that before entering upon the subject in debate, he would notice a rebuke he had received from his Colleague who had last spoken (Wise) for the omission to offer the usual Resolution that the House should go into mourning for the decease of John Randolph, who at the time of his Death, had been a member elect of this House (Randolph died last June, and Bouldin was chosen to succeed him —) He said he had no disposition to take to himself any general reflections which might equally apply to others, but thought he could not avoid some reply to a censure, which could apply to no other person than himself — That it would have been kind if his colleague instead of this public animadversion upon his omission had enquired of him privately the reason for it — That another of his Colleagues had done so in the most delicate manner, and through a third person, at the commencement of the Session — And now to justify himself before this House, his Colleagues and his Constituents it was necessary for him to say, what he should have said, if he *had* offered such a Resolution — At this instant, Mr. Bouldin shook, staggered and fell, and never spoke another word — He was taken as soon as possible without the bar, laid on the carpet close to a window which was thrown up — The House was instantly adjourned. Two or three physicians, members of the House, and Dr. Naudain of the Senate hastened to his aid. He was immediately bled, but died within fifteen minutes — His wife was in the Gallery where she had come to hear him speak — She came down immediately after he fell, quite in a state of distraction — There was a moment of interval when he had an appearance of returning life, which was told her to compose her agitation, but two minutes after, he expired — her friends were obliged to take her away, screaming in agony. I saw him within five minutes after the Spirit had departed; and the corpse was soon after removed into the Speaker's chamber — I had gone over from my Seat, to say a word to Mr. Beardsley, while Mr. Bouldin was speaking, and had my eyes upon him as he was speaking his last words — I had but just turned from looking in his face, when I heard a member say — "he is greatly agitated" — I looked towards him, and he was already fallen — As I walked home, I mused on the frailty of human life, and the vicissitudes of human passions and fortunes, but especially on the tenderness with which the feelings and judgments and motives of others ought to be treated in political debate — Mr. Bouldin was a man of good dispositions and sterling integrity; warped sometimes into great curvature by the political prejudices of the Virginia School. He had been bitter as gall upon all the Tariff questions, and the Proclamation and the removal of the deposits had brought him round to determined opposition to the present Administration — His Speech would have been one of the severest against the administration to which the debate has given rise; and the Catastrophe which intercepted it is but one of the symptoms of intense excitement spreading over the community.

———

16. III:30. Sunday. ≈ I heard this morning at the Presbyterian Church Mr. Smith from Daniel 5:27 — "Thou art weighed in the balances and art found wanting." After the Sermon he gave notice that there would be a monthly sale of effects, next Saturday to pay the debts of the Church, and he called most earnestly upon the members of the Society for contributions. There was an approach to an intimation that if they should neglect this intimation, he would be forced to leave them, and he particularly requested every individual member of the Society to pray every evening for a revival of the Spirit of Religion — There is great need of it — Indifference to religion and infidelity are vices which naturally spring from general peace and prosperity — We are deeply infected with them, and they are spreading with frightful rapidity. May God in his Mercy and in his own due time provide the remedy!

———

18. IV. Tuesday. Passing in my way to the Capitol this morning, by the house where Mr. Wirt had lodged, a crape tied to the knocker of the door announced his decease; and thus pass away in succession the glories of this world — He has not left a wiser or better behind — At the last election of President of the United States, he was one of the Candidates who received the suffrages of the People, and a very little difference in the

state of the public mind at that time would have effected his election — He had never been in public life, excepting in connection with his profession, which was the Law, but for twelve years during the Administration of James Monroe, and mine, he was Attorney-General of the United States — His death was announced to the Supreme Court by Mr. Webster, with an appropriate Eulogy.

———

[March 1834]
17. V:45. Monday. ≈ When Massachusetts was called, I presented the Resolutions of the Legislature, upon the Currency, and the removal of the Public Deposits from the Bank of the United States, with a very few remarks; touching somewhat personally upon the President — and I moved that they should be read, printed, and laid on the table to be referred to a select Committee with Instructions to report a plan for continuing to the People the advantages resulting from a National Bank — Polk started up, and fell into an idolizing and mawkish glorification of Doctor Andrew Jackson, with some coarse and equally dull invective against me — I rose and said I should not reply to his Speech; and gave notice once for all, that whenever any admirer of the President of the United States, should think fit to pay his court to him in the House, either by a flaming Panegyric upon him, or by a rancorous invective upon me, he should never elicit one word of reply from me

> "No! — let the candied tongue, lick absurd pomp,
> And crook the pregnant hinges of the knee,
> Where *thrift* may follow fawning."

Polk shrunk back abashed into his shell, and said not a word — The lines from Hamlet struck the House like a spark of electricity; and D. J. Pearce said to me laughing that if Polk had not enough of that, he was too unreasonable.

———

20. V. Thursday. ≈ Mr. Burges continued his Speech upon Mardis's Resolution till one O'Clock, when the special order of the day was called, and Henry L. Pinckney made his Speech in favour of Wildes proposed amendment to the first of the four Resolutions reported by the Committee of Ways and Means — While Pinckney was speaking James Blair of South-Carolina

came, and took a seat near and in face of him, looking steadily
and intently at him for some time — And at the moment when
Pinckney said that the whole South, was united against the
removal of the Deposits, Blair with a loud voice exclaimed "*Its
a lie.*" — There was a momentary pause — Pinckney stop'd,
and said — "I claim the Protection of the House." No movement was made by the House — One of the members friendly
to Blair, went round to the seat where he was and whispered to
him; upon which Blair rose, and went with him out of the
house — Pinckney had already resumed, his Speech, which he
concluded without appearing to have been at all disconcerted
by this singular interruption. Blair is an honest and very intelligent man ruined by habits of intemperance and maddened
with opium.

21. V. Friday. At the House, upon the motion of William H.
Ashley of Missouri, the Committee of the whole House were
discharged from the consideration of two Bills, which had
been referred to them, one for the continuation of the Cumberland road, from the river Mississippi to the city of Jefferson
in the State of Missouri, and one, for the survey and location
of the Cumberland road from Vandalia, in the State of Illinois,
to the Mississippi, and the Bills, were committed to the Committee of the whole House on the State of the Union — There
is by the rules of the House a distinction between a Committee
of the whole House, and a Committee of the whole House on
the State of the Union — the latter being reserved for subjects
considered of the highest importance — It is always in order
to move to go into Committee of the whole on the State of
the Union, and it always has precedence in point of time, over
the ordinary Committees of the whole House — The practice,
with the ordinary routine of Bills, when they are reported, to
read them a first and second time, by their titles, which is a
constructive reading, and refer them to the Committee of the
whole House, and make them the order of the day for *to-
morrow*. But this to-morrow, for multitudes of Bills never
comes — It is to-morrow, and to-morrow and to-morrow —
for the Bills thus referred must when the House go into
Committee of the whole be taken up in the order of their
commitment, and there are many which the Committee never

reach. Ashley's motive therefore in getting the two Bills transferred from the Committee of the whole House, to the Committee of the whole House on the State of the Union, was to obtain for them a chance of being considered, at the present Session of Congress. — This Cumberland Road, from Vandalia, in the State of Illinois to the Mississippi, and from the Mississippi, to the City of Jefferson, in the State of Missouri — how it sounds! what a demonstration of the gigantic growth of this Country in population and in power is contained in these few words — and how insignificant in comparison with them is the subject which occupied the whole time of both Houses of Congress this day — In the House, Mr. Burges consumed the first hour with another driblet of his Speech upon Mardis's Resolution — Then George R. Gilmer of Georgia made a Speech of an hour and a half against the amendment proposed by his Colleague Wilde, to the first Resolution reported by the Committee of Ways and Means. — After which C. C. Clay of Alabama took the floor and the House adjourned. I went into the Senate chamber, and heard Thomas H. Benton of Missouri till 4 O'Clock.

———

30. VI. Sunday. Easter. Heard this morning at the Presbyterian Church Mr. Skinner, from Ephesians 3:14 "For this cause, I bow my knees unto the father of our Lord Jesus Christ." Took Louisa with me to Church — After dinner I attended at St. John's, where the Evening service for Easter day was read by an Irishman, I believe named M'Calla, who preached from 2 Peter 2:20 "For if after they have escaped the pollutions of the world through the knowledge of the Lord and Saviour Jesus Christ, they are again entangled therein, and overcome, the latter end is worse with them than the beginning." — In this discourse there was no reference made to the festival of the day, which would seem of all other days in the year to be most highly deserving of celebration with religious fervour by Christians — In Roman Catholic Countries and in the Greek Church, it is solemnized with the most animated devotion, and as the day of the Resurrection of the Saviour is more emphatically the Christian's day, than that of his birth, which is not very precisely ascertained, and if it were, could only be commemorated, as the day of promise, while that of Easter is

the day [of] consummated life and immortality. — The Resurrection of Christ, was the accomplishment of the purposes for which he came into the world — Its extraordinary and mysterious connection of coincidence with the Jewish Passover, gives it great additional interest, and the occasion it has given for ascertaining to the minutest second of time the extent of the annual revolution of the Earth round the Sun, has made it important to the scientific history of Astronomy. For these reasons I have regretted that in the general abolition of religious holidays by the Protestant Churches of the purest doctrine, they had not made an exception for this day; with which I would also have included Christmas day — In this Country the Catholics, and especially the Episcopalians, keep Christmas with much more earnestness than Easter, the cause of which may be that Christmas is a day for feasting, and Easter is not — The minced-pies and Plum pudding of the Christmas dinner form for the great multitude of worshippers the keenest incentive to their piety, and the most rapturous of their extasies.

—

[April 1834]

2. V:30. Wednesday. James Blair a member of the House of Representatives from South-Carolina shot himself last Evening at his lodgings at Dowson's N. 1 after reading part of an affectionate Letter from his wife to Governor Murphy of Alabama who was alone in the chamber with him, and a fellow lodger with him at the same house.

At the Meeting of the House, George M'Duffie, announced the decease of Mr. Blair; alluding to the Catastrophe of the death of Thomas T. Bouldin, and said that the decease of Mr. Blair had been equally sudden — He expressed his disapprobation of the practice of pronouncing panegyrics upon members who have ceased to live, and are beyond the reach alike of censure and of praise — That panegyrics were useless to those to whom the person was known, and uninteresting to those who knew him not — He moved that the usual Resolutions on similar occasions should be adopted — That the members of the House would attend the funeral at 4 O'Clock this afternoon — That they would testify their respect for the memory of James Blair, by wearing crape thirty days. That a Message be

sent to the Senate, announcing the Event; and that a Committee of Arrangements be appointed to superintend the funeral
— The house then adjourned. Poor Blair — The indifference
and insincerity of M'Duffie's remarks were as unfeeling as if his
heart had been of marble. There is a gloomy churlishness in
the character of M'Duffie averse enough to Panegyric, but if
Blair had been of his own political party, he would have lauded
him to the skies. Blair was a man of amiable natural disposition
of excellent feelings, of sterling good sense, and of brilliant
parts, unredeemably ruined by the single vice of intemperance,
which had crept upon him insensibly to himself, till it had
bloated his body to a mountain — prostrated his intellect, and
vitiated his temper to madness. He had paid three hundred
dollars fine, for beating and breaking the bones of Duff Green,
because he had charged the Union party of South-Carolina
with being Tories — He had discharged a pistol, at an actress
in the Theatre at Washington, from one of the boxes — He
had within the last ten days given the lie to Henry L. Pinckney
while speaking in his place in the House of Representatives,
and he was in the constant habit of bringing a loaded pistol
with him to the House — The chances were quite equal that
he should have shot almost any other man than himself. Yet he
was one of the most kind hearted men in the world; a tender
and affectionate husband and father, and has left a wife devoted
to him, and children to whom his death is perhaps a blessing
— It was no doubt a difficult task for M'Duffie to announce
his decease to the House in an appropriate manner — But the
expedient of evading all note of sympathy with the feelings of
his friends, by an affected and hollow pretence of dislike to all
obituary panegyric was not felicitous.

———

7. VI. Monday. — I finished the preparation of my manuscript
so far as to send by my Son John to the National Intelligencer
office, about half of my intended Speech, with the extracts —
Weather yet stormy — At the House, it being the weekly day
for receiving Memorials and Petitions, I found Dutee J. Pearce
of Rhode-Island presenting Petitions from that State against
the Bank of the United States, and against the restoration of
the Deposites — The call for the States was carried from
Rhode-Island Southward through the Union — States and

Territories — one hundred and forty eight Memorials Petitions, and authenticated Proceedings of public Meetings were presented — nearly one half of them being for or against the recharter of the Bank of the United States, and for or against the removal of the Deposites — In presenting these many of the members introduced them with short Speeches, and not unfrequently the Speech was against the purport of the Petition which it introduced. This is a singularity confined entirely to the Memorials and Petitions relating to the Bank of the United States — a subject of great party excitement and controversy — The other subjects upon which the memorials are most numerous, are for Post-Offices and Post-roads, and Petitions for Pensions for Services during the Revolutionary War and since — Uriah Tracy thirty-years ago, used to say that the Soldiers of the Revolution claimants never died, that they were immortal. Had he lived to this time he would have seen that they multiply with the lapse of time. As Petitioners they are more numerous at every Session of Congress than before. And of late as some of them have died, their widows have begun to Petition, and this day there was a Petition from the Son of a deceased Pensioner praying that the Pension may be continued to him — There were also sundry Petitions from various parts of the Country for the abolition of Slavery in the District of Columbia. These are always turned over to the Committee on the District, with a Chairman and a Majority of the Committee Slave-holders; and the House hear no more about them. W. W. Ellsworth of Connecticut this day presented one or two of these Petitions, and with much solemnity of manner said he wished the house to understand, that he concurred entirely in the views and Sentiments of the Petitioners, on this subject, and then moved that the Petition without reading should be referred to the Committee on the District of Columbia — There are Petitions for Appropriations for Roads and Canals, and other works of internal improvement — little encouraged at this time. Resolutions of State and Territorial Legislatures — among which Lucius Lyon, the territorial Delegate from Michigan presented Resolutions of the Legislature Council requesting that a census of the Territory may be taken, and that they may be authorised to hold an extra Session — referred to the Committee on the Territories — Also

a Memorial concerning the Southern Boundary of the Territory, in controversy with the State of Ohio — lies on the Table
— Mr. Gales called me out, and spoke of the manner in which
he proposed to print my intended Speech, in the Intelligencer,
in such sort that it may be made up into a pamphlet. He gave
me as a sample a copy of Mr. Wilde's Speech. Mr. Corwin of
Ohio called me out and said he believed, if I wished to make
my Speech on the deposits question, one of the members from
the State of Ohio who voted with the majority would move a
reconsideration of the second Resolution to give me the opportunity to speak — I declined for various reasons — one,
that I was unwilling to accept a privilege not to be extended to
others. Another, that I would be under no obligation, which
the member making the offer might reproach me with, if he
should dislike my Speech — A third reason was the useless
waste of time in delivering a Speech which would not change
one vote, after the question to which it applies has been decided by yeas and nays.

———

9. VI. Wednesday. ≈ The House went into Committee of the
whole on the state of the Union upon the general Appropriation Bill. The amendment moved yesterday by me to strike out
the Appropriation for a temporary additional Clerk in the Department of State for one year was debated till half-past four
O'Clock — Several propositions were made to amend the
clause: one by John W. Brown of New-York, which after being
much discussed he withdrew, upon a motion of H. Binney to
strike out the word preserve and insert the words "to make an
index" with reference to the papers of the Department — Mr.
Binney spoke twice in favour of the Appropriation, intimating
that he did so, having assented to it in the Committee of Ways
and Means — Governor Lincoln made a long Speech in favour
of my amendment, and was bitterly replied to, by Hawes of
Kentucky and by Mann of New-York — Polk spoke three or
four times, and Archer of Virginia made a warm Speech in
honour of the Secretary of State Louis M'Lane. I made a final
reply after two or three abortive motions for the Committee to
rise — the question was taken, and the vote to strike out the
clause as amended by Mr. Binney's motion was 89 to 70. The
Committee rose, and the House, near 5 adjourned — My mind

was deeply moved by these two days of debate — The immediate object of which was very small, but the principle which it
involved I thought of the deepest importance — Within the
last five years Congress has been led into an irregular confused
mode of connecting with the Appropriation Bills a multitude
of other objects, which are surreptitiously introduced to authorize expenditures which Congress would not directly sanction — I made this motion, as a first step of an attempt to
arrest this practice, and to bring the Legislature back to the
true principles of making Appropriations — It is an arduous
undertaking and must be perseveringly pursued — The success
of the first movement is encouraging; but the evil usage will be
constantly returning; and some nice discrimination will be necessary, to avoid excluding small expenditures of no importance,
without admitting others — I took Stansbury the Reporter to
the National Intelligencer Office, and found upon enquiry that
they had no Press-copy ready for me. Mr. Gales told me that they
could not get my intended Speech into the Newspaper till
Saturday Morning. — Evening at Whist.

———

17. V:30. Thursday. ≈ The President of the United States this
day sent to the Senate a Protest, against their Resolution, of
censure upon him for his recent interferences with the public
revenues; and he calls upon them to enter his protest upon
their Journals — Great excitement — Poindexter moved that
it should not be received — Clay, Webster and Preston are
absent — The correction and revisal of the second and third
sheets of my suppressed Speech absorbed all my time at home.

———

[June 1834]
2. V:30. Monday. ≈ At the House, immediately after the reading of the Journal, Andrew Stevenson the Speaker addressed
the House, and resigned his Office; stating that he had this day
addressed a Letter to the Executive of Virginia, resigning his
seat as a member of the House. He then took leave of the
House in a Speech of 15 minutes full of good principles and
good feeling, in elegant language, very handsomely delivered.
The House immediately proceeded to ballot for Speaker.
There were ten ballots taken, at the last of which John Bell of
Tennessee was chosen by 114 of 215 votes. He was conducted

by me, and Richard M. Johnson to the Chair, whence he made a short address to the House, and took the Oath to support the Constitution of the United States administered by Lewis Williams of North-Carolina the person who has been longest in continuance a member of the House; immediately after which the House adjourned. The competitors for the Chair, were Wilde and Wayne of Georgia, Polk of Tennessee, and Sutherland of Pennsylvania.

———

21. V:30. Saturday — Wasted the morning of the Summer Solstice — Just before going to the House I heard that intelligence had been received of the death of General La Fayette. At the Meeting of the House I moved a joint Resolution for the appointment of a Committee to consider and report what measures it may be proper for Congress to adopt, honorary to the Memory of General La Fayette. The Resolution was unanimously adopted ≈ Two Messages were received from the President; one announcing the decease of La Fayette, and communicating the general Order to the army and navy, issued on the occasion — The other, communicating a memorial from the granddaughters of the Count de Rochambeau, claiming remuneration for his Services in the revolutionary War — It was referred to the Committee on foreign Affairs — The House adjourned, near 9 in the Evening.

———

[July 1834]
4. V. Friday. Independence day — My Son John's birth-day — He is 31 — Day of my father's death — This threefold anniversary impresses me with an awful solemnity which I cannot waste in frivolous banqueting; and still less in mere political party carousals — I would rather devote it partly to humiliation and prayer, partly to useful occupation and the remainder to family social conviviality — I had invitations to whig celebrations at Philadelphia and at Boston, both of which I declined — My wife spent the whole day at her brother's; he is convalescent but yet very ill; and Mr. Frye has also been suddenly seized, and is confined to his bed.

———

15. V. Tuesday — Quincy — I resume the Diary in this Book after interruption from the 5th of March, during which it has

been kept on sheets which I could take with me to and from
the house from day to day — Perhaps that is the best form in
which a Diary can be kept — It is certainly the most convenient, at the time of keeping; though not the best for preservation ≈ I visited my Garden, and found amidst the enormous
growth of weeds, a number of seedling plants of the last year,
and many that have come up the present Season — But a large
portion of those that I had set out last October, and among
them several very fine trees are dead — I have much anxiety
for the proper disposal of my time, until the approach of Winter shall call me again to Washington — and a deep, though
most fruitless impression of the duties of advancing age.

16. V. Wednesday. Weather still above Summer heat. Fahrenheit at 84; and time wasted, I know not how. ≈ I wrote a short
Letter to Midshipman Joseph H. Adams concerning one to
him from his Guardian Phineas Foster — But that which absorbed the largest portion of the day, was a research respecting
the Origin of Committees of Correspondence, in the approach
of our War for Independence. George Tucker professor of
Moral Philosophy at the University of Virginia recently wrote
me a Letter of enquiry upon this Subject. He is writing the
Life of Thomas Jefferson, and enquires whether any Commit-
tees of Correspondence were appointed by the Legislature of
the Colony of Massachusetts Bay before 1773 — Jefferson
claims the invention of Committees of Correspondence for
Virginia, and it has become a controverted point of History.
Tucker cites in his Letter to me Marshall's life of Washington
— Gordon, Mrs. Warren, and Samuel A. Welles. I referred to
Gordon and Marshall, to Hutchinson's third Volume, the
Massachusetts State Papers from 1764 to 1775, Tudor's life of
Otis and Alden Bradford's History — And as almost univer-
sally happens upon a consultation of books to verify a fact, or
authenticate a recital I became so much engaged in the re-
search that it nearly consumed the day.

17. IV:45. Thursday — From Quincy to Boston and Medford.
≈ At ten I went with Wilson and the Coach into Boston —
The first person whom I met in the Street was Dr. George
Parkman, who invited me to dine with him, but I was engaged

to go to Medford. I called at my Son Charles's Office and saw him — Then went to the State-House, and in the Secretary's Office. I saw Mr. Bangs, and extracted from the Journal of the House of Representatives of the Province of Massachusetts Bay, of the 6th of November 1770 the entry of an order for the appointment of a Committee of Correspondence; to correspond with the Agent of the Province and others in England, with the Speakers of the several Assemblies, and with Committees of Correspondence appointed, or who might be appointed by them ≈

18. V. Friday — From Medford to Boston and Quincy. I took a shower bath this Morning, and walked round the grounds of Mr. Brooks's Garden — After Breakfast I came with my Son Charles to Boston — Called upon Dr. George Parkman who shewed me seventy-five plates which he has just received from England of Audubon's work upon American Ornithology — He related to me also several anecdotes concerning Audubon himself. He then walked with me into State Street where I viewed the front of the Suffolk Bank, a new Building with four fluted Pillars of Quincy Granite, of the Ionic Order. In State Street I met Mr. Abbott Lawrence, with whom I went to the U.S. Branch Bank, and saw Mr. N. Biddle. He came yesterday from Newport, and proposes to return to-morrow. He was with a convocation of Bank President's and Directors, with whom after a few minutes I left him.

—

21. V. Monday. ≈ I wrote two Letters — one to Samuel Brown, and one to E. Kirby, both at Brownville, and in answer to Letters from them, relating to the Monument to be erected over the remains of General Brown at Washington — They urge me to write the obituary Inscription; a task from which I should have been glad to be relieved, but which I have nevertheless consented to undertake. — General Brown is one of those men, who have rendered eminent services to this Country, and to whom full Justice has not been rendered in return. He was a native of Pennsylvania, and it is a very remarkable fact that the People of that State, whose fanatical passion for Andrew Jackson can be compared to nothing but that of Titania Queen of the Fairies, for Bottom, after his Assification,

never manifested the slightest regard, or gave a single token of gratitude to *him*. He made this remark once, himself, with deep and indignant feeling, to me — He said nothing of Jackson, or of the senseless devotion to him of the Pennsylvanians — But he knew that his own services had been more arduous, and his sufferings infinitely more severe in the Cause of the Country than those of Jackson — But such is the nature of popular applause — General Brown died Commander in chief of the Army; and probably Jackson would never have been any thing more, had not Congress, by reducing the army dismissed him from his Military Station — My Son Charles came out from Boston, to dine and spend the night here — I employed the afternoon in reading over that part of Marshall's life of Washington, which preceded the commencement of our Revolution. I resumed also the sketch introductory to the Discourse upon the life and character of La Fayette, which I had begun, on the 4th of this month, and which since that day has remained untouched — I fear the thought is too unwieldy to be fully carried out by me — I find in the newspapers notice of the death of Edmund Charles Genet, to whom I was once, forty years ago, a political antagonist.

23. V. Wednesday. I wrote a serious Letter to my Son John — made a copy of it, and despatched it by the mail — So little of any thing that I ever deliberately projected in my life has ever succeeded, that I cannot indulge a hope of success on this occasion. The Circumstances of the time impose a duty upon me, which I must discharge — My own Life, has been upon the whole fortunate down even to the present time — or rather I would say that a kind and indulgent Providence has shaped my fortunes more auspiciously than I could have done by any Prudence of my own — As my years advance my prospects decay; my hopes are blasted with disappointment; my trials sharpen with severity, and the forethought of what is to come after me, bears me down with a burthen beyond endurance — Solitude quickens my fears — I have lost my appetite. I am losing my sleep. I feel as if heavy calamities were impending over me, and the Letters from my wife aggravate all my apprehensions — If not a Sparrow falls to the ground but by the decree of superior goodness and wisdom, may I not ask for mercy or for

resignation? what I do, will come to naught — may not a ray of comfort and relief beam from a quarter where it cannot now be foreseen?

———

30. V. Wednesday. ≈ There is at present a great calm in the political world; and no prospects upon which I can dwell with satisfaction — The system of Administration for the Government of the Union, is radically and I believe irretrievably vitiated — Vitiated at the fountain. The succession to the Presidency absorbs all the National Interests, and the electioneering contests are becoming merely venal — My hopes of the long continuance of this Union are extinct — The people must go the way of all the world, and split up into an uncertain number of rival communities enemies in War, in Peace Friends — Were it otherwise, and were the future destinies of the Nation to be as prosperous and as glorious as they have been hitherto, my lease of life is so near its close that I should live to witness little of it — My own system of Administration, which was to make the National domain the inexhaustible fund for progressive and unceasing internal improvement has failed — systematically renounced, and denounced by the present Administration, it has been undisguisedly abandoned by H. Clay — ingloriously deserted by J. C. Calhoun, and silently given up by D. Webster — These are the opposition aspirants to the Presidential succession, not one of them having a system of Administration which he would now dare to avow, and at this time scarcely linked together by the brittle chain of common opposition, to the unprincipled absurdities of the present incumbent.

———

[August 1834]
10. V. Sunday ≈ I read the 11th Sermon of the 5th Volume of Saurin, upon the Eternity of God — said to have been delivered in the French Church at Rotterdam the first Sunday of the year 1724 — It gave me no satisfaction. The subject is above human comprehension, and so he declares it to be — I can follow no train of reasoning on this topic a single step without stumbling — My own existence and the world around me, bespeaks an intelligent first cause, not temporary. The authentic history of the human species is traceable back not more

than 4 – 5 – or at most 6000 years — a drop of water to an Ocean, in comparison with a conceivable portion of time — But eternity has neither past nor future, while time has no present — Eternity cannot be measured by time — The phenomena of physical nature, would seem to indicate that matter is not destructible, but only changeable — It is unceasing mutability — Eternity is immutable. I must wait for light, and hearken to human reason upon more comprehensible things.

———

28. IV:30. Thursday — Cambridge — Boston — Quincy. I went to Cambridge with Wilson in Carr's Chaise with Wilson and one of the Carriage horses — I attended a few minutes after nine in President Quincy's Study — The judges of the Boylston prize Declamations present were twelve — we proceeded to the new Meeting House ≈ The auditory was assembled for the Φ.B.K. performances, and the house was crowded. The Oration was delivered by William Howard Gardiner, a lawyer in Boston, son of the late Dr. John Silvester John Gardiner and was an admirable defence and vindication of the Study of classical learning — It was two full hours in the delivery, and not much too long. It was admirably well spoken, and rivetted the attention of the auditory almost to the last moment. Never was the cause of classical Literature pleaded with more eloquence and beauty — The Poem by Ralph Waldo-Emerson was a slovenly performance, the only merit of which was its brevity. It was five minutes past 3 when the performances closed, and I went immediately into Boston, walked round the Borders of the common reflecting on the various turns of fate below, and especially on all the vicissitudes which have befallen me since on the 5th of August 1809 I left the House at the Corner of Boylston Street where Charles was born, and embarked for St. Petersburg — what an age of hope and disappointment — of good and evil fortune I have since gone through — Prosperous on the whole beyond the ordinary chances of human life — but with how many deep afflictions, with how many cruel humiliations! ≈ A weary day.

29. IV:30. Friday. ≈ I went immediately after dinner to my Garden; but was called back to two other visitors from Charleston South-Carolina — Mr. Yeadon, Editor of the Charleston

Courier, who brought me a Letter from Joel R. Poinsett, and Mr. Levi, whom he introduced to me, as a Citizen of Charleston — Mr. Yeadon spoke with some concern of the political condition of South-Carolina, where the nullification and Union parties are still at issue with each other, and still mutually inveterate — I observed that in that controversy, the Union party had conceded too much to their adversaries. — Levi said that if so, Mr. Jefferson's doctrine was the cause of it; and that if the Union party had not held out a strong adhesion to State rights, they would have been officers without an army — Mr. Yeadon said they had much anxiety about the appointment of a judge of the Supreme Court, in the place of Judge Johnson, and hoped it would be Mr. Pettigru — Col'l Drayton having by his removal to Philadelphia, ceased to be considered a citizen of South-Carolina. He said further that when President Jackson's first Cabinet was broken up, he offered the Office of Secretary of War to Col'l Drayton, by whom it was declined — and that Drayton was the real head and founder of the Union party — He said too that at the next Session of the Legislature, the nullification party would call a convention of the People, and thereby procure an Amendment to the Constitution of the State, prescribing the test Oath to establish the State authorities as the only Sovereign powers in this Union — And he alluded to the apprehension always prevailing in the South, that the People of the North have a perpetual propensity to promote the abolition of Slavery in the South — This Ghost I believe will haunt them, till they bring it up in reality — I said I had no longer the confidence in the long duration of the Union that I once had — but did not say why.

———

[September 1834]

6. V. Saturday. Early this morning I went into Boston with my wife, and Walter Hellen. At Charles's House, we found him and his wife — At ten O'Clock I went to the Council Chamber in the State House where I met a few acquaintance, and many Strangers — It was the anniversary of La Fayette's birth day and the day fixed for the Commemoration of his Life and Character, by the young men of Boston. A large procession civil and military was formed, which went from the State House to Faneuil Hall, where a splendid Oration of an hour

and fifty minutes was delivered by Edward Everett — He
commenced precisely at two O'Clock, and for lack of time,
abridged his discourse, perhaps nearly an hour. It was received
with universal applause, and in the delivery was often interrupted by long protracted shouts and hand-clappings, of exulting approbation — It was delivered, every word from
Memory — His manuscript lying on the table, and he never
once recurred to it — The Oration was preceded by a dirge of
Handel, with appropriate words in prose adapted to the Music
— An admirable prayer by Mr. Frothingham — A Requiem in
verse — the Words by Grenville Mellen — Music by Lowell
Mason — and was followed by a Hymn — words by Isaac
M'Lellan jun'r Music by G.J. Webb. — It was past four
O'Clock, when the ceremonies closed. ≈ I received at Boston
this morning a Letter from C. W. Pasley Col'l of Royal Engineers in England, dated Chatham 20 June 1834 — He has
been publishing a work upon Weights and Measures, of which
he presents me with a Copy (but that was not with the Letter)
and says he has done Justice to my Report made to the Senate
of the United States in 1821 acknowledging that my historical
account of English Weights and Measures, is more correct
than any that has been given by any English writer; including
the Reports of Committees of the House of Commons — This
acknowledgment thirteen years after the publication of my
Report was very gratifying to me — If either of my children or
any of theirs should ever read this page, let me tell him that
Col'l Pasley's testimonial to that single point, the accuracy of
my historical investigation of English weights and measures, is
but one of many discoveries which he will find in my Report, if
he will have the courage and perseverance to read, and examine it as he reads — He will find the History not only of English, but of Hebrew, Greek, Roman, and French weights and
measures, traced to their origin, in the natural history of man
and of human Society, such as he can find in no other writer,
antient or modern — He will find a philosophical discussion of
the moral principles involved in the consideration of weights
and measures, and of the extent and limitation of its connection with binal, decimal and duodecimal arithmetic, for which
he might look in vain elsewhere; and if he should remark that
not one of his Countrymen ever noticed these peculiarities of

that Report, he may amuse himself by enquiring why and how it has happened — The Report from the day of its publication, has in this Country scarcely been known to exist; and this commendation of it, coming back from England is therefore the more welcome to me.

———

[October 1834]

9. III:45. Thursday. ≈ This was another day of disappointment to my occupations. Charles found me the Volumes of La Cretelle's History of France containing the period immediately preceding the French Revolution — The weakness of my eyes allowed me to read only a few pages of it, and I could read nothing else — I wrote nothing. Mr. Plumer's conversation was chiefly upon New-Hampshire Politics, in which or in any other Politics at this time, there is nothing of absorbing interest — The Prosperity of the Country, independent of all agency of the Government, is so great that the People have nothing to disturb them, but their own waywardness and corruption — They quarrel upon dissensions of a doit, and split up into gangs of partizans of A. B, C, and D, without knowing why they prefer one to another — Caucusses, County, State, and National Conventions Public dinners, and dinner table Speeches two or three hours long, constitute the operative power of electioneering, and the parties are of working men, temperance reformers, Antimasons, Union and State rights men, nullifiers, and above all Jackson men — Van Buren men, Clay men, Calhoun men, Webster men, and M'Lean men — whigs and Tories, Republicans and Democrats, without one ounce of honest principle to chuse between them — New-Hampshire is governed by a knave of the name of Isaac Hill, Editor of a newspaper, mail contractor and now a Senator of the United States — just cunning enough to grow rich by railing against the rich, and to fatten upon the public spoils bawling Democracy — This is the besetting Sin of popular governments, and it is now as it always has been — Van Buren is a demagogue of the same School, with a tincture of Aristocracy, an amalgamated metal of lead and copper. There are five or six Candidates for the succession to the Presidency; all of them demagogues; and not one of them having any consistency of system for the Government of the Union. Plumer asked, as others have asked, whether they might not go back to

the last Administration. They might as well ask the resurrection of one dead man to life by touching the bones of another — a miracle never repeated since it was seen at the Sepulchre of Elisha. I have nothing henceforth to look to but the grave, and if possible to withdraw from the public Scene, without waiting to be pushed from it — May it please the giver of all good from the disgrace of dishonouring my last days, by loitering too long upon the Stage.

———

18. IV:15. Saturday. ≈ I went with Kirk to the Mount Wollaston farm, and examined the Orchard of Apple-trees which I set out in 1830; and the grove of chesnut and Oak trees growing from nuts and acorns then planted round its borders. I agreed with Spear to set out some more trees, and to plough up the ground on the Eastern border where none of the plants from the seed of 1830 has survived; though there are nearly three hundred trees on the three other sides — I came home and dined — Immediately after dinner, Charles came in from Boston, having a Letter from Walter Hellen, written Wednesday Evening, saying that my Son John was extremely ill, and urging that if his mother could not come on, Charles or I should come immediately — It was necessary to communicate this to my dear wife, whose distress was agonizing, and who though unable to walk across her chamber long insisted upon going immediately, herself to Washington — I determined to go myself to-morrow; to take the Boat from Providence on Monday; and I sent immediately for Dr. Holbrook, who came, and assured my wife that it was impossible she should go to Washington, in the present state of her health, and that the attempt would be at the hazard of her life. She became herself convinced it would be so, and was partially tranquilised. The Doctor did not apprehend any further effect upon her of this dreadful shock, but he had not been an hour gone, when she was seized with excessive sickness, faintings and cramps — I sent for him again and he came at nine this Evening. After some time the extreme sickness subsided and he promised to come again early to morrow Morning ≈

19. IV. Sunday. ≈ I wrote a page, for occupation, if possible to relieve the deep affliction of my Soul. I feel the duty and the

difficulty of resignation to the Will of God — I invoke his mercy, profoundly conscious as I am of my own unworthiness to obtain it — And still cherish hope, where hope is without rational support.

20. V. Monday — From Boston to Providence. Steamer Benjamin Franklin ≈ There was much conversation this evening among the Passengers upon religious and political topics in which I took a part. Much discussion upon the controverted character and divinity of Christ, and much upon the Slave question, the prospects of universal emancipation, and the intellectual capacity of the African race. These Conversations were continued till past midnight — to the annoyance of one whom they roused from sleep in his cot.

———

22. V:30. Wednesday — From Philadelphia to Washington. ≈ it was just ten O'Clock, when I alighted at the House of my Son John, at Washington — William C. Greenleaf came to the door, and as I came out of the Carriage, I asked how my Son was — he said — very low. Mrs. Frye received me in the drawing-room; and Mr. Frye in my chamber. — Mrs. Frye advised me at first not to see him till the morning, but afterwards changed her mind, and thought it best I should see him before retiring to bed — I sent for Dr. Huntt in the middle of the Night. He came, and advised me to see him — I went to his bed-side twice, and saw and heard him; he had no consciousness of any thing on Earth — His wife was in bed in the upper chamber; very sick herself — on seeing me she burst into tears — I promised her that I would be a father to her and her children — Finding myself much exhausted and unwell, I retired at 2 in the morning to bed.

23. IV:30. Thursday. At half past four I rose again, and going into the bed-chamber where my Son lay, found Mr. Frye, closing his eyes — He had just ceased to breathe — May God in his infinite mercy have received him to the joys of Heaven! Of the day from that time I have no distinct recollection — In a state between stupefaction, and a nervous irritation aggravated by the exertion to suppress it, the effort of my Soul was a deep, and earnest and unceasing supplication to God, for the

Spirit and the will to fulfil all the duties devolving upon me, by this event; and for the blessing of Almighty God upon this purpose — Mr. Frye, whose devotion to my dear child, during all his illness has been unbounded, undertook to make all the necessary arrangements for the funeral — My dear Son had been in a declining and drooping state of health more than three years — Several times afflicted with severe and acute disease; often so far recovered as to be out — able to travel and attend to business but never well ≈ I wrote to my beloved wife, and to my only surviving Son, communicating to them this heavy dispensation of the Providence of God. I controuled as far as I was able the unutterable anguish of my own Soul, endeavouring to sooth the yet more aggravated affliction of his widowed wife. Reduced and emaciated by sickness herself, she suffers in body and in mind; above all at her own inability to render to her beloved and affectionate husband in the extremes of his last illness the tender attentions and good Offices which smooth the pillow of death ≈

24. V. Friday. The day passed like that of yesterday almost unconsciously to myself, with an agonizing heart, a perpetually aggravating sense of the calamity that has befallen me — an inability to realize its extent — a galling consciousness that it can never be repaired, and an unceasing recollection of all the precious services that my darling child had rendered me — his discharge of all his filial duties, his kindness, his affection, his devotion to all my interests, and all my desires — the uncomplaining patience with which he has endured misfortune, sickness and disappointment, the hardness of his fate, and the meekness with which he has submitted to it — even his infirmities — Oh! let me not murmur at the will of God — Let me cast myself and him upon the mercies of an omnipotent creator and preserver; let me believe, that for suffering upon Earth there is compensation in Heaven, and that there, the tears of sorrow are wiped away, and that every virtue shall be blessed with its reward — My child — my child — In the bosom of your God, may never-ending joys — joys unspeakable and full of glory, cancel all the sufferings, of which your portion was so great here below, and may it one day be the blessed destiny of your Parents to enjoy them with you.

—

27. V Monday. I had not been out of the house, since my arrival in the City, excepting yesterday to go to Church — This morning I walked round the Capitol hill and garden for exercise. Mr. and Mrs. Frye were here the greater part of the day: and also W. C. Greenleaf. We began to make the collection of my dear deceased Son's manuscript Books and Papers, and the examination of them occupied me near the whole of the day — I received and answered a Letter from my dear wife of the 23ᵈ. I received also a Letter from Solomon Lincoln of Hingham, enclosing a copy of Resolutions adopted at the Meeting on Monday last of the whig Convention of the 12ᵗʰ Congressional District of Massachusetts — Approving the course I have held in Congress and nominating me, as a candidate for re-election as a member of the 24ᵗʰ Congress — In the calamities which oppress me and call for submission to the Will of Heaven, it is cheering consolation to me that the kindness and good will of my neighbours are yet left me — That my public conduct is approved by those who have entrusted their interests to my charge, and that they still have confidence in me.

———

[December 1834]

12. V:15. Friday ≈ Morning visit from Mr. Webster, which made me a quarter of an hour belated at the meeting of the house. The call for Petitions was in progress, soon succeeded by that for Resolutions. These are almost numberless, for the plunder by wholesale and retail of the Public Lands — I am more and more convinced it will be impossible to save them from the grasp of the western People, aided by the abandonment of the South, and the treachery of Northern traffickers for the Presidency — There was much discussion about fixing a day for debating the Bill for reducing and graduating the price of Public Lands; that is to say for giving them away.

———

24. VI:45. Wednesday. Overslept myself till broad daylight, which in my present state of occupations was a heavy loss of time — I had hoped to finish by this day my second and abridged Oration upon the Life and Character of La Fayette; but am disappointed, and have yet work for three or four days — At the House, the concurrent Resolution fixing the 31ˢᵗ inst't for the delivery of the Oration upon La Fayette had been

yesterday ordered to be engrossed for a third reading; but this morning the Speaker said it was a concurrent, and not a joint Resolution and did not require three readings. He should therefore consider it as passed, and send it to the Senate for concurrence. When the Resolution offered yesterday by Mr. Lincoln to call upon the President for information of the State of the Negotiation respecting the North Eastern boundary came up, Gorham Parks opposed its passage in a long, acrimonious Speech against its passage, professing at the same time to be altogether indifferent about it and objecting especially to the latter part of it — His object seemed to be to vent his spleen against the State of Massachusetts, and to rouse the party feeling of the Administration men to put down the Resolution. Evans of Maine answered him with a mild, temperate, playful and cutting severity, exposing the inconsistencies and profligacy of the party in Maine, which have used this controversy as an Engine against the last Administration, and are now tamely sacrificing the territory of the State itself in servile submission to the present Administration. Evans among other things noticed the boisterous nullification doctrines of the party in Maine, until the President's Proclamation of December 1832, referring to debates in the Legislature in which he had opposed in vain those doctrines, and to the tameness with which they have been abandoned since the Proclamation — T. F. Foster of Georgia followed Evans with a spirited speech in honour of nullification. Lincoln replied fully to the objections of Parks — F. O. J. Smith, makes a Speech against that of Evans, but says he shall vote for the Resolution — The Orders of the day were called for at the expiration of the hour; but the house were so much amused by the debate on Lincoln's resolution that they refused to pass to the orders, and the debate continued till past 3 when the house adjourned over to Saturday. Beatty of Kentuckey, nettled at the failure of his motion yesterday for a joint Resolution to adjourn over to Monday now opposed the motion to adjourn over Christmas day at-all; and called for the yeas and nays, but the house denied them. There is no trial of temper more provoking than that of conflicting with a majority of a deliberative Assembly; and none where a manifestation of temper is more useless and unwise — I have fallen into this error more than once, and occasionally made myself exceedingly obnoxious by it — The manifestation of temper must be most carefully distinguished from resistance to the will of a Majority, which is sometimes a duty of the highest order.

———

[January 1835]

Sunday 18 Jan'y 1835. V:15. ≈ I paid a morning visit to Miss Harriet Martineau and Miss Jeffery her companion — She had brought me Letters of Introduction from Mr. Furness of Philadelphia, and Mr. Charles Brooks of Hingham; in company with whom Miss Martineau came from England — She is the author of Conversations upon political Economy, which I have not read or seen — She is a young woman, I suppose about 30 — deaf, and hearing only through an Ear trumpet — Her conversation however is lively and easy, and she talks politics English or American — I met there Mr., Mrs. and Miss Webster, and Mr. I. C. Bates.

———

V:15. Friday 30 Jan'y 1835. Rode to the Capitol, and attended the funeral of Warren Ransom Davis, a member of the House of Representatives from South-Carolina. The Service was performed by Mr. Hatch, the Chaplain of the Senate, according to the forms of the Episcopal Church — Mr. Preston the Senator from the State said to me that I had lost in Davis a devoted friend — and I believe it was true. Nearly the last words he ever spoke in the House were, that he hoped God would forgive him for the part he had taken in 1828 against me; for he never should forgive himself — I rode to the grave-yard with Charles G. Ferris from New-York — As we were descending the broad flight of steps from the Rotunda, on the Eastern front of the Capitol, I heard the snap of a Pistol — sounding like a squib — It was aimed at the president of the United States, by an insane man named Lawrence, and it was said he snap'd a second pistol, but I heard only one report — They both missed fire. The incident occasioned some commotion; but the funeral procession was not delayed — The number of the members who followed it however was not so great as usual — From the grave-yard I returned with Mr. Ferris to the Capitol, where there came only the Speaker, and one or two other members — He took the Chair, and at my motion adjourned the House.

CHAPTER XII ❦ 1835–1838

Twenty-Fourth and Twenty-Fifth Congresses

[March 1835]

7. VI:30. Saturday. Fahrenheit 32–36. Snow, Sleet, Hail and rain, the whole day, which confined me to the house — I endeavoured to take up the thread of my Diary, which has broken several times and which it is impossible for me wholly to repair — I have written Letters to my Son Charles, to judge Hopkinson at Philadelphia, and to B. F. Hallett — The position which I now occupy before the public resembles much that which I held in 1807 and 1808 — The forced unanimous vote in the House on Monday Evening last in favour of my Resolution is the exact counterpart of the forced town meeting, called by the federalists in Boston, upon the affair of the Chesapeak, after they had refused calling one at my request; and of the forced Resolutions then adopted; for which they took ample vengeance of me afterwards — My conduct then expelled me from the Senate of the United States, as it has excluded me from it now — It afterwards sent me for eight years on important Missions in Europe; made me eight years Secretary of State, and four years President — I have not life before me for such another Career now, and with the same Ordeal to pass through, I have nothing before me but the prospect of a desperate struggle and political ruin — I shall not live to see as before the day of reparation — The french chamber of deputies will reject the Bill for paying the five Millions of Dollars, stipulated by the Treaty. Some rash and foolish act of President Jackson will follow, and if the two Countries should be saved from a War, it seems as if it could only be by a special interposition of Providence. The Presidential succession has mingled itself with all the important transactions of the recent Session of Congress; broken up the administration party, and laid the foundation for an entirely new organization of parties at the next Session — Standing alone as I do, disconnected from all parties, and having at the recent Session taken upon the French question a stand so conspicuous, so desperately contested; so

triumphant in its result, and so sure to combine against me *all* the Candidates for the Presidency, what can save me from destruction at the next Session, if the French quarrel should continue, but an unseen protecting power? — Be thou faithful unto death.

———

25. VI. Wednesday. ≈ My occupation is almost exclusively upon the Patronage Bill — To the passage of this Bill, through the Senate, all the powers of Calhoun, Clay and Webster have been devoted; joined by Hugh L. White who since he has been nominated a Candidate for the Presidency has wheeled to the right about, from East to West, without notice or at least without public censure; the Jackson party not yet daring to assail him, and the whigs hailing him with a hearty welcome — I have examined this subject with much attention, but not yet so thoroughly as I ought before committing myself to the desperate chance of encountering all these Giants — They were very feebly resisted by the Administration members of the Senate, who understood little of the Subject. — I fear it will not have justice done it in the House, and am above all distrustful of my own ability to do it Justice.

26. VI:15. Thursday. I finished this morning the draught of a Speech upon J. C. Calhoun's patronage Bill; which would fill eleven columns of the National Intelligencer, and would take between three and four hours to deliver. Upon reading it over, I find it is without method, and in a great measure without point — A desultory discussion upon the debate in the first Congress on the President's power of removal from Executive Offices, with a severe and cutting review of Daniel Webster's speech in the Senate, in favour of the Bill — That Speech is indeed so shallow, so unprincipled, and so subversive of all Constitutional doctrine, that I could not possibly treat it with respect: but this is not wise. Some time past noon, I walked to the Capitol, and looked into two volumes of Swift's works — Scott's Edition, for the passage cited in Johnson Dictionary under the word Executive, but could not find it — I found however several references to Hobbes's opinions, and examined the Folio Volume of Hobbes's Works, till 3 O'Clock when I was obliged to leave the Library, which is closed at that

hour — I did not find the word Executive in his Book — He speaks of Legislative Power, but scouts all ideas of mixed Monarchy and rejects with the utmost disdain all ideas of a division of Powers — His Leviathan was published in Paris in 1751 — three years after the execution of Charles the 1st. His book was exceedingly obnoxious; more however for its anti-religious than for its monarchical principles — He insists upon the Sovereign power to levy Soldiers and taxes as he may need them. It seems to me there is nothing in the book worth retaining — Historically it may be considered as an exposition of the political doctrines of the Cavaliers of that time — This afternoon the Telegraph contained J. C Calhoun's last Speech on his Patronage Bill — as shallow as Webster's and much more dogmatical — There are plausible arguments in both — but not one that is sound — After reading that of Calhoun, and analyzing the main stay of his argument I found it ended in empty sophistry — His conclusion impudently overstretches his premises — I began this Evening a reply to his Speech which employed me till near eleven O'Clock — Dr. Huntt here — Fanny yet very sick.

27. V:30. Friday. I finished this morning the remarks on J. C. Calhoun's speech, on his Patronage Bill as additional to mine; and now on reviewing my own, I find it like a tape-worm, without beginning or end — all desultory — I want Patience to write it over again, and methodize it — There is a great defect running through all the arguments in reply to the Speeches of Calhoun and Webster — it is contemptuous and disdainful; which I could not help — Calhoun's tone, is so self-sufficient and overbearing, and Webster's reasoning so utterly ignorant or unprincipled that they provoked my temper, and I answer them with cutting sarcasm; the use of this weapon is seldom politic — In the present case it would certainly not be so. I should write my Speech over again to say in mild, courteous, inoffensive language, what I have said in consuming caustic — I can make no use of my Speech as now written, and yet it contains matter to grind up into dust, Calhoun's and Webster's Speeches and also Calhoun's Patronage Report — Mr. Fendall was here and I had near two hours of conversation with him — He appeared to incline to the opinion that the

Grand-jury of the Circuit Court now in Session, ought to in-
dict Andrew Jackson, the President, and a man named Coltman, a member of the Common Council of the City — for a
conspiracy and subornation of perjury, to charge Poindexter
with having employed Lawrence to shoot the President —
Coltman is a member of the Common Council, and that body
have passed Resolutions branding him with infamy — The
whole transaction is inexpressibly base, and approaches much
too near to the President, for the good of his reputation —
The Committee of the Senate however exonerate him from
the guilt of the conspiracy — Fendall has been lately to Richmond, Virginia, where he says the whig members of the Legislature had two Caucuses, and postponed the nomination of a
candidate for the Presidency — The whigs are to have a Convention at Baltimore next December to nominate a Candidate
for the Presidency. I walked round the Capitol before dinner,
and in the Evening began an answer to a Letter from Dr.
George Parkman of Boston; which from drowsiness I could
not continue.

28. VI. Saturday. In the search for the History of the Doctrine
respecting the separation of the Legislative and Executive
Powers of Government, I visited this morning the Congress
Library, and examined Locke on Government, and the works
of Sir Robert Filmer — Locke's Treatise was written expressly
to refute the Doctrines of Filmer, and the principal question
between them was this separation of the Legislative and Executive Powers — Filmer insisting as Hobbes and all the writers
of that age on the monarchical side had done, that Government implied absolute power, and that there could be no separation of powers, without a dissolution of the Government.
Locke lays down very distinctly the division of the powers, and
in the 12th Chapter of the second book, treats expressly of the
Legislative, Executive and federative power of the Commonwealth, meaning by the federative power, the Executive with
reference to the Laws of Nations — This division is more
complete than that of Montesquieu. I think Locke was the in-
ventor of this theory of the division of powers; and of the reasoning which considers liberty, as depending upon their
separation — Montesquieu has taken the argument of Locke,

and applied it to the particular organization of the English Government. I took out from the Library the volume of the works of Sir Robert Filmer — It is a small octavo Volume, containing several Tracts upon Government published at different times. That, to which Locke's Treatise is the reply, is the last in the volume — entitled Patriarcha; and was first published in 1680 — This was doubtless the doctrine of Charles the second, and of his Court. — It has fared with Sir Robert Filmer, and the Tory writers of that age, as it did with the Sophists of the age of Socrates and Plato — Men of great and powerful minds, assuming erroneous first principles, and erecting upon them plausible and stupendous systems of morals and Politics, overwhelmed not by the greater skill or talent, but by the purer fountain of elementary principle, and rendered odious to all time.

———

31. VI. Tuesday. I walked this morning to the Capitol, and spent there between two and three hours in examining Marchamont Nedham's right Constitution of a Commonwealth, Harrington's Oceana and Sydney's Discourses on Government, for their views of Legislative, Executive and Judicial Power — There is very little in either of them upon the last, but all of them mark the distinction between Legislative and Executive power — There are seven pages of Nedham's work, of argument and historical illustration to prove the absolute necessity of separating these two powers; and there is nothing in Montesquieu or in Locke on this subject, but what is quite as well said in these seven pages — Harrington's Oceana, is a sort of political romance, dedicated to Oliver Cromwell Lord Protector, and being an Allegorical exposition of the English Commonwealth under his Government. Montesquieu charges Harrington with building a Chalcedon, with a Byzantium before his eyes — But Harrington's book was published in 1656 and his Byzantium then was Cromwell's Protectorate. Nedham's book was also published in 1656 as Hobbes's Leviathan had been published in 1651. Sidney's Discourses were unpublished until his trial, but they are entirely confined to the refutation of Sir Robert Filmer's Patriarcha; which was afterwards taken in hand by Mr. Locke — Filmer's reasoning appears now so utterly absurd that one can hardly conceive how two such elaborate

works as those of Sidney and Locke should have been thought necessary, to answer them — Filmer solves all civil Government into paternal authority, and spurns at every idea of limitation upon it. Hobbes does the same — I looked also into Fortescue de laudibus legum Angliae, but found nothing there upon Legislative or Executive power.

———

[April 1835]
3. VI. Friday. The child Fanny, is recovering from her severe intermittent fever, but her mother and grandmother are much indisposed with heavy colds — I called at Mrs. Wolfenden's for a settlement of her rent and she gave me a bill of half her quarters rent for putting up a coal grate — Walking round the Capitol, Franklin E. Plummer, a member of the late House of Representatives from Mississippi was starting from Mrs. Dunn's in a Carryall, and asked me to take a seat with him which I did; he was driving to the War Department, where I left him — He said he thought Poindexter had been imprudent in his great dinner Speech at Philadelphia. — The whigs of Philadelphia have made a magnificent Banquet at the Arch-Street Theatre; in honour of Mr. Poindexter; against whom, the basest conspiracy ever witnessed in this Country has been defeated and exposed — growing out of the attempt of Richard Lawrence to assassinate the President; at the Capitol, on the 29th of January, the day of Warren R. Davis's funeral. Immediately after Lawrence's two pistols missed fire the President said it was a Poindexter affair — Soon after a man named Coltman a member of the Common Council, suborned two men named Foy and Stewart to make affidavit's that they had seen Lawrence go to Poindexter's house, and talking with him, a day or two before the attempted Assassination — The President was treasuring up these Affidavits, when they were communicated to D. J. Pearce when visiting at the House, and by him to Southworth, a newspaper correspondent and Reporter — The facts got thus into the newspapers — Poindexter, wrote to the President demanding an explanation but received no answer. Poindexter demanded an investigating Committee of the Senate; and there was one appointed who detected and exposed the conspiracy, so far at least as to fasten the Subornation by Coltman; and the falsehood of the two affidavits — They reported a

triumphant vindication of Poindexter's innocence, and the report was unanimously accepted by the Senate — The public indignation is thus transformed, from the Assassin of the person to the Assassin of character, and Jackson himself bears no small portion of the public odium. The Philadelphia whigs turn it to political account; and give a great festival to Poindexter, to celebrate his escape from the conspiracy — Poindexter avails himself of the occasion to make a flaming opposition Speech, which may be excusable in him but which seems to me not well judged — The whole affair is sickening to me, and looks too much as if we were running into the manners of the Italian Republics.

———

19. VI. Sunday — Easter-day. ≈ In the pursuit of my enquiries concerning this Patronage Bill, I got engaged with Gales and Seaton's Register of debates Vol. 6 part 1 upon the debates in the Senate of the Winter of 1829–30 the first Session of the 21st Congress; and of Jackson's Administration — It absorbed my attention so intensely that the day was gone, and I had done nothing — It seemed a trial of strength between the makers of long Speeches, who could hold out longest, and wander widest from the proper subject of discussion — A very large portion of the debate upon Executive patronage was wasted upon Foot's Resolution respecting the Public Lands — That debate was one of the earliest results of that coalition between the South and the West, to sacrifice the manufacturing and free labour interest of the North and East to the Slave-holding interest of the South, by the plunder of the public Lands surrendered by the South to the new Western States — This was the secret of that combined, and simultaneous attack of Hayne and Benton upon the Eastern Section of the Union, so manfully and ably met and repelled by Webster and Sprague — The Jackson Administration had been formed upon this combination, and had drawn New-York and Pennsylvania into its vortex — It is rather surprising that the sacrifice of the public Lands was not then entirely consummated — Benton was the founder of this project — Clay had built his reputation as a Statesman and raised his ladder to the Presidency upon internal improvement, of the Western Country — He had connected himself with the free labour interest of the North in this

pursuit; Benton who had been one of his partizans till then saw he could supplant him, by purchasing of the South the plunder of the public Lands, and selling to them the Western interest of internal improvement — This was the governing impulse of the joint movement of Hayne and Benton, against the East and North in that debate — Why can I pursue this subject no further? Mary was seized violently this morning with a return of chills and fever, and was confined the whole day to her bed.

20. VI. Monday. Mary was still confined all day to her bed — Her brother Johnson was here this afternoon, but did not come in to visit me — Dr. Huntt was here. This occurrence has disconcerted all my arrangements for returning to Quincy, as I cannot go and leave her ill here, and as these returns of chills and fevers are apt to be exceedingly obstinate — I received a Letter from the Rev'd Dr. Sprague of Albany, which I answered — Walked round the Capitol Hill before dinner; and to alleviate my anxiety and distress, gave up as much as possible my mind to my researches upon Executive Patronage. I read over most of the debates in the Senate, through the memorable Session of 1829–30 and made out a list of all the Speakers on the numerous questions involving this Constitutional principle — I perused also the Executive Journal of that Session, published as an Appendix to the Legislative Journal of the same Session — It was Webster's Speeches and replies to Hayne in that Session, in the debates on Foot's Resolution, which raised his reputation to the highest pitch, and not without reason — They are monuments of eloquence and debateable power — Neither he nor Hayne in their Speeches on that Resolution introduced the Patronage question, but Foot himself and others did — particularly Clayton, Johnston, Grundy, Livingston and Bibb — The great effort of every member was to shew that he could make a tiresome long Speech — Webster however, putting his whole stake upon the answer to Hayne, rather affectedly avoided noticing Benton, who was the great and real assailant — The Policy of this is extremely doubtful — It seems to me upon a review of the whole debate that Webster should have answered Benton as well as Hayne — that he should have assumed the offensive against both, and

exposed the profligate combination between Nullification and
the Robbery of the Public Lands which urged the joint attack
of Benton and Hayne upon the East — This he did not do —
He kept wholly on the defensive as to the East; and suffered
Hayne to sacrifice, all the rights of the old States to their portion of the public Lands, with impunity — This was the deadly
poison of that league which brought in the Jackson Administration, and it has never yet been exposed — The failure of
its consummation hitherto has been owing to the breach between Jackson and Calhoun, brought about by Van-Buren —
to the consequent precipitation of the nullification rebellion of
South-Carolina — to the compromise between Clay and Calhoun, and to Clay's Land-Bills, which though defeated by
Jackson's veto have yet defeated or rather delayed the total
sacrifice of the public Lands, which yet Jackson openly recommended in his message of December 1832 — My wife and two
Grand-children, narrowly escaped severe injury if not worse,
by the slamming to of a window blind, which smashed four
squares of large window-glass in the dining room, where they
were standing — Fanny escaped with a slight scratch on the
head — the others were unhurt — blessed be God.

———

24. VI. Friday. My speculations upon the Patronage Bill have
all of a sudden met with a check, from a slackening of thought
in the midst of the argument, and from a call to other objects
— Alfred this day left us, and I returned him to his mother; by
whom he had been bound by an Indenture to my Son. I have
not been able to find the deed. There were yet four or five
years of his time to run; but we were so much dissatisfied with
him, that we thought it best to discharge him; and have taken
a young black man named Augustus in his place — I was much
occupied in making out a list of Postmasters in the Towns of
the 12th Congressional district of Massachusetts, and answered
a Letter from Frederick Kretschman a German at Philadelphia,
who has made a German Translation of my Oration, on the
Life and Character of La Fayette, and wishes me to read it, and
advise him whether to send it to Germany for publication. Mr.
Van Buren, the Vice-President paid me a morning visit — Our
conversation was upon the surprizing growth and increase of
the City and State of New-York, in the half century since I

landed there from France in July 1785, when the population of
the City was less than twenty-thousand Souls. It is now little
short of two hundred and forty thousand, and still increasing
with unexampled rapidity — He remarked that very few persons had made fortunes by this course of Events, although the
rise in the price of Lands had kept full pace with the growth of
population — That John Jacob Astor, had systematically in-
vested his property in Lands and had now an Estate worth
thirteen or fourteen, some said fifteen Millions of Dollars. He
said he himself had foolishly two or three years since sold the
greater part of his own Estate in Lands, and that now the same
lands were worth at least forty per cent more than he sold
them for. I observed that the creation of Banks and of Bank
paper, aggravated heavily the price of Lands — He said that
was true, and very obvious; and it was surprizing that People
would not see it — This was the nearest approach that we
made to politics.

———

[July 1835]
10. IV. Friday. ≈ John Marshall, Chief Justice of the United
States died at Philadelphia last Monday the 4th inst't. He was
one of the most eminent men that this Country has ever
produced — He has held this appointment thirty-five years —
It was the last act of my father's Administration, and one of the
most important services, rendered by him to his Country —
All Constitutional Governments are flexible things — And as
the Supreme Judicial Court is the tribunal of last resort for the
Construction of the Constitution and the Laws, the Office of
Chief Justice of that Court is a station of the highest trust, of
the deepest responsibility; and of influence far more extensive
than that of the President of the United States. John Marshall
was a federalist of the Washington School — The associate
judges, from the time of his appointment have generally been
taken from the democratic or Jeffersonian party — not one of
them excepting Story has been a man of great ability. Several
of them have been men of strong prejudices, warm passions,
and contracted minds — one of them occasionally insane —
Marshall, by the ascendency of his genius, by the amenity of
his deportment, and by the imperturbable command of his
temper has given a permanent and systematic character to the

decisions of the Court and settled many great constitutional questions favourably to the continuance of the Union. Marshall has cemented the Union, which the crafty and Quixotic Democracy of Jefferson had a perpetual tendency to dissolve — Jefferson hated and dreaded him — Marshall kept Jefferson much under the curb; some times, as perhaps in the case of Aaron Burr's conspiracy too much so — but Marshall's mind was far better regulated than that of Jefferson — It is much to be feared that a successor will be appointed of a very different character — The President of the United States now in Office has already appointed three judges of the Supreme Court; with the next appointment he will have constituted the Chief Justice, and a majority of the Court — He has not yet made one good appointment — His Chief Justice will be no better than the rest — The death of Judge Marshall has occurred under Circumstances of deep melancholy — His disease was the stone — he had been saved and relieved about three years, by the operation of lithotomy performed with consummate skill by Doctor Physick — He had now been brought, a few days before his death to Philadelphia, for a further and last resource to save him — His eldest Son, a man of more than forty years of age, having a wife and family of six children, was at Baltimore, on his way to Philadelphia, to sooth with filial affection and tenderness the last moments of his father's life, when by the falling of the timber of a house in a Tornado, upon his head he was mortally wounded, and died after being trepanned three or four days before his father. Oh! how much suffering is in the best and happiest condition of human existence.

———

[August 1835]

11. III:50. Tuesday. ≈ I received a Letter from Mr. Frye at Washington about my private business; and in great distress and agony at an attempt of a negro slave of Mrs. Thornton, at Washington, to murder her, and her mother Mrs. Brodeau. There is a great fermentation upon this subject of Slavery, at this time in all parts of the Union. The emancipation of the Slaves in the British West India Colonies — The Colonization Society here, the current of public opinion running every where stronger and stronger into democracy and popular

supremacy, contribute all to shake the fetters of Servitude —
The theory of the rights of man has taken deep root in the soil
of civil Society. It has allied itself with the feelings of humanity
and the precepts of Christian benevolence. It has armed itself
with the strength of organized association. It has linked itself
with religious doctrines and religious fervour. Anti-Slavery
Associations are formed in this Country and in England, and
they are already co-operating in concerted agency together —
They have raised funds to support and circulate inflammatory
Newspapers and pamphlets gratuitously — and they send
multitudes of them into the Southern Country, into the midst
of the swarms of Slaves. There is an Englishman, by the name
of Thompson, lately come over from England, who is travelling about the country holding meetings and making eloquent
inflammatory harangues, preaching the immediate abolition of
Slavery. The general disposition of the people here is averse to
these movements and Thompson has several times been routed
by popular tumults. But in some places he meets favourable
reception, and makes converts — There has been recently an
alarm of Slave-insurrection in the State of Mississippi, and
several white persons have been hung, by a summary process
of what they call Lynch's Law. That is Mob Law — Add to all
this the approach of the Presidential election, and the question
whether the President of the United States shall be a Slave-
holder or not. They never fail to touch upon this key in the
South, and it has never yet failed of success. Rouse in the heart
of the Slave-holder, the terror of his Slave, and it will [be] a
motive with him paramount to all others never to vote for any
man, not a Slave-holder like himself — There are now Calls in
the Atlas the Webster paper, and the Morning-Post, the
Jackson-Van-Buren-paper at Boston, for a Town-meeting, to
put down the abolitionists; but the disease is deeper than can
be healed by Town-meeting Resolutions.

12. IV. Wednesday ≈ At two O'Clock I went in the Carriage
alone to Boston, and dined with Mr. Benjamin Gorham —
The party consisted of Mess'rs Flournoy and Foster of Georgia
— Charles Codman, Isaac P. Davis, Edward Everett, Abbott
Lawrence, Joseph Russell, David Sears, Mr. Truman, and
myself — Mrs. Gorham was the only Lady at Table — Mr.

Sears has lately returned from France, with his family. He went with the expectation of procuring for his children advantages of superior-education. He returns disappointed and convinced that the Schools whether for boys or girls at Paris are not so good as those of this Country — Davis had a hand bill from the Atlas Newspaper Office, containing an account of continued riots at Baltimore, on Saturday and Sunday last, in which the Houses of Reverdy Johnson, John Glenn, and John B. Morris were destroyed by the mobility — In those two days, the authorities of the City and of the State appear scarcely to have made an effort to sustain the Laws and the rights of property — The riotous spirit manifested itself also last Night at Charlestown, and Roxbury, by an attempt to celebrate in a tumultuous manner the anniversary of the destruction of the Roman Catholic Nunnery at Charlestown — It is said this was suppressed, but Edward Everett says there were riotous assemblages in the Streets very noisy till late last Night. The Baltimore riot was directed against all the persons implicated in the fraudulent failure of the Bank of Maryland which happened, nearly 18 Months ago. Mr. Abbott Lawrence told me that they were going to have a very great meeting at Boston to put down the Anti-Slavery abolitionists; but he said there was no diversity of opinion, upon that subject here — That I think will depend upon the measures to be proposed. If the measures are vapouring Resolutions they will pass unanimously and be inefficient — If the measures are efficient, there will be diversity of opinion — I returned home immediately from Mr. Gorham's, and reached my House shortly before the nine O'Clock bell — Charles and his wife spent the Evening at Mr. Lunt's. George Whitney has taken his dismission from the Church and Congregation where he was settled — I took with me to Boston the first Volume of the Letters from Horace Walpole to Sir Horace Mann — The Letters are of the winter of 1741 and 1742 and are very interesting, by containing the detailed account of the breaking up of the ministry of Sir Robert Walpole — The Letters from the Minister's Son, living with him, and himself a member of Parliament, witnessing and reporting from day to day the successive votes marking the decline and fall of a great man from power, afford a melancholy but instructive picture of human nature, in the high political relations of Society — The picture has strong resemblances to others of which I have had more knowledge and experience.

———

14. IV. Friday. ≈ The accounts of the riots in Baltimore continue. In the State of Mississippi mobs are hanging up blacks suspected of insurgency, and whites suspected of abetting them — At Charleston South Carolina Mobs of Slave-holding Gentlemen intercept the Mails, and take out from them all the inflammatory pamphlets, circulated by the abolitionists, who in their turn, are making every possible exertion to kindle the flame of insurrection among the Slaves. — We are in a state of profound Peace, and over pampered with prosperity — Yet the elements of exterminating war seem to be in vehement fermentation, and one can scarcely foresee to what it will lead.

———

18. IV:45. Sun rose 5:11. My Son Charles's birth-day — His age twenty-eight ≈ I received from Washington a Richmond Enquirer, containing the Address of the Baltimore Van Buren Convention to the Democratic Republicans of the United States. There is something extraordinary in the present condition of parties throughout the Union. Slavery and Democracy, especially the Democracy founded as ours is upon the rights of man, would seem to be incompatible with each other — And yet at this time, the Democracy of the Country is supported chiefly, if not entirely by Slavery — There is a small shallow and enthusiastic party, preaching the abolition of Slavery upon the principles of extreme democracy — but the democratic Spirit, and the popular feeling is every where against them — There have been riots at Washington, not much inferior in atrocity to those at Baltimore — A Slave of Mrs. Thornton, made an attempt to murder her and her mother with an axe in the Night — He was prevented from accomplishing his purpose by his own mother; and in revenge for this, mobs of white people at Washington have destroyed sundry Negro houses, school-houses and a church — In the State of Mississippi, they have hanged up several persons for circulating abolition pamphlets — In Charleston South-Carolina the principal men of the State, with the late Governor Hayne at their head, seize upon the Mails, with the co-operation of the Postmaster himself, and purify it, of the abolition pamphlets — and the Postmaster

General, Amos Kendall, neither approves nor disapproves of this proceeding — At Washington a man named Crandall has been imprisoned for circulating incendiary pamphlets and in Halifax County, Virginia, a man named David F. Robertson, a Scotch Teacher was in danger of his life; because another man named Robertson was suspected of having dropped in a Steam-boat, the first number of a newspaper, printed at New-York with the title of Human Rights — In Boston, there is a call for a Town-Meeting, signed by more than five hundred names, with H. G. Otis, and P. C. Brooks at their head. This meeting is to be held next Friday, and is to pass Resolutions against the abolitionists, to sooth and conciliate the temper of the Southern Slave-holders. All this is Democracy and the Rights of Man.

———

22. III:45. Saturday — Saw Sirius — Sun rose 5:16. The Rev'd. Samuel Nott jun'r Minister of a Congregational Church and Society at Wareham in the County of Plymouth, with his wife paid me a morning visit, of kindness and curiosity, and gave me a small volume of Sermons published by him and entitled Sermons from the fowls of the Air, and the Lilies of the Field. He told me that he had been some time a Missionary in India, and that he had seen me once in London at a Meeting of the British and foreign School Society in the year 1816 (13 May) We had some conversation upon the most agitating topic of this time — Slavery and its abolition. He thought that the abolition of Slavery must come — but that it should be gradual; beginning by attaching the slave to the soil, like the Serfs in the North of Europe. I said Mr. Rufus King had expressed a similar opinion in a Speech on the Missouri question, in the Senate of the U.S. but I believed the Slave-holders would never consent to it — My own opinion is that the Planters of the South will separate from the Union in terror of the emancipation of their Slaves, and that then the Slaves will emancipate themselves by a servile War. This consummation may be yet remote, and must be preceded by the sacrifice of the Public Lands to the Western States, effected by the co-operation of the South, to purchase that of the West, in perpetuating the Servitude of their Negroes — This Coalition accomplished the election of Andrew Jackson as President of the United States, and is now in full vigour to secure the election of his successor.

This is the under current, with the tide of Democracy at the Surface.

———

[September 1835]
1. III:45. Tuesday. Neponset Bridge Proprietor's annual Meeting Squantum. Harvey Field brought me a printed Petition to the Legislature of the Commonwealth for the abolition of Capital punishment — He asked if I would sign it. I declined, and told him I had not brought my mind to the conclusion that it would be for the good of the community — We have by the Laws of the Commonwealth only five crimes punishable with death — Treason, Murder, Burglary, Arson, and Rape — Now a Law to save the precious lives of men guilty of either of those crimes has in my judgment little claim to the merit of humanity. They are a class of People with whom humanity cannot sympathize — A law to prohibit the killing of Rattlesnakes would be as rational, and might be urged also upon principles of humanity — There is another point of view in which the abolition of capital punishment at this time is specially objectionable — While such exceeding tenderness is felt for the lives of Traitors, Murderers and Robbers, here is the Sovereign people, hanging up without judge or jury, gamblers, and even the mere circulators of printed papers recommending the abolition of Slavery. On one hand we have the most reckless disregard of human life, and the punishment of death summarily inflicted for offences comparatively light — and even for that which is no offence at all, on the other Traitors and Murderers, are taken into peculiar favour — and their lives must be preserved and guarded, as if they were the very jewels of the Land. The signs of the times are portentous — All the tendencies of Legislation, are to the removal of restrictions from the vicious and the guilty, and to the exercise of all the powers of Government, Legislative, judicial and executive, by lawless assemblages of individuals — I have however no doubt that the punishment of death will be abolished in this Commonwealth — and in all probability throughout this union.

———

[November 1835]
23. IV:15. Monday. Rain and Sleet almost the whole of this day — There seems to be an impulse more powerful than my will

which engrosses and swallows up my Time in some one object of occupation to the exclusion of all others — The Rule for the House now forms that object, and I can neither get through with my reflections upon it, nor abstract myself from them — Before dinner I walked to Mr. A. Guista's, and asked him to call with the note that I gave him about this time last year which he promised to do. After dinner I had a visit from Mr. Fendall, and had much conversation with him respecting Jonathan Russell's Ghent conspiracy against me — a full account of which I gave him from his private Letter of 24 December 1814 to Mr. Monroe to his triplicate Letter in Walsh's Gazette of May 1822. Among the dark spots in human nature which in the course of my life I have observed, the devices of rivals to ruin me have been sorry pictures of the heart of man — They first exhibited themselves at College — but in the short time that I was there, their operation could not be of much effect — But from the day that I quitted the walls of Harvard, H. G. Otis, Theophilus Parsons, Timothy Pickering, James A. Bayard, Henry Clay, Jonathan Russell, William H. Crawford, John C. Calhoun, Andrew Jackson, Daniel Webster, and John Davis, W. B. Giles and John Randolph, have used up their faculties in base and dirty tricks to thwart my progress in life and destroy my character — Others have acted as instruments to these and among these Russell was the most contemptible because he was the mere Jackall to Clay — He is also the only one of the list whom I have signally punished — To almost all the rest I have returned good for evil. I have never wronged any one of them, and have even neglected too much even my self defence against them.

———

[December 1835]
IV. VII:15. Friday. ≈ I made minutes of preparation for presenting 2 Petitions at the meeting of Congress next week; but from the crippling of my hands I cannot be prepared as I had intended and flattered myself I should be — I read the Message of George M'Duffie, Governor of South-Carolina, to the Legislature of that State — It is a bold uncompromising exposition of the Southern Slave-holding policy and opinions — Its insolence towards the free States is in even pace with its doctrines upon Slavery — I wait to see how long this tone is to be endured. Semper ego auditor tantum? It would at this time be

of no earthly use for me, to resist this torrent of moral depravity on one side, and of craven cowering on the other. My duty for the present is silence — Whether it may ever come to be my duty [to] speak, is in the darkness of futurity.

———

13. V. Sunday ≈ I read in the Knoxville Register the long dramatic narrative of John Howard Payne — He has suffered an abominable outrage, but I fear it is without prospect of a remedy — There is no security for the right of Life, of Liberty, of property or of reputation, in any of the Slave holding States with reference to Negroes, or Indians — I can at least give no aid to procure for him a remedy, or satisfaction.

———

18. V. Friday. ≈ At the House, the meeting of this day was held for the purpose of receiving private Bills from the Committee of Claims; but the Speaker called the States for the presentation of Petitions — N. B. Borden, presented a petition from Wrentham, for the abolition of Slavery in the District of Columbia, and moved its reference to a select Committee — Hammond of South Carolina moved that the petition should be rejected — This proposition which was wholly unexpected to Polk the Speaker disconcerted him, and he blundered in the tangles of the Rules — a debate of four hours arose between the fury of the Southern Slave-holders and wiley compliances of the Kinderhook school, in which the rest of the House took no part — Granger of New-York came to me and asked me if this was to be tolerated — I told him it would be tolerated — That the Presidential Election was crushing every elementary principle of Freedom, in the free States, and that I saw no prospect of useful resistance at this time — I should say nothing — I believed no one else would say anything — There was a perfect snarl of debate upon a multitude of questions succeeding each of other one only of which was taken by yeas and nays. This was the identical question to lay on the table; carried triumphantly by the South two days ago as a test question; now voted down by themselves 121 to 95 to get a vote of rejection — The House adjourned about 4 without closing the debate ≈

———

19. VI:30. Saturday ≈ I returned the visit of Mr. Martin — His servant told me that he was with Mr. Van Buren, and I left a

Card — I then returned the visit of Mr. Abbott Lawrence at Gadsby's, and found Mr. Granger with him: but they were carrying his dinner in just as I entered his chamber — They were conversing upon the calamitous fire at New-York last Wednesday night, in which nearly seven hundred houses were burnt down and from fifteen to twenty Millions of dollars of property was destroyed — Dr. Huntt who came this morning to visit Fanny had first mentioned it to me. Mr. Lawrence, and Mr. Granger spoke also of the debate yesterday in the House upon the petition to abolish Slavery in the District of Columbia, and both urged me to address the House on the subject — I fear I must.

21. VII:30. Monday ≈ Joab Lawler of Alabama, offered a Resolution that Congress had not the Constitutional right to abolish Slavery in the District of Columbia, and another that the House would receive no petition, praying therefor — Wise offered the same Resolutions otherwise expressed —   moved a suspension of the Rules that he might move to lay on the table Hammond's motion to reject the Petition, and offer his Resolutions — He called for the yeas and nays which were 115 to 101 against suspending the rules — Then came the motion to reconsider the reference of a petition from Cummington presented by Briggs, to the Committee on the District of Columbia — against which I addressed the house and was answered by Bouldin, and by   An adjournment was then moved, but suspended for a Message from the President with Documents relating to a bequest from an Englishman named Simonson for the establishment of a learned Institution in the City of Washington — The Message was at my motion referred to a Committee of Nine ≈

22. V. Tuesday ≈ In the House Lane of Indiana came to my Seat, and claimed the Smithson bequest Message as appurtenant to the Committee on the District of Columbia — I told him I did not know whether it did or not, but that I should call the Select Committee together, and if they should find it appertaining peculiarly to the District, they would ask to be discharged, and that it should be referred to that Committee — Upon the reading of the Journal the Select Committee were

announced, and I am the Chairman — The Speaker then said the unfinished business of yesterday was the reconsideration of the reference of the Petition from Cummington for the abolition of Slavery in the District of Columbia to the Committee on the District — The debate was then continued by Speeches from Wise of Virginia, Dromgoole of Virginia, Granger, Mann, and Beardsley of New-York, and Ingersoll of Pennsylvania. After 3 O'Clock Slade of Vermont moved an adjournment, announcing his intention to speak upon the subject to-morrow. Granger's Speech was short but spirited and pungent — Wise and Dromgoole made frequent and direct allusion to what I said yesterday — Wise maintained that Congress had no right to abolish Slavery in the District of Columbia, and quoted the provision that private property shall not be taken for public uses without compensation — and he complained that runaway Slaves should not be recovered in the North notwithstanding the Constitutional provision, that they should be restored — Joseph R. Ingersoll proposed a Resolution declaring in the broadest terms that the Constitution of the United States recognizes the right of the People of the Southern States to hold Slaves — A strange concession for a Pennsylvanian.

———

[January 1836]
4. V. Monday. I attended the house with feelings of no small anxiety. After the reading of the Journal, the Speaker called the States for Petitions, beginning with Maine — when he came to Massachusetts I presented the Memorial of F. C. Gray, and others, praying for an Act similar to that which passed the Senate at the last Session of Congress to indemnify them for French Spoliations prior to the year 1800. The memorial was at my motion without reading referred to the Committee of foreign Affairs — I next presented the petition of Albert Pabodie and 153 inhabitants of Millbury in the County of Worcester and Commonwealth of Massachusetts praying for the abolition of Slavery and the Slave-trade in the District of Columbia. This Petition was couched in the same language, with that which Briggs had presented last week, and which after it had been referred to the Committee on the District of Columbia, was by a reconsidered vote laid on the table together with the motion that it should be printed — I therefore

now after stating the contents of the petition from Millbury, said it was my intention to move that without reading it should be laid on the table — I was instantly interrupted by my next neighbour John M. Patton, who inquired whether the Petition had been received, to which the Speaker answered that it had not, whereupon Thomas Glascock, a new member from Georgia moved that it be not received, and was proceeding to make a Speech, when I called him to order, and appealing to the 45th rule of the House which prescribes that there shall be no debate upon Petitions on the day when they are presented, I demanded that the debate should now be postponed to a day certain, that this day might be free for the receipt of Petitions from all the States. The Speaker decided that as the Petition had not been received, it was not in possession of the House, and that the 45th rule of the House interdicting debate did not apply; from this decision I appealed, and asked for the yeas and nays which were ordered, and a debate arose upon the appeal, which consumed the day — I spoke twice; the second time after a clamorous call for the question, but after I had spoken Vinton of Ohio, moved an adjournment which was carried, leaving the question undecided — We had a family party to dine, with whom I invited this morning Mr. Jeremiah Bailey, member of the House of Representatives from Maine, and the husband of Dr. Welsh's eldest daughter, Charlotte, Mr. Abbott Lawrence with Professor Palfrey of Cambridge, and Mr. Stephen C. Phillips, and they all came. After they went away in the Evening we had a family party at whist.

5. VI:30. Tuesday. ≈ The call for Petitions proceeded as far as Virginia, when Wise enquired of the Clerk of the House what was the cause of the delay which had occurred in the printing of the Public Documents — Gillett offered to answer, but the Speaker said it was not in order, and a motion to adjourn was made and carried — In the Evening I finished my observations upon Othello, in a Letter to Dr. George Parkman.

6. V. Wednesday. Mr. James came this morning and paid a Quarter's Rent for his Mother; and with a bill for groceries, and Borland brought a Bill for Carpenter's work upon houses — Other Bills were also brought in, and the cares and troubles

of a household establishment are superadded to those of the public service. At the House, the thirty days from the commencement of the Session having expired, the business of the day commenced by a call of the States for Resolutions — Jarvis of Maine, offered as he said at the request of Owens of Georgia, a Resolution, declaring that the House will not entertain any Petitions for the abolition of Slavery in the District of Columbia; and he said that it was almost the universal opinion at the North that Congress have no right to interfere with Slavery — He read Resolutions apparently to that effect, adopted at some meeting last Summer in the State of Maine — I asked him to consent that the consideration of his Resolution should be postponed, to give an opportunity to other members to offer Resolutions; but he declined — Huntsman of Tennessee came to my Seat and asked me to move to lay the Resolution on the Table, and said they would support that — I made the motion accordingly and it was rejected by yeas and nays 123 to 66 Huntsman himself voting with the majority — Wise then moved two or three Resolutions as substitutes for those offered by Jarvis — and they declared that Congress had no power to abolish Slavery in the District of Columbia. Owens had said last week that he would move the Resolution now offered by Jarvis, and would immediately call for the previous question upon it — Wise now in offering his substitute said he should like to see who would move the previous question, upon it — Glascock, offered a Resolution as an Amendment to those of Wise; but Wise accepted it as a modification of his Resolutions — Cambreleng had been some time calling for the orders of the day; the hour for Resolutions having expired — He now succeeded.

———

8. V:30. Friday ≈ I answered a Letter from James C. Doane of Cohasset, and read part of a pamphlet on Slavery, by the Rev'd. Dr. Channing of Boston — He treats the subject so smoothly that some of the Southern Slave-holders have quoted it with approbation, as favouring their side of the question; but it is in fact an inflammatory, if not an incendiary publication. There is a chapter containing an exposition of the nature, and character of Slavery — Then one upon rights — and then one of explanations — These have a very jesuitical complextion. The

wrong, or crime of Slavery is set forth in all its most odious colours, and then the explanations, disclaim all imputation of criminality upon the Slave-holders. — There are some remarks certainly just, upon the relaxation of the moral principle in its application to individual obligation necessarily resulting from antient and established institutions. — But this is an exceedingly nice and difficult line to draw, and belongs at least as much to the Science of casuistry as to that of Ethics.

9. IV:30. Saturday. At ten O'Clock, or as soon after as I could get out of my house and reach the Capitol I met the Committee, on the President's Message relating to the Smithsonian bequest — The members present were Garland of Virginia, M'Kennan of Pennsylvania, Pearce of Rhode-Island, Thomas of Maryland, and Chapin of New-York — The absent members were Garland of Louisiana, Hannegan of Indiana, and Speight of North-Carolina, who is still confined by illness — The members now present had got over their scruples with regard to the acceptance of the bequest and directed me to prepare a Report and a Bill to that effect — A Committee of the Senate the Chairman of which was Benjamin Watkins Leigh of Virginia have already reported to that effect, and presented a joint Resolution authorising the President to obtain the funds, and making an appropriation of 5000 dollars to defray the expenses which may thereby be occasioned — Mr. Leigh's report contains a short and satisfactory argument for the competency of Congress to accept the bequest, and shewing it to be their duty — But as money cannot constitutionally be appropriated by Resolution, my direction from the Committee is to prepare a Bill, and to make the appropriation 10000 instead of 5000 dollars ≈

10. V:30. Sunday. Morning service at the Presbyterian Church. Mr. Bishop preached from Matthew 5:16 Let your light so shine before men, that they may see your good works, and glorify your father which is in heaven — Mr. Wardwell was in my pew, but the congregation was very thin — This young man preaches good works too much for the taste of a Presbyterian Calvinistic Society — His discourses are all practical. They rivet the attention of his hearers, and are never tedious — He

preaches more to my satisfaction than any other person whom for many years I have heard in this City — After Church I called successively upon Mr. Bankhead, the Charge d'Affaires from Great-Britain, and upon Col'l Aspinwall, who is at Fullers, to enquire if either of them could give me any further information respecting Mr. James Smithson, but they could not — I was desirous of obtaining it for the purpose of introducing into the Report of the Committee upon his bequest some complimentary notice of the donor. But so little are the feelings of others in unison with mine on this occasion, and so strange is this donation of half a million of dollars, for the noblest of purposes, that no one thinks of attributing it to a benevolent motive. Vail intimates in his Letter that the man was supposed to be insane. Bankhead thinks he must have had republican propensities, which is probable — Col'l Aspinwall conjectures that Mr. Smithson was an antenuptial son, of the first duke and duchess of Northumberland; and thus an elder brother of the late duke — But how he came to have a nephew named Hungerford, son of a brother named Dickinson and why he made this contingent bequest to the United States of America, no one can tell — The report if it hazards any reflection upon the subject must be very guarded. Mr. Bankhead thought it was a fine windfall for the city of Washington, and hoped if a professor of divinity should be wanted, we should remember his friend Hawley. Mrs. Bankhead was in admiration of the splendid edifice that might be erected with the money — Col'l Aspinwall said it would be easy to obtain the information which I desired in England; but that he had made no enquiries at the time when he had procured, and forwarded to the Department of State a copy of the Will, because, the bequest was then contingent, and it was very uncertain whether it would ever take effect — The will was made in 1826 — The year before which the Testator's nephew, the present Duke of Northumberland, had been upon a magnificent Embassy Extraordinary, at the Coronation of Charles the 10th of France. There seems to have been a determination, in the mind of the Testator, that his Estate should in no event go to the Duke of Northumberland or to any of his family — But certainly in the bequest itself there is a high and honourable sentiment of philanthropy, and a glorious testimonial of confidence in the

Institutions of this Union. A stranger to this Country, knowing it only by its history, bearing in his person the blood of the Percy's and the Seymour's, brother to a nobleman of the highest rank in British heraldry; who fought against the Revolution of our Independence at Bunker's Hill, that he should be the man to found at the City of Washington for the United States of America an establishment for the increase and diffusion of knowledge among men, is an event in which I see the finger of Providence compassing great results by incomprehensible means — May the Congress of the Union, be deeply impressed with the solemn duties devolving upon them by this trust, and carry it into effect in the fulness of its Spirit, and to the increase and diffusion of knowledge among men.

———

12. IV:30. Tuesday. ≈ At the House, my appeal from the decision of the Speaker that the 45th Rule of the House does not apply to a motion that a petition be not received was the special order of the day — Before calling the House to order Mr. Polk came to my Seat, and spoke somewhat doubtingly whether he should first announce it to be taken up, or the unfinished business of yesterday — I said I supposed the special order would come up of course. He did accordingly announce it — Ward of New-York moved that it should be postponed till next Monday, which gave rise to a short debate — The postponement was a Van Buren or majority measure; upon which the division was not sectional but political — I opposed the postponement, on the grounds that the question to be decided on the appeal was not confined to Petitions upon the subject of Slavery, but to all petitions; but that it must be decided before the question could be taken whether the petition presented by me, should or should not be received — As the Petitioners had thought proper to send their Petition to me, I wished to be able to inform them, what disposition of it has been made by the House. — I objected also to the postponement to next Monday because that being the day for receiving petitions, the debate if renewed would again interfere with the performance of that duty — The postponement was however carried ≈ I walked home with Jarvis and with a young man, a new member from the City of New-York named M'Keon — He spoke to me, of a quotation that I had made from Lear.

13. IV. Wednesday. I began the draught of a Report upon the Smithsonian bequest, which absorbed the morning till breakfast time and the journal dropped of course in arrears ≈ Jarvis called up his Resolution declaring that the subject of abolishing Slavery in the District of Columbia, ought not to be entertained by Congress, and that all petitions that may be presented demanding it should be laid on the table without printing. This was Jarvis's Resolution, but he had borrowed it from Owens of Georgia, who had given notice that he would move it and then immediately move the previous question. But when Jarvis moved his Resolution, Wise immediately moved as an amendment a declaration that Congress have no power to abolish Slavery; and said he would see, who would move the previous question on that — Glascock moved as an Amendment to Wise's Amendment a declaration that any attempt to agitate the question of abolishing Slavery in the District of Columbia would lead to the danger of a servile War — He meant this as a substitute for Wise's Amendment, but Wise disconcerted him by accepting the Amendment as a part of his own — Chilton Allen, now moved to lay the whole triad of Resolutions upon the table — but this was rejected by yeas and nays 58 to 155 — Holsey of Georgia then claimed the floor — Cambreleng told him he should in five minutes call for the orders of the day — Holsey moved to postpone till next Tuesday — Parks moved to postpone till to-morrow — No decision was made by the House; but the vote to postpone till Tuesday was carried. ≈

14. V:30. Thursday ≈ Mr. Granger of New-York came to my Seat, and said that Mr. Thompson of South-Carolina was desirous of being introduced to me, but felt some scruple under an apprehension that I might have taken offence, at some remarks made by him in one of his speeches censorial upon me — I told Granger, that I scarcely ever noticed in any manner; any personality bearing upon me, by any member of the House, and that nothing said by Mr. Thompson had given me the slightest offence — Granger afterwards brought Thompson to my seat and introduced him; I found him much of a Gentleman — Mr. Lane of Indiana told me there was a young

Lady by the name of Sealy who wished me to write my name in her Album, which he promised to send me.

———

18. V:15. Monday. Petition day at the House — My appeal from the decision of the Speaker had been postponed to this day, and was now at the motion of Hawes postponed again till Thursday next — The States are called over for Petitions — Maine had scarcely been gone through, when a Message from the President was announced, and by unanimous consent was immediately read. It was the final statement of the dispute with France with the latest correspondence between our Chargé d'Affaires Barton, and the Duke de Broglie, and between our Secretary of State Forsyth, and the French Chargé d'Affaires Pageot until these diplomatic subalterns were on both sides recalled — Immediately after the Message was read M'Keon of New-York started up and sent a paper of Resolutions to the Clerk. The Speaker said some disposal must first be made of the Message. There was a call for the reading of the Correspondence and it was read — John Y. Mason, Chairman of the Committee of Foreign Relations moved the reference of the Message and Documents to that Committee which was done. M'Keon insisted upon offering his Resolutions, but the House would not permit them even to be read — He gave notice amidst loud calls of order that his Resolutions were to approve the course of the President, and that he should take the earliest possible opportunity to present them. At the motion of Hawes twenty thousand extra copies of the Message and Correspondence were ordered to be printed — The call for Petitions was then resumed — When the turn of Massachusetts came, I presented first a petition from sundry persons, sent to me under a blank cover, praying for the construction of a Harbour, at the Mouth of the river St. Joseph in the Territory of Michigan which was referred to the Committee of Commerce — Then a Petition from 366 inhabitants of Weymouth in my own Congressional District praying for the abolition of Slavery and the Slave trade in the District of Columbia — Hammond of South Carolina interrupted me and moved that the Petition be not received — He had no right to interrupt me and the Speaker said I was entitled to the floor — Pinckney of South-Carolina then

intreated me to allow a motion to postpone the question of the receipt of the Petition, so that the reception of other Petitions might have free course this day, to which I consented, and for which he thanked me. The question of reception was then postponed, and I presented another petition to the same effect of 158 Ladies, Citizens of the Commonwealth of Massachusetts for I said I had not yet brought myself to doubt whether females were Citizens — The question upon the reception of this Petition was also postponed — A great number of other Petitions with the same prayer were presented by many members; and all were postponed on motions of Hammond that they should not be received and by a new motion by Gideon Lee of New-York that the motion not to receive be laid on the table — The Speaker varied the manner of putting the question, some time that it should not be, and sometimes whether it should be received, and finally put it upon the preliminary question; which he has decided is debateable; but that a motion to lay it on the table is in order, and that is not debatable — M'Kennan of Pennsylvania on presenting an abolition petition moved its reference to a select Committee; and upon the motion to lay that motion on the table, called for the yeas and nays — Wise moved a call of the House which was refused — the yeas and nays for laying on the table were 177 to 37 and I was obliged to vote with the affirmatives, by the consent I had given that the petitions presented by me should be so disposed of.

———

[February 1836]
4. VI. Thursday. — Severe cold — Fahrenheit — At the House — Cambreleng moves a suspension of the rules of the House to move a Resolution for referring all the abolition Petitions, and Resolutions now before the House to a Select Committee with Instructions to make a long report, question taken by yeas and nays   to   not two thirds.
Motion by Mann of New-York, to suspend the rules to take up the report of the Select Committee on the Rules 102 to 103 not two thirds.

———

15. V:30. Monday. ≈ At the House several motions were made to dispense with the reading of the Journal, but without

success — After the reading of the Journal, Franklin Pierce of New-Hampshire asked the permission of the House, to make a statement; upon which objection being made, he moved and carried the suspension; and made his Statement, which was an attack upon him in a New-Hampshire Newspaper, for an assertion made by him at an early day of the Session that not one person in 500 in New-Hampshire was in favour of the abolition of Slavery — which had been read by Mr. Calhoun in the Senate — Pierce defended the accuracy of his former assertion, with severe remarks upon the Paper — After which Petitions were called for — and Briggs presented a Petition from the State of New-York for the abolition of Slavery and the Slave-trade in the District of Columbia — Wise objected to the receipt of the Petition, which the Speaker decided was in order and that the question was debatable — upon which Wise commenced a furious Slavery Speech, and speaking of H. L. Pinckney's Resolution, said he hissed him as a Deserter from the principles of the South on the subject of Slavery. He was called to order and a snarling debate of two hours followed — It was finally decided by yeas and nays — That he was out of order — and then a motion was made that he should have permission to proceed which was granted, 111 to 92. Then Vinton made a point of order, whether after the adoption of the Resolution of H. L. Pinckney, this Motion against receiving the Petition was in order — This started a new debate which continued till 4 O'Clock, when the house adjourned — I took Jarvis home to his lodgings, and passed the Evening in writing.

———

[April 1836]

13. V:45. Wednesday ≈ Dr. Huntt was here and by his direction the poultices on my leg are discontinued. It is apparently and very slowly healing — I still drag through the writing of my daily Diary, and wrote this day part of a Letter to Robert Walsh — Finished reading Holland's Life of Martin van Buren, a partizan electioneering work written with much of that fraudulent democracy by the profession of which Thomas Jefferson rose to power in this Country, and of which he set the first successful example — Van Buren's personal character bears however a stronger resemblance to that of Mr. Madison than

to Jefferson — They are both remarkable for their extreme caution in avoiding and averting personal collisions — Van Buren, like the Sosie of Moliere's Amphitryon, is "l'ami de tout le monde" — This is perhaps the great secret of his success in public life, and especially against the competitors with whom he is now struggling, for the last step on the ladder of his ambition. Henry Clay and John C. Calhoun — They indeed are left upon the field for dead — and men of straw, Hugh L. White, William H. Harrison and Daniel Webster, are thrust forward in their places — Neither of these has a principle to lean upon. Van Buren's principle is the Talisman of Democracy, which so long as this Union lasts can never fail.

———

[May 1836]

8. V:30. Sunday ≈ I employed the leisure of the day in answering a Letter of the 14ᵗʰ of January from E. Price Greenleaf; and in reflections upon the debate of yesterday, and the condition of our public affairs especially of our relations with Mexico — The prospect of more comprehensive and momentous discussion, and my own condition — so infirm — so helpless — So nearly hopeless — The last Night was not to me a night of repose — nor of much refreshing sleep. I shall henceforth speak in the House of Representatives, at the hazard of my life.

———

15. IV:30. Sunday ≈ My time and attention and Sentiments are becoming absorbed in the danger of a War with Mexico. — I read a Speech of a Col'l Wharton, one of the Texian Commissioners, at a great meeting at New-York — and for the second time the address of S. F. Austin another Texian Commissioner to a very large meeting at Louisville ladies and gentlemen.

———

17. IV:30. Tuesday. The change from Winter to Summer has taken place in 24 hours — Sunday and yesterday morning we had fires in our dining room, and wanted them in our chambers — This day we have high Summer heat — Mary and her children rode with me to the Capitol — At the House immediately after the reading of the Journal I asked the consent of the House to offer two Resolutions calling upon the President for copies of any overture made by his authority since the 3ᵈ of March 1829 to the Government of Mexico for the acquisition of any

territory, of that republic, by the United States and any question of boundary between the two Countries; and for copies and Translations of any Law, Ordinance or Decree of the Mexican Government, abolishing Slavery within the Territories of that Republic — Objection was made, and after several attempts to postpone my question I insisted on its being taken and the permission was refused by yeas and nays 74 to 85 ≈

18. IV:30. Wednesday. Immediately after the reading of the Journal, H.L. Pinckney, presented the Report of the select Committee to whom all the abolition Petitions were referred and said that the report had the unanimous assent of the Committee — He moved that 5000 copies of the report should be printed for the use of the House — It was immediately attacked with extreme violence and a fiery debate arose which continued until one O'Clock, and then by a suspension of the rule for another half hour. Motion was made to print ten thousand and twenty-thousand copies, and Waddy Thompson said that he would commit it to the flames or to the hang-man — Ben Hardin who was a member of the Committee declared his dissent to the main Sentiment of the report, and protested against it — At half past one the order of the day was called, and in Committee of the whole, Mann of New-York in the Chair, Forrester of Tennessee, made his White electioneering Speech of about one hour — then the Bill for the Defence of the Western frontier, amended by the Senate so as to turn a militia levy into a ten thousand men addition to the army — M'Kay objected to this amendment, and I made a warm Speech against it, and was answered with much virulence by Lawler of Alabama, and by Glascock of Georgia — The previous question was called by Mann of New-York who refused to withdraw the motion to allow me to reply to Lawler and Glascock. The previous question was carried; but the Senate's amendment was rejected 102 to 104. Then after an abortive attempt to adjourn, Cambreleng presented a Bill appropriation of half a million of dollars for the suppression of the hostilities of the Creek Indians, which passed through all its stages with some skirmishing debate, for information of the causes of the War — The House adjourned after 6 — My wife was very ill, and bled by doctor Huntt.

———

24. V. Tuesday. ≈ At the House, judge Jeremiah Smith asked me specially to make a speech, which I promised him to do if the House would permit me — Immediately after the reading of the journal, I asked the unanimous consent of the House to offer the two Resolutions of call upon the President for information concerning our Affairs with Mexico, which I moved last week, and I asked the permission of the House to assign my reasons for offering the Resolutions. objection was made, and Chambers of Kentucky moved to suspend the Rules, to enable me to assign my reasons, which was rejected — I then moved the suspension of the Rules to enable me to offer the Resolutions — and asked for the yeas and nays — Huntsman said he would vote for my introducing the first Resolution, for he knew that the President was perfectly willing to communicate the information — I then modified my motion for leave to offer the first Resolution — Waddy Thompson said he would vote for my Resolution with an amendment asking the opinion of the President as to the acknowledgment of the Independence of Texas — The vote for suspending the rule was 82 to 68 a majority but not two thirds — The printing of Pinckney's Slavery report, and Robertson's motion to recommit the report with Instructions followed, and Robertson continued his argument till eleven O'Clock, when the fortification Bill was resumed in the Committee of the whole on the Union — Abijah Mann in the chair. ≈ Then a squabble between Jenifer and Thomas, and battling till one O'Clock in the morning, when the Speaker adjourned the House til ten O'clock Wednesday Morning.

25. V. Wednesday. Mrs. A. Adams, and Mary rode with me to the Capitol — At the House, the motion of Robertson, to recommit Pinckney's Slavery Report, with Instructions to report a Resolution, declaring that Congress has no Constitutional Authority to abolish Slavery in the District of Columbia, as an amendment to the motion for printing an extra number of the report was first considered — Robertson finished his Speech which was vehement, and he read the Letter from Mr. Van Buren on the subject of the Power of Congress to abolish Slavery in the District, and he charged him with evading the question. I asked that so much of the Letter as he had referred

to should be read and it was — immediately after the conclusion of Robertson's speech I addressed the Speaker, but he gave the floor to Owens of Georgia, one of the signing members of the Committee, who moved the previous question, and refused to withdraw it — It was seconded and carried by yeas and nays 110 to 89 — I asked what the main question would be — the Speaker decided that it would be the adoption of the Resolutions of the Committee, which have not been in the slightest degree discussed — I appealed from the decision which the house confirmed. — The question on the first Resolution was taken 168 to 9. — Glascock asked to be excused from voting — I required that the reasons for excusing him should be entered on the Journal — The Speaker was doubtful — the hour of one came and the order of the day was called — A joint Resolution from the Senate authorising the President to cause rations to be furnished to suffering fugitives from Indian hostilities in Alabama and Georgia. Committee of the whole on the Union, and a debate of five hours, in which I made a Speech of about an hour; in which I opened the whole subject of the Mexican, Indian, Negro and English war — Answered by Lawler, Haynes, Waddy Thompson and Wise — The Resolution was carried through all its Stages, and passed and the House adjourned between 7 and 8 O'Clock, and I came home much exhausted, and soon sought my bed.

26. V. Thursday. I had a very indifferent Night, and little sleep — At the House the first subject was the question upon Glascock's assigning the reasons for his asking to be excused from voting on the Slavery Report Resolutions — The Speaker announced that he had recurred to the only precedent on the Journals of the House, which was in my own case; and that the House then determined to proceed in the call of yeas and nays, and announce the decision without waiting first to decide any question on the refusal of the member to vote — But that such question would remain to be afterwards decided by the House — I rose and began to prove that the case was totally different from that of 1832, which could not therefore apply as a precedent; but I was called with great vociferation to order and not permitted to proceed. The Speaker went on and announced the result of the vote on the 1st Resolution — On the call of

yeas and nays upon the second Resolution, I asked to be excused from voting, and the call was continued passing me by. — Others declined voting and they were also passed by. On my name's being called on the third resolution I answered I hold the Resolution to be a direct violation of the Constitution of the United States of the Rules of this House and of the rights of my Constituents — They passed on — Granger asked to be excused from voting on the second Resolution, because the Resolution is different from that which the Committee was instructed to report — He was passed over and not allowed to offer his reasons — A Scene of great disorder ensued — Glascock claimed the floor to assign his reasons — The Speaker gave him the floor, and then took it away from him by arbitrary, absurd and inconsistent decisions, all of which were sustained by the House by large majorities by yeas and nays; as were the three Resolutions reported by the Committee.

—

29. IV:30. Sunday.

> Just in the last distressing hour
> The Lord displays delivering power;
> The mount of danger is the place
> Where we shall see surprising grace.
> Watts. Book I. Hymn 129.

≈ After dinner I attended at the Presbyterian Church, and heard Mr. Farrar a young Clergyman from Albany — His Sermon was from 2 Timothy 2:12 "If we suffer, we shall also reign with him." There was nothing remarkable in the discourse; but the lines at the top of this page are the closing verse of one of the hymns which he gave out to be sung — There is scarcely a Sunday passes over my head, but in attendance upon divine service, I hear something of which a pointed application to my own situation and circumstances occurs to my thoughts — It is often consolation; Support — encouragement. — Sometimes warning and admonition. Sometimes keen and trying remembrance of deep distress. The lines above cited are of the cheering kind — I was occupied all the leisure of the day and evening in writing out for publication my Speech made last Wednesday in the House of Representatives, one of the most hazardous that I ever made, and the reception of which even by the People of my own district and State is altogether uncertain.

———

[June 1836]
2. V. Thursday. My Speech on the distribution of rations to the fugitives from Indian hostilities in Alabama and Georgia was published in the National Intelligencer of this morning, and a subscription paper was circulated in the House for printing it in a pamphlet, for which Gales told me there were 2,500 copies ordered — Several members of the House of both parties spoke of it to me; some with strong dissent — After the reading of the Journal several propositions for the receipt of petitions — and several by consent were received. G. Lee offered a Resolution to which I objected unless the House would allow me to present twenty Petitions, remonstrances and memorials against the admission of Arkansas, as a Slave State.

———

19. IV:30. Sunday. ≈ I have been some days occupied in preparing my Report of the proceedings in Committee of the whole, and in the House upon my proposed amendment to the Bill for admitting the State of Arkansas into the Union — My correspondence consequently falls into arrears again. My Speech on the rations, comes back with echoes of thundering vituperation from the South and West, and with one universal shout of applause from the North and East — This is a cause upon which I am entering at the last Stage of Life, and with the certainty, that I cannot advance in it far — My Career must close leaving the cause at the threshold — To open the way for others, is all that I can do. The cause is good and great.

———

[July 1836]
9. V:30. Saturday. Atlee, Edwin B.; Barton, Isaac; Semple, Matthew; Buffum, Arnold ≈. The four persons first named, came this morning as Committees — 1. Of the Pennsylvania Society for promoting the abolition of Slavery. 2. Of the Philadelphia Anti-Slavery Society, with votes of thanks to me and to the other members of Congress who at the late Session of Congress opposed the influence of the Slavery predominant party in that body. I desired them to return my thanks to the respective Societies for the honour they had done me by these

Resolutions, and to assure them of the grateful sentiments
with which I received them — One of the Resolutions contained also an invitation of attendance at a public meeting,
which I declined; and I gave them a full and candid exposition
of my own principles and views with regard to the Institution
of Domestic Slavery differing from theirs under a sense of the
compact and compromise in the Constitution of the United
States. I declined attendance at any public meeting of the Societies, and said I believed the cause itself would be more
benefited by such Service as I could render to it, in the discharge of my duty in Congress than by giving notoriety to
any action on my part in support of the Societies, or in connection with them — They acquiesced in these determinations,
and declared themselves well satisfied with the result of this
interview.

———

11. VI. Monday. With praise and prayer to God, and a solemn
sense of my earthly condition, and hopes of a better world, I
enter upon the seventieth year of my pilgrimage. Benjamin
Lundy came this morning and in a conversation of about two
hours, made me acquainted with his principles, prospects and
purposes relating to Slavery. He was heretofore the Editor
of the Genius of Universal emancipation; and has now the intention of commencing the publication of a Newspaper devoted like that to the extinguishment of Slavery — A cause
which within the last two or three years has fallen into great
discouragement — He solicited assistance from me, for the
matter of his proposed publication but I thought best not to
give him any expectation of it. Mr. John Vaughan called, and
invited me to breakfast with him to-morrow morning with
Captain La Place, Commander of the French Frigate L'Arte-
mise, now lying in the Harbour of New-York — But I had
made my arrangements to go in the six O'Clock morning
boat, and was obliged to decline Mr. Vaughn's invitation.
Judge Hopkinson with Commodore Biddle, and Mr. Huntt
Dr. Huntt's brother successively came, and engaged me in
conversation till I was called to dinner so that I was unable to
pay the visit I had intended to Charles J. Ingersoll. Mrs. Biddle
came in from the Country before dinner with her daughter
Mata — After dinner Mr. William B. Reed came in, but I had

no time to converse with him — Benjamin Lundy came at six, and I walked with him to the house of his friend James Mott, N. 136, North Ninth Street, where the[re] was a large tea and evening party of men and women, all of the Society of Friends — I had free conversation with them till between ten and 11 O'Clock upon Slavery — the abolition of Slavery and other topics, of all which the only exceptionable part was the undue proportion of the talking assumed by me, and the indiscretion and vanity in which I indulged myself — Lucretia Mott the mistress of the House, wife of James Mott is a native of the Island of Nantucket and had heard of my visit there last September. She is sensible and lively and an abolitionist of the most intrepid School — Benjamin Lundy and another Friend came home with me to Mr. Biddle's, and Lundy came in and conversed with me nearly another hour. Mr. Biddle the[n] came in, and I completed the day with him till Midnight.

————

22. IV:15. Friday. ≈ This afternoon Aldermen Greele and Hunting and the members of the common Council of the City of Boston came out as a Committee and invited me in the name of the City Government to deliver before them an Eulogy upon the life and character of the late James Madison — Mr. Greele delivered to me a Letter of Introduction from the Mayor Samuel T. Armstrong — I accepted this invitation with an aching heart; under a deep feeling of my incompetency to do the subject Justice; and a consciousness of the hours of anguish which opens before me till the work shall have been performed — The day is hereafter to be fixed — the last week in August, or first in September — I am destitute of almost all the indispensable materials.

————

[August 1836]
8. III:45. Monday. ≈ Mr. Edward Everett, now Governor of the Commonwealth, and Mrs. Everett paid us a morning visit; and he gave me a Volume of his Orations and Speeches, recently published — They are among the best ever delivered in this Country, and I think will stand the test of time. — The custom of delivering Orations, on public occasions was introduced into this Country by the Boston Massacre of 5 March 1770 of which there were thirteen delivered successively till

1783 in Boston Town meeting — The 4th of July was then substituted for the yearly town Oration, and these have been continued till the present time. Other towns and cities have followed
the example, and other occasions have been taken for the delivery of similar discourses till they have multiplied so that they
now outnumber the days of the year — Of the thousands and
tens of thousands of these Orations which teem in every part of
this Country, there are perhaps not one hundred that will be
remembered, alteri Seculo; and of them, at least one half have
been or will be furnished by Edward Everett — He has largely
contributed to raise the Standard of this Class of compositions,
and his eloquence has been the basement story of his political
fortune; as yet one of the most brilliant ever made in this union
≈ I received from Mrs. D. P. Madison, a Letter, with a summary
statement by her brother of the principal events in the life of Mr.
Madison; but it contains little if any thing that I can use for the
Eulogy which I am preparing.

———

29. V. Monday. ≈ Mr. Greenleaf brought me a message from
Mr. Armstrong the Mayor, requesting me to fix a day for the
delivery of the Eulogy on Mr. Madison — This is rather em-
barrassing, as I do not see the end of my work and have yet
much to write, and more to revise — I have come now to Mr.
Madison's course of conduct relating to the alien and Sedition
acts; a subject of extreme difficulty to manage, inasmuch as it
forms in the opinion of his party friends, perhaps the greatest
of his merits and services; while I myself believe him to have
been in error throughout the whole of those transactions. —
To refresh my memory on these subjects and to retrace the
history of those controversies more accurately I read over the
portion of Jefferson's correspondence during that period,
published by his Grandson — It shews his craft and duplicity
in very glaring colours — I incline to the opinion that he was
not altogether conscious of his own insincerity, and deceived
himself as well as others — His success through a long life, and
especially from his entrance upon the Office of Secretary of
State under Washington, until he reached the Presidential
chair, seems to my imperfect vision a slur upon the moral
government of the world — His rivalry with Hamilton was
unprincipled on both sides — His treatment of my father was

double dealing, treacherous and false beyond all toleration — His Letter to Mazzei and his subsequent explanations of it and apologies for it, shew that he treated Washington, as far as he dared no better than he did my father — but it was Washington's popularity that he never dared to encounter — His correspondence now published proves how he dreaded and detested it — His letter to my father at the first competition between them for the Presidency — The fawning, dissimulation of his first address as Vice-President to the Senate, with his secret machinations against him from that day forth, shew a character in no wise amiable or fair; but his attachment to those of his friends whom he could make useful to himself was thorough-going and exemplary — Madison moderated some of his excesses, and refrained from following him into others. — He was in truth a greater, and a far more estimable man.

30. III:30. Tuesday. ≈ I wrote little, and continued reading the Letters of Jefferson, from 1793 till August 1803 published by his Grandson — His duplicity sinks deeper and deeper into my mind — His hatred of Hamilton was unbounded — Of John Marshall most intense — of my father, tempered with compunctious visitings, always controuled by his ambition — They had been cordial friends, and co-operators in the great cause of Independence; and as joint Commissioners abroad after the Peace of 1783, there had then been a warm and confidential intimacy between them, which he never entirely shook off, but which he sacrificed always to his ambition, and at the last stage of his life to his envy and his poverty — for he died insolvent, and on the very day of his death received eleemosinary donations from the charity of some of those whom he had most deeply injured — This circumstance is not creditable to his Country — She ought not to have suffered a man who had served her as he had to die, with his household wanting the necessaries of life — But it was the natural consequence of the niggardly doctrines which his political system had imposed upon him, and which he had passed off upon the Country for Patriotism — Among his slanders upon the administration of my father was the charge of extravagance in diplomatic expenditure; and when he sent Mr. Monroe on the Louisiana mission to France, he wrote to him that he could not have an outfit;

and that the refusal of outfits was one of his reforms upon extraordinary missions — The end of all which was that Mr. Monroe obtained not only the outfit, but gratuities and allowances more than any other minister abroad has ever had, and died leaving still unsatisfied claims — I am compelled to draw many other harsh conclusions against this great man, from his now published Letters.

31. V. Wednesday — Commencement day at Cambridge ≈ I set apart two seedling circles in the Seminary for my Granddaughters Georgiana Frances and Louisa Catherine, each with a Stake and stone bearing their respective names and in which they planted peach and plum stones; and apple and grape seeds — They take a fancy to this themselves, and I wish to encourage them in it — Simple and innocent pleasures, are not only enjoyments but virtues. An interest in the Life of Plants is more rational than in that of cats, dogs, Parrots or monkies and by its capability of being made useful deserves to be cherished, and cultivated ≈ The preparation for the Eulogy of Mr. Madison occupies my time with much reading, and my progress in writing upon it is slow and very irksome — There are circumstances in the Life of Mr. Madison, of which I cannot speak with praise, and of which I would therefore gladly not speak at-all — But I cannot pass them over in silence — Nor will it be possible for me to treat them without giving offence to a large portion of the People of this Union — Should I suppress the truth?

———

[September 1836]

2. IV. Friday. ≈ I looked this day into Mr. Wirt's Life of Patrick Henry, to see his account of the debates in the Virginia Convention upon the Constitution of the United-States, and of Henry's opinion and conduct on the occasion of the alien and Sedition Laws — It seems difficult to reconcile them together — His opposition to the Constitution was founded perhaps on the peculiarity of his situation — His opinions then were in the highest tone of republican doctrine, and his aversion to the consolidation of the union deeply rooted — This makes his approbation of the Alien and Sedition Laws the more extraordinary. But in truth the opposition to those Laws was merely

factious — The main argument of Mr. Madison's report against the alien Law was that it applied to alien friends, when such measures should be applied only to alien enemies — But there was a fallacy in it — The foreign emissaries against whom the alien act was pointed were in no wise *friends* of this Country — They were chiefly Frenchmen. Jefferson in his correspondence says its principal object was Volney — The relative situation of the United States and France, at that time not a state of amity, but of hostility, though not of declared war. It was such that measures of defence against French secret emissaries were more necessary than they would have been in avowed and open War. The Sedition act was an ineffectual attempt to extinguish the fire of defamation — but it operated like oil upon the flames. Patrick Henry was elected a member of the Legislature of Virginia in 1799 but he died in June of that year, and before their meeting.

———

27. IV:15. Tuesday — Boston ≈ I delivered an Eulogy upon the life and character of James Madison. Two hours and a half were occupied in the delivery, and yet I omitted much of the abridgement of my discourse in the copy made chiefly by my Son — The House was crowded to the utmost of its capacity — I had undertaken this task with a most painful anxiety and fear that I might be disabled from performing it altogether. An anxiety much sharpened by the illness which for the last three days had almost extinguished my voice — I did get through but with extreme difficulty, with frequent imperfections of delivery; without being able to raise my voice to be heard throughout the house, and with entire conviction, that I must never again engage to address such an auditory, on a day fixed before hand — or indeed upon any day or any occasion. Forty three years and more have passed away since I first spoke to a crowded audience in Boston — My voice is now gone. My eyes are in no better condition. ≈ I closed the day with Gratitude to Heaven for my deliverance from this trial, and with a firm determination never again to expose myself to the same hazards.

———

29. V:30. Thursday. ≈ I read the Article from the North American review upon nullification, sent to me by Mr. Edward

Everett, and written by him in 1830 — I read also the Letters from Mr. Madison to him, upon the subject, of the same dates — I have undertaken to mark in very explicit terms, the difference between the opinions, the purposes, and the conduct of Mr. Madison and Mr. Jefferson with reference to the alien and the Sedition acts — They were very remarkably different. I foresee that this may engage me in a controversy with the Jeffersonian School of the South; and that it will be specially unpalatable in Virginia — There are many considerations which make this exceedingly hazardous at my time of life, but after long deliberation, I have concluded that there is a duty for me to perform — a duty to the memory of my father — a duty to the character of the People of New-England — A duty to truth and Justice — If controversy is made, I shall have an arduous, and probably a very unthankful task to perform, and may sink under it; but I will defend my father's fame — I will vindicate the New-England character, and I will expose some of the fraudulent pretences of Slave-holding democracy. — I pray for temper, moderation, firmness and self-controul; and above all for a pure and honest purpose — and if it so please Heaven for success.

———

[November 1836]

3. IV. Thursday. Storm all night and the whole of this day with alternation of Sleet, rain and Snow. Towards evening it held up without clearing up — I was confined all day to the house; and yet idled away my time, chiefly in directing copies of the Eulogy on James Madison to sundry persons, and correcting the errata — I received a Letter from S. S. Southworth expressing in terms of extravagant applause his opinion of the Eulogy and requesting a copy of it — Quite probably he may publish a bitter and sneering critical review of it — Jefferson paid Callender for reviling and slandering my father, and called it charity — Webster paid Southworth, or at least promised to pay him for reviling and slandering me, and may call it Charity, if he has paid. Southworth is one of the best representatives of the class of political writers for hire in this Country. He has been one of the most virulent lampooners upon me of the whole tribe and has written me many Letters full of kindness and veneration.

———

11. IV:15. Friday. Washington. ≈ The excitement of the Presidential Election is here as we have found it all along on the road — The remarkable character of this election is that all the candidates are at most third-rate men, whose pretensions rest neither upon high attainments, nor upon eminent services, but upon intrigue and political speculation. The Presidency has fallen into a joint stock company — Jackson came in upon the trumpet-tongue of military achievement — His Presidency has been the reign of subaltern knaves, fattening upon land jobs and money jobs, who have made him believe that it was a heroic conception of his own to destroy the Bank of the United States, and who under colour of this have got into their own hands the *use* of the public monies at a time when there is a surplus of forty Millions of Dollars in the Treasury. Two political Swindlers Amos Kendall, and Reuben M. Whitney, are the Empson and Dudley of our Solomon, and by playing upon his Vanity, and his thirst of petty revenge have got into their own hands the overflowing revenue of the Country; with the temporary and illegal *use* of which they are replenishing their own Coffers and making princely fortunes. — Jackson has wearied out the sordid subserviency of his Supporters, and Van Buren has had the address to persuade him that he is the only man who can preserve and perpetuate the principles of his administration — And as his term of eight years has run through, and his gang are weary of his sway, he has set his heart upon bringing in Van Buren as his Successor, and has successfully exercise[d] all his influence to promote that result. The opposition divided between three talented aspirants to the Presidency, neither of whom would yield subordination to either of the others, have been driven in mere desperation to set up men of straw in their places, and they have taken up Hugh Lawson White and William Henry Harrison as the Israelites set up a calf, and as the Egyptians worshipped oxen and monkies. White and Harrison are men of moderate capacity, but of varied public service, and of long experience in the affairs of the Nation — They are as competent for the Presidency at least as Jackson, and like him, if elected to his Station, would rule by the proxy of subalterns — By party management and political love-potions, White and Harrison are now the golden calves of the People, and their dull sayings are repeated for wit, and their grave inanity is

passed off for wisdom — This bolstering up of mediocrity
would seem not suited to sustain much enthusiasm; but a
practice, has crept in of betting largely upon the issue of elections, and that adds a spur of private personal and pecuniary
interest to the impulse of patriotism — This is the exciting
cause of all the ardour which we have met with throughout
this Journey.

———

25. VI:30. Friday. My Time is slipping away, and I am doing
nothing — I rose this morning two hours later than my regular
time, because I had spent the last Evening abroad, and because
the morning was so cold, that I could not write before breakfast
— This is an incurable infirmity of the Winter, which has
begun this Season earlier than usual — The consequence is
that I must write between breakfast and dinner, a time when
numberless unforeseen, and for the most part trivial calls
dissipate the day till it is imperceptibly and irretrievably gone.
≈ There is in the Boston Courier which Gales this day sent me,
such a Review of the Eulogy on Madison by a blue-light
federalist of the Hartford Convention School, while in the
Telegraph Newspaper of this day, there is a deadly onset upon
me, from the clanking Chains of a Southern Slave-holder, for
my Speech upon the Texian Imposture, last June. The idea this
Evening occurred to me, of making a collection of as many of
my writings which have been published in pamphlets, to have
two or three sets of them bound up in Volumes, for gifts to my
grand-children — The three Eulogies may be literary and political curiosities, in a century from this day; but of most, perhaps all my other writings, no trace will remain, unless in some
such collection, made by myself.

———

[December 1836]
5. VII:30. Monday. Second Session, Twenty-fourth Congress
commenced. Precisely at Noon, James K. Polk, Speaker of the
House of Representatives of the United States, took the Chair
of the House. and announced that this was the day fixed by the
Constitution of the United States for the annual Meeting of
Congress ≈ Many cordial greetings from members of all parties. I went into the Library, and took a minute from the first

Edition of the Federalist. Mary Louisa, and Georgiana Frances went to School to Mrs. Brechard.

6. VI:30. Tuesday. ≈ At the Meeting of the House, D. J. Pearce Chairman of the Committee on the part of the House to notify the President that the two Houses were ready to receive any Communication from him said they had performed the Service, and that he was requested by the President to inform the House that he would make a written communication to both Houses at 12 O'Clock this day. The Message was accordingly brought in immediately afterwards; and took the Clerk nearly an hour and a half to read. The message repeatedly alludes to the fact of its being the last annual Message that will ever be addressed to Congress by him — It teems with glorification upon the prosperous condition of the Country; with a considerable spice of piety; a hasty and not very satisfactory view of the State of our foreign Relations — an unsettled boundary question with Great-Britain, long-standing claims of indemnity upon the Belgian Government; no reference to the quarrel with Buenos Ayres; but a boastful notice of a commercial Treaty with Siam — A very lame account of the wanton disregard of the rights of Nations, in the invasion of the Mexican Territories — There is excuse, apology, extenuation, and a flimsy argument to justify the invasion, a recommendation to pass the act for settling the boundary between the United States and Mexico, and earnest caution to preserve a strict and faithful neutrality between Texas and Mexico — with expressions of much regret that Gorostiza the Mexican Minister had returned home. But three fourths of the Message consisted of a Dissertation upon Banks, banking and the currency with a new tribunitian invective against the Bank of the U. States, a Lamentation over the excesses of money in the Public Treasure — A direct thrust at the Compromise Tariff, and abundance of verbiage about gold and silver and the injustice of bank paper to the labouring poor ≈

7. VI:30. Wednesday. This is the day of the Meeting of the electoral Colleges for the choice of a President and Vice-President of the United States for four years from the 4th of March next

— It is already well ascertained that a Majority of the whole number of the votes will be for Martin Van Buren of New-York as President and almost certain that Richard M. Johnson of Kentucky will be the Vice-President.

———

22. V. Thursday. ≈ A Message was received from the President, concerning the new Republic of Texas — the recognition of her Independence, and her application to be annexed to the United States — This Message, was in a tone and Spirit, quite unexpected to me, and certainly to a large portion of the House — A total reverse of the Spirit, which almost universally prevailed at the close of the last Session of Congress, and in which the President notoriously shared. This Message discourages any precipitate recognition of Texas, and speaks with due caution and reserve of its annexation to the United States. Motions were made to print ten thousand and twenty thousand copies of it, which occasioned some debate. Whittlesey of Ohio objected to the largest number, upon the principle of economy. But after some discussion withdrew his objection — Briggs, Hoare, D. J. Pearce and even Boon of Indiana, the thickest skull, the narrowest mind, and the pettiest teazle in the house supported the largest number — The Message itself was referred to the Committee on foreign relations, of which Howard of Baltimore is now Chairman.

———

24. VI:30. Saturday. A succession of visitors from almost immediately after breakfast till past 3 O'Clock kept me at home ≈ I asked Cushing if there would be a Report from the Committee of Foreign Affairs on the President's Message concerning Texas — He had some doubts. Cushing as a member of that Committee concurred in their excellent senseless Report of the 4th of July last on Texas, screwed through the House by the previous question, without allowing one word of discussion — The tone is now totally changed. Waddy Thompson told me yesterday that he would give me the Report of Gen'l James Hamilton, to the Senate of South-Carolina upon the subject; which spoke the sentiments of the People, of that State — The Message of Governor M'Duffie did not — Hamilton's report was published in the Telegraph of last Evening. It represents the Texians as a

People struggling for their Liberty and therefore entitled to our Sympathy — The fact is directly the reverse — They are fighting for the establishment and perpetuation of Slavery; and that is the cause of the South-Carolinian sympathy with them — Can this fact be demonstrated to the understanding, and duly exhibited to the Sentiment of my Countrymen? with candour — with calmness with moderation, and with a pencil of phosphoric light? — Alas! No! — Mr. Samuel H. Smith called on me and amused me with some of his antediluvian fancies, about the high Salaries and corrupting patronage of the federal Government. He thinks that the President's Salary should be reduced to ten thousand dollars a year; and all the rest in proportion.

———

26. VI:15. Monday. Rain almost all night and this morning which made it necessary for me to ride to the Capitol — At the House W. C. Dawson a member from Georgia who comes in the place of Coffee, deceased since the close of the last Session was qualified and took his seat. Petitions called for, by States. I presented the petition of Joseph Page, and 26 citizens of the town of Silverlake, Susquehannah County, Commonwealth of Pennsylvania, praying for the abolition of Slavery and the Slave trade in the District of Columbia — Pickens of South-Carolina, attempted to raise a question upon the reception of the Petition; and appealed to the Resolutions of the last Session — The Speaker said, it was too late — the petition being already in possession of the house; and he considered the Resolutions of the last Session, as expired with the Session itself. Davis of Indiana called up the Resolution that he had offered and which was on the Speaker's table, that all Petitions which may be offered praying for the abolition of Slavery in the District of Columbia or in the Territories shall be laid on the table, without reading or being printed, and without debate. Davis had not the wit to see that his Resolution instigated the very debate that he wanted to suppress — I said the Resolution deserved a full and thorough consideration, and I hoped would have it — But I suggested to him the expediency of moving to postpone, and make it the special order of some future day, to avoid interrupting the presentation of petitions — Davis's friends, moved to lay his Resolution, and the whole

subject on the Table which was done — by yeas and nays 116
to 36.

———

31. VI:30. Saturday ≈ *Year* — The year 1836 has been a year of
some vicissitude in my public life, and in my private concerns
— strewed with roses, and beset with thorns; for the results of
which, I bow in grateful homage to the Disposer of all Events
— A year of severe trials, which I have sustained without sinking, by the aid of a merciful protector, but which in the course
of Nature I cannot expect to sustain me much longer — The
year began by a desperate and furious, yet insidious and crafty
onset upon my character, by Daniel Webster in the form of a
Speech in the Senate on the 14th of January — published with
great flourishes of trumpets in the National Intelligencer of
the 18th — I answered by the offer of a Resolution of enquiry,
and a Speech on the 22d of the same Month; it demolished the
Speech of Webster; drove him from the field, and whip'd him
and his party into the rank and file of the Nation, in the quarrel
with the French king — but it opened upon me the whole
pack of the Presidential opposition candidates, and their abet-
tors, in and out of Congress, who would have sunk me into
perdition temporal and eternal, if they had had the power — I
weathered this storm, and was re-elected to the next Congress
without formal opposition, but almost without whig votes —
The delivery of the Eulogy upon President Madison was the
principal incident of the year — and was successful — I have to
bless the giver of all good for improved health — not only my
own, but that of my dearest friend.

———

[February 1837]
6. VI:15. Monday — At the House — Petition day — I
presented Petitions of Joseph Rolette, Crawford County, Wisconsin Territory — of Huldah Pennyman — Petition Letter
of Elias Ward, and Petition of David Loud, a Soldier of the late
War — all referred — Then 32 Abolition Petitions, laid on
the Table — Stated the liability to imposition occasioned by
the order of 15 Jan'y and my suspicions of the genuineness
of the two last petitions that I had in my hands — Petition of
9 women of Fredericksburg — laid on the table — Petition
from Slaves — I asked the Speaker whether it came within the

order of 15 Jan'y — Said he must consult the House — Stormy debate succession of motions to bring me to the bar — Haynes, Waddy Thompson, Lewis, Dromgoole, Granger, Abijah Mann, Cambreleng — adjourned between 5 and 6. Patton's motion by suspension of the Rules — to take the Petition of the women off the files and return it to me — superseded by the privileged question — Struggle to prevent me from presenting Petitions, other than from my own State — decision of the Speaker, confirmed.

———

[April 1837]

2. VI. Sunday. Heard this morning at the Presbyterian Church Mr. Fowler from Isaiah 53:6 — "and the Lord hath laid on him the iniquity of us all." A discourse thoroughly calvinistical upon the doctrine of vicarious atonement by sacrifice of blood. A doctrine to me so utterly senseless and absurd, that I cannot without effort sit and hear it preached with Patience. ≈ I wrote to Mr. Biddle, and read the printed Letter of Gerrit Smith, to the Rev'd. James Smylie late stated Clerk of the Presbytery of Mississippi, author of [a] book in defence of Slavery to which this Letter is an answer — I have read scarcely any thing upon this controversy, and am quite incompetent to discuss it myself — I come to the conclusion, without examining the premises. — I have an abhorrence of Slavery; but how bad it is no one can imagine without understanding the details — Smylie defends Slavery as an institution sanctioned by the Scriptures. — But the extermination of the Canaanitish Nations was also sanctioned by the Scriptures — The punishment of death was prescribed for a multitude of what we should consider very trivial offences — The theory of the rights of man was then utterly unknown — And Mr. G. Smith shews that the servitude of that time was a milder condition than the Slavery of the present age and of this Country — This subject of Slavery, to my great sorrow and mortification is absorbing all my faculties.

———

8. V. Saturday. I read this morning in the Manuscripts of Mr. Madison the Report of the Speech of Alexander Hamilton, in the Convention of 1787 upon presenting *his* plan for a Constitution of the United States — The Speech occupied a whole

day, and was of great ability — The plan was theoretically better than that which was adopted — But energetic and approaching the British Constitution far closer, and such as the public Opinions of that day never would have tolerated — still less would it be endured by the democratic spirit of the present age, far more democratic than that — For after half a century of inextinguishable wars between the democracy of the European race and its Monarchy and Aristocracy, the democracy is yet in the ascendant and gaining victory after victory over the porcelain of the race — If Hamilton were now living he would not dare in an assembly of Americans, even with closed doors to avow the opinions of this Speech, or to present such a plan even as a speculation.

———

13. VI:15. Thursday. The children, recommenced their morning reading to me, with the 17th chapter of Numbers — their mother was taken unwell and confined to her chamber all the day — The Rev'd. Dr. Follen, the German Unitarian Clergyman, paid me a morning visit, and I had a long conversation with him upon the unitarian doctrines, and upon the Covenants of the old and new Testaments, which seem to me to sanction the political principle that by the Law of Nature all legitimate Government is founded in compact — I asked him if he had considered the influence first upon the History of the Jews through the old and new Testament, next upon the Christian Religion — thirdly upon the theory of human rights and the foundations of Government of this primary historical fact — He said he had not, and that it opened to him an entirely new view of the Scriptures — I believe this is the case with many others, and that I should do well to write a Dissertation or Lyceum Lecture upon it. The Scriptures represent man, as having at his creation a Law prescribed to him by his Creator — He is placed in Eden there to remain in a happy state of connubial felicity, upon one condition — This is not a covenant, but a Law — The consent of Adam was not required to this Law — there is permission given him to subsist upon the fruit of all the trees, excepting one — but no promise is made to him; no covenant contracted with him. He violates the condition imposed upon him, and suffers expulsion from Paradise — There is no mention of a Covenant till after the

Deluge, but immediately after that there is a Covenant, express and formal with Noah — This however is of a general character, and Noah himself by his curse upon Ham, deprived one third part of his descendants of the benefit of it. But the Covenants with Abraham are the most remarkable both for their solemnity and for their import — They were covenants of Religion and of Government — The first was at Sichem, Gen: 12:7, the second at Bethel — Gen 13:14 — The third and most solemn covenant is related in the 15th chapter with all its particulars and specially stated, in the 18th verse — The 4th is related in the 17th Chapter when Abraham was 99 years of age; and the covenant was sealed by the rite of circumcision — In the 22d chapter, verses 17–18 the covenant is again renewed, after the call for the sacrifice of Isaac and its release. In Chapter 26, v. 2 the Covenant is repeated with Isaac — The blessing was afterwards transferred to Jacob, and the covenant renewed with him, in the dream at Bethel — ch. 28, v. 13–20, 22 — and again ch. 35, v. 10 where his name is changed to Israel — and in ch. 46 v. 3 when he is ordered to go down to Egypt — The subsequent covenants were with the whole People, from that of Mount Sinai, down to the Babylonian captivity — and then came the New covenant of the gospel of Christ — all this to be elucidated — I walked before dinner, stopped at the Office of the National Intelligencer where I saw Mr. Gales, with whom was Mr. Featherstonhaugh — Seaton afterwards came in — Evening disoccupied — There was a gathering this morning of perhaps a hundred labourers in the front yard of the President's House — It was said their object was to remonstrate against working more than ten hours a day — It was said the President sent them word that he could not parley with them so long as they should present themselves in that manner.

———

15. V:30. Saturday ≈ I met Mr. Leonard Jarvis, who turned and walked with me to the Capitol. Mr. Burch was not there, but confined to his house with a pulmonary complaint and a relapse. They gave me the sheets of the Journal of the House for the first fortnight in February. In the library, I took up the second Volume of Matthias's Edition of Gray's works, and wandered over it till the clock struck three and warned me to depart — I found in it the analysis of the writings of Plato,

which I had no time to examine, but which I hope to find time
to look into hereafter — I read some of his Letters to his
mother, to his father, and to his friend West; and mused over
that affecting incident that Gray's Ode to Spring was sent by
him when first written, in a Letter to West, who died just before he should have received it — I have literary tastes peculiar
to myself, and the correctness of which I distrust, because they
differ from the general voice — There is no Lyric Poet of antient or modern times, who so deeply affects my feelings as
Gray — Every one of his Odes, is to me an inestimable jewel,
and nothing in all Dr. Johnson's writings is so disgusting to
me, as his criticisms upon them — The progress of Poesy and
the Bard are the first and second Odes that ever were written
— Dryden's Alexander's feast, Horace's Carmen Seculare and
Collins's Passions pari passu come after — Pindar's Pythics are
admirable and Anacreon is charming as a songster — But the
progress of Poesy, is the point of the Pyramid — the first of
Odes — as the Church yard is the first of Elegies — Yet I have
read scarcely any thing of Gray, except the very small collection
of his Poems, and these two thick Quarto's of his works are
almost all news to me — Why is it that I must reproach myself
for an hour given to them as wasted time?

———

19. VI. Wednesday. I answered a Letter from John G. Whittier
inviting me on the part of the managers of the Massachusetts
Anti-Slavery Society, to attend the meeting of the New-England
Anti-Slavery Convention at Boston, to be held on the last
Tuesday of May. I have not absolutely declined to attend, but
have assigned reasons for not attending which will probably be
decisive to my own mind. Upon this subject of Anti-Slavery,
my principles and my position make it necessary for me to be
more circumspect in my conduct than belongs to my Nature
— I have therefore already committed indiscretions of which
all the political parties avail themselves to proscribe me in the
public opinion — The most insignificant error of conduct in
me at this time would be my irredeemable ruin in this world,
and both the ruling political parties are watching with intense
anxiety for some overt act by me, to set the whole pack of their
hireling Presses upon me. It is also to be considered that at this
time the most dangerous of all the subjects for public conten-

tion is the Slavery question — In the South it is a perpetual agony of conscious guilt and terror, attempting to disguise itself under sophistical argumentation and braggart menaces. In the North, the People favour the whites and fear the blacks of the South — The Politicians court the South because they want their votes — The abolitionists are gathering themselves into Societies increasing their numbers and thriving upon persecution — But in proportion as they increase in numbers and in zeal they kindle the opposition against themselves into a flame; and the Passions of the Populace, are all engaged against them — The exposure through which I passed at the late Session of Congress was greater than I could have imagined possible: and having escaped from that fiery furnace, it behooves me well to consider my ways before I put myself in the way of being cast into it again — On the other hand may God preserve me from the craven Spirit of shrinking from danger in the discharge of my duty — Between these two errors let me pursue the path of rectitude unmov'd, and put my trust in God.

————

27. V:30. Thursday ≈ I have cleared off the arrears of my correspondence, with the exception of several Letters from strangers asking for Autographs, a recent fashion like that of keeping Album's — The Album is I believe a German invention, never introduced till of late years into this Country, and now perverted by its multiplication, and its degeneracy into a mere catalogue of insignificant names — Those in which sentiments are added are records of human imbecility — bushels of chaff without the two grains of wheat — Ashamed to write my bare name in answer to a request for an Autograph, I have usually added a few lines of rhyme without reason — Casting about for a thought, two days ago, I looked into Horace and fell upon the 6th Ode of the 3d Book, ad Romanos — I took the thought of the first lines — modernized it — localized it and paraphrased it, till I turned it into an Ode as long as the original, but so little like it that no one would ever recognize it — This day I finished it, and call it a prophecy, addressed to the sons of the Pilgrims — a poor thing and not fit even for an autograph or an Album — This has happened to me five or six times — I angle for a thought, and after four or five nibbles

catch one, and when the line brings it up it turns out to be a sculpin for a mackerel or a cod. My prophesy is upon a grave and solemn subject.

———

[May 1837]
6. V:15. Saturday. I had a Letter this morning from my Son, and concluded to take the chance of going home alone next week, leaving my family to follow me, if it may-be after the first of next Month. To assist in effecting which I wrote short Letters to Dr. James Laurie, and to Mr. George Wood the Treasurer of the Columbian College which I left at their respective Offices — Before leaving the City I thought it a decent mark of courtesy to visit Mr. Van Buren at the President's house — I went accordingly, and was received by him in his Cabinet, alone. I had not before set my foot, in the house since I left it on the evening of the 3^d of March 1829 — The conversation with Mr. Van Buren was upon subjects of a general nature, and not at-all upon the public affairs of the Country — Upon the inconvenience of a Summer residence in this city, and on my custom heretofore when under that necessity of bathing and swimming every morning in the Potowmack — Then upon the general state of European Politics — He spoke of unfriendly relations existing between Great-Britain and Russia, and between Russia and Prussia — Of the character of the Crown-Prince of Prussia, as violent, and of his reputation as unpopular — Of dissensions between the present king of England, William the 4th and the Duchess of Kent, mother of the Princess Victoria, presumptive heiress to the Crown, and coming of age on the 24th of this Month — I mentioned my intention to leave the City next Tuesday, and he asked me to remember him respectfully to my Son, and his wife.

———

[June 1837]
1. IV:15. Thursday. Thayer, Minott; Turner, Samuel A.; Fogg, Ebenezer J.; Little, Edward P.; Field, Harvey. These Gentlemen came as a Committee of the delegation in the House of Representatives of the Commonwealth from the towns composing the 12th Congressional District of Massachusetts. Mr. Thayer on their part read to me an Address and left it with

me, expressing their approbation of my conduct as their Representative in Congress, especially at the last Session, and presented me a Cane made of the timber of the frigate Constitution. I answered Mr. Thayer's address orally, and accepted the cane, as a token of their esteem, the value of the Article not being of sufficient pecuniary value to be declined upon a general principle. Mr. Thayer made on his account a second Address, which I also answered. In the Evening, with Louisa C. Smith, Charles and his wife, we visited at Mr. John Greenleaf's, and afterwards at Mrs. T. B. Adams's — both houses were full of company — Mr. and Mrs. Angier were at Mrs. Adams's.

———

6. IV. Tuesday. Charles went with Midshipman John Q. Adams to Boston, and returned to dinner — I am falling into a waste of time which I fear I have not strength of mind to resist — Much of the day was spent in examining my plants, and inspecting the Garden, Nursery and Seminary. Visited also my Orchard in which there is much to do — The two Misses Grimke of South-Carolina, with Mr. and Mrs. Fuller, and had much argumentative conversation with me upon Slavery and abolition. And after dinner Rev'd. Mr. Lothrop, minister of the Brattle Street Church in Boston, with his Son, and his relation Mr. Westmore of Utica N.Y. just returned, from a Southern and Western tour.

———

[August 1837]
23. IV:30. Wednesday. ≈ The District Convention of delegates from the towns of the 12th Congressional district of Massachusetts, convened to pass resolutions, approving of my conduct at the last Session of Congress, in the discussions upon the right of petition, and against the annexation of Texas to the United States ≈ I addressed them for about an hour and a half on their Resolutions — I was frequently interrupted by cheering applause, and although my speech was far below mediocrity it was very favourably received.

———

[September 1837]
1. V. Friday. Philadelphia. Employed the morning before breakfast in writing to my wife. Breakfasted at the Lady's

ordinary, to which Judge Baldwin of the Supreme Court of the United States had recommended me, and who was the only person present whom I knew ≈ I found Mr. Biddle, in bed — much flushed, and with a feverish hand ≈ I had a long conversation with him upon the affairs of the Banks, banking and the currency; but found him fully convinced that the resumption of specie payments by the Banks will for an indefinite period of time be impracticable ≈ I then went to the Anti-Slavery Office 223 Arch Street — thence to Samuel Webb's house, and afterwards to Benjamin Lundy's Office — I saw and had long conversations with them both, and with two or three others whom I found with them — of whom was Mr. Buffum who told me he was a hatter — Lundy returned with me to my lodgings. He and the abolitionists generally are constantly urging me to indiscreet movements which would ruin me and weaken and not strengthen their cause — My own family on the other hand that is my wife and Son and Mary exercise all the influence they possess to restrain and divert me from all connection with the abolitionists, and with their cause — Between these adverse impulses my mind is agitated almost to distraction. The public mind in my own district and State is convulsed between the Slavery and abolition questions and I walk on the edge of a precipice in every step that I take.

———

9. IV:30. Saturday. ≈ I called at the President's House, and spent half an hour in conversation with him respecting the weather, the climate, and Queen Victoria, the girl of 18 sovereign of all the British dominions — "Youth at the prow, and pleasure at the helm" — I had been told that in these troublous times, Mr. Van-Buren was so deeply affected by them, that he looked extremely wretched; but I found no such thing. He had every appearance of composure and tranquility — He spoke indeed of the cares and afflictions of the Station which he now occupies, and said it was surprising how universal the delusion was that any one could be happy in it, and he spoke of the calm, philosophical Spirit of Dr. Franklin and of Mr. Madison — who he said had expressed to him a very high esteem for me — There are many features in the character of Mr. Van-Buren strongly resembling that of Mr. Madison — His calmness — his gentleness of manners, his discretion — his

easy and conciliatory temper — But Madison had none of his obsequiousness — his sycophancy — his profound dissimulation and duplicity — In the last of these he much more resembles Jefferson, though with very little of his genius — The most disgusting part of his character his fawning servility belonged neither to Jefferson nor to Madison.

———

14. III:30. Thursday ≈ H.R.U.S. I presented the Petition of Sherlock S. Gregory of Sandlake, Rensselaer County, New-York, for an act of Congress declaring him an alien or stranger in the land, so long as Slavery exists, and the wrongs of the Indians are unrequited and unrepented of — The Petition lies on the table, but together with two or three remarks which I made on presenting it, it roused the wrath of Cushman of New-Hampshire, the man of previous questions, [who] moved a resolution "that the operation of the 16th rule of the House, in relation to the call of the States for the presentation of Petitions be suspended during the present Session of Congress." I saw his drift and immediately assailed his resolution as an attempt to abridge the right of petition. Tillinghast and Mercer came also to the rescue — Cushman was so confounded that he knew not what to say. Polk the Speaker, said he probably meant only to suspend the call of the States, and not the presentation of Petitions, and advised him to modify his Resolution accordingly. I objected to that, observing that it totally changed the character of the Resolution — I insisted upon the preservation of the form — The call of the States, and demanded the yeas and nays — Cushman was at his wits end. He said he was the last man in the world to abridge the right of petition — he was interrupted by calls from his own party to withdraw his Resolution, and awkwardly did withdraw it.

———

18. III:30. Monday ≈ H.R.U.S. — At my motion 2000 extra copies of the revised rules, with Jefferson's Manual and the Constitution of the United States be printed and by a suggestion of G. N. Briggs, suitably bound — I presented 90 Petitions and remonstrances against the annexation of Texas to the United States. Governor Lincoln presented the Resolves of the Legislature of Massachusetts concerning the franking privilege, and Mr. Cushing, the Resolutions respecting the order of 18

January 1837 and Slavery in the District of Columbia. After presenting my Petitions, I offered a Resolution — That the power of annexing the People of any independent foreign State to this Union is a power not delegated by the Constitution of the United States to their Congress, or to any department of their Government, but reserved to the People. The Speaker refused to receive this motion or to allow it to be read; on the pretence that it was not in order — I appealed to the uniform practice of the House to receive with Petitions, Resolutions relating to the subject of them; but in vain.

———

28. III:15. Thursday. H.R.U.S. — I presented   Petitions for the abolition of Slavery in the Territories   for refusing the admission of any new Slave holding State into the Union — and   for the prohibition of the interstate Slave trade — With the last I asked leave to offer a Resolution, calling upon the Secretary of the Treasury to report at the next Session of Congress the numbers of Slaves exported from, and imported into the several Ports of the United States, by the Coasting trade. There was what Napoleon would have called a superb NO! returned to my request, from the servile side of the House. ≈

29. III:30. Friday. H.R.U.S — I reached the House, at the instant of time to present 51 petitions and remonstrances against the order of the House of Representatives of the 18th of January 1837, which was to lay on the table without printing or further action of the House upon them all Petitions, Resolutions and Papers in any manner relating to Slavery. Most of these were received by me during the last Session, but the majority of the House by evading after the 6th of February the reception of all Petitions, excluded the reception of these, and of 150 others, all of which I have now presented and they have all been received and laid on the table.

———

[October 1837]
1. IV. Sunday. ≈ Evening at home — I found in Niles's register of yesterday a correspondence between Governor Schley of Georgia, and Governor Dunlap of Maine, of grave import — Schley demands that two citizens of Maine should be delivered up, to be tried in Georgia, for felony in stealing a Slave

— Dunlap answers that he is no abolitionist, and will carry into full effect the Constitutional provision for the restitution of fugitive Slaves — But that the case is not made out, for surrendering citizens of Maine. Schley replies — insists that the case is made out, and threatens War.

———

3. III. Tuesday ≈ H.R.U.S. This being the last of the thirty days, from the commencement of the Session, for the presentation of Petitions, I presented two against the annexation of Texas — but I reserve a considerable number for the Winter Session. F. O. J. Smith obtained leave of absence for his Colleague George Evans, from next Monday for the remainder of the Session — Evans is one of the ablest men, and most eloquent Orators in Congress. His powers of reasoning and of pathos, his command of language and his elocution are not exceeded by any member of this Congress, much superior to the last. The last effort that he made was in January 1836, was the most furious personal philippic against me that ever was delivered — afterwards printed in a pamphlet, and circulated by thousands in my own district — I never answered him, though I wrote a full and complete answer which I was prepared to deliver, had the occasion presented itself — He is now under a dark cloud; publicly charged with having debauched the wife of Bellamy Storer, a member of the last Congress from Ohio, but a native of Maine — This charge [he] has made fruitless attempts to repel. His denials have only fastened upon him the charges of prevarication and falsehood in aggravation of that of seduction and double adultery — He has a look of wretchedness and conscious shame which moves my compassion — I have not spoken to him since his outrageous and unprovoked attack upon me, with whom he had always before been upon terms of professed friendship. But the other day he silently rose and offered me a Chair in which he was sitting and I can hardly forgive myself for not offering him, as I had a strong impulse to do, my hand.

———

6. III:15. Friday. I find it very difficult to reach the House before the Speaker takes the Chair which is precisely at ten O'Clock — The prayer of the Chaplain occupies but two minutes — the reading of the Journal seldom takes more than

three, and by five minutes after ten the Speaker plunges into the business of the day. While Petitions were received every morning, and I had multitudes of them to present, a necessity was imposed upon me to be there at the stroke of the Clock, and I was there. Since the expiration of the 30 days, leaving only one day in the week for the receipt of Petitions, my punctuality has almost insensibly to myself fallen off, and this morning I found Thomas, Chairman of the judiciary Committee, moving that the Committee of the whole should be discharged from the Bill to continue the expiring Laws, that it might be taken up and passed in the House, which was done — Wise presented a petition from 37 Ladies and Gentlemen of Halifax County Virginia, praying Congress to furnish husbands, at public expence, to all female petitioners upon subjects relating to slavery, thereby giving a direction to their minds calculated to make them good matrons, and averting the evils with which the fanaticism of the Eastern States threaten the people of the South — It was received and laid on the table — I propose to notice it hereafter.

———

10. IV. Tuesday ≈ Committee of the whole on the state of the Union — The Divorce, or Sub-treasury Bill from the Senate, was called up, not by Cambreleng, but by Pickens of South-Carolina, who made in support of it a prepared Speech of two hours with which he has been swelling like a Cock-turkey, ever since Calhoun's bargain and sale of himself to Van Buren, at the commencement of this Session — Pickens is a fixture to the House of Calhoun, and Van Buren bought him with Calhoun — Cambreleng tickles his Vanity by pushing him forward as the champion of this Bill, and saving himself the trouble and the odium of this task — which indeed he could not have performed himself — Pickens is a coarse sample of the South-Carolina school of Orator Statesmen — pompous, flashy and shallow — Legare is another — much more polished; better educated and better disciplined — A fine speaker; a brilliant scholar; but yet a shallow bottom — He opposed the taking up of this Bill; but it was carried against him. Pickens's speech was a jumble of indigested political economy, of abuse upon Jackson for his war against the Bank — of abuse repeated from Calhoun, upon Banks, banking, and the Bank

— of South-Carolina nullification, of Slave-driving autocracy and of ranting radicalism — He said if the abolitionists of the North would preach insurrection to the Southern Slaves he would retort upon them by preaching insurrection to the labourers against the Capitalists of the North — He said he supposed he should pass for a Loco foco; but he had recently heard it said that John Milton was a Loco foco — Then he passed a panegyric upon John Milton, as the intrepid supporter of the *rights of man*, and concluded that if John Milton was a Loco-foco, he was content to be called so too — All this was delivered with an air of authority, and a tone of dogmatism, as if he was speaking to his Slaves.

———

14. VI:30. Saturday. I had no time to write this morning, and my Diary is running into arrears I fear inextricable. — Nor had I time to read my Letters and papers by the morning Mail. Scarcely time for breakfast, and yet I found the House already in Session. ≈ I retired to the chamber of the Committee of manufactures and wrote a Letter to my wife — I have found this so agreeable, and so useful a manner of transacting the business in the house and disposing of the time in the recess, that I regretted the single exception of the day when by the invitation of Elisha Whittlesey, I went and dined with him at his lodgings. Five or six small crackers and a glass of water, give me a sumptuous dinner. I consume an hour and a quarter in writing a Letter, and the time passes like a flash of lightening — I am calm and composed for the Evening Session; and far better prepared for taking part in any debate than after the most temperate dinner at home or abroad ≈

15. VII:30. Sunday. ≈ I had a visit from Edward Wyer; who after years upon years wasted in pursuit of subsistence by public office, has by dint of perseverance and importunity obtained at last the appointment of door-keeper to the Senate — I prevailed upon him to stay and dine with me. As did Mess'rs Borden, Hastings, Parmenter and Phillips of the Massachusetts delegation in the House — And thus on this and the two preceding Sundays, I have had to dine with me all the members of the Massachusetts delegation in the House. For the last three winters I have been from various causes unable to entertain

company at dinner, much to my sorrow; for one of the choicest enjoyments of this life to me is the practice of liberal hospitality — But the death of my dear and ever lamented Son John, the sicknesses of my wife, my own occasionally disordered health, embarrassments in my pecuniary concerns, and sometimes a state of feeling between a large portion of the members of the delegation and me have deprived me of the means, and even of the desire to associate with them at convivial meetings. By the continual evolution of political opinions, and passions, I happen at this moment, to be again upon terms of good understanding and good fellowship with them all — and I have taken the opportunity afforded me by this momentary calm, and this extraordinary Session of inviting them all to dine with me — It may be the last time I shall ever have the opportunity of meeting my political associates and adversaries in the intercourse of mutual good will at the social board — and for this purpose I have been obliged to take the Sunday, the rest of the week being wholly absorbed by public duties — It has deprived me of the power of attendance on public worship in the afternoon; which I have regretted, but could not avoid.

—

23. V. Monday ≈ There was in the National Intelligencer this morning an advertisement, signed James H. Birch, and Edward Dyer Auctioneer — headed Sale of Slaves — A sale at public auction at 4 O'Clock this afternoon, of Dorcas Allen, and her two surviving children aged about 7 and 9 years (the other two having been killed by said Dorcas in a fit of insanity as found by the jury who lately acquitted her) — The advertisement further says that the said Slaves were purchased by Birch, on the 22^d of August last of Rezin Orme, warranted sound in body and in mind — That the terms of sale will be cash, as said Slaves will be sold on account of said Rezin Orme, who refuses to retake the same and repay the purchase money, and who is notified to attend said sale, and if he thinks proper to bid for them or retake them, as he prefers, upon refunding the money paid, and all expenses incurred under the warranty given by him — I asked Mr. Frye, what this advertisement meant — He seemed not to like to speak of it, but said the woman had been sold with her children to be sent to the South, and separated from her husband — that she had killed

two of her children, by cutting their throats, and cut her own to kill herself, but in that had failed — That she had been tried at Alexandria, for the murder of her children, and acquitted on the ground of insanity — And that this sale now, was by the purchaser, at the expense of the seller, upon the warranty that she was sound in body and mind — Mr. Frye brought me ten numbers of Niles's Register, which has been sent to his house while I was absent last Summer, and of which I had obtained another set, supposing that they had been stopped during the recess. I took them to Niles's Register Office, but he was not there — I called at the Office of the National Intelligencer and saw Mr. Seaton — enquired of him concerning the advertisement of the Sale of Slaves, in the paper of this morning. He answered with reluctance, and told me the same story that I had heard from Mr. Frye — adding that there was something very bad about it, but without telling me what it was — It is a case of Conscience with me, whether my duty requires or forbids me to pursue the enquiry in this case — to ascertain all the facts, and to expose them in all their turpitude to the world — The prohibition of the internal Slave-trade is within the Constitutional power of Congress, and in my opinion is among their incumbent duties — I have gone as far upon this article, the abolition of Slavery, as the public opinion of the free portion of the Union will bear — and so far that scarcely a slave holding member of the House dares to vote with me, upon any question — I have as yet been thoroughly sustained in my own State; but one step further, and I hazard my own standing and influence there; my own final overthrow, and the cause of Liberty itself for indefinite time — certainly for more than my remnant of life — Were there in the House one member capable of taking the lead in this cause of universal emancipation, which is moving onward in the world, and in this country, I would withdraw from the contest, which will rage with increasing fury, as it draws to its crisis, but for the management of which my age, infirmities and approaching end totally disqualify *me*. There is no such man in the House ≈

24. IV:45. Tuesday. Fahrenheit at 82. — The weather has been several days very fine, but at high Summer heat. This morning I visited Mrs. Madison, who has come to take up her residence

in this city — I had not seen her since March 1809 — The
depredations of time are not so perceptible in her personal
appearance, as might be expected — She is a woman of placid,
equable temperament, and less susceptible of laceration by the
scourges of the world abroad, than most others — The term of
her husband's presidency was tempestuous, and turbulent; but
he weathered the storm by that equanimity which carried him
also through an eventful period, and a boisterous age — The
two closing years of his presidency terminated his political life,
with honour, and tranquility, eminently successful in its general result, and glorious individually to him — The succeeding
twenty years she has passed in retirement — so long as he
lived, with him, and now upwards of a year since his decease
— She intended to have removed to this place last Autumn,
but was prevented by an inflammatory disease in her eyes,
from which she has almost wholly recovered — There is no
trace of it in her appearance now.

———

28. VI. Saturday ≈ There was in the National Intelligencer of
this morning an Advertisement again of the Sale of a Woman
and two children at 11 O'Clock. I went between 11 and 12
O'Clock to the room — the woman and children, girls of 7
and 9 years of age were there, the woman weeping and wailing
most piteously. I enquired of Dyer if they were sold. He said
no — That they had been sold last Monday, and bought in
by the husband of the woman who was free, and a waiter at
Gadsby's — he had bought them in for 475 dollars, but was
unable to raise the money, which was the reason why they
were to be sold again — They were waiting for the man, who
was endeavouring to procure by subscription, upon his own
engagement to repay the money, the means of paying for his
purchase last Monday — Mr. F. S. Key the District Attorney
came in, and appeared to interest himself in favour of the man.
I learnt from Dyer, that the woman had been the Slave of a
white woman who had married a man named Davis who lived
at Georgetown, and was a Clerk in the War Department —
That this white woman had died, and had before her death,
promised Dorcas her freedom. That on her death bed, she had
made her husband Davis promise her that he would emancipate Dorcas — That he did actually liberate her, but gave her

no papers — That she lived twelve or fifteen years at large — married, and had four children — That in the meantime Davis married a second wife, and afterwards died without granting to Dorcas her papers of freedom — That Davis's widow, married a man by the name of Rezin Orme, and that he sold Dorcas and her four children, on the 22^d of August last for 700 dollars to Birch who is an agent for the negro Slave-traders at Alexandria. That Dorcas and her four children, were on the same day removed to one of the Slave prisons in Alexandria. That in the Night of that day, she killed the two youngest of her children, one a boy four years of age, and the other a girl under twelve months — That she attempted to kill the other two, but was prevented; their screaming having roused some person in the house, who went into the cell where she was confined, and took her surviving children from her — That she was tried at Alexandria for the murder of her two children and was acquitted by the jury on the ground of insanity — These were stated as the facts, and it was said to be doubtful whether Rezin Orme, had any right to sell them at all. Mr. Key made some enquiries about Orme, who it was said had left the District, and was not to be found — and about Mrs. Orme, who he said was under obligations to him; but who Dyer said had shut herself up in her chamber and would be seen by no person on the subject. Mr. Key called me out of the Auction-room to speak in private with me on the subject; he said he thought a subscription might be raised to enable Allen to pay for the purchase of his wife, and children; and I told him I would give fifty dollars towards it — I then called upon judge Cranch at his Office in the City Hall, and enquired of him concerning the trial of this woman at Alexandria. He read to me his Notes at the trial — There were two Indictments against her; one for the murder of each of her children — She was tried only upon one — That of the boy — The evidence of her killing them was complete — The defence was insanity — Not the slightest evidence of insanity at the time, except the mere fact of her killing the children — There was evidence of her being subject to fits, which sometimes lasted an hour. That she is passionate, and violent, and some times wild in her talk — The jury acquitted her as insane. The prosecutor entered a noli prosequi upon the second indictment — Upon being asked why she had killed her children, she said they were in Heaven — that if they had lived she did not know what would have become of them — That her mistress had been wrong — that her mistress was a methodist; and so she was herself— There was no evidence before the court, of any thing preceding the acts for which she was tried.

———

30. V:45. Monday ≈ I called at Dyer's auction room to enquire what had been done with Dorcas Allen and her two children on Saturday. He was not there; but a man in his place told me that Mr. Key and Birch had made some arrangement by which the woman had been taken by her husband, and the two children had been taken away by Birch.

———

[November 1837]

1. V. Wednesday. Cold Night and Morning, so finger pinching that it robs me of my best writing time ≈ Nathan Allen, the husband of the woman and children sold last week, came this evening with the subscription paper, to pay Birch for them — They are now in the Jail waiting for this money to be raised to have them delivered over to the Husband and father — I subscribed fifty dollars to be paid if the sum be made up to complete the purchase — I enquired of Allen, apparently an active, but very ignorant man how Dorcas came to be the property of Rezin Orme; he said some people thought she was not — She had originally belonged to a woman in Baltimore named Emery, who married Gideon Davis. on her death bed she made Davis promise that he would give Dorcas her freedom, but Davis never did — He married a second wife named   belonging to Georgetown — Davis himself died without emancipating Dorcas and his widow married Rezin Orme — who sold her and her four children — Dorcas is subject to epileptic fits very violent after which she is sick ten or twelve days. She has been repeatedly sold and turned back on account of these fits and often turned upon her husband's hands to be maintained and doctored at his charge, because her owners would not incur the expense — The eldest of the surviving girls is 12 years old, and named Maria — the youngest 9. He says he shall easily find a place for Maria, who is a smart child — It is very doubtful whether I have not imprudently engaged myself in

this matter, which I must pursue further. The emancipation of the woman and children is not yet secured — I finished the draught of my Speech of 14 October, but was obliged to close the Evening soon after nine.

2. V. Thursday. ≈ I called at Mr. Dyer's auction room to enquire about Dorcas Allen and her children — Dyer had been misinformed that they would be liberated by the giving of a note to a man who would lend Allen the money, which Mr. Key was to endorse. He said the woman and children were *not* at the Jail, and that Mr. Key had gone to Mrs. Orme, in her sick chamber, she having been lately confined; and had frightened her so by threatening her with the Law that it was not expected she would live — He pronounced a panegyric upon Orme, who he said was one of the best and most respectable men in the world — And as to the Slaves, he had a right to sell them — they were his property. I asked him by what authority he had sold them — He said by Mr. Birch's — that he had not asked him for any proof that they were his — he had trusted to his word. I said I understood they were not Orme's property — He said they were his by his wife — I said I had heard they were not his wife's — Well, he said he had heard so too — They were really part of Gideon Davis's Estate. He died insolvent, and they belonged to his creditors, and if he was one of them he would claim them as such — Here then is another danger to which these unhappy beings are subjected — If their freedom from Birch's sale should be purchased, they might still be reclaimed by Davis's creditors.

———

9. IV. Thursday. The black man Nathan Allen came again, about the contribution to purchase his wife and children, which he finds it very difficult to accomplish. He said General Smith of Georgetown had agreed to endorse the balance of the sum which was to be paid for the redemption of his wife and children; but the doubt remains whether they will be emancipated — I told Allen to ask Mr. Key to call on me.

———

13. III:45. Monday. Nathan and Dorcas Allen were here this morning. He had not yet made up the subscription for the balance between 330 and 475 dollars. General Walter Smith of

Georgetown having promised to endorse Allen's note for the former sum, if he could procure the remainder to pay Birch for a Bill of Sale of the woman and the two children — But he said that General Smith had examined at the Registry of Wills, Davis's Will, and that by the Will the woman and children were bequeathed to Davis's wife, and therefore her second husband had an undoubted right to sell them — I told him that whenever the Bill of sale should be ready, I would give the check for 50 dollars which I had promised — He came again twice in the course of the day — once while I was out, and again after I returned — He then told me that Birch had again taken the two children, and put them into the jail, and would carry them away, if the money was not paid — That General Smith now said, if I would pay the fifty dollars, he would undertake with the other subscriptions, to pay the whole sum and take the bill of sale. — He repeated that General Smith was entirely satisfied with the validity of Birch's title, and that he had the right to make the sale — I then gave him the check for 50 dollars in Bills payable in Bills at the Bank of Washington to Walter Smith Esq'r or his order; and told him when the affair should be completed to bring me the Bill of sale that I may see it — I could pursue the question of Birch's title no further, without becoming liable to the imputation of shrinking from my own promise, and prevaricating upon the performance of my engagement. Yet I still doubt the legality of the sale to Birch, and whether the complete emancipation of the woman and children will be effected — I could not take the course of the Law, for Mr. Key told me that if upon a writ of Habeas Corpus Birch's title should be disproved, still as they were slaves they could not be discharged — Such is the condition of things in these shambles of human flesh, that I could not now expose this whole horrible transaction, but at the hazard of my life. Any attempt to set aside this purchase for illegality would be stigmatized as mean and *dishonourable* — Iniquity must have its whole range — I therefore made the promise of 50 dollars, for their emancipation, and have now paid it, without even being sure of effecting it — rather than attempt, to bereave the man-robber of his spoils.

—

22. V. Wednesday. There was a riotous assemblage of people, perhaps 300 in number with a Cannon, who went round last

Night to the President's House, and the House of some of the Heads of Departments, discharged their cannon, and made much disturbance, in celebration of the whig victories in the late elections; especially in the State of New-York — I heard little of it myself, though it once awaked me out of sleep; and I knew not what it was — This effervescence of popular feeling is too common, and too little discountenanced by any of the predominating parties — both of them use the populace to glorify their triumphs and to depress their enemies; and both of them suffer for it in turn — The most atrocious case of mob rioting which ever disgraced this Country happened on the Night of the 7th of this Month at Alton in the State of Illinois, where a man by the name of Lovejoy, one of the leading abolitionists of the time has been striving to establish a Newspaper — Three times he had imported printing presses in the place; and three times they had been destroyed by mobs, and once or twice, the Offices in which they were placed — The fourth time, the press was imported, and deposited in a Merchant's warehouse. The mob assembled in the Night; surrounded the warehouse, and demanded that the press should be delivered up to them. It was refused. They assailed the house with musquetry — forced their way into it; set fire to the roof of the building; shot Lovejoy dead, wounded several others, till the press was delivered up to them, which they broke to pieces and threw into the river — One of the assailants also by the name of Bishop was also killed in the affray — This Lovejoy wrote me a Letter last January, which I answered in April — He was a man of strong religious, consciencious feeling, deeply indignant at what he deemed the vices and crimes of the age — Such men are often fated to be martyrs, and he has fallen a martyr to the cause of human freedom — I went and sat again to Mrs. Towle for my portrait. Her husband was there, and inclined to talk politics, from which however I preferred to divert the conversation.

———

30. IV:15. Thursday. I am endeavouring to finish the biographical sketch of my father for my [son] but my subject swells as I proceed, and here is the Session of Congress again close at hand. Mr. G. W. Cherry was here again this morning, and I had a long conversation with him upon his project of Colonization. He is one of the most benevolent visionaries, of that fraudulent

charitable institution the Colonization Society. His plan is to
raise a fund for purchasing a number of Slaves, and locating
them in small villages where they may in a given time purchase
their freedom by their own labour — I freely gave my opinion
to Mr. Cherry that the whole colonization project was an
abortion — That as a system of eventual emancipation of the
Slaves of this Country, it was not only impracticable, but
demonstrated to be so — That as a scheme for relieving the
Slave States of free Negroes, its moral aspect was not comely,
and it was equally impracticable. I held this opinion when the
existence of the Colonization Society was first made known
to me in September 1817 — every day's experience had confirmed me in it, from that time to this — I have never taken
any part against the colonization Society — But I never joined
it — never attended any of its meetings and never believed in
its usefulness. I observed that by the very last accounts published by the Society itself, it appeared that even now, after
twenty years of continual migration to the settlements it appeared they were starving for want of bread; with a fertile soil,
and a Latitude close upon the equator. And the cause assigned
of it is that the colonists waste their time in idleness and will
not work — Mr. Cherry had little to say in reply to this, but he
took my remarks in kindness, and thanked me for the attention
that I had given to his plan in the African Repository, which I
returned to him.

———

[December 1837]
5. III:45. Tuesday. ≈ The House at Noon was called to order,
and Mr. Muhlenberg of Pennsylvania reported from the joint
Committee to wait on the President, that he had informed
them he would make a Communication to both Houses of
Congress this day at 12 O'Clock — The Message was immediately afterwards delivered by his Son, and private secretary   Van Buren — The reading of it by the Clerk took an
hour and a quarter ≈ The Message gave me a fit of melancholy
for the future fortunes of the Country — Cunning and duplicity pervade very line of it. The sacrifice of the rights of Northern freedom to Slavery and the South, and the purchase of the
West by the plunder of the public Lands, is the combined

system which it discloses; — It is the system of Jackson's Message of December 1832 covered with a new coat of varnish. Jackson was dashing and daring. This man is insinuating and plausible. Their characters are comprized in the names of Shakespear's two catch-poles Phang and Snare.

6. III:45. Wednesday. ≈ Between one and two O'Clock the House adjourned. I enclosed to Mr. Charles Sumner at New-York three Letters of Introduction to Paris and London. In the Evening I wrote to Mr. Philip Ammidon, and read in the second Volume of Burr's life — Matthew L. Davis, its author is here, as he has been during several late Sessions as a Correspondent of the New-York Courier and Enquirer. He writes under the signature of the Spy in Washington. He came to my seat this morning, and I told him I was reading his book. His account of the origin of the political parties in New-York, during the revolutionary War, and of their subsequent bearing on the fortunes of Burr, throws some light upon the history of the time. The failure of my father's re-election in 1801 was the joint work of Burr and Alexander Hamilton, and it is among the most remarkable examples of divine retributive justice that the result to them was the murder of one of them by the other in a duel, and the irretrievable ruin of the murder[er] by the very accomplishment of his intrigues — Even handed Justice never held a better balanced scale — Between my father and Jefferson, the final decision of that same Justice was reserved, for a higher state of being — The double-dealer succeeded in this world; yet his death bed was less tranquil and composed than that of him whom he had wronged — Jefferson's hypocrisy and duplicity in the scenes of his election as President, are exposed, in glaring colours in these Volumes; which apparently intended to vindicate the character of Burr do but set the Seal upon his condemnation — But they fix an indelible stain upon that of Jefferson.

———

20. VI. Wednesday. ≈ Slade's motion of Monday, to refer a petition for the abolition of Slavery and the Slave-trade in the District of Columbia to a select Committee came up — Polk the Speaker by some blunder had allowed Slades motion for leave to address the house in support of the petition, without

putting the question of laying on the table — So Slade to-day
got the floor; and in a Speech, of two hours on Slavery —
shook the very Hall into convulsions — Wise, Legare, Rhett,
Dawson, Robertson, and the whole herd were in combustion
— Polk stopped him half a dozen times, and was forced to let
him go on — The Slavers were at their wits end — At last one
of them *objected* to his proceeding on the pretence that he was
discussing Slavery in Virginia — and on this pretence which
was not true — Polk ordered him to take his seat. A motion to
adjourn made half a dozen times before out of order was now
started and carried by yeas and nays — Formal notice was immediately given, by a member of a meeting of all the slave-
holding members in the Chamber of the Committee on the
District of Columbia — Most, if not all of the South-Carolina
members had left the Hall ≈

21. VI. Thursday ≈ H.R.U.S. — The Journal had disfigured
and falsified the Transactions — Slade moved to amend the
Journal so as to state the facts correctly — but his motion was
rejected — Patton had a resolution ready drawn agreed upon
at the Slavery meeting of yesterday; a resolution like that of the
16th of January last, that no petitions relating to Slavery or the
trade in Slaves in any State, District or Territory of the United
States shall be read, printed, committed or in any manner
acted upon by the House — I objected to the reception of the
Resolution, and Patton moved to suspend the rules, which was
carried 136 to 65 and after a Speech, he moved the previous
question which was carried as was the Resolution
When my name was called I answered I held the Resolution to
be a Violation of the Constitution of the right of petition of
my constituents and of the people of the United States, and of
my right to freedom of Speech as a member of this House — I
said this amidst a perfect war-whoop of order. In reading over
the names of the members the Clerk omitted mine. I then
mentioned it and the Speaker ordered the Clerk to call my
name again. I did not answer but moved that my answer when
first called should be entered on the Journal. The Speaker said
the motion was not in order, that the only answer that could
be given was aye or no. I moved that my motion might be

entered on the Journal with the decision of the Speaker that it was not in order — to which he made no answer ≈

22. VI. Friday. H.R.U.S. On the reading of the Journal, I found my motion yesterday made to insert on the Journal my answer to the gag resolution — I moved to amend the journal by inserting that when my name was called I rose and said I hold the resolution to be a violation of the Constitution of the United States, of the right of petition of my Constituents and of the People of the United States, and of my right to Freedom of Speech as a member of this House — Boon asked if my motion was debatable; I said I hoped it was, and that the house would allow me to debate it — Boon moved to lay my motion on the table — I asked for the yeas and nays, but they were refused and the motion was laid on the table — but my answer was entered on the Journal. Patton had come charged with a speech to prevent this entry upon the Journal — Boon's motion to lay mine on the table balked him; and I bantered him on his Resolution, till he said that if the question ever came to the issue of War, the Southern people would march into New-England and conquer it — I said I had no doubt they would if they could, and that it was what they were now struggling for with all their might — I told him that I entered my Resolution on the Journal because I meant his name should go down to posterity, damned to everlasting fame — He forced a smile and said we should then go down together — I replied precisely — side by side — that was what I intended. So conscious was he of the odious character of his Resolution that he dared not resent these remarks — but he dared not object to Boon's motion to lay mine on the table; which precisely answered my purpose of having my answer entered upon the Journal. He soon after rose from his seat and left the House.

———

[January 1838]
1. V. Monday. The new year began with one of the most beautiful days that the course of the Seasons ever brought round — A clear sky — a bright Sun, a calm atmosphere, and all physical Nature moving in harmony, and Peace — The President's House was open as usual from 11 in the morning to 3 in

the afternoon; and was crowded with visitors innumerable — I
was not among them — I have found it necessary to assume a
position in public towards him, and his administration which
forbids me from any public exhibition of personal courtesy,
which would import a friendly feeling. Mr. Clay whose public
position, not precisely the same as mine differs little from it
went and escorted Mrs. Bell of Tennessee, wife of the late
Speaker of the House, who was also there — They afterwards
came here, as did about 300 ladies and gentlemen, of those
who had been at the Presidents House — Mr. Clay told me
that he had twice during his visit spoken to Mr. Van Buren;
and the second time congratulated him upon his happiness in
being surrounded by *so many of his friends* — to which Mr.
Van Buren answered; the weather is very fine — No insignificant answer — for it implied his conscious assent to the satirical
reflection, implied in Clay's remark — Fair weather friends —

> Donec eris felix, multos numerabis amicos
> Tempora si fuerint nubila, solus eris.

I snatched a quarter of an hour before noon to call on Mrs.
Madison who also received many visitors, just before reaching
her house, I met Lewis Williams and Mr. Graham, and Joseph
L. Williams of Tennessee, and thought they were going to my
house; but from a feeling of awkwardness at asking them the
question, and the fear of losing my chance to visit Mrs. Madison, I passed by them with a slight salutation, when I believe
I ought to have stopped, and enquired if they were going to
my house, turned back with them, and waited for another
chance to visit Mrs. Madison — Upon what slight shades of
difference depends propriety of conduct in social intercourse
— These three men intended me a civility. There are no three
men more entitled to a kind and courteous return. Yet they
must have felt themselves slighted, and I might have returned
their kindness in a manner which would have gratified them
— Am I too old to learn? — Among our visitors whom I did
not expect, were Mr. Forsyth, Secretary of State, with his wife
and two daughters, and Mr. Poinsett, Secretary of War, alone.
I have never had any personal misunderstanding with either of
them — They are both under great political obligations to me,
in return for which no two men have been more active or

effective political adversaries to me. Politically they have returned me unmixed, unqualified evil for good — So has their chief — Martin Van Buren; though his obligations to me personally, are incomparably less than theirs — His Predecessor Jackson's obligations to me, were incomparably greater; and were returned by still fouler and baser ingratitude — Forsyth and Poinsett first as partizans of Crawford and Calhoun, deadly enemies to each other afterwards as partizans of Jackson, my competitor did every thing in their power to ruin me in fortune and reputation; but always bore to me a smooth face, and gave me fair words — This is the hypocrisy of Politics, to which I am obliged to submit as to the fashion of the world — but which I cannot and never could practise.

———

15. V. Monday. My wife is confined to her bed with a very severe attack of Erisypelas, and had a restless night. Mrs. Goods watched. She was this day better. Dr. Huntt was here, himself dying with a consumption — H.R.U.S. — Petitions beginning with Virginia; going South and West; and then back from Wisconsin through to Maine — There were a great multitude of Abolition and Anti-Texas petitions from all the free States — all laid on the table — I presented nearly sixty myself. Also the Petition of Benoit Henri Klimkiewitz a Polish exile, for a grant of land — Mr. Ungerer had brought it to me at the door of the Hall — It was referred to the Committee on the public Lands. The Petition of 54 citizens of Ohio that Congress would carry into execution the 10th Article of the Treaty of Ghent. Haynes instantly moved to lay it on the table, but I asked that the Article should be read by the Clerk and it was read. Petition laid on the table — A Petition that Congress would repeal the Law in the District of Columbia, by which Freemen are liable to be sold for Jail fees — I moved its reference to the Committee on the District of Columbia with Instructions to report a Bill to abolish imprisonment for debt in the District — The Speaker entertained this motion. Haynes, moved to make it an enquiry into the expediency but for once the House deserted him, and the petition was referred with the Instruction.

———

28. V. Sunday. ≈ I received this day 31 Petitions, and consumed the whole evening in assorting, filing, endorsing and entering

them on my list, without completing the work — With these
Petitions I receive many Letters which I have not time to
answer — Most of them are so flattering; and expressed in
terms of such deep sensibility, that I am in imminent danger of
being led by them into presumption, and puffed up with vanity
— The abolition Newspapers, the Liberator, Emancipator,
Philanthropist, National Enquirer and New-York Evangelist,
all of which are regularly sent to me, contribute to generate
and nourish this delusion, which the treacherous, furious,
filthy and threatening Letters from the South on the same
subject cannot sufficiently counteract — My duty to defend
the free principles and Institutions is clear, but the measures by
which they are to be defended are involved in thick darkness.
— The path of right is narrow, and I have need of a perpetual
controul over passion.

———

[February 1838]
11. VI. Sunday. Fanny continues so unwell that she could not
read with me in the Bible; but Louisa read her four chapters
— I attended Church this morning at the Presbyterian, and
heard Mr. Fowler, preach from Hosea 4:17 "Ephraim is joined
to idols — let him alone." — Mr. Fowler is a young, warm
hearted, sincerely pious calvinist, feeling intensely for the salvation of the sheep of his flock and possessing more of the will
than of the powers of pathetic eloquence — He laboured exceedingly to alarm his hearers in his commentary upon this
text; but from the moment that he read it, a reminiscence occurred to me that in the year 1808 at a time when I had committed the unpardonable sin against the federal party, by
sustaining the administration of Jefferson in his quarrel with
England, and the federal wrath was boiling over against me,
this very text from Hosea, was given at a federal party public
dinner on the 4th of July some where in the County of Worcester, as a toast, annexed to my name — This recollection gave
an irresistibly ludicrous turn to all Mr. Fowler's exertions to
give a terrific exposition to his text.

———

13. VI. Tuesday. Both the children and Elizabeth are very sick,
confined to their beds — A projector from Baltimore named
Pennington was here, with an invention for navigating through

the air, and an engraved plate representing his machine which is in the form of a boat — He wants an appropriation by Congress to try his experiment upon a large scale, and as I did not encourage him to expect my assistance to obtain this appropriation he talked flippantly enough about the propensity of the world in general to discountenance all great inventions and discoveries. I preserved my good humour, and did not discompose his, nor yet trust my faith to take passage in his airy boat. ≈

14. IV. Wednesday. ≈ The call commenced with me, and I presented 350 Petitions, of which 158 were for the rescinding of the Patton gag, or Resolution of 21 Dec'r 65 for the abolition of Slavery and the Slave trade in the District of Columbia, in the Territories   for the prohibition of the internal Slave trade   against the admission of any new State whose Constitution tolerates Slavery, and   against the annexation of Texas to the Union — Besides these there were several Petitions for various objects of anomalous character, which could be included in neither of these Classes — One or two were claims for Pensions — one of a deaf mute editor of a newspaper, praying for the privilege of sending his paper by mail free of postage, and a petition of   of his neighbours that the prayer of his Petition might be granted — Mr. Ratcliff's Memorial from Aaron Clark, Mayor of the City of New-York, and sundry others, praying for the aid of Congress to obtain the making a ship Canal across the Isthmus of Panama. I moved its reference to a Select Committee, but a motion was made and carried to refer it to the Committee on Roads and Canals — A Petition from a man named Judson that Congress would appropriate money to build a Wall, like the Wall of China, between the free and the slave holding States. I asked the Speaker if that came under the Resolution of 21 December — he said it did not. I then moved its reference to a select Committee — but a motion was immediately made and carried to lay it on the table — The Petition for an Appropriation for the relief of Mrs. Lovejoy shared the same fate — Several of the strange Petitions from Sherlock S. Gregory were treated in like manner. But there was one praying that Congress would take measures to protect Citizens of the North going to the South

from danger to their lives — When the motion to lay that on the table was made, I said that in another part of the Capitol, it had been threatened that if a Northern abolitionist should go to South-Carolina, and utter a principle of the Declaration of Independence — here a loud cry of order — order — burst forth, in which the Speaker yelled among the loudest — I waited till it subsided and then resumed; that if they could catch him they would hang him — I said this so as to be distinctly heard throughout the Hall, the renewed deafening shout of order-order notwithstanding — The Speaker then said, the Gentleman from Massachusetts will take his Seat — which I did, and immediately rose again, and presented another Petition — He did not dare to tell me that I could not proceed without permission of the house and I proceed[ed] — The threat to hang northern abolitionists was uttered by Preston in the Senate within the last fortnight.

———

[March 1838]
5. VI:15. Monday. Copious rain last night, and all the fore-part of this day — Mr. Ratcliff was here this morning. His memorial for negotiating a ship Canal across the Isthmus of Panama has been referred to the Committee of Roads and Canals. Mr. Ratcliff has conferred with the Chairman of that Committee Mr. Mercer, and wishes me to confer with him — He asked my opinion also whether he could with propriety call on the President, Van Buren, to converse with him on the subject — I advised it — I received by the Mail this morning from Rocky Mount, Franklin County Virginia, signed by John V. Brown and 12 others, a Letter and Petition to Congress, to arraign at the Bar of the House and expel forever John Quincy Adams — At the House it was the day for calling up the States, for Resolutions — The Speaker began with Wisconsin and Florida, going through the Territories and new States, then North and East, concluding with Maine — When Massachusetts was called after all the other members of the delegation who had resolutions to offer had finished, I offered a Resolution, that the Letter and Petition, with the names of the signers be printed and referred to a Committee of nine members, to consider and report thereon, with liberty to send for persons

and papers — The Speaker said the Petition could not then be received — Resolutions having then the exclusive right to reception. I claimed the reception of the Petition, as involving the privilege of the House and its members — It was accordingly received and read, with the names. Stuart, the representative from that district said he did not know one of the signers and believed the names all fictitious — Patton asked if the question of *reception* could not be made. The Speaker said it was too late — Mercer moved the question of consideration. Another moved to lay the whole on the table, and that was carried. The Resolutions of the Legislature of Alabama, for the annexation of Texas were introduced by Lawler and at his motion ordered to be printed and laid on the table — I moved their reference to a select Committee, and barely obtained a vote by yeas and nays.   Waddy Thompson told me that he had received last winter a petition numerously signed, praying for my expulsion, but he never presented it. After the call for Resolutions had gone through the Speaker began again at Wisconsin the call for Petitions. Proceeding as far as Virginia, when after several unsuccessful attempts, a motion to adjourn, about 4 O'Clock was carried. I walked home, accompanied to the parting point by Mr. Kemble.

———

10. VI:30. Saturday. ≈ A call of the house was ordered and proceeded just far enough to make a quorum, when a motion to adjourn was carried, before two O'Clock. I went into the Senate chamber where I found John C. Calhoun, discoursing to his own honour and glory, and vituperating Henry Clay; upon which delicious topics he had already been two hours occupied and used up another hour after I went in — It was the settlement of accounts which Calhoun had threatened when Clay attacked him, a fortnight or three weeks ago — Clay replied instanter, saying that though much indisposed, he would not take three weeks to concoct a retort upon the Senator from South-Carolina — He was from a half to three quarters of an hour and had manifestly the advantage in the debate — Calhoun had affected to consider himself as on the defensive in this contest — But between the special and the present Session of Congress he had written a Letter at

Fort Hill, his residence, to vindicate himself for his change of
party, in which he declared that he had no reason to confide in
the firmness or Patriotism of the whigs, and that if he continued to act with them, the fruits of victory would all go to them
and not to him and his friends — Clay took his text from that
Letter, and drove him from his defensive ground irrecoverably
— There was rejoinder, surrejoinder, rebutter and surrebutter
— The truth and the victory were with Clay, who closed with
a taunting hope that the settlement of accounts was as satisfactory to the Senator from South-Carolina, as it was to him —
Clay spoke of the South-Carolina Nullification with such
insulting contempt, that it brought out Preston, who complained of it bitterly — Preston's countenance was a portraiture
of agonizing anguish — These personal oratorical encounters
between Clay and Calhoun are Liliputian Mimicry of the Orations against Ctesiphon and for the Crown — or the debate of
the second Philippic.

———

[May 1838]
21. V:30. Monday. Attended at the chamber of the Committee
of Manufactures, at ½ past 9, but the only other member who
attended there, was Mr. Slade, and of course we could do no
business — H.R.U.S. — The States beginning with Maine
were called for Petitions; of which I presented 35 being exactly
the number of days since the last presentation — 24 of these
were against that abomination the fraudulent Treaty of New
Echota, and for justice and mercy to the Cherokee Indians — I
presented them all at once, knowing that every one of them
would be separately laid upon the table — Multitudes of other
Petitions to the same effect were thus laid on the table at the
motion of the members from Georgia — Calvary Morris afterwards presented one from 177 citizens of Marietta, Ohio,
which with a short Speech he moved should be referred to a
select Committee — Owens moved it should be laid on the
table — Morris called for the yeas and nays — Chapman of
Alabama moved a call of the House, but it was denied, and the
Petition was laid on the Table 107 to 71 — I presented the
petition of Stephen Toller and 38 inhabitants of Jeffersonville,
Goochland C. Virginia, praying for my expulsion, as a nui-
sance, which I moved should be referred to the Committee on

the judiciary — Dromgoole said he supposed it was a Quiz — or if not, it was a question of privilege, and must be decided by the House — He moved it should be laid on the Table unless the Gentleman from Massachusetts wished to give it another direction. I said the Gentleman from Massachusetts cared very little about it — and it was laid on the table — Of the Resolutions of the Legislature of Massachusetts those concerning the militia were presented by Gov'r Lincoln, and referred to the Committee of the Whole on the state of the Union — those on the Subtreasury Bill, to the Committee of Ways and Means — presented by Mr. Fletcher — Those on the Northeastern boundary, by Mr. Cushing; referred to the Committee of the whole, upon George Evans's Bill — Those on our Indian Relations by Mr. Reed, and at the motion of a Georgia member laid on the table — They objected also to their being printed — and that question was laid over. Those against the annexation of Texas were presented by George N. Briggs, who moved their reference to the Committee of foreign Relations, and that they be printed — Haynes was just moving to lay them on the table, when I appealed to his candour, and generosity and also to his State rights principles, to let them be referred; observing that I hoped and trusted the questions relating to Texas and Mexico, would now cease to be causes of division, among us — That the Mexican proposal for an arbitration of our differences has been accepted. That the Texian proposal for annexation has been, or is about to be withdrawn. That all objection to a fair consideration of these Memorials and Petitions seemed to be removed; and the Gentleman from Georgia, might be well assured that no report from the Committee of Foreign Relations on this subject, unfriendly to his views was to be expected — Haynes then said that to shew his generosity since I appealed to it, he would withdraw his objection to the reference and the printing of these Resolutions — No other person made objection and the Resolutions were referred. This point being gained I moved the reference to the same Committee of all the petitions this day presented against the annexation of Texas; of which there were several — Some uneasiness was manifested by several members, and particularly by C. F. Mercer, who objected to the reference of one Memorial, but upon being told by the Speaker that several had been referred withdrew his objection, not without muttering. — W. C. Calhoun presented the Massachusetts Legislative Resolution against the admission of any new Slave-State into the Union — The first Resolution was half read, until the clerk came to the word Slavery, when he was stop'd by the Speaker, and the Resolutions were laid on the table under the order of 21 Dec'r 1837. Grennell presented the Resolutions on the subject of duelling which were referred to the Committee of the whole House on the state of the Union, to which the Bill from the Senate against duelling has been referred. There remain three sets of Resolutions of the Massachusetts Legislature to be presented hereafter — Among the petitions which I presented was one with documents, which I found on my table, from Lianah Kibbey for a widows pension — The Speaker presented several petitions, and I reminded him of one from the workmen employed here on the public buildings thrown out of employment by the suspension of the work on the Treasury building — He presented it, and it was referred to the Committee on the Public Buildings.

—

27. VII. Sunday. Dissipation always encroaches upon tomorrow — The Supper party of the Evening before last, and the Dinner party of yesterday, took large tribute from the morning hours of this day, and consequently from the punctuality of this Diary. ≈ After dinner, at St. John's Church Mr. Hawley read Evening prayers, with only the second lesson, for the fifth Sunday after Easter, and a Stranger preached from John 8:51 "Verily, verily, I say unto you, if a man keep my saying, he shall never see death." There were scarcely thirty persons in the House — The neglect of public worship in this City is an increasing evil; and the indifference to all religion throughout the whole country portends no good. There is in the Clergy of all the Christian denominations, a time-serving, cringing, subservient morality, as wide from the Spirit of the Gospel, as it is from the intrepid assertion and vindication of truth — The counterfeit character of a very large portion of the Christian ministry, in this Country, is disclosed in the dissensions growing up in all the protestant Churches, on the subject of Slavery — The abolitionists assume as the first principle of all their movements that Slavery is *Sin* — Their opponents halting

between the alternative of denying directly this position, and of admitting the duty binding upon them, to bear testimony against it, are prevaricating with their own Consciences, and taxing their learning and ingenuity to prove that the Bible sanctions Slavery — That Abraham, Isaac, and Jacob were Slave-holders, and that St. Paul is the apostle of Man-Stealers because he sent Onesimus back to his master Philemon — These preachers of the gospel might just as well call our extermination of the Indians, an obedience to divine commands because Jehovah commanded the children of Israel to exterminate the Canaanitish Nations. This question of Slavery is convulsing the congregational churches in Massachusetts. It is deeply agitating the Methodists. It has already completed a Schism in the presbyterian Church, two separate bodies of which are now in Session at Philadelphia, each pretending to be the general Assembly of the whole Church — From all this present evil, may the fountain of all truth draw future and transcendent good.

———

30. IV:30. Wednesday. My Son Charles, with his wife, his daughter Louisa Catherine, and the Nursery maid Catherine   left us this morning, by the Cars for Baltimore, to return home. They have spent with us the Month of May, and have made it the most pleasant month of the year — We wished them to remain longer, but Charles could not be persuaded ≈ H.R.U.S. ≈ The Indian hostility Bill followed in Committee of the whole on the Union, Howard in the chair. Holsey of Georgia, finished his speech commenced last evening; chiefly a heavy, dull invective against me and my administration, and a glorification of Georgia, for having set me at defiance — Holsey affects to be a systematic lawyer — he said to day, referring to the decision of the Supreme Court of the United States against the Legislative Robbery by Georgia of the Indian Lands, which decision, Jackson prevented being executed. Holsey said that *Law*, consisted of the co-operating action of three departments of Government. The Legislative, the Judicial and the Executive — That wherever the concurrence of either of those Departments was wanting, there was no Law — That in the case alluded to there was against Georgia the concurrence only of the Legislative and the Judiciary,

and so long as the Executive was on the side of Georgia, she would laugh to scorn the decision of the Supreme Court of the United States — And such is the composition of the House of Representatives of the United States, that discourse like this passes for argument — This same Holsey said on a former day that there were two kinds of Justice — Moral Justice and Political Justice — That the People of Georgia were at all times willing to dispense Political Justice, but would never suffer that *moral* Justice should be secured to them — And this like the laughing to scorn of the decision of the Supreme Court of the United States, he said boastfully, to the honour and glory of the People of Georgia — Holseys Laws of Justice and of Nations, stung Naylor, who followed him with a vehement denunciation of Georgia, and especially of that ne plus ultra of rascality the Treaty, so called of New Echota of December 1835. Naylor proved by numerous references to the Documents, the nefarious villainy of that whole transaction — but the Senate of the United States by the vote of two-thirds of the Senators present, advised and consented to its ratification — The frauds were all then exposed — But Holsey's principle is the practical Law of the Land — Moral Justice — laudatur et alget. He was followed by Dawson, a far more intelligent and plausible man, who said he was considered in Georgia, as belonging to what was called the Indian party. He had always been the friend of the Indians, and was for doing them full Justice — But he attempted to justify the conduct of Georgia, by, the principles of my Plymouth Oration, and by the practise of all the older States — Dawson, was followed by Bell of Tennessee, who began a long Speech, as the sun was setting, but about 8 O'Clock, from mere weariness the Committee rose, and the House adjourned — I got home about nine — There is a panic rumour abroad, artificially gotten up; of Slave insurgency, amounting to nothing.

———

[June 1838]
3. V:30. Sunday. I took Mary and her daughter Fanny with me this morning to the Capitol, where in the Representative Hall, Harriet Livermore preached from Luke 23–34 "Then said Jesus, Father, forgive them, for they know not what they do" — A discourse on the absolute and unqualified forgiveness of

injuries — Indirectly only against duelling, not even indirectly against Slavery — Eleven years have passed away since I first heard her in the same Hall; more than six since I had heard her last ≈ I reminded her that when I heard her at the Capitol in 1832 she had announced her intention of going to the western Indians. She said she had been there with the approbation of the Government, and the warm recommendation of President Jackson — But the Schermerhorn's of that region, by which I understood the male missionaries had forced her away, and robbed her of all her property ≈ She said she had since been at Jerusalem, and had only three weeks since returned to the United States — She spoke with great kindness of the converted Jew missionary Joseph Wolff, who she said was the greatest man living and of whose prediction that the Millennium is to commence in 1846 she declared her entire belief — Tis rather too soon — There is a permanency in this woman's monomania, which seems accountable only from the impulse of vanity, and the love of Fame — The religious Spirit easily allies itself to these Passions, and they, eagerly grasp the garb of religion. — The holy Spirit avails itself of these purposes to promote its own cause — When Harriet Livermore preaches in the Representative Hall of the United States the forgiveness of injuries — alas! how few converts, will she make! and yet? is there no blessing of God, for a word spoken in Season? Is there no avenue to improvement in the heart of man? There is — Harriet Livermore towards the close of her discourse, upon the absolute, unqualified and irremissible command of Jesus Christ to his disciples to practice the duty of mutual forgiveness, said there was no portion of mankind, upon whom that obligation was more imperiously binding than upon those who filled the Seats in that Hall — May some of those who heard her lay it to their hearts, and Harriet Livermore will have worthily fulfilled her destiny upon earth.

———

6. IV:15. Wednesday ≈ The Bill constituting the Territory of Ioway was largely debated — Downing, the delegate from Florida moved the Previous Question, but it was not sustained. Bond had moved to reduce the Salary of the Governor proposed in the Bill at 2000 dollars as Governor, and 1500 dollars as Superintendent of Indian Affairs to 1500 as Governor, and

1000 as Indian Superintendent — The sums reported in the Bill were declared by the Chairman of the Committee, Bronson, to be the same established by Law, and now received by the Governor of Wisconsin. Bond called for the yeas and nays, and intending to vote against the reduction, I gave my reasons for the vote; and commented upon the spurious economy which vents itself in charges of extravagance and declamations against executive patronage, and contents itself practically with nibbling at the Salaries of subordinate Officers — I took the occasion while up of answering Waddy Thompson's declaration that he would vote for no new Northern Territory, while Northern fanatics were pouring in Petitions against the annexation to this Union of the great and glorious Republic of Texas — I objected to the peculiar glory of Texas which consisted in having made of a Land of Freemen, a land of Slaves — I said we had too much of that sort of glory already, and was proceeding to illustrate by the atchievements of the late Philadelphia Mobs when the stunning cries of order emboldened the Speaker to order me to take my Seat — Thompson intreated that I might be allowed to proceed, insisting that I was strictly in order — But I had said as much as I wished to say then and I did not appeal from the Speaker's decision — I had some sparring with Mercer, about the size of the new Territory — It was finally found that Bond's amendment put the Salary of the Governor of the Territory of Ioway at the same sum now allowed to the Governor of Wisconsin — The amendment was accepted and the Bill after further discussion passed by yeas and nays 113 to 51.

———

12. IV:30. Tuesday. ≈ Returning to the House, I found Mason of Ohio, still speaking on the pre-emption Bill — Casey of Illinois, and Crary of Michigan followed Mason, and gave the whole theory of the Settlers on the public Lands — which is that the only just right to land is occupancy and labour, and that this right is individual as well as social — That every man has a right to take up unoccupied land; and having taken it up has the right to purchase the right of the community at the lowest price, and in preference to all others. Crary compared the right of the Squatter on Land, to the right of the fisherman upon the Ocean — It was a common right, and the

fisherman was a squatter upon the water, just as the Settler is a squatter upon the land — This is the tone of opinion throughout the new Western States, and so thoroughly is the sense of right and wrong in the human heart subservient to the physical wants of the human animal, that this utter perversion of the elementary principle of property passes throughout the western region for irrefragable logic — I take no part in this debate — The public Lands are irrecoverably lost, and it were a worthless and a thankless task to intermeddle in the scramble for the spoils.

——

24. V:15. Sunday. Attended at St. John's Church. Mr. Hawley read the morning service for the 3^d Sunday after Trinity by mistake for the 2^d. A stranger preached from John 11:40 "Jesus saith unto her, said I not unto thee, that if thou wouldest believe, thou shouldest see the glory of God?" — a well written, and affecting discourse upon that transcendently wonderful miracle, the raising of Lazarus from the dead — of which event the preacher gave a narrative with commentary as he went along; dwelling emphatically upon the fact that it was performed at the petition of a woman — I spoke to President Van Buren, and asked half an hour's conversation with him at 6 O'Clock this evening to which he acceded ≈ I went to the President's, and putting into his hand the Letter which I have received in duplicate from R. Rush, of 15 May requested him to read it — I then had a conversation of nearly two hours with him upon the Smithsonian bequest — referring to my report; and intreating him to have a plan prepared to recommend to Congress for the foundation of the Institution, at the commencement of the next Session of Congress. I suggested to him the establishment of an Astronomical observatory — with a Salary for an Astronomer and Assistant — for nightly observations and periodical publication — Then annual courses of Lectures, upon the natural, moral and political Sciences — And above all no jobbing — No Sinecures — No monkish Stalls for lazy idlers — Mr. Van Buren received all this with complacency, and apparent concurrence of opinion. Said he would look into my report — Wished me at leisure to name any persons who I thought might be usefully consulted — Appeared very favourably disposed to the Establishment of

an Observatory, and willing to do right. I urged upon him the deep responsibility of the Nation to the world, and to all posterity worthily to fulfil the great object of the Instuton. I only lament my inability to communicate half the solicitude, with which my heart is on this subject full

___

[July 1838]

7. V:30. Saturday. Com'ee of Manufactures — no Meeting. I alone there — H.R.U.S. Morning hour. 15th day, Texas. I read A. Jackson's Letter to W. Fulton 10 Dec'r 1830 Howard's Agitation — His Letter to W. Fulton, and Fulton's answer. He gives them to me to be communicated to the House. Dromgoole moves suspension of the rules to answer me. Refused ≈ At 20 minutes past Midnight I left the House and came home, sick at heart, exhausted and faint with weariness and excessive heat — knowing that nothing further would be done by the House to any useful purpose.

8. VI:30. Sunday. Just before 8 O'Clock this morning my Granddaughter Mary Louisa came in to my chamber and told me the flag of the House of Representatives was still flying. They sat all night — had a call of the House and adjourned about 8 this morning. Lewis day a Negro 54 years old a Slave of John West Minor living in this district on the Virginia side of the Potomack, came to enquire if I could obtain for him relief or mercy — One of 15 four of whom his master has already sold to go to Georgia — and the rest are to be sold in a few days — I could afford him no relief, but commended him to mercy and Patience — He was broken hearted.

___

19. III:45. Thursday. ≈ We came on immediately, and at nine of the morning, just sixteen hours from New-York I alighted at the Rail-way Depot, below the bottom of the Common. I had my two Trunks laden upon a Hack with the name of the Marlborough Hotel upon it, and deposited at that House, where I breakfasted. A great revolution has occurred in that establishment, since I dined there in 1835 with poor Alexander Townsend, then its proprietor, and whose melancholy death so soon afterwards ensued — It is now a religious and temperance House, and I found the Gentleman's Parlour, with a central

table covered with Bibles, Prayer-books and Psalm-books — Upon the ground adjoining the House where formerly stood the Stable, there now stands a Chapel — the officiating Minister at which is Mr. Fitch — After breakfast I went to my Son's Office in Court-Street; and found a notice on his door that he is in Town on Tuesday's and Friday's till 1 P.M. Then I went to Elm Street and engaged a passage in the Quincy Stage this afternoon, with directions to Mr. Gillett to take me up at the Marlborough Hotel. I next went to my Son's House N. 3 Hancock Avenue, but found it shut up — Called at Mr. Frothingham's, and was engaged by him and Mrs. Frothingham to dine. At Governor Everett's but found a notice on the door "out of Town" ≈ At 2 I went and dined with Mr. Frothingham — At 4 returned to the Marlborough Hotel, where Gillett soon took me up and landed me before 6 at my house in Quincy — Here, I found my wife, and family, and my Son, his wife and children all in comfortable Health, and it seemed to me like an entrance into Paradise ≈

20. V. Friday. My indisposition continued all this day, and kept me confined to the house; feeble and almost helpless. Louisa C. Smith is here, having come out from Mr. Foster's last Tuesday with Charles — Mr. Francis Jackson was here with his daughter. Charles and his wife were here more than once, and all their children, including the youngest Son, Henry Brooks, born   .

———

[August 1838]
23. IV. Thursday. ≈ I despatched a dozen Letters enclosing the Quincy Patriot of last Saturday which contains my Letter to my Constituents, and Legare's report on the Peace Society Petitions, to one member from each town in the District represented at the Convention of this day last year — I finished my Letter in answer to that of President J. Edwards, with his queries concerning the abolition of Slavery in the District of Columbia. Four of the Letters which I have written since I returned home from Washington have already been published in the Newspapers. This practice renders my correspondence irksome, because I never can be sure that what I write will not be published and of course I should be cautious to write

nothing unfit for publication — It gives an air of constraint to my Style; and makes the writing of a Letter, a laborious task.

———

[September 1838]

4. IV:30. Tuesday ≈ The Pic Nic and Ball given by the Ladies of Quincy was on this day, with great formality, and with the intention of shewing respect to me and to my wife. The hour fixed in the printed invitation was four in the afternoon. The place was a lot of Land given by my father to the Town of Quincy, and called the Hancock lot, because the cellar still remains upon it of the House in which John Hancock was born. Soon after four Mr. Ibrahim Bartlett, and Mr. Lloyd G. Horton came as a deputation from the company to enquire at what time it would suit me to join them — I said immediately — My wife with Mrs. W. S. Smith, Louisa C. Smith and Mary had already gone — Mr. Bartlett and Mr. Horton returned to the company, and then came back and escorted me to the entrance of the lot where I was received by six young unmarried Ladies between whom I was conducted to the large Lime-tree in the centre of the lot — there received by two married Ladies who presented me to Mrs. Baxter the Lady hostess of the party — who conducted me and my wife to a couple of chairs under an Arch of Evergreens overshaded by the widespreading branches of the Lime tree — There was an inscription over the arch, which I did not see — The Rev. Mr. Peter Whitney stood near; and all around was a circle of women young and old to the number of about two hundred, with very few exceptions all inhabitants of Quincy — Mr. Whitney in the name of the Ladies addressed me by name, and said they had invited me to that party in token of their respect for my long and eminent public services — Much to my relief he said no more — for more according to the custom which has lately crept in among us from England of beplastering a man with flattery to his face, more would necessarily have been fulsome and unmeaning adulation in the shape of praise — I then addressed the Ladies for about five minutes; thanking them for their kindness, and alluding to the testimonials of approbation and confidence which I had received last Summer from the men of this Congressional District after the fiery trial of the preceding winter. I

said, that this had made a deep and abiding impression upon my heart; but that at the two Sessions of the present Congress new trials of a different character, in which the rights and the reputation of the women of my Country, and particularly of the district, were involved. I stated the number of Petitions which I had received from the several towns in the district from women; the violent outrage by the Chairman of the Committee of foreign Affairs Howard, upon the Petitioners, and the insult upon the sex, which I had felt myself called upon to repel, and the defence of the rights and fair fame of women which ensued — It was to this, I presumed, that I was indebted for the present kind notice of approbation, from the Ladies of Quincy, and to another of a similar nature, in another town of the District. I then made some remarks on the right of Women, to Petition, and on the propriety of their taking a part in public affairs — This was a point to be left to their own discretion, and there was not the least danger of their obtruding their wishes upon any of the ordinary subjects of Legislation — Banks, Currency, Exchange, Sub-treasuries, internal improvement, tariffs, manufactures, public Lands, Revenues and Expenditures, all which so profoundly agitate the men of the Country; the women, so far from intermeddling with them, could scarcely be prevailed upon to bestow a thought upon them; and knowing that it was scarcely consistent with civility so much as to name them in their presence, I now alluded to them only to discard them. But for objects of kindness, of benevolence, of compassion, women so far from being debarred by any rule of delicacy from exercising the right of petition or remonstrance, are by the Law of their nature fitted above all others for that exercise — I said I hoped their right would never again be questioned. I was sure if the Gentleman who I believed in an unguarded and inconsiderate moment had indulged himself by casting the reflection which I so earnestly reprobated, could be present to witness the Scene now before me, he would never again be tempted to express so ungentle a sentiment — I hoped no member of the House of Representatives of the United States would ever again be found to treat with disrespect the sex of his mother, but would feel for every woman the sentiment which I would now tender, in thanks to every female present, whether Mother, daughter, wife or sister, as expressed in the beautiful lines of an English Orator and Poet

"Had I a heart for falsehood fram'd — I ne'er could injure you;
For though your tongue no promise claim'd — Your charms
    would keep me true.
To *you* no Soul can bear deceit   No Stranger, offer wrong,
But Friends in all the aged you'll meet — And Lovers in the
    young."

Thus I closed, and then the collation followed — With many of the women, I was acquainted and they introduced me to others — As the Sun went down there was a dance upon the green — The morning had been cold — The Sun had warmed the atmosphere and it was very comfortably warm — Immediately after Sunset however it became again chilly, and the party adjourned to the Ball-room at French's Hotel, now called the Hancock House — Invitations to the Ball were given us on the ground — I came home and between 7 and 8 accompanied the Ladies to the Ball. The Hall was crowded to excess, and fifty couples were dancing at one country dance — The dancing was universally good, and far more animated than I had seen at private Balls for many years. We remained about half an hour after the Evening Bell; and then though much urged to stay to the Supper, came home — The dances were Cotillions, Country dances and fancy dances. No Waltzing — The Ball was continued till between one and two of the morning.

———

7. IV. Friday ≈ While I am waiting for a further supply from Gales and Seaton of my pamphlet speech, it occurred to me to send a copy of it to the first petitioner of all the petitions and remonstrances against the annexation of Texas to this Union, which were committed to my charge, at the two Sessions of the present Congress — For this purpose it becomes necessary to make out an Alphabetical list of all the Petitioners, at the head of the Petitions; a work upon which I began, with the Petitions presented at the Special Session; of which there were about 400 — of which ninety against the annexation of Texas, and the rest, for the abolition of Slavery — It is slow work and will take me two hours a day for nearly three weeks to com-

plete the Lists for both Sessions — It occupies time too which ought perhaps to be devoted to more intellectual occupations. But there appears to be a duty of obligation to give to the Petitioners who entrusted their Petitions to me, some information of what disposal was made of them — and I propose to send one copy of my pamphlet to the first petitioner of every petition that I presented against the annexation of Texas.

———

[November 1838]
8. IV:15. Thursday. Cloudy starless morning — I read Pearson § 48 on the reading Microscope — 49. On the plumbline 50. On the Spirit-level and 51. On Artificial Horizons — These are all inventions for improving and perfecting the great instrument of astronomical observation, the Telescope. — The practical usefulness of this Science seems confined to Navigators, on the Ocean; and they generally know little more of it than to take the Altitude, of the Sun upon the Meridian, and with the help of tables in the Nautical Almanac, to work out their Longitude. — To me, the observation of the Sun, Moon and Stars has been for a great portion of my life a pleasure of gratified curiosity, of ever returning wonder, and of reverence for the creator and mover of these unnumbered worlds — There is something of awful enjoyment, in observing the rising and setting of the Sun — That flashing beam of his first appearance upon the horizon. That sinking of the last ray beneath it, that perpetual revolution of the great and little bear round the Pole — that rising of the whole Constellation of Orion from the horizontal to the perpendicular position, and his ride through the Heavens with his belt, his nebulous sword, and his four corner stars of the first magnitude, are sources of delight to me which never tire. Even the optical delusion, by which the motion of the Earth from West to East, appears to the eye as the movement of the whole firmament from East to West, swells the conception of magnificence to the incomprehensible infinite — There is indeed intermingled with all this a painful sensation of desire to know more of this stupendous system, of sorrow in reflecting how little we ever can know of it, and of almost desponding hope that we may know more of it hereafter.

———

10. V. Saturday. Fahrenheit 22. From Quincy to Boston. ≈ While packing up for my departure, I had a morning visit from Dr. Channing, Dr. Tuckerman, Mr. Phillips, Son of the late Lieut't. Governor Phillips, and Dr. Channing's Son — They were here nearly two hours, and I had a long conversation with them upon Slavery and Anti-Slavery: abolition Societies and Slave-holding policy — Doctor Channing asked my opinions upon two points — One the present test question of the abolitionists — the immediate abolition of Slavery in the District of Columbia and the territory of Florida; and the other whether in the event of the adoption of those measures the Southern States would secede from the Union — I said first, that to make a test question upon the *immediate* abolition — was absurd and had something captious in it, because it was notoriously impracticable — There is in the present House of Representative[s a majority] of nearly two to one opposed to the consideration or discussion of the subject; and if the proposition should be made they would refuse to consider it — Mr. Phillips said he wished I would take some method of publishing this opinion — I told him of the Letter I wrote to Mr. C. P. Kirkland, and said I should probably take some occasion to express similar opinions at the approaching Session of Congress — But that my opinions will have no influence upon the abolitionists; who have already given me repeated warnings that they will desert and oppose me, if I do not come over to *them*, in the creed of *immediate* abolition — I said, it was necessary to consider the Spirit of abolitionism, as a fact as well as a theory — As a phenomenon to be studied; and over which no individual can have much controul — As to the second question, I did not believe that the South would dissolve the Union, if Slavery should be abolished in the District of Columbia and in Florida. South Carolina might perhaps secede, but she could not carry the South with her — Dr. Channing appeared to entertain great apprehensions for the Union and deep concern at the violence of the abolition Spirit — We had also some conversation upon the currency, Bank and Subtreasury questions. Mr. Phillips expressed himself strongly averse to a National Bank. I said I thought a National Bank, indispensable for the safe collection and disbursement of the revenue, and if I had the power, that is if I could prevail upon

Congress and the People to be of the same opinion, I would establish one to-morrow. But now there is a prejudice against it in the opinions of a large portion of the People throughout the Union — It is a bone of party contention, and therefore not now expedient — Nor should I have the same confidence in a National bank, to furnish a sound currency to regulate exchanges, and to check the over-issues of all the State Banks as did the two former Banks of the United States each for twenty years — The main difficulty would now be to make up a Capital, for a National Bank; four fifths of the Capital of the last Bank having consisted of public securities, bearing an interest of 6 per cent, to which the faith of the Nation was pledged, and which now no longer exist — I promised to call and see Dr. Channing in Boston, before my departure, for Washington.

———

12. IV:30. Monday ≈ Between Breakfast and dinner I visited Dr. Channing, Mrs. S. A. Otis, Mr. Samuel Armstrong Mr. Abbott Lawrence and Mrs. Dexter. Saw only Dr. Channing and Mrs. Dexter. None of the rest were at home — I had a conversation again of two hours or more with Dr. Channing upon the subject of the abolition of Slavery. — The Doctor [who] was heretofore an idol of the party now calling themselves whigs, has become very obnoxious to them — They had almost worshiped him as a Saint — They now call him a Jacobin. He is deeply sensitive to this change in his worldly fame, and exceedingly fearful that the abolition cause will go to ruin, or that the abolitionists will stir up an insurrection of Slaves, and lead to a dissolution of the Union — In his youth he resided some time in Virginia and is well acquainted with the character of the planters in that State, which he thinks has undergone a great and remarkable change since he lived there; that is, within the last forty years. He was then struck with the great, and unbounded security in which they lived in the midst of their Slaves and surrounded by them, and nightly at their mercy for their lives — They were also then a people careless of property, improvident and thriftless and generally wasting their estates in expenses beyond their means. He thought them now at least as economical, thrifty and parsimonious as the people of the North. He spoke of the family in which he lived, the heads of which had been at one period

while he was there been absent some time from home, leaving
him in charge of the domestic establishment — And there was
then one Slave who slept not in the house himself, but came
regularly every evening and locked him in for the night and
carried away the key — Much of this security was owing to the
fact that among the household Slaves there was almost always
one or more profoundly attached to their masters, and if ever
any project of insubordination or disorder was formed among
the field-Slaves, the House Servants always, disclosed it to
their Masters — The Doctor said there were now at the South
many women, inclined to favour the abolition of Slavery —
That in the course of the last Summer, he had travelled in
company with a Lady of Baltimore, who told him that she was
herself an abolitionist, and that multitudes of Southern women
were so at their hearts. But he recurred continually to the fear
that the Southern Slave-holders would dissolve the Union —
Said he had heard it had been remarked by Mr. Cushing that
there was a growing coldness, on the part of the Southern
members towards those of the North; and asked me how the
Southern members treated me — I said they all treated me as
gentlemen, and most of them with kindness and courtesy —
That Mr. Cushing had been desirous of a very intimate personal intercourse with the Southern members, and perhaps
had seen some change in their deportment towards him — I
had thought it apparent that they generally held in contempt
the Northern members who truckled to them, such as John
Randolph had nicknamed dough faces — But there was so
marked a difference between the manners of the South and of
the North, that their members could never be very intimate
personally together. — The Doctor appeared to entertain a
great distrust of the political action of the abolitionists; and
feared they would ruin their own cause and its friends. He
asked me to write to him which I promised to do.

———

18. V:15. Sunday. I omitted the mention yesterday of a morning
visit from Harriet Welsh, and some conversation with her,
upon the claim of the granddaughter of Col'l Richard Gridley
to a pension, which I ought not to forget at Washington. I
omitted also to notice the most affecting incident of my visit to
mount Auburn. It was the solitary inscription, of the name of

Maria Osborne Sargent, wife of Charles P. Curtis; born in 1804, deceased at the age of 30 in 1835 — daughter of Daniel Sargent and Mary Frazier once to me the most beautiful and most beloved of her sex — In the 15th year of her age she gave me, then 22 the assurance of her affection and the pledge of her faith — A year afterwards she withdrew them, from distrust instilled into her mind, by an envious cousin — Twelve years afterwards She married Daniel Sargent, and in 1804 at the age of 30 died of a consumption consequent upon the birth of this only child — This child I never saw — She too closed her career at the early age of 30 and upon meeting unexpectedly here the inscription of her name upon the grave-stone, a mingled emotion of tenderness, of melancholy, and yet of gratitude to Heaven, affected me to tears — I imagined to myself what would have been her fate and mine, had our union been accomplished — That in all probability I should have lost her in the prime of life, and lost perhaps a child like this, cut off like this in the blossom. Dearly! — how dearly did the sacrifice of her cost me, voluntary as it was — for the separation was occasioned by my declining to contract an unqualified engagement, forbidden by my father, and by the advice of her cousin to her, to insist upon a positive engagement or a separation — Four years of exquisite wretchedness, followed this separation, nor was the wound in my bosom healed, till the Atlantic Ocean flowed between us — till all the faculties of my Soul, were absorbed in the politics of a revolutionary period, and the incidents of a wandering and adventurous life, led me to the formation of other and more propitious ties — by which I am yet happily bound.

———

24. VI. Saturday. ≈ I had met Edmund Quincy in the street, and he had promised to come, and have some conversation with me this Evening. He came, and I conversed with him freely on the political movements of the Anti-Slavery and abolitionist party — They interrogate all the candidates for the General and State Legislatures, what their opinions are upon sundry questions relating to the abolition of Slavery, and if the answers are not exactly conformable to their opinions they vote against the candidate or scatter their votes to defeat his election — Very few of the candidates answer the questions to

their satisfaction, and they shew their power by marring the Elections. The result of their interposition has been hitherto mischievous, and I believe injurious to their own cause. I urged this as strongly as I was able; but apparently without making any impression upon his mind. — The moral principle of their interference, to defeat elections when they cannot carry them, appears to me to be vicious; and I think the first result of their movements will be to bring the two parties together against them. — As yet their political action has only tended to break down the barriers between the parties, the natural consequence of which is to strengthen the administration which they abhor.

———

[December 1838]

10. VI:15. Monday. A black man came this morning to my house and sent in a note signed William Lodge, asking money for rent; and with the note, a Bible — I told my waiting man, Moses Smallwood that it must be a mistake, and that the man must be enquiring for some other person. He then sent in word that he wanted to see me. He came in, and said that he had got a white man named Reynolds to write the note for him, but that it was only to get the means of seeing me — That he had a message to me from the Lord, who had appeared to him, and commanded him to say to me that the Negroes must be made free — I enquired of him his name. He said the name given him by his Parents was that subscribed to the note — William Lodge — But the Lord had given him the name of John — I asked him of his occupation, and he said that until last Thursday he had been working with a shoemaker in the Pennsylvania Avenue — but he had then left him and was now without work — On further enquiry I found that he had formerly lived with me, and in the Summer of 1830 went with the family to Quincy. He was then not more than eighteen or nineteen years old, and I was obliged to turn him off for gross misconduct in the house — The summer afterwards while my Son John was living with his family in the House on the President's Square, in this City, the House was broken open in the Night and robbed, by a gang of which this Messenger from the Lord was the pilot and perpetrator — He was taken up, and lodged sometime in jail; but was finally released for want

of positive proof to convict him — I had not heard of him since, and did not recognize him now, till upon pressing enquiries he acknowledged that he had lived with me — And he said that the Lord had told him that after my father's death, his Estate at Quincy belonged to him — I told him to go away, and to deliver no more such Messages from the Lord to any one, for so sure as he did, he would be taken up, and committed to jail, and sold — That I would not complain of him to the police but others would if he should make any more revelations from the Lord.

———

13. V. Thursday ≈ I doubt if there are five members in the House who would vote for a Bill to abolish Slavery in the District of Columbia, at this time — The conflict between the principle of liberty, and the fact of Slavery is coming gradually to an issue. Slavery has now the power and falls into convulsions at the approach of Freedom. That the fall of Slavery, is predetermined in the counsels of omnipotence, I cannot doubt — It is a part of the great moral improvement in the condition of man, attested by all the records of History. But the Conflict will be terrible, and the progress of improvement perhaps retrograde before its final progress to consummation. ≈

14. V:30. Friday. ≈ Howard enquired if the call for Petitions, would be in order, this being one of the days devoted by the Rules of the House to private business. The Speaker said the call for Petitions was the business first in order every day of the first thirty of the Session, upon which Howard moved to proceed to the call of Petitions — The Speaker Commenced with New Hampshire, where the House had been left by Atherton's Resolutions. Then passing to Massachusetts, Cushing offered two Resolutions, recommitting to the Committee of Foreign Affairs certain petitions, Resolutions and other papers, which had been referred to them at the last Session, and he gave notice that he should ask leave to introduce a Bill for the protection of Citizens of the United-States in the territory of Oregon — W. B. Calhoun presented several Slavery-abolition petitions all at once; upon which Mr. Wise objected to their being received — The Speaker said that under the Resolutions which had been adopted by the House

the question of reception could not be made — From this decision Wise took an appeal, and a debate of nearly two hours
ensued, all between the Slave holders whether a question of
the reception could be made of a paper which the house had
predetermined should be laid on the table — The Speaker recurred to the precedents for the three last Sessions of Congress;
and Wise and Pickens, groped about to find a distinction, between the Resolutions of Atherton, and those of Patton and
Pinckney. At last Taylor of New-York called for the previous
Question which was carried, the main question being whether
the decision of the Speaker should stand — When my name was
called by the Clerk, I rose and said, "Mr. Speaker — considering
all the Resolutions, introduced by the Gentleman from
New-Hampshire as" . . . . the Speaker roared out — the
Gentleman from Massachusetts must answer ay or no, and
nothing else — order! — With a reinforced voice, "I refuse to
answer, because I consider all the proceedings of the House as
unconstitutional" — While in a firm and swelling voice I pronounced distinctly these words, the Speaker and about two
thirds of the House cried Order! — Order!! Order!!! till it became a perfect yell — I paused a moment for it to cease, and
then said — A direct violation of the Constitution of the United
States — While speaking these words with loud distinct and
slow articulation, the bawl of Order! Order!! resounded again
from two thirds of the House — The Speaker with agonizing
lungs screamed, "I call upon the House to support me in the
execution of my duty!" — I then coolly resumed my Seat —
Waddy Thompson of South Carolina, advancing into one of
the aisles, with a sarcastic smile, and silvery tone of voice said —
what aid from the House, would the Speaker desire? — The
Speaker snarled back — the Gentleman from South Carolina is
out of order! — and a peal of laughter burst forth from all sides of
the House. The Clerk will proceed with the call, said the Speaker
and the yeas and nays 185 to 6, Wise refusing also to answer.

19. V. Wednesday. Attended the meeting of the Select Committee on the duelling Bill — Present Adams, Toucey, Grennell, Rariden, Grantland, Henry, Coffin — Absent Elmore and
Clark — The Bill and the Amendments of the former Committee were thoroughly discussed, and all the amendments of

the old Committee, but one, were adopted with slight modifications — I disapproved most of the Amendments, because they reduced the penalties of the Bill, as it came from the Senate, instead of which they should in my opinion have been increased ≈ A message was then received from the President, with copies of the correspondence, called for by Fry's Resolution, relating to the call of the Governor of Pennsylvania, on the President and Government of the United States for aid to quell the mob at Harrisburg which prevented the organization of the State Legislature. The papers were all read — Naylor moved that they be read and referred to a Committee of the whole on the State of the Union — Underwood moved that they be printed and laid on the table, which was finally carried without a division — Naylor made an ardent and passionate Speech and Potter an adverse one, in which he said that the difficulties at Harrisburg were likely to be all amicably settled. That is to say that three members of the whig house of Representatives have gone over to the Democratic House, leaving the whigs without a Quorum, and making one for the Democrats without counting the members from Philadelphia, whose Seats are contested, but who will now be secured to them by their compeers — The correspondence shews a refusal by the President to give the aid called for by the Governor of Pennsylvania, and a concurrence of all the Departments of the general Government to countenance and support the popular movement to overawe the Legislature — The whole series of these Events, is a development of our condition, of no good omen to the future operation of our political institutions. Charges of gross fraud and corruption in the election returns from Philadelphia, were made by both parties against each other, neuter falso — both true — The result was two sets of 8 members returned to the Legislature — The elections for the remainder of the State were so equally divided, that the eight members thus contested form the majority of the House — Both sets repair to Harrisburg claiming their Seats, and divide into two parties, each numbering a Quorum of the House, and each organizing itself as a House — At this juncture a number of individuals proceeding from Philadelphia and other place, occupy the Halls of both Houses of the Legislature, and by threats of personal violence, intimidate the members and interrupt the deliberations of the body. The Governor of the State calls upon the Militia for the restoration of Law and order, and also upon the President of the United States for aid to suppress the Insurrection. The call on the militia was answered — An armed body of them were conveyed to Harrisburg, and order was restored — But three members of the regularly constituted House, went over to the other, and thus the party, which resorted to the direct interposition of the People has prevailed, and the mock democracy becomes the democracy of numbers — Fraud and violence have thus been introduced into our elections, and have signally triumphed. And the Government of the United States, called to interpose for the preservation of the Laws and of order, refuses its aid; affects a great abhorrence at interfering in the political divisions of the people in the States, and thus gives its real aid and support to fraud and violence against order and Law — But a precedent is established by which in the event of a servile insurrection, all aid to suppress it may be explicitly refused by the General Government, and by all the free States.

CHAPTER XIII ❦ 1839–1843

Twenty-Sixth and Twenty-Seventh Congresses

[March 1839]

23. IV:45. Saturday. I have determined to accept the invitation of the New-York Historical Society, to deliver, if I possibly can, an address before them on the 30th of next Month, the 50th Anniversary of the inauguration of George Washington, as first President of the United States. I have brought myself to this conclusion with extreme repugnance, and under a sense of obligation to that Society which I cannot repress. The subject is rugged with insurmountable difficulties — My reputation, my age, my decaying faculties have all warned me to decline the task — Yet I cannot resist the pressing and repeated invitations of the Society. The day was a real epocha in our history; but to seize and present in bold relief all its peculiar characters would require a younger hand, and brighter mind.

———

[April 1839]

20. V:30. Saturday. I received from Mr. Joseph Blunt an answer to my enquiries concerning the time and place for the delivery of the historical Dissertation before the New-York historical Society — The Place a large Church — The time Noon. The Duration from an hour to an hour and a half. I read over my discourse and selected from the beginning, the middle and the end three fragments, the delivery of which need not exceed an hour and a half; and is just about one third of what I have written. But whether my voice or the patience of the auditory will hold out for that time must remain for trial. Col'l Thomas paid me a morning visit; full as he always is of political gossip, and the small caballing for place. He says that Mr. Clay himself got up, and he believes, wrote the anti-abolition petition from this District, upon which he made his anti-abolition speech at the last Session of Congress, and that its effect has been to demolish his last possible chance for the presidency — I said I supposed he expected to propitiate Southern votes by it. He

said he would not get them — That his only prominent supporter at the South now was Mr. Preston, but yesterday the
most furious champion of nullification. It is indeed curious
that Preston has avowed in a speech at a whig meeting, and in
a published Letter, that he was one of a small party of friends
to whom Clay read his anti-abolition speech before he delivered it in the Senate — Thomas said he had no doubt of the
re-election of Mr. Van Buren — I gave my seventh and last
sitting for my Portrait to Mr. Charles, who told me that he was
forming his style upon the model of Sir Joshua Reynolds; but
that he was a young man — This is the thirty-fifth time that my
likeness has been taken by Artists for Portrait, miniature, bust,
or medal, and of the whole number Parker's miniature.
Copley's portrait in 1796 and Stewart's head in 1825, with
Persico's bust now in the library room of Congress are the
only representations of my face, satisfactory to myself.

———

[May 1839]
24. IV. Friday. Foul weather. A cold Northeast storm confined
me to the house almost the whole day. I ought to have done
much. Mais helas! il n'en est rien. There is such seduction in a
library of good books that I cannot resist the temptation to
luxuriate, in reading, and [it is] because I have so much to write
that I count all time lost, that is not spent in writing — I finished
reading Dr. Channing's Letter to Jonathan Phillips upon Slavery
— He demolishes all the argument of Clay's Speech, which is
indeed nothing at all. — The remark of Junius that the arguments of tyranny are as despicable as its power is dreadful applies
especially to all arguments in behalf of Slavery.

———

[July 1839]
6. IV. Saturday. I am yet unable to accomplish any thing beyond keeping up the current record of my diary, and bringing
up the arrears of the index, at the rate of a month in three days;
and I am yet more than four years in arrear. ≈ Here I begin, to
be continued from day to day, till completed, a List of papers
relating to the title to Mount Wollaston, and to John Quincy
my ancestor its proprietor.

———

14. II:30 and V:5. Sunday. ≈ I have answered a very earnest invitation of Joshua Leavitt and H. B. Stanton to attend a great National Anti-Slavery Convention to be held at Albany, on the 31ˢᵗ of this month. I have declined attending on the express ground of my dissent from the Declaration of Sentiment of the American Anti-Slavery Society of 1835, and especially to the belief and affirmation "that every American citizen who retains a human being in involuntary bondage as his property is (according to Scripture) Exodus 21:16 a <u>Man Stealer</u>." I have taken a direct issue upon that affirmation, with the American Anti-Slavery Society and all its affiliated associations — The conflict is fearful but certain as I am that this declaration is neither true nor just, I have no doubt of ultimate success in the encounter.

15. IV:10. Monday. The Diary of yesterday, consumed too much time; and occupies too much space; and in retrieving my arrears of index I found a record of three days 26, 27, and 28 September 1835 which I had forgotten, and thought I had made no record of them at all. I had even made that entry yesterday in my index, and was now obliged to deface the book by erasing it, and making the proper entry. — There came this afternoon a man by the name of Samuel Goodhue, a Soldier of the Revolution, 74 years of age, now residing in Boston, who said he had heretofore entertained a strong desire to see and talk with my father, but had been disappointed — That he had only once seen me in company with Mr. Armstrong when I delivered the Eulogy on James Madison. But he had long wished to converse with me, and to ask sundry questions, a paper of which he had in his pocket. He said he had been a member of the Common Council, with my dear departed Son George, but was not a member of that body now. I listened to his questions and answered them as well as I could. He kept throughout for at least two hours the style of interrogation, affirming nothing himself, but disclosing clearly enough his own opinions by the character of his enquiries — He is an ardent patriot of our revolution, and now a whig abolitionist head over ears — He abhors Andrew Jackson, for his Bank war, and his removals from Office — He thinks slave

holding a crime, which ought to be abolished though it should cost the dissolution of the Union; and he thinks as it was wrong in the representatives of the free States to stipulate for the delivery up of fugitive Slaves, a bad promise is better broken than kept, and that we ought to consider that pledge in the Constitution null and void — Here is the Roman Catholic principle that faith is not to be kept with heretics, in all its glory. Mr. Goodhue is sincere and honest in these opinions, and to warrant his opinion that a breach of faith with Slave holders is an obligation of duty he instanced the case of St. Paul who upon his conversion at Damascus, broke his promise to the high priest, to bring all the Christians he could find, in bonds to Jerusalem — I told him the conversion of St. Paul was by a miracle — a special command from Heaven — and until we should receive a like command, it would be best for us to keep our faith — He was not satisfied with this reasoning, and insisted still on the enquiry whether a wrongful promise were not better broken than performed.

———

23. IV:30. Tuesday ≈ Dr. Frothingham has sent me the 4th Volume of Maclaine's Mosheim, in which I read part of the chapter of History of the Anabaptists or Mennonites — And I read some pages of Mr. Buxton's book which he has sent me on the African Slave-trade — The cruelties of that trade are heart sickening — So are the details of Theodore D. Weld's book — American Slavery as it is — The stomach heaves at the perusal of the numberless cases of human suffering inflicted by human hands. — I went to see the setting of the Sun, from the Porch of Charles's house, and he and his wife spent the Evening with us.

———

[August 1839]
3. IV. Saturday. ≈ Dr. John Codman of Dorchester was here with two Scottish gentleman — Mr. Tawse an Advocate and Mr. Lyon a Writer to the signet, or Attorney at Edinburgh — They came out in the Great Western, upon her last passage, as agents for the trustees of some charitable fund appropriated for Indians at Dartmouth College — They feel a particular solicitude for the remnant of the Seneca tribe, still lingering in the western part of the State of New-York; but upon whose

lands a land company in that State have fixed their fangs, and whom the Government of the United States by a Schermerhorn Treaty are driving like a herd of cattle beyond the Mississippi. Dr. Codman had been with these two Gentlemen to Hanover, New Hampshire, and had seen at Dartmouth College two Indian Students, one of them in the Senior Class, a Chief of the Seneca tribe quite an interesting young man named Pearce — I told them that the case of the Seneca Indians was hopeless. That a fraudulent Treaty coaxed, and bullied and bribed out of perhaps one tenth part of their chiefs and Warriors, was already sweeping them away beyond the Mississippi, and that there would soon be no trace of them left in the State of New-York as there is nothing left of the most powerful tribe of the Cherokees in Georgia. Such is the inexorable Law of the white man, and the administration of the Government of the United States is moulded upon it — I mentioned the recent accounts in the Newspapers of the Execution according to Indian Law, that is the murder of Major Ridge, and his Son, and Elias Boudinot, by the party of their old Associate John Ross — They had been bullied, and bribed away beyond the Mississippi — had sold their Lands, themselves and their tribe to the abomination of Schermerhorn Treaty, and had paid the forfeit of their treachery with their lives — But the expulsion of the tribe from Georgia has been consummated, and they have gone to be finally exterminated beyond the Mississippi — They said the young chief at Dartmouth College, had expressed the same apprehension, and had told them that he had himself been offered five thousand dollars for his assent to the cession to the New-York land company and to the removal of the tribe West of the Mississippi — They seemed inclined to flatter themselves that the case was not quite so desperate as I believed it; but they were not sanguine in hope. I told them it was painful to me to speak of the treatment of Indians by my countrymen; but it was in vain to disguise or suppress the truth — An inflexible determination to extirpate the race of Indian Savages was the white mans law on this continent, and I feared would be so till the race itself shall be exterminated from the face of the Earth.

18. IV:30. Sunday. ≈
    List of Mount Wollaston papers continued

Will of John Quincy
John Quincy died on the 13th of July 1767.

Bequeaths his personal Estate to Elizabeth his wife, and one half the profits and improvement of the mount Wollaston farm, for her life, and with this reservation, the same Estate in fee to his Son Norton Quincy ≈ To his Son Norton two Negro Man Servants and to his wife one Negro woman Servant, the profits of their labour to be enjoyed equally between his wife and Son.

———

[September 1839]
23. IV:15. Monday. ≈ Mr. Francis Jackson brought me a Letter from Mr. Ellis Gray Loring, requesting my opinion upon the knotty questions involved in the case of the Spanish ship Amistad recently taken by a vessel of the U.S. engaged on the survey of the Coast and brought into New-London, having on board about 40 African Slaves, and two Spaniards of the Island of Cuba their owners — The Slaves having been charged with murder and piracy, for taking the ship and putting to death the Captain and one or two other white men — Judge Smith Thomson of the U.S. Circuit Court has decided that his Court has no jurisdiction to try the offence of piracy committed on the high Seas in a Spanish vessel; but his opinion is not yet published; and the newspaper account of his decision I think incorrect. I desired Mr. Jackson to say that I felt some delicacy about answering his Letter until judge Thomson's opinion shall be published and until the final decision of the Government upon the whole case in the mean time I requested him to ask Mr. Loring to look up and examine the records of the Circuit Court upon the trial of the Pirates convicted and executed there in   and I mentioned to him the refusal of President to deliver up a man charged at Charleston S.C. with Piracy committed on board of a British Vessel.

———

28. IV:45. Saturday ≈ I received some weeks since a Letter from Sidney Peirce dated East Marlborough Chester County Pennsylvania the 9th of this month, requesting as a favour some thought

or sentiment of mine, written with my own hand — The writer represents herself as the daughter of a farmer, having just passed from the fairy dreams of childhood to the sober realities of life, residing beneath the paternal roof, in the South-eastern part of Chester County Pennsylvania — The hand-writing, the spelling, and composition of the Letter, all indicate a cultivated mind and liberal education; the only deduction from the estimate of which is the fulsome flattery with which her request is urged — But this I suppose emanates from the enthusiasm of Anti-Slavery; not yet refrigerated, as with the great mass of the Abolitionists it has been by the dampers which I have put upon their senseless and overbearing clamour for the immediate, total, uncompensated abolition of Slavery in the District of Columbia — I have sent to Miss Peirce copies of my Oration upon the life and character of La Fayette, of the fragment Speech of June and July 1838 and of the Jubilee of the Constitution, with the following thought or sentiment of mine written with my own hand on a blank leaf before the Oration on La Fayette

To Miss Sidney Peirce, Hamorton Post-Office Chester County Pennsylvania

> Fair Maiden — my Career on Earth is run:
>> For I have wintered three score years and ten —
>> This world, to me, is but the Lions den —
> My term is closing — thine has just begun.
> My thread of life from mingled yarn was spun
>> The motley web of praise and blame from men
>> But Truth and Freedom have inspir'd my pen
> And now from thee a nobler prize have won
> Thy voice for me shall fill the trump of Fame,
> For thou hast wreath'd a chaplet round my name
>> Of pure, bright, incorruptible renown
> More precious than Golconda's sparkling gem —
> More glorious than the Monarch's diadem
>> The hero's laurel or the Martyr's crown.

——

[October 1839]
1. IV:30. Tuesday ≈ I answered an invitation of a Committee of the Citizens of Springfield, to a public dinner to be given

there on the 3ᵈ of this month upon the occasion of the opening
of the railroad from Boston to that place, through Worcester;
and the project of which imports a continuance of it to the
Hudson river — I declined this invitation. But that which now
absorbs great part of my time, and all my good feelings is the
case of 53 African Negroes taken, at sea, off Montauk point, by
Lieut't. Gedney in a Vessel of the United States employed
upon the survey of the Coast; and brought into the Port of
New-London — These Negroes were a fresh importation of
Slaves from Africa into the Havana, against the Laws of Spain;
and her Treaties with Great-Britain — purchased there under
the nose of the joint Commission of Britain and Spain sitting
there for the suppression of the Slave-trade — Shipped from
the Havana, for another port in the Island, by two Spanish
Subjects, Ruiz and Montes, the purchasers of the Slaves —
When four days out, the Negroes revolted; killed the Captain
and Cook of the ship; took possession of the ship; spared the
lives of Ruiz and Montes, and ordered the latter, skilful in
Navigation of, which they were ignorant, to steer for Sierra
Leone. He deceived them by changing the course of the ship
every night from that which they understood enough of navigation to make it necessary for him to steer by day — By this
double process, they had as it were finally drifted upon our
coast, and being finally boarded by Lieut't. Gedney, he at the
request of the two white men took possession of the vessel,
without resistance from the negroes, and brought her into
New-London. 49 of the Negroes were claimed by Ruiz as his
property. 4 Children, 3 girls and a boy, by Montes as his property. But they charged the Negro men, with murder, and Piracy, for killing the Captain and cook and taking the ship; and
yet claimed all the Negroes as their property; and Lieutenant
Gedney libelled the ship and Cargo, including the Negroes
for Salvage — The Spanish Minister too, at Washington, has
laid claim to the whole ship, Cargo and Negroes, to be restored to the owners, by virtue of the 9ᵗʰ Article of the Treaty
with Spain of 27 October 1795 — the District judge Judson
received the charge of Piracy, and committed the 49 negro
men to be tried at the Circuit Court at Hartford on the 17ᵗʰ of
September, and the four children to appear as witnesses — and
at the same time he admitted the claim of the Spaniards to the

Negroes as their property, and the Libel of Captain Gedney. When the Circuit Court met, on the 17ᵗʰ Judge Thomson, upon a statement of the facts by the grand-jury charged them that the Court had no jurisdiction of any crime committed on the high seas, in a Spanish vessel — but he refused to liberate the Negroes, upon Habeas Corpus; because they were claimed by the Spaniards as property, and he held that the District Court had jurisdiction upon this claim — More upon this subject to-morrow.

———

6. IV:30. Sunday ≈ I have heretofore noticed my correspondence with Mr. James H. Hackett upon Shakespear's Tragedy of Hamlet — I this day received a Letter from him dated London   August 1839 — on opening of which the first thing that met my eye was as I thought my own Letter to him of 19 February last from Washington, but which on examination and on reading his Letter I found was a lithographic copy of mine, which he says he had taken, because he had lent the original to so many of his numerous friends and acquaintances that it had been nearly used up — The lithographic copy of my Letter is so perfect a facsimile that if it had been presented to me as the original I should have acknowledged it without an instant of hesitation as my own ≈ Mr. Hackett in his Letter mentions also that he has very recently heard of an analysis by me of the tragedy of Othello, and enquires where he can procure it. — This extension of my fame is more tickling to my vanity than it was to be elected President of the United States. I pray God to forgive me for it; and to preserve me from falling in my last days into the dotage of self adulation — There are indications enough of the censorial Spirit of the world, and still more of its indifference, if I will but take note of them.

———

26. IV. Saturday ≈ I have chosen the Smithsonian bequest as my subject for a Lecture to the Quincy Lyceum which I last Wednesday promised Mr. John A. Green now its President to deliver deo adjuvante on Wednesday the 20ᵗʰ of next Month — This subject weighs deeply upon my mind — The private interests and sordid passions into which that fund has already fallen, fill me with anxiety and apprehensions that it will be squandered upon cormorants or wasted in electioneering

bribery — The apparent total indifference of Mr. Van Buren, to the disposal of the money, with his *general* professions of a disposition to aid me — the assentation of all the heads of department without a particle of assistance from any one of them, excepting the Attorney General Grundy, whose favourable opinion Cambreleng at the last Session contrived to nullify — the opposition open and disguised of Calhoun, Preston and Waddy Thomson, even to the establishment of the institution in any form, the utter prostration of all public Spirit in the Senate, proved by the encouragement which they gave to the mean and selfish project of Asher Robbins to make a University for him to be placed at the head of it, the investment of the whole fund, more than half a Million of dollars in Arkansas and Michigan State Stocks; and the dirty trick of filching ten thousand dollars from the fund last Winter to pay for the charges of procuring it, are all so utterly discouraging, that I despair of effecting any thing for the honour of the country or even to accomplish the purpose of the bequest the increase and diffusion of knowledge among men — It is hard to toil through life for a great purpose with a conviction that it will be in vain; but possibly seed now sown may bring forth some good fruits hereafter — In my report of January 1836 — I laid down all the general principles upon which the fund should have been accepted and administered. I was then wholly successful — My Bill passed without opposition, and under its provisions the money was procured and deposited in the Treasury in gold — If I cannot prevent the disgrace of the Country by the failure of the testator's intention by making it the subject of a Lecture, I can leave a record for future time of what I have done, and what I would have done to accomplish the great design, if executed Well — And let not the supplication to the author of all good, be wanting.

———

28. IV. Monday. Mr. Albert Smith of North-Bridgewater came with a Letter from Eliab Whitman, Chairman of the Town Committee of whigs of that town, stating that for several weeks past their whole community has been disturbed and agitated by the discussion of political subjects, and as the annual State election approaches, the excitement increases and pervades more or less the whole community — That the

democratic party having been for several years past in a minority, have of late become exceedingly active in making proselytes, and that they have recently procured a gentleman to
lecture on the currency; and that there is to be a second, and a
third Lecture — That the whig citizens of North-Bridgewater
have recently determined to meet their enemies in their own
way, by a lecture touching the general features of the National
Administration and also those of this State, and that immediate application should be made to me to perform this Service
— He refers me for particulars to Mr. Smith, who for the last
two years has been a Representative of the Town in the general
Court, and urged me very earnestly to comply with this invitation. I said to Mr. Smith that I was grateful for the confidence
manifested by my fellow-citizens of North-Bridgewater; and
regretted that my engagements, and the short time within
which it would be necessary for me to proceed to Washington
made it impossible for me to comply with their request — I
said further that I approved generally of the principles and
measures of the Administration of the State; and disapproved
of almost every thing done by the federal Administration —
But that I had always professed not to be a party man, and
wished to preserve that character to the end — That I had
sometimes supported important measures of the administration against the general opinions of the whig party; and that
even now upon the subject of the license Law, to which they
were devoted, I had already given the opinion that it would be
desirable it should be modified — I made sundry other observations to shew that some other person would be more suitable
for this service than me. He then asked me if I could recommend any person, but I knew of none. He finally said he would
go and consult Mr. Robert C. Winthrop, and I thought he
could do no better.

———

[November 1839]
20. IV:30. Wednesday. ≈ It has pleased Almighty God, in the
wise and good dispensations of his Providence, this day to
dispose of my Granddaughter Georgiana Frances Adams,
daughter of my dear deceased Son John, and of his wife, Mary
Catherine Hellen. The child died at ten minutes before six
O'Clock this afternoon, in the same chamber and bed in which

on the 10th of September 1830 she was born. At the hour of her birth I addressed a prayer to God for her worldly and eternal welfare — That she might be blessed with a long life of prosperity usefulness and virtue. That prayer has not been all denied — She has been upwards of nine years one of the chief delight of the lives of both her Grandparents — of her father while he lived, and of her widowed and now disconsolate mother.

——

[December 1839]
25. V:15. Christmas — Wednesday ≈ I received this afternoon from James F. Otis a Newspaper published at New-York called Brother Jonathan, in which is printed, announced as from the original manuscript, a poem by me called the Vision, written in 1789 or 1790 while I was a student at Law in the Office of Theophilus Parsons at Newbury-Port. It is nearly fifty years since I had seen this effusion of my early love; and on reading it now the first impression upon my mind is that I have never since written any thing equal to it. But I had no copy of it myself, and knew not that a copy of it existed in the world. My next feeling was curiosity to know whence the publication now came, and through whose hands the manuscript had passed. This I suppose I can ascertain. ≈

26. V:30. Thursday. ≈ Before dinner I visited President Van Buren, and while I was there, the Vice-President Richard M. Johnson came in with another Kentuckian whom I did not know — Col'l Richard M., whose Vice-Presidential Chair, it is said is to be gently drawn from under him at the next Presidential election appeared much elated at his success in effecting his passage over the snow-choked mountains, so as to reach this city the evening before last — He thought it a fair parallel to Napoleon's passage over the Alps — It cost him fifty dollars for extra carriage hire; an inflexible determination to achieve, what all the Stage drivers and Inn holders pronounced impossible; and sundry bumps in the head, having been twice overset — Mr. Van Buren is growing inordinately fat.

——

[January 1840]
1. VI. Wednesday. From 11 in the morning till 4 P.M. there were a succession of friendly visitors, as has been usual on the

New Year's day since we left the President's House. Neither my wife nor Mary received visitors, and I was left to entertain the Ladies as I could — This ceremony grows more and more irksome to me every year. The young and the prosperous may take pleasure in the recollections of the past and the anticipations of the future which associate themselves with the commencement of the year, but the idea which ought first and last to present itself to the mind of one who has already past through so many new years days as I have, is the great probability that it will be the last — Among the visitors of this day were Gen'l Scott, who has been recently talked of as a whig candidate for the Office of President of the United States — William H. Harrison was however preferred both to him and to Henry Clay. A very curious philosophical history of parties might be made by giving a catalogue raisonné of the Candidates for the Presidency voted for in the electoral Colleges since the establishment of the Constitution of the United States — It would contain a History of the influence of the Presidential Office upon the Government of the United States, and the reaction of the Government upon the President's Office — Would not the retrospect furnish as practical principles in the operation of the Constitution — 1. That the direct, and infallible path to the Presidency is military service, coupled with demagogue policy — 2. That in the absence of military service, demagogue policy is the first and most indispensable element of success, and the art of party drilling is the second. 3. That the drill consists in combining the Southern interest in domestic Slavery with the Northern riotous democracy — 4 That this policy and drill first organized by Thomas Jefferson first accomplished his election, and established the Virginia dynasty of 24 years a perpetual practical contradiction of its own principles — 5. That the same policy and drill invigorated by success and fortified by experience has now placed Martin Van-Buren in the Presidential chair, and disclosed to the unprincipled ambition of the North the art of rising upon the principles of the South and 6. That it has exposed in broad day the overruling influence of the institution of domestic Slavery upon the history and policy of this Union — How this power may be counteracted is no deep mystery but I have not time to set the machine in motion, and shall say nothing about it; but leave it to posterity to wait the good time of the Lord.

___

19. VI. Sunday ≈ Much of the day was consumed in reading in the New-York Emancipator of last Thursday, a series of Letters from Lewis Tappan to the Committee in behalf of the captured Africans, detailing from day to day the proceedings of the U.S. District Court at New-Haven, in the case and the decision of the judge Andrew Judson, that the Africans except one shall be delivered to the President of the United States to be sent home to Africa; and that one, the boy Antonio, to be sent home to Cuba.

20. V:30. Monday. ≈ On entering the House I found Mr. Slade on the floor upon Waddy Thompson's Resolution for a rule to exclude abolition Petitions; into the vortex of which he had drawn the whole subject of Slave-trade, Slavery and abolition — He took nearly three hours to conclude the Speech that he had commenced on Saturday, and delivered himself of the burden that has been four years swelling in his bosom. The house was nearly deserted before he finished.

___

28. IV:30. Tuesday ≈ Going to the House; I met in the Capitol Yard Daniel Webster, and greeted him upon his recent return from his visit to England — I found the House in Session, and W. Cost Johnson, upon the floor concluding his anti-abolition Speech, which took him between two or three hours — He was about half tipsey, and in his merriest and wittiest mood — In undertaking to answer my last speech, he took the course under the form of nauseous and fetid flattery, to make me as ridiculous before the house and the country as he possibly could — He closed with offering a resolution as an amendment to mine, providing that no petition resolution or paper relating to slavery or the abolition of Slavery or the Slave trade in any State, District, or Territory should be received or in any manner entertained by the House — I objected to this as not in order, my own resolution being an amendment to an amendment, beyond which in the uniform practice of the house are inadmissible — But Thompson accepted Johnson's Resolution as an addition to his own, and Linn Banks who had been put

by the Speaker into his chair expressly for the occasion declared the combined Resolutions in order; — Vanderpoel made a short and furious Speech which he closed by calling the previous question — The main question was on the combined Resolutions, carried by yeas and nays 116 to 106 and then carried as amended 114 to 108 and thus it is made a rule of the house that no abolition petitions shall be received — Davis of Indiana then moved a reconsideration of the resolution adopted yesterday about the printing — Carried.

29. VI. Wednesday. Morning visits from John G. Whittier, Isaac Winslow, and Samuel Mifflin, all of the Society of Friends and all abolitionists — Whittier is now the Editor of the Pennsylvania Freeman Newspaper published weekly at Philadelphia: Whittier said he thought this last outrage upon the right of Petition, the establishment of a rule refusing to receive or entertain any abolition petition, might perhaps be the best thing that could have been done to promote the cause of abolition — It was at least casting off all disguise. I said it would depend upon the impression which it would make on the people; and I had little expectation from that — They had been familiarized to the privation of the right, and could not be roused to take an interest in it. The difference between the Resolutions of the four preceding Sessions of Congress, and the new rule of the house, is the difference between petty larceny and highway robbery. — I had much conversation with these men upon the dissensions among the anti-slavery men, and abolitionists, and concerning the late Benjamin Lundy.

———

[February 1840]
16. V:30. Sunday. Mr. Meehan the Librarian of Congress yesterday told me that in the violent storm of the Night before last, one arm of the emblematical statue of America, in the Pediment over the entrance door of the Hall of the House of Representatives, my design so beautifully executed by Persico, had been blown away, and came down with a tremendous crash — He said the group was of free stone — I said it was ominous — He said he hoped not — But he was mistaken as to the Statue mutilated. It is not the figure, but that of Justice which has lost her right arm, nearly to the elbow — Still more

ominous, and painfully significant of the condition of the Hall within, where Justice has emphatically lost her right arm.

———

[March 1840]

1. IV:45. Sunday. I walked to the Capitol, and heard Mr. Cookman, the chaplain of the Senate. An English Methodist; settled here within the last two years, and celebrated for his eloquence. His text was from 1 Timothy 4:16 — First clause of the verse "Take Heed unto Thyself" which words he pronounced with a loud voice — a deep emphasis upon each of the underscored words and a semicolon pause between each of them and the next. He then began by some general remarks upon the characteristic of the present age — which he said was excitement — association — movement in masses — the power of numbers — which he exemplified by alluding to the multitudes of Meetings, of Conventions, of Societies for Political, Religious or benevolent purposes — But he was now about to address his auditory individually, in a solitary capacity; and in the words of the Apostle Paul, to say to each man, woman and child who heard him Take — Heed — unto Thyself — What an easy, natural, beautiful introduction! He made no formal division of his subject; but it divided itself; and he had the skeleton always in his head — First guarding against any imagination that his object was to inculcate selfishness, but only the spirit of that self-love, which is implied in the precept to love thy neighbour *as* thyself — he successively repeated Take heed what thou thinkest — what thou sayest — what thou doest with obvious considerations of the relative importance of thoughts, words and actions — upon each of which he descanted at considerable extent — Then still repeating the Instruction take heed to thyself, applied it to the several relations with others, he finished with words of exhortation, particularly addressed [to] the younger part of his hearers. Hast thou ever done a good action? I hope thou hast — many — what thinkest thou of them now? do they not afford thee an inexhaustible source of pleasure? Hast thou never sinned? I know thou hast — what thinkest thou of that sin now? — I will tell thee what thou thinkest — with regret — with regret! if not with remorse — thy habitual thought is — I wish I had not committed that sin — Oh think then that on thyself depends whether thy destiny

after this life shall be an eternity of blessedness or of woe —
Then after a somewhat overcharged and hyperbolical declamation upon eternal punishment; he closed with saying Oh! think
of that dying admonition of a pious father — think of that
angel voice of a beloved sister, urging thee to virtue — and
Take — Heed unto Thyself! — He closed, and the tears were
streaming down my cheeks.

—

[April 1840]
6. VI. Monday. The morning was devoted principally to the
perusal of the despatches from N. P. Frist, Consul of the
United States at the Havana, concerning the fraudulent use of
the flag of the United States for carrying on the African Slave
trade — They are voluminous, and manifest either the vilest
treachery or the most culpable indifference to his duties —
For the last three years it is apparent that there has been the
most shameful prostitution of the American flag to carry on
that traffic — That it has been openly, notoriously practised
before his face — That as Consul of the United States, and at
the same time acting Consul for Portugal, he has actively lent
his aid to it; and when detected in malpractices by the members of the British and Spanish mixed Commission, held a
most grossly insulting and insolent correspondence with them;
and then in a long series of Letters to the Secretary of State
charges all this unlawful and unhallowed trade to defects in the
Laws. There is a very long Letter from Mr. Fox to the Secretary of State denouncing both the abuse of the flag, and the
conduct of Trist, and Forsyth's answer is as if one of the gang
of pirates were appealed to to pass sentence upon the rest ≈

7. IV:30. Tuesday. I read this morning Horace Everett's Speech
delivered in the House of Representatives in Committee of the
whole upon the Indian annuity Bill on the 3^d of June 1836. It
gives a perfectly clear and distinct exposition of the causes and
origin of the Florida War, and demonstrates beyond all possibility of being gainsaid that the wrong of the War is on our
side — It depresses the Spirits, and humiliates the soul to think
that this War is now running into its fifth year; has cost thirty
millions of dollars; has successively baffled and disgraced all
our chief Military Generals, Gaines, Scott, Jessup, Macomb,

and that our last resources now are bloodhounds and no quarters. Sixteen Millions of Anglo-saxons, unable to subdue in five years by force and by fraud, by secret treachery and by open war sixteen hundred Savage Warriors — Mr. Everett's speech refers to Executive Documents 267 and 271 of the 24th Congress 1st Session 23 May and 3 June 1836 — There is a previous Message of the President to the Senate of 9 Feb'y 1836 Senate Document 152 of the same Session, containing a report from the adjutant General giving a summary account of the causes of the War. There is a disregard of all appearance of right in all our transactions with the Indians, which I feel as a cruel disparagement of the honour of my country.

———

13. IV:30. Monday. I answered a Letter from Gen'l Towson, enclosing Resolutions from the horticultural Society of this City, calling upon me for a Report from a Committee appointed in June 1838 to taste a great many samples of American wines, and compare them with some of the finest European wines, and to judge of their relative merits — I have found it impracticable to perform this service, and have now given Gen'l Towson the reasons of the failure. With the Diary of yesterday it fully occupied last Evening and this morning — At the House the sitting began by a reception of Petitions and Memorials — The call began with Maine and just reached me. I presented twenty received since the last petition day. Three of my Petitions, were excluded from reception by the rule of 28 January — One for the release of Mackenzie was referred to the Committee on the judiciary. A series of Resolutions of the Legislature of Massachusetts, concerning the foreign Slave trade, were read, ordered to be printed and referred to the Committee of Commerce, to which so much of the President's annual message as relates to that subject was already referred. — A series of Resolves against the ill treatment of Citizens of Massachusetts in certain other States was read, and I moved that they should be printed and referred to a select Committee. They were laid on the table by yeas and nays 102 to 49: The motion to print was also laid on the table. The Series of Resolutions on the violation of the Constitution by the House of Representatives in rejecting petitions was a laid on the table by 105 to 54, and the motion to have it printed was also laid on

the table. There was a short petition from the interior of New-York, praying Congress to repeal the Laws in the District of Columbia which authorise the whipping of women. I was requested by a Letter from one of the Petitioners to read this Petition in the House which I did. Linn Banks said, no good could come from such a petition; and moved to lay it on the table; which was accordingly done. I got through with the presentation of my petitions just as the morning hour expired. Randolph moved a suspension of the rules to continue the call for Petitions — lost by yeas and nays 74 to 83.

———

17. V:15. Good Friday. A dark coloured mulatto man named Joseph Cartwright a preacher of a coloured methodist church, came this morning with a subscription book to raise 450 dollars to purchase the freedom of his three grand children, two girls and one boy, all under three or four years of age. He told me that he had been upwards of twenty years in purchasing his own freedom, that of his three Sons — that after this Henry Johnson late a member of the House of Representatives from Louisiana had bought his sons wife and her three children with many other slaves, to carry them away to Louisiana — That after the purchase he had been prevailed upon to consent to leave them here for a short time, in the charge of a man to whom he had ostensibly sold them, but with the consent that this Joseph Cartwright should purchase them for 1025 dollars — He had actually purchased and paid for the mother and was now endeavouring to raise 450 dollars for the three children. There were in the subscription book, certificates of two white methodist ministers Hamilton and Cookman to the respectability of this man — a preacher of the gospel! what a horrible exemplification of Slavery!

———

26. IV:30. Sunday. I attended public worship this morning with my wife, Miss Cutts and my Granddaughter Mary-Louisa. Mr. Cookman preached from Psalm 72:16 "There shall be a handful of corn in the earth upon the top of the mountains; the fruit thereof shall shake like Lebanon; and they of the city shall flourish like grass of the earth. 17 His name shall endure forever; his name shall be continued as long as the Sun; and men shall be blessed in him: all nations shall call him blessed.

18 Blessed be the Lord God, the God of Israel, who only
doeth wondrous things. 19 And blessed be his glorious name
forever: and let the whole earth be filled with his glory. Amen
and amen. 20 The prayers of David, the son of Jesse are
ended." — And it was a good ending said Mr. Cookman. —
He analyzed and commented with great ingenuity and fervour
upon every part of this text as prophetic of the Messiah's
kingdom — of that blessed time, when War shall be banished
from the earth — The theme is to me delightful — These
promises of the Scriptures — these transcendantly sublime
prophesies of the old covenant, and these practicable means
and irresistible tendencies to their fulfilment in the new are the
most precious pledges of my faith — If I did not believe them,
I should be compelled to reject the whole Book — I do most
faithfully believe them. Peace — perpetual Peace! what an inexpressible blessing to the race of Man! Not that I deem it
necessary to believe that the nature of carnivorous beasts shall
be changed — These I suppose to be figures of speech — but
that the murderous and treacherous passions in the heart of
man shall be so far eradicated or restrained that there shall be
no more public or private War — With the practice of War
Slavery must of course be extinguished. Mr. Cookman was
sufficiently enthusiatic in this belief to gratify me; and my faith
and hope in the future advent of the kingdom of the Messiah,
to pass among my friends for insane. That Christianity has already made immense progress in checking and controuling the
anti-social passions of man is undeniable. A religious principle
that man has no right to take the life of man, will soon accomplish the abolition of all capital punishments, and the principles
of Liberty are daily rendering the life of man more and more
precious. Mr. Cookman quoted Maundrell for the size of the
enormous Cedar of Lebanon, and spoke of what kings would
do in the Millennium; if there should be kings; at that time,
which was very doubtful. — The hall was more crowded than
I had seen it for many years.

———

[May 1840]
3. V:30. Sunday. When I came home last Evening, I found Miss
Cutts here, but she soon went away. I know not how to describe the effect upon my body and mind of such a week as I

have just past — labouring day and night in legislative deliberation, upon a measure the final consummation of which was
scarcely susceptible of divided opinion. War against an administration upon the petty details of an appropriation bill suits
neither my taste nor my principles — I was ready to pass it as it
went into Committee of the whole on the state of the Union
— Its worst feature was a pitiful attempt to filch about 100 000
dollars from the sums indispensable for the completion of the
public buildings, by defrauding the poor workmen upon them
at daily wages, of their dues. This attempt I contributed to
defeat, and the appropriations in the bill are sufficient to pay up
all the arrearages, and to continue the works. They had actually
suspended them, and left the workmen without employment
— Several of them yesterday morning accosted me as I was
walking to the Capitol, intreating me to use my influence with
Mr. Noland to set them to work again. I spoke to Petrikin,
who told me that both he and Governor Lincoln had advised
Noland to set the men to work. I sent for Noland himself and
intreated him to do so. He said he was willing, but Mr. Keim,
an Administration member of the Committee on the public
buildings had told him it was doubtful whether the appropriation would pass. I asked him to set the men to work on my
responsibility, and he said he would.

———

6. V. Wednesday. The members of the Baltimore whig convention of young men, are flocking to this city by hundreds. The
convention itself consisted of thousands; an immense unwieldy
mass of political machinery to accomplish nothing ≈ and in the
midst of this throng Henry Clay, Daniel Webster, William C.
Preston Senators of the United States and four times the
number of members of the House of Representatives, have
been two days straining their lungs, and cracking their voices
to fill this multitude with windy sound — for the glorification
of William Henry Harrison and the vituperation of Martin Van
Buren.

———

9. V:30. Saturday. The weather is so cold and raw with much
rain that we have been obliged to rekindle the fires in the dining room and in my own chamber — I finished last Night
almost sleepless and this morning my verses on the wants of

man. I suppose it is my intense anxiety for the Bill now under my charge which bereaves me of sleep, and the composition of verses, trifling upon another is the only mode of relieving myself from the continual pressure upon the brain of thought upon one subject, through a sleepless Night.

———

20. V. Wednesday. I had a night of quiet repose, but the soreness and pain in my shoulder was more troublesome this day than yesterday. This was a day of constant rain, and although convinced that I should have suffered less by attending at the House upon my duty than by staying at home, I yielded to the intreaties of my wife, and confined myself at home. Dr. Thomas called this morning. I had time to ruminate upon my accident, and could scarcely refrain from repining at the peculiar untowardness of the disability just at this moment of my right arm — One of the first questions asked me by Dr. May was whether the shoulder had ever been dislocated before. I had no recollection of any such event; but remembered having been told by my mother, that when a child two or three years old, I was straying out into the street, when the nursery maid ran out after me, and seizing me by the right hand, gave it an involuntary sudden jerk, and dislocated the shoulder. My right hand has, consequently I suppose upon this early disability, been weaker than the left all my days. Always unable to write fast, and for the last twenty-five years unable to write at all as other men do with the forefinger and the thumb. My right hand has been many times further disabled by casualties of various and different kinds; against all which I have struggled to the utmost of my ability, considering it as the business and duty of my life to write; and receiving as admonitions and chastisements of Providence these occasional disabilities.

———

[June 1840]

12. IV:45. Friday. ≈ This was a day devoted by the rules of the house to private business — but the rules were suspended by a bare majority vote, for the subtreasury — Botts of Virginia threw into the house a hand-grenade, which exploded to the great alarm of the Slavers — Sometime last winter, a Lieutenant in the Navy named Hooe, a Virginian was tried by a Court Martial at Pensacola; and two black men, the Steward

and Cook of the vessel were admitted by the Court as witnesses against him. He protested against their admission; but he was convicted of the offence charged against him and sentenced to some partial suspension from the service. The Secretary of the Navy Paulding confirmed the sentence, and President Van-Buren endorsed upon the proceedings that he saw no reason for his interference in the case — Botts asked leave to introduce a Resolution, calling for copies of the proceedings on this Court-Martial, with a preamble of bitter censure upon the Court for admitting the testimony of the two Negroes. Botts came to my seat before he offered the Resolution, and asked if I should object to it. I said certainly not as a call for papers. But I said I should not view the transaction in the same light that he did. He said nothing to me of his preamble. Objection was made to his Resolution — he moved a suspension of the Rules — He carried a majority to suspend but not two thirds, 95 to   The servile phalanx was broken — All the whigs North and South voted to suspend — Stragglers north and Semi South deserted from the Kinderhook ranks — Pickens swore like uncle Toby's armies in Flanders, and bolted to dodge the vote — Frank Thomas Snake number one, could not think of admitting such a Resolution, without time to reflect — M'Kay, snake number two voted against suspending, and then offered himself a Resolution calling for the papers without preamble — But the house would not receive it, and he gave notice that he would offer it again to-morrow — The rules for the consideration of private business were then suspended. Committee of the whole on the state of the Union — Banks in the Chair. Daniel D. Barnard took the floor and spoke till the recess without concluding, against the Bill — He spoke as usual admirably well: but he spoke to the stone pillars. The debate is so hacknied that the voice of one from the dead could not rouse attention to it.

———

[July 1840]

12. V. Sunday. I entered yesterday upon the seventy-fourth year of my age; and I have now lived as long since the decease of my mother as she had lived when I was born — I am deeply sensible of the duty of beginning in earnest to wean myself from the interests and affections of this world, and of preparing

myself for my departure to that which is to come — and yet
the day of yesterday was so absorbed in worldly business, and
worldly pleasure that not a moment of it was left for self-
admonition or for meditation — The truth is I adhere to the
world, and to all its vanities from an impulse altogether involuntary, and cannot by any exercise of my will realize that I can
have but very few days more to live, and that I have nothing
better or more urgent to do than to pack up and make ready
for my voyage — I might have taken another warning to the
same effect by attendance this morning at the Presbyterian
Church — where it was Communion-day, and where Mr.
Wood preached from Luke 22:19 And he took bread, and gave
thanks, and broke it, and gave unto them saying, "This is
my body which is given for you: this do in remembrance of
me." A strictly adapted communion discourse, but not very
impressive — The communicants were very few — the members of other churches present were invited to partake, but as I
knew this was not intended to include the members of Unitarian Churches, I did not avail myself of the invitation — Mr.
Wood invited also the members of other Churches present
who might abstain from joining in the Communion service to
stay while it should be performed; but if any should find that
inconvenient, they would have the opportunity of withdrawing
while a hymn, which he gave out should be sung — I accordingly withdrew.

———

25. IV:30. Saturday ≈ I finished the day in drudgery to assort
and file my papers. I have hundreds of Letters unanswered,
and not even duly filed — Loose public documents and pamphlets and newspapers innumerable — I am packing up four
large boxes of them, and of books to send by water round to
Boston, which is another grievous trouble — At least 49 50^{ths}
of my unanswered Letters, are from total strangers, and utterly
worthless. — Multitudes of Applications to attend public
meetings; and to deliver Orations, Addresses, Lectures, to Ly-
ceums, Literary Societies and political gatherings of the People
— Household cares are superadded more and more burdensome with the advance of years — Anxieties for the journey for
the return home, and for those I am to leave behind — An
hourly reminded and daily deepening consciousness of decay

in body and mind; an unquenchable thirst for repose, yet a motive for clinging to public life; till the last of my political friends shall cast me off, all this constitutes my present condition — These are my cares and sorrows — but with them I have numberless blessings for which I cease not to be grateful to the author of all good, and I have the cheering hope of a better world beyond the grave. The late Session of Congress has been painful to me beyond all former experience by the demonstration which it has given of degenerating institutions. Parties are falling into profligate factions. I have seen this before, but the worst symptom now is the change in the manners of the People — The continuance of the present Administration, will if accomplished open wide, all the flood-gates of Corruption — Will a change produce reform? Pause and ponder! Slavery — the Indians — The public Lands — The collection and disbursement of public monies — The Tariff, and foreign Affairs — What is to become of them?

———

[August 1840]

2. V. Sunday. Communion day at Meeting. Mr. Lunt preached this morning Sermon, from Acts 17:21 "For all the Athenians and Strangers which were there, spent their time in nothing else but either to tell or to hear of some new thing." It is the doom of the Christian church to be always distracted with controversy; and where religion is most in honour, there the perversity of the human heart breeds the sharpest conflicts of the brain — The Sentiment of Religion is at this time perhaps more potent and prevailing in New-England, than in any other portion of the Christian world. For many years since the establishment of the theological school at Andover the Calvinists and Unitarians have been battling with each other upon the atonement, the divinity of Jesus Christ and the Trinity — This has now very much subsided — but other wandering of minds takes the place of that, and equally lets the wolf into the fold. A crack-brained young man named Ralph Waldo Emerson, a son of my once loved friend, William Emerson, and a Classmate of my lamented son George, after failing in the every day avocations of a Unitarian preacher and schoolmaster, and starts a new doctrine of transcendentalism, declares all the old revelations superannuated and worn out, and announces the

approach of new Revelations and prophesies. Garrison and the Non-resistant abolitionists, Brownson and the Marat Democrats, Phrenology and animal Magnetism all come in furnishing each some plausible rascality as an ingredient for the bubbling cauldron of religion and politics — Pearce Cranch ex ephibis preached here last week, and gave out quite a stream of this transcendentalism, most unexpectedly — Mr. Lunt's discourse this morning was intended to counteract the effect of these wild and visionary phantasies, and he spoke with just severity of the application of this Spirit of hurly burly innovation to the most important and solemn duties of the Christian faith — He treated the subject but in part, and promised to discourse further upon it hereafter. Mr. Lunt's opinions favour a compromise between the past and the future; disapproving alike the obstinate and bigoted adherence to establishments and dogmas, merely because they are old; and the restless and reckless pursuit of mere innovation.

———

13. IV:30. Thursday ≈ The Boston Papers, Courier, Daily Advertiser, and Atlas, are now filled with election returns from North-Carolina, Kentucky, Indiana, and Alabama — All for the State Governments and all hitherto more or less favourable to the whigs, as the opposition to the present Administration of the General Government call themselves. The imposture of Jackson and Van-Buren democracy would seem to be drawing to its Catastrophe — and yet falsehood, injustice and wrong are permitted by divine Providence to have such sweeping sway over the affairs of men that I scarcely dare indulge the hope that the day of retribution will come even when it seems to approach. Twelve years I have submitted almost in silence to the foulest and basest aspersions upon myself, my administration and my father, of which Jackson took the lead by denouncing me, in his inaugural speech; while at the same time the remnants of the old Hamilton federalists assailed me with a furious onset here in my native Commonwealth. It would have been a waste of time and toil, to have attempted my defence, hitherto. The public ear was not open to me and I have lived slumbering under a cloud — Is the time arriving for me to speak? or must I go down to the grave and leave posterity to do Justice to my father and to me? In humble submission I

prostrate myself before the footstool of God, and implore the aid of his Spirit, to nerve my will and to prescribe my path.

———

29. III:45. Saturday ≈ Mr. Thomas P. Beal alighted from the Plymouth stage and spent an hour with me under great political excitement — The whole country throughout the Union is in a state of agitation upon the approaching presidential election such as was never before witnessed. — From the organization of the Government under the present Constitution of the United States, the nominations of Candidates for the Office of President were made in Caucus Conventions by members of Congress, and by the members of the State Legislatures. The Congressional Caucus nomination of 1824 was in favour of William H. Crawford, and signally failed — The State Legislature nominations produced only cross purposes, and have been superseded by party popular conventions, increasing in numbers till that of last May at Baltimore of the young men, to confirm the nomination of W. H. Harrison made before, by a select Caucus Convention at Harrisburg, Pennsylvania, last December, amounted it was said to twenty thousand delegates. This has been followed by numerous assemblages in all the States where the opposition is in any strength, and not a week has passed within the last four months without a convocation of thousands of people, to hear inflammatory harangues against Martin Van Buren and his administration, by Henry Clay, Daniel Webster, and all the principal opposition Orators in or out of Congress — I received earnest invitations to attend these Meetings and address the People at Nashville, Tennessee, Chillicothe Ohio, Wheeling Virginia, Baltimore, Alexandria, Georgetown, and many other places, all of which I declined both from general principles and from considerations specially and peculiarly applicable to myself. One of these assemblies was held yesterday by a public dinner given to Caleb Cushing by some of his constituents at Newburyport, and a Ball in the evening by him to them. I was invited also there but did not attend. Mr. Webster and Mr. Saltonstall were there, and a stump speech scaffold, and it is said a procession of 6000 people or more, and a dinner of 1800. Here is a revolution in the habits and manners of the people — Where will it end? These are party movements and must in the natural progress

of things become antagonistical — At the Baltimore meeting one of the marshals of the procession was killed upon the spot — These meetings cannot be multiplied in numbers and frequency without resulting in yet deeper tragedies — Their manifest tendency is to civil war.

———

[September 1840]

24. IV:30. Thursday. ≈ Charles attended a Meeting of the democratic party this Evening, at which George Bancroft, Collector of the Customs at Boston, Superintendant of Lighthouses within the Commonwealth, and Commissioner for building a Custom house at Boston, delivered an electioneering democratic address — This practice of itinerant speech-making has suddenly broken forth in this Country to a fearful extent — Electioneering for the Presidency, has spread its contagion to the President himself — to his now only competitor; to his immediate Predecessor — to one at least of his Cabinet Counsellors, the Secretary of War — to the Ex-candidates Henry Clay, and Daniel Webster, and to many of the most distinguished members of both Houses of Congress — Immense assemblages of the People are held — of 20, 30, 50,000 souls, where the first Orators of the Nation, address the multitude, not one in ten of whom can hear them, on the most exciting topics of the day — As yet the parties call and hold these meetings separately and seldom interfere with each other — But at the Baltimore convention last May one of the Marshals of the procession, a respectable mechanic of the city was killed, by an attempt of individuals of the opposite party to break it up — At a meeting a few days since on long Island, Mr. Webster in a speech of two hours and a half, observed that there was to be held a meeting of the opposite party another great meeting at the same place on the next day; and he gave what was equivalent to a challenge to Silas Wright and all the administration leaders to meet him on the stump — A hand bill was this day circulated in this town, severely reflecting on Mr. Bancroft, for coming to deliver this address — Charles says that at Medford there has already been hostile collision between the parties — and the tendency of all this undoubtedly is, to the corruption of the popular elections, both by violence and fraud — Charles came in after hearing Mr. Bancroft's

address, which was delivered at the Universalist Meeting house — Bancroft is an apostate federalist, as are almost to a man the leaders of the mock democracy of this State — Most of them, have cast off their caterpillar skin within the last five years — My father used to say of such "Flectere si nequeo superos, Acheronta movebo."

27. IV:30. Sunday. ≈ I had heard Mary Louisa read two chapters of the Book of Judges in Saci's french Bible, and had read the 6th chapter of the first Volume of Bancroft's History of the United States. This chapter is entitled restrictions on Colonial Commerce — It is a very lame account of the English Navigation Act, and a florid panegyric upon the first settlers of Virginia; upon the soil, and climate of that Country — upon the Indian Monarchs, Powhatan and Opechancanough in equal measure. Bancroft is that combination of sycophant and slanderer, which formed Shakespears Iago. The "flatteur dehonté, et calomniateur au besoin" of Mirabeau. With all this he has transcendent talents and indefatigable industry. Every page of his history teems with evidences of profound research, quick perception and brilliant imagination — It is extremely entertaining — The style diffuse and declamatory; far less chaste, though more fascinating than that of Irving or of Prescott. The morality ostentatious, but very defective.

[October 1840]
1. IV. Thursday ≈ My early rising enabled me to effect more this day than usual, though three hours of it were occupied in reading Mr. Webster's Speech to a great meeting of Merchants last Monday, at New-York — One of the most remarkable peculiarities of the present time is, that the principal leaders of the political parties, are travelling about the Country from State to State, and holding forth like methodist preachers, hour after hour to assembled multitudes, under the broad canopy of Heaven. Webster and Clay, W. C. Rives, Silas Wright, and James Buchanan, are among the first and foremost in this canvassing Oratory, while Andrew Jackson, and Martin van Buren with his heads of Departments are harping upon another string of the political Accordion, by writing controversial electioneering Letters — Besides the prime

leaders of the parties numerous subaltern officers of the administration, are summoned to the same service, and instead of attending to the duties of their Offices Rave, recite and madden round the land.

———

8. III:45. Thursday. ≈ Yesterday morning I waked up not knowing the hour, and upon lighting my lamp, and coming into my chamber found it was two O'Clock — It was warm so I sat down at my desk in my loose gown, and wrote upon my lecture till four, then went to bed again, and dozed till six — broad daylight, and just before Sun rise. Brownson's defence of his Article upon the labouring classes, and my mother's Letters, occupy my reading time for the present — Brownson covers his attack upon religion, by pointing it against the priests — under which denomination he includes all regularly settled clergymen. He professes the Quaker creed, and greatly admires their meetings of silent meditation. But his greatest of all abhorrencies is poverty, as a remedy for which he proposes to abolish all hereditary property — Men are to dispose of their property at their pleasure while they live, but when they die it is to revert to the community — This he deduces as an irresistible consequence from the natural equality of men, and from the principles of Democracy. Brownson, has a petty Office, given him by the Collector of the customs at Boston George Bancroft, whom he accordingly bedaubs with fulsome flattery — The drift of all his discourse is to inflame the passions of the poor, against the rich, and as Van Buren's policy must be to sustain the institution of Slavery, Brownson stoutly affirms that Slavery is better than the system of free labour. — Some of his opinions are so odious that the leaders of his party dare not endorse them — they complain that he has brought them out too soon. He replies to this objection by repeating the doctrines, and blustering about his Independence.

———

27. V. Tuesday. ≈ Mr. Ellis Gray Loring of Boston, and Mr. Lewis Tappan of New-York, called on me this morning, and earnestly intreated of me to assume as assistant Counsel to Mr. Baldwin of Connecticut, the defence of the Africans captured in the Amistad, before the Supreme Court of the United States at Washington, at their next January term — I endeavoured to

excuse myself upon the plea of my age and inefficiency — of the oppressive burden of my duties as a member of the House of Representatives, and of my inexperience after a lapse of more than thirty years, in the forms, and technicals of argument, before judicial tribunals, and said I would cheerfully do, what I had heretofore offered, that is give any assistance of Counsel and Advice to Mr. Baldwin, and any other person charged with the argument before the Court — But they urged me so much and represented the case of those unfortunate men as so critical, it being a case of life and death, that I yielded, and told them that, if by the blessing of God my health and strength should permit, I would argue the case before the Supreme Court; and I implore the mercy of Almighty God, so to controul my temper, to enlighten my Soul and to give me utterance that I may prove myself in every respect equal to the task — They promised that Mr. Baldwin would furnish me with a complete brief, and Mr. Tappan left with me two scrap books, containing in slips from the Newspapers all the publications relating to the trials from the time of the capture by Lieutenant Gedney.

———

[November 1840]

17. IV:45. Tuesday ≈ At 8 A.M. we arrived at New-Haven, and I took lodgings at the Tontine Hotel — Breakfast — Immediately after, Mr. Roger Sherman Baldwin called on me, and invited me to his office in his house, whither I went with him. He read to me sundry papers, and gave me one containing an argument, drawn up, by him — all, relating to the Negro prisoners taken in the Amistad. We had two hours of conversation upon the whole subject, in which he exposed to me his views of the case; the points which had been taken before the District and Circuit Courts; and the motion to dismiss the appeal which he supposes the proper course to be taken before the Supreme Court. He read to me numerous authorities on the several points which he proposes to urge at the trial; and said he hoped the Supreme Court would take up the case in the first or second week of the Session. — I visited the prisoners, with Mr. Baldwin — Mr. Wilcox the Marshal of the District, Mr. Pendleton, his deputy, and keeper of the house where they are confined together — The three girls are in a separate

house, and I did not see them. There are 36 men, confined all in one chamber perhaps 30 feet long by 20 wide — sleeping in 18 crib beds in rows two deep on both sides the length of the chamber — They are all but one young men, under 30 and of small stature — none over 5 feet 6. Negro face, fleece and form, but varying in shades of colour from ebon black to dingy brown — One or two of them are almost mulatto bright. Cinque and Grabow, the two chief conspirators, have very remarkable countenances — Three of them read to us part of a chapter in the English New Testament — Very indifferently — One boy writes a tolerable hand — Mr. Ludlow teaches them; but huddled together as they are, and having no other person to talk with but themselves their learning must be very slow.

—

22. V. Sunday. I was able this morning to write for a couple of hours before breakfast. Met at the breakfast table Mr. Charles Fenton Mercer who after 22 years of service in the house of representatives of the United States, last Winter in a fit of despair accepted an Office as Cashier of a Bank at Tallahassee in Florida; and is now going to England I suppose to raise the wind for that institution. Mercer is one of the most respectable natives of Virginia, and has devoted his life to the internal improvement of the Country, and to the gradual extinction of Slavery in the State — In both of these benevolent and exalted purposes his exertions have been abortive — The Savage and barbarous genius of Slavery has not only baffled them all, but has kindled a flame of popular odium against him, from which he has shrunk into the cashier of a bank at Tallahassee — A noble Spirit doomed to drudge in the mines! I called at Mr. John Sergeants and walked with him and Mrs. Sergeant to the Episcopal Church where Mr. Odenheimer read the morning service for the 23ᵈ Sunday after Trinity, and preached from Ephesians 6:17 "And take the helmet of Salvation" — he observed that there was some obscurity in the text as to what the helmet of salvation was, but that from another text 1. Thessalonians 5:8 it was ascertained to be Hope; and thus opened the general subject of all the encouragements of religion. The discourse was apparently one of a series, upon the several weapons of the whole armour of God — The preacher is a young man,

moderately eloquent, and his amplification of the virtue and efficacy of Hope as a Christian virtue was instructive and might have been specially useful to me — Particularly his quotation from St. Paul, who had *hope*, because he had fought the good fight; and had kept the *faith* — As I was coming out of church Mrs. Middleton spoke and named herself to me. I had not seen her for more than twenty years — She had then several young children, but was young and beautiful. Now she has the remains of beauty blended with the marks of deep affliction upon her face — I should not have recognized her. She is English born, and bears an excellent character — I dined with Mr. N. Biddle, en famille, with no other addition save judge Hopkinson. — We sat after dinner, settling the Nation till near 8 in the Evening, little satisfied with the result — Hopkinson is snug in port. Content with his office of District judge — Undisturbed by Ambition or fear — Biddle broods with smiling face and stifled groans over the wreck of splendid, blasted expectations, and ruined hopes. A fair mind — a brilliant genius, a generous temper an honest heart, waylaid and led astray by prosperity — suffering the penalty of scarcely voluntary error — 'tis piteous to behold.

28. IV. Saturday. My old Piedmontese man servant Giusta, whom I picked up at Amsterdam in June 1814 a stray deserter from Napoleon's army in his disastrous Russian campaign, who served me faithfully till the 3ᵈ of March 1829 when I left him as steward of the President's house to my successor there, Andrew Jackson, called to see me this morning — Antoine's life with a little embroidery from the hand of an imaginative novelist, would make an amusing and instructive tale — He married at our house in 1818 an English girl who from our kitchen at Ealing came over with us to this country, and has been to him an excellent wife. Tis pity they have never had a child — They lived two or three years with President Jackson; but could not abide his negro slaves and his savage temper — They left him and kept five or six years a small oyster and coffee house, in which he amassed a fund sufficient for them to live comfortably on its income — he purchased a small lot and tenement upon which they live, and where like Diocletian he cultivates cabbages, and lettuce, and celery. He went home

two years ago to visit his relations and was gone more than a year. He found them poor and miserable, and his brother ruined by habits of intemperance — Good humoured and social, Antoine had acquired in this Country a habit of free speaking which on his return home soon brought him under the surveillance of the police — He came back and brought one of his nephews with him. But he casts lingering looks towards the natale solum and intends to dispose of all his property here, and go back to spend his last days in the land of his birth.

———

[December 1840]

4. IV:30. Friday. Morning visits from Col'l Henderson of the Marine Corps, and Mr. Cazenove of Alexandria. Mutual gratulation at the downfall of the Jackson–Van Buren Administration is the universal theme of conversation. One can scarcely imagine the degree of detestation in which they are both held — No one knows what is to come — In four years from this time the successor may be equally detested. He is not the choice of three fourths of those who have elected him — His present popularity is all artificial — There is little confidence in his talents or his firmness — If he is not found time-serving, demagogical, unsteady and western-sectional, he will more than satisfy my present expectations. — Jackson's Administration commenced with fairer prospects and an easier career before him, than had ever before been presented to any President of the United States — His personal popularity founded exclusively upon the battle of New-Orleans, drove him through his double term and enabled him to palm upon this Nation the Sycophant, who declared it glory enough to have served under such a Chief for his Successor. Both the men have been for twelve years the tools of Amos Kendall the ruling mind of their dominion — Their edifice has crumbled into ruin by the mere force of gravitation, and the wretchedness of their cement — But what is to come? No halcyon days — One set of unsound principles for another. One man in leading strings for another — Harrison comes in upon a hurricane — God grant he may not go out upon a reck!

———

7. VI:30. Monday ≈ It was broad daylight when I rose. The sky had cleared away cold, and I lay abed shrinking from the task

of pinching my feet with cold water, and of making a wood fire in a chilly chamber; which after all, I was obliged to perform, having in the meantime lost the two best hours of the day for work. This day commenced the second Session of the 26th Congress — The heavy fall of snow compelled me to ride to the Capitol and a quarter before 12 I took my seat, being that which Rice Garland transferred to me the morning after the close of the last Session. Precisely at Noon, the Speaker Robert M. T. Hunter took the chair and the names of the members were called over by States. ≈

8. V:30. Tuesday. Sharp head-ache almost the whole night, and very little sleep. Rode to the Capitol. The Speaker took the Chair at Noon, and the roll was called over of members who had not answered — Fifty additional members now answered to their names. A message was sent to the Senate, to inform them that a Quorum of the house were assembled, and ready to proceed to business ≈ I gave notice of my purpose to offer to-morrow a Resolution that the standing rule of the house, numbered 21 adopted on the 28th of January last be rescinded — It is the rule that abolition petitions shall not be received or in any manner entertained by the house — No other business was transacted — The Senate did not form a Quorum, five additional members only to those present yesterday having appeared, one of whom was the President pro tem W. R. King — The house adjourned about half past 12. Of the members who came in this day John Sergeant, W. B. Calhoun, Millard Fillmore and Daniel D. Barnard who travelled with his wife and two children, left Philadelphia on Saturday morning in the Cars, and at 9 O'Clock that evening found themselves 23 miles from Baltimore, in the middle of the road with the snow falling and the storm howling around them, and unable equally to proceed or to recede — There of eighty passengers in the train, thirty of whom were women, the greater number remained, the whole night of Saturday, the whole day and Night of Sunday, and Monday till near noon; when fresh engines came and took them up, and brought them last night into Baltimore. A small part of their company found a refuge in two or three hovels near the place where they were arrested, but fared worse than those who adhered to

the Cars. These made themselves comfortable by shutting out the tempest, keeping up good fires, and foraging successfully round the neighbourhood, for a supply of provisions — Sergeant says there was in all this not much of hardship — The passengers from the South brought an account that Waddy Thompson just beyond Petersburg in Virginia, was knocked down between the two rails, and the whole train of five cars, engine and all passed over his body without hurting him much, or perhaps at all. He did not come on however in the cars ≈

9. VI. Wednesday. ≈ A Quorum of both houses was this day formed — The joint committee waited upon the President, who informed them that he would send forthwith a Message to the two houses. It was accordingly received and read — ready printed for the Senate — Atherton of New Hampshire moved that the Message should be referred to the Committee of the whole on the state of the Union and that 15000 copies of it with the documents, and 5000 copies without the documents be printed for the use of the members of the house, which was carried — I had offered my resolution to rescind the 21st standing rule of the house — Jenifer moved to lay it on the table. Lewis Williams that it be postponed — I said I was willing to take the question immediately without debate — I offered the Resolution, at the earliest possible moment for two reasons — first because the commencement of the Session is the time for receiving petitions — and secondly because so far as the discharge of my duty was concerned I would not suffer that rule to stand one hour as the Law of the house. Linn Banks moved that it should be laid on the table — I said that if the house did not choose to take the vote directly on the resolution, I should prefer next the question of laying on the table, because it could then be called up at any time — I asked for the yeas and nays and they were 82 to 58 — all the South, and Northern serviles voting in the affirmative — The house adjourned about 3.

———

11. VI:30. Friday ≈ I paid morning visits to Mr. Henry Clay lodging at Mrs. Arguelles's and to Mr. Solomon Lincoln, at Brown's Hotel — While I was at Mr. Clays, numerous other visitors came in, among whom the Russian Minister Bodisco,

whom Mr. Clay bantered coarsely about his marriage last
Spring with a young girl at Georgetown, daughter of a clerk in
one of the public offices named Williams. Bodisco took Clay's
greasy jokes very good humouredly, and with no small self
complacency assured him that all was right. Clay said he had
visited Mr. Van Buren yesterday and had an hour's conversation with him on the issue of the Presidential Election — Mr.
Clay further told us that before leaving home he had seen the
President elect Harrison, and that he looked well, though
some what shattered — At Mr. Lincoln's room I met Mr.
Webster, Governor Lincoln, and Robert C. Winthrop. I called
at the Office of the Attorney General Gilpin who informed me
that he had seen the President of the United States, concerning the case of the Amistad negroes, and he had concluded
that the case could not be dismissed from the Supreme Court
without an argument because the Spanish Minister insisted on
the delivery up of the men as slaves to be sent to the Havana,
as Slaves, and further that the motion to dismiss the case was
made in the Circuit Court, and there refused — I said that the
refusal of the Circuit Court to dismiss the cause seemed no
reason for precluding the dismission of it from the Supreme
Court, and that the Spanish Minister had not only not demanded the delivery of the men as Slaves, but had explicitly so
demanded them as Assassins — He said there was a subsequent
Letter from the Spanish Minister in April last insisting upon
the delivery of the men as Slaves, upon the principles of certain
Resolutions of the Senate, adopted at their last Session — I
denied the right of the Spanish Minister to claim them as
property — the pretended owners having claimed them — and
not having appealed from the decision. Mr. Gilpin had also the
papers from the Secretary of the Treasury respecting the purchase of the Schooner Amistad before him but did not appear
to understand the question. Mr. Solomon Lincoln, Mr. Barnard and Mr. Winthrop dined with us. My wife keeps her
chamber. Mr. Hallowell, and Mr. Stabler were visitors from
Alexandria, to solicit a Lecture.

12. V. Saturday. ≈ I thought it necessary to look into the case
of the Amistad captives, to prepare for the argument before
the Supreme Court in January; of which I dare scarcely to

think — I read especially the Article in the American and foreign Anti-Slavery Reporter of 1 October 1840 entitled the Amistad case p. 48–51 with deep anguish of heart, and a painful search of means to defeat and expose the abominable conspiracy executive and judicial of this Government against the lives of those wretched men. How shall the facts be brought out? How shall it be possible to comment upon them with becoming temper — with calmness — with moderation — with firmness — with address — to avoid being silenced, and to escape the imminent danger of giving the adversary the advantage in the argument, by over heated zeal. Of all the dangers before me, that of losing my self possession is the most formidable — I am yet unable to prepare the outline of the argument, which I must be ready to offer the second week in January. Let me not forget my duty.

———

27. VI. Sunday ≈ In attempting to resume this evening the preparation for the case of the Amistad captives, I meet immediately the questions what right Lieutenant Gedney had to seize them on the shore of New-York, or the vessel on the high Seas — I can find no such right; and yet I foresee too clearly that I shall either not be allowed to make the question or that it will be suppressed without even being answered — Oh! how shall I do justice to this case, and to these men?

———

[January 1841]
2. VI. Saturday. ≈ Governor Lincoln came alone, and I had a long conversation with him on the present state and prospective movements, of parties — The Governor gave me to understand that he knew Webster was to be Harrison's Secretary of State, but left it rather uncertain whether he had it from himself or from good authority. He said Mr. Stephen C. Phillips had told him he had it directly from Webster — I asked him whether Mr. Webster had consulted or communicated with him concerning any measures which were to indicate the principles upon which the administration would be conducted. He said Mr. Webster had once commenced a conversation with him, in which he had answered some enquiries, by assurances that all would be right — that the expectations of the friends of General Harrison would be gratified, but that he had

not then time to enter into details and thus avoided all specification — I enquired if he knew who was to be the Secretary of the Treasury and whether John Sergeant or Thaddeus Stevens was to be the representative of Pennsylvania, in the new administration — He did not know ≈ Mr. Thaddeus Stevens is now here, and has been for some days, and there is much said of his claims to notice and distinction from General Harrison and his friends ≈

3. V. Sunday. ≈ Evening so cold that I could not write — I was obliged to employ it in reading, and nearly read through the record prepared for the Supreme Court in the case of the Amistad Negroes.

———

6. V:30. Wednesday. ≈ I went in to the Library and borrowed the 14th Volume of Peters's Reports, a Volume of the Laws of New-York, containing the Constitution of the State and Jefferson's Notes on Virginia ≈ I rode home, and spent the Evening in writing — oppressed with trivial researches.

———

10. VI. Sunday. ≈ After the service, Jonathan Elliot at the request of Mr. Braxton, introduced him to me — He enquired if I had been acquainted with his father or grandfather. I had not — but I said his grandfather was universally known as one of the signers of the Declaration of Independence — Of his father I had never heard. His father he said must have been about of my age — He said that his father and forefathers had been episcopalians, but he had become a dissenter, and a member of the baptist church which he preferred to all the other denominations — He said he was pleased to find that many of the members of Congress were religious men. That they had prayer meetings every Saturday Evening; and that many of the members attended them. This was news to me ≈ Evening consumed in reading Amistad Documents.

11. V:20. Monday. ≈ There was this Evening a meeting of the Institution for the promotion of Science and the Arts, at which I intended to have been present, but was deterred by unfavourable weather, and by necessary to the Amistad negroes case — I employed the whole Evening in reading and

writing upon it — But it presents itself every day to me in a
new aspect — and I still know not how to present it to the
Court.

12. VI. Tuesday. Landis, John. This John Landis styles himself
a painter of sacred history. A Dunker with a long thick coal
black beard. A Poet in his own estimation quite equal to
Milton — A Painter of two wretched daubs, which have been
suspended in the Rotunda, for sale, and which he urged me to
purchase — I told him I could not afford to purchase pictures
— he said it might be a very profitable investment of money;
for that pictures, for example of Raphael, Titian, Rubens or
West increased greatly in price, the older they grew. The man
is poor, and feeds upon his fancies ≈ Mr. Roger Sherman
Baldwin, of New-Haven, Counsel for the Amistad Prisoners
came into the House, and I had a long conversation with him,
first without the Bar, and then in the chamber of the Committee of Manufactures, concerning their case — He read me his
brief, which I signed with him — He proposes to begin with a
motion to the Court to dismiss the case, on the ground, that
the United States having no interest in the case have no right
to appeal from the decision of the District judge. I must follow
him; but know not yet how to order my Speech aright —
When I came home I found my wife much indisposed with an
attack of Erisypelas — She soon took to her bed.

14. VI. Thursday. Another dull and gloomy day — my wife
continuing better, but still confined to her bed — Mary rode
with me to the Capitol where I went in to the Supreme Court
room just before the judges came and opened the court. F.
Key, the District Attorney came to me and enquired when the
case of the Blacks was to come on — I said we had filed a motion to the Court to dismiss the cause, which I understood was
to come up for arguments, on Saturday — He said he was
afraid there was not any chance for the poor creatures — That
the case of the Antelope, was precisely in point against them.
He had argued that case for the freedom of the Negroes, but it
had been overruled — Yet it never would do to send them
back to Cuba — The best thing that could be done was to
make up a purse and pay for them and then send them back to

Africa. I said we hoped to prove that the case of the Antelope, would not be conclusive in its bearing upon our clients; but he continued very positive in the impression that it would — I went therefore into the Supreme Court Library room: and took out the volume of Wheaton's Reports containing the case of the Antelope — I read as much of it as I could — and longed to comment upon it as I would — but I have neither time nor head for it — nothing but the heart.

———

16. V. Saturday. This day the motion signed by Mr. Baldwin and myself, and filed by him in the Supreme Court, to dismiss the appeal by the United States from the Decree of the District and Circuit Courts, in the case of the Amistad captives, was to have been argued — Saturday being by the rules of the Court the weekly day for the argument of motions — I was not half prepared, and went to the Court with a heavy heart, full of undigested thought — sure of the justice of my Cause; and deeply desponding of my ability to sustain it — When the Court was opened the Chief Justice, Roger B. Taney said that the Court had thought it best to postpone the Amistad case, to await the arrival of judge Story, who was expected to be here on Monday or Tuesday. It was desirable that there should be a full Court for the hearing of the case.

———

20. VI. Wednesday. ≈ By an agreement this day between Mr. Baldwin, and the Attorney General Gilpin the Supreme Court, postponed the Amistad Captives case till the 16th of February; and Mr. Baldwin left the City this afternoon to return home — This gives me a long respite for further preparation but my senseless distribution of time leaves me none for this all important claim — I went into the Senate chamber and heard a closing debate on Benton's pre-emption Bill — Sharp shooting between Henry Clay, and the sneaking scrivener Buchanan — My whole Evening was engrossed till Midnight with two heavy Mails of Letters legible and illegible, and dull pamphlets and newspapers — Not five minutes for the Amistad.

———

26. V:15. Tuesday ≈ Luther C Peck a Member from the western part of New-York called me out into the lobby and introduced to me two Chiefs of the Seneca tribe of Indians. A

young man educated at Dartmouth college named Pierce; and an elderly pure Indian speaking no English, named two Guns — They gave me, two petitions which they requested me to present — And they wished to have some conversation with me; for which they are to call at my house to-morrow Morning — Adjourned at half past three and walked home. Evening consumed in reviewing the case of the Antelope, which I did not half finish; a desperate, dangerous and I fear useless undertaking.

27. V:30. Wednesday. The two Seneca Indian Chiefs, who were introduced to me yesterday came this morning, according to appointment, to converse with me concerning their grievances, and especially to urge the presentation of their petition that no appropriation may be made to carry into effect the fraudulent Treaty, by which they are to be driven like a herd of swine from their homes to a wilderness west of the Mississippi — I told them I would present their petitions as soon as I could possibly get the ear of the house to receive them — That I had already presented a petition from Andover, Massachusetts, praying in their behalf that no appropriation may be made to carry into execution that swindling Treaty. That petition had already been referred to the Committee of Indian affairs; and I advised them to see Mr. Bell, the chairman of that committee; to communicate to him the purport of their petitions, and converse with him concerning them. I promised to speak for them, myself to Mr. Bell; but he was absent the whole of this day from the house — I was twice in the Supreme Court library room, to get at the whole case of the Antelope, upon which I want to open a Steam-battery, upon the argument in the case of the Amistad captives — but Oh! how impotent is my voice to fulfil the purpose of my heart!

———

[February 1841]
4. VI:15. Thursday. ≈ On my return to [the] House, I found Charles Shepard on the floor, discussing the topics of the Treasury Note Bill, as a Southern planter for an hour; followed by James Garland of the same interest — I then took my turn for an hour, and arraigned before the Committee, the Nation and the World, the principles avowed by Henry A. Wise and his three coloured standard of Overseer black,

duelling blood red, and dirty cadaverous nullification white — Of its effect I will not now speak. I have discharged what I believe to be a solemn and sacred duty — At the close of his reply his gang of duelists clap'd their hands and the gallery hissed. William Cost Johnson began his usual rhodomontade, but the whole committee was in fermentation; they rose and the house adjourned at half 4 — My wife dined with her brother Thomas B. Johnson whose health is very bad. The episode of this day has so completely absorbed all my feelings that my usual occupations were suspended.

5. V. Friday. Sleepless Night. The step that I have taken yesterday absorbs all the faculties of my Soul — Deliberately taken, to have any useful effect, it must be calmly, firmly, judiciously, perseveringly, alas! skifully, pursued — I fear I have estimated too highly its importance — I fear my own incompetency to sustain it effectively and successfully — I know not what support I shall receive in or out of the house — I stand alone in this undertaking. Few if any of my colleagues appear to understand my purpose and from their deportment yesterday, I should conclude they thought it one of my eccentric, wild, extravagant, freaks of passion — Trumbull of Connecticut alone came to me after it was over, took me by the hand, and thanked me — Mr. Barnard thought I ought to have dwelt more emphatically upon the disclaimer of all motive personally offensive to Wise; though he admitted I had disclaimed them. Brockway this day asked if my speech would be printed, and ascertained that Wheeler had taken full and accurate notes of it — Mr. Merrick Senator from Maryland and David Hoffman of Baltimore visited here this day, and told my wife that Mr. Webster had been highly delighted at hearing of my speech — but all around me is cold, and discouraging, and my own feelings are wound up to a pitch that my reason can scarcely endure — I trust in God to controul me. ≈

VI. 6. Saturday. I attended at the Hall of the house, half an hour before Noon, the stated time of the house's meeting, and went into the Office of the Clerk of the Supreme Court, and read several pages more of the Record of the Antelope case in the U.S. Circuit Court for the District of Georgia — Returning to the house, they had no sooner commenced upon business than I was called out of my seat to see a Mr. Bacon of New-Haven a brother of the Clergyman who was here with Dr. Parker, and who has lived some time on the Coast of Africa — I had some conversation with him, respecting the manner in which this Slave-trade is carried on in the interior of Africa itself. He says that they are divided into small tribes, each with chiefs who [a]re called by Europeans, kings — That they are constantly at War with each other for the express purpose of making Slaves for sale. That the Europeans at the factories on the Coast advance money or goods to them with a credit of three, four or six months, in which time they are to procure and bring down for delivery at the factory a given number of Slaves, and when they deliver them they recieve another credit in advance — That great numbers of the Slaves by nightly expeditions were taken and their villages were burnt — That considerable numbers were sold by judicial sentences for crimes, particularly for adultery: an offence for which they are particularly sensitive — He says he asked Sinqua who sold him, and he answered the son of his king; whom he Bacon well knew, as one of the most active African traders.

———

8. V:30. Monday ≈ I went to the house at 11. Theodore Talbot rode with me. I went into the Office of the Clerk's Office of the Supreme Court, and waded neck deep into the Record of the Circuit Court in Georgia, of the case of the Antelope — but could not reach the first decree of the Court — In the house this was the day for the reception of Petitions — The only one for several weeks past — The only one for the re-mainder of the Session — John W. Jones Chairman of the Committee of Ways and Means, moved to go into Committee of the whole on the state of the Union, upon the Pension ap-propriation Bill — Waddy Thompson, chairman of the Military Committee had Letters from the Secretary of War, and from General Armistead asking an appropriation of 100 000 dollars to buy a surrender of the remaining Indians in Florida, and wanted to go into Committee of the whole upon the Union for that — Jones told him that he might move it as an amend-ment to his pension bill — I supplicated for this day, for the reception of petitions: of which I said I had in my draw — ten

of which might possibly be received. — I spoke in vain. I called for the yeas and nays which were 92 and 92 and the Speaker decided to go into Committee of the whole, and called Clifford of Maine to the Chair — The Pension Appropriation Bill was read — Waddy Thompson then moved his appropriation-bill to buy an Indian surrender — Petrikin objected to it as not in order, as it certainly was not, by the 50th rule — Clifford was muddily bothering his trickster invention to get over this rule, when Briggs suggested to him the last patch upon the 76th rule; he snap'd at it like a mackerel at a red rag, and said the amendment was in order — Waddy Thompson made a frothy speech upon the amendment and when he had done, I objected that the amendment was not in order — he said it was too late; and the debate proceeded — Giddings of Ohio in a speech of three hours opposed the amendment, assuming to prove that the Florida War originated and has been conducted throughout, for the support of Southern Slavery — He laid down too narrow a basis for his superstructure, but he proceeded step by step citing his documentary proof as he went along to the exquisite torture of the Southern duelists and Slave-mongers. Georgians, Carolinians and Virginians. — They interrupted him every five minutes by calls to order, and Clifford who has neither eyes to see nor a heart to feel what is or is not in order, according to his caprice, sometimes sustained and sometimes silenced him — When he finished Mark A. Cooper one of the Apostate and dismounted whigs of Georgia took the floor and argufied without losing his temper till half past 4 when the Committee rose and the house adjourned.

———

19. VI. Friday. ≈ I left the house; and went into the Supreme Court, and heard the argument of Mr. Webster on the second Mississippi Slavery case; and the closing argument of Mr. Walker the Senator from Mississippi in reply — The question is whether a State of this Union can constitutionally prohibit the importation within her borders of Slaves as merchandize. Mr. Walker threatened tremendous consequences if this right should it be denied to the States, all of which consequences sounded to me like argument for the constitutional authority to prohibit it in all the States, and for the exercise of it.

———

22. VI. Monday. ≈ I walked to the Capitol with a thoroughly bewildered mind — So bewildered as to leave me nothing but fervent prayer, that presence of mind may not utterly fail me at the trial I am about to go through — At the opening of the Court, Judge Thompson read a decision of the Court on a certain case, Mr. Norvell, and S. T. Mason both of Michigan were admitted as Attorneys and Councellors of the Court — The Attorney General Henry A. Gilpin then delivered his argument in the case of the Amistad Captives — It occupied two hours and after a summary statement of the facts as developed in the documents from which he had copiously read on Saturday, he contended that the Amistad was a regularly documented Spanish Schooner employed in the coasting trade, between the different ports of the Island of Cuba. That the Passports of the passengers were regularly signed by the Governor General of Cuba and proved beyond all controversy that the blacks were the property of Ruiz and Montez — That the Court, by the Comity of Nations could not go behind or enquire into the validity of these documents, for which he cited many authorities in the Law books. — He attempted no argument to show that the right of property remained unimpaired by the insurrection, and insisted that all the negroes ought to be restored to their owners, and that the Circuit Court erred in pronouncing the negroes free — Mr. Baldwin followed in a sound and eloquent but exceedingly mild and moderate argument in behalf of the captives till half past 3 when the Court adjourned ≈

23. VI. Tuesday. With increasing agitation of mind, now little short of agony I rode in a hack to the Capitol, taking with me in confused order a number of books which I may have occasion to use — The very skeleton of my argument is not yet put together. When the Court met, Judge Wayne, and Judge Story, read in succession two decisions of the Court, and Mr. Baldwin occupied the remainder of the day, four hours in closing his argument in behalf of the Amistad Captives, and in the support of the decision of the District and Circuit Courts. The point upon which he dwelt with most emphatic earnestness was the motion to dismiss the appeal of the United States, on the contest of their right to appear as parties in the cause they

having no interest therein — His reasoning therein was powerful, and perhaps conclusive — But I am apprehensive there
are precedents, and an executive influence operating upon the
Court, which will turn the balance against us on that point. In
commenting upon the insurrection of the blacks, Mr. Baldwin
firmly maintained their right of self-emancipation, but spoke
in cautious terms to avoid exciting Southern passions and
prejudices, which it is our policy, as much as possible to asswage
and pacify — When he came to the point of questioning the
validity of the Governor General's Ladino Passports, he left a
good deal still to be said — He closed at half past 3 and left
the day open for me to morrow — I went into the Congress
Library, and took out for use the 37th volume of Niles's register
containing the speech of James Madison, in the Virginia Convention, on the double condition of Slaves in that State as
persons and as property. I did not wait to attend at the meeting
of the house after the recess ≈

24. V. Wednesday. ≈ I was busied in preparation in the Clerk
of the Supreme Court's room, nearly an hour to the moment of
the meeting of the Court — When that was opened Josiah
Randall, and Mr. Polk now a Clerk in the Department of War,
were admitted as Attornies and Counsellors of the Court, and
Chief Justice Taney announced to me, that the Court were
ready to hear me. The judges present were Taney, Story,
Thompson, M'Lean, Baldwin, Wayne, Barbour and Catron.
Judge M'Kinley has [not] been present during any part of this
trial. The Court room was full, but not crowded, and there
were not many Ladies. I had been deeply distressed and agitated till the moment when I rose, and then my Spirit did not
sink within me — With grateful heart for aid from above,
though in humiliation for the weakness incident to the limits
of my powers, I spoke four hours and a half, with sufficient
method and order to witness little flagging of attention, by the
judges or the auditory; till at half past 3 O'Clock, when the
Chief Justice said the Court would hear me further to-morrow
— Mr. Baldwin mentioned that he would stay and hear me
to-morrow, but that he should be obliged to leave the City on
Friday to return home. The structure of my argument — so far
as I have yet proceeded is perfectly simple and comprehensive

— needing no artificial division into distinct points, but admitting the steady and undeviating pursuit of one fundimental principle, the ministration of *Justice* — I then assigned my reason for invoking *Justice*, specially, aware that this was *always* the duty of the court; but because an immense array of power, the executive administration, instigated by the Minister of a foreign Nation has been brought to bear in this case on the side of *injustice* — I then commenced a review of the Correspondence between the Secretary of State, and the Spanish Ministers Calderon and Argaiz, which I analyzed with critical research as far as I was able, but with not half the acuteness nor with a tenth part of the vigour which I would have applied had they been at my command — I did not I could not answer public expectation — but I have not yet utterly failed — God speed me to the end. After the adjournment of the Court, I went for a few minutes into the house, but they were yet in recess.

———

[March 1841]
1. V. Monday. ≈ I went to the Supreme Court and concluded my argument in the case of the Amistad captives — I spoke about four hours, and then closed somewhat abruptly; leaving almost entirely untouched the review of the case of the Antelope, which I had intended and for which I was prepared — It would have required at least an hour, and I had barely reached it when the usual time of the Court's adjournment came — I was unwilling to encroach upon the the time of the Court for half of a third day, so that I cramped into a very brief summary, what I had to say upon that case, and finished with a very short personal address to the Court. They immediately adjourned, and [I] went into the hall of the house of Representatives.

———

4. VI:30. Thursday. ≈ The inauguration of William Henry Harrison as President of the United States was celebrated with demonstrations of popular feeling, unexampled since that of Washington in 1789, and at the same time with so much order and tranquility, that not the slightest symptom of conflicting passions occurred to disturb the enjoyments of the day. Many thousands of the people from the adjoining and considerable numbers from distant States had come to witness

the ceremony: the procession consisting of a mixed military and civil cavalcade and platoons of volunteer Militia companies, tippecanoe clubs, students of colleges and school boys, with about half a dozen veterans who had fought under the hero in the war of 1811, with sundry aukward and ungainly painted banners and log cabins, without any carriages or showy dresses was characteristic of the democracy of our institutions, while the perfect order with which the whole scene was performed and the absence of all pageantry was highly creditable to them — The numbers were not comparable to those of the military assemblage at Baltimore upon the reception of La Fayette in 1824, nor was there any thing now of the pride pomp and circumstance of that day. The coup d'oeil of this day was showy-shabby — The procession passed before the windows of my house — General Harrison was on a mean looking white horse in the centre of seven others, in a plain frock coat or surtout, undistinguishable from any of those before, behind, or around him. He proceeded thus to the Capitol; where from the top of the flight of steps at the eastern front, he read his inaugural address, occupying about an hour in the delivery; and before pronouncing the last paragraph of which the Oath of Office was administered to him by Chief Justice Taney. The procession then returned to the Presidents house, and he retired to his chamber, while an immense crowd of people filled for an hour or more all the lower rooms of the house. I saw the procession pass from my chamber windows. Mr. Leavitt was with me, and we were reading the opinions of the judges Davies and William Johnson, in the case of the Antelope.

———

9. V. Tuesday. ≈ I waited upon tenterhooks, half an hour for the meeting of the Court. A young man named Charles Hopkins from Vermont came and requested me to present him for admission as an Attorney and Counsellor of the Court, which I did. He told me he had already been admitted to the Circuit Court — He was accordingly admitted and sworn — Judge Story delivered the opinion and decree of the court in the case of the United States Appellants vs. the Schooner Amistad. It affirms the decision of the District and Circuit Courts excepting with regard to the Negroes — It reverses the decision

below placing them at the disposal of the President of the United States to be sent to Africa; declares them to be free and directs the Circuit Court to order them to be discharged from the custody of the Marshal — Judge Baldwin expressed some dissent from the opinion which I did not hear nor did I learn what it was — I went to the chamber of the Committee of Manufactures and wrote to Mr. Roger S. Baldwin at New-Haven, and to Mr. Lewis Tappan of New-York to inform them of the decision of the Court, and gave the Letters to Mr. M'Cormick the Postmaster of the House ≈ I went to the Office of the Clerk of the Supreme Court and wrote a motion for a mandate to the marshal of the District of Connecticut to discharge forthwith the Amistad captives from custody ≈

10. V:15. Wednesday ≈ I withdrew the motion for a mandate to the Marshal of the District of Connecticut, forthwith to discharge the Africans of the Amistad, at the suggestion of judge Thompson who assured me that he would see to it, and that they should be discharged within three or four days.

———

18. VI:30. Thursday. Leonard Adams is an inhabitant of this City about 65 years of age, originally from Massachusetts, but who has resided many years, here and raised by laborious industry a family of ten children, five of whom are yet living. He has been these two years working as a labourer at the Patent Office, and came now to ask my influence to obtain for him some place in one of the Departments as a watchman or Messenger — I might as well undertake by my influence to obtain for him the Office of Porter at the gate of Heaven.

———

21. V. Sunday. ≈ In the afternoon at St. John's Church, I heard Mr. Hawley read the service for the 4th Sunday in Lent, and preach from Revelation 22:12 "And, behold, I come quickly; and my reward is with me, to give every man according as his work shall be." The preacher remarked how universally all men worked for reward, which he illustrated by sundry specifications, but never bethought himself of the Slave — If he had thought of it, he would not have ventured to take the verse for a text. The courtly preacher never mentions hell to ears polite.

Massillon sometimes preached to the conscience of Louis 14 but no minister of the word of God South of Mason and Dixon's line, ventures to preach one word against Slavery — Not a few preach Slavery itself ≈ I am yet, and shall be I scarcely know how long absorbed in the drudgery of assorting filing and endorsing Letters which I have been receiving, during the whole Session of Congress, and two thirds of which when received I had not even time to read — I am compelled to read them now and groan under the waste of time consumed upon such trash. There is not one in fifty of them worth the paper upon which it is written; and if I begin to read any thing else, daylight fades into twilight and twilight into darkness before I am aware that the day is gone and I have done nothing. I this day took up and made a minute of 8 folio pamphlet documents containing about 1300 pages of papers communicated to the British Parliament in 1839 and 40 relating to the Slave trade divided into Classes, A. B. C. D. two sets of each. What can I do with them? — It is impossible to separate the discussion upon the African slave-trade, from the moral and political aspects of Slavery; and that is with us a forbidden topic — I apprehend this is the rock upon which the Harrison administration will drift and go to pieces; as it is the Quicksand upon which that of Van Buren was stranded — The tariff and the bank are but suckers from the root.

22. IV:30. Monday. ≈ Mr. Jocelyn called here while I was out, and in the Evening again when I had a long conversation with him respecting the Amistad Africans — They are now discharged from prison and have been sent to be employed and instructed at Farmington, about 25 miles from New-Haven. I advised that they should be sent home as soon as could be done with convenience and safety. ≈

23. V:30. Tuesday. Chilly rain all the morning — I had a very bad night and feel as if my Constitution was breaking up. I received two days since a Letter from a Stranger advising me now to retire from the world, the only reason for my postponing which is that I cannot afford it. There is another which I

should have much trouble to overcome, but which I would encounter — That is the vacuity of occupation, in which I could take an interest — More than 60 years of incessant intercourse with the world has made political movement to me as much a necessary of life as atmospheric air — This is the weakness of my nature, which I have intellect enough left to perceive, but not energy to controul — And thus while a remnant of physical power is left me to write and speak, the world will retire from me before I shall retire from the world.

———

29. IV:30. Monday ≈ I completed the assortment and filing of my Letters received since the beginning of this year, and find myself with a task before me perfectly appalling. I am yet to revise for publication my argument in the case of the Amistad Africans, and in merely glancing over the Parliamentary Slave-trade papers lent me by Mr. Fox, I find impulses of duty upon my own conscience, which I cannot resist, while on the other hand, the magnitude, the danger, the insurmountable burden of labour to be encountered in the undertaking to touch upon the Slave-trade. No one else will undertake it — No one but a Spirit unconquerable by Man, Woman or Fiend, can undertake it, but with the heart of Martyrdom — The world, the flesh, and all the devils in hell are arrayed against any man, who now, in this North-American Union, shall dare to join the standard of Almighty God, to put down the African Slave-trade — and what can I, upon the verge of my seventy-fourth birthday, with a shaking hand, a darkening eye, a drowsy brain, and with all my faculties, dropping from me, one by one, as the teeth are dropping from my head, what can I do for the cause of God and Man? for the progress of human emancipation? for the suppression of the African Slave-trade? — Yet my conscience presses me on — let me but die upon the breach.

———

[April 1841]
2. V:30. Friday. The condition of the President's health is alarming. He was seized last Saturday with a severe chill; and the next day with what his physicians called a bilious pleurisy; since that time he has been very ill, with symptoms varying from day to day and almost from hour to hour. The porter at

the door answers all enquirers that he is better; while Mr. Chambers and Mr. Todd report that there is no change, and the physicians agree to answer all alike. Yesterday during the day time the answer was much better — last evening not so well — this morning, quite out of danger.

———

4. V. Sunday. At 30 minutes past midnight this morning of Palm-Sunday the 4th of April 1841 died William Henry Harrison, precisely one calendar month as President of the United States, after his inauguration. The first impression of this event, here where it occurred is of the frailty of all human enjoyments, and the awful vicissitudes woven into the lot of mortal man — He had reached but one short month since the pinnacle of honour and power in his own country — He lies a lifeless corpse in the Palace provided by his Country for his abode. He was amiable and benevolent. Sympathy for his sufferings and his fate, is the prevailing sentiment of his fellow-citizens — The bereavement and distress of his family, is felt intensely, albeit they are strangers here, and known to scarcely any one. His wife had not yet even left his residence at North-bend, Ohio, to join him here. An express was sent for her two or three days since, but the tidings of death must meet her before she can reach this city. The influence of this event upon the condition and history of the Country, can scarcely be foreseen — It makes the Vice-President of the United States, John Tyler of Virginia, acting President of the Union, for four years, less one Month — Tyler is a political sectarian of the Slave-driving, Virginian Jeffersonian school — Principled against all improvement — With all the interests and passions, and vices of Slavery rooted in his moral and political constitution — with talents not above mediocrity, and a spirit incapable of expansion to the dimensions of the station upon which he has been cast by the hand of Providence unseen through the apparent agency of chance — To that benign and healing hand of Providence I trust in humble hope of the good, which it always brings forth out of evil — In upwards of half a century, this is the first instance of a Vice-President's being called to act as President of the United-States, and brings to the test that provision of the Constitution which places in the Executive

Chair a man never thought of for it by any body. — This day was in every sense gloomy — Rain the whole day. ≈

5. V:30. Monday. ≈ The corpse of the late President Harrison was laid out in a plain coffin covered with black velvet, on a table in the middle of the entrance Hall at the President's house — At 2 O'Clock P.M. I went with my wife and Mrs. Smith, and took a last look at the face of the Patriot Warrior, taken away thus providentially from the evil to come. ≈

6. V:15. Tuesday. The arrangements for the funeral of the late President of the United States, William Henry Harrison, were published in this day's National Intelligencer — The Vice-President John Tyler of Virginia, arrived here at 5 O'Clock this morning, and took lodgings at Brown's Hotel. At Noon the heads of Departments waited upon him. He requested them all to continue in their Offices, and took the Official Oath of President of the United States, which was administered to him by William Cranch Chief Justice of the Circuit Court of the District of Columbia — The judge certifies that although Mr. Tyler deems himself qualified to perform the duties and exercise the powers and Office of President, on the death of President Harrison, without any other Oath than that which he had taken as Vice-President, yet as doubts might arise, and for greater caution he had taken and subscribed the present Oath — And may the blessing of Heaven upon this Nation attend and follow this providential revolution in its Government — For the present it is not joyous but grievous — The moral condition of this country is degenerating; and especially that part of its institutions, which is organized by the process of unceasing elections — The spirit of the age and country is to accumulate power in the hands of the multitude, to shorten terms of service in high public office; to multiply elections and diminish executive power — to weaken all agencies protective of property or repressive of crime — to abolish capital punishments, imprisonment for debt, and even the lien upon property of contracts — Slavery, Temperance, Land-jobbing, Bankruptcy, and sundry controversies with Great-Britain, constitute the materials for the History of John Tyler's administration — But the improvement of the condition of man will form no part of his

policy, and the improvement of his Country will be an object of his most inveterate and inflexible opposition — May the omnipotence of God overrule the depravity of man — Of human purpose or human energy I despair.

———

15. V:45. Thursday. I finished my letter to the Governor of New-York, which I marked private, but wrote with a constant anticipation, that it may be published very soon; and in all probability will be sooner or later. — I have laid down the principle, of international Law, upon which I concur with him in his controversy with the executive authorities of Virginia. I take what I believe to be the impregnable position, the right of each Sovereign party to a contract to construe its provisions for itself, but not to impose its construction upon the other — I have not touched upon the policy or impolicy of delivering up fugitives from Justice — nor upon the usages among civilized Nations, nor upon the degree of transgression embraced in the definition of the word crime. Upon all these points there is much debatable ground — But the independent right of construction on both sides, the necessity that both parties should understand the words constituting obligation in a compact, in the same sense, and the basement story of the controversy the conflict between Freedom and Slavery are parts or auxiliaries of Seward's argument which cannot be shaken. Prudence has warned me to stand aloof from this contest, but I cannot. The leading men of the North are all truckling to Southern Slavery — They are all ready to desert Seward in the stand that he has taken. I see what it will cost me to stand by him; but I have so little political capital left, that the remnant is not worth saving — Especially at the cost of base desertion from the cause ≈

16. V:45. Friday. ≈ I paid a visit this morning to Mr. Tyler who styles himself President of the United States and not Vice-President acting as President, which would be the correct style — But it is a construction of the Constitution, in direct violation both of the grammar, and context of the Constitution, which confers upon the Vice-President on the decease of the President, not the Office, but the powers and the duties of the said Office — There is a dogmatical article in the National

Intelligencer, asserting this false construction, which is not worth contesting, but which to a strict constructionist would warrant more than a doubt whether the Vice President has the right to occupy the President's house or to claim his Salary without an act of Congress. — He moved into the house, two days ago, and received me in the old South-east Cabinet chamber. He received me very kindly, and apologized for not having visited me without waiting for this call — To this I had no claim or pretension. My visit was very short, as there were several persons in attendance and among them Mr. Southard now President of the Senate.

————

20. VI. Tuesday ≈ In my conversation with Mr. Bell last evening, I had reason to conclude, that the policy of Mr. Tyler will look exclusively to his own election for the next four years term as President; and that of Webster will be to secure it for him. That Mr. Clay will be left to fight his own battle with the Land Bill, without aid or support from the administration, and that between Tyler and Webster there will be a concert of mutual concession between the North and the South — Clay will soon be in unequivocal opposition, and the administration will waddle along, living from hand to mouth — for as to any great commanding and compact system, Webster is "a great baby" and Ewing is another — Of course, this Administration will be a failure, and a general bankruptcy is impending.

————

27. IV:30. Tuesday. I had hoped in the short visit to my children during the interval between the last, and the approaching Session of Congress to pursue the most necessary occupations with which I am burthened with little interruption; but when I came to luxuriate in the Study of my Son, with his classical Library, I find myself every moment enticed away, by the fragrance of one blossom after another, till the day has passed off and I have done nothing. ≈

————

28. V. Wednesday. Clear, vernal day — the first of a fortnight — Morning devoted to writing, and commenced the revisal of my speech on the case of the Amistad Africans. Received two Letters having reference to that subject — one from Simeon S.

Jocelyn, Joshua Leavitt and Lewis Tappan the Committee at New-York, which has supported them through all their trials, expressing a grateful acknowledgment of my services in their behalf. The other from Arnold Buffum, dated the 19th inst't at New-Garden Indiana, complaining bitterly of the act of Congress of 1793 prescribing the process for taking up fugitive Slaves; and of certain proceedings of the colonization Society; with a postscript suggesting an amendment to the Constitution changing the mode of electing the President of the United States — This election of a chief magistrate for the whole Union, will never be settled to the satisfaction of the People. The theory of elective Monarchy is that the choice may fall upon the wisest, and the best — The theory of frequent elections is that power cannot be long trusted to the same hands even of the wisest and the best. The two parts can be reconciled to each other only by the inconsistency and corruptibility of human nature in its best estate; and never, never will any great people be satisfied with the result of their own elections of an executive head — We have now the tenth President of the United States brought into Office, in the space of 52 years that the Constitution has been in operation — One amendment has already changed the mode of election prescribed by that instrument — A second practical alteration has limited the term of service to two periods of four years — And a third is growing upon the impatience of the people, for a further limitation to one term of 4 years, while the office itself is falling into hands incompetent to the management, and upon heads inadequate even to the conception of any comprehensive system of administration for the affairs of a great confederated Nation — There is not a mind now occupied in the executive administration of this Government, and the only change yet accomplished, is of one set of low and miserable expedients for another — The only prospect now is of recoiling to the last with aggravation of a shameless failure of the apparent extrication of the Country from the fangs of a worthless and profligate faction.

———

[June 1841]
10. IV. Thursday ≈ It was half past 12 before I reached the house. C. J. Ingersoll resumed and in three hours concluded

his speech, all *at* and against me. J. C. Clarke then moved the previous Question. He yielded however to the earnest and importunate solicitation of Thomas F. Marshall of Kentucky, upon his promise to review it. Marshall then made a splendid two hours speech, at and against me, and closed by renewing the demand of the Previous Question — A motion was made to lay the whole subject on the table — lost by yeas and nays. — The previous question was then carried by yeas and nays and the question to reconsider the vote adopting my amendment to Wise's motion for adopting the old rules — "except the 21st" was lost by yeas and nays 116 to 110 — a second deliverance as by fire — Wise then called up Fornance's motion to reconsider the vote of the House adopting the old rules, with my amendment excluding the 21st upon which he said, he had *a word to say*. It was half past 5 O'Clock — he said he was ready to go on now, or to adjourn as it should please the house. A motion was immediately made to adjourn, and carried by yeas and nays ≈

11. IV. Friday. ≈ At the house, Hiram P. Hunt a mellow whig member from New-York who occupies the seat immediately before mine gave notice of his intention to ask leave to bring in a bill to repeal the act of 2^{d} October 1837 to postpone the fourth instalment of deposits with the States — Hunt is a busy body Marplot in the morning, and always fuddled after dinner — The fourth instalment has been long since used up and wasted by the Van-Buren Administration, and it is too late to call for it now. — To raise money from the people, by taxation now, merely to deposite with the States, will not meet with much encouragement from Congress. But it will consume time — Sundry other members asked Wise to allow them a minute or two to offer resolutions, but he was biting his curb bit, and rudely refused. After much solicitation he permitted Botts to enquire of the Speaker, whether a reconsideration of the vote adopting the rules would not annul all the proceedings of the House under the rules. — Without waiting for the Speaker's answer Wise began in a tone, which I saw would break him down — Loud — vociferous — declamatory — furibund — he raved about the hell-hound of abolition, and at me as the leader of the abolitionists throughout the

Union, for a full hour till his voice had broken into childish treble two or three times. Arnold of Tennessee came to my seat, and with deep earnestness intreated me not to reply to him, and I promised that I would not. Without abatement of his vehemence Wise came to speak of the controversy between the States of Virginia and New-York; and then his tone suddenly fell, he became bewildered in his argument; his voice failed him, he became ghastly pale; said he felt himself unwell, sank into his chair and fainted. Several of his friends flew to his assistance, led him out of the Hall, and took him to his lodgings. The house postponed the further consideration of the Subject till to-morrow.

———

14. IV. Monday ≈ At the House immediately after the reading of the Journal Mr. Wise resumed his speech in support of Fornance's motion to reconsider the vote adopting the old rules except the 21st and spoke for upwards of six hours a continued invective upon me. He was apparently recovered from his fainting fit of last Friday, and he had sufficient self controul to avoid the bawling, brawling tone with which he then broke himself down — but beginning every successive sentence with a loud and vehement clatter, he immediately bowed down over his desk till his head and chest became horizontal, his mouth pouring out all the time his words in a whisper. Abolition — abolition — abolition — was the unvarying cry, and he represented me as a fiend, the inspirer and leader of all abolition — He gave a history in his own way full of misrepresentations of all the gag motions, orders and resolutions down to the Rule of 28 January 1840 — from Pinckney's gag in 1835 — He finished about half past six when half a dozen members started up and Botts moved the previous question. Rayner of North Carolina intreated him to withdraw the motion, and promised that he would renew it — but Botts persisted — there was a call of the house, but only 210 members answered to their names — The previous question was then put and carried, and then the reconsideration was carried by a vote of 106 to 104 and the House was again left without rules — Several motions were then made with great confusion and disorder till a motion was made to adjourn and carried by yeas, and nays. I came home about 8 O'Clock in great tribulation,

and perplexed in the dilemma between firm perseverance, intemperate retaliation and tame submission. What I most need and fervently pray for, is controul over my own temper.

———

30. IV. Wednesday. Bath and Swim. Morning visit from John Ross, Chief of the Cherokee Nation with Vann and Benn two others of the delegation. Ross had written to request an interview with me for them, on my appointment as Chairman of the Committee on Indian Affairs. I was excused from that service at my own request from a full conviction that its only result would be to keep a perpetual harrow upon my feelings, with a total impotence to render any useful service — The Policy from Washington to myself of all the Presidents of the United States had been Justice and kindness to the Indian tribes, to civilize and preserve them — With the Creeks and Cherokees it had been eminently successful — Its success was their misfortune — The States within whose borders their settlements were took the alarm, broke down all the Treaties which had pledged the faith of the Nation. — Georgia extended her jurisdiction over them — took possession of their Lands, houses, cattle, furniture, negroes, and drove them out from their own dwellings — All the Southern States supported Georgia, in this utter prostration of faith and justice, and Andrew Jackson by the simultaneous operation of fraudulent treaties and brutal force consummated the work — The Florida War is one of the fruits of this policy; the conduct of which exhibits one [un]interrupted scene, of the most profligate corruption — All resistance against this abomination is vain. It is among the heinous sins of this Nation for which I believe God will one day bring them to judgment — but at his own time, and by his own means. I turned my eyes away from this sickening mass of putrefaction, and asked to be excused from serving as Chairman of the Committee. Ross and his colleagues are here, claiming indemnity for the household furniture, goods, and cattle stolen from their people, when they were expelled from their dwellings; and a new treaty to give them some shadow of security for the permanent possession of the lands to which they have been driven. They complain of delays, and neglect by the new Secretary of War, Mr. Bell, and I promised

to speak to him in their behalf — and I told them to call upon me freely, if upon any occasion I could be serviceable to them.

———

[July 1841]

11. IV. Sunday. My birth day happens this day upon the Sabbath. Every return of the day comes with a weight of solemnity more and more awful. How peculiarly impressive ought it then to be, when the annual warning of the shortening thread, sounds in tones deepened by the Church bells of the Lord's day? The question comes with yearly aggravation upon my conscience — what have I done with the seventy-four years that I have been indulged with the blessing of life? and following close upon it, another, what can I do, what shall I do with the scanty and perilous remnant of life before me?

———

24. IV:30. Saturday. Edward Southwick the man who visited me yesterday told me that he was a native of Massachusetts but now resided in the western part of New-York, that he was an abolitionist, and was now going to the South, to discuss the matter with them there. He asked me what I thought of it — I said the best thing he could do, was to turn round and go home — He asked if I thought there would be danger of harm to him. I said the least he could expect to get was a ducking. He said the late Governor of North-Carolina, had written to him that there was not the slightest danger for him in that State — I said North-Carolina was not so fanatical as some other Southern States, but he had better not trust himself even there — I would advise him too to be very cautious in his conversation here, and to go home as soon as possible.

———

28. IV:30. Wednesday. I was obliged this morning to hasten to the Capitol, to be there at the meeting of the house — As soon as the Journal of yesterday had been read, I rose to present the residue of the Petitions which I had on hand. The Speaker said there was an appeal from his decision that I had the right to present them. He took the question whether the decision of the Speaker should stand as the judgment of the house, and nearly all the members present rose in the affirmative — not ten in the negative — I presented them accordingly — one for

a bankrupt Law was received and referred to the committee of the whole on the state of the Union — One from Wheeling, signed by 130 Citizens of Virginia, praying Congress to enact Laws that all the free coloured population may be sold as Slaves, or expelled from the Country — I said I had long hesitated whether I would present this petition; to the prayer of which nothing could be more abhorrent to my disposition — My respect for the right of petition was my only motive for presenting this. I asked the Speaker if this was one of those, which would be suspended by the rule of this Session — he said it would. Stanley objected to its being received, and said it was as inhuman and unjust as would be the general emancipation of Slaves.

———

[August 1841]
14. IV. Saturday. The President of the United States, the members of his Cabinet, and all the members of both houses of Congress had received invitations to visit the line of battle ship Delaware lying off Annapolis, this day — Commodore Morris who is going out in command of her, had given me an additional verbal invitation, and I had concluded to go, until the feud between the President, and the two houses of Congress, festering ever since a special Providence placed John Tyler in the Presidential Chair came to an issue, by the passage of the Bank Law, which it is known he intends to negative — The excitement in both houses, and in public is so great that I thought it no time for festivity or hollow hearted pageantry. The President himself appears to have become sensible, that this exhibition of himself to public gaze and outward display of adulation was ill suited to the real feelings of the time, and did not go. — The house yesterday, adjourned over to Monday for this frolic, but the Senate refused to adjourn and sat this day as usual.

———

16. V. Monday ≈ At last the house went into Committee of the whole on the state of the Union, upon the Bankrupt Bill. Tillinghast in the Chair. Isaac E. Holmes of Charleston S. Carolina made a long-studied hour speech against the Bill — Holmes is a pompous Orator fancying himself a very profound statesman — he has a pickpocket habit of looking askance

from the corner of his eyes, while he is speaking, and he affects deep logical deduction — Francis James of West-Chester Pennsylvania, a plain, downright wet quaker followed him for the bill, succeeded by John Sergeant, and he by Jacob M. Howard of Michigan. Their speeches were made with less than 40 members in the hall — The flock were in the Senate to hear the veto upon the Bank-bill, delivered there this day at Noon. ≈ When the veto message was read in the Senate there was some slight disorder in the galleries, whereupon T. H. Benton made a ridiculous scene, till a man was taken into custody, and the doughty knight of the stuff'd cravat abated his manly wrath — The veto message and its inevitable consequences will utterly prostrate the administration, and the party by which it was brought in. It surrenders the Country to the profligate political swindlers so recently driven from power! There is a Providence in the fall of a sparrow.

————

[September 1841]
3. IV. Friday ≈ Col'l Hayne of S.C. came to my seat to request a conversation with me at some convenient time, about a plan which he has formed for settling by a compromise the great Slavery question, and he wishes me to undertake — His views are pure and benevolent; I promised cheerfully to see and hear him on the subject without fixing the time.

————

11. V:30. Saturday. The meeting at Mr. Webster's last evening was at his request. He stated that the Secretary of the Treasury Thomas Ewing, the Secretary of the Navy, George E. Badger of North Carolina and the Attorney General John J. Crittenden of Kentucky had called on him this day and informed him that they, and John Bell of Tennessee, had determined to send in their resignations of their respective Offices (the latter of Secretary of War) to President Tyler at 11 O'Clock to-morrow Morning — Mr. Webster then addressing me, said, that being thus placed in a peculiar position, and seeing no sufficient cause for resigning his office he had requested this meeting to consult with the members of the delegation and to have the benefit of their opinions, assuring them that as to the Office itself it was a matter of the most perfect indifference to him whether he retained or resigned it — a declaration which it is

possible he believed when he made it — But he had prefaced it by stating that he saw no cause sufficient to justify his resignation. It was like Falstaff's recruit Bullcalf. "In very truth, sir, I had as lief be hang'd, sir, as go; and yet, for mine own part, sir, I do not care: but, rather, because I am unwilling, and for mine own part have a desire to stay with my friends: else, sir, I did not care, for mine own part, so much." ≈ We all agreed that Mr. Webster would not be justified in resigning at this time, but we all felt that the hour for the requiem of the whig party was at hand.

———

17. V:45. Friday. After a long spell of dry weather we had a moderate cool rain nearly all this day, and the settling in of autumn. I received the proof slips of my Speech delivered on the 4th inst't on the M'Leod Resolution, the language of which wholly extemporaneous is mean and tautological, full of repetitions and desultory, but has the merite de l'apropos. The Speech has for the time saved Webster from the catastrophe which has befallen his colleagues — It has given him the means of saving himself from ruin, and his country from a most disastrous and cruel War — My reward from him will be professions of respect and esteem, speeches of approbation and regard for me to my friends, knowing that they will be reported to me; secret and deep laid intrigues against me, and still more venomously against my son — Such is human nature, in the gigantic intellect, the envious temper, the ravenous ambition, and the rotten heart of Daniel Webster — His treatment of me has been, is, and will be an improved edition of Andrew Jackson's gratitude — But these are things according to Plutarch, not to be told in the biographies of great men.

———

[October 1841]

12. IV:45. Tuesday. ≈ Mr. Kirkland Lothrop, Minister of the Brattle-street Church was here this afternoon — He spoke of the trial of Alexander M'Leod, at Utica in the State of New-York; before judge Greely, of the Supreme Court of that State, and a jury; for the murder of a man named Durfee, and the burning of the Steamboat Caroline in the night of the 29th and 30th of December 1837 — This trial, which commenced on Monday the 4th of this Month continued through the last

week, and is probably not yet concluded —All the Newspapers have been full of reports of the progress of the trial; which involves at once a question of Peace and War with Great-Britain, and of civil War, and the existence of the Union between the General Government, and the Government of the State of New-York. This is one of the consequences naturally flowing from the Jeffersonian doctrine of nullification, and of State rights — And that doctrine had its origin in that root of all evil Slavery — This in the case of M'Leod, and the burning of the Caroline is complicated with the convulsive condition of Canada, the fermenting spirit of insurrection against the British Government in that Country — the sympathies and antipathies, always existing between the bordering population of rival nations, and the reckless spirit of adventure avarice and ambition burning in the bosoms of multitudes, especially of young men, having little or nothing to lose, and in imagination every thing to gain by war and confusion — Mr. Lothrop spoke of a Letter from Mr. Roebuck to Captain Napier, and of his answer dated in August last in England, and republished here in the New-York Herald — They discuss the question of collision between our general Government, and that of the State of New-York, whereby the Government of the United States, though admitting the obligation to release M'Leod, from the time when the British Government avowed the act of burning the Caroline as their own, have yet been disabled from effecting his release by the refusal of the Government of New-York to deliver him up — whence Mr. Lothrop says, Captain Napier gravely concludes, that there must be War, whether M'Leod shall be finally released or not — A military conclusion.

———

15. IV:30. Friday. ≈ My library and house are choked up with pamphlets, newspapers and voucher papers public and private — all in such disorder that a search for any one book, paper or document is almost without exception an irretrievable waste of time — I spend now hour after hour of almost every day in fruitless search for papers none of which I can find. The only alleviation for this is that I some times find what I am not looking for, but which I want as much as I do the object of my search. In hunting over this day the pamphlets in one of my closets, I found a number of packages of the Returns of

Commerce and Navigation, from 30 September 1838 to 1839, reported to Congress 1 July 1840 but not printed and received here till last May, when in the very few days that I spent here, I had no time to direct them to the proper persons — I left them here therefore, and thought no more about them, till on rummaging over the closet, the last two or three days, I find them encumbering the shelves. I have also multitudes of my own Orations, Addresses, Eulogies and other pamphlets for want of having distributed, when they were fresh and readable, have now got to be classed with old lumber, and with which I know not what to do — This confusion in my library, leaves me no time for my necessary correspondence, and I receive great numbers of Letters which I never answer. We have this day the account that on the trial of Alexander M'Leod at Utica, in the State of New-York, for the murder of Durfee, in December 1837 at the destruction of the Steamboat Caroline, the verdict of the jury pronounced him not guilty, and he was immediately discharged — This relieves us from all immediate danger of hostile collision with Great-Britain, but leaves the Negotiations with that Country upon the Maine boundary, the South-Sea boundary; the Slave-trade, and the seizures of our vessels on the coast of Africa, thorns to be extracted by purer and more skiful hands than are to be found in the administration of John Tyler.

———

[November 1841]
5. IV:15. Friday ≈ After breakfast, I called on Mr. Abbott Lawrence, and had an hour of conversation with him upon the electioneering politics of the day. The whig party, as they call themselves is splitting up into a thousand fragments — Mr. Lawrence is struggling to sustain it, and Rufus Choate, and Robert C. Winthrop, and Leverett Saltonstall are haranguing whig caucus-meetings throughout the State in vain to support it — The general expectation is that Marcus Morton will again be elected Governor of the Commonwealth, and that democracy will ride rough shod over the whole Country — The ambitious politicians are trimming their sails to the breeze — Webster has been spending several weeks at Marshfield, fishing, shooting, ut olim, leaving his son Fletcher to act the Secretary of State, and affecting the Stoic to the still recurring

rumours that he is to be discarded, or hoisted out of his department into some foreign mission. He has avoided and evaded all conversation with Mr. Lawrence upon the thorny questions of Bank, Tariff and negotiation with England, and Lawrence has lost all confidence in him — Caleb Cushing has taken a Lover's leap over to the Tyler territory, and makes his court (fait sa cour) to the Lady Elizabeth — This as Burke says is a curious show, but unsafe to stand upon — The prospects of the Country so far as government is concerned are dismal, but its prosperity continues unabated and increasing — God and Nature are still bountiful; but Providence as if to reserve to itself its supremacy of beneficence, and to baffle and disconcert all human exertion to promote its purpose, scattered to the winds of Heaven all the plans of improvement in the condition of the Country, by clipping the thread of Harrison's life at the very moment when he had been raised to the summit of power, and when all the hopes of a liberal administration of the National Government were concentrated upon him.

———

19. IV:5. Friday. ≈ I received last week a splendidly bound quarto bible presented to me, with an address in manuscript, fronting the title page, signed by Cinque, Kinna and Kale for the 35 Mendian Africans of the Amistad. Mr. Lewis Tappan has been extremely desirous of having this done by a public exhibition and ceremony, which I have repeatedly and inflexibly declined, from a clear conviction of its impropriety, and an invincible repugnance to exhibiting myself as a public raree show — but as in common civility, an answer was due to the present and the address, I wrote one this day to the address, and one enclosing it to Mr. Tappan. There was last night, a northern light of surpassing Splendor. This morning was clear, but the clouds were gathering all day and a copious rain came on at night.

20. IV:30. Saturday. ≈ I walked out before dinner, and called at the Office of Mr. Ellis Gray Loring, with whom I had about an hour's conversation. He is under no small concern, from apprehension upon two points at the approaching Session of Congress, one the rule, excluding the reception of all petitions, resolutions and papers relating to Slavery — And the other,

upon a revived project of annexing Texas to the United States — a project, of which formal notice has been given in newspapers devoted to the interests and aspirations of President Tyler. I look forward to both these designs with alarm and anguish — not for the power of the South which can effect nothing by itself; but from experience of the treachery of the Northern representation both to Northern interests and principles.

———

[December 1841]

18. V:30. Saturday ≈ This afternoon Mr. Leavitt, called on me with Mr. Gates, member of the house from the State of New-York — They are alarmed at numerous indications of a design to revive the project of annexing Texas to the United States. They said there was a long article in the New-York Courier and Inquirer recommending it, by arguments addressed first to the abolitionists, and then to others — And they asked if any thing could now be done to counteract this movement — I know of nothing, but to make it as soon and as extensively known as possible — There is apparently in this movement a concert of long standing between Andrew Jackson, Samuel Houston recently elected for the second time President of Texas, and Santa Anna now re-instated as President of the Mexican Confederation; and that the project is to be consummated by a cession of Texas from the Mexican to the North American confederacy. The developements of this project are not yet sufficiently clear and explicit to know how to meet and counteract it.

———

27. V:15. Monday. Mr. Leavitt brought me a New-York evangelist, a Newspaper of which he said he was formerly the editor. It contained the protest made at New-Orleans of Zephaniah C. Gifford, acting Master, and of the Officers and crew of the American brig Creole a Slave-trader, bound from Norfolk Virginia, to New-Orleans with a cargo of tobacco, and 135 slaves — On Sunday the 7th of November at 9 PM, the cargo mutinied, and after a fight in which one Slave trader and one mutineer were killed, and several others on both sides were wounded, the mutineers prevailed, and compelled the white crew to navigate the vessel into Nassau New Providence

— where 19 of the self emancipated cargo were arrested and imprisoned upon charges of mutiny and murder, and the rest were received and landed as free; except five who refused their freedom, and returned to the brig, and were landed at New-Orleans — This is a remarkable event, and will be followed by momentous consequences.

———

[January 1842]

1. IV. Saturday. This was the thirtieth New-Year's day that in the course of my life, I have passed at the city of Washington; and the 25th in succession; and of the physical atmosphere was without exception the finest of those days. One of the consequences of which was that the President's house was thronged with visitors beyond all former example. So thronged as we heard from many of those who went there, that the crowd in the house was so great that to avert the danger of suffocation, the porter at the outer door was obliged to lock out hundreds who were rushing to it for admission, and that among the excluded were both the General's Scott and Gaines — I say visitors to the house, for it is the house, and not the President who is visited — From the first establishment of the Government of the United States to this day, there never has been a time, when the personal sympathies of the people of all parties were so utterly indifferent as they are this day to John Tyler.

———

4. IV:30. Tuesday. ≈ In the house, the question of reference to a select committee of the petitions and remonstrances against the gag-rule, came up, but, by the shameless prevarications of the Speaker and of about twenty members of the northern democracy, it was laid on the table, which on the 14th of December had been refused by yeas and nays 87 to 92 — The baseness of these proceedings is too severe a trial of my temper — Oh! for restraining grace — for inflexible firmness — for untiring perseverance — for suavity of manner, and for self-controul!

———

18. V. Tuesday. ≈ At the house the day was occupied in calling the States for Petitions — The progress made was northward from Kentucky to New York — The delay was chiefly caused by the presentation of petitions — abolition, anti-slavery and for

and against the repeal of the bankrupt law. After much desultory discussion, these last were all referred to the Committee on the judiciary. The abolition petitions which came within the gag-rule were all quietly excluded; and every anti-slavery petition which could not be disposed of thus, when presented. Wise, Hopkins, and Campbell of South-Carolina, interchangeably, move the question of reception, and then move to lay that question of reception on the table — The yeas and nays were taken several times, and the vote to lay on the table always prevailed. At last Granger presented a petition praying Congress to secure by Law to the free citizens of the United States, the benefits of the Post-Office — The question of reception, and the motion to lay on the table followed and Granger called for the yeas and nays — This question brought the practice of excluding petitions one step beyond all former precedent and Mallory of Virginia moved to adjourn, though it was but just after 3 O'Clock. The adjournment was carried by Tellers — Joseph R. Ingersoll succeeded in getting sundry petitions against the repeal of the Bankrupt act, referred to the Committee on the judiciary, referred with instructions to enquire into the expediency of reporting a bankrupt bill free from the defects and supplying the deficiencies of the one just repealed — Sundry other Resolutions were offered, but objected against and not received — Mr. Augustus Young a member of the house from Vermont and Mr. Whitcomb, now a clerk in the Treasury Department, spent the Evening with me, in general conversation upon political subjects. Mr. Young feels deeply the degradation of the free and especially the eastern portion of the Union, by subserviency to the insolent domination of the Southern, slave-traders and slave-breeders; but he sees and I see no prospect of breaking the yoke in my life-time.

———

21. III:15–IV:15. Friday ≈ I presented a petition from sundry citizens of Massachusetts praying that the benefits of the naturalization Laws may be extended to persons of colour — Wise made objection to its reception and moved to lay his own objection on the table, carried by yeas and nays 116 to 68 — A Petition to Congress to secure to each of the States a Republican Government was in like manner laid on the table — A

Resolution of a Pennsylvania Anti-Slavery Society against a War with England to hold native Americans in Slavery — Wise objected to this as not *presentable*, because it was not a petition, but the Speaker overruled that. He then attempted to prevent me from reading it; but did not succeed in that — but it was laid on the table — I finally presented the petition from Georgia for my own removal from the Office of chairman of the Committee of foreign relations, and demanded to be heard in my own defence which produced a fractious debate, which was cut off after 4 O'Clock, by the adjournment of the house — Marshall of Kentucky had moved that I should have leave to be heard in my own defence — Wise moved to lay the motion on the table — rejected 82 to 84. The whole subject laid on the table 94 to 92.

———

24. IV:45. Monday ≈ At the house the curious decision of the house on Saturday, sustaining the Speaker in pronouncing me out of order, upon a point made by Rayner, which the Speaker himself said was not the point decided by him came up — I claimed the right to proceed; but the house by yeas and nays decided that I should not. This arbitrary decision was no sooner announced than Wise started up and swaggeringly said — and now is *my* turn! and he demanded to be heard in defence of himself against charges, which he pretended I had made against *him* — The rabid democrats of the north were all for allowing him, but his motion was finally laid on the table — by yeas and nays 101 to 78, and most of those who voted for silencing me voted also against silencing him. I then renewed the motion to refer the petition to the Committee with instructions to choose a chairman if they think proper — debate arising thereon it was laid over; and I presented sundry other petitions — One from Benjamin Emerson and 45 others of Haverhill, Massachusetts, praying Congress, to take measures for peaceably dissolving the Union with an assignment of three reasons — I moved its reference to a select Committee with instructions to report an answer assigning the reasons why the prayer of the petition ought not to be granted — Then came another explosion, and after snarling debate a Resolution offered by Thomas W. Gilmer, that I deserved the censure of the house, for presenting a petition praying for the dissolution of

the Union — Hot debate arose upon this, in the midst of which the house adjourned. ≈ Walk home — Evening in meditation.

25. IV:30. Tuesday. ≈ At one Gilmer's resolution of censure upon me was taken up — Thomas F. Marshall offered a much more violent one with a flaming preamble charging me in substance with subornation of perjury and high treason; and resolutions that the house might well expel me, but would only pass upon me the sentence of their highest indignation, and turn me over for the rest to my own conscience and the contempt of the world — The Speaker received this Resolution, and when Marshall finished his speech in support of it called upon me for my answer to it, and said the question would be on the adoption of the Resolution — I said I thought it impossible the house should entertain the Resolution and after a few remarks postponing my defence till it should be ascertained that I stand accused, I finished and was followed by Henry A. Wise [who] in a speech of personal invective upon me, took nearly two hours, and then at the motion of his colleague Hopkins, the house adjourned ≈

26. III–IV:15. Attended this morning the Committee on the Smithsonian bequest. Present Adams, Underwood, Houston, Randall and Truman Smith — The Documents requested from the Secretary of the Treasury had not been received — The Committee sat about half an hour and then adjourned — After which Mr. Habersham came in — Absent, Charles J. Ingersoll, Hunter, and Bowne — I am convinced that nothing will be done of any use by this Committee. In the house, Fillmore made an attempt to take up the Treasury Note-bill, returned from the Senate with an amendment striking out Gilmer's additional section; but Wise objected the question of privilege — I addressed the Speaker referring to the Letter from Wise from which I was reading —— Wise resumed his philippic against me, and kept it up about three hours before he finished — I then said that I had determined not to interrupt him till he had disgorged his whole cargo of filthy invective, but I thought it impossible that the house should entertain the resolution which charged me with subornation of perjury and consequential high treason — crimes for which I could

only be tried by a regular circuit Court, by an impartial jury — and I claimed the benefit of the sixth Article Amendatory to the Constitution of the United States — The Speaker required me to reduce my point of order to writing which I did, and congratulated the Speaker upon his discovery of the expediency of having points of order reduced to writing, a favour which he had repeatedly denied to me — He said it was a power exclusively possessed by the Speaker. But that my demand was a question not for him to decide but for the house. I then addressed the house and denied their power to try me for the crimes with which I was charged, and that they had no right to assume the guilt without allowing me the privilege of a trial — And as to the Resolution itself I denied the right of at least one hundred members of the house, to sit in judgment upon me, their personal and pecuniary interest in the question carrying such a bias against me, as would make them challengeable as jurors in a Court of Law. Marshall replied, by a County-court subterfuge of argument that the charges of subornation, of perjury and consequential high Treason were not against me, but against the petitioners; and he argued that I might be punished for the contempt of the house, although for the same crime I might be tried by the judicial tribunals of the Country. — Fillmore finally moved to lay the whole subject on the table which was rejected by a vote of 90 to 100, and the house adjourned ≈

27. IV:30. Thursday. ≈ Mr. Weld came with a kind offer of assistance, in the search of documents, books or papers. Francis W. Wilcox is brother to a clerk in one of the Departments who wrote and published a book about Slavery. He had a new tricksy folio general Atlas, a copy of which he wanted me to buy, but I declined. Mr. Weld spoke of the temper of the people here, highly excited against me, by these motions of censure upon me, and the inflammatory harangues of Wise and Marshall against me; but he said he thought the tide was turning in my favour. ≈

28. Friday. IV. Mr. Weld was again here, and undertook to mark the passages in Marshall's life of Washington, recounting the charge against him of being under English influence — At

the house, immediately after the reading of the journal Fillmore enquired of the Speaker what was the business before the house, and was answered that it was the question of privilege, on my trial. Lewis Williams moved a call of the house, which was carried and pursued until 201 members answered to their names, after which the call was superseded — The question was upon the motion of Richard W. Thompson of Indiana, to lay Marshall's Resolutions of censure upon me, on the table — Marshall now with intense importunity, urged Thompson to withdraw his motion, to give Marshall the opportunity to explain and to justify himself, that Thompson after much struggling yielded upon condition that Marshall after delivering his few words, would renew the motion to lay the whole subject on the table — Marshall then commenced a violent declamatory and most eloquent philippic of nearly two hours against me — He laboured with agonizing energy to answer the speeches of Underwood and of Botts delivered yesterday and was particularly resentful against Underwood — I interrupted him occasionally to rectify gross misrepresentations of facts, and sometimes to provoke him into absurdity; as for example at one part of his speech that the northern abolitionists knew nothing about the condition of the Slaves he assumed a courteous tone, and invited me to visit the western Country — "To be lynched?" said I — "very likely" — said he and proceeded — When he closed he renewed according to his pledge to Thompson, the motion to lay the whole subject on the table, but said he earnestly hoped it would not prevail; and voted against it — when the roll was called upon the question to lay on the table Botts rose, and asked if I wished to reply to Marshall; I said I would not be responsible for the consumption of one hour of time upon concerns merely personal to me — That Marshall had occupied two hours in a personal invective upon me found upon principles totally unfounded and unjust. Here I was stopped by calls to order and not allowed to answer the question — The motion to lay on the table was rejected by yeas and nays 96 to 110, and I arose to make my defence. Gilmer interrupted me to enquire whether he could not have an opportunity to make a speech in support of *his* resolutions of censure — The Speaker said he would unless the whole subject should be laid on the table or the previous question taken. Gilmer then apologized to me for interrupting me, and I entered upon my defence. I was soon interrupted by Wise to defend himself for his share in the Cilley duel, and challenged him to name any colleague of mine who ever told him that I had defended at a public meeting his innocence in that affair. He said there were two or three of them, they were now present — he would not name them, but leave them to answer for themselves — and a dead silence followed — I caused to be read at the Clerk's table extracts from the report of the majority of the Committee, on the Cilley duel case, and from the minority report of Elmore in the same case. It was now past 4 O'Clock, and [at] the request of Botts and many others I yielded the floor to him for a motion to adjourn which he made and it was carried — I came home to a sick family, and to musings for the further defence of myself against this persecution.

29. V. Saturday. Mr. Choate, one of the Senators from Massachusetts came this morning, and offered me any assistance that it might be in his power to render me, in my present strait; for which I thanked him and may perhaps avail myself of his offer — My means of defence requiring searches of books and documents, multiplying upon me as I proceed — At the House Fillmore moved with my consent that the question of privilege should be suspended to take up the amendments of the Senate to the Treasury Note Bill — I said I consented because I would not be answerable for one moment of time consumed on matters merely personal to me. Joseph R. Ingersoll offered a Resolution to suspend my trial, to afford me time to obtain information necessary for my defence. 2 — To instruct the Committee on the judiciary to consult and report upon precedents applicable to the case — The Resolutions were objected to by Mallory and others — But Fillmore's motion to take up the Treasury Note bill finally prevailed against the earnest remonstrances of Sprigg of Kentucky who when it was taken up made a two hours Speech against it — Stanly then moved the previous question. Roosevelt then made a question of privilege that the amendment of the Senate made it a bill for raising revenue which it was not when it went from the house; and that the Senate could not convert an ordinary bill into a

revenue bill, because all bills to raise revenue must originate in the house. The Speaker overruled this objection — Roosevelt appealed from the decision which was sustained by the house 112 to 73 — and immediately afterwards Atherton repeated it as a point of order. — The Speaker again overruled it — Atherton again appealed and again the Speaker's decision was again sustained 117 to 76 — Hopkins moved to lay the Bill on the table — Rejected by yeas and nays 96 to 101 — The final question of concurring with the Senate, in striking out Gilmer's section, was carried by a tie 100 to 100 and the casting vote of the Speaker. I was deeply fearful that a reconsideration would be moved; but it was not and the bill was passed. Fillmore moved immediately to adjourn, but Nathaniel G. Pendleton of Cincinnati Ohio, started up with a Resolution as a substitute for Marshall's Resolution of censure upon me. Pendleton's Resolution was a frothy declaration of abhorrence of a petition for the dissolution of the Union — That the petition was presented by me, and that it be not received. Proffit and Mallory two of the most inveterate of my persecutors, objected to receiving Pendleton's motion — Nothing but the vengeful malignity of Marshall's Resolution will satisfy them, and yet Proffit to throw me off my guard said to me that there would be a majority of fifty against Marshall's Resolution in the house.

———

31. VII:15. Monday. The pressure upon my mind in the preparation for my defence is so great that for several successive nights I have had little sleep ≈

Day — My occupations during the month have been confined entirely to the business of the house, and for the last ten days to the defence of myself against an extensive combination and conspiracy in and out of Congress to crush the liberties of the free people of this Union, by disgracing me, with a brand of censure, and displacing me from the Chair of the Committee of foreign affairs, for my perseverance in presenting abolition petitions. I am in the midst of that fiery ordeal, and day and night are absorbed in the struggle to avert my ruin — God send me a good deliverance!

———

[February 1842]
3. IV:30. Thursday. ≈ Gilmer consumed nearly two hours in his

long meditated and bitterly rancorous speech against me —
when he closed, Cushing started up, but the Speaker said I was
entitled to the floor in my own defence. I spoke accordingly
about an hour and a half; and brought to light the conspiracy
among the Southern Members of the Committee of foreign
Affairs to displace me as Chairman, and to elect Cushing in my
stead — I produced the anonymous letter from Jackson N. C.
20 Jan'y 1842 threatening me with assassination; and the engraved portrait of me, with the mark of a rifle ball on the
forehead, with the motto to stop the music of John Quincy
Adams 6th President of the United States

> who in the space of one revolving moon
> Is statesman, poet, babbler and buffoon —

These were Gilmer's own words excepting the word fiddler
which his echo changed to babbler — I produced also, and
read the minutes of the proceedings in the Committee of foreign Affairs — I reviewed my relations with the Virginian
Presidents of the United States heretofore Washington, Jefferson, Madison, Monroe, and contrasted them with this base
conspiracy of three Virginians banded here, together with numerous accomplices in and out of the house for my destruction. Near four O'Clock, I closed for the day, with an apt
quotation from Moore's Love's of the Angels, and came home
very much exhausted.

4. V. Friday. I occupied the whole of this day in continuing my
defence before the house — I began by renewing the charge
upon Gilmer of having tampered with my colleague Cushing
by the offer to choose him chairman of the Committee of
Foreign Affairs in my place. He denied it positively, and called
upon Cushing as positively to deny it; which with no small
blustering he did — I then called upon Cushing to say who it
was that had made the overture to him, which after some
shuffling he declined to do, upon the pretence of not revealing
private conversation but R. B. Rhett was forced to come out
and acknowledge that *he* was the man, who on the same day
when Gilmer gave notice in the house that he should move in
Committee to chuse another Chairman, went to Cushing, and
told him that they would elect him chairman in my place.

Cushing repelled the advance, and said he would not serve, and intreated Proffit to dissuade them from the attempt which he did for two days, without success — After bringing out all this, I returned to the Haverhill petition — and to the external conspiracy against me. To the Gilmer and Marshall Resolutions of Censure, and the intervening Southern Caucus, I brought out Triplett to acknowledge that he called the Caucus; Marshall that his resolutions had been submitted to them, and that there were forty members and more at the Caucus — I paid my tribute of thanks to Lot Warren of Georgia for his manly Declaration of yesterday, that he would give no countenance whatever to these proceedings against me, and I returned with warm acknowledgments the kindness of the members from Kentucky, Maryland and Virginia who have refused to join in this conspiracy against me, and I charged the Newspapers of this City and District, with injustice to me; the Globe being daily filled with abuse, and invective upon me, while I am here on my trial; and the reporters of the intelligencer suppressing the most essential parts of my defence. I specially refuted the pretence that the Union could be dissolved only by force, and cited the example of the peaceable dissolution of the confederation Union, by the present Constitution of the United States ≈

5. V:15. Saturday. No report of my yesterday's speech in the National Intelligencer; but a blustering Notification that as I have chosen to complain of their reporters, they will report no more, without my own authority. This is a mere subterfuge, to suppress the publication of my defence, and the exposure which I made of the conspiracy in and out of the house against me — I read the paragraph in this morning's Intelligencer merely stating that I had continued my defence, and the sturdy notification that [they] would report nothing further, unless furnished by myself and I commented freely upon them, as proof demonstrative of the servile submission of the Press in this District to the Slave tyranny of the South — And I requested a postponement of further proceedings on my trial till next Thursday week for time to receive answers to my calls on the executive Departments, and to prepare for my defence so that it may be reported without delay — Marshall made a

bitter and spiteful speech against the postponement; and Arnold moved the previous question upon the Resolutions. I saw that would cut me off from all further defence, and preferred going on at once. Arnold at my request withdrew his motion for the previous question. I withdrew mine for postponement and proceeded. I was not well prepared; having expected that there would be no opposition to my motion for a postponement; but I found no lack of matter for discourse till the motion between 3 and 4 for adjournment which was carried — My last missile upon Marshall, was an exquisite blast upon Slavery, by himself in his pamphlet Letters to the Commonwealth Newspaper in Kentucky; which pamphlet he himself had given me some weeks since. He writhed under it in agony. Before I had read the extract half through, Romulus M. Saunders started up on a point of order on the old pretence that I had no right to discuss the subject of Slavery. The Speaker ruled the point against him. He appealed and demanded the yeas and nays which were refused and the decision of the speaker sustained 97 to 25. I saw my cause was gained and Marshall was sprawling in his own compost. I came home scarcely able to crawl up to my chamber, but with the sound of Io triumphe! ringing in my ear — Doctor Frye dined with us, and Miss Cutts was here this Evening — Marshall sent to me and demanded the return of his pamphlet.

6. IV:30. Sunday ≈ My attention, morning and afternoon involuntarily wandered from the preachers and their discourses to the critical nature of my own position, confident of my deliverance from this particular assault upon me, so senseless, that its malignity merges by its stupidity, not into innocence but into harmlessness, but always distrustful of my own controul over my own Spirit — One hundred members of the house, represent Slaves, four fifths of whom would crucify me, if their votes could erect the cross — forty members representatives of the free in the league of Slavery and mock democracy, would break me on the wheel if their votes or wishes could turn it round — And four fifths of the other hundred and twenty are either so cold or so lukewarm, that they are ready to desert me at the very first scintillation of indiscretion

on my part. The only formidable danger with which I am beset is that of my own temper ≈

7. V. Monday. Mr. Weld was here this morning with a cheering report of the impression of my defence of Thursday Friday and Saturday, upon the current of popular opinion out of the house — A Mr. Dorsey, a Stranger, brought me a document which he supposed might be useful to me, in my defence — and Robert Reeves the Scotch ex-custodian of the Treasury building came and took back his manuscript dialogue between a Calvinist and an Arminian which he had lent me to read, and in which he is sure that he has definitively settled the knotty problem of pre-destination and free will. I prepared a minute of the outlines of the continuance and conclusion of my defence, which would have occupied at least a week — But I saw on Saturday that the house was tired of the whole subject; and that to close it now would afford relief to all parties. I went to the house therefore prepared to proceed; but willing to stop short and dismiss the subject from the consideration of the house forever. I was be-lated, and the house had been about ten minutes in session when I entered and took my Seat — Other business was under consideration, but the question of privilege, or my trial was soon called up. I then observed that having perceived on Saturday some impatience on the part of the House to get rid of this subject, and persevering in the determination not to be respon-sible for one hour of time unnecessarily consumed on this sub-ject, if the house was ready to lay it on the table forever, I would acquiesce in that decision without requiring further time for my defence; of which I should need much, if required to proceed — Botts then moved to lay the whole subject on the table for-ever, carried by yeas and nays 106 to 93. Meriwether of Georgia, asked to be excused from voting because he hotly lusted for a vote of the severest censure upon me, but despaired of obtaining it. The house refused to excuse him, and he voted to lay on the table the whole subject. They then took in hand the Haverhill petition and refused to receive it 166 to 40 — Briggs, Baker, Cushing, and Hudson voting with the majority — I then pro-ceeded with my budget of which I presented nearly two hun-dred; till the house adjourned — Most of them were excluded by the rule, or laid on the table by objections to their reception

— And thus ended the second prosecution of me, by the despotic process of contempt. D. D. Barnard offered sundry Resolutions denouncing this prosecution in its true character, but they were not in order, nor received by the house.

———

17. V:15. Thursday. Mr. Angier rode with me this morning to the Capitol. I introduced him into the Library of Congress, and to the Librarian Meehan — And I went with him to the room where the Supreme Court of the United States were in Session — This room I re-entered with a silent thrill of delight; for the first time, since I was there at this time last year, under such an heavy pressure of responsibility, and with so glorious a result! I dare not trust myself with the exultation of my own heart on this occasion, so fearful I am of incurring the guilt of presumptuous vanity, for the feeling of deep humility.

———

[March 1842]
3. VI:15. Thursday ≈ Mr. Giddings came, and to my satisfaction somewhat abridged the Monday lecture against capital punishment. He came to enquire the precise extent to which I hold the subject of Slavery in the States subject to the jurisdiction of the National Government, and I explained it to him. In the case of a servile War involving the free States of the Union, the question of emancipation would necessarily be the issue of the conflict — All war must end in peace, and peace must be concluded by Treaty — Of such a Treaty, partial or universal emancipation would probly form an essential, and the power of the President and Senate of the U.S. over it would be co-extensive with the War.

———

10. IV:30. Thursday. ≈ Mr. Nathaniel Tallmadge one of the Senators from New-York came into the house with Charles Dickens and called me out from my seat and introduced him to me — I dined with Robert C. Winthrop and John P. Kennedy — They went expressly to Dickens's lodgings at Fuller's to prevail on him to come and dine with them; but he was at dinner and they did not see him.

———

14. VI. Monday. ≈ Dinner at Boulanger's to Charles Dickens; to which I was invited by Aaron Ward. G. M. Keim presided. Mr.

St. C. Clarke Vice-President — I. E. Holmes — Sutton a Reporter — Roosevelt — French — Robert Tyler — Toasts — Speeches. Songs — It was near Midnight when I came home.

---

19. V:30. Saturday. ≈ The Meeting of the Committee on the Smithsonian bequest was fixed for 10 this morning, but it was 11 when I reached the chamber of the Committee and found there, Underwood, Habersham, Truman Smith, Benjamin Randall and Charles J. Ingersoll — Absent Bowne, Houston and Hunter. Of my tardiness, I failed not to be reminded — We took up the old bill, and debated it from the third to the sixth Section inclusive. Every provision, of every section was contested; and the only sound principle settled was that the principal sum of the bequest should be preserved unimpaired as a perpetual fund, from which no appropriation shall be made — Habersham of Georgia opposed the parts of the Bill providing for the establishment of an Astronomical Observatory — His argument was the danger and difficulty of carrying it through Congress — And he said that only yesterday one of the members from the South urged in conversation with him that Congress had no constitutional power to accept the bequest, and that the money ought to be sent back to England. I saw the finger of John C. Calhoun and of nullification; and said that the objection against the power of Congress to accept the bequest would not be removed, by striking out the observatory — That Mr. Calhoun and his co-adjutors had urged it from the beginning and it had been time after time settled against them — That any application of the fund to the purposes of the testator would be resisted by them, and if any thing was to be done it must be carried against their stubborn opposition.

---

21. IV:30. Monday. ≈ In the call for Resolutions, Andrews of Kentucky moved an inquiry of the President and heads of Departments for the names of all the members of Congress who have applied for offices by themselves or their friends, of the 25th or 26th Congresses; and specifying the office applied for in each case — Giddings of Ohio offered a series of resolutions relating to Slavery and the Creole case — Ward, moved the previous question. Everett moved to lay them on the table

— lost by yeas and nays 52 to 128 — Everett moved a call of the house, refused — After much turbulence and confusion, Giddings withdrew the Resolutions. Botts then moved a suspension of the rules to offer a Preamble and Resolution of censure upon Giddings, yeas 128 nays 68 not two thirds. Weller of Ohio then offered the same resolution it being still the turn of the State, and he moved the previous question — The question whether Giddings should be heard in his defence was unsettled at the adjournment.

22. V:30. Tuesday. ≈ In the house the resolution of censure upon Giddings, with a preamble, first moved yesterday by Botts, then moved by Weller, moving at the same time the previous question was taken up, and after two full hours of twistings, decisions by the Speaker, reversed by the house, motions that he should have permission to be heard in his defence, by reconsideration; by suspension of the rules, by general consent the resolution of censure was actually passed by yeas and nays 125 to 69. And then the preamble was adopted 119 to 66 — I can find no language to express my feelings at the consummation of this act — Immediately after the second vote, Giddings rose from his seat, came over to mine; shook cordially my hand; and took leave — I had a voice only to say — I hope we shall soon have you back again. He made no reply, but passed to the seats of other members, his friends, and took leave of them as he had done of me — I saw him shake hands with Arnold, who voted against him. He then left the house, and this evening the City.

———

26. V:30. Saturday. Mr. Sprague and Mr. Robbins called on me this morning, and said they were desirous of having some conversation, concerning the duties on cordage to be fixed on the revisal of the Tariff. But the conversation immediately became general concerning the present aspect of affairs in Congress and in the Country, which is deplorable. I told them that Slavery, the support, the perpetuation, and the propagation of Slavery was at the root of the whole system of policy of the present administration — That an essential part of this system was hostility to the manufactures, and to the free labour of the North — That this Spirit, in alliance with the mock democracy

of the free States exercises now absolute controul over the majority of both houses of Congress, and if unable to carry all its purposes into execution now, will at least defeat every measure which could contribute to promote the manufacturing interest or the domestic industry of free labour.

———

[April 1842]
3. V:45 Sunday. ≈ As we were returning home we met a carriage laden with two travelling trunks; part of the baggage of Lord Ashburton, once Alexander Baring, who arrived last Evening in the Warspite from England — whence he now comes as Envoy Extraordinary and Minister Plenipotentiary upon a special mission.

———

[May 1842]
5. V. Thursday. Morning visit from Mr. Lay who has been recently appointed Chargé d'Affaires, to Sweden, but complains much of ill treatment from Mr. Webster ≈ Next came Mr. Joshua Leavitt with the gratifying intelligence that Joshua R. Giddings was here — re-elected by a majority of upwar[d]s of 3000 of his old constituents of the 16ᵗʰ Congressional District of Ohio.

———

11. V. Wednesday. Mr. Giddings had yesterday requested an interview with me at my house this morning to which I had agreed and he came. He said that the army appropriation bill would shortly come up for the consideration of the house. There was an item of appropriation in it of 100 000 dollars for the prosecution of the War in Florida, which he thought should be struck out — Mr. Slade with whom he had conversed upon the subject, was of the same opinion; and they had thought it best to consult with me, concerning the expediency of making the motion. I said I concurred entirely in the opinion that the item ought to be struck out, but I was not sure that it would be advisable at the present time to make the motion — It would undoubtedly breed a tempest — The whole system of policy of the Country, foreign and domestic, War and Peace, Slavery and the Slave-trade would be opened for debate on this motion, and the public feeling on this topic was so lukewarm, and so perverted even in the free States, that

I could not ward off the doubt of the expediency of agitating it at-all, by starting the game ourselves.

———

21. V. Saturday. The chill North-easter continues; but this day without rain — I wrote lines in the album of Anna Payne, Mrs. Madison's niece — and in the Boston Mercantile Journal, edited by a man characteristically named Sleeper Mr. G. Brown has published with a puff, my paraphrase of the 1st and 2^{d} verses of the 61st chapter of Isaiah written at his request. Not a day passes but I receive Letters from the North and sometimes the West asking for an autograph, and a scrap of poetry or of prose, and from the South almost daily Letters of insult, profane obscenity and filth — These are indexes to the various estimation in which I am held in the free and servile sections of this Union. Indexes to the moral sensibilities of free, and of Slavery tainted communities. Threats of Lynching and Assassination, are the natural offspring of Slave-breeders and Slave-traders — profanity and obscenity are their natural associates; — such dross the fire must purge — But the perpetual calls for autographs and Album scraps, are scarcely less annoying in another way — They set in motion the rhyming maggot in my brain and breed swarms of May-flies as prolific as the dead herrings that line the banks of the Potomac.

———

[June 1842]
12. V:45. Sunday. The party at the President's house last evening consisted of about 100 persons, invited by Mrs. Robert Tyler. Mrs. Madison, with her niece Anna Payne, my family and my self, and all the remnants of President Monroe's family — The bride, Mrs. Heiskell being the only surviving grandchild of Mr. Monroe — There was dancing in the now gorgeously furnished East room, and an elegant supper — The courtesies of the President and of Mrs. R. Tyler to their guests, were all that the most accomplished European Court could have displayed — The President led the bride into the supper table, and requested me to escort Mrs. Robert Tyler. Lord Ashburton followed with Mrs. Madison, and Mr. Webster the Secretary of State with my wife — After supper I had a long conversation with Lord Ashburton; and went into the room, where Mr. Healy is copying the full length portrait of President

Washington and where the portrait of Mr. Guizot painted by him, is deposited. He has also the President's daughter Alice, painted by him. — It was within 5 minutes within of midnight when we came home.

———

18. V:45 Saturday. ≈ At the House Edward T. White by an explosion of indignant eloquence, and a suspension of the rules, introduced and drove through by a headlong impulse a bill taking away the power of holding to bail on mesne process a debtor unless upon affidavit of the debt by the creditor — He declaimed about Liberty and the natural, inalienable rights of man, as if there was not a Slave in his State or in this District — If I had said one word about Slavery I should have had the whole pack of Southern Doulocracy and Northern Servility upon me; produced merely a brawl, and been branded as a firebrand, in my own land of the pilgrims — I retired in utter disgust without the bar, and suffered this paroxism of frenzy for the rights of man, to liberate one Louisiana constituent of Edward D. White, from imprisonment for want of bail, leaving six thousand Slaves to drag their lengthened chain for life, and as inheritance for their children forever.

———

[August 1842]

19. II. IV:30. Friday. I was roused twice in the Night by severe cramp in the legs, and feel that my body and mind are rapidly falling into decay. The position that I have taken is arduous enough to crush any man in the vigour of youth; but at 75 with failing senses, and blunted instruments, surrounded by remorseless enemies and false and scary and treacherous friends, how can it end but in my ruin? — But I must meet the shock.

———

[September 1842]

1. V:15. Thursday. ≈ I called at the Treasury Department — The Secretary, Mr. Walter Forward has been several weeks absent, at the Bedford Springs, convalescent from a bilious fever — I read from the National Intelligencer, and the Globe the reports of the passage through the house of the joint resolution from the Senate appropriating 6000 dollars for the expense of liberating Citizens of the United States, from Mexican captivity taken as Texan prisoners of War, in the expedition against Santa

Fé last Summer; and desired him particularly to mark my earnest and repeated remonstrances against it, as unconstitutional. I said I knew not whether the President had signed the resolution or not, but I objected to the drawing of any money from the Treasury under its authority — I requested Mr. M'Clintock Young the Chief Clerk to inform the President of my objection; and to say that I wished to give no unnecessary trouble to the Department, or notoriety to the transaction, and would be satisfied with an assurance that no money should be drawn from the Treasury upon this resolution before the next Session — but I should otherwise address and publish a Letter to the Secretary of the Treasury on the subject. ≈

2. V:15. Friday. My mind is in the condition of a ship at Sea in a hurricane suspended by an instantaneous calm. The brain heaves. — The head swims — The body totters, and I live in a perpetual Waltz — The presentiment of a sudden termination to my life is rather cheering to me, than painful, and a man conscious of no sin upon his Soul, which repentant tears could wash out, may wash out, can dispense with the deprecation of the episcopal litany against sudden death — The apprehension however of such a close to my life ought to, and does admonish me to set my house in order, to be prepared as much as a prudent forecast can provide for whatever event may by the will of God befall me — I see my duty, but I procrastinate — I had determined to devote the interval between the Session of Congress just closed and the next, in all probability the last I shall ever attend, in settling all my private concerns so that I may be ready for the summons at a minute's notice to appear before my maker, but I have not felt myself at liberty to decline engagements to attend two public meetings in my own district, and to address them; and last Evening I received a Letter from Dutee J. Pearce of Newport, Rhode-Island indicted for Treason against the State soliciting my aid in his defence — I could not hesitate an instant to undertake it, though it comes upon me like a thunder-clap — No one can imagine what I suffered, when I engaged to defend before the Supreme Court of the United States the lives and liberty of 36 Africans of the Amistad, nor with what gratitude to heaven, I heard the decision of the Court pronouncing them free — And with what

delight I dwelt upon the confident hope that it was the last occasion upon which I should ever be called to stake my personal, moral, intellectual and political character upon issues involving the lives, fortunes, and characters of others as well as my own — I have now on hand a controversial warfare with John Tyler President of the United States; bitter personal hatred of five of the most depraved, most talented, and most influential men of this Country, four of them open and undisguised — C. J. Ingersoll, Wise, T. F. Marshall, and W. Cost Johnson; the fifth under a mask — nameless. — And now, this trial for Treason — which will be at least as much a trial of me as of Pearce himself — The Mercy of God is the only anchor of my Soul for deliverance from this ordeal.

———

5. V. Monday. ≈ I received this day an impertinent Letter from Fletcher Webster, bloated with self-sufficiency as an Executive Officer, maintaining that an appropriation by Resolution is quite as proper and valid as if made by Law, and that he has already made the requisition at the Department of the Treasury for the 6000 dollars appropriated by the Resolution. Fletcher Webster, the first exploit of whose manhood was to debauch and get with child his own cousin under the desecrated protection of his father's roof is by that same father's appointment chief clerk and now acting Secretary of the Department of State, strutting about with all the insolence of Office, and blundering on with all the ignorance of an unschooled boy — He says in his Letter that there are numerous precedents of this course — I answered him this Evening, and called for a specification of his numerous precedents — I went also to the Capitol, and examined the journal of the Senate; and traced up the fraud to the South-Carolina Senator, W. C. Preston, connived at by George Evans, Chairman of their Committee of finance — as arrant a piece of sheer knavery, as ever was perpetrated at East-cheap or found its reward at Tyburn. And Preston and Evans are two of the ablest men, and most efficient whigs in Congress. ≈

6. V:30. Tuesday. ≈ I received this day from Fletcher Webster a reply to my answer as impertinent, as ignorant and as insolent

as the former; — Into what hands have the Presidency, the Departments of State and of the Treasury fallen! ≈

7. IV. Wednesday. From short as usual and disturb'd repose I was up this morning at 4 O'Clock, and after the final preparations for departure, My wife, my Son John's widow Mary Catherine, her daughter Mary-Louisa, Walter Hellen, Mrs. John Adams's half brother, and Miss Mary Estelle Elizabeth Cutts at precisely six O'Clock took seats in the Rail-road Cars for Baltimore — The weather warm but pleasant — Among our fellow travellers not more than 30 was Robert Tyler the President's son, who cold spoke to the Ladies with me, but upon enquiry of some one whether he had spoken to me, answered no, because I had abused his father. Captain Tyler's two sons, are to him, what nephews have usually been to the Pope — and among his minor vices is nepotism — He has quartered both of them upon the public for salaries, and made old Cooper, the broken down stage-player, father of his Son Robert's wife, a military store keeper — The son John was so distended with his dignity as Secretary that he had engraved on his visiting cards "John Tyler jun'r Private and confidential Secretary of his Excellency John Tyler, President of the United States." Robert is as confidential as John, and both of them divulged all his cabinet secrets to a man named Parmelee and John Howard Payne, hired Reporters for Bennett's Herald Newspaper at New-York, who by their intimacy with these upstart Princes crept into the familiarity of domestic inmates at the President's House.

———

[October 1842]
9. III:45. Sunday. ≈ Mr. Lunt preached, this forenoon from Psalm 57:6 "Behold, thou desirest truth in the inward parts" — It was a funeral discourse on the decease of Dr. William Ellery Channing, and a noble tribute of honour to his Memory. — He spoke in general terms of his early writings, and of the general character of his mind and of his compositions. He was one of the most eminent writers upon religion, morals and politics that this country has produced — Writing always in the genuine spirit of Christianity, with the tenderness of a

father to his children; and always looking to the improvement and purification of the human character, especially in the humbler and indigent classes of the community — His recent labours have been chiefly confined to promoting the cause of universal liberty, and the extinction of Slavery and the Slave-trade throughout the Earth — Mr. Lunt did him ample justice on this point. He gave a short extract from the last Address delivered at Lenox on the first day of last August and spoke of it in terms of enthusiastic applause — This was very creditable to Mr. Lunt, inasmuch as Dr. Channing's course has on this subject been too bold and anti-servile for the timid and the time-serving friends of freedom — Dr. Channing never flinched or quailed before the enemy — But he was deserted by many of his followers, and lost so many of his parishioners that he had yielded to his colleague E. S. Gannett, the whole care of his pastoral office, giving up all claim to salary, and reserving only the privilege of occasionally preaching to them at his convenience. The loss of Dr. Channing to the anti-slavery cause is irreparable.

———

24. V. Monday. ≈ Just before dinner, five very respectably looking men of colour, three negroes and two light mulattos, came as a delegation from a meeting of the People of colour in Boston, at which they told me, upwards of 500 persons were present, to solicit me, to act as council in behalf of George Latimer, arrested and claimed as a slave, by James B. Gray of Norfolk, Virginia — They delivered to me, a Letter from S. E. Sewall, and Amos Binney Merrill, lawyers of Boston engaged as counsel for Latimer, recommending to me them and the object of their mission. I answered them, expressing my grateful sensibility to the coloured people of Boston, for this mark of their confidence in me, and said I would cheerfully comply with their invitation, if I were still in the practice of the Law — but that for more than 30 years, I had been withdrawn from it by other occupations, and except in one instance about 2 years ago, when I argued before the Supreme Court of the United States the Cause of the captive Africans of the Amistad, I had never resumed the practice — I had now one contingent engagement to defend Mr. Dutee J. Pearce upon an Indictment against him for Treason, but I hoped he would not be

tried at all — This too was a very extraordinary occasion, and upon no other should I feel myself justified in attempting to address a Court and Jury. But they might say to Mr. Sewall, and Mr. Merrill that if any point of Law should occur upon which they might think that my opinion could be of an[y] service to their client I would cheerfully give it at their request — They asked me to write a word of answer to Mess'rs Sewall and Merrill, which I promised to do and did.

———

[November 1842]

7. IV:30. Monday. ≈ I finally made out to take the 14ᵗʰ quarto volume of my diary to Mr. Gill the book-binder to be bound. But I have not been able to assort about 50 volumes of loose pamphlets which incumber my rooms. — I added to the volume sundry fragments, for I have found it impossible to keep my diary unbroken — Since 1 June 1839, there is no chasm; a page a day and rarely two pages have been my continual task: but the keeping of a diary that I would recommend would be Quarto volumes of one size, of 500 pages each — every page divided by two red lines into 3 equal parts — The entries to be made in abridged style and form of memoranda — never to exceed or fall short of one third of a page — Each volume to contain the record of 4 years — In 60 years this would make 15 volumes of 500 pages each — quite enough for the autobiography of one man. — I have already more volumes and multitudes of fragments — Trash inexpressible which I pray to God may never be exposed; but which I leave to my Son to be used according to his good judgment for a memoir of my life; and if by the Mercy of God, the manuscripts should be preserved, to be left with those of my father to one of my grandsons who may be worthy of possessing and passing them down to future generations.

———

12. V. Saturday. ≈ I received as usual a number of Letters requesting me to deliver Lectures in sundry places, and among them one from Joseph L. Tillinghast of Providence Rhode-Island, requesting a copy of my Lecture upon Democracy for publication. This has occasioned no small embarrassment in my mind, for the topic is as sharp with quills as the fretful porcupine; and the same opinions, which have been very

favourably received here may be very obnoxious there. I need a guiding Spirit as much as I ever did at any period of my life — My present position is one of great popularity with a falling party; and in falling with them the prospect for me is of a sudden, and overwhelming reverse in which case persecution may come not only upon myself which I can bear with fortitude, but upon those to whom my good name is not only dear but necessary for their comfort. I have deliberately assumed an aggressive position against the President, and his whole executive Administration — against the Supreme Court of the United States, and against the commander in chief of the army — I am at issue with all the organized powers, of the Union — with the twelve hundred millions of dollars of associated wealth, and with all the rabid democracy of the land. I do not mistake my position, nor disguise to myself its perils — But my cause is the cause of my Country, and of human liberty. It is the cause of Christian improvement — the fulfilment of the prophesies, that the day shall come when Slavery and War shall be banished from the face of the Earth.

———

[December 1842]

5. V:30. Monday. Third Session of the 27ᵗʰ Congress commences. I was absorbed in reading the Letters and papers received by the mail this morning till I was belated in reaching the Hall of the House of Representatives — The house had been in Session ten minutes when I took my seat, and they were occupied in calling the roll of members by States when I entered. 174 members answered to their names. Caleb Cushing moved the message to the Senate, and the appointment of a joint-committee to wait on the President and inform him that the two houses are assembled, and ready to receive any communication from him — Tillinghast moved the appointment of a joint library Committee — The usual orders were passed for the supply of newspapers equal to 3 daily to each member. Horace Everett gave notice that he would to-morrow or as soon as may be move to introduce a bill to repeal the bankrupt act — I gave notice that I would to-morrow move a resolution to rescind the 21ˢᵗ rule, which excludes abolition petitions from reception. Henry A. Wise objected to the reception of my motion but as it was only notice of my intention

to offer a resolution, he could not exclude it — W. Cost Johnson also manifested a disposition to object to the reception of the resolution, and Turner of Tennessee told me I began early with my hot shot — The order for the appointment of Chaplains was passed — The Clerk came back from the Senate chamber with notice that they had not formed a Quorum and at half past 12 the house adjourned till 12 to-morrow. Some 30 members, all but one or two of them whigs came and shook hand with me at my seat, and the mutual greeting appeared all round friendly and good humoured ≈

6. IV:45. Tuesday ≈ At the house — No Quorum of the Senate yet. I now offered my Resolution that the 21st rule, excluding abolition petitions from reception should be rescinded — Wise objected again to the reception of the resolution. The Speaker decided that it was in order; Wise protested against the decision, but did not venture to appeal — Weller of Ohio moved to lay the resolution on the table, lost by yeas and nays 84 to 93. Horace Everett moved the previous question — There was a second; but the house refused to take the main question now, that is, this day — by yeas and nays — 84 to 99 — The old game is playing over again by the Northern democratic alliance with Southern Slavery. ≈

7. IV. Wednesday. At the meeting of the House this morning W. Cost Johnson moved that 5000 copies of a document of the last Session, called upon a resolution offered by me, containing a statement of the debts of the several States, should be printed — but his motion was laid on the table — I called up my resolution for rescinding the 21st rule — The Speaker decided that although the house had yesterday decided that they would not then put the main question, to rescind, it was still under the operation of the previous question, which must now be put again. I did not appeal from the decision but observed that I had always understood that the refusal to put the main question *now*, exhausted the previous question, and left the main question debatable. Other members were more refractory than I was. Everett remonstrated. W. Cost Johnson moved to lay the Resolution on the Table, lost by yeas and nays 90 to 91. Then the previous question was again put and

lost 91 to 93. Underwood still contested the decision of the
Speaker who said the subject must lie over till to morrow, and
then the majority will lay the resolution on the table. Bidlack
asked to be excused from voting on that question and then de-
fined his position. — He said he had always voted with the South
on this delicate question, and believed he should still; as long as
the South held together — but he saw that this day, some of the
members from Virginia and Kentucky voting the other way.

———

12. V. Monday. ≈ At the House — My Resolution to rescind
the 21st rule was laid on the table by yeas and nays 106 to 102.
Absent 31, dead 2. Speaker 1. Of the 34, 19 would have voted
ay, 15 no. The vote of the whole House would have been 125 to
117 or possibly 122 to 120.

———

16. V. Friday. The assortment, and filing and endorsement of
my papers in monthly files of my Letters received from last
March till September yet absorbs all my leisure time; and the
unassorted papers are yet in so many heaps that I do but just
begin to see my way clear out of the tangle — In the mean
time every day brings new trashy materials for large files of the
present Session. I am however, the first time for six years relieved from the burden of unreceivable petitions — The
Speaker has decided that the mode of receiving petitions
adopted upon a resolution offered by me at the last Session is
yet in force; by this and the practice of the Speaker under it,
every member not only introduces any and every petition that
he pleases but has it referred to any Committee that he thinks
appropriate — I had ten petitions which I should have presented if the States had been called; but after the speaker's
present decision, I made out the list; directed the committee
to which each of them should be referred, and gave the list,
after it was entered on the Journal of the house, to Mr. Gales,
to be published in the National Intelligencer, and it was published in the paper of this day — The Speaker's decision was, I
believe unwarranted, and the chance is that it will terminate in
an explosion.

———

23. IV:30. Friday. A spell of cold weather came on so that I
could not write early this morning, and that occasioned an

arrearage. I slept in the upper chamber, and after making my fire was obliged to resort to reading by lamplight to employ the time till breakfast — I read a pamphlet, entitled Martial law, by a Kentuckian in four numbers of republication from a Kentucky Newspaper. Its author is said to be a man named Nicholas of the old Virginian family of that name, and is or has been a judge in the State of Kentucky. — In the form of a Dissertation upon martial Law, it is a violent invective against General Jackson for declaring Martial Law at New-Orleans, which he contends was Treason against the United States — Then against me for having asserted in the house of representatives that by the same martial law which Jackson declared at New-Orleans, he might have emancipated all the Slaves in Louisiana. The Senators Buchanan and Berrien come in for a share of his abuse — The Legislature of Rhode-Island — and the minority of the judiciary Committee of the House, in their report on the bill for refunding Jackson's fine have also their share, but the motive at the bottom of it all is the panic terror at my exposure of the danger to Southern Slavery of eventual emancipation by martial law.

———

[January 1843]
2. VI. Monday. Visitors, from 10 to 3 by hundreds. Morning absorbed in reading the Newspapers of the last Night's Mail and the Globe of Saturday evening upon my table — It contains the speech of John C. Calhoun in the Senate of the United States last August in favour of advising and consenting to the ratification of the Webster and Ashburton Treaty. Calhoun is the High Priest of Moloch — The embodied Spirit of Slavery — He has resigned his Seat in the Senate of the United States to take effect from the close of the present Congress the 3^d of March next — and immediately upon the acceptance of his resignation by the Legislature of South-Carolina, they unanimously nominated him as a Candidate for election, as President of the United States for four years from the 4th of March 1845. His speech is remarkable for one of those glaring, unblushing dare devil inconsistencies, which as far as I know are peculiar to the doctrinal school of Slavery — He begins by a broad, explicit, unqualified declaration that he has always believed the claim of Maine upon the Northeastern boundary

question just; and then proceeds with an elaborate argument to prove, that on that same identical boundary question the title of Great-Britain is clear to more than she has ever claimed — On the subject of Slavery and the Slave-trade, the negotiation itself was a Scapinade — a struggle between the Plenipotentiaries to outwit each other, and to circumvent both countries by a slippery compromise between freedom and Slavery. Calhoun crows about his own success in imposing his own bastard Law of Nations upon the Senate by his preposterous Resolutions, and chuckles at Websters appealing to those Resolutions now after dodging from the duty of refuting and confounding them then — Calhoun concludes upon the whole to put up with the ticklish truce, patched up between the Treaty and the correspondence; and this was what in fact reconciled him to the ratification — There is a temperance in his manner obviously aiming to conciliate the Northern political sopranos who abhor slavery, and help to forge fetters for the Slave — My wife is still confined to her bed, and was more unwell this day than yesterday. There were however none the less of female visitors, who were well received by Mrs. John Adams. Our late minister to France Lewis Cass, was among them; and told me that shortly before he left France he had a conversation with *my old friend the king*, concerning me, which he wished to tell me; and he was beginning to do so, when other visitors came up and interrupted him. He said he would call again some evening and tell me — They say the crowd at the President's this day was unexampled — I did not go out.

———

6. V:30. Friday. ≈ Mr. Leavitt, who has been quite unwell came and borrowed a file of the Richmond Whig. He has published in the Emancipator only a part of my address at Braintree, and for omitting other parts of it alledged that he did not approve them. I asked him, what were the parts which he disapproved. He said the parts which had a political party aspect. I said they all had indirect reference to the Slavery questions. ≈

7. IV. Saturday. I sit up so late at Night reading the Newspapers and Letters, which come by the Mail from 9 to 10 in the evening, that I seldom reach my bed before midnight, which

necessarily delays for two hours at least that of my rising. Sex horas somno — says Lord Coke, quoting from I know not whom — and that has been for more than forty years my rule of life — and the six hours are from ten at night to four in the morning — But the rule of life must be modified, by external causes, and by social relations with others. If I sit up till Midnight I cannot rise before six, and that irregularity leads to the laxity of the rule itself — to indulging in morning laziness encroaching upon the best hours of the day.

—

12. V:30. Thursday ≈ General Cass came in last evening after dinner at Webster's, and told me what he had spoken of at my house on the second of this month — General Cass said that shortly before he left France, the king Louis Philippe asked him what in nature had got into Mr. Adams, with whom he recollected to have formed a very pleasing acquaintance in England; and whom he had ever since considered as a friend. Mr. Cass said he was surprized, and asked the king to what he alluded — Why — says Louis Philippe — he denies my title — The General said he knew not what to say in reply — I told him that in a lecture delivered before a literary Society, speaking of the dangerous and convulsed condition of Europe, and referring to France, I said that its king held his crown neither by the monarchical title of heredity succession, nor by the republican title of popular election, but I spoke it as of a historical fact without evil intention to him, and without imagining that it would have been remembered by any one the next day — Well, said Mr. Cass — but it was *true*.

—

14. V. Saturday. A black man named Moses Bell came this morning, and sent me a paper narrative of gross personal abuse by whipping and *cobbing* with which he has been treated by a white man claiming him as a Slave; In March 1841 Bell sued the white man named Rhodes in the circuit Court for his freedom. The trial was procrastinated about 18 months, till last August — on the 20th of August he was adjudged on the special verdict of a white jury to be free — from this sentence Rhodes appealed to the U. S. Supreme Court now in Session. Mr. Hoban and Mr. Wallach have been Bell's lawyers in the Circuit Court, and he said he had been advised to apply to me

to assist him in the Supreme Court — I promised to do for him what I could.

—

25. IV:15. Wednesday. John Davies, a coloured man, came this morning with a Letter from himself to me — asking my advice in behalf of his wife's son, named Joseph Clark, sold some years since by Mrs. Hellen to some one, who sold him to the Senator Berrien, who sold him to a Col'l Curry, an agent or sub-agent employed in the removal of the Cherokee Indians. Currey took him to the State of Arkansas, employed him as an interpreter, and promised him his freedom. Currey afterwards died, and by his Will, declared Clark *free*, after 3 years service to his brother — The rascal brother sold him for 900 dollars, and he is now in irredeemable Slavery for life — The mother of this poor man, Jenny lived sometime with us, and at her instance her husband Davies came to ask my advice what can be done for him — But he has neither means to sue for his freedom, nor evidence to prove the Will. He is now living with a Dr. Davis Flint, Cherokee Nation, and is acting as interpreter — Can I not possibly do something for this man?

—

[February 1843]
9. VI. Thursday. The cold weather produces perturbation in my daily occupations, and particularly in the more irremissible of them all the Diary ≈ Mr. Leavitt called on me, and spoke of the underhand movements to carry by springing a mine, the annexation of Texas to this Union — He suggested that some of the members thought of uniting in an address to the people of the free States against it. Mr. Giddings had intimated to me yesterday a similar purpose, in which I told him I would very readily concur — but that I had no confidence in the firmness of any one member from the free States, to put their names to any such address.

—

15. VI. Wednesday. Snow — Sleet — Glassy Streets and hard frost. Adjourned Meeting of the Committee of foreign Affairs — Present Adams, Cushing, Meriwether, Caruthers, Stuart, Shepperd — Absent Everett, Granger and Holmes. Cushing resumed and concluded the reading of his report on the Ashburton Treaty — The part of the report relating to the

boundary questions was all unexceptionable; but all the remainder, and particularly the part relating to the Article of compromise, with regard to the suppression of the African Slave-trade was so full of bad temper and absurd reasoning, that I objected to it, altogether; and said if it was to be presented to the house at all, I should move many amendments to it, and to strike out nearly the whole of it. Mr. Meriwether also objected to it, and said he had written out his views on the execution of the treaty, also in the form of a report — We had no time for further discussion, and adjourned to Friday Morning 10 O'Clock — Before going to the house, I had a quarter of an hour's conversation with Cushing, and told him there was a War now in parturition between Freedom and Slavery, throughout the globe. That it would be a War for the abolition of Slavery — at the head of which would be Great-Britain. That in this War I could take no part — I was going off the Stage; but he was coming on to it — and I conjured him, as he cherished his own and his Country's honour, not to commit himself in this great controversy to the side of Slavery — And to return to the cause of liberty from which he had not yet irrevocably strayed. He heard me without taking offence, but apparently without conviction.

———

22. V. Wednesday. ≈ After the reading of the journal I moved to suspend the rules to enable me [to] present 53 petitions upon a variety of subjects among which was the great Massachusetts Latimer Petition ≈ My Latimer petition so entirely covered my table that it left me no space for writing at it and Brockway lent me his table for the day. I made out a list of 33 petitions, with the objects prayed for by them, and the Committees to which they should be referred, which I delivered to Mr. Burch in the Clerk's Office, demanding that they should be entered on the journal of the house, and that my list be returned to me for publication in the National Intelligencer. The Latimer Petition is among them; and there are two others for the dissolution of the Union.

———

27. III–VII. Monday. ≈ I had prepared resolutions to be offered to the house with a view to call the attention of the people of the free States to the disproportion of slave-holding judges on

the bench of the Supreme Court of the United States ≈ Fillmore moved to go into Committee of the whole on the state of the Union, to take up the civil and diplomatic appropriation Bill — I called for the regular order of the day — The call for Resolutions. The house decided to go into Committee — I asked leave to present my Resolutions respecting the Slaveholding and free State judges on the bench of the Supreme Court. Multitudes of objections were heard. I asked a suspension of the rules and the yeas and nays. The Speaker said the house had voted to go into Committee, and my Resolutions were returned to me. I gave them to Stansbury to be published in the National Intelligencer.

CHAPTER XIV ❧ 1843–1848

Twenty-Eighth, Twenty-Ninth, and Thirtieth Congresses

[March 1843]

10. IV:15. Friday. ≈ I spent much of this day in transiently read-ing the report of the trial in the Supreme Court of the United States of the case of Edward Prigg against the Commonwealth of Pennsylvania, otherwise called the fugitive slave case — Seven judges — every one of them dissenting from the reason-ing of all the rest, and every one of them coming to the same conclusion: the transcendent omnipotence of Slavery in these United States, riveted by a clause in the Constitution that persons held to labour, escaping from one state to another shall be delivered up on the claim of the person to whom the labour is due.

———

18. II, IV–VI. Saturday. Twice up in the night, and convulsed the whole day in casting off phlegm from the stomach — what a disgusting object to himself is a man? It is difficult to con-template the infirmities of our physical nature philosophically. Every thing about sickness is odious to the sufferer and annoy-ing to those around him. There is a consolation in the kindness of nursing friends; but the primary grief and self-reproach to me is the loss of time — I am idle — As the hours pass in suc-cession I know, I might be working — I brood over projected labours and never commence working — As morning dawns, I have a long day before me, and think I shall use it to some good purpose. It slips away, I know not how — Approaching midnight summons me to repose — and I have lost a day.

> I've lost a day — the Prince who nobly said —
> Had been an Emperor without his crown.

The globe of earth has not space for the surface of Empires over which I should be worthy to rule if I could proclaim the record of my lost days. ≈

19. IV–VI. Sunday. I have this day been debarred by my disease from the privilege of attendance upon public worship; and felt it with deep mortification. The time has been, chiefly in foreign countries when I have too long intermitted the duty of that attendance — Of this I charge myself especially when in Holland, in Berlin, in St. Petersburg, and last in France — I have lost by it rich opportunities of obtaining instruction; not only religious, but worldly, moral, political, intellectual — For this I blame myself; but the importance of regular attendance upon the duties of the Christian Sabbath in social communion has impressed itself more deeply on my mind in proportion as I have advanced in years. I had neglected to become a member of the church, till after the decease of my father — another omission which I now regret. I have at all times been a sincere believer in the existence of a supreme creator of the world, of an immortal principle within myself responsible to that creator for my conduct upon earth; and of the divine mission of the crucified saviour, proclaiming immortal life and preaching peace on earth, good will to men, the natural equality of all mankind, and the Law, thou shalt love thy neighbour as thyself. Of all these articles of faith, all resting upon the first, the existence of an omnipotent Spirit, I entertain involuntary and agonizing doubts, which I can neither silence nor expel, and against which I need for my own comfort to be fortified and sustained, by stated and frequent opportunities of receiving religious admonition and instruction — I feel myself to be a frequent sinner before God; and I need to be often admonished of it and exhorted to virtue. This is administered in all the forms of Christian worship, and I am sure of receiv[ing] it with whatever denomination of Christian worshippers I associate to obtain it — Of late years I have deemed it my duty to attend the weekly morning performances of the Chaplains of Congress in the Hall of the House of Representatives; and I hold pews at St. John's episcopal church and at the second Presbyterian church, at which I attend alternately when Congress are not in session, and in the afternoon when they are — This forms a regular portion of my habits of life, and I cannot feel the privation of it without painful sensibility.

—

21. V:45. Tuesday. ≈ The controversy between Lewis Cass and Daniel Webster, about the Ashburton Treaty, the rights of

visitation and of search and the Quintuple Treaty, still with the comet, the Zodical light and the Millerite prediction of the second advent of Christ, and the end of the world within five weeks from this day continue to absorb much of the public and of my attention — The intelligencer of this day announces another Letter from Cass to Webster who in his last Letter declares the correspondence closed. This strange correspondence — The debates in the French Legislative chambers, and in both houses of the British Parliament and in both houses of Congress, but especially in the Senate — This Slave trade and right of search complicated with the quintuple Treaty, with Texas, Mexico, California, Oregon, and the next Presidential election, breed teeming fancies in my brain till I grope to find my way out of the thicket.

———

23. V:45. Thursday. Another Letter from Lewis Cass to Daniel Webster, about the Ashburton Treaty, the right of visitation and search, and the offended dignity of the aforesaid Lewis Cass at the Lordly tone assumed by the Secretary of State in the previous part of this correspondence — I am thinking if there is any thing parallel to this correspondence in our diplomatic history. Silas Deane came home from France and made a rumpus (that word is not in Webster's Dictionary — what a pity!) for several years; blew up a flame which kept this union long in a phease (another Websterless word) and has left a large claim of his heirs and legal representatives, against the United States of which not a dollar is due, but which on some lucky day they will recover — Mr. James Monroe was recalled by President Washington, through Timothy Pickering, wire worked by Alexander Hamilton — Mr. Monroe published a volume of his correspondence — against the administration of Washington by whom he had been appointed and recalled — which book largely contributed to the fall of Washington's Administration as continued by his successor. It helped to bring in the Jefferson Administration, which laid the foundation for the dissolution of the Union. Cass and Webster are both New-Hampshire adventurers, who have made their way in the world, by mere dint of talents, Figaro fashion, making a trade of politics, and a Lottery prize of their Country. ≈ In this controversy Cass is outrageously wrong from beginning to

end: but in permitting Tyler to approve Cass's protest, Webster put into Cass's hand a scourge which Cass now plies against him with merciless dexterity.

———

[April 1843]

3. IV:30. Monday. North-east wind — chill — damp — snow. Morning call from Mr. Heman Lincoln. He is connected with the Baptist missions, and has been on an excursion to Virginia — He was inquisitive upon the prospects of the approaching Presidential election — He asked my opinion of the chances, and agreed with me that the prospects were in favour of Martin van Buren. He thought the prospects of Henry Clay as irretrievably gone: as I have no doubt they are — Those of Tyler, Calhoun, Cass, are equally desperate. Buchanan is the shadow of a shade, and General Scott is a Daguerrotype likeness of a candidate — all sunshine, through a camera obscura. Mr. Lincoln's partiality was for Theodore Frelinghuysen, or judge John M'Lean. I had never heard the name of Frelinghuysen as a candidate before; and M'Lean, is but a second edition of John Tyler — vitally democratic, double-dealing and hypocritical — They will all go into the democratic convention, and all melt into the Corinthian brass of Kinderhook. ≈

4. V:15. Tuesday. ≈ At home I took up the Message and documents relating to the seizure of Monterey by Captain Thomas ap Catesby Jones — There is no warrant for it in any of his written instructions from the Navy Department — But I remark, with no small concern 1. the special charge of exploring the coast within the gulph of California and as high as the Port of San Francisco — one of the reasons of which is the weakness of the local authorities, and their irresponsibility to the distant government of Mexico. 2. The tone of intercourse both military and diplomatic, bearing upon Mexico — It would never have entered into the head of Jones to commit such an outrage upon a Nation whom he believed able to resent it — Waddy Thompson's diplomacy is in perfect keeping with this temper — Even his apologies are insolent, insulting, and contemptuous; and there is far too much of the same spirit in the notes of our Secretary of State — The spirit of encroach-

ment upon Mexico, is stimulated and nourished by this settled and but too well founded conviction of her helpless weakness in conflict with the gigantic energy of our national avarice and ambition — When I contemplate the prospect before us, my heart sinks within me for the cause of human freedom, and for our own.

———

11. IV:15. Tuesday ≈ To concentrate my reflections upon one of the numerous projects floating in my brain I began yesterday an address to my late constituents of the 12th late, and my future constituents of the present 8th congressional districts of Massachusetts, which, if I have the courage and perseverance to finish it, I may deliver as a Lecture before the commencement of the next Session of Congress. I know not how this may succeed — the time is not propitious for me to speak to my countrymen unpalatable truths — but I wish to leave behind me something which may keep alive the flame of liberty and preserve it in that conflict between Slavery and freedom which is drawing to its crisis and which is to brighten or to darken the condition of the human race upon earth — I wrote this Evening a short Letter to Washington Irving at Madrid, and received one from Mrs. Stewart, to General Rodil; and requesting that her mother might see my letter to Mr. Irving before I send it.

———

14. IV:30. Friday. ≈ In the midst of all her vices, difficulties and troubles, Texas is swelling with incredible rapidity into a formidable Slave State which Mexico can never recover, and from the contamination of whose Slavery nothing can save this Union, short of a special interposition of Providence.

———

29. V. Saturday. Summer heat — Lassitude and 76. I walked out this morning to the meeting of the Pennsylvania and Louisiana avenues, and sat to Mr. West for two Daguerrotype likenesses; one of which he took for David L. Child, and one for himself — I did not see either of them, nor do I feel any curiosity to see them — They are resemblances too close to the reality and yet too shadowy to be agreeable — I had once before been painted by Mr. Charles in the same chamber. Childs

left the City this morning — Not without danger of being
Lynched I hear for his pamphlet on the Texan Revolution —
The pamphlet smacks of abolition.

———

[May 1843]
6. V. Saturday. I have accepted an invitation from the Massachusetts historical Society, to deliver on the 29th of this month
a discourse before them, on the second centennial anniversary
of the confederation of the New-England Colonies, and I have
come here without and before my family, for the purpose of
preparing it — I have paid so little attention to that portion of
our history that I scarcely knew the sources at which the principal facts relating to it were to be found — nor have I any clue
to the aspect in which it should be viewed for any useful purpose at the present time — Pope makes it a point of self-
glorification, that not in fancys maze he wander'd long, but
stoop'd to truth and moraliz'd his song — I believe that moral
principle should be the alpha and omega, of all human composition — poetry or prose scientific or literary written or spoken
— and emphatically of every discourse. An Epic Poem, a
Drama, Pastoral, Georgic or Fable, Ode, Sonnet or epigram
should alike spring from one vital seminal principle of morals
and so should every History Dissertation, Treatise, Discourse
or epistle — Pen should never be put to paper, but for the
discharge of some duty to God or man.

———

8. IV:45. Monday. ≈ I went to the Emancipator Office, and had
a long conversation with Mr. Leavitt. He is to embark next
Tuesday in the Steamer for Liverpool, to attend as a delegate
from the American anti-Slavery Society the second triennial
meeting of the World's convention for the promotion of the
abolition of Slavery and the Slave-trade throughout the Earth
— I urged him very earnestly to observe with unremitting care
the movements of the British Government with regard to
Mexico and Texas — I told him I distrusted them altogether
— I believed their real policy far from desiring to favour the
abolition of Slavery either in our Southern States, or in Texas.
I suspect on the contrary that for a suitable equivalent they will
readily acquiesce both in the annexation of Texas to this
Union, and to the perpetuation of Slavery here to weaken and

to rule us. Mr. P. C. Brooks and his Son, dined with us at my Sons house, and I began at a perfect hazard to write my discourse.

———

11. I, III, IV:30. Thursday ≈ I passed the day as with a mill-stone about my neck, working invita Minerva upon my address for the historical Society, unable even to get through with my daily task of two pages and seeing as yet no point of departure for the discourse — hitherto I stumble one after another upon preliminary points of doubtful propriety to the occasion and more doubtful adaptation to the taste and prejudices of the day — I find continual occasion to resort to books which I have not at hand. In discussing a confederacy of New England Colonies the subject leads to remarks upon the propriety of the name upon the special sympathies with the condition and characteristic properties of the mother Country, old England and to a comparative notice of the elementary composition of the other colonies which now constitute jointly with us the North American Union. This has already brought me upon debatable ground, and upon the accursed domain of Slavery. What shall I do with it? I am upon the breakers, and know not how to draw off from them. The relations of the Colonies with the Indians also constitute another shoal which I have not yet reached but upon which I shall be in imminent danger of stranding — I can scarcely express how in my weakened condition these thoughts weigh me down.

———

19. IV. Friday. Having no time to spare for the composition of my address for the Massachusetts historical Society, and deeming it necessary for the filling of the time allotted to the discourse, that it should consist of 32 pages, occupying two hours or thereabouts I begin the day with that labour, and prescribing to myself to write two pages each day till I get through — I began therefore this morning as soon after rising dressing and making my fire was practicable, and with the interval of half an hour for breakfast kept incessant alternate reading and writing, till the village bell rung for noon before my task for the day was completed — In the course of my treatment of the subject I was this day brought to the consideration of the character of Roger Williams and the establishment of

the Colony of Rhode-Island — It has in recent times become a sort of literary fashion to extol the character of Roger Williams, by disparaging those of the Massachusetts [leaders] with whom he contended. I have suspected that there is in this much injustice; and the more minutely I examine his controversy with them, the more firmly this opinion fixes itself in my mind — Roger Williams was a Welshman — He came sharpened for controversy, a polemical porcupine from Oxford, an extreme puritan quilled with all the quarrelsome metaphysical divinity of the age — He arrived eight months after Winthrop and his company and began by preaching at Salem that the Charter was of no avail, because the king had no power to grant the lands because they belonged to the Indians, and that the Church was no true Church because she had not proclaimed her repentance for having held Communion with the Church of England before the Emigration — These doctrines struck at the vitals of the Massachusetts Colony, civil and ecclesiastical — If there is any thing surprizing in their treatment of him, it was their lenity towards him. His principle of liberty of conscience admirable in itself, was utterly at variance with itself in his excommunication of the colonial church for not excommunicating the episcopal church of England — Altogether he was a mere boute-feu and they were amply justified in getting rid of him. I see that Bancroft tells his Story with extreme partiality to puff him up — not only to a Saint and Hero; but to a transcendent Genius — A Newton, Kepler, or Copernicus. His principle of Toleration was the inspiration of a strong mind, and his success in settling a small colony where it was carried into practise gives lustre to his name. The recent revolution in Rhode Island, is the Euthanasia of his system.

———

27. V:15. Saturday. ≈ I came in my address to the parallel between the New-England confederacy of 1643 and the North-American confederacy of 1774 — I had some hopes on approaching this topic to bring up some interest with it — but it sinks under me — Not one of the motives which stimulated the puritans to their confederacy of 1643 had the slightest influence in actuating the Confederacy of 1774. The parties to the New-England Union were homogeneous. Those of the North-American Union were not only of heterogeneous but

of hostile elements; and in the latter there was the ingredient of Slavery which poisoned the whole composition — I have touched upon it in this address; but on revisal propose to strike out all that I have written relating to it — This afternoon I rode with my daughter and her son Charles to Weymouth to enquire of the state of Mrs. Mercy Tufts who has been very dangerously ill with the Erisypelas — We saw her two daughters Mercy and Susan, who told us she was somewhat better, though still confined to her bed — We rode home with a sprinkling rain and the evening was wintry cold — This family of Tufts are all that now remain of my childhood's remembrance of Weymouth — Some of the earliest of my recollections are there, and the localities which remain unchanged bring them back, with a pungency for which I scarcely know how to account. I have no such reminiscences in Boston, because every thing there is changed; but spots of the old road through Braintree and Weymouth are precisely as they were seventy years ago, and a return to them seems to sweep away the interval of time, and to make me again a child — But there is not one individual of my grandfather Smith's blood now living in Weymouth.

———

[June 1843]

12. IV. Monday. ≈ I answered a Letter from William Pitt Fessenden, a member of the last Congress from Portland Maine, who has been charged in an abolitionist address to the people of that State, with lukewarmness in the support of the right of petition. He wrote to me requesting my testimony, as to his course in the house on this subject. I have given him my testimony — The abolitionist charges against him are unjust — but zeal in support of the right of petition can do nothing in the Congress of the United States — I wrote this answer with great difficulty, much hesitation, and not a little imprudence in lifting up one corner of the curtain which covers the hideous reality of the Slave ascendancy in the Government of this Union — The double representation of the Slave owners in the House of Representatives and in the electoral colleges for the choice of President and Vice-President. — Semper ego auditor tantum?

———

16. III:45. Friday. ≈ This was the [day] of the reception of the President of the United States by the city of Boston. He comes with his cabinet and a ridiculous parade of ostentation to attend the celebration of the completion of the Bunker hill monument; a costly pageant first got up by Joseph Tinker Buckingham President of the Bunker hill Monument association and Editor of the Boston Courier, the most respectable of Webster's Trumpeters — The corner stone of the monument was laid by La Fayette on the 17th of June 1825, on which occasion [he] delivered an eloquent Discourse. He is to deliver another. The object now is to glorify him — A formal invitation was sent to him last fall immediately after the completion of the monument inviting him to the performance of this service, which he then accepted; and the invitation and acceptance were published in newspapers all over the country — The invitation to the President and his Cabinet to attend is a political device of Webster's own — a gull-trap for popularity, both for himself and for Tyler, by which he hopes to whistle back his whig friends whom he had cast off as a huntsman his pack, and who now threaten to hunt him like the hounds of Acteon. The reception of the President this day had all the appearances of cordiality, notwithstanding a drenching rain to cool it. He is lodged at the Tremont house at an enormous expense to the city; was entertained there with a sumptuous dinner, by the City Council, and went to the theatre and to an evening party at the Postmaster Gordon's house. I was invited to the dinner, but sent an excuse ≈

17. IV. Saturday. This was the day of the great celebration of the completion of the monument on Bunker hill; and never since the existence of the three hills was there such a concourse of strangers upon their sides as has been assembled on the banks of "Majestic Charles" this day. What a name in the annals of mankind is Bunker hill? — What a day, was the 17th of June 1775? and what a burlesque upon them both is an oration upon them by Daniel Webster, and a pilgrimage of John Tyler and his Cabinet of Slave-drivers, to desecrate the solemnity by their presence! And then a dinner at Faneuil Hall in honour of a President of the United States hated and despised by those who invited him to it, themselves as cordially hated and

despised by him. I have throughout my life had an utter aversion to all pageants, and public dinners, and never attended one, when I could decently avoid it — I was a student at Cambridge when on the 17th of June 1786, Charles river bridge was opened. The colleges were emptied on that day of the Students who flocked to witness the procession and the pageant — I passed the day in the solitude of my Study, and dined almost alone in the Hall. I had then no special motive for my absence. But now with the ideal association of the thundering cannon which I heard, and the smoke of burning Charlestown which I saw on that awful day, combined with this Pyramid of Quincy granite, and Daniel Webster spouting, and John Tyler's nose with a shadow outstreching that of the monumental column; how could I have witnessed all this at once without an unbecoming burst of indignation or of laughter? Daniel Webster is a heartless traitor to the cause of human freedom. John Tyler is a Slave-monger — what have these to do with the Quincy granite pyramid on the brow of Bunker's hill? — What have these to do, with a dinner in Faneuil hall, but to swill like swine and grunt about the rights of man? I stayed at home and visited my seedling trees; and heard the cannonades of the rising, the meridian and the setting Sun — and answered a letter from the Rev'd Joseph Emerson, dated at New-London Connecticut making enquiries about a translation of Voltaire's philosophical dictionary, published under the name of John Quincy Adams, and secretly circulating as he says, about the country, as my work — I saw the Sun set from the front of Charles's house, at the extremity of his north western declination, and as I heard the cannonade salute of the closing day, and saw the smoke ascending from the side of the pyramid, the top of which was full in view; then came in forcible impulse to my memory the cannonade, and the smoke and the fire of the 17th of June 1775 — I waited to see the revolving fire of the Boston Lighthouse kindled, and then returned to my peaceful home.

18. IV. Sunday. ≈ The Rev'd Benjamin Kent now keeper of a school for girls at Roxbury preached for Mr. Lunt this morning with a double text. Romans 7:24 "O wretched man that I am! who shall deliver me from the body of this death?" and

Philippians 4:13 "I can do all things through Christ which strengtheneth me." The doctrine of the discourse was that the will of a perfect Christian fortified by conscience is omnipotent. That nothing is impossible for it to atchieve; and to elucidate the principle, he presented a parallel between these two passages from the writings of St. Paul, first in the epistle to the Romans in the agonies of despair and then four years later to the Philippians in the exultation of a glorious victory and triumph by the strength of Christ assisting him — The first written in the midst of the terrible struggle of his conversion, and while he was yet uncertain of its success. The last was written after his conversion was consummated, and his confidence in himself with the strength imparted to him by Christ his lord and master was unbounded. Upon this theme Mr. Kent amplified and dilated until he reminded me of the story which I once heard Dr. Franklin tell of a convent of monks who had a very inconvenient hill in front of their monastery, and upon their faith like a grain of mustard seed's being sufficient [to] cast the mountain into the sea, set up a general onset of prayer to remove the mountain, which they perseveringly pursued till tired of the obstinate adherence of the mountain to its place one of the friars gave out that there was a mistake in the translation of the text, and that the true reading should be that with faith like a mountain it is possible to move a mustard seed — Mr. Kent and Mr. Lunt dined with us. They were both at the Bunker hill celebration yesterday; which went off admirably well. Webster's Oration was brilliant and eminently successful. Two hours and seven minutes — Suitable to the occasion, and often rapturously cheered. The dinner at Faneuil hall was also very well ordered and passed off agreeably. — The cheering of Webster was hearty and general — that of the President feeble and cold.

———

[July 1843]
4. III:30. Tuesday ≈ My only surviving Son, Charles Francis, delivered the annual Boston City Oration on the Anniversary of Independence; an incident of the most intense interest to me, it being this day fifty years, since I performed the same service to the town. ≈ The hall was crowded to its utmost capacity, with a very respectable and highly intelligent auditory. There was a station assigned in the procession to the members

of the Massachusetts delegation in Congress; in which I walked with Robert C. Winthrop. ≈ The last time I had been in Boston on the 4ᵗʰ of July was in 1809. I went up the hill at Sunset. Mrs. Frothingham returned with her children to Boston — We witnessed the fire works on the Common of Boston. No language can express the agitation of my feelings, and the remembrances of this day.

———

6. IV. Thursday. ≈ My Son went this morning to Cambridge to attend a greek examination. At 10 O'Clock, I left home with his wife, and her Son John Quincy — we went into Boston, and dined at Dr. Frothingham's; meeting there her father Mr. Peter Chardon Brooks — Immediately after dinner we proceeded to the depot of the Western Railroad, where after taking leave of Charles who had just come in from Cambridge, we started in the Cars at half past 3 — The weather was fine — clear sunshine yet comfortably cool — We passed through the towns of Natick, Southborough, Westborough, Worcester, Brookfield, Charlton and several others which I neglected to ascertain, and at a quarter before 9 landed at Warriner's United States Hotel in Springfield 90 miles from Boston. Among our travelling companions were the Rev'd Alexander Young, Minister of the New South Church, Boston; going by the way of Hartford and New-Haven to preach two Sundays at New-York. Mr. and Mrs. Joseph Grinnell of New-Bedford, and Mr. Henry Sargent, going to visit his son, settled at Newburgh opposite to Fishkill landing on Hudson's river — The Season is delightful. The face of the Country like the garden of Eden — It is the Season of hay-making and throughout our way, the mower with his scythe, the cocking of the grass, or the spreading it from the cock to dry, followed in alternate succession, and the atmosphere was charged only with varieties of fragrance. Fields of Indian corn, Rye, Potatoes and Oats interchangeably with pastures covered with grazing cattle, neat and comfortable houses and kitchen gardens and Orchards laden with ripening fruit, attested a genial climate a fruitful Season and a region of Peace, plenty and contentment.

———

25. IV:30. Tuesday. This morning I delivered to professor Mitchell my answer to the Resolutions of the Cincinnati

Astronomical Society of the 18th inst't inviting me to lay the corner Stone of the observatory which they propose to erect; and to deliver an Oration on the occasion — I have accepted the invitation, and promised to perform the duty; if in my power on some day in the month of November next, to suit the convenience of the Society. This is a rash promise, and in faithfully analysing my motives for making it I wish I could find them pure from all alloy of vanity, and self-glorification. It is an arduous, hazardous and expensive undertaking, the successful performance of which is more than problematical and of the event of which it is impossible for me to foresee any thing but disappointment. Yet there is a motive pure and elevated and a purpose benevolent and generous, at least mingling with the impulses which in this case I obey, and upon which I may without irreverence invoke the blessing of Heaven as I do, for fortitude, energy and perseverance to accomplish what I have promised — Mr. Mitchell after receiving my answer, took his departure to return to Cincinnati. Mr. Millard Fillmore and Mr.   Love, heretofore members of Congress came this day, deputed from the City of Buffalo to invite me to visit that place, and Mr. Fillmore delivered to me a similar written invitation signed by 13 citizens of Syracuse — I went this morning with Gen'l Porter to Goat Island to bespeak a warm bath at the bathing house just above the single sheeted fall from which it borrows the stream that supplies the bath — They had then no heated water, but promised to have some ready for me this evening. I then walked about an hour before breakfast with the General to re-inspect all the points from which the cascades and the rapids are seen to the best advantage. The sky was unusually clear, the Sun shining in cloudless splendour and the snowy foam of the spray reflected the burning beams in a constantly shifting rainbow adding exquisite beauty to the awful grandeur of the falling flood.

—

27. Thursday. IV:15. ≈ We arrived at Rochester between 2 and 3 — and found Guns firing, Bells ringing and an immense crowd of People — Shouting — Mr. Brooks with Mrs. Charles F. Adams, and John Quincy proceeded this Evening to Canandaigua — The first person whom I saw before I alighted from the Car was Francis Grainger, who had come in deputation

from Canandaigua to invite me to stop a day there; and he brought me a kind and friendly invitation from Mr. John Greig; late member of Congress chosen to supply Grainger's place, when he was appointed Postmaster General, and who when Grainger retired from the Tyler Cabinet, resigned to bring him again into the house — I consented to stop and dine to-morrow with Mr. Greig at Canandaigua: to have an interview and hand shaking with the inhabitants; and then proceed on to Auburn in the Evening — With Mr. and Mrs. Grinnell, Cornelia, and Miss Otté I remained for this day at Rochester. We dined at the Eagle Hotel. After dinner rode round the city, and to the cemetery of mount Hope, a copy from that of Mount Auburn superior to the original. At 6 P.M. was the public meeting. The Mayor Isaac Hills, addressed me from a stage in front of a public building. I answered him by a speech; and Grainger being called out made a short one — Then came the shaking of hands. In the Evening I received the Ladies at the Eagle Hotel, and made them a short Speech. The firemen's torch-light procession closed the day.

28. V:30. Friday. ≈ we proceeded in the Cars, to Auburn, accompanied by the Ex-Governor William H. Seward and another deputy from Auburn, with an invitation to me to stop there — At Geneva, and several other places on the road crowds were collected to shake hands with me; to hear me speak a few words, and shout me onward — We arrived at Auburn between 9 and 10 at Night, and by the torch light procession of the firemen I was transported to Governor W. H. Sewards house for the Night.

———

[August 1843]
1. V:15. Tuesday. I received yesterday a Letter from David Thompson, Benjamin Anderson, and Tucker Woodson, a Committee appointed by the coloured citizens of Utica, to wait on me, and return their thanks for my efforts, in protecting the right of petition, and promoting the abolition of Slavery, and proposing to come, if it would be agreeable to me in the Evening. I accordingly received them about 8 O'Clock, and one of them addressed me in a short, but formal speech, modest and well delivered. I answered them with equal brevity;

thanking them for their kind attentions to me; assuring them that I had no claim to gratitude from them for services in which I had performed no more than my indispensable [duty] — That I should still and ever be happy to serve them to the utmost extent of my power, and commend them to the protection of our common father and creator — My first visit this morning immediately after breakfast was to the female Seminary, where I was introduced to the assembled teachers and pupils, and addressed in behalf of the trustees of that institution by Mr. Spencer in a manner so affecting that it made a child of me. It consisted chiefly of extracts which he read from my mothers published Letters of 19 August 1774 to my father, and of June 1778 to me. — I actually sobbed as he read, utterly unable to suppress my emotion. Oh! my Mother! Is there any thing on earth so affecting to me as thy name? so precious as thy instructions to my childhood? so dear as the memory of thy life? I answered, I know not what — My thoughts were all upon my mother — My heart was too full for my head to think, and my presence of mind was gone — At the close of his address, Mr. Spencer presented to me, at the request of the Ladies 12 numbers of a monthly publication, from August 1842 to July 1843, called the Young Ladies Miscellany the original productions of the Utica female Academy — At 10 O'Clock the reception took place, on a stage erected in front of the Bleecker house; where Mr. Bacon addressed and welcomed me in the name of the citizens of Utica: I answered him in a speech of about half an hour, sufficiently cheered for my hopes or wishes, but of mortifying inanity to myself — The shaking of some hundred hands then followed, and on my way, returning to Mr. Johnson's I stop'd and four Daguerrotype likenesses of my head were taken: two of them jointly with the head of Mr. Bacon, all hideous. Then a visit to the dwarf, C. F. Stratton called General Tom Thumb, 11 years old, 25 inches high; weighing 15 pounds. Dressed in military uniform, mimicking Napoleon. Dinner party at Mr. Johnson's. Ride after dinner to the Lunatic hospital. John M. Niles, U.S. Senator from Connecticut is there. Thence we went to the York Mills Cotton Factory, where there was a crowd — a reception a procession, an address and speech; and a present of several pieces of the cotton cloth which I declined accepting. Elegant evening party and supper at Mr. Johnson's.

2. V. Wednesday. ≈ From Utica to Schenectady the distance is 77 miles and from Schenectady to Albany 16 — At Herkimer 14 miles — At Little Falls 22 from Utica, and at every place in the valley of the Mohawk where the Cars stop'd 5 minutes for wood and water, crowds of people were assembled, received me with three cheers, and manifested a desire to see and hear me, with which I complied by descending from the Cars, shaking hands with as many of them as could reach me, and addressing them, till the passing bell called me back to my seat — At Little Falls, I was addressed and welcomed by Arphaxed Loomis an ex-member of the 25th Congress whom I did not recognize till after I had answered — In the valley of the Mohawk we saw the fortress dwelling house of Sir William Johnson, and that of the Indian chief Brant; said to be his Son. About an hour before we reached Schenectady the wind raised by the rapid motion of the Car, lodged on the ball of my left eye, beneath the underlid, a small sharp-angled pebble of the entrance of which I was not conscious when it happened, but which fretted the eye to torture, produced considerable inflammation, and made it impossible for me to look in the face of those whom I was to address. A sumptuous dinner had been provided for us at Schenectady. I was in anguish unutterable — I retired to a private chamber and washed the eye in cold water without relief. Dr. Duane who had observed my suffering followed me to the chamber; examined the eye, discovered the offensive pebble; wiped it out with the corner of a towel, and I was well. Mr. De Graff a member of former Congresses presided at the cold water dinner — After dinner an address of welcome from the porch of a dwelling house was answered by me, as the moment inspired. Mr. Daniel D. Barnard and two other gentlemen from Albany, met us at Schenectady were at the dinner and accompanied us to their home — There we were received after sunset with firing of cannon — ringing of bells, a procession and cavalcade of butchers, and many thousand citizens, and after announcing from the steps of the capitol that I would meet them at 10 to-morrow morning, I came

with Mr. Barnard to his house, and received an Evening
Serenade.

———

7. V:15. Monday. ≈ Lewis Tappan was here with his wife and
two daughters, but the Ladies declined alighting from his carriage, and he stayed with me but a few minutes — The day
after he was here on the 31ˢᵗ of last May, he embarked for England, and has just now returned — He attended the second
World's convention held at London from the 18ᵗʰ to the 22ᵈ
of June, and gave me a brief and rapid summary of their
proceedings — He said he had a Letter to me from Thomas
Clarkson, and sundry papers containing full and detailed reports
of the proceedings of the Convention — But they were at Brook-
line and he would send them to me — He was to go for New-
York this afternoon. He said he had told Lord Aberdeen of my
distrust of the British Government on the subject of Slavery,
and particularly on the surrender of fugitive Slaves. He said
Lord Aberdeen was startled at the suggestion, and utterly disclaimed all intention of suffering the tenth Article of the Ashburton Treaty to be made the instrument of reclaiming Slaves
— This Article is a pattern example of diplomatic swindling
— There is hope that its purpose may be defeated by the alarm
of the English abolitionists and their remonstrances against it
before the enact[ment] of it by Parliament as English Law —
A grosser fraud was never practiced upon nations than was intended by that article — The apologies for it, by Lord
Ashburton, and by the British Ministers are lame and prevaricating — and from the statements of Mr. Tappan, all my suspicions of the duplicity of the British Ministers, on the subject of
Texas and Slavery are but too strongly confirmed — The policy
of the British Government is to cherish sustain and protect the
institutions of Slavery in our Southern States, and in Texas,
and their task is to do it by humbugging the abolitionists in
England into the belief that they intend directly the reverse.

———

19. III:30. Saturday. ≈ I went this evening to the town Hall,
and heard an Anti-Slavery Address of about an hour delivered
by Wendell Phillips; an intimate friend of my youth was his father John Phillips, afterwards the first Mayor of Boston — I
had heard much of Wendell as an Abolitionist enthusiastic

Orator, but had never seen or heard him. He was now introduced to me by one equally a stranger to me, but who introduced himself — named J. W. Pendleton. Mr. Phillips spoke to
me about his fathers intimate acquaintance with me; which I
confirmed; and assured him of the respectful and affectionate
memory that I retain of him — He said he was so young when
his father died that he had but a faint recollection of him; but
that a friend of his who had known him had told him if his father had lived to this time, he would not have followed the
course which he does — I said I thought that was probable;
the great characteristic of his father having been prudence and
discretion in the avowal of his opinions — and boldness that of
Wendell himself — His address this evening was extemporaneous, and very handsomely delivered — Its topics were censure
upon the church for coldness or lukewarmness to the cause of
anti-slavery, and a fervid argument for the total and immediate
abolition of Slavery throughout the world.

———

26. IV:30. Saturday. ≈ At Sunset I walked up the hill to
Charles's house but was belated for seeing the Sunset. — As I
passed by the seedling wild cherry I saw that the mushroom
or toadstool had shot up its stem till it became top-heavy,
broke down and turned black as a sooty chimney — Mr.
Edward Brooks jun'r came out from Boston to take tea with
Mrs. Charles, and I went to the town hall, and heard Wendell
Phillips deliver a second Anti-Slavery Address. — He spoke
without Notes, as all the Lecturers now do — His argument
was the incumbent duty of every abolitionist is to tramp under
foot the article of the Constitution which requires the surrender of fugitive Slaves — He assumes the position that this
is null and void; as a compact contrary to the Law of Nature
and of God — He thanked God that he was not a citizen of
the United States — and goes the extremest lengths of the
abolitionists — After his lecture he came and spoke to me, and
I told him I could not concur in his doctrines. He took me
home in his Carry all. — His auditory was small.

———

[September 1843]
19. III:45. Tuesday. ≈ I received a second Letter from Mr.
Giddings, with one of the same date (13 September) from him,

James M. Bloss, and Gaius N. St. John, as a Committee of the People of Ashtabula County, Ohio inviting me to visit them on my way to or returning from Cincinnati — This afternoon I answered the invitation and the Letter from Giddings; but it left me in the evening only the power to finish the page I had begun yesterday of my discourse. In the distribution of my time, it is distressing to be so exceedingly straitened for hours to read; and I feel it cruelly now, when I want to compress a history of Astronomy into a discourse of three hours delivery. My task is to turn this transient gust of enthusiasm for the Science of astronomy at Cincinnati into a permanent and persevering national pursuit which may extend the bounds of human knowledge, and make my country instrumental in elevating the character and improving the condition of man upon Earth — The hand of God himself has furnished me this opportunity to do good — But O! how much will depend upon my manner of performing that task? and with what agony of soul must I implore the aid of almighty wisdom for powers of conception, energ[y] of exertion and unconquerable will to accomplish my design.

———

[October 1843]

11. V. Wednesday. ≈ I received a Letter from Mr. Henry Clay, with a kind and cordial invitation to Kentucky, and to Ashland his house, on the occasion of my approaching tour to Cincinnati — And the invitation is extended equally to Mrs. Adams — I receive it with a full sense of the generous and friendly feeling of Mr. Clay; but under equal embarrassment whether to accept or to decline it. I had intended not to protract my journey beyond the absolute necessity required for the performance of the duty which I have engaged to perform; and that becomes more formidable as I approach the day of performance. Even now it brings me to the borders of distraction — There are numerous reasons why I should not step beyond the State of Ohio, and my deliberate judgment is that I should adhere to that determination — Yet there are considerations of great weight prompting to my acceptance of the invitations to Kentucky and especially that of Mr. Clay. I must wait for Counsel.

———

14. IV:10. Saturday. ≈ After dinner Isaac H. Adams and his Sister Mrs. Angier were here. Also Dr. Fisher of Dorchester and Mr. Edward Jarvis who said that they proposed to memorialize Congress, to demand a revisal of the returns of the last census especially with regard to the number of persons returned as insane. From these returns it is made to appear that there is an immense disproportion of insane persons, of the free coloured class, over every other portion of the population. The Slavemongers are building upon it a systematic argument in support of Slavery. Mr. Jarvis has published in the Boston Courier an Article, proving that the census returns have been falsified to give this appearance to the facts — He believes that the falsification of the Document was made at the Department of State, and therefore proposes this memorial to demand the revisal of it — I told him that if they would send the memorial to me I would present it.

———

30. IV:15. Monday. We embarked this morning before 8 in the Steamer Gen'l Wayne, Captain   with falling snow which began about 5 — We had many opinions of the great imprudence of going out in that state of the weather but the depu[ta]-tion from Erie were impatient to get home and I was not less impatient to reach as soon as possible the point of my destination Cincinnati.

———

[November 1843]
2. IV–VI:30. Thursday. I came on board of the Canal Packet boat Rob-Roy, yesterday very unwell with my catarrh, hoarseness and sore-throat and some fever. this boat is 83 feet long, 15 feet wide, and has besides the persons here named about 20 other passengers. It is divided into 6 compartments; the first in the bow with two settee beds for the ladies, separated by a curtain from a parlour bed chamber, with an iron stove in the centre and side settees, on which four of us slept feet to feet — then a bulging stable for four horses two and two by turns and a narrow passage with a side settee for one passenger to sleep on, leading to the third compartment a dining hall and dormitory for 30 persons; and lastly a kitchen and cooking apparatus with sleeping room for cook, steward and crew, and necessary conveniences. So much humanity crowded into such

a compass was a trial such as I had never before experienced, and my heart sunk within me, when squeezing into this pillory I reflected that I am to pass 3 nights and 4 days in it. We came on board the boat at 2 O'Clock the time when she was to depart, but it was 4 before she left the wharf. We were obliged to keep the windows of the cabins closed against the driving snow, and the stoves heated with billets of wood made the rooms uncomfortably warm. It was a comfortless evening, but before its close I found that our fellow travellers who shared the after cabin with us were well bred persons, and pleasant companions. Mr. John B. Macy resides at Cincinnati. His brother Francis at Portsmouth Ohio. His daughter Charlotte, a handsome and amiable young woman from 17 to 20, and Miss Langdon of Buffalo, from 25 to 30 with fascinating manners substitutes for beauty relieved the tediousness of the evening. Mr. Russell, grandfather of Charlotte Macy was also of the company, and Mr. Chamberlin a young man who had met me at Cleveland with an invitation from the inhabitants of Akron to me to visit that place — About 11 O'Clock I took to my settee bed, with a head ache, feverish chills, hoarseness and a sore throat, and my tussis senilis in full force. After a restless sleepless night, I rose twice; first at 4 and again at half past 6 — As soon as daylight came I was taken in a carriage to a hotel, where we had a plentiful breakfast. I was then taken again in a carriage to the town hall, where I was addressed, and answered by a short speech after which I shook hands with the men, women and children. Among the women, a very pretty one, as I took her hand kissed me on the cheek. I returned the salute on the lip and kissed every woman that followed, at which some made faces, but none refused. — We returned to the boat, and continued all day our progress through the canal at the rate of about 2 miles and a half an hour — I was able to occupy part of the day morning and afternoon with writing in this diary. There was snow great part of the day — no encouragement to open the windows or to view the country through which we pass.

———

8. IV–V:45. Wednesday. ≈ The arrangements for laying the corner stone of the Observatory, and for the delivery of my Oration to-morrow were concerted, with Professor Mitchel,

judge Burnet, and Mr. Greene — but the address on the spot, in the act of laying the corner stone, was not yet prepared — Worn down with fatigue anxiety and shame as I was, and with the oppression of a catarrhal load upon my lungs, I sat up till one in the morning writing the address, which from utter exhaustion I left unfinished and retired to a sleepless bed. I fear I am not duly grateful to divine Providence for the blessing of these demonstrations of kindness and honour from my Countrymen; but I dread still more the danger of being pampered and elated into vanity by them.

———

14. IV:30. Tuesday. ≈ The Night was nearly sleepless, and I was of course unfitted through this day for reading. I had received warm invitations from Maysville Kentucky, and from Portsmouth Ohio to visit them and receive a welcome. — Immediately after breakfast this morning, we reached Maysville 65 miles from Cincinnati — On landing, we proceeded with a dense crowd of people to a hotel where we breakfasted again, and then repaired with the Mayor and a large deputation of the citizens to the Methodist Church. There, I was welcomed to the city and introduced to the people in a highly complimentary address by the Mayor, which I answered, and as I had done at Covington, included in my remarks a just tribute of respect to Mr. Clay. And here I solemnly declared that the charges of corrupt bargaining which had been trumped up against him and me were utterly without foundation. There has been a cordiality in my reception at Covington, and here, not surpassed even at Cincinnati. But the impulse is from the friends of Mr. Clay, and all the affectionate part of their caresses are meant for him — The mayor thanked me warmly for my answer and requested me at my leisure to furnish him with a copy of it for publication.

———

24. III–IV:45. Friday. I have performed my task, I have executed my undertaking, and am returned safe to my family and my home. It is not much in itself — It is nothing in the estimation of the world. In my motives and my hopes it is considerable. The people of this Country do not sufficiently estimate the importance of patronizing and promoting Science as a principle of political action and the Slave oligarchy systematically struggle

to suppress all public patronage or countenance to the progress of the mind — Astronomy has been specially neglected
and scornfully treated — This invitation had a gloss of showy
representation about it, that wrought more on the public mind
than many volumes of dissertation or argument. I hoped to
draw a lively and active attention to it among the people, and
to put in motion a propelling power of intellect which will no
longer stagnate into rottenness. I indulge dreams of future
improvement to result from this proclamation of popular
homage to the advancement of Science, and am willing even to
see my name perhaps ostentateously connected with a movement to which I so long and so anxiously strove to give an
impulse in vain — For whatever of vain-glory there may be in
this self approving reflection I pray to be forgiven — But I return to my home with the symptoms of of speedy dissolution
upon me — I had no conception of the extent to which I have
been weakened by this Tussis Senilis — or Pneumonia Notha,
or Old Mans cough — My strength is prostrated beyond any
thing that I ever experienced before — even to total impotence
— I have little life left in me, but it is my duty to cherish that
which God has given me till it shall be his pleasure to take it
back.

---

29. IV:45. Wednesday. I made this morning the draught of a
Resolution, which I propose to offer to the House of Representatives at the approaching Session of Congress — A Session
at which a trial of character more severe than I ever before experienced awaits me; and from which may the Mercy of God
deliver me to the judgment of the after age, pure and unsullied.
Clouds and darkness are before me.

[December 1843]
10. VI:30. Sunday. ≈ Walking home I stop'd at the House of
the Mexican Minister, General Almonte, and was introduced
to his wife, and his Sister, her mother — He spoke of the recent re-election of General Santa-Anna as President of the
Mexican Republic, and of the relations between Mexico and
this Country. A subject upon which I want Prudence and
Fortitude to think, and still more to act — After dinner I attended at the second Presbyterian Church, and heard Mr.

Knox, from 1 Corinthians 15:16. "The sting of death, is Sin."
— Mr. Knox's Sermons are all comminutions — It is well for
Christians to be often warned of their responsibilities, their
imperfections and their Sins. — But Sin is a term of so indefinite
a meaning, that to declaim against it is to brandish a sword in
the air — I spent this evening in preparing for the duties of the
coming week, and in meditating purposes never to be performed
— On full deliberation I conclude that the whole course of my
conduct in this Congress must be defensive, even of the cause of
Liberty, and above all things to endure mortification.

———

16. IV:30. Saturday. I expended all the leisure of this morning
in copying a list of the yeas and nays on my motion to except
the 23^d or anti-petition rule, from the adoption by the house of
the rules of the last Congress. Two hundred members of the
present house have taken their seats — The vote of the whigs
has never exceeded 65, that of the democracy has not passed
130. The democratic majority may be set down as averaging
just two thirds — Yet on my motion the vote stood 91 to 94 a
majority of only 3 to retain the rule — 27 members from
New-York voted for my motion — only 5 against it — 12 from
Pennsylvania for and 8 against it. Ohio 13 for and 5 against it
— This morning, immediately after the reading of the journal
the Speaker said the first business in order was the call of the
States for Petitions — This caused surprize, the practice of
presenting petitions openly in the house having been superseded in the last Congress, by that of presenting them silently
at the clerks table, and having them referred to the appropriate
Committees — The Speaker was now reminded of this practice, which he explicitly recognized, but called out Petitions
are in order from the State of Maine — Mr. Barnard first urged
to proceed immediately to the election of a chaplain, and cav-
illing objections being made, moved a suspension of the rules,
which was carried by a vote of two thirds.   had moved a
resolution that the house would dispense with the election of a
chaplain for the present Session; but this proposition was immediately shouted down — At the first viva voce vote for
chaplain, there was no choice; at the second   Tinsley was
chosen — M'Kay, chairman of the Committee of Ways and
Means moved the reference of the annual report of the

Secretary of the Treasury on the finances, in parcels to four separate Committees. I objected to this and insisted that the whole Report should be referred to the Committee of Ways and Means, which after a short and spirited debate was done — Then the Speaker called again for petitions, for which no one seemed prepared — The States of Maine and New Hampshire were quickly despatched — Massachusetts was called — Parmenter and D. P. King offered Resolutions of the Legislature which were ordered to be referred and printed. The Speaker hurried on and called Rhode-Island and Connecticut till Winthrop called him back — I then rose and presented a memorial from   Appleton and Co. and 96 Booksellers and traders praying for an international copy right Law, which was after some discussion ordered to be printed — and referred to a select Committee. My next presentment was a petition from James B. Cooper and 585 citizens of New[-York] praying Congress to separate the People of New-York, from all connection whatever with Slavery — and this produced a blow up and adjournment.

17. IV:30. Sunday. The explosion which took place in the house, on my presenting yesterday the anti-slavery petition of 585 citizens of Western New-York is a premonitory symptom of the desperation with which the Slave power will be exercised in the present Congress — The Latimer petition, signed by upwards of 50 000 names was received at the last Session of Congress, and referred to the judiciary Committee. The Petition from New-York which I presented yesterday contains the same prayer in the same identical words — The Speaker instantly decided — that it was excluded from reception by the gag-rule now the 23^{d}. I remonstrated, that on the Journals of the last Session, it was recorded that petitions in the same words were received and referred to the judiciary Committee. Half a dozen Slave breeders were already on their feet — The Speaker coolly said — "does the gentleman appeal from the decision of the chair?" I said I had already too much experience not to be aware of the fate of any appeal from the decision of the chair — but that I intreated the Speaker to revise his own decision so far as to look at the precedent on the Journal of the last Session. The Speaker said he considered the petition

excluded by the rule — I then said that if the Speaker refused to look at the precedent, I had no other alternative, and *must* take an appeal from his decision — At this instant T. W. Gilmer started up in a panic and moved to adjourn, which after a short respite to receive communications from the Executive departments was carried without opposition; the Speaker saying in the most courteous tone that he would very cheerfully examine the precedents.

———

21. VI. Thursday. ≈ In the house, the life and death struggle for the right of Petition was resumed — The question of reception of the petition from Illinois was laid on the table 98 to 80 after a long and memorable debate. I then presented the Resolves of the Massachusetts Legislature of   March 1843 proposing an Amendment to the Constitution of the United States, making the Representation of the People in the house proportioned to the numbers of free persons — and moved it should be read, printed and referred to a select Committee of 9, and now sprung up the most memorable debate ever entertained in the house; in the midst of which the house at half past 3 adjourned. — I can give no account of it — Wise formally surrendered at discretion his citadel rule, to the right of petition — Then came a cross fire between Holmes, Beardsley, Weller, and French — till at the motion of Belser of Alabama, the house adjourned — R. D. Davis of New-York had taken the floor — The crisis now requires of me coolness, firmness, Prudence, Moderation, and Fortitude beyond all former example. I came home in such a state of agitation that I could do nothing but pace my chamber.

22. IV:30. Friday. Pilgrim Anniversary — The agony continues. ≈ The occurrences in the house yesterday and this day have been so extraordinary that they would require a narrative which it is impossible for me to write out, but a brief summary of which I must borrow a supernumerary page to record. Yesterday after the long snarling debate to suppress the enthusiastical petition from the State of Illinois, finally read, and upon question of its reception, laid on the table, when I presented the Resolves of the Legislature of Massachusetts, and moved the reference of them to a select Committee of 9.

Jameson moved the Committee on the Judiciary,   a
Committee of one member from each State, Wise rose, called
upon the Reporters to take note of what he was about to say,
asked the particular attention of the house, and declared once
for all, and forever that he renounced this <u>War</u> against Southern rights which had been several years waged in the hall. He
would vote for my motion to refer these Resolves to a select
Committee and hoped I should be the chairman of it that the
whole Committee should be of the same complexion; and that
the whole mass of abolition petitions should be referred to the
same Committee, that we might make a report in our own
way, and the house and the country might see what we were
after — Whereupon Holmes, Beardsley, Weller and French,
made frothy and foaming speeches about abolition. R. D. Davis
rose to take the floor, and I said I hoped I should be indulged
with an opportunity to say a few words, when the house
adjourned — This day, when the Speaker announced the call
for petitions, as the order of the day — R. D. Davis rose again to
take the floor, but Preston King one of the five members from
New-York, who clings to the gag-rule, made a feeble attempt
to deprive me of the floor to reply to the slave mongers licensed
all day yesterday — He charged me with arresting the progress
of the presentation of petitions — I said I would not move a
suspension of the rules to obtain permission to address the
house, but only demanded a decision upon my motion to refer
the Resolves of the Legislature of Massachusetts to a select
Committee — Hudson moved to suspend the rules to enable
me to address the house and Hunt of New-York called the yeas
and nays on the motion — The vote was 123 to 46 and I spoke
about an hour in reply to Wise, Holmes, Weller and French.
Desultory, weak, and superficial — but effective — Belser
moved to lay the Resolves of Massachusetts on the table —
Lost 64 to 104. Jameson withdrew his motion to refer them to
the Committee on the judiciary, and my motion to refer them
to a select Committee of 9 was carried without a division.

———

[January 1844]
I. V:30. Monday. I begin the new year as I closed the old one
with praise and prayer to God — With grateful thanksgiving
for the past — with humble supplication for the future —

Physical Nature never was more kindly adapted to the enjoyment of man in commencing the year, than it was this day, at this place. The close of the last year was serene, mild, and beautiful — The entrance of the new annual portion of everlasting ages, was yet more auspicious and cheering — The morning, noon and night of it was delightful — I rose an hour and a half later than my time — but closed before breakfast the diary of the departed year. From ten till 3 O'Clock, an uninterrupted stream of visitors, absorbed the time, and exhausted my patience — It is generally meant in kindness, always in civility — and for a succession of 15 years since I left the Presidents house, has greeted me in still increasing numbers. Among the visitors of this day were some of the bitterest political enemies, North and South, that I have in the world — Holmes and Campbell of South-Carolina — Burke and Hale of New-Hampshire were of the number; and Charles Jared Ingersoll the cunningest, and most treacherous cat of them all — Holmes however could not cover his sore with Court Plaister. He made a merit of his visit by saying he had come to see me, "notwithstanding the sword of Orlando" — A dash of ridicule that I cast upon him for his hectoring bravadoes of battle against the abolitionists — An hour of argument he could answer with blustering sophistry — An impregnable syllogism with rodomontade, but Durindana cut so deep that he will never recover from the wound — Of all weapons in debate sarcasm is the lethalis arundo. Immediately after I got disengaged from the throng, about 3, I walked to Mrs. Madisons house and paid her a visit. Found with her several ladies: of whom were Miss Legaré, sister of the late Attorney General: two misses Bryant, daughters of another sister and Anna Payne who live with her ≈ I have piles of Letters unanswered and which I never shall find time to answer. To-morrow recommences the struggle which for me can terminate only with my life. May the Spirit from above in life and death sustain me!

2. III:45. Tuesday. ≈ At ten I met the Committee on the revisal of the rules. Present Adams, Beardsley, C. J. Ingersoll, White, Chapman and Vinton — Absent, Wise, Davis and Dromgoole, the last of whom has not once attended the Committee. Before the Quorum was formed this morning, Beardsley told me that

he thought the house would not confirm the vote of the Committee to strike out the gag rule, and he intimated that Davis of Indiana had changed his opinion and would move to reverse the decision of the Committee — But Davis did not attend — The members present, after a final cursory revisal of the whole report, instructed me to present it, this day to the house, and to move that it be printed, and made the order of the day for this day week. — I told Beardsley that the action of the house upon the gag would depend entirely upon the perseverance of the 27 members of the New-York delegation; and that I was told the Richmond Enquirer had threatened that if they did persevere, Van Buren's claim to the Presidency would be forfeited. He admitted the fact and said that he hoped the members would not be moved by any such consideration — Two or three weak minded men might be.

———

4. V. Thursday. I have named in the margin all the members including myself of the select Committee on the Massachusetts Resolves, all of whom met this morning in the room of the Committee of Commerce, and, when that Committee met, passed into the room of the Committee on the Militia — I moved that the Committee should take minutes of their proceedings, and that when any member should present any resolution or motion in writing the question upon it should be taken if he desired it — Which was agreed to and Joseph D. Ingersoll consented to keep the minutes, at my request. I then moved the two Resolutions, which I asked the Committee to instruct their chairman to offer to the house instructing the Committee to enquire and ascertain as far as may be practicable the number of owners of Slaves, and the amount of the chattel property represented in the house. Gilmer insisted upon taking immediately the question upon the motion submitted by him at the last meeting in writing that the amendment to the Constitution proposed by the Resolves of the Legislature of Massachusetts ought not to be recommended — I first moved as an amendment to that resolution, to strike out the word *not* and then moved to postpone the consideration of it to discuss my Resolutions looking for calls for information and to give time for argumentative reports on both sides to be prepared and submitted to the Committee and

then to the house if so decided by the committee. The question on postponement was carried by vote 7 to 2 — Gilmer and Burt only voting no — Gilmer then invited me to state candidly my views in support of the amendment proposed by the Massachusetts Legislature, which I did in a very summary manner — disclaiming all intention of saying any thing offensive to any member of the committee compelled as I was to state the feelings of my constituents under their sense of the wrongs endured by them, resulting from the Slave representation in Congress — Burke and Gilmer said my father had contended that the Slaves should be represented equally with the whites — But that was in the confederation of States without any representation of the people. Garrett Davis suggested that if information of the number of owners of Slaves, and of the amount of their value was to be sought — similar information of the numbers of other proprietors and of the value of other property would be equally necessary. From this I dissented no other property being represented in Congress.

———

21. V. Sunday. Light snow, all the morning. I attended public worship at the Capitol, where the Rev'd Justin Edwards said to be from Boston preached a discourse upon the sanctity of the Sabbath from Mark 2:27 "The Sabbath was made for man." This question about keeping the Sabbath holy, as a day of rest is one of the numerous religious and political excitements, which keep the free people of this union in perpetual agitation — They seem to be generated by the condition of the country — in a state of profound peace — There are in this country as in all others a certain proportion of restless and turbulent spirits, poor, unoccupied, ambitious, who must always have something to quarrel about with their neighbours — These people are the authors of religious revivals — They formed in the days of Washington's administration the germ of the Jacobin clubs — During the last War with Great Britain, they generated the Washington benevolent Societies and Peace Societies. In later times, they have bred the Masonic and anti-masonic Societies, the Temperance Societies, the Colonization, abolition, and anti-Slavery Societies, and they are now beating the drum and blowing the trumpet for a holy Sabbath Society — A numerous Convention is already advertised to

promote the cause, and Mr. Edwards has come to preach for it in the Representative Hall ≈

22. V:15. Monday. ≈ Giddings presented several anti-slavery and abolition-petitions; among the rest one from 381 citizens of Hampshire County, Massachusetts, praying Congress by law to prohibit the officers of the United States from assisting to arrest persons suspected of being fugitives from Slavery. There was much fluttering among the Slavers. The Speaker decided that this petition was not within the 25th rule — From which decision Black of Georgia appealed — I called for the yeas and nays — Saunders attempted to raise the question of reception, but the Speaker said it was too late — Jameson enquired if laying the appeal on the table would carry the petition with it. The Speaker said no — Wilkins said there was just such a petition referred to the Committee on the judiciary — Payne moved to lay the appeal on the table — carried 113 ayes. He then made the question of reception and Cave Johnson moved to lay that on the table — This is the wooden nutmeg form of rejecting a petition, without refusing to receive it — The question to lay on the table was lost 85 to 87 and then the question to receive was lost 85 to 86. In the interval between the two takings of yeas and nays Freedom lost two votes, Slavery gained one, and the majority was changed — Beardsley presented a petition praying for the repeal of the act of February 1793 for catching fugitive Slaves — Thompson moved the question of reception, and Weller moved to lay it on the table — Beardsley moved a call of the house — and Hopkins moved to adjourn, and it was carried. Another slip of the rattlesnake Slavery from the grasp of Freedom ≈

23. V. Tuesday. ≈ A poor Negro came in a state almost of distraction, to implore me to save his wife from being sold away. I asked him how I could do that? He said by purchasing her myself; for 400 dollars — I told him that was impossible. The poor fellow went away in despair.

———

30. V:30. Tuesday. ≈ Between the preparation of my report on the Massachusetts Resolves, and keeping time with my daily record the labour is more than Herculean, and my correspon-

dence is almost entirely suspended — Five days in the week the
Report of the Committee on the rules is the first business in
order to be transacted by the house; and if I were to be absent
one day when it would be called up; it would be laid upon the
table without redemption. When I call it up scance a day passes
but some dirty trick is devised to postpone the taking of the
question ≈

31. IV:30. Wednesday ≈ I hurried up to the Capitol to be there
at the meeting of the house — The report on the rules was immediately taken up, and Andrew Johnson a new member from
Tennessee made an hour speech in support of the gag-rule, and
especially abusive upon me. So they all are. — I am compelled
not only to endure it with seeming insensibility, but to forbear
so far as I can restrain myself from all reply. This man took at
once the ground that Congress have no power to abolish Slavery in the District of Columbia, because the Legislatures of
Virginia and Maryland had no such power, before their cessions
of the two parts of the district to the United States — All the
arguments of the speech were upon a level with this.

———

[February 1844]
7. V:40. Wednesday. At the house, before the chaplain appeared
Mr. Hudson came to my seat and told me that he had heard the
democracy had in a new caucus determined to take immediately
the question on the restoration of the gag rule — That Dromgoole would withdraw his motion to recommit the report and
will move the previous question — The New-York democrats
have been whipped in, by the threat that the South will desert
Van Buren, if his friends join to rescind the rule, with a promise
of Calhoun and his party to support Van Buren if the rule is retained and the tariff broken down — I have been prepared for
this reverse, and must bear it with patience.

———

14. V. Wednesday. ≈ At the house Stephen A. Douglass of Illinois, the author of the majority Report from the Committee
of Elections, had taken the floor last Evening, and now raved
out his hour in abusive invectives upon the members who had
pointed out its blunders, and upon the whig party. His face
was convulsed — his gesticulation frantic; and he lashed

himself into such a heat, that if his body had been made of combustible matter it would have burnt out. In the midst of his roaring to save himself from choking he strip'd off and cast away his cravat, unbuttoned his waistcoat and had the awkward aspect of a half naked pugilist — and this man comes from a judicial bench, and passes for an eloquent Orator.

———

23. VI. Friday. ≈ I answered this morning a Letter from my Son, and see by the Boston Courier of Wednesday morning that the Resolves reported by him against the annexation of Texas passed on Tuesday, in the Senate of Massachusetts, unanimously with one exception upon the first Resolve 34 Senators present. Six absent — among whom was Levi Lincoln — My Son's speech is in the Courier, and shews that he is aware of his position — which he has deliberately assumed, explicitly declared, and will firmly maintain — My heart aches at the prospect of the dangers and trials that await and already beset him. May the God of Justice be his guide and guard — and the God of Mercy protect him.

———

28. VI. Wednesday. ≈ While we were at dinner John Barney burst into the chamber; rushed up to general Scott and told him with groans that the President wished to see him — That the great gun on board the Princeton, the Peacemaker had burst and killed the Secretary of State Upshur, the Secretary of the Navy T. W. Gilmer, Captain Beverley Kennon, Virgil Maxcy, a Col'l Gardiner of New-York and a coloured servant of the President, and desperately wounded several of the crew — General Scott soon left the table — Mr. Webster shortly after — also the Senator Bayard — I came home before 10 in the Evening.

———

[March 1844]
25. IV. Monday. I approach the term, when my daily journal must cease, from physical disability to keep it up. I have now struggled nearly five years without the interval of a day while mind and body have been wearing away under the daily silent but unremitting erosion of time ≈

———

26. V. Tuesday. ≈ The Commissioner of Patents H. L. Ellsworth, came with Jeremiah E. Cary of Cherry valley, member

from the 21st congressional district of New-York, Otsego and Scoharie, and delivered to me a Letter from himself, with one from Julius Pratt and Co. Manufacturers at Meriden Connecticut, and a present of a milk white Ivory cane, one yard long made of one elephant's tooth, tip'd with silver and steel, with the American eagle inlaid in gold on its top and a ring under the pommel, inscribed with my name, and the words Justum et tenacem propositi virum — The Letter requests that on the day when the gag rule shall be finally abolished I will insert the date after the inscription on the ring — After expressing my deep sensibility to this testimonial of kindness and approbation of my public conduct, I promised a written answer to Mr. Pratt's Letter, and alluding to my custom of declining valuable presents from individuals for public service, I accepted the cane as a trust to be returned when the date of the extinction of the gag-rule shall be accomplished.

———

[April 1844]
8. V:30. Monday. Mr. Walter Forward of Pittsburgh called on me this morning deeply concerned, and anxiously adverse, as I had found him last November at Pittsburgh against the annexation of Texas to this Union — To his enquiries as to the prospects of this event at present I could give no answer — though I now see it doomed beyond the reach of all but almighty power, and despair of that — The impulse of national aggrandizement, spurred by private avarice and corruption cannot be resisted; and it will now be consummated even without a War — with the connivance, if not with the aid of England.

———

11. V:30. Thursday. ≈ This morning the Rev'd R. R. Gurley called on me with the Rev'd Aaron Foster, from whom I had received a queer letter on the 24th of last October the day before I left Quincy for Cincinnati. He came now with a small Album, blank excepting a creed in half a dozen lines that Permanent and universal peace is the genius of Christianity and promotive of the prosperity of Nations and claims the prayers and exertions of all philanthropists. He wished my name as first subscriber to this creed. I reinforced the creed by declaring peace the Law of Nature and of Natures God — the vital

spirit and genius of Christianity, and essential to the Liberty, Justice and Prosperity of Nations — I subscribed to this, and left him to find other subscribers as he may.

———

14. V:30. Sunday. ≈ Immediately after dinner I received visits from the Minister of Great Britain Mr. Pakenham, and his Secretary Mr. Bidwell — With Mr. Pakenham I had some conversation. I enquired if his negotiation with our Government on the subject of the Oregon territory had commenced. He said it had not — But he said that he had made an explicit declaration to our Department of State that the British Government would in no respect interfere in the affairs of Texas; and he spoke of it as some what extraordinary that the fact had been publicly denied in the Madisonian, the official daily journal of the Executive — He said he had thought of addressing a note to the Secretary of State on the subject. But he manifested no feeling on the signature of the Treaty for the annexation of Texas to the United States, and left me with the impression that Great Britain would oppose no resistance to its consummation.

———

17. V. Wednesday. ≈ Numerous Reports of Committees were received almost all pernicious — The Western harbour Bill was taken up, and the previous question was withdrawn, for the homunculus Douglass to poke out a speech in favour of the constitutionality of appropriations for the improvement of Western rivers and harbours. — This brought out Rhett in all his fury and Holmes in all his casuistry, against Douglass and against the whole system of Internal improvement, federalism, consolidation and despotism — The debate was continued between the conflicting absurdities of the Southern Democracy which is Slavery and the Western democracy which is knavery, till Kennedy of Indiana slumped into a motion to strike out the whole bill, and inserting the bill first reported by the Committee omitting the Illinois river. Hopkins Quasi speaker pronounced this not in order. Kennedy appealed. Adjourned.

———

22. V. Monday. ≈ This was a memorable day in the annals of the world — The Treaty for the annexation of Texas to this

Union was this day sent in to the Senate; and with it the freedom of the human race — In the house it was a no less disastrous day. M'Kay chairman of the Committee of Ways and
Means made his long fore-announced motion to suspend the
rules to go into Committee of the whole on the state of
the Union, to take up his anti-tariff bill; and after a call of the
house upon which 194 members answered to their names, the
motion was carried by a vote of 104 to 94, the majority consisting of that floating class of Janus-faces, who decide all great,
and critical questions, by holding themselves at market till the
last hour, and then let the hammer fall to the highest bidder
— The vote against reconsidering the passage of the Western
harbour bill had been 73 to 111 — The number voting on the
motion to take up the anti tariff was 198, probably the largest
vote of the Session — The standing supremacy of the Slave
representation is 112 a bare majority of the whole house consisting of 80 Slaveholders and 32 free trade auxiliaries — This
is the average allowing 8 Slaveholders for occasional defection
from their iron rule, and an equal number of Laodicean freeman neither hot nor cold, and ever wavering between Slavery
and Freedom.

———

[May 1844]
1. IV:30. Wednesday. ≈ This was the day of the first whig convention at Baltimore to nominate Henry Clay as their candidate for the Office of President of the United States for four
years from the fourth of March next and to agree upon a
Candidate for the Office of Vice President — They met accordingly 275 in number from the 26 States, equal to the
Constitutional number of the two houses of Congress; and
what never has happened in either house of Congress, the
whole number from every State was present.

———

4. IV:30. Saturday. The stream of visitors, returning delegates
from the Baltimore conventions is yet copious and unabated.
many of my old acquaintances come to shake hands with me as
they pass, and many others ask to be introduced to me for the
same purpose. Their names are seldom pronounced by their
introducers so that I distinctly hear them, and their names and
their persons slip alike from my memory the moment they part

from me. But they consume time, and multiply subjects of excitement tending to distraction. At the same time the Treaty for the annexation of Texas to the United States, with the President's message transmitting it to the Senate, and the accompanying documents, prematurely published, and the conflicting opinions of the leading men of the Union, disclosed in Letters and speeches at public meetings, all indicate the immediate crisis of a great struggle between Slavery and Freedom throughout the world. I must retire from this contest, or perish under it probably before the close of the present year, or even of the present Session of Congress — The issue is precipitated by its bearing on the approaching Presidential election. It is John Tyler's last card for a popular whirlwind to carry him through, and he has played it with equal intrepidity and address. He has compelled Clay and Van Buren to stake their last chance upon opposition to the measure *now*, and has forced himself upon the whole democracy as their exclusive candidate for the Presidency next December.

———

9. IV:15. Thursday. A new subject of political excitement is opening upon this country, the extent and duration of which it is impossible for me to foresee, but which must have great influence for good or evil (God grant it may be for good) upon the future history and fortunes of this Union — It is a deadly feud between the native american poor population, and the Roman Catholic Irish multitudes gathered in the city of Philadelphia — The animosities between these two classes of people have been fermenting in all our atlantic cities for several years, and have been much aggravated by the pernicious factious influence of these Irish Catholics over the elections in all the populous cities — The reaction of the native American population effected a total revolution in the recent election of the City Government of New-York — They have now broken out in furious riots at Philadelphia, where from the first of this week a succession of bitterly exasperated mobs, have destroyed multitudes of human lives, dwelling houses, schools and churches, unrestrained by the Government of the City or of the State.

———

31. V. Friday. I finished the draught of a Report from the select Committee on the Smithsonian bequest, but in the process of

preparing it changed my purpose from the design of reporting two bills, to that of including the whole subject in one — At the house I presented by leave of the house a petition of Tarr and 179 citizens of Pennsylvania, native americans, praying for an alteration of the naturalization laws to require of 25 years of naturalization, residence for the admission of foreigners to the political rights of native Americans — The petitioners not one of whom is personally known to me requested me in presenting it to the house to give my opinion upon its merits — This required of me a painful operation, for I do not approve the change of the Law petitioned for and know that an odious colouring will be given to the mere presentation of the petition — But I did not feel it becoming in me to refuse to present the petition, nor yet to shrink from the avowal of my opinion against it — I therefore presented the petition, stated the facts and said as the petitioners had chosen to call for my opinion, I felt myself obliged to say that I could not support its prayer — I moved its reference to the judiciary committee. J. W. Brown of Indiana and Hammett of Mississippi moved to lay it on the table which was carried by yeas and nays 128 to 26. Charles J. Ingersoll voted first no, and after the close of the call changed his vote.

———

[June 1844]

2. V. Sunday. I received yesterday a printed note of invitation — "Rachel Priestman a minister of the Gospel in the Society of Friends, has appointed a meeting for Divine Worship, to be held in the Capitol to-morrow morning at 11 O'Clock to which thou art respectfully invited." I attended accordingly. She preached from the Clerk's table where two men and two women of her company were seated with her. After sitting about 20 minutes in silence she took off and laid aside her black bonnet and rising began rather suddenly, "This is a faithful saying, and worthy of all acceptation, that Christ Jesus came into the world to save Sinners." from this text 1 Timothy 1:15 without so naming it, she discoursed nearly an hour in the peculiar canting tone of Quaker Oratory, slow, distinct and loud articulation without a moment's loss of words, but within almost every sentence, a pause and hitch to take breath, repeating almost every verse in Paul's epistles impressing the

doctrine of Salvation by Faith in Christ Jesus — Her exhortations were full of unction and intensity — She finished as abruptly as she had begun, and sat down, apparently exhausted — The house was well filled and and attentive. Some of the auditory thinking the service over began to move, but a man of her company requested them not to depart, and they resumed their Seats. After an interval of about 5 minutes she kneeled and made a fervent affectionate and passionate prayer in behalf of her hearers, not omitting a supplication to God to turn their hearts to dissolve the ties of bondage, and let the oppressed go free. After the service was over, she came with her husband I suppose, to my seat and shook hands with me.

———

8. V. Saturday. ≈ My morning hours after rising are so constantly absorbed by newspaper reading and the evening hours by company or disability that I have no time except during the Session of the house to make up my record from day to day, which in the course of six hours I am usually just able to do.

———

10. V. Monday. The vote in the U.S. Senate on the question of advising and consenting to the Texian Treaty was
Yeas Atchison, Bagby, Breese, Buchanan, Colquitt, Fulton, Haywood, Henderson, Huger, Lewis, M'Duffie, Semple, Sevier, Sturgeon, Walker, Woodbury   16.
Nays. Allen, Archer, Atherton, Barrow, Bates, Bayard, Benton, Berrien, Choate, Clayton, Crittenden, Dayton, Evans, Fairfield, Foster, Francis, Huntington, Jarnagin, Johnson, Mangum, Merrick, Miller, Morehead, Niles, Pearce, Phelps, Porter, Rives, Simmons, Tallmadge, Tappan, Upham, White, Woodbridge, Wright.   35.
Hannegan absent.

I record this vote as a deliverance, I trust by the special interposition of almighty God, of my Country, and of human Liberty; from a conspiracy comparable to that of Lucius Sergius Catilina — May it prove not a mere temporary deliverance, like that only preliminary to the fatally successful conspiracy of Julius Caesar — The annexation of Texas to this Union is the first step to the conquest of all Mexico, of the West India

Islands, of a maritime colonizing slavery tainted monarchy, and of extinguished freedom. ≈

11. V. Tuesday. ≈ Two messages were received from the President one communicating the Treaty for the annexation of Texas, recently rejected by the Senate with all the documents relating to the Treaty published by the Senate, and others with a message of 16 May, not published by the Senate, and calling on Congress to accomplish the annexation. J. P. Kennedy moved to lay this message on the table, lost 59 to 118 by previous question it was referred to the Committee of Foreign Affairs. — Weller moved to suspend the rules for a motion to print 15 000 copies of the message lost 108 to 79, not two-thirds. I moved to suspend the rules to offer two resolutions declaring the exclusive Constitutional power of Congress to declare War — and that any attempt by the President to negotiate the Country into a War by Treaty would be a violation of the exclusive constitutional authority of the house — lost 78 to 108.

———

16. VII. Sunday. ≈ After the morning service I had a visit from Daniel D. Barnard to take leave; and a long conversation with him. This Texas annexation we deem the turning point of a revolution which transforms the North-American Confederation into a conquering and warlike Nation. Aggrandizement will be its passion and its policy. A military Government, a large army, a costly navy, distant Colonies, and associate islands in every sea will follow of course in rapid succession — a President for four years will be a laughing stock. A Captain General for life and a Marshal's truncheon for a Scepter will establish the law of arms for the constitution, and the skeleton forms of War and Slavery will stalk unbridled over the land — Blessed God deliver us from this fate! ≈

17. V. Monday. Close of 28 Congress, 1 Session. The first shock of Slave Democracy is over. Moloch and Mammon have sunk into momentary slumber — The Texas Treason is blasted for the hour, and the first Session of the most perverse and worthless Congress that ever disgraced this confederacy has

closed. This last day, from 10 in the morning till Noon was a continuation of tumult from the adjournment of yesterday morning. The joint Resolution of the two houses, had fixed the adjournment, by their respective presiding Officers at 12 O'Clock Meridian this day. There were numerous bills public and private still pending before them both, and the 37th joint rule forbids the sending of any bill to the President for his approbation on the last day of the Session — This rule was rescinded and bills were sent to him and signed by him at least until the moment of adjournment.

———

[July 1844]
6. IV:15. Saturday ≈ At the Office of the National Intelligencer, I took 6 copies of the paper of this day, containing my closing list of Petitions, presented by me at the recent Session of Congress to the house of Representatives, with the note upon the memorial of A. de Kalb Tarr and 179 citizens of Pennsylvania, praying for alteration of the naturalization Laws. I enclosed one of these papers in my Letter to W. D. Barnes, and A. de Kalb Tarr; and one to my Son, for the long Letter of Waddy Thompson jun'r against the annexation of Texas, and the annexation Treaty. — I met Mr. Thompson at the Intelligencer Office, and had a long conversation with him and Mr. Gales, on the subject — Thompson is a South-Carolina planter, owner of 100 Slaves, and religiously believes that Slavery was made for the African race and the African race for Slavery — He opposes the annexation of Texas on Southern grounds as a Southern man — So did Calhoun — so did M'Duffie. So did Hamilton, all now rabid annexationists — Thompson will be converted like them. He knocks down Walker, Wilkins and C. J. Ingersoll with their own Maul. But he smuggled through Congress the acknowledgment of Texas, prematurely — He is as cunning as four yankees, as sly as four quakers, and just now admires the People of Massachusetts too much — I hope his Letter will be eminently useful at the present crisis, and devoutly pray that he, and Benton, and the Princeton gun, may be instruments for the deliverance of my Country.

———

11. IV:30. Thursday. I enter this day on the 78th year of my age; and but for a blessed dispensation of almighty God, it would

have been the last day both of my own life, and of that of my dear and ever beloved wife. We both escaped as if by miracle, and neither of us are hurt ≈ We left Baltimore at 9 A.M. in the train of Cars for Philadelphia, which city we reached about 4 in the afternoon, and found yet in amphibious state between mob and martial Law — We concluded to proceed immediately to New-York. At 5 in the afternoon we left Walnut Street wharf in the Steamer New Philadelphia and came to Bristol 20 miles — there landed, and proceeded in the train of Cars through Trenton, New Brunswick, Elizabethtown and Newark to Jersey City — The Sunset between Trenton was glorious, equal to anything I ever beheld. As I witnessed the departing luminary, and the peace and quiet and felicity of all around me, I thought of Washington and Trenton and the 25th of December 1776 and a feeling of inexpressible joy, filled my Soul — Between 10 and 11 we alighted from the cars on an unrailed floor, raised about 4 feet above the ground, walking on this floor, dark as midnight I stept unawares off the floor, and pitched over, and drew my wife, whose arm was linked in mine over after me. Blessed by God neither neck nor limb of either of us was broken — We were enabled after an hour of delay to cross the ferry to New-York, and reached the Astor house before midnight.

12. V:30. Friday. The sensation which I suffered last night by the shock of my own fall, instantly succeeded by that of my wife was such as I never in my life experienced before, and which I have no words to describe: while falling I had the distinct idea that I was killed — A shriek from my wife, and the consciousness that she too was killed had in it a thrill of horror of which I knew not that the human frame was susceptible. My fall was so disposed that my left hip first met the earth tip'd me over upon the right side and laid me sprawling, but neither my head nor my body struck the earth — I instantly rose, feeling pain only on the hip and that not severe — but the terror for my wife, no pang of death could surpass. She had fallen forwards. Her cloathing had protected her from any shock to the body, but her left wrist was sprained and the recoil from the ground struck her breast; broke the glass of the breast pin, and slightly bruised a spot on the upper side of her chin

below the lip. She had fainted and was senseless. Several men came to our assistance — They took her up and carried her into one [of] the house sheds of the railroad company where were benches to sit upon. A physician was sent for, but as she soon came to and appeared not to be much hurt that order was countermanded — The other passengers had crossed the river in the Steam-ferry boat, and that boat in about half an hour returned. My wife had then so far recovered that she was able to be led to the boat; we crossed the river, and a hack took us to the Astor House. They gave us two bed-rooms on the first floor, and before midnight we were lodged for the Night, still unknowing how much we were injured but grateful that our lives and limbs had been spared.

———

[August 1844]
27. III:45. Tuesday. No sight of morning stars, or of rising or setting Sun — My Son went to Boston, and returned to dine. Mr. Withington is a young student of divinity recently from the theological school at Cambridge — A native of Dorchester and now residing there — He assigned two motives for his call to see me — one, as a manifestation of personal respect for my character — The other to ask my opinions upon some scruples which troubled him with regard to his voting at the presidential election — He was an abolitionist in principle, though not of the abolition party, nor of any abolition Society. He was also a whig and strongly desirous of voting for the whig candidate. But the Liberty party charged him with being an avowed duelist — and not only a Slave holder, but a decided partizan for perpetual Slavery. A gambler — intemperate, and otherwise of loose licentious life — There was no satisfactory refutation of these charges made public, and he was much perplexed what to do. He needed advice and came to ask it of me — I said that his doubts were of no easy solution. That I took no part as a partizan in the presidential election. I deemed it my duty to abstain from canvassing for any one for that office, and to leave it to the people to fix their choice for themselves — But as to matters of fact I would say what I knew or believed and as to principles, what I think — Mr. Clay is a Slave holder and a supporter of Slavery — I believe him in error upon those points; and hope he will revise and reform his opinions. He is

a man of the world, of self-indulgent habits; but not as I believe a gambler or intemperate — He abhors dueling, and has been engaged in several duels — A rigorous puritanical principle of morals cannot be applied to the exercise of the right of suffrage — There must be some reference to the result — Mr. Clay's chief competitor is vastly more exceptionable than he — To vote for a third candidate who cannot be elected is in effect to vote for the worst of the three — Mr. Withington thanked me. My reasoning evidently failed to convince him.

———

[October 1844]
2. IV. Wednesday. ≈ My visitors yesterday from the Committee of the Liberty party were apparently not of one mind when they came, nor yet when they left me. My opposition to the immediate abolition of Slavery in the District of Columbia, and in the Territories, they all disapprove, and Mr. Howe the late Senator from Norfolk County in the State Legislature pressed me specially with the question whether Congress have not the power to repeal the Laws of the District which allow and sanction Slavery. With regard to the inter-state Slave trade I told them I had no doubt of the power of Congress to prohibit that, and would vote for a bill to that effect to-morrow, though it would not be possible to prevail upon the house to receive such a bill — I told them I regretted that I could not concur with them in all their opinions, and still more the dissensions prevailing among themselves — The Colonization Society — The Anti-Slavery and abolition Societies — the no-government, non resisting and women membered Societies. I grieved also at their classing in the same level of exclusion the whig and democrat parties. — I thought there was a great difference between them; and that placing them on the same level was to secure the triumph of the worst party — This tendency of all private associations to settle into factious cabals is the besetting sin of all elective governments.

———

7. V. Monday. This was one of the epochal days of my life — On the 26th of last month my son brought me the Boston Post of 25 March containing Andrew Jackson's Letter to Aaron Vail Brown of 12 Feb'y 1843. The next morning I found on my file the semi-weekly Globe of 21 March 1844 containing

Brown's Letter to the Editors of the Globe, with Jackson's
Letter for publication. I determined to make them the text of
the address which I had promised to deliver to the young
men's whig club of Boston this Evening — I thought this a
suitable occasion for opening my defence before the country
and the world, against the conspiracy of Andrew Jackson,
Aaron Vail Brown, George W. Erving and Charles J. Ingersoll,
with their co-adjutors and tools, to ruin my good name, and
fabricate a fable to justify the robbery of Texas from Mexico,
by the pretence that Texas had been by me treacherously surrendered to Spain — I began the address that day and finished
it this day just in time for dinner — The composition therefore
is excessively hurried and unskilfully put together, with sundry
repetitions, which needed a pruning hand; but I had no time
to give — At 6 O'Clock this afternoon I rode into Boston with
my Son and Walter Hellen, and precisely at 7 alighted at the
Tremont Temple — I was there received with the utmost simplicity by the Committee of the young men's whig club, in a
private room adjoining the hall which was already crowded as
full as it could hold — Several of my elderly friends were assembled in this private room and I was specially greeted by Samuel
T. Armstrong, Jeremiah Mason, Abbott Lawrence, Stephen C.
Phillips, Robert C. Winthrop, Josiah Quincy jun'r, Samuel H.
Walley jun'r, and several others. Mr. Hayden Editor of the
Boston Atlas, Erastus Brooks of the New-York Evening Express, and the younger Buckingham, applied for the use of my
manuscript for immediate publication in their respective papers
— I gave it with a pledge that I should have a proof sheet to
revise before publication, to Mr. Hayden the first applicant. At
precisely half past 7 I entered the Hall with my Son, who is
President of the club, and with the chairman of the Committee
of the Club. The reception was complimentary and enthusiastic, and my Son said that after such a reception, it would be
superfluous for him to do more than announce to them the
name of his father John Quincy Adams — whereupon another
shout of welcome shook the house — A young Mr. Coffin at
my request read the Letters of Aaron Vail Brown and of Andrew Jackson, and I discoursed upon them two hours and
ten minutes much to the amusement of the auditory — The
closing Apostrophe to the young men of Boston was specially

well received. As soon as the crowd was cleared away we re-entered the Carriage, left my son at the United States Hotel and with Walter Hellen I returned to Quincy, reaching home at eleven.

———

24. III:40. Thursday. ≈ This afternoon Miss Catherine Thaxter called here with a cousin of hers, apparently of a later generation whom she introduced as Miss Susan Thaxter. Catherine spoke of my father and mother, and said she was here at the fiftieth anniversary of their marriage — which was of course the 25th of October 1814, and she well remembered hearing my father say then to my mother that he loved her as dearly as he did on the wedding day. ≈

25. IV:40. Friday ≈ Again as the Sun went down, I walked up the Hill to Charles's house to see the Sun set. But although it was not quite 5 O'Clock the Sun was already behind Mount Ararat. — I went further over the hill and surveyed the village, the surrounding country; the harbour and bay of Boston. The State house of Boston itself and the shaft of the Bunker-hill Monument; and Memory returned to the fact that this day 80 years ago, my father and mother were united in marriage — What an ordo seculorum commenced for me from that day. What was then the condition of the People who then consti- tuted the town of Braintree — What is the condition of the People of the three towns of Quincy, Braintree and Randolph now? And what will be the condition of the occupiers of the soil of these three towns in 80 years from this day? The recol- lection of the past is pleasing and melancholy — The prospect of the future — Oh! how gloomy it is! Not a soul now lives, who was then in the bloom of life — Not a soul now living will be here in 1924 — My own term — how soon it will close! And to whom will all this belong in 80 years from this day? Will prayer to God preserve the branches and shoots from my father's Stock? What a phantasmagoria is human life!

26. IV. Saturday. ≈ Mr. Loring was here this morning alarmed at the double opposition of the democracy and the Liberty party, each playing into the other's hands to defeat my elec- tion, each holding up an ex-Senator from the County of

Norfolk in the State Legislature against me; neither expecting
to elect their own candidate, but purposely combining to exclude me — I have no doubt of their success, and only ask to
meet the exigency with a proper spirit. Leavitt in the morning
Chronicle, hints that the object of the Liberty party in defeating my election is to force me upon the Legislature as a candidate for the Senate and then to give a chance for Appleton
Howe's election as the member for the District — The electioneering of the Liberty party, from Birney their head down,
is more knavish than that of either of the others.

———

29. IV:45. Tuesday. ≈ This morning as the floods of rain were
falling a young man named Seymour, came on horseback from
Boston, where he had arrived, by the night passage from
New-York — He brought me a Letter from J.R.S. Van Vliet,
Chairman of the Committee of arrangements of the whigs of
New-York, who are to have another great procession of trades
to-morrow among which will be the Printers; and they want
me to write a short address to the People which they may print
with my name, while they are moving — I told this young man
it was impossible, being engaged day and Night in preparing
an Address to be delivered to the People of my own district to
morrow — He asked for a written answer, but I thought a
verbal one sufficient — The poor young man said he was very
unwell and had not slept last Night. I pitied him.

———

[November 1844]
5. IV:30. Tuesday ≈ I received from Nashville, Tennessee a
Newspaper, containing Andrew Jackson's first Answer to my
address to the young men of Boston. — He is in great fury,
but totally abandons the charge of the Erving Treaty — I had
been all the morning commenting upon James K. Polk's Letter
declaring his opinion in favour of the immediate annexation of
Texas in which he assails me directly by name — And the remainder of the day and evening till 11 at night I was absorbed
in writing a reply to Jackson's letter to Robert Armstrong —
The paper was enclosed to me by Boyd M'Nairy — Jackson
denies positively that he ever advised the acceptance of the
Sabine for the western boundary. Whether he equivocates
upon the word *advised*, or has totally forgotten his interview

with me of 2 and 3 February 1819. The memory of violent men, is always the slave of their passions. Jackson pledges himself to answer my charge further as soon as he can procure the Erving Manuscripts from Washington.

———

7. IV:30. Thursday. ≈ I called at my Son's office, and learnt that there is a second Letter from Andrew Jackson in answer to my address to the young men of Boston. This last is addressed to Blair the Editor of the Globe, and calls upon him for help in this controversy — There was great agitation in the streets, especially in State Street on the opposite sides of which are the Atlas and Times Newspaper Offices, before the doors of which crowds were collected awaiting the election returns from New-York — They were then highly favorable to the whig party ≈

8. IV:30. Friday. I understood the meaning of the guns fired last night, on receipt of the election returns, from the western Counties of New-York, by the train of Cars from Albany. They settle the Presidential election, and James K. Polk of Tennessee is to be President of the United States for four years from the 4th of March 1845 — What the further events of this issue may be — but it will be the signal for my retirement from public life — It is the victory of the Slavery element in the Constitution of the United States. Providence I trust intends it for wise purposes and will direct it to good ends — From the sphere of public action, I must at all events very soon be removed — My removal now is but a few days in advance of the doom of Nature, and gives me time if I have energy to improve it, which will not be lost.

———

12. V. Tuesday. The following is the copy of the whig ticket voted for yesterday at Quincy, and for which I voted after tearing from it my own name, and pinning to the remnant of the paper the strip bearing the name of Samuel Curtis ≈ The practice is for each voter to put into the ballot box the whole printed ticket, but every individual strikes out or effaces any name for which he chooses not to vote and substitutes another name in its place — Candidates usually strike out their own names, but not always. There is no law, authorising the rejection of any man's vote for himself. — The majority in the

town of Quincy at the autumnal elections has been for several years democratic, consisting of transient Stone-cutters from New Hampshire. There were taken yesterday 719 votes, the number of registered voters in the town being 7   Of the returns I only know that there were 345 for me, not a majority of the whole. The Boston Atlas and Courier of this morning did not come by the regular mail, but I received a Courier under a blank cover — My Son came out from Boston with the Atlas, which has the returns from the whole Commonwealth except six towns. The whig ticket has been sweepingly successful — The vote in the 8th Congressional District is 8041 for me 5322 for Wright 850 for Howe and all others. A result which I dared not expect and upon which I dare not attempt to express my feelings.

———

25. V:15. Monday. I arrived here on Saturday Evening with a clear sky, bright moonlight, and the atmosphere of May rather than of November. Yesterday Morning it was yet warm; but the wind came round to the North west and it was all day growing cold; and as I was returning from church last evening between 5 and 6 O'Clock, I saw the moon just risen with the shadow of the earth already encroaching upon her disk — The eclipse was total and lasted upwards of three hours but the cold was so pinching that I could look at it only once or twice, and then less than five minutes at a time — This day has been of bright clear disqualifying cold. I unpacked my trunks, and immediately missed one or two articles, precisely those I wanted and left behind. It made a day of fruitless search and of wasted time. I walked out for exercise, and at the National Intelligencer Office saw Mr. Gales in deep distress at the issue totally unexpected issue of the Presidential election. He is in despair and foresees that it must prove his irretrievable ruin. It has been accomplished by fraud through the Slave representation. The partial associations of native americans, Irish catholics, abolition Societies, Liberty party — The Pope of Rome, the Democracy of the sword, and the dotage of a ruffian, are sealing the fate of this Nation, which nothing less than the interposition of omnipotence can save.

———

[December 1844]

2. IV:45. Monday. 28 Congress, 2ᵈ Session ≈ I gave notice that I should to-morrow move a Resolution, to rescind the 25ᵗʰ rule which excludes the reception of abolition petitions. Drom-goole said my motion was not in order; but it was entered on the journal — Giddings thought they would trip me up on the point of order, and thought it would be necessary to move an amendment of the rules — but I assured him that rescind was the word. ≈

3. III–VI:45. Tuesday ≈ In pursuance of the notice I had given yesterday, I moved the following Resolution — "Resolved that the 25ᵗʰ standing rule, for conducting business in this house, in the following words — 'No petition, memorial, res-olution or other paper, praying the abolition of Slavery in the District of Columbia, or any State or Territory or the Slave trade between the States or Territories in which it now exists shall be received by this house or entertained in any way whatever' — be, and the same is hereby rescinded." I called for the yeas and nays. Jacob Thompson of Mississippi moved to lay the Resolution on the Table — I called for the yeas and nays on that motion — As the Clerk was about to begin the call, the President's Message was announced and received. A member called for the reading of the Message. I said I hoped the question upon my resolution would be taken. The Clerk called the roll, and the motion to lay on the table was rejected 81 to 104 — The question was then put on the reso-lution and it was carried 108 to 80 — blessed ever blessed be the name of God!

———

19. V. Thursday. ≈ Pollock gave notice of his intention to ask leave to introduce a bill or resolution, to submit the question of the annexation of Texas to the People — A Message was received from the President, with the brawling correspondence between Calhoun, Shannon and the Mexican Minister of for-eign Affairs Manuel Cresencio Rejon. The Message rails at the Mexican Government with the temper of a common scold, and concludes by saying that although we should be fully jus-tified, in declaring War against them, he will not recommend

that, but only that we should take Texas and then if Mexico makes war upon us, all the responsibility of it shall rest upon her. The Message was referred to the Committee of foreign Affairs. ≈

20. IV:45. Friday. I read this morning the whole correspondence communicated yesterday with the message of the President, and see the subjugation of the Union to the double slave representation with deplorable certainty of proof — John C. Calhoun and South-Carolina are in the ascendant, and an internal convulsion in Mexico happens at this moment as if by interposition of the evil principle to help him to consummate his abominable purpose — The prospect is deathlike.

———

31. III:30–V:30. Tuesday. The closing day of every year is the special season for retrospection, for thanksgiving, for self-examination; for repentance — It bears every year with increasing gravity upon the conscience and at the stage of life which I have attained, every year with more irresistible demonstration of the decay of body and mind. I am sinking under them — yet I struggle to keep my head above the surface of the flood. My last night's repose was disturbed, I know not from what cause. I rose between 3 and 4 with an aching head; and returned for two more hours of waking dreams — Mr. Daniel R. Tilden a member of the House of Representatives from Ohio, brought me some days since a small album with a note saying that he had purchased it for his little daughter Sarah, and requesting me to write something in it. These requests thicken upon me greatly to my annoyance; and the time they consume, and the impotence of mind which they disclose is a continual source of self reproach and mortification — A Sonnet for Miss Tilden's Album occupied the morning.

———

[January 1845]
1. IV:45. Wednesday. The whig members of the Massachusetts delegation in the house of Representatives had agreed to meet at my house this morning at 10 O'Clock, before the crowd of visitors should be coming to consult together upon what we shall do in the critical state of public affairs, and whether any joint action on our part may be advisable — Six of them, came,

all of the right complexion, except Daniel P. King, and we had some desultory conversation, without coming to any satisfactory result. We were soon interrupted by the entrance of other visitors; a stream of whom came and went for the space of 3 hours. The weather betokened May rather than January, and all the world was abroad — Great numbers of members of both houses of Congress were here, and among them several of the bitterest political opponents that I have in the world — The personal hatred of the Southern Slave holders against me is evidently much envenomed by the extinction of the petition gag rule, and my position as the head of the anti-Slavery movement in this Country, disavowed by the whole body of abolitionists, and bound hand and foot, and chained to a rock as I am by the Slavemonger brood linked together with the mongrel democracy of the North and West. When the throng had passed away, about 3 O'Clock I walked out and paid a visit to Mrs. Madison. ≈ In the evening I had a visit from Commodore Jesse D. Elliott, who gave me a bronze medal which he has had struck in honour of J. Fenimore Cooper, for his vindication of the Commodore's character in his naval history of the United States.

———

22. VI. Wednesday ≈ Till this Texas question is decided I can think of nothing else. I am crushed between the upper and the nether millstone of the question to speak or not to speak in this debate — If possible Speak I must — Yet I make no progress in my preparations ≈ Douglass of Illinois introduced a Bill of which he had given notice yesterday, for establishing military posts in the Territories of Nebraska and Oregon — Twice read and referred to the Committee of Military Affairs. Orville Robinson a New-York Van-Burenite asked leave to introduce a Bill for the annexation of Texas to the United States. I called for the reading of the Bill, and upon its being read, quite a commotion rose among the Southern members. Payne of Alabama objected to its reception — It proposes to admit so much of Texas now as will constitute one Slave holding State now, and no Slavery in all the rest of the territory no slavery but by the consent of Congress hereafter. Payne was frantic about it. Andrew Stuart on the other side moved to reject the Bill at the first reading to make an issue with the Slavers. The

house refused to reject the bill by yeas and nays 68 to 119. The bill was referred with all the rest to the Committee of the whole on the state of the Union — Tilden of Ohio presented Resolutions of the Legislature of that State against the annexation of Texas, and for the occupation of Oregon.

___

25. V:20. Saturday. "Why should I grieve, when grieving I must bear." ≈ At the house, as soon as the journal was read, I asked the permission of the house to make an explanation of an expression which I had used yesterday, and which had been by some persons misunderstood — No objection was made — I had said that if Slavery were totally abolished forever in Texas and the voluntary consent of Mexico could be obtained I would vote for the annexation of Texas to-morrow — This expression had been snap'd up by the slave-mongers, that it admitted the Constitutional power of *Congress* to annex Texas — the whole drift of my speech had been exactly the reverse — I had not been three minutes speaking, and was referring to my argument of yesterday, founded on my whole course on the Louisiana purchase in 1803 in the Senate, when Saunders of North-Carolina, interrupted me; said I had made my explanation, and objected to my proceeding further — The Speaker would have put me down. I did not give him time, but concluded, and Saunders moved to go into Committee of the whole on the state of the Union, and Hopkins took the chair. Stephens of Georgia made a sophistical speech for and against the annexation, and Woodward of South-Carolina, who got the floor unfairly, made as stupid a speech for annexation — I say stupid for so he insolently called a speech made by a member from Vermont. Douglass of Illinois was in the chair. Rathbun rose and asked if that epithet of Woodward's was in order. Douglass said it was not strictly in order, but that so much latitude of reflection had been allowed throughout the whole of this debate, that he had forborne to notice it in this particular case — Rayner complained that by the management of the chairman none of the Southern whigs had been allowed to explain their reasons for opposition to the annexation, which Hopkins resented — Causin closed the debate and at 2 came the hour of doom. All the propositions were successively rejected, till that offered simultaneously by Milton Brown in the

House and Foster in the Senate, which was carried in Committee 107 to 102 and by yeas and nays in the house 120 to 98. Let the will of God be done.

———

[February 1845]
19. V:15. Wednesday. I read a series of 12 letters printed in the Boston Atlas, addressed to me on the subject of the annexation of Texas to the United States; well written, though I know not by whom; well reasoned, and conclusive against the measure; but without avail; for it is now apparent that it will be consummated, and is written in the book of Fate — The only insurmountable objection against it, the perfidious robbery and dismemberment of Mexico is lost in the Anarchy and civil war into which precisely at this moment Mexico has fallen. She cannot maintain her own identity — She is falling to pieces, and if Texas were restored to her she could not hold it — The opposition is now confined to the mere mode of making the acquisition, and the question of power will be finally decided by the Will — The Constitution is a menstruous rag, and the Union is sinking into a military monarchy to be rent, asunder like the Empire of Alexander or the kingdoms of Ephraim and Judah.

———

27. VI. Thursday. ≈ The Senate this Evening by a vote of 27 to 25, adopted the Resolutions of the House of Representatives, for admitting Texas as a State into this Union — with two additional Resolutions giving the President an alternative, as to the manner of consummating this transaction — This addition was proposed by Robert J. Walker, Senator from Mississippi, and is in substance the plan of Thomas H. Benton. It is a signal triumph of the Slave representation in the Constitution of the United States.

———

[March 1845]
3. VI. Monday. Close of the 28th Congress, and of the Administration of John Tyler, Vice-President of the United States acting as President — Memorable as the first practical application of the experimental device in the Constitution of the United States, substituting the Vice-President as the Chief Executive Magistrate of this Union in the event of the decease

of the President ≈ The day was consumed in the convulsive agitations, and fraudulent devices usual on the closing day of a Congress. The Session was protracted till 3 in the morning of Tuesday and the time was passed in shuffling bills and amendments between the two houses, in concurring and non-concurring with amendments — in receiving reports from the Committee of enrolled bills — in messages between the two houses and from the President announcing his signature of Bills. ≈ President Tyler vetoed a Bill prohibiting payment for certain armed steamers for which he had contracted without Law. He sent the Bill back to the Senate, which upon reconsideration passed the bill with only one opposing vote — It came to the house, and was there passed again 126 to 31 — The first Law passed in defiance of the veto precisely as Midnight came — Adjourned at 3 A.M. of

4. VIII. Tuesday. Inauguration of James Knox Polk as P. U. S. The day after the closing scene of a dying Congress reminds me of what is said of Typhon in the Asiatic Seas, and of a West India hurricane, when it often happens that the transition from the most terrific fury of the tempest to a dead and breathless calm is instantaneous — Such is the change of ones personal existence between the whirlwind of yesterday, and the tranquility of this day — There was an unusual degree of pomposity paraded in the inauguration of James Knox Polk as President of the United States, by the democracy but I witnessed nothing of it — A Committee of arrangements for the reception and inauguration of the President-elect had been appointed by the Senate consisting of Levi Woodbury of New-Hampshire, Sidney Breese of Michigan, and Walter T. Colquitt of Georgia, all rank democrats, who in a very polite note, enclosed to me, three printed copies of the arrangements, with a notification that a position had been assigned to the Ex-Presidents which the committee would be happy to have me occupy. I did not avail myself of the invitation — There was a procession of 10 or 11 military companies who escorted Mr. Polk and Mr. Tyler, who rode together, in an open carriage, from Coleman's National Hotel to the Capitol — They first assembled in the Senate, chamber where George Mifflin Dallas, Vice-President elect was qualified as President of the Senate, and whence they proceeded to a platform protruding from the

portico at the top of the flight of stairs ascending the eastern front to the entrance of the Rotunda — There Mr. Polk delivered his inaugural address, half an hour long, to a large assemblage of umbrella's for it was raining hard all the time. The official oath was then administered to him by Chief Justice Taney, and the draggle-tail procession thinned in numbers escorted him back to the President's house — At night there were two balls, one at Carusi's hall, at 10 dollars a ticket of all parties — the other of pure democrats at 5 dollars a ticket at the National Theatre — Mr. Polk attended both but supped with the true blue 5 dollar democracy. My family and myself received invitations to both, but attended neither.

———

13. V:30. Thursday. ≈ At the Patent Office I applied to the Commissioner Henry L. Ellsworth, for the Ivory cane made from a single tooth, presented to me by Julius Pratt and Co. of Meriden, Connecticut, and which on the 23^d of April last I deposited in the Patent Office. — There is on the top of the cane a golden Eagle inlaid, bearing a scroll with the motto "Right of Petition Triumphant" engraved upon it — The donors requested of me, that when the gag rule should be rescinded I would cause the date to be added to the motto, which I promised to do if the Event should happen in my lifetime — Mr. Ellsworth sent the cane to my house. There is a gold ring immediately below the pommel of the cane, thus engraved

To JOHN QUINCY ADAMS
Justum et tenacem propositi virum.

I crave pardon for the vanity of this memorial.

———

17. V:45. Monday of Passion week — St. Patrick's day. Mr. Campbell dined with us, but I had the whole day without interruption for the performance of my daily task. This consists of writing the journal of yesterday and two pages for publication — Besides this I undertook this day to despatch to the several Historical Societies in the United States the medals in honour of James Fenimore Cooper, which I promised him to distribute and which he sent me several weeks since, for that purpose

≈ In the afternoon I took the Ivory cane to Fischer's shop and directed the date 3 December 1844 to be engraved on the breast of the Eagle directly under the words Right of Petition Triumphant on the scroll; that being the day on which the gag rule against the reception of Petitions touching the abolition of Slavery [was rescinded]. — I walked round over the Tyber Creek, and by the Potomack bridge, reflecting how strange it is that the recent Session of Congress began with a silent vote by yeas and nays 106 to 84 to rescind the rule excluding anti-slavery petitions, and ended by receiving the Resolutions of the Legislature of Ohio, rescinding the Resolutions of censure upon me of the Legislature of 1842, for having presented to H.R.U.S the Haverhill petition — And yet this is the same house which together with the remnant ruin of a whig Senate, passed the Resolutions for the Robbery of the Mexican Provinces, and the admission of Texas as a State, and future States into this Union.

———

[April 1845]
29. IV:30. Tuesday. ≈ President Wayland of Brown University has sent me a copy of his correspondence with the Rev'd Richard Fuller of Beaufort South-Carolina, upon domestic Slavery considered as a Scriptural Institution — I am trying to read it. I suppose it conformable to the meek and gentle Spirit of Christianity, to consider Slavery as an institution, but it is impossible for me to consider it in moral principle any other than an institution of burglary, arson or parricide. I suppose a Feejee islander could calmly discuss the institution of eating his father or his son — but a Christian minister of the word of God, who undertakes to prove from Scripture that Slavery is not a moral evil, is in my estimate of his man character one degree lower than the Feejee Cannibal.

———

[June 1845]
26. III:45. Thursday ≈ I saw the Sun rise and set, clear, from Charles's house on the hill. The pleasure that I take in witnessing these magnificent phenomena of physical nature, never tires. It is a part of my own nature, unintelligible to others, and I suppose a singularity which I should suppress or renounce. The sensations which affect me at the rising and setting Sun,

are first, of Adoration to the power and goodness of the creator of this wonderful universe mingled in the morning with thanksgiving for the return of the great luminary of heaven, the source of life and of light — in the evening with sadness at the departure of this greatest of blessings with a conscious sense of the dependance of all animated nature, upon the constant beneficence of the creator, and with humble supplication for forgiveness of my own errors, and infirmities, and for the continuance of the never ceasing bounties of the omnipotent and all seeing God — These sentiments are always the same, and are rather quickened than deadened by repetition — I take pleasure in indulging them, and wish that my conscience could testify to the influence of these sentiments on my conduct in life.

———

28. IV:15. Saturday. ≈ I am drawing to the conclusion of the Correspondence between President Wayland, and Dr. Richard Fuller upon the sinfulness of Domestic Slavery — The ingenuity and intense anxiety of Dr. Fuller to escape from this principle indicates the last resort of the Slaveholder to evade the wrath to come — There is one remark in the last Letter of President Wayland, at the simplicity of which I could not choose but smile — After lavishing upon his correspondent all the language of endearment, and all the vocabulary of admiration on the temper and talent of his correspondent's defence of Slavery, he tells him there is one thing which throughout the whole discussion he has entirely forgotten or overlooked — namely the distinction between right and wrong. It is so.

29. IV:15. Sunday. Mr. Lunt preached this morning from Ecclesiastes 3:1 "To every thing there is a Season, and a time to every purpose under the heaven"; — He had given out as the first hymn to be sung the 138th of the Christian Psalter, his compilation, and the hymn book now used in our church. It was my version of the 65th Psalm, and no words can express the sensations with which I heard it sung — Were it possible to compress into one pulsation of the heart the pleasure which in the whole period, of my life I have enjoyed in praise from the lips of mortal man, it would not weigh a straw to balance the ecstacy of delight which streamed from my eyes, as the organ

pealed and the choir of voices rung the praise of almighty God
from the soul of David adapted to my native tongue by me —
To this thrill of rapture the composition of which I dare not
analyse there was one drawback — In the printed book, the 5th
line of the second Stanza reads "The morning's dawn, the
evening's shade" and so it was sung — but the corresponding
7th line of the same Stanza reads
"The fields from thee the rains receive" totally destroying the
rhyme. I instantly saw that the 5th line should read "The morning's dawn, the shades of eve" — but whether this enormous
blunder was committed by the copyist or the pressman I am left
to conjecture — That it was committed by me is scarcely possible. The correction is so obvious, that it could scarcely escape
the notice of any intelligent reader of English versification —
The Sermon was ingenious and eloquent, but somewhat eccentric, embracing remarks upon the melancholy paroxysms of
Swift and Cowper, and a critique and commentary upon
Shakespear's Hamlet. The specifications of the opposite objects
for which the royal preacher says there are appropriate times
has one item which the purer morality of Jesus Christ has reformed. He says there is a time to love and a time to hate —
The precept of Christ, forbids hatred at all times, and probably
with reference to this very passage commands his disciples to
love their enemies.

—

[July 1845]
7. IV. Monday. We have the first news that the Congress of
Texas assembled on the 17th of last Month immediately and
by unanimous votes of both houses accepted the terms prescribed by the joint Resolution of the Congress of the United
States of the first of March last for annexing Texas to the
United States; and that the Senate of Texas have unanimously
rejected the Treaty, negotiated for them by the ministers of
France and Great Britain with Mexico. If the voice of the
People is the voice of God, this measure has now the sanction
of almighty God — I have opposed it for ten long years, firmly
believing it tainted with two deadly crimes. I. The leprous
contamination of Slavery and 2. Robbery of Mexico. — Victrix
Causa deo placuit. The Sequel is in the hands of Providence,
and the ultimate result may signally disappoint those by whom

this enterprize has been consummated — Fraud and Rapine, are at its foundation — They have sown the wind — If they reap the whirlwind, the being who left to the will of man the improvement of his own condition, will work it out, according to his own good pleasure.

———

26. IV. Saturday. ≈ Anniversary of my marriage 48 years have since passed away. A small remnant only can be before us. A Merciful Providence has hitherto conducted us along the path of life — We have enjoyed much — We have suffered not a little — Good and Evil have followed us alternately — The thread has been of checkered yarn. Altogether my lot has been a happy one upon Earth, and every feeling of my heart ought to be a sentiment of Gratitude to him who is the disposer of events — I have met with bitter disappointments. Heavy calamities have befallen me — All my children with one exception have been taken from me — One in infancy — two in the prime of life, and this bereavement has once been extended to the second generation — The successive decease of my brother Charles, of my Sister, of my mother of my father and of my brother Thomas, have for the last thirteen years left me the only member of the family of the past and the present generation, surviving on this earth — The common theme of reason is death of fathers, and it is one of the fatalities of old age, to follow to the tomb all the joys of cotemporary kindred and friendship.

> As those we love decay, we die in part;
> String after string, is sever'd from the heart.

With regard to what is called the wheel of Fortune, my career in life has been with severe vicissitudes, on the whole highly auspicious. With advantages of education perhaps unparalleled, with principles of integrity, of benevolence, of industry, and frugality, and the lofty Spirit of patriotism and Independence taught me from the cradle, with the love of Letters and the arts useful and ornamental, and with aspirations of Science, limited only by the scanty spark of etherial fire in the soul, my intercourse with my cotemporaries, has in all its fluctuations been more successful than I deserved — My life has been spent in the public service — Washington, Madison, Monroe were my friends and benefactors — Jefferson a hollow and treacherous friend — Jackson, Charles J. Ingersoll, George W. Erving, Jonathan Russell, base, malignant and lying enemies, a list to which I might, but will not add other names — I have enjoyed a portion of the favour of my country at least equal to my desert, but have suffered and yet suffer much from that Slander which outvenoms all the worms of Nile — But I am wandering from my wedding day.

———

[September 1845]
2. IV:15. Tuesday. A black man by the name of Joseph P. Humphries came this morning to visit me, and ask for advice. He comes from Charleston South-Carolina, with certificates of conduct and character from white men of whom I know nothing, but who I suppose pass for respectable persons in that region — He comes from Charleston, because being free, having learnt to read and write, and being a taylor by trade he cannot live in that glorious exemplification of democracy the State of South-Carolina — He comes to settle in Massachusetts, and apprehensive of the prejudices against his colour in Boston, said his inclination was to fix himself in some small country town — I told him that I thought the prejudice against his colour would be more annoying to him in any country town than in Boston. That in country towns he would find very few if any of his own colour, with whom to associate, or from whom to derive countenance and support — In Boston he might exercise his trade and the people of his colour of whom there are many of respectable standing would afford him society and employment. He thanked me for the advice, and said that several of his friends in Boston had given him the same.

———

17. IV. Wednesday ≈ My practice of rising at 4 O'Clock in the morning was commenced in the Summer of 1796 at the Hague — I had never before been an early riser upon principle, though I had been taught from a child that early to bed and early to rise was the way to be healthy, wealthy and wise — I had been very late to bed and late to rise the preceding winter and spring at London — Returned to the Hague, and no longer stimulated by the same motive to sit up late, I chanced to

read in an English Review of the Life of John Wesley, the founder of the episcopal Methodist church a statement that at a certain period of his life he formed the deliberate determination to rise every morning at 4 O'Clock. That the morning after coming to this resolution he commenced the practice, and continued it through his whole life — Profoundly struck with this narrative, the first thing I said to myself was — what John Wesley accomplished, cannot I undertake? I was not sure of my perseverance; but I thought I could try it for a time — I began it by going to bed in June 1796 at the Hague before 9 O'Clock in the Evening — I slept sound, and after a refreshing night awoke and rose with the Sun — The experiment was cheering; I continued it through the Summer and autumn and when winter came with its long and cold nights, I still took to an early bed with provision made for a lamp to be lighted and a fire to be kindled at four O'Clock the next morning. The fiftieth year has now commenced since I went through this process, and I rose this morning, at 4 O'Clock, and lighted my lamp and kindled my fire — I have not perhaps so inflexibly adhered to the rising hour of four as he did, but the average of my rising hour for the fifty years has not exceeded half past 4. One consequence has been that the hours before breakfast have been the most contented the most active and most efficient hours of the day — My habitual practice of Summer Sea and river bathing and swimming began much later, and I have of late years been obliged to abandon them altogether. The Shower bath was my last resource and I must now give up that — The jar is too racking, and I can not recover the composure of the hand through the day.

———

[December 1845]

*6. V. ≈ With Mr. Bancroft I had a free and long conversation on Politics and especially on the parts of the Message of the President of the U.S. relating to the controversy with Great-Britain concerning the Territory of Oregon — He appeared anxious to know my opinion on that subject which I freely gave him. I said that I approved entirely of Mr. Polk's repeated assertion of the principel first announced by President James Monroe in a Message to Congress, that the Continents of

———

*Indicates entry recorded by an amanuensis.

North and South America were no longer to be considered as
scenes for their future European colonization. He said he had
heard that this part of the Message of Mr. Monroe had been
inserted by him at my sugestion. I told him that was true, that
I had been authorized by him to assert the principal in a Letter
of instruction to Mr. Rush then Minister in England and had
written the paragraph in the very words inserted by Mr. Monroe in his Message. It was Mr. Monroe's custom and has been
I believe that of all the Presidents of the United States to prepare their Annual Messages and to receive from each of the
Heads of Departments, paragraphs ready written relating to
their respective Departments; and adopt them as written or
with such modifications as the writer of the Message deemed
advisable. That this principle thus inserted was disagreeable to
all the principle European Sovereigns I well knew and that those
of Great Britain, France and Russia had explicitly expressed their
dissent from it; notwithstanding which I adhered to it and was
glad that Mr. Polk had so emphatically referred to and repeated
it. I hoped he would adhere to it, but I must in candor say that
with it I believed it indispensably necessary to make large expenditures for preparation by Sea and land, to maintain it if necessary by force of arms, but had not been entirely without
apprehension that Mr. Polk would ultimately recede from it. He
asked me if I disapproved of Mr. Polk's repeating the offer of
assuming the forty-ninth degree of Latitude as the boundary
line between us and the British Possessions to the Pacific Ocean.
I said that I did not disapprove it as the refusal of the British to
accept it would strengthen our final adherence to our whole
claim, but that I should not have repeated it myself at this time.

———

*14. III:45, VI. ≈ My chief occupation was to read the discus-
sion between the successive Secretaries of State, Daniel Webster,
Abel P. Upshur, John C. Calhoun and James Buchanan with
the British Ministers Henry S. Fox and Richard Pakenham
concerning the contest of title between the United States and
Great Britain to the Oregon Territory. The most remarkable
reflection to which this correspondence gives rise in my mind
is, that not withstanding the positive declaration of Mr. Polk in
his Inaugural Speech of the unquestionable title of the United
States to the whole Oregon Country to Latitude 54.40,

notwithstanding a repetition of the same declaration in his recent Message to Congress and notwithstanding the constant professed inflexibility of his Official Newspaper in the support of this Claim he has actually repeated the offer heretofore made by Mr. Monroe and repeated by me, of continuing the Boundary Line between the British Possessions and the United States in the Latitude of 49, from the Mississippi to the Pacific Ocean and that it has again been rejected by Great Britain. This offer was formerly made under the impression that it would not be accepted, but that its effect would be to preserve the Peace between the two Countries, and postpone the issue of the Controversy until the time should come when we should be able to maintain our Claims by an appeal if necessary to arms. My own opinion is, that this offer ought never again to be made, nor accepted if offered by Great Britain herself but, it is too clear to me, that Mr. Polk, will finish by accepting it.

———

*25. V:30. Christmas day. ≈ I had a visit from Mr. James Buchanan, Secretary of State. He told me, that he had formerly visited my father at Quincy, and said that in speaking to him of some of the Tories during our Revolutionary War, he [said they] were men of great respectability, fine talents, and excellent private character but that they were all dep[l]orably loyal, an epithet which, Mr. Buchanan said, had greatly diverted him.

———

[February 1846]
*13. V:30. ≈ On the day after the passage of the Resolution, for giving notice, of the Oregon Convention, Charles J. Ingersoll, came to my seat, and had some conversation with me, respecting an Amendment, which I had proposed to him, to insert in the resolution, and which he had promised to move, but had not the opportunity so to do. After he left my seat, W. P. Thomasson of Kentucky, with a smile said to me, that another member of the House on remarking, the conversation of Mr. Ingersoll with me, had observed, that it was the meeting of Pilate and Herod — I said that this was not very complimentary, but that if it was intended as a censure upon me, for inconsistency, I would answer as Cicero had done before me, upon his reconcilliation after the death of Caesar, with some of

the loco-foco tribunes with whom he had long been in violent
opposition and hostility, that I would wish my enemies to be
transient, and my friendships to be eternal. Thomasson was
much amused at this answer and circulated it freely in whispers,
around the House.

———

[May 1846]
*11. V. War with Mexico. A message from the President of the
United States to both Houses of Congress, was received this
morning, after the House had been one hour in session. It
occupied about half an hour, in the reading, recommending,
not in direct terms, but by circumlocution a declaration of
War against Mexico. It begins with a reference to the state of
the relations, between the two Countries, presented in the
Annual Message, at the commencement of the Session; and
then relates, the series of events, diplomatic and military, which
have since occurred, and brought on a state of hostility now
existing between them. A voluminous correspondence, accompanied the message. When it was received, the House was
in Committee of the whole on the state of the Union, Samuel
Gordon, of the tenth Congressional District of New York, in
the Chair, upon the Military Academy Appropriation Bill —
against which William Sawyer, of the fifth Congressional District of Ohio, was playing off, his democratic artillery. On the
receipt of the message, the Committee immediately rose. —
The Message, and part of the accompanying Documents were
read, and after some altercation as to the mode of disposing of
them, they were ordered to be printed and referred to the
Committee of the whole on the state of the Union — The
House went immediately into that Committee, at the motion
of Hugh A. Haralson, of Georgia Chairman of the Committee
on Military Affairs — George W. Hopkins of Virginia, in the
Chair. They immediately took up Bill No. 145, reported from
the Committee authorizing the President to accept the service
of volunteers, not exceeding fifty-thousand men, with an Appropriation of ten millions of dollars. A long debate ensued,
numerous Amendments were proposed, a distinction between
War and hostilities much discussed and numerous efforts
made, to shape into a declaration of War against Mexico, one
of which finally succeeded. A motion was soon made, by Jacob

Brinkerhoff of Ohio, that the Committee rise, for a resolution to close the debate in two hours, upon which resolution the yeas and nays were demanded and refused. At the end of the two hours, the Bill was reported to the House, with the Amendment declaring War, by a long preamble adopted at the motion of Lynn Boyd, and was passed by yeas and nays, 174 to 14. Amos Abbott, and Robert C. Winthrop of Massachusetts voting for this declaration of War. Of the 14, besides myself, Ashmun, Grinnell, Hudson, and Daniel P. King were five — Benjamin Thompson and Julius Rockwell, were absent. There is one vacancy in the delegation from Massachusetts. Thus only one half of the delegation from Mass voted for this most unrighteous War. Garrett Davis of Kentucky, asked, to be excused, from voting, for which he assigned reasons, perfectly conclusive, against the War, and finally withdrew his motion to be excused, and voted for the Bill. Thomas H. Bayly of Virginia did the same. Elias B. Holmes of New York, Albert Smith, of the same State, also voted for the Bill, protesting against the preamble, as base, fraudulent and false — which preamble contained the declaration of War. And thus the Bill was passed, and the House adjourned.

—

*13. V. Morning employed, in writing, with a view to retrieve if possible the arrears of this Journal, which are growing, like the leak in an unseaworthy ship. At the House, Isaac E. Holmes of South Carolina, Chairman of the Committee of Naval Affairs, presented a communication from the Secretary of the Treasury in relation to the Engineers, for the Revenue Marine Service. Holmes moved, to discharge the Committee of the whole House from the consideration of a Bill upon this subject, referred to them, and take it up and pass it, in the House, which was accordingly done, though in direct defiance, of a rule of the House, that all matters touching appropriations of money, shall be first considered in Committee of the whole — This Committee of the whole, is in our theory of Legislation, the great security for the freedom of Speech, and of debate, upon all subjects before the House, but it is becoming little more than a dead Letter by this evasive practise, of referring subjects to the Committee, and then discharging the Committee from the consideration of them, without any

consideration at all. This, together with the other recent practise, of limiting the time, for debate in Committee of the
whole, takes away, all the benefit of free debate intended, by
that organization of the rules.

———

[July 1846]
*11. IV:30. I enter upon my eightieth year — with thanksgiving
to God, for all the blessings, and mercies, which His Providence has bestowed upon me, throughout a life extended now,
to the longest term allotted to the life of man. With supplication for the continuance of those blessings and mercies, to me
and mine, as long as it shall suit, the dispensations of His wise
Providence, and for resignation to His Will, when my appointed time shall come.

———

13. IV. I rose this morning with the dawn, and drawn by an irresistible impulse walked over the lower Tiber bridge, to my
old bathing spot, on the margin of the Potomac, and there,
under the shelter of the high bluff yet remaining, I bathed and
swam, from five to ten minutes, came out, dressed myself, and
walked home. As I went down the Hill, to the edge of the
water, I found three young men, neither of whom I knew, already in the river, and heard one of them say, there is John
Quincy Adams. They had their clothes, at one of my old standard rocks, but without noticing or disturbing them, I found
another rock, a few rods higher, towards the Potomac bridge,
where I left my clothes. The tide was low, and the time not
convenient, for entering the river, but I succeeded, in obtaining
the bath, for which I panted. The time consumed, was as in
former days, about one hour and a half — half an hour going
to the river, ½ an hour to bath, swim, and dress, and half an
hour to return — The thermometer was at 84, the water
warm, the atmosphere calm, and the Sun clear.

———

[August 1846]
*Quincy. Sunday, 16 August, 1846. V. Blessing, praise and
supplication to God on first rising from bed, on returning to
my earthly home, after an absence of nine months in the public
service of my Country — Some discouragement of Soul follows the reflection, that my aspirations to live in the memory,

of after ages, as a benefactor to my Country, and of mankind, have not received the sanction of my maker — That the longing of my Soul through a long life, to be numbered among the blessings bestowed by the Creator on the race of man is rejected, and after being trammeled and counteracted and disabled, at every step of my progress, my faculties are now declining from day to day into mere helpless impotence. Yet — of the will of my heavenly Father, which should I repine?

———

[September 1846]

14. II:55–IV. ≈ This afternoon Mr. Charles Sumner and Dr. Howe came out from Boston, and invited me to attend, and preside at a public meeting proposed to be held at Boston, a week from to-morrow Tuesday the 22^d of this month, with a view to pass Resolutions expressing the public feeling at the recent kidnapping and abduction of a negro man, who had escaped from his master at New-Orleans and landed in the neighbourhood of Boston. He was pursued, captured and ship'd off for New-Orleans, by the Captain of the vessel in which he made his escape, unknown to the captain — But for retaking him the Captain had no authority from the owner of the Negro. There was a meeting last evening of a few persons indignant at this outrage upon the Laws of the Commonwealth and upon the rights of human nature, who resolved to call upon this meeting, and these gentlemen came out as a Committee from this primary meeting to give me the invitation. After expressing my sense of the honour done me, I suggested some difficulties owing to the state of my health, and especially the near extinction of my voice, disqualifying me, if not from attending at least from presiding at such a meeting, I finally promised to attend the meeting if my health would permit, and to preside, if I should be able to rely upon my voice for a hearing. From my house the Gentlemen went up the hill to my Son's but he was out for a Sea bath, and they did not see him. Mrs. John and Mrs. Charles went to Boston, this afternoon, and came back at 9 this Evening with my granddaughter, Louisa Catherine who finally comes home from Mrs. Sedgwick's school at Lenox, where she has passed two years in the course of her education. She was 15 on the 13th of last Month.

———

[October 1846]

31. I, IV:15. ≈ On the 30th of September 1845 I was compelled to desist from the practice which I have maintained with some few intervals of exception for more than half a century of keeping in my own hand a daily journal of the incidents of my life — Unwilling to give it up entirely, I continued it with the assistance of my two daughters, and especially of my granddaughter Mary Louisa, through the last winter, and until the close of the Session of Congress on the 10th of August. As the Summer came on I recovered partially the use of my right hand, and with untiring labour have brought up my Diary to this day. But I have lost again the command of my right hand and cannot hope to recover it again. I have but a few days more to live, and the record of that remnant can be of little interest even to my Son, and to those of my family whom I am about to leave behind. There has perhaps not been another individual of the human race, of whose daily existence from early childhood to four score years has been noted down with his own hand so minutely as mine — At little more than twelve years of age I began to journalize, and nearly two years before that on the 11th of February 1778 I embarked from my maternal uncle, Norton Quincy's house at Mount Wollaston on board the Boston Frigate Captain Samuel Tucker then lying in Nantasket roads, and bound to France. I was then ten years and seven months old, and the house whence I embarked had been built by my great grandfather John Quincy — upon his marriage with Elizabeth Norton in 1716. There he lived to the age of 77 years, and there he died on the 13th of July 1767 — the day after I had received his name in baptism — If my intellectual powers had been such as have [been] sometimes committed by the creator of man to single individuals of the species, my diary would have been next to the holy scriptures the most precious and valuable book ever written by human hands, and I should have been one of the greatest benefactors of my Country and of mankind — I would by the irresistible power of Genius, and the irrepressible energy of will and the favour of almighty God, have banished War and Slavery from the face of the earth forever — but the conceptive power of mind was not

conferred upon me by [my] maker, and I have not improved the scanty portion of his gifts as I might and ought to have done. May I never cease to be grateful for the numberless blessings received through life at his hands — never repine at what he has denied, never murmur at the dispensations of his Providence, and implore his forgiveness for all the errors and delinquencies of my life.

———

[November 1846]
4. V. ≈ Mrs. Charles and Mary Louisa went to Boston in the Carriage, but returned to dinner. There was a steady and soaking rain all morning which cleared off towards night. The weather confined me to the house, and I forgot the invitation of Mr. Edmund Quincy, to the meeting of the Norfolk County Anti-Slavery Society, held at the Town-Hall — It was my intention to have attended. I have no communion with any Anti-Slavery Society, and they have disclaimed all confidence in me: but I sympathize with all their aversion to Slavery.

———

[March 1847]

Washington. Sunday 14 March 1847.
Posthumous Memoir

On Friday the 20th of November 1846, being at my son's house in Mount Vernon Street Boston, I rose as I had for many years been accustomed to do between 4 and 5 O'Clock in the morning, and went through the usual process of ablution and friction with a horse hair strap and mitten, given me in the summer of 1843, and which from that time I had used from day to day — and after breakfasting with the family, I attempted to walk out with Dr. George Parkman to visit the new establishment of the Medical College — I suddenly found myself unable to walk and my knees sinking under me — With the help of Dr. Parkman I staggered back to my Son's house. Dr. Jacob Bigelow my physician was called in. Dr. Jackson accidentally was in consultation with him, and I was put to bed to which I was several days and nights confined, with a suspension of bodily powers, with little or no pain, and little exercise of intellect — From that hour I date my decease, and consider myself for every useful purpose to myself or to my fellow creatures dead — and hence I call this and what I may write hereafter a posthumous Memoir.

I was confined for several days, I know not how many to the bed; my sudden and extraordinary seizure was noticed in the Boston Newspapers of the following day. On Friday the 17th my Son had left Boston with my wife, my son John's widow Mary Catherine Adams and her daughter Mary Louisa Adams — he went with them as far as Philadelphia and then returned to Boston where he found me ill in bed at his house. He had heard of my being taken ill, before he reached home, in the cars of the long Island Railroad.

On Sunday the 22[d] my wife who had arrived at Washington was informed of my sudden illness, by two Letters from Mrs. Charles Adams, and by the newspaper paragraphs. The next morning she left Washington accompanied as far as Baltimore by Isaac Hull Adams, and thence she proceeded alone by Railroad and Steamboat alone, and reached Boston on Tuesday Evening the 24th having made the passage from New-York in the Steamer Atlantic, the last passage which she made before that in which she perished.

From that time until the 8th of February 1847, we lived at my Sons house, N. 57 Mount Vernon Street Boston, and with his family — On the first of January 1847 I was first able to take a ride in a carriage of about an hour with my daughter Mrs. Charles F. Adams, which ride was as thenceforth daily repeated till the 22nd of January when I made the experiment of walking in the Street in Boston ≈ My sleep was variable — some times quiet with little disturbance, but generally restless uneasy and feverish — My convalescence was slow — scarcely perceptible, but without any painfull attack, and without any substantial restoration of health — The shaking palsy continuing unabated, and becoming more aggravated — in proportion as I seemed to recover the use of my limbs. ≈

Friday 12 February 1847. My dear wife's seventy-second birthday. We came by the Railway from Philadelphia to Baltimore where we dined at the United States Hotel and after dinner proceeded by the Railway to Washington. We found our

carriage waiting for us, at the depot, and about 8 O'Clock in
the evening landed at our house in F Street.

———

[October 1847]
*8. V. I had a more comfortable night, but the day threatened
a turn. Mr. Emmons called here, with two Volumes of Rogers
Poems, which he proposes to present to Mr. Meredith, and he
requested me to write some lines, but without saying what by
way of Autograph. I wrote accordingly a very few lines expressing my opinion of Rogers, as the most pleasing English
Poet of the present Century. I remember reading the Pleasures
of memory at the time of its first publication. I think as early as
1793, and they gave me more pleasure than any of the Poems
of Cowper, Burns or any of the De la cruscan writers of the
same period, and much more than Southey or Peter Pindar at
that time more popular than all the rest, and now almost totally forgotten: I was personally acquainted with Mr. Rogers at
that time and met him several times in society, though not at
his own house. Campbell was of rather a later date, Walter
Scott still later. Byron and Shelley last of all. Coleridge and
Wordsworth are hardly to be included in the Catalogue and of
some later Poet tasters I cannot charge my memory with their
names. I ask the pardon of Mr. More, upon the whole the one
who will last the longest of them all.

———

[November 1847]
*1. V. ≈ I returned to my Son's house No. 57 Mount Vernon
Street and from thence we returned to Quincy to dine. At five
P.M. we took the Railroad train of Cars for Fall River, J. Q. Adams,
Louisa Catherine Adams, Mrs. John Adams, Mary Louisa & Isaac
Hull Adams. Mrs. Eleanor Goods, Margaret Delaney and William
Wheeler, Coachman, eight persons. Lieut. Joseph Harrod Adams
goes with us as far as New York. It seemed to me on leaving home
as if it was upon my last great journey.

———

[December 1847]
1847 — Wednesday, 1 December.
"Glory to almighty God — His Will be done — He that justi-
fieth the wicked, and he that condemneth the just, even they

both are abomination to the Lord."   Proverbs 17:15. This quotation from scripture was repeated to me in the year 1787 by Theophilus Parsons, with whom I was then a student at Law at Newbury Port — In the course of my daily reading of the Scripture this morning I came to it again — Fifty years have passed away since it was impressed upon my Memory and committed to my heart as a precept of heavenly Wisdom.

I called this morning at the Treasury Department and recommended to the Secretary Mr. Robert J. Walker Captain Charles Swift of Quincy for the appointment of keeper of the light-house newly constructed at Minot's ledge on Cohassett rocks ≈ I had a long conversation of speculative politics, with Mr. Walker and I consider every word henceforth issuing from my lips as my last words and dying speech.

———

[February 1848]
1848. 20 Feb'y.

> Fair Lady, thou of human life
>   Hast yet but little seen.
> Thy days of sorrow and of strife
>   Are few and far between.

CHRONOLOGY

NOTE ON THE TEXTS

NOTES

INDEX

Chronology

1767 Born July 11 in Braintree, Massachusetts, the second child of John Adams, a lawyer and rising patriot leader, and Abigail Smith Adams. (Father, born 1735, Harvard 1755, is the great-great-grandson of Henry Adams, who immigrated to Massachusetts from Somerset, England, in 1638. Mother, born 1744, is the daughter of the Reverend William Smith of Weymouth, and the granddaughter of Colonel John Quincy, a former speaker of the Massachusetts House of Representatives. Parents married October 25, 1764. Sister Abigail "Nabby" born July 14, 1765.) Baptized July 12 and named for his ailing great-grandfather, who dies the next day.

1768 Father declines reelection as a Braintree selectman and moves family to a rented house on Brattle Street in Boston to accommodate increased legal practice and political activities. The first of five British regiments lands at Boston on October 1 to quell unrest arising from newly imposed imperial taxes and trade regulations. Sister Susanna born December 28.

1770 Sister Susanna dies on February 4. British soldiers under the command of Captain Thomas Preston fire on an aggressive crowd on March 5, killing five civilians in what becomes known as the Boston Massacre. Father agrees to defend Preston and eight soldiers after they are indicted for murder. Brother Charles born May 29. After trials in the autumn, Preston and six of the soldiers are acquitted, while the other two are convicted of manslaughter.

1772 Brother Thomas Boylston born September 15.

1773 In Boston, the ongoing imperial crisis escalates when on December 16 a large crowd boards East India Company ships carrying taxed tea—"that bainfull weed," as mother refers to it—and tosses 342 chests worth an estimated £10,000 into the harbor.

1774 In February father purchases his father's homestead (now known as the John Adams Birthplace) and the family again returns to Braintree. In response to the Boston Tea Party, the British Parliament passes Coercive Acts abrogating the Massachusetts colonial charter and closing the port of Boston effective June 1. Massachusetts House of Representatives calls on June 20 for a "Meeting of Committees from the several Colonies on this Continent" to address the crisis and elects father and four others as delegates. First Continental Congress opens in Philadelphia on September 5. In October, father is elected to Second Continental Congress to meet in May 1775. John Quincy, who is principally educated by his parents, also begins to be tutored by his father's law clerks, John Thaxter, a cousin of his mother, and Nathan Rice. During his long absences from home, John Adams writes exhortatory letters to Abigail Adams about the education of "our lovely Babes": "Let us teach them not only to do virtuously but to excell. To excell they must be taught to be steady, active, and industrious."

1775   Parliament declares Massachusetts to be in a state of rebellion on February 9. Hostilities begin with skirmishes at Lexington and Concord on April 19. Second Continental Congress convenes on May 10. Father nominates George Washington as commander-in-chief of Continental Army, June 14–15. With mother at Penn's Hill in Braintree, John Quincy observes fires in Charlestown and hears the report of cannons at the battle of Bunker Hill on June 17, and is later grieved to learn of the death that day of the family's friend and "beloved Physician," Dr. James Warren, who has recently saved his badly fractured forefinger from amputation. Father signs Olive Branch Petition to George III, adopted by Congress on July 5.

1776   Father supports resolution introduced on June 7 stating that all political bonds with Great Britain ought to be dissolved and is appointed to committee to draft a declaration. Congress approves independence on July 2 and the Declaration of Independence is adopted on July 4. George III proclaims the thirteen colonies in rebellion on August 23. On July 12 John Quincy travels to Boston with mother and siblings, family servants, and several relatives to receive inoculation against smallpox, returning to Braintree in September. Father obtains leave from Congress, and reaches home in early November.

1777   Father leaves to rejoin Congress in January. On July 11,

John Quincy's tenth birthday, mother gives birth to a sister, Elizabeth, who is stillborn. American forces achieve their first major victory of the Revolutionary War at Saratoga, New York, on October 17, bolstering American appeals for financial support from the French. Father again obtains leave from Congress, and in November returns to Braintree intending to resume his law practice; instead he is nominated by Congress to replace Silas Deane as commissioner to France, joining fellow envoys Benjamin Franklin and Arthur Lee.

1778   France and the United States sign treaties of alliance and commerce in Paris on February 6. John Quincy sails for France with father on February 15; they land at Bordeaux on April 1 and join Franklin at Passy on April 9. He attends Monsieur Le Coeur's boarding school along with Benjamin Franklin Bache, Franklin's grandson, studying French (in which he will become fluent), Latin, dancing, drawing, music and fencing. War begins between Great Britain and France on June 14. Congress abolishes the three-member diplomatic commission and appoints Benjamin Franklin sole minister plenipotentiary to France on September 14.

1779   Father learns of the termination of his mission on February 12 and leaves Passy with John Quincy on March 8, traveling to Nantes and Lorient in search of passage to America. In Nantes, they make the acquaintance of American merchant Joshua Johnson and his family before finally sailing for Massachusetts on June 17 aboard the French frigate *La Sensible*, arriving in Boston on August 3. Father is promptly named by Congress minister plenipotentiary to negotiate treaties of peace, amity and commerce with Great Britain. On November 12, John Quincy begins first diary as he prepares once more to accompany his father to Europe, sailing again on *La Sensible*, this time also with brother Charles, his father's private secretary John Thaxter, and legation secretary Francis Dana. Leaks force the ship to land at El Ferrol, on the northeast coast of Spain, on December 8, and the party travels overland to Paris.

1780   Arrives in Paris on February 8. Father is stymied in his diplomatic efforts by the French court and resolves to leave Paris on July 27 and travel with John Quincy and Charles to the Netherlands in search of support for the

American cause. The boys are enrolled at Amsterdam's Latin School on September 30, then withdrawn in December to attend public lectures at the University of Leyden under the supervision of tutors Thaxter and Benjamin Waterhouse, an American medical student at the university. Congress appoints father to negotiate a treaty of amity and commerce with the Dutch Republic, December 29.

1781   Formally admitted as a scholar to the University of Leyden, January 10. On July 7, departs Holland with Francis Dana, who has been commissioned envoy to the court of the Russian Empress Catherine the Great at St. Petersburg. Having passed through Berlin and Riga, arrives at St. Petersburg on August 29 and serves as Dana's private secretary and interpreter, French being the official language of the Russian court. (Catherine withholds recognition of the United States.) Brother Charles, desperately homesick, is sent back to the United States on August 12. French and American forces achieve a decisive victory over the British at Yorktown, Virginia, on October 19.

1782   Departs St. Petersburg for The Hague on October 3, traveling through Stockholm, Copenhagen, and Hamburg. On October 8, father signs Treaty of Amity and Commerce with the Dutch Republic, which had earlier recognized American independence, on April 19.

1783   Arrives at The Hague on April 21 and reunites with father there on July 22. Proceeds with him to Paris, where on September 3 John Adams signs definitive treaty of peace between Great Britain and the United States of America along with Benjamin Franklin, John Jay, and British negotiator David Hartley. Travels with father to England in October where they pass two months in and around London before visiting Bath in December.

1784   Accompanies father to The Hague, arriving on January 12. Mother and sister depart Boston, June 20, and arrive in London July 21. John Quincy is reunited with them there on July 30, carrying a letter from his father to his mother that reads, "I Send you a son who is the greatest Traveller, of his Age, and without Partiality, I think as promising and manly a youth as is in the World." Father arrives in London on August 7, and the family travels to Paris and settles in Auteuil, where John Quincy becomes acquainted with Thomas Jefferson, who like his father has been commissioned by Congress to negotiate commercial treaties with states in Europe and North Africa. (John Adams will recall this period in an 1825 letter to Jefferson in which he refers to John Quincy as "our John": "I call him our John, because when you was at Cul de sac at Paris, he appeared to me to be almost as much your boy as mine.")

1785   On January 1, begins new diary ("Ephemeris. Volume 1.") in which he inscribes Voltaire's maxim "*La mollesse est douce et sa suite est cruelle*" ("Indolence is sweet, its consequences bitter"). Departs from Lorient for the United States aboard *Courier de l'Amérique*, May 21; arrives at New York on July 17 and at Boston on August 25. Meets with Harvard College president Joseph Willard on August 31, who grants admission but advises him to wait until the spring to begin classes. Resides with mother's sister Elizabeth and her husband, the Reverend John Shaw of Haverhill, Massachusetts, who have been caring for younger brothers Charles and Thomas.

1786   Matriculates on March 15 as a junior at Harvard, which waives tuition fees for him and his brother Charles, a freshman, in recognition of their father's public service. In London, where father is the first U.S. minister to the Court of St. James's, sister Nabby marries Colonel William Stephens Smith, secretary to the American legation, on June 12. Adams is alarmed in the autumn by reports of the wave of agrarian protests in the western part of Massachusetts that becomes known as Shays's Rebellion.

1787   Graduates from Harvard on July 16 as a member of Phi Beta Kappa. Delivers senior oration on "The Importance and Necessity of Public Faith to the Well Being of a Nation." Dr. Jeremy Belknap publishes the oration in the *Columbian Magazine* in September. Begins clerkship in the law offices of Theophilus Parsons in Newburyport, Massachusetts, in September. Expresses skepticism regarding the proposed U.S. Constitution in October. Parents arrange for the purchase of the Vassall-Borland house in the North Precinct of Braintree, known as the "Old House," in preparation for their return from Europe. (North Precinct reincorporated as Quincy in 1792, in honor of maternal great-grandfather.)

1788   Massachusetts ratifies the U.S. Constitution, February 6. Parents arrive in Boston on June 17, and John Quincy joins them at their new estate in Braintree in October.

1789   On February 4, George Washington is elected president of the United States, receiving the votes of all sixty-nine electors, and John Adams is elected vice president with thirty-four electoral votes; they are sworn in at New York City, the temporary federal capital, on April 21.

1790   Becomes increasingly enamored with sixteen-year-old Mary Frazier of Newburyport. Admitted to the bar on July 15 and opens law office at 23 Court Street in Boston on August 9.

1791   The first American edition of Thomas Paine's *Rights of Man* is published in May with a prefatory letter by Thomas Jefferson referring to "political heresies which have sprung up among us," an obvious allusion to "Discourses on Davila," a series of newspaper essays (April 1790–April 1791) in Philadelphia's *Gazette of the United States* highly critical of the French Revolution and unbalanced democracy; though anonymous, the Discourses are widely understood to be the work of Vice President Adams. John Quincy responds by publishing under the pseudonym "Publicola" eleven letters critical of Jefferson and Paine in Boston's *Columbia Centinel*, June 8–July 27; these are soon reprinted throughout the country.

1792   On December 5, George Washington is reelected as president, again unanimously, with 132 electoral votes, and John Adams is reelected as vice president with seventy-seven votes. John Quincy publishes three essays as "Menander" in defense of theatrical performances, then prohibited in Massachusetts, in the *Columbia Centinel*, December 19–22. He writes, "no obedience is due to an unconstitutional act of the legislature."

1793   Revolutionary France declares war on Great Britain and the Netherlands on February 1; President Washington issues proclamation of neutrality on April 22. John Quincy writes three essays as "Marcellus" in defense of American neutrality published in the *Columbia Centinel*, April 24–May 11. Delivers annual Fourth of July oration in Boston, which is published as a pamphlet. Publishes five more essays as "Columbus" in the *Columbia Centinel*, November 30–December 18, denouncing "the intrusion of a foreign influence into the administration" of American affairs. Like his December "Barneveld" essays, in which he defends the president's right to "receive and dismiss foreign ministers and consuls," these essays are written in response to the controversial mission of Edmond-Charles Genêt, the first minister sent to the United States from the new French Republic; their authorship is widely known, and they bring John Quincy to the president's attention.

1794   Nominated minister resident to the Netherlands by President Washington on May 29 and unanimously confirmed by the Senate the following day. Departs Boston for Philadelphia, June 30. Receives commission from Secretary of State Edmund Randolph on July 11, at Philadelphia. Sails with brother and secretary Thomas Boylston aboard *Alfred* from Boston to England en route to The Hague, September 15. In London in October, meets with and delivers papers to Chief Justice John Jay, who has been dispatched by the president to negotiate a treaty with Great Britain amid rising tensions over neutral rights and other unresolved issues between the two countries. Arrives at The Hague on October 31. Presents credentials to Stadtholder Prince William V, November 15. Jay's Treaty signed November 19.

1795   William V flees to England on January 18 in the face of a French-supported uprising that results in the proclamation of the Batavian Republic the following day. Brother Charles marries Sarah Smith, sister of William Stephens Smith, in New York, August 29. John Quincy departs for London October 22 to ratify Jay's Treaty in the absence of the U.S. minister to Great Britain, Thomas Pinckney. Regularly visits the family of Joshua Johnson, now American consul at London, and becomes acquainted with his daughters.

1796   Attends audience with George III, January 9. Sits for portrait by John Singleton Copley, begun February 11, which he will regard as one of the few successful likenesses taken of him. Courts and becomes engaged to Louisa Catherine Johnson, born February 12, 1775, daughter of Maryland native Joshua Johnson and Englishwoman Catherine Nuth, but declines to set a wedding date. Departs London on May 28 and arrives at The Hague on May 31. Nominated by President Washington to be minister plenipotentiary to Portugal, May 30. On December 7, John Adams receives seventy-one electoral votes and is elected president of the United States; Thomas Jefferson, leader of the opposition party, receives sixty-eight electoral votes and becomes vice president.

1797   Father is inaugurated as president on March 4. Receives final orders to depart for Portugal. On July 26, marries Louisa Catherine Johnson at the parish church of All Hollows Barking, London. Though many of his belongings have already been dispatched to Lisbon, is nominated by his father to serve instead as minister plenipotentiary to Prussia and is confirmed by the Senate 19–9. Former schoolmate Benjamin Franklin Bache accuses the Adamses of nepotism in the Philadelphia *Aurora*. Johnson family leaves for the United States; Joshua Johnson's bankruptcy is revealed as creditors dun his new son-in-law, who does not receive promised marriage settlement. John Quincy, Louisa Catherine, and Thomas Boylston arrive at Berlin on November 7, just nine days before the king of Prussia, Friedrich Wilhelm II, dies. On November 30, Louisa Catherine suffers the first of many miscarriages. John Quincy is elected to the American Academy of Arts and Sciences.

1798   Louisa Catherine loses pregnancies in the spring and summer. Amid ongoing violations of American neutral rights by the warring European powers, the revelation of the "XYZ" Affair stirs American public opinion against France. Congress authorizes the navy and armed merchant vessels to capture armed French ships, July 9. John Quincy devotes much time to the study of German. Louisa Catherine succeeds charmingly at the Prussian court, while John Quincy and his mother Abigail worry that she will be "allured by the splendor."

1799   Signs renewed Treaty of Amity and Commerce with Prussia on July 11 before embarking with Louisa Catherine on four-month tour of Bohemia and Saxony. Begins work on a translation of *Oberon*, German epic poem by Christopher Martin Wieland; it will be completed the following spring, but remain unpublished until 1940. George Washington dies on December 14.

1800   Louisa Catherine endures another miscarriage in January. President Adams persists in his determination to avert open war with France by dispatching a peace mission to Paris, provoking the anger of Federalists, especially those in the cabinet. Ensuing protests result in the president demanding the resignations of Secretary of State Timothy Pickering and Secretary of War James McHenry. In June, Alexander Hamilton meets with New England Federalists to persuade them to support Charles Cotesworth Pinckney for president rather than Adams. From July 23 to September 24, John Quincy and Louisa Catherine tour Silesia. Hamilton publishes pamphlet on October 24 calling John Adams "unfit for the office of chief magistrate." Brother Charles dies of complications from alcoholism in New York on November 30. Presidential electors meet December 3. Aaron Burr and Thomas Jefferson each receive seventy-three electoral votes, defeating John Adams who receives sixty-five votes. John Quincy publishes translation from the German of Friedrich von Gentz, *The Origin and Principles of the American Revolution*, which argues that the American and French Revolutions had nothing important in common.

1801 "Letters from Silesia" and a translation of "The Thirteenth Satire of Juvenal" are published in the inaugural issue of *The Port Folio*, January 3, 1801; the former will be reprinted as a book in 1804. Jefferson is elected president by the House of Representatives after thirty-six ballots and Aaron Burr becomes vice president. Recalled by father from Prussia. Jefferson is inaugurated March 4; John Adams does not attend. In Berlin, on April 12, the Adamses' first child is born, and named for George Washington: "I know not whether upon rigorous philosophical principles it be wise to give a great and venerable name to such a lottery-ticket as a new-born infant." The family departs Berlin June 17 and sails from Hamburg to Philadelphia aboard *America*. While Louisa Catherine and George proceed to her family in Washington, John Quincy continues on to Quincy, where on September 21 he is reunited with his parents for the first time in seven years. In October dines at Executive Mansion with President Jefferson and visits Martha Washington and family at Mount Vernon, October 27–28. Moves to Boston to reestablish law practice in November. Louisa Catherine travels to Boston later, and meets the Adams family for the first time on November 25.

1802 Joins Society for the Study of Natural Philosophy and attends his first meeting on January 7. Elected to the Massachusetts state senate as a Federalist in April. Writing in the guise of Thomas Paine, publishes in the October 30

edition of *The Port Folio* a mock-Horatian ode ridiculing
Thomas Jefferson's relationship with Sally Hemings. Pub-
lishes *An Address, to the Members of the Massachusetts
Charitable Fire Society* and *An Oration, Delivered at
Plymouth, December 22, 1802, on the Anniversary of the First
Landing of Our Ancestors.* Loses election to U.S. House of
Representatives for the Boston district by fifty-nine votes
in November.

1803   Appointed United States senator by the Massachusetts
            senate on February 3 to fill an unexpired term lasting until
            1809, joining fellow senator Timothy Pickering in the
            Massachusetts delegation. Son John Adams II born July 4.
            After his parents lose $13,000 in the failure of a London
            bank, Adams works tirelessly to compensate against these
            losses, selling various family properties in installments.
            Great Britain declares war on Napoleonic France on May
            18, once again bringing the issue of American neutral
            rights to the fore. Senator and Mrs. Adams arrive at Wash-
            ington, October 20, and board with Louisa Catherine's
            sister Ann and her husband, Walter Hellen. Supports
            House bill funding the necessary bonds to purchase Loui-
            siana in November, breaking with Pickering and other
            Federalists.

1804   Sides with Federalists against Republican efforts to im-
            peach federal judges. Spends the summer in Quincy re-
            viewing the record of U.S. laws enacted since 1789, while
            Louisa Catherine and children remain in Washington near
            her Johnson and Hellen relations. Writing as "Publius
            Valerius," publishes "Serious Reflections, Addressed to the
            Citizens of Massachusetts," a series of articles in the Bos-
            ton weekly *The Repertory*, October 26–November 16,
            critical of the three-fifths clause of the Constitution and
            the resulting disproportionate power of southern slave-
            holders in the federal union.

1805   Family moves with Louisa Catherine's sister Eliza to
            Quincy when the Senate goes into recess. Brother Thomas
            Boylston marries Ann Harrod of Haverhill, May 16. Adams
            becomes first Boylston Professor of Rhetoric and Oratory
            at Harvard, June 26.

1806   Sons George and John remain in Quincy with grandpar-
            ents. Member of committee that presents, on February 5,
            three resolutions to the Senate protesting British captures

and condemnations of American vessels, calling on President Jefferson to demand restoration and indemnity and recommending nonimportation of British goods. Supports Non-Importation Act of April 15. Begins lectures at Harvard during the long congressional summer recess (May to October). Louisa Catherine, pregnant, remains in Washington; on June 22 she delivers a son, stillborn. Adams receives honorary Doctor of Laws degree from the College of New Jersey (Princeton).

1807   Proposes resolution for a national plan of internal improvements in February. Again as "Publius Valerius," publishes a series of articles in *The Repertory* concerning the *Chesapeake-Leopard* affair of June 22, when the USS *Chesapeake*, in international waters having just departed from Norfolk, Virginia, was fired upon and four of its crew were seized by HMS *Leopard*; he is the sole Federalist to participate in a meeting at the Massachusetts State House that resolves to support the Jefferson administration in response to the affair, which, he will later recall, marks the beginning of "the really important period of my life." Son Charles Francis born, August 18, named for his deceased uncle, and for Francis Dana. Departs, with Louisa Catherine and infant Charles for Washington in October. Professing to place the country's welfare over partisan or sectional interests, Adams is the sole Federalist to vote for the administration's Embargo Act, December 18.

1808   Attends the Republican party caucus in Boston, January 23. Discusses foreign affairs with President Jefferson, March 15. On June 3, six months ahead of schedule, the Federalist-controlled Massachusetts state legislature elects James Lloyd to replace Adams at the end of his term, and forwards positive instructions to vote to repeal the Embargo; faced with this clear repudiation, Adams resigns from the Senate, June 8. Publishes *A Letter to the Hon. Mr. Harrison Gray Otis . . . on the Present State of our National Affairs*, explaining his support of the Jefferson administration. Continues lectures at Harvard.

1809   Leaves for Washington to represent clients before U.S. Supreme Court. In March, serves as one of three chief lawyers for the appellee in *Fletcher v. Peck*, a dispute over the validity of the Georgia law abrogating the Yazoo Land Act of 1795, by which the state legislature had previously granted some 54,000 square miles in present-day Alabama and Mississippi. The case results in a landmark decision in which the Court strikes down a state law for the first time. Attends the inauguration of James Madison on March 4; meets with the new president two days later and learns he will be nominated minister to Russia. Publishes *American Principles. A Review of the Works of Fisher Ames* in the *Boston Patriot* in April and as a pamphlet in June; its vigorous critique of Federalism, as embodied in the career and writings of the deceased Massachusetts senator, marks his final break with the party that had elevated him into national politics. Appointment as the nation's first minister plenipotentiary to Russia confirmed by Senate, June 27. Departs for Russia aboard *Horace* on August 5, accompanied by his wife, youngest son Charles, sister-in-law Catherine "Kitty" Johnson, and nephew and secretary William Steuben Smith; his two oldest sons, George and John, remain in Massachusetts in the care of relatives. The party arrives at St. Petersburg, October 23. Begins cordial diplomatic relationship with Russian chancellor Count Nikolai Petrovich Rumiantzov. Has first audience with Czar Alexander I on November 5.

1810   As Adams settles into the diplomatic routine in Russia, a two-volume edition of his *Lectures on Rhetoric and Oratory, Delivered to the Classes of Senior and Junior Sophisters in Harvard University* is published in Cambridge. (John Adams will send a set to Thomas Jefferson as a kind of peace offering on January 1, 1812, renewing their correspondence after years of estrangement.)

1811   At mother's behest, Adams is appointed by President Madison an associate justice of the Supreme Court on February 22, and confirmed by Senate. But he declines the appointment when he learns of it, preferring to remain at his post in St. Petersburg. Daughter Louisa Catherine Adams born August 12.

1812   Over united Federalist opposition, the Republican majority in Congress votes to declare war on Great Britain, June 17, citing impressment of American sailors under the British orders-in-council as the principal grievance, and President Madison signs the act the following day. Napoleon invades Russia, June 24. An American army invades Upper Canada, July 12, but is repelled by British forces and their

Indian allies, who in turn take possession of Detroit and other key posts in the Old Northwest. Undersupplied French forces occupy Moscow on September 14, and shortly after are forced to begin a disastrous retreat. Daughter Louisa Catherine dies, September 15. Last French troops depart Russia, December 14.

1813   In March, the Madison administration embraces a Russian offer of mediation with Great Britain and dispatches Secretary of the Treasury Albert Gallatin and Federalist senator James A. Bayard of Delaware to St. Petersburg to join Adams for negotiations; the pair are en route before news arrives that British cabinet has declined the mediation. Sister Nabby dies of cancer at the Old House on August 15. In the autumn another major American offensive into Canada, this time aiming for Montreal, ends in failure.

1814   When Britain signals its willingness to enter into direct talks, Adams is appointed in January as chief negotiator of a five-member commission comprising Gallatin, Bayard, Henry Clay of Kentucky, and Jonathan Russell of Massachusetts. Travels alone from St. Petersburg to Ghent, April 18–June 24. Negotiations begin on August 8, and the British plenipotentiaries lay down aggressive terms reflecting their stronger military hand. On August 24 and 25, British forces occupy Washington and burn the capital's public buildings. A similar assault on Baltimore is repulsed by American defenders, September 13–14. That same month, British naval and land forces take control of more than a hundred miles of the Maine coast, from Eastport to Castine, but a large British invasion of northern New York is turned back at Plattsburg. By early December, pressed by bad news from North America and by demands for tax relief at home, the British government resolves to extricate itself from the American war. The Treaty of Peace and Amity between His Britannic Majesty and the United States of America, signed on December 24, does not address the issue of impressment and restores the status quo between the two nations prior to the war. Federalists convene in Hartford, Connecticut, December 15–January 5, to protest the war and a decade of Republican policies, and dispatch a delegation to Washington to present their grievances.

1815   On January 8, American forces led by General Andrew Jackson overwhelmingly defeat a British invasion force at

New Orleans in the last major action of the War of 1812. Word of Jackson's victory and of the signing of the peace treaty at Ghent reach Washington in the second week of February, at the same time as the delegation from Hartford arrives, a coincidence that serves to greatly discredit Federalist opposition to the war. Adams is appointed minister plenipotentiary to the Court of St. James's in February. He is reunited with Louisa Catherine and Charles Francis, who have made a hazardous overland winter journey from Russia, in Paris, March 23, and witnesses Napoleon's brief return to power (the Hundred Days). On May 7, receives word of his new commission. The family departs Le Havre for London, May 23; two days later they are reunited with sons George and John, just arrived from America, who have not seen their parents in almost six years. Presents credentials to Prince Regent, June 8. With fellow commissioners Clay and Gallatin, concludes commercial convention with Great Britain, July 3, the first accord between the two nations signed on the principle of diplomatic equality. Settles family at Little Ealing, a village outside London. Suffers a near-fatal injury while instructing George and John how to handle a pistol in October. In December, nephew John Adams Smith arrives in London to serve as private secretary.

1816   Begins negotiations with British foreign secretary Lord Castlereagh on northern borders and armaments, January 25. Brother-in-law William Stephens Smith dies, June 10.

1817   Named secretary of state by new president James Monroe, March 6. Nomination confirmed by the Senate with only one dissenting vote. Receives notification of his appointment in a letter from the president, April 16. The Rush-Bagot agreement, limiting naval armaments on the Great Lakes, signed in Washington on April 29. Sails from Cowes on the Island of Wight aboard *Washington* on June 15 and arrives at Sandy Hook Lighthouse on August 6. Louisa Catherine suffers final miscarriage while at sea. Passes a month in Quincy before setting forth for Washington on September 9. Son George enters Harvard in August. Arrives at Washington on September 20 and swears oath of office two days later. Begins service in President Monroe's cabinet along with Secretary of the Treasury William H. Crawford, Secretary of War John C.

Calhoun, Secretary of the Navy Benjamin Crownin-shield, and Attorney General William Wirt. In December, Monroe orders General Andrew Jackson to subdue Seminole and Creek Indians in Georgia. American forces occupy Amelia Island, on southern border of Georgia, December 23.

1818   The new secretary of state and his wife become embroiled in a "visiting controversy" when members of Congress and their wives insist upon being called on at home before accepting invitations to parties at the Adamses' residence. Eventually, Louisa Catherine will become a leading hostess and serve effectively as her husband's "campaign manager" in Washington. Begins negotiations with Luis de Onís y González-Vara, Spain's envoy to the United States, to settle status of Florida and boundaries in the West. Andrew Jackson pursues his Indian targets into Florida, occupying Pensacola, St. Augustine, and St. Marks, and executes two British subjects, James Armbrister and Alexander Arbuthnot, believed complicit in fomenting Seminole attacks on American interests. In a July 15 cabinet meeting, Adams is alone in his defense of Jackson's actions. Instructs Richard Rush and Albert Gallatin in negotiations with Great Britain resulting in the Anglo-American Convention of 1818, which settles disputes relating to the status of enslaved people who escaped to the British during the War of 1812, American access to Canadian fisheries, and transatlantic commerce, and which establishes free and open access to the Oregon Country for both nations for ten years. Mother dies of typhoid fever on October 28. In November, sends and publishes letter of instruction to U.S. envoy George W. Erving in Spain, justifying Jackson's actions in Florida and demanding that Spain police Florida or sell it to the United States. In his diary, Adams begins to record emerging intrigues in the cabinet surrounding which of the officers will be put forward to succeed Monroe.

1819   Signs Transcontinental Treaty with Spain, alternatively known as the Adams-Onís Treaty, February 22, acquiring Florida for the United States and defining the boundary between the Spanish Viceroyalty of New Spain and the United States. Treaty is ratified unanimously by the Senate, but Spain's King Ferdinand VII withholds ratification to pressure the United States not to recognize the revolutionary states of South America. Son John enters Harvard in August. Controversy over admission of Missouri with slavery erupts in Congress. In cabinet, Adams declares the restriction of slavery in the territory to be constitutional, but avoids the issue in public. The young nation experiences its first major financial crisis, now known as the Panic of 1819, when, as foreign demand for American agricultural goods wanes with a return to normalcy in Europe, the postwar land boom collapses, and the country's overleveraged banking system follows suit. The poorly managed Second Bank of the United States has contributed to the situation first through inflationary lending and then by initiating a severe credit contraction in the summer of 1818.

1820   January to February, debates in Congress over admission of Missouri continue. Missouri Compromise admitting the district of Maine as a free state, the state of Missouri with slavery, and banning slavery north of 36°30′ passes March 2. Purchases house on F Street in Washington in April. King Ferdinand VII ratifies Transcontinental Treaty on October 24. James Monroe, who is effectively unopposed, is reelected with 228 of 229 electoral votes. The sole dissenting vote, cast by New Hampshire elector William Plumer, is for Adams.

1821   On February 19, the Senate ratifies Adams-Onís Treaty for a second time, this time after rejecting a proposal by Henry Clay demanding that Spain cede Texas. Treaty proclaimed on February 22. Submits his exhaustive "Report Upon Weights and Measures" to the Senate on the same day, and it is later published. Asserts the justness of colonial revolutions for independence in a Fourth of July oration delivered in the House, later published as *An Address, Delivered at the Request of a Committee of the Citizens of Washington . . . on the Fourth of July, 1821*, while warning of British designs and defending policy of neutrality against calls by Clay and others for the United States to involve itself in liberal movements in South America and Europe. Son George graduates from Harvard in August. On September 16, Czar Alexander issues an ukase restricting to Russian subjects whaling, fishing, and all other industry in Russian territory on the northwest coast of America, and prohibiting the approach of foreign vessels within one hundred Italian miles of Russian claims, at a degree of latitude farther south than the United States or Great Britain has ever conceded.

1822 On March 8, President Monroe signals to Congress his desire to recognize the independence of South American states. Congress appropriates funds for missions therewith, May 4. Treaty of commerce signed with France, June 24. Through spring and summer Adams engages in a newspaper controversy with fellow Ghent commissioner Jonathan Russell, a political ally of presidential aspirant Henry Clay; the exchange culminates in September with his publication of *The Duplicate Letters, the Fisheries, and the Mississippi*, which reveals that Russell has faked a letter purporting to show that Adams had sold out the interests of the West in favor of New England during the Ghent negotiations.

1823 On February 23, House of Representatives passes resolution calling upon President Monroe to negotiate with maritime powers for the abolition of the African slave trade. Congress also passes resolution calling American ships to be granted equal standing in British colonial ports, after the British impose a discriminatory tax on U.S. tonnage. Adams sends a proposal to London for convention to discuss freedom of the seas, July 29, which the British government rejects. Attempting to make provision for a return to private life after the coming presidential elections, purchases Columbian Mills, a grist and flour mill in the District of Columbia, from wife's cousin George Johnson. At the request of President Monroe, Adams draws up general instructions for American ministers to South America directing them to uphold republicanism against monarchy, to support their separation from Europe, to be open to discussing a Pan-American congress, and to offer them favored-nation status in commercial treaties, April 30. Son John is expelled from Harvard for participating in a student rebellion. In August, Thomas Jefferson expresses his preference for William H. Crawford in the next presidential election. Crawford suffers a debilitating stroke in September. Adams receives on November 17 a note from the Russian government announcing its resolution, shared by other members of the Holy Alliance (Austria and Prussia), to strive against republican movements worldwide. In a series of cabinet meetings in

November he outlines the principle that European powers must abstain from interfering in the independent states of the Americas, which the president incorporates into his December 2 addresses to Congress and which becomes known as the Monroe Doctrine.

1824   The Adamses host a ball in honor of General Andrew Jackson on the anniversary of the battle of New Orleans. Anglo-American Convention on the African slave trade concludes on March 13 with both parties agreeing to punish slave traders as pirates, to allow a reciprocal right of visit and search of merchant ships, to render captured ships to their home country, to leave individuals belonging to crews on accused vessels, and to hold ships' officers responsible for the prevention of resistance to the right of search and visit. William Crawford leads opposition to the convention, successfully attaching an amendment stipulating that ships on the American coast be exempt from search. Great Britain is unwilling to accept this amendment and the convention fails. Russo-American Convention signed on April 17. Russia agrees to abandon its claims in the Pacific Northwest south of 54°40′N and the United States agrees to prohibit sale of alcohol and firearms to native peoples in the region, a point first raised by Count Rumiantzov during Adams's residency at St. Petersburg. Negotiates new commercial treaty with France, June 24. In the November presidential election Andrew Jackson receives ninety-nine electoral votes, Adams eighty-four, Crawford forty-one, and Clay, now Speaker of the House, thirty-seven. No candidate receiving a majority, the election is sent to the House of Representatives, where members will vote by state for one of the top three candidates. John C. Calhoun is elected vice president.

1825   Clay, whose support as Speaker is widely seen as decisive in the forthcoming presidential election in the House, calls on Adams in Washington, January 9. Representative George Kramer anonymously accuses Adams and Clay of having struck a bargain in the January 28 edition of Philadelphia's *Columbia Observer*, and the *National Intelligencer* quickly picks up the story. Adams is elected president of the Unites States on February 9, receiving the votes of thirteen of twenty-four state delegations in the House of Representatives. Illinois, Maryland, and Louisiana defect from Jackson and Clay brings the votes of

Kentucky, Ohio, and Missouri to Adams. On March 3, Senate consents to Treaty of Indian Springs, signed by two United States commissioners and a rump group of Creek leaders; it stipulates the exchange of all Creek lands in Georgia for equal acreage west of the Mississippi, plus a bonus of $400,000 and annuities. Adams is inaugurated on March 4 and appeals for national unity and the final extirpation of the "baneful weed of party strife." Cabinet consists of Secretary of State Henry Clay, Secretary of the Treasury Richard Rush, Secretary of War James Barbour, Attorney General William Wirt, Postmaster General John McLean, and Secretary of the Navy Samuel L. Southard. Son John serves as private secretary. Ratifies the Treaty of Indian Springs despite charges by Creek leaders that it is unjust and fraudulent. Sends orders to Major General Edmund P. Gaines, already in Georgia to investigate, to impose a moratorium on the survey of Indian lands. Georgia governor George Troup demands the recall of Gaines. After meeting with a delegation of Creek leaders, Adams determines that a new treaty must be negotiated to supplant the previous. Almost drowns while taking morning swim in Potomac River, June 13. First of several acts passed by Parliament nearly shuts down U.S. trade in the British Caribbean, June 27. Spends part of the summer with father in Quincy. Charles Francis graduates from Harvard in August. Sends message on State of the Union to Congress, December 5. "Liberty is power" he tells Congress, recommending, among other measures, the establishment of a Department of the Interior, the founding of a national naval academy and a national university, a uniform national bankruptcy law, more effective patent laws, and a vigorous system of internal improvements. Nominates a mission to attend the Congress of Panama, December 26. Congressional opposition delays confirmation of appointments; in the end, one U.S. delegate arrives after the conclusion of discussions, while the other dies en route.

1826   Creek leaders sign Treaty of Washington on January 24. This second treaty cedes all Creek lands east of the Chattahoochee River and guarantees to the Creeks lands not ceded. Resolution introduced by Senator Martin Van Buren condemns Adams for accepting invitation to Panama Congress without consulting Senate, February 15. Nominates Robert Trimble of Kentucky to the Supreme

Court, April 11. Son George, who struggles with alcoholism and depression, is elected to the Massachusetts House of Representatives, and serves only one year. Both John Adams and Thomas Jefferson die on July 4, the fiftieth anniversary of independence. Adams spends part of summer and early fall vacation arranging father's estate in Quincy. Governor Troup ignores the Treaty of Washington and sends surveyors to Creek lands immediately after September 1, the date prescribed in the Treaty of Indian Springs. In a cabinet meeting, Adams is advised to order troops to Georgia, but demurs in the face of Troup's pledge to resist. William Morgan, a disgruntled Mason from Batavia, New York, is abducted and likely murdered by a band of Masons on September 18. The Masonic Order fails to condemn the act and an anti-Masonic movement begins in western New York. Adams becomes a communicating member of the Congregational Church of Quincy, October 1. Convention signed with Great Britain to pay for enslaved people "carried off" during War of 1812, November 13.

1827 On February 5, Adams sends a message to Congress explaining his desire to avoid violent conflict in Georgia and calling upon Congress to enact expedient legislation. Congressional committee proposes to purchase title to all Indian lands in Georgia and to maintain the Treaty of Washington in the interim. Governor Troup declares Georgia will fight federal troops if sent to Georgia. Controversy over the administration's tariff bill, which increases the schedules in place since 1816, ends with a tie-breaking vote by Vice President Calhoun in the Senate against the tariff, March 1. On May 5, Andrew Stevenson of Virginia is elected Speaker of the House, cementing the loss of pro-administration majorities in both houses of Congress.

1828 On February 25, son John marries his cousin Mary Catherine Hellen, who had previously been engaged to older brother George. On April 8, delivering documents to Congress in his capacity as his father's secretary, John has his nose pulled by journalist Russell Jarvis, an assault that nearly precipitates a duel. Signs into law on May 19 a protective tariff initiated by Van Buren and anti-tariff Democrats, called the "tariff of abominations" because its schedule was designed to be so prohibitive as to ensure its defeat. Breaks ground for Baltimore and Ohio Railroad, July 4. Presidential election is held from October 31 to November 5. Andrew Jackson receives 178 electoral votes, while Adams receives 83. Granddaughter Mary Louisa, first child of John and Mary Catherine, born December 2. Engages in public controversy with Virginia senator William Branch Giles over his actions as a senator during Jefferson's administration. Letters between Adams and his antagonists in New England are published by Federalists as *Correspondence Between John Quincy Adams, Esquire . . . and Several Citizens of Massachusetts* early the next year. Writes but withholds from the press a lengthy review of the actions of Massachusetts Federalists before and during the War of 1812; it is eventually published with the correspondence by grandson Henry Adams as *Documents Relating to New England Federalism, 1808–1815* (1877).

1829   Charles Francis is admitted to the Massachusetts bar in January. The Adamses move from the Executive Mansion to a residence on Meriden Hill, a mile to the north. Drafts the beginning of history of political parties in the United States and commences work on a biography of John Adams, both left incomplete. Traveling from Boston to Washington to join the family, son George disappears from a steamship in New York harbor on August 30, an apparent suicide. His body is discovered on City Island, New York, on June 10. Adams returns to Quincy. Charles Francis marries Abigail Brooks, daughter of wealthy Massachusetts merchant Peter Chardon Brooks, September 3. Returns to Washington, joining Louisa Catherine, John, Mary Catherine, and Mary Louisa, December 5.

1830   Elected to Board of Overseers of Harvard University. Writes lengthy essays on the Russo-Turkish War and on Greece for *The American Annual Register*. Returns to Quincy with Louisa Catherine in May. Granddaughter Georgiana Frances, John and Mary Catherine's second child, born September 10. Nominated as a candidate for the House of Representatives at a National Republican convention in Halifax, in Plymouth County, Massachusetts, October 12. Election is held on November 1. Adams receives three fourths of all votes cast and is elected to represent Massachusetts's Eleventh District in the Twenty-Second Congress.

1831   Publishes epic poem *Dermot Mac Morrogh, or The Con-
            quest of Ireland; An Historical Tale of the Twelfth Century.
            In Four Cantos* in April. Attends an Anti-Masonic Con-
            vention at Faneuil Hall in May. Responding to the national
            crisis that has arisen from South Carolina's stated intention
            to nullify the Tariff of 1828 as unconstitutional, delivers
            Fourth of July address at Quincy in which he refutes the
            doctrine of state nullification. Arguing that the Union
            began with the Declaration of Independence, which codi-
            fied a previously existing Union and never granted sover-
            eignty to the separate states, he declares "Independence
            and Union Forever!" From August through September,
            writes a series of letters to various correspondents confirm-
            ing his anti-Masonic leanings. Louisa Catherine, first child
            of Charles Francis and Abigail Brooks, is born August 13.
            Delivers a eulogy to James Monroe at Boston, August 25,
            subsequently published, in which he further defines his
            nationalist interpretation of the Constitution. Has an in-
            terview in September with William H. Seward in which he
            expresses his willingness to accept the Anti-Masonic nomi-
            nation for president, though he later declines the nascent
            party's nomination for governor of Massachusetts. Meets
            twice in October with Alexis de Tocqueville and Gustave
            de Beaumont on their investigative tour of America. In
            November, Adams sells his shares in the Bank of the
            United States to divest himself "of all personal interest in
            it" before entering Congress, where he will argue for the
            renewal of its charter. Twenty-Second Congress begins,
            December 5. Reluctantly accepts appointment as chair of
            the Committee on Manufactures and uses position to
            advance a balanced solution to the emerging sectional
            crisis over the tariff dispute. Presents fifteen petitions
            from citizens of Pennsylvania calling for the abolition of
            the slave trade and slavery in the District of Columbia,
            December 12.

1832   Brother Thomas Boylston dies, March 13, the second sib-
            ling to succumb to the effects of alcoholism. Serves on
            special committee to investigate the Bank of the United
            States. Writes supplement to committee's minority report
            defending the Bank against charges of usury and other vio-
            lations of its charter. President Jackson signs compromise
            tariff bill on July 14; drafted by Adams, it becomes known
            as the Adams Tariff. On December 10, Jackson issues

proclamation denouncing the doctrine of nullification and declaring acts of disunion treasonous.

1833   Speaking on February 4 against efforts to revise the 1832 tariff, Adams decries the "protection" of Southern interests inherent in the Constitution's three-fifths and fugitive slave clauses and in the safeguards provided by the federal army against servile insurrection and hostile Indians. "My constituents possess as much right to say to the people of the South, 'We will not submit to the protection of your interests,' as the people of the South have the right to address such language to them." Writes minority report on the President's annual message, later published as the *Report of the Minority of the Committee on Manufacturers, Submitted to the House of Representatives of the United States, February 28, 1833*, in which he examines the philosophical underpinnings of the tariff debates and those on other controversial issues, including internal improvements, the management of federal lands, and the national bank. He warns that continued acquiescence to Southern control over the federal government threatens "not only the prosperity but the peace of the country" and will lead to "the most fatal of catastrophes—the dissolution of the Union by a complicated, civil, and servile war." At the urging of President Jackson, Congress, with Adams voting in the affirmative, passes the Force Bill on March 1, empowering the president to compel South Carolina to comply with federal law; South Carolina repeals its Nullification Ordinance on March 15, defusing the constitutional crisis ffor the moment. Adams is reelected to Congress on April 1, now from Massachusetts's Twelfth District, which he will represent in the Twenty-Third through Twenty-Seventh Congresses, increasingly aligning himself with the Whig caucus. John Quincy II, second child of Charles Francis and Abigail Brooks, is born on September 22. Adams survives derailment on the Camden and Amboy Railroad without injury, November 8. Stands as Anti-Masonic nominee for governor of Massachusetts. After no candidate receives a majority of votes, Adams withdraws to support the National Republican candidate, John Davis.

1834   Publishes a speech critical of President Jackson's intention to withdraw public deposits from the Bank of the United States in the *Daily National Intelligencer*, April 12. By the summer, John Adams II's descent into alcoholism has

become painfully evident to the family. Under his misman-
agement the Columbian Mills is an increasing drain on his
father's finances. When John dies, October 23, Adams becomes guardian of his two daughters. Delivers an address
to Congress on December 31 in honor of the recently deceased Marquis de Lafayette.

1835   Grandson Charles Francis Adams Jr. is born on May 27. In
December, Adams is appointed chairman of a special
House committee established to make provision for the
$500,000 bequest of Englishman James Smithson to the
United States government "to found at Washington,
under the name of the Smithsonian Institution, an Establishment for the increase and diffusion of knowledge
among men." For several years following Adams will play a
leading role in ensuring that the United States applies the
legacy to Smithson's desired end.

1836   On January 22, in a three-hour speech on the House floor,
defends Andrew Jackson's policy toward France regarding
reparations for spoliations that occurred during the Napoleonic Wars and criticizes Daniel Webster and the Senate
for their unpatriotic opposition. This speech earns Adams
the sobriquet "Old Man Eloquent." On March 2, Texas
declares independence from Mexico. On May 25, in remarks later published as *Speech of John Quincy Adams on
the Joint Resolution For Distributing Rations to the Distressed Fugitives from Indian Hostilities*, again raises the
possibility of wartime slave emancipation and denounces
the Second Seminole War and the threat of a war with
Mexico in defense of Texas as manifestations of a larger
proslavery agenda. Also in May, Henry Laurens Pinckney
of South Carolina proposes three resolutions denying the
constitutional power of Congress to interfere with slavery
in the states, suggesting Congress ought not interfere with
slavery in the District of Columbia, where its power to do
so is acknowledged, and advocating that all petitions, memorials, and resolutions relating to slavery be peremptorily
tabled and not acted upon. Denied an opportunity to
speak against these proposals, Adams demands "Am I
gagged or am I not?" During a roll call vote on the third
resolution Adams protests, "I hold the resolution to be a
direct violation of the Constitution of the United States,
of the Rules of the House, and of the rights of my constituents." For each of the next four Congresses, despite

his efforts and over his protests, the House will successfully reintroduce what becomes known as the gag rule. Delivers at Boston, September 27, and later publishes a much longer version of *A Eulogy on the Life and Character of James Madison*. In the presidential elections, Vice President Martin Van Buren, a Democrat, easily defeats Whig candidates William Henry Harrison and Hugh L. White.

1837   On February 6, Adams presents an abolitionist petition from nine ladies of Fredericksburg, Virginia, and asks Speaker James K. Polk to consider another petition "purporting to come from slaves" before presenting it; outraged Southern members seek a motion of censure. When Representative John Mercer Patton of Virginia claims that the Fredericksburg petitioners were free blacks or mulattoes of "infamous character," Adams, observing "great resemblances between the progeny of the colored people and the white men who claim possession of them," levels the charge of infamy "on those who made it, as originating from themselves." On March 3, in the last act of the Jackson presidency, the United States recognizes the Republic of Texas. Gives *An Oration Delivered before the Inhabitants of the Town of Newburyport* on July 4, expanding on his interpretation of the Declaration of Independence and the Constitution. Writes and publishes a series of letters to his constituents defending his introduction of antislavery petitions. On August 4, Texas presents the Van Buren administration with a formal offer to annex itself to the United States. With the nation once again in the throes of a financial crisis, Congress convenes in special session on September 4 to consider a measure, known as the Sub-Treasury bill, to remove government funds from state banks, which were widely seen as contributing to the ongoing economic panic, and assign control of these monies to designated federal agents. In the autumn, involves himself in the controversial slave auction of Dorcas Allen and her children, and eventually contributes fifty dollars toward the purchase of their freedom; for Adams the episode exposes with new clarity the byzantine cruelty of slavery. Delivers an anti-Texas annexation speech in the House on December 13, describing the Texas revolution as in reality a revolt against Mexico's abolition of slavery in 1829, and prods the president to accept arbitration with Mexico.

1838   Grandson Henry Brooks, fourth child of Charles Francis and Abigail Brooks, is born on February 16. Overcoming long-held suspicions of the movement, Adams grows closer to abolitionists; Louisa Catherine corresponds with abolitionist Sarah Grimke. By parliamentary strategy, Adams seizes control of the House floor during the morning hour for committee business for three weeks from June into July, delivering a speech in which he describes a plot to annex Texas, upholds the propriety of women petitioning Congress, and declares slavery to be a sin.

1839   Introduces and sponsors an anti-dueling law for the District of Columbia originated in the Senate by Samuel Prentiss of Vermont. The Prentiss-Adams law is enacted on February 20. On February 25, asks leave of Speaker Polk to present resolutions for three constitutional amendments outlining his preferred program of emancipation: (1) to end hereditary slavery and for every child born after July 4, 1842, to be born free, (2) with the exception of the Territory of Florida, to henceforth never admit a slave state, and (3) to prohibit the slave trade in the District of Columbia after July 4, 1845. Writes and presents *The Jubilee of the Constitution. A Discourse Delivered at the Request of the New-York Historical Society* on April 30. In May and June, publishes letters explaining why he presents petitions on behalf of the abolition of slavery in the District of Columbia but will not support legislation for its immediate effect, citing the dictates of "justice, the Constitution, and prudence." On August 26, Thomas R. Gedney, commander of the USS *Washington*, boards and captures *La Amistad*, a Spanish schooner under the control of Mende captives (forty-nine adults and four children) recently transported from Africa, who have seized the ship and killed the captain and crew, sparing only José Ruiz and Pedro Montes so they could navigate the ship back to Africa. The ship is interned in New Haven, Connecticut, and the Mende captives are placed under court jurisdiction. Louisa Catherine and Mary Hellen continue to read, record, and file the large number of petitions directed to Adams. Elected to the American Antiquarian Society on October 23. Granddaughter Georgiana Frances dies November 20. In December, serves as Speaker of the House for ten days during a controversy over the organization of the House for the session.

1840   District Court trial of the *Amistad* case is heard in New Haven and results in a January 23 ruling that the majority of the captured Africans be freed. Decision is appealed to the Supreme Court of the United States, scheduled to convene in January 1841. Suffers fall in the House chamber on May 18, dislocating his shoulder and badly wounding his head. In October, Adams agrees to help argue the *Amistad* case before the Supreme Court. In November, Charles Francis is elected to the Massachusetts House of Representatives. In the presidential election, the Whig candidate William Henry Harrison easily defeats the incumbent Martin Van Buren. The Whigs also gain control of the House of Representatives and the Senate for the first time.

1841   *United States v. The Amistad* begins on February 22. Adams closes for the defense on February 24 by focusing on the underlying issue of whether the Africans were slaves under Spanish law. Adams is set to conclude his argument the following day but Justice Philip Barbour dies that night. The Court reconvenes on March 1 and Adams concludes by arguing that rendering the Africans to Spanish authorities would "disable forever the effective power of *habeas corpus*." On March 9, Supreme Court rules in favor of the captured Mende and frees them. Just a month after his inauguration, President Harrison dies of pneumonia on April 4 and for the first time in the nation's history the vice president assumes the presidency. After the euphoria of Harrison's election, the unexpected advent of John Tyler of Virginia to the presidency, and his subsequent repudiation of Whig principles, leave the Whig Party in disarray. Grandson Arthur Adams, fifth child of Charles Francis and Abigail Brooks, is born on July 23. On September 4, Adams defends the British position in the extradition case of Alexander McLeod, a Canadian who participated in the sinking of the *Caroline*, an American vessel, during a cross-border action related to the 1837 rebellion against British rule in Upper Canada (Ontario). When the House rejects the British demand for McLeod's repatriation, Adams warns his colleagues not to allow a point upon which the United States is wrong to be entangled with one upon which it is right, the northeast boundary. Publishes poem, *The Wants of Man*.

1842   Speaks, January 4–6, against the bellicose rhetoric aimed at Mexico and Great Britain regarding the Texas question and again warns that slave emancipation could come by martial law. Presents a petition, January 25, from forty-six citizens of Haverhill, Massachusetts, requesting that Congress adopt "measures peaceably to dissolve the Union of these States" so that they might no longer be complicit in the perpetuation of slavery. An attempt is once again made to reprimand Adams, who vigorously defends the right of petition over several days of intense debate. Finally, on February 9, the motion of censure is tabled. This most recent effort to silence Adams draws national attention to the gag rule and to the right of petition as a matter of constitutional principle. Debates possibility of congressional emancipation during wartime with Henry Wise and Charles Jared Ingersoll, April 14. Elected to the Twenty-Eighth Congress as a Whig nominee in November, now representing Massachusetts's Eighth Congressional District; in the House as a whole, the Whigs lose their majority in dramatic fashion, with the Democrats gaining forty-nine seats. Publishes *The Social Compact, Exemplified in the Constitution of the Commonwealth of Massachusetts*, laying out his beliefs about democracy and his opposition to women's suffrage.

1843   Delivers address to the Massachusetts Historical Society on the seventeenth-century confederation of New England colonies on May 29. Tours western New York and Ohio in July to September on trip to lay cornerstone at the new observatory of the Cincinnati Astronomical Society; celebrated by crowds at many towns en route and also on return trip through Kentucky and Pennsylvania, October to November.

1844   In February, Adams proposes, as he had in 1838, resolution denying the power of the government to annex a foreign state or people, and to declare any attempt by "act of Congress or treaty" to annex Texas unconstitutional. On March 3, Adams and twelve other antislavery congressmen sign a public circular of protest, written by Adams, against Texas annexation. World Antislavery Convention of June 1843 in London adopts a resolution in his honor, citing "the moral heroism with which he has thrown himself into the breach." On October 7, Adams delivers an antislavery and anti-Texas address at a Whig rally at Tremont Temple in Boston and refutes the long-standing charge that he gave away Texas in the 1819 treaty with Spain. Adams's speech is reprinted around the North on the eve of the national election. Charles Francis is elected to the Massachusetts state senate. In the presidential election, Democratic candidate James K. Polk defeats the Whig Henry Clay. On December 3, Adams introduces a resolution to rescind the 25th Standing Rule (the gag rule), which the House adopts by a vote of 105 to 80. Writes in his diary that night, "blessed ever blessed be the name of God!"

1845   Granddaughter Mary Gardner, sixth child of Charles Francis and Abigail Brooks, is born February 19.

1846   Grandson Arthur Adams dies from diphtheria on February 9. On February 19, Texas is formally annexed to the United States. Adams votes for the Wilmot Proviso, August 8, an attempt to ban slavery from any territory gained in the war with Mexico, which has begun in April. On August 27, he presides over a civic meeting protesting the rendition of a fugitive slave at Faneuil Hall. Is reelected to Congress in November. Suffers a stroke on November 20 that leaves him partially paralyzed.

1847   Speaks in the House against proposal to provide indemnity to the owners of the *Amistad* in March and the proposal is defeated 94–28. On May 11, Adams is one of only fourteen congressmen to vote against a bill authorizing President Polk to pursue war with Mexico. Presents two petitions for peace with Mexico on December 20.

1848   Suffers a cerebral hemorrhage and collapses in the House of Representatives on February 21. He is carried to the Speaker's chamber where he dies on February 23. His last words are variously reported as "This is the last of earth. I am content." and "This is the end of earth, but I am composed." His remains are interred temporarily in a vault in the Congressional Cemetery in Washington before being removed in March to Quincy, to be buried next to his parents. Brooks Adams, seventh child of Charles Francis and Abigail Brooks, born June 24. In November, Charles Francis runs as vice presidential candidate of the Free-Soil Party, an alliance of antislavery Whigs and Democrats.

Note on the Texts

This volume presents selections from twenty manuscript volumes of the diaries of John Quincy Adams, beginning with the entry for March 4, 1821, the first day of the second term of the administration of James Monroe, and concluding with the last recorded entry, written three days before his death in 1848, a short piece of verse for a young admirer. (A companion volume presents selections from 1779 to 1821.) Adams wrote his diary in a total of fifty-one manuscript volumes, amounting to almost 15,000 pages, which are housed today in the offices of the Adams Family Papers at the Massachusetts Historical Society in Boston. Some of these volumes are bound journals or repurposed almanacs, others are pinned or stitched collections of loose sheets. Thanks to careful preservation by the author and his descendants, the editors of the Adams Family Papers conclude that all but a very few loose leaves of the diaries have survived. Collectively, they form an unrivaled personal record of historical events from the Revolution to the Mexican War by a figure prominently involved in them. As his son Charles Francis Adams, the editor of the first published edition of Adams's diary, rightly observed, "It may reasonably be doubted whether any attempt of the kind has ever been more completely executed by a public man."

Adams was a prolific diarist throughout his long life, but the degree of faithfulness with which he made entries varied over time, as did the manner in which he recorded them. As this volume begins, Adams was nearing the end of a twenty-six-year run of consecutive daily entries begun in 1795, a remarkable feat that testifies to his extraordinary discipline and dedication. This accomplishment is more noteworthy still when one considers that he found writing physically difficult because of a hand injury suffered in his youth.

Adams often composed his diary "in arrears," as he called it, especially during the busy years of his service as secretary of state from 1817 to 1825, using memoranda and abbreviated draft entries to help him reconstitute longer entries some days afterward. In 1816, he also began to compose, both retroactively and moving forward, a volume of line-a-day entries that acted as a monthly index to the larger work. So, for many dates there exist three different diary records: a detailed long-form entry fully composed in polished prose; a draft or short-form entry written in a more telegraphic style for future elaboration; and a highly abbreviated, single-line recap. The present edition generally presents Adams's long-form entries, though some draft entries are included for dates for which a long form does not exist.

As he suggests more than once in the diary, the burden of bringing the record up to date in this way could be overwhelming. From May 6 to August 21, 1821, there is a gap of several months in his long-entry diary, signaling that he fell unusually far behind and was never able to make up the dates. Other gaps followed: January 7–April 1, 1822; January 12–June 1, 1823; February 16–July 1, 1826; August 6–December 1, 1828; and March 25–December 1, 1832. On returning to the diary after the first of these gaps, on April 1, 1822, Adams wrote: "I make one more effort to resume my diary which has now suffered repeated and irreparable interruptions — I abandon definitively the attempt to keep it, minute and circumstantial." In the final years of his life, as his ability to write grew increasingly impaired, Adams had recourse to amanuenses, particularly his wife, Louisa Catherine, his daughters-in-law Mary Hellen and Abigail Brooks, and his granddaughter Mary Louisa. Entries not written in Adams's own hand are indicated by an asterisk in the present volume.

The diary served several purposes for Adams. Most practically, it was a resource to which he could return to confirm his own recollections and to substantiate, refine, or refute the claims of others about political events he witnessed or participated in. On January 15, 1831, for example, Adams wrote in his diary that "on further examination of my Diary of 1818, I thought it advisable to have extracts from it made of all those parts of it relating to the Seminole War, and the cabinet meetings concerning it. As the copy must be made by an entirely confidential hand, my wife undertook the task; she has often assisted me in the same manner before." Confidentiality was required because observations and expressions of a frank and personal nature are interspersed throughout the diary. These were not meant to be read by anyone, at least not anyone outside of the immediate family.

After Adams's death in 1848, his massive papers, including the diaries, were left to his sole surviving child, Charles Francis Adams, who at first granted limited access to the diaries to scholars and biographers, but who grew increasingly cautious about doing so as controversial entries began to circulate. Over time, as the younger Adams began to conceive plans to prepare a published edition, further restrictions were imposed. It was not until his own public career ended in 1873 that Charles Francis Adams was able to turn to editing the diaries full-time, and when he did he adhered to a protective distinction between the public and the private. In the preface to the resulting twelve-volume edition, *Memoirs of John Quincy Adams, Comprising*

Portions of His Diary from 1795 to 1848 (Philadelphia: J. B. Lippincott & Co., 1874–77), Adams laid out his editorial philosophy:

> After careful meditation over the materials of this great trust . . . [i]t was very clear that abridgement was indispensable. Assuming this to be certain, it became necessary to fix upon a rule of selection which should be fair and honest. To attain that object I came to the following conclusions: 1st. To eliminate the details of common life and events of no interest to the public. 2d. To reduce the moral and religious speculations, in which the work abounds, so far as to escape repetition of sentiments once declared. 3d. Not to suppress strictures upon contemporaries, but to give them only when they are upon public men acting in the same sphere with the writer. . . . 4th. To suppress nothing of his own habits of self-examination, even when they might be thought most to tell against himself. 5th. To abstain altogether from modification of the sentiments or the very words, and substitution of what might seem better ones, in every case but that of obvious error in writing.

"Guided by these rules," Adams concluded, "I trust I have supplied pretty much all in these volumes which the most curious reader would be desirous to know."

Curiosity is inherently subjective, of course, and susceptible to change over time. Charles Francis Adams Jr., for one, found that his grandfather's diary from the late 1780s, when John Quincy Adams was a young law clerk in Newburyport, Massachusetts, "greatly interested" him, notwithstanding his father's decision to exclude it from the *Memoirs* because it "contains little of, so-called, historical value." This led the younger Adams to publish *Life in a New England Town: 1787, 1788. Diary of John Quincy Adams, While a Student in the Office of Theophilus Parsons at Newburyport* (Boston: Little, Brown and Company, 1903). Charles Francis Adams Sr.'s selection of John Quincy Adams's diary was by any standard generous—the twelve volumes present, in terms of word count, roughly half of the entire diary manuscript —but its excision of his father's private and family concerns ("the details of common life") can be said to have resulted in a one-dimensional picture of the man in the public mind, one that would predominate for a century or more.

By returning directly to the manuscript diaries and incorporating entries and passages excluded from the *Memoirs*, the current edition seeks to present a more rounded portrait than has heretofore been available to the general reader. The previous reader's edition of the diary, prepared by the historian Allan Nevins in 1928, arose from his concern that the *Memoirs*, this "unrivalled treasury for the social and political history of the time, has long been out of print and is now rather rare and extremely costly. Its ponderous bulk, moreover, makes it forbidding to the general reader, and difficult of use by the ordinary student." To remedy this, Nevins "selected from it those passages which seem of the greatest permanent worth, giving emphasis to the materials which throw light on the social background of the period, on J. Q. Adams's character, and on the more dramatic political and diplomatic events of the time." *The Diary of John Quincy Adams, 1794–1845: American Political, Social and Intellectual Life from Washington to Polk* (New York: Longmans, Green and Co., 1928), his 600-page volume of selections from the *Memoirs*, was reissued in 1951 by Charles Scribner's Sons. Excerpts from the *Memoirs* were also included in Adrienne Koch and William Peden, eds., *The Selected Writings of John & John Quincy Adams* (New York: Alfred A. Knopf, 1946).

When Charles Francis Adams died in 1886 he left his papers, and those of John and Abigail Adams, and of John Quincy and Louisa Catherine Adams, to his four sons, one of whom, the aforementioned Charles Francis Adams Jr., later became president of the Massachusetts Historical Society. In 1902 Charles Francis Adams Jr. had the family papers moved from the Stone Library, a separate fireproof building his father had built on the grounds of the family estate in Quincy, to the Massachusetts Historical Society building in Boston, and in 1905 he created the Adams Manuscript Trust to ensure continued family ownership and control of the papers for the next fifty years. In 1954 the Adams Manuscript Trust entered into an agreement with the Massachusetts Historical Society and Harvard University Press to publish the family's papers through the year 1889. The Adams Manuscript Trust was dissolved in 1956 after it transferred ownership of its papers to the Massachusetts Historical Society, which began to identify and photocopy Adams documents in repositories outside of the family archive. The collection was microfilmed from 1954 to 1959. Publication of the Adams Family Papers began in 1961 and has proceeded in several series since, including a letterpress edition, *Diary of John Quincy Adams*, David Grayson Allen, Robert J. Taylor, Marc Friedlander, and Celeste Walker, eds., 2 vols. (Cambridge, MA: The Belknap Press of Harvard University Press, 1981), which presents Adams's diaries from November 1779 to December 1788.

In 2005, the microfilm of the entire diary was scanned and published online as *The Diaries of John Quincy Adams: A Digital Collection*: http://www.masshist.org/jqadiaries/php/, the source for texts used here. The present edition replicates as closely as possible the manuscript original, in ways that depart slightly from the approach taken in the 1981 letterpress edition, and substantially from that taken in the *Memoirs* and the works derived from it. Judging by his own editorial guidelines, Charles Francis Adams found many instances of "obvious error in writing" in the diaries, for he systematically emended his father's more idiosyncratic eighteenth-century style, characterized by capitalization of common nouns, liberal use of dashes, and British spellings, to bring it into conformity with the prevailing Victorian style. The current edition, by contrast, retains John Quincy Adams's spelling, capitalization, and punctuation, including his use of dashes to separate sentences or sentence fragments. These dashes, which in the manuscript can vary in length, have been standardized as em-dashes. The editors of the 1981 edition chose to interpret the combination of a period and a dash as a paragraph break; this edition does not. It has been necessary in certain instances to supply punctuation for clarity, as for instance with Adams's casual and inconsistent use of quotation marks when rendering dialogue. The end of the page often served for Adams as a marker of medial or terminal publication, and commas and periods have been added accordingly. To minimize hand lifts, Adams sometimes incorporated commas into the preceding words, as slight dots, bulges, or, if the word ends in an r, overhangs. When it is unclear whether a comma was intended, one has been added only if it improves clarity. Commas and periods are often indistinguishable in the manuscript and are rendered here in the way most conducive to clarity. Except for the suffixes to numerals, and M^r·, M^{rs}·, and D^r·, superscripts have been converted to contractions (Col^l· becomes Col'l). Other contractions, such as altho' and return'd, have been retained, as have ampersands. Given the length and complexity of Adams's diary, it is remarkable how rarely he crossed out or otherwise corrected his manuscript. On the rare occasions when he did, the current edition slightly adopts his correction. It also silently omits inadvertent repeated words and adds dropped words in brackets, in the latter case only if the omission affects clarity.

For more on the diaries and their history, see *Diary of John Quincy Adams*, David Grayson Allen et al., eds., 2 vols. (Cambridge, MA: The Belknap Press of Harvard University Press, 1981), 1:xvii–l and David Waldstreicher, "John Quincy Adams: The Life, the Diary, and the Biographers," in Waldstreicher, ed., *A Companion to John Adams and John Quincy Adams* (Malden, MA, and Oxford: Wiley-Blackwell, 2013), 241–62.

Notes

In the notes below, the reference numbers denote page and line of this volume (the line count includes headings, but not rule lines). No note is made for material included in the eleventh edition of *Merriam-Webster's Collegiate Dictionary*, except for certain cases where common words and terms have specific historical meanings or inflections. Biblical quotations and allusions are keyed to the King James Version; references to Shakespeare to *The Riverside Shakespeare*, ed. G. Blackmore Evans (Boston: Houghton Mifflin, 1974). For further historical and biographical background and references to other studies, see David Waldstreicher and Matthew Mason, *John Quincy Adams and the Politics of Slavery: Selections from the Diary* (New York: Oxford University Press, 2016); Samuel Flagg Bemis, *John Quincy Adams and the Union* (New York: Alfred A. Knopf, 1956); Leonard L. Richards, *The Life and Times of Congressman John Quincy Adams* (New York: Oxford University Press, 1986); Daniel Walker Howe, *What Hath God Wrought: The Transformation of America, 1815–1848* (New York: Oxford University Press, 2007); Fred Kaplan, *John Quincy Adams: American Visionary* (New York: Harper, 2014).

CHAPTER VIII: 1821–1825

1.22–24 the Marshal of the District . . . the late Speaker of the House.] Tench Ringgold of Maryland was U.S. marshal for the District of Columbia from 1818 to 1831. Thomas Dougherty of Kentucky was the clerk of the House of Representatives from 1815 to 1822. John W. Taylor of New York was Speaker of the House from November 15, 1820, to March 4, 1821.

2.4–5 The Secretaries . . . and the Navy] Adams, William H. Crawford, John C. Calhoun, and Smith Thompson.

2.17 The Chief Justice] John Marshall was chief justice of the U.S. Supreme Court from 1801 to 1835.

2.39 Brown's Hotel.] The Indian Queen Hotel, Jesse B. Brown proprietor, located on Pennsylvania Avenue between Sixth and Seventh Streets.

3.10–11 the case of Levett Harris against W. D. Lewis.] Levett Harris had been U.S. consul at St. Petersburg during Adams's tenure as minister there and hoped eventually to become minister himself, but his reputation had been damaged by charges of official misconduct and corruption as consul. In 1819, Harris sued Philadelphia merchant William D. Lewis, who had represented the Lewis family's commercial firm in Russia, for libel for suggesting that Harris had accepted bribes to permit illicit trade through customs.

7.4 they have wasted of their time at Cambridge] Adams's eldest son George, a bright but erratic student, would graduate from Harvard in the Class of 1821. Middle son John was concluding his second year, but would be expelled before graduation for participating in a student rebellion. (Youngest son Charles Francis would not matriculate until September.)

7.31–33 the Barracks at St. Augustine . . . Fromentin] As Florida underwent a complicated transition from Spanish to American control under the terms of the Adams-Onís Treaty, there was controversy about the housing of U.S. troops in public buildings in St. Augustine. There were also persistent tensions between General Andrew Jackson, military governor of the new Florida Territory, Colonel José Callava, the last governor of Spanish West Florida, and former Louisiana senator Eligius Fromentin, newly installed as U.S. judge for the territory. The three clashed in August and September over claims against the estate of a deceased Spanish official by his illegitimate daughter, who appealed to the new American authorities for redress. Jackson used the judicial powers granted to him under his commission as military governor to intervene and ultimately arrested Callava to force him to release papers relevant to the case. Outraged when Fromentin then issued a writ of habeas corpus for the former Spanish governor, Jackson wrote to Adams demanding the judge's removal.

8.22–23 lost a number of Slaves . . . during the late war] Over the course of the War of 1812 some five thousand American slaves escaped to British ships or lines, responding to offers of freedom and resettlement in British colonial possessions in Canada and elsewhere.

9.14 Oakhill] President Monroe's estate in Loudoun County, Virginia.

9.25–26 "close ambition varnished o'er with zeal."] *Paradise Lost*, II.485.

10.32 the case of La Jeune Eugénie] Writing for the U.S. circuit court for Massachusetts in the case of *U.S. v. La Jeune Eugenie*, Supreme Court Justice Joseph Story held that the African slave trade violated both natural and international law, and that federal courts had the authority to confiscate ships employed in the trade. The case arose out of the capture by a U.S. revenue cutter of the French ship *La Jeune Eugenie* off the coast of West Africa on the suspicion that it was an American ship covertly engaged in the slave trade. Discovering their mistake, the revenue cutter's crew then claimed an award available under the law prohibiting the slave trade with Africa. Both the French consul in Boston, where the vessel was brought, and the French owners of the ship submitted claims for its return. Though Story determined that the ship was indeed French-owned, he refused to return it to its owners because they had clearly been involved in an illegal trade. The ship was instead returned to the French government for further adjudication.

10.35   the case of the Apollon] In 1820, before the Adams-Onís Treaty had gone into effect, the French ship *Apollon* was seized by American authorities in the St. Marys River, between Georgia and Spanish Florida, on suspicion of evading customs collection. When both the French and the Spanish ministers protested that the ship had been taken in Spanish waters, Adams had suggested that in the absence of effective Spanish control of the border, the United States was forced to intervene.

11.12–13   Newfoundland fishing vessel piracy] Canning had first brought this case to Adams's attention on October 13:

> He came to enquire, whether we could deliver up a certain Captain of a British fishing vessel, belonging to the Island of Newfoundland; who ran away with his vessel, and her fare of fish, and after disposing part of his Cargo by smuggling on our coast, entered one of our Eastern ports, and was there seized for a breach of our revenue Laws — The crime of which this man is impeached is a Statute piracy, both by the British Laws, and our own. But our tribunals can take cognizance only of offenses against our own Law, which can operate only upon offences within our jurisdiction; they cannot try this man, either upon our Statute, which he has not, or upon the British Statute, which he has transgressed. I told Mr. Canning that I thought we could not deliver up this man.

12.5–6   both these writers, as well as Grotius] Adams refers to the three major authorities on international law in the eighteenth century: Jean-Jacques Burlamaqui, *Principes du droit naturel* (1747; *The Principles of Natural Law*, 1748) and *Principes du droit politique* (1751; *The Principles of Politic Law*, 1752); Emmerich de Vattel, *Le droit des gens* (1758; *The Law of Nations*, 1759); and Hugo Grotius, *De Jure Belli ac Pacis* (1625; *The Laws of War and Peace*, 1654).

12.9   Barbeyrac's Notes] French jurist and translator Jean Barbeyrac prepared an annotated edition of Grotius's work in 1729.

13.3   the mere mint and cummin of the Law] Cf. Matthew 23:23.

14.4   the death of the Queen] Caroline, Queen Consort of the United Kingdom as the wife of George IV, died on August 7, 1821.

15.18   Dr. Floyd's Resolution] Here begins the so-called duplicate letter controversy, which will engross much of Adams's time and attention. In January 1822, Congressman John Floyd of Virginia introduced a resolution calling upon President Monroe to release to the House "all the correspondence which led to the Treaty of Ghent, which has not yet been made public, and which, in his opinion, it may not be improper to disclose." Pursuant to the resolution, Russell, who had served with Adams on the five-member American commission at Ghent, submitted a letter to then Secretary of State Monroe, dated December 25, 1814, the day after the treaty ending the War of 1812 was signed. In the letter Russell intimated that he would be sending a subsequent letter explaining in detail his reasons for objecting to any linkage in the treaty between British navigation rights on the Mississippi and U.S. fishing rights off Newfoundland. In April, the House adopted another resolution by Floyd, this time calling for the second letter to which Russell had referred, which was missing from the State Department files that had been released. Russell then submitted, on April 22, what he said was a duplicate of that letter, originally written from Paris on February 11, 1815. The letter seemed to suggest that Adams, as head of the U.S. commission, had acted in contravention of diplomatic instructions at Ghent. Subsequently the president found Russell's original letter to him in his personal files, and on comparison it was revealed that Russell's copy deviated significantly from the original. Adams then launched a newspaper campaign to expose Russell's duplicity.

16.7   his daughter at Mendon] Russell's wife Sylvia had died in 1811. His daughter Amelia lived with her mother's family in the town of Mendon in Worcester County, Massachusetts.

17.32   the experiment of cradling] By means of an inclined plane or marine railway system adapted by Commodore John Rodgers from a design by English naval engineers John Thomas and Henry Steers, enabling 140 men to haul the 1,726-ton U.S.S. *Potomac* out of the water at the rate of four feet per minute, a remarkable feat witnessed by President Monroe and other dignitaries.

19.38–39   Five years have this day passed since Dr. Tillary . . . congratulated me] New York physician James Tillary was a fellow passenger with the Adamses on their return to America in 1817.

24.40   Virginius and the Highland Reel.] *Virginius*, five-act tragedy (1820) by Irish playwright James Sheridan Knowles. *The Highland Reel*, comic opera (1788) by Irish playwright and librettist John O'Keeffe.

25.2   Bertram.] *Bertram; or The Castle of St. Aldobrand*, five-act tragedy (1820) by Irish playwright and novelist Charles Robert Maturin.

25.2–3   the Roman History.] As Livy's *History of Rome* was generally called in the eighteenth and nineteenth centuries.

25.13   brevier type] A small type of approximately eight-point size.

26.4   "With a bare Bodkin."] Cf. *Hamlet*, III.i.77.

26.8–9   The proposition of Mr. Sanchez] Cuban agent Bernabé Sanchez was floating a plan to incite a revolt in Cuba as a prelude to annexation by the United States.

27.37–38   the holy Alliance] The coalition formed by Alexander I of Russia, Franz I of Austria, and Friedrich Wilhelm III of Prussia in the wake of the defeat of Napoleon, formalized by treaty in Paris on September 26, 1815.

30.19   the case of the Danish Slave] When John Barry, a slave owned by a woman on the Danish possession of St. Croix, escaped and stowed away to

New York, the Danish minister demanded his return. In his opinion Wirt concluded that he could "see no difference between the President's authority to restore this slave and his authority to restore a ship or any other property belonging to a subject of a foreign prince, which has been improperly taken from his possession by our citizens, or by force furnished from the United States."

32.31 Robert Smith] Smith had been U.S. secretary of state from 1809 to 1811.

33.12 Gales and Seaton] Joseph Gales Jr. and his brother-in-law William Winston Seaton were publishers of the pro-administration *National Intelligencer* and for many years the official printers to Congress.

38.14–15 Antoine was with me.] Antoine Giusta had been Adams's valet and steward since they met at Ghent in 1814.

40.1 Bladensburg] Town approximately eight miles northeast of Washington.

40.14–16 the Quirpon Islands . . . to Cape Ray] Quirpon Island is located off the northern tip of Newfoundland, at the entrance to the Gulf of St. Lawrence. Cape Ray is some 425 miles to the southwest, on the opposite end of Newfoundland. Adams and Menou were consulting the widely reprinted 1755 map of North America by American cartographer John Mitchell.

40.28–29 the War between France and Spain] French forces had invaded Spain in April 1823 to crush a revolution there and restore the Bourbon Ferdinand VII to the throne.

40.30–32 Jefferson's answer to Genet . . . Pickering's Instructions] Secretary of State Thomas Jefferson to French minister Edmond Genêt (July 24, 1793): "by the general law of nations, the goods of a friend found in the vessel of an enemy are free, and the goods of an enemy found in the vessel of a friend are lawful prize." As Adams suggests, this principle was echoed in the July 15, 1797, instructions of Secretary of State Timothy Pickering to U.S. commissioners to France John Marshall, Charles Cotesworth Pinckney, and Elbridge Gerry.

43.32 the first Treaty with Prussia.] Negotiated by John Adams, Thomas Jefferson, and Benjamin Franklin in 1785. Its most seminal provision for Adams was Article 12:

> If one of the contracting parties should be engaged in war with any other power, the free intercourse & commerce of the subjects or citizens of the party remaining neuter with the belligerent powers, shall not be interrupted. On the contrary, in that cases as in full peace, the vessels of the neutral party may navigate freely to & from the ports and on the coasts of the belligerent parties, free vessels making free goods, insomuch that all things shall be adjudged free which shall be on board any vessel belonging to the neutral party, although such things belong to an enemy of the other; and the same freedom shall be extended to

persons who shall be on board a free vessel, although they should be enemies to the other party, unless they be soldiers in actual service of such enemy.

45.15–16   "it is not in Man that walketh to direct his steps."] Cf. Jeremiah 10:23.

46.6   his Declaration in the Treaty] See for instance the preamble to the treaty of the Holy Alliance:

> [Their Majesties] solemnly declare that the present Act has no other object than to publish, in the face of the whole world, their fixed reso- lution, both in the administration of their respective States, and in their political relations with every other Government, to take for their sole guide the precepts of that Holy Religion, namely, the precepts of Jus- tice, Christian Charity, and Peace, which, far from being applicable only to private concerns, must have an immediate influence on the councils of Princes, and guide all their steps, as being the only means of consoli- dating human institutions and remedying their imperfections.

46.32   Fuller's] Hostelry operated by Stephen Fuller Jr. in Walpole, Massa- chusetts, approximately halfway between Providence and Boston on the stage road.

47.6–7   Mr. Southard] Senator Samuel L. Southard of New Jersey was se- lected by Monroe to replace Smith Thompson as secretary of the navy in Sep- tember 1823 after Thompson was elevated to the Supreme Court.

49.20–21   Cadiz has surrendered to the French] French forces captured the rebel stronghold of Cádiz, in southwestern Spain, on August 23, 1823.

51.14   the Greeks as an Independent Nation] Greek revolutionaries were en- gaged in a long struggle to free their country from Ottoman rule.

55.27   at Governor Barbour's.] Virginia senator James Barbour lived at "Fra- scati," his family's estate in Orange County.

56.34   G.M. Dallas] Philadelphia lawyer and former diplomatic secretary George Mifflin Dallas was being considered for the post of minister to Mexico.

63.14–21   Lord of all . . . bless my native Land!] This is Adams's own verse.

64.30–31   the Resolution offered by me to the Senate on the 23^{d} of February 1807] "Resolved, That the Secretary of the Treasury be directed to prepare & repeat to the Senate at their next Session, a plan for the application of such means as are within the power of Congress, to the purpose of opening roads & making canals together with a statement of the undertakings of that nature, which, as objects of public improvement, may require & deserve the aid of governments, and also a statement of works, of the nature mentioned, which have been commenced, the progress which has been made in them, &

the means & prospect of their being completed; & all such information as, in the opinion of the Secretary, shall be material in relation to the objects of this resolution."

64.33   his brother in the State of Ohio.] Ohio congressman William McLean.

65.4–5   who can hold a fire . . . of the frosty Caucasus] Cf. *Richard II*, I.iii.295.

68.31   Edwards's charges] Ninian Edwards was a senator from Illinois from December 3, 1818, to March 4, 1824, when he resigned to accept an appointment as U.S. minister to Mexico. Writing as "A. B." while still a senator, he published a series of articles in the *Washington Republican* accusing Crawford of corruption in the management of public land revenues. Early in 1824 he lodged formal charges against Crawford in the House of Representatives. As Plumer predicted, the House committee charged with investigating the charges found them without merit, and the affair cost Edwards his diplomatic post.

69.12   n'importe.] French: whatever.

69.34–35   Bishop Burnet's History of his own Times] Having spotted Adams's diary, Hay playfully likens it to the popular multivolume memoir of Gilbert Burnet, Bishop of Salisbury, which offers a vivid, journalistic portrait of events in England from the Restoration to the reign of Queen Anne.

73.28   P. U. S.] The president.

76.27–28   my old School-mate Jesse Deane] In 1778, thirteen-year-old Jesse Deane traveled to France with John and John Quincy Adams to join his father, Silas Deane, whom John Adams was to replace as American envoy to France. The three arrived at Paris just days after the elder Deane had departed to return to America, and Benjamin Franklin assumed custody of his departed colleague's son. Jesse Deane was tutored at Passy together with John Quincy and Franklin's grandson, Benjamin Franklin Bache.

77.7–8   Mr. John Vaughan] Philadelphia merchant and philanthropist John Vaughan was the librarian and treasurer of the American Philosophical Society.

80.22   what they call the *Relief* party] Foreclosure and indebtedness were rampant in the wake of the Panic of 1819 and in several state legislatures, especially in the West, pro-debtor coalitions formed to advocate for relief.

81.31   Mr. Welles] Elijah Gardner Welles, compiler and publisher of *The Orator's Guide, or, Rules for Speaking and Composing: From the Best Authorities* (Philadelphia, 1822).

82.33–34   a public insult to Mr. Edwards.] Adams and other members of the cabinet were reluctant to be seen as taking a side in the so-called A.B. Controversy (see note 68.31).

83.13–14 the Act of Congress establishing the Cumberland Road] Signed into law by President Jefferson on March 29, 1806.

84.10 "Incedo super ignes"] Horace, *Odes,* II.i.7–8: "[A dangerous Work you write, and tread] / O'er Flames by treacherous Ashes hid." From 1722 translation by Thomas Creech.

85.34 Mr. Baker's] Washington's Second Presbyterian Church, Daniel Baker, pastor.

85.34 a Son of Dr. Mason] Presbyterian minister Ebenezer Mason, eldest son of theologian and educator John Mitchell Mason.

87.21 the Hero] Jackson.

89.4 the Massachusetts claim] During the War of 1812, Federalist-controlled Massachusetts had resisted calls by the Madison administration to mobilize its militia and make it subject to control by, or at least coordination with, federal authorities planning invasions of Canada. The situation was further complicated later in the war when parts of the state (which still included Maine) were occupied by the enemy, requiring extensive and costly defensive measures. In an 1817 audit of Massachusetts's claims upon the federal government for compensation for its contributions to the war effort, most of the requests were denied because such services "were rendered independently of the authority of the United States, and that the Militia were withheld from the command of the officers of the United States." In 1824, the Massachusetts state government, now under Republican control, dispatched Adams's friend George Sullivan, son of former governor James Sullivan, to Washington to attempt again to resolve the claims. This time the effort had the support of the Monroe administration, which saw a generous resolution of the claims as a way of strengthening the party in New England.

89.22–23 the Ladies] That is, wives Rachel Donelson Jackson and Floride Calhoun.

90.5 Samuel Phillips Lee] From this first commission as midshipman, Lee would rise to become a rear admiral in the U.S. Navy, remaining loyal in the Civil War even as other members of his famous family, including cousin Robert E. Lee, joined the Confederacy.

93.27–29 certain passages . . . had been offensive to the Roman Catholics.] Lee likely had these passages about the Protestant Reformation in mind:

> The religious reformation was an improvement in the science of mind; an improvement in the intercourse of man with his Creator, and in his acquaintance with himself. It was an advance in the knowledge of his duties and his rights. It was a step in the progress of man, in comparison with which the magnet and gunpowder, the wonders of either India, nay the printing press itself, were but as the paces of a pigmy to the stride of a giant. . . . The corruptions and usurpations of the church were the immediate objects of these reformers; but at the foundation

of all their exertions there was a single plain and almost self-evident principle—that man has a right to the exercise of his own reason. It was this principle which the sophistry and rapacity of the church had obscured and obliterated, and which the intestine divisions of that same church itself first restored.

94.35 Carusi's Rooms] Carusi's Assembly Rooms, a dining and dancing venue operated by Italian immigrant Gaetani Carusi and located at C Street between Eleventh and Twelfth Streets.

96.6–7 Ingham's . . . siege upon D. P. Cook] From the diary entry for February 5, 1825:

D. P. Cook called this morning as he had promised. I reminded him of what he had told me of [Pennsylvania congressman Samuel] Ingham's conversations with him respecting the Government of Arkansas; and of [South Carolina congressman George] M'Duffie's talk with him in Ingham's chamber. . . . The substance was that Ingham knowing Cook to be a Candidate for the appointment of Governor of Arkansas, urged him to declare openly that he would vote for Jackson, and intimated that he should then have the appointment. Cook says he offended Ingham by his answer to this proffer; and Ingham has said nothing of it since — M'Duffie's argument was to the same purpose. That General Jackson's election would depend upon his, Cook's, vote. That there was a moral obligation to vote for him who had the greatest number of electoral votes. That if I should be elected it would only be by Clay's corrupt coalition with me — and that the People would be so disgusted with this that there would be a systematic and determined opposition from the beginning so that the Administration could not get along — It would be overthrown and he would be involved in its ruin.

96.8 Benton's screw upon Scott] John Scott, Missouri's lone representative in the Eighteenth Congress, was being pressured to support Jackson by Thomas Hart Benton, one of the state's senators, who insisted that "nine tenths of the people" in the West supported the general. In the end, Scott cast Missouri's vote for Adams.

96.15–16 It is not in man that walketh to direct his steps.] See note 45.15–16.

CHAPTER IX: 1825–1829

100.14 Williamson's] Hotel located at Pennsylvania Avenue and Fourteenth Street.

101.38–102.1 Scott's Bible and . . . commentary of Hewlett] Adams was consulting multivolume Bible commentaries by English theologians Thomas Scott (first published 1788–92) and John Hewlett (1816).

102.13 my Diary-Index] A monthly line-a-day recap of events. See the Note on the Texts in this volume.

105.24 the Treaty of Indian Springs] Treaty negotiated by commissioners of the U.S. government and a minority faction of Creek Indians led by William McIntosh, signed on February 12, 1825, and ratified by the Senate on March 7, 1825. Alabama stood to gain some three million acres of Creek lands under its terms. A large majority of Creek chiefs and warriors objected, insisting that McIntosh did not have authority to sign treaties or cede territory. Adams appointed Brevet Major General Edmund P. Gaines to investigate the Creek claims.

106.27–28 The Clark party in Georgia] Anti-Crawfordite supporters of John Clark, governor of Georgia from 1819 to 1824.

107.23 Seest thou a man diligent *in his* business?] Cf. Proverbs 22:29.

108.31–32 Dr. Caldwell's Lecture upon the organ of amativeness] Charles Caldwell of Lexington, Kentucky, was the author of *Elements of Phrenology* (1824). In phrenology, the organ of amativeness refers to the cerebellum.

109.1–2 Van Ness's Poplars . . . the Tiber] John Peter Van Ness, a former congressman from New York and future mayor of Washington, had a large estate near the president's house, located at the site of the present-day headquarters of the Organization of American States on Constitution Avenue and Seventeenth Street. Enclosed in a tunnel, the Tiber Creek flows today underneath Constitution Avenue.

111.39 Van Zandt] Nicholas Van Zandt has presented Adams with a copy of the just-published *Life and Character of the Chevalier John Paul Jones, a Captain in the Navy of the United States during their Revolutionary War.* The work consisted primarily of Jones's letters and naval logs, compiled by John Henry Sherburne, a clerk at the Navy Department.

112.9 from my own memory.] In the spring of 1779 Adams and his father waited for two months at the French port of L'Orient for return passage to America. There they encountered John Paul Jones, who entertained them aboard the *Bonhomme Richard.*

112.14 Johnson's Sermon 18] Samuel Johnson ghostwrote sermons for "sundry beneficed clergymen that requested them," especially his friend John Taylor, cathedral canon at Westminster Abbey. Sermon number 18 treated 1 Corinthians 6:8: "Nay, you do wrong and defraud, and that your brethren."

112.18 La Grange] The Château de la Grange-Bléneau, located approximately forty miles southwest of Paris, was Lafayette's home from 1802 until his death in 1834.

112.35 having lost two daughters] Twelve-year-old Eliza Clay died in Lebanon, Ohio, as the Clay family was traveling back to Washington. Her twenty-year-old sister Susan Clay Duralde died in New Orleans five weeks later.

113.20–23 by persisting in a Law . . . in direct violation of the Constitution] The Negro Seaman's Act of 1822, which stipulated that any free black sailor who arrived in a South Carolina port must be jailed during his stay and, if the state was not reimbursed for the expense of the incarceration by his captain, the individual could then be sold as a slave. The Supreme Court justice Adams refers to was South Carolina Unionist William Johnson.

114.15–16   the claims of our Citizens upon France] For compensation for seizures of American shipping, dating in some cases to the 1790s.

118.11   W. Elliot's Son] Seth Alfred Elliot, publisher of *Elliot's Washington Pocket Almanac*, issued annually from 1823 to 1832.

118.27   Patrick Henry's prophesy] At the Virginia ratifying convention, on June 5, 1788, Henry had delivered a long speech in opposition to the proposed new constitution, which he predicted would create an unrestrained federal government destined to "oppress and ruin the people."

118.34–35   a convert to Captain Symmes] In 1818 U.S. Army officer John Cleves Symmes Jr. had publicized an inventive theory about the nature of Earth's core, announcing in his *Circular No. 1* that "the earth is hollow, and habitable within; containing a number of solid concentrick spheres, one within the other, and that it is open at the poles 12 or 16 degrees; I pledge my life in support of this truth, and am ready to explore the hollow, if the world will support and aid me in the undertaking."

120.12–13   the Columbian Institute] The Columbian Institute for the Promotion of Arts and Sciences, a learned society founded in 1816 and chartered by Congress in 1818.

121.21–23   It resembles . . . the last days of Queen Anne.] When, in July 1714, Tory ministers Henry St. John, Viscount Bolingbroke, and Robert Hartley, Earl of Oxford, vied angrily with one another at the ailing queen's bedside. Swift likened it to a "ship's crew quarrelling in a storm." Anne died shortly thereafter and the Whig-engineered succession of George I of Hanover to the English throne resulted in Oxford's imprisonment and Bolingbroke's exile.

124.1   Ɋↄↄↄↄↄ] Adams developed his own shorthand to record both thoughts of an especially personal nature (as at 313.2) and more mundane recurring features of the diary, like meteorological observations, as possibly here. The editors of the Adams Papers are still deciphering Adams's system.

125.33–34   the Panama Mission] Adams's proposal to send a U.S. delegation to the Panama Congress of 1826, the first international gathering of American countries, provoked fierce controversy in both houses of Congress, in the Senate over the confirmation of Adams's nominees, and in the House over appropriation of funding for the mission.

127.2   round by S. H. Smith's] Samuel Harrison Smith owned a large country seat at Sidney, approximately five miles northwest of the President's House, the site today of the campus of The Catholic University.

127.4   Michaux's first Volume] From the three-volume *Histoire des arbres forestiers de l'Amérique Septentrionale* (1810–13; *The North American Sylva*, 1819) by French botanist François André Michaux.

127.9 Hawley's] St. John Episcopal Church, Lafayette Square, William Dickinson Hawley, rector.

127.20–21 a discourse to be published] Isaac Darneille, *A Discourse or Lecture on the Subject of Civilizing the Indians, in which is exhibited a New Plan to Effect their Civilization and to Meliorate their Condition* (Washington D.C., 1826).

131.10–11 Merrill's at Waterloo] Tavern operated by John A. Merrill, located approximately fifteen miles southwest of Baltimore.

131.32 Fuller's at Waltham] A slip of the pen: in the diary draft for July 12 Adams correctly notes that he "Dined at Fuller's in Walpole," not Waltham. See note 46.32.

134.12 the Pastor by whom I had been baptized] Anthony Wibird, Congregational minister at Braintree.

137.21 Mather's Magnalia, and Hutchinson's History] *Magnalia Christi Americana: or, The Ecclesiastical History of New-England, from its First Planting in the Year 1620, unto the Year of Our Lord, 1698* (London, 1702) by Boston minister Cotton Mather and *The History of the Province of Massachusetts-Bay*, 2 vols. (Boston, 1764, 1767) by Massachusetts colonial governor Thomas Hutchinson.

137.30–31 But knowledge . . . did ne'er unroll] Thomas Gray, "Elegy Written in a Country Churchyard" (1751), ll. 49–50.

139.17 two other women and two men] Listed in the margin as Eli Ruth, Avis, Isaac Bassett, and Wistar, the last probably being Thomas Wistar, a leading Philadelphia Quaker.

140.10 an old Saturday's club] A Boston literary and social club in which Adams had been a member.

140.35–36 the subject of the Colonial Trade] In 1822, Parliament had opened West Indian ports to some American trade but retained mercantilist duties in favor of staples from within the British Empire. The United States, in turn, continued to impose discriminatory duties on British goods coming into American ports.

140.37 the Slave indemnity question] The United States sought compensation on behalf of slaveholders affected by the exodus described in note 8.22–23.

141.30–31 the Court-Martial upon Lieutenant Constantine Smith] Smith was charged with killing fellow marine lieutenant William T. Bourne in a duel in Washington on June 27, 1826.

142.2 the short-hand] Adams wrote the poem in the margin using a short-hand system of his own devising (see note 313.2). The translation provided here is from Charles Francis Adams's edition of the diary.

142.23   Dr. Lane came for my decision upon his claim] In the case of slave ships seized by the United States the federal government contracted with individuals to hold the enslaved people involved while the case was being adjudicated, leading to claims for compensation such as this one by Robert Carr Lane of Mobile, Alabama.

144.17   a powerful exposure of him in the newspapers] Eight articles by "Curtius" highly critical of Benton for allying himself with his once-inveterate enemy Andrew Jackson had appeared in the *Missouri Republican* and were collected in a pamphlet entitled *Torch Light, An Examination of the Origin, Policy, and Principles of the Opposition to the Administration, and an Exposition of the Official Conduct of Thomas H. Benton* ([St. Louis], 1826). The articles were republished in pro-administration newspapers around the country.

145.9   for the Richmond Enquirer to take hold of.] Thomas Ritchie's newspaper was the mouthpiece for Old Republican opposition to the Adams administration in Virginia.

149.6–7   the Proclamation.] As related in the diary for the previous day:

> Cabinet Meeting at 10 — Mr. Clay had sent me yesterday a draught of a Proclamation, declaring, that the trade and intercourse between the United States, and Certain British Colonies, which had been opened by an Act of Parliament of June 1822, was now prohibited by two Acts of Parliament of 5 July 1826 and an Order-in-Council of 27 July 1826 — I had made some slight alterations in the draught, and abridged it by one half. Some further alterations were made, and it was determined that it should be issued, to-morrow or the next day.

150.8   flints from Barataria.] That is, from the smuggling depot organized by French-American privateer Jean Lafitte on an island in Barataria Bay, approximately thirty miles south of New Orleans.

151.34–36   Not wanting . . . sorrow, and pain] *Paradise Lost*, I.556–58.

160.5–6   The names in the margin] Congressmen: John Bailey of Massachusetts, David Barker of New Hampshire, Daniel D. Barnard of New York, John Barney of Maryland, George O. Belden of New York, Richard A. Buckner of Kentucky, John C. Clark of New York, James Clarke of Kentucky, Henry W. Connor of North Carolina, William Creighton Jr. of Ohio, Benjamin W. Crowninshield of Massachusetts, John Davis of Massachusetts, John D. Dickinson of New York, Clement Dorsey of Maryland, William Drayton of South Carolina, Henry W. Dwight of Massachusetts, Jonas Earll Jr. of New York, Edward Everett of Massachusetts, James Findlay of Ohio, Benjamin Gorham of Massachusetts, John Hallock Jr. of New York, Joseph Healey of New Hampshire, James L. Hodges of Massachusetts, Martin Hoffman of New York, Peter Little of Maryland, John Maynard of New York, Thomas Metcalfe of Kentucky, Thomas Newton Jr. of Virginia, Joseph Richardson of Massachusetts, Henry R. Storrs of New York, Aaron Ward of New York, Thomas Whipple

Jr. of New Hampshire, Austin E. Wing of Michigan Territory, Silas Wood of New York, David Woodcock of New York, John C. Wright of Ohio, and Silas Wright Jr. of New York. Senators: Samuel Bell of New Hampshire, Nathan Sanford of New York, and Nathanial Silsbee of Massachusetts.

161.8–9   "je vois que les Calomnies s'accréditent toujours,"] French: "I see that slander is always believed."

162.16   spoke as to the ears of an Adder] Cf. Psalm 58.4.

163.36–37   like a Partridge upon the Mountains.] Cf. 1 Samuel 26:20.

164.15   imperium in imperio] Latin: government within a government.

164.27–28   video meliora proboque; deteriora sequor] Latin: I know and approve better things, but incline to things which are worse.

165.2   the worms of Nile] Cf. *Cymbeline*, III.iv.35.

167.19   alieni appetens, sui profusus.] From Sallust, *Bellum Catilinae*, sec. 5: "[His mind was daring, crafty, fickle, capable of the most profound dissimulation, and of acting any part whatever,] greedy of what was not his own, and lavish of what was, [extremely eager in the gratification of his desires.]" Translation from John Clarke, *Bellum Catilinarium et Jugurthinum* . . . *i.e. The History of the Wars of Catiline and Jugurtha, by Sallust* (London, 1734).

167.27–28   the China-Jordan] The Erie Canal, which was modeled on China's large state-sponsored artificial waterways and which Clinton did more than anyone else to make a reality. By opening the west to the Atlantic trade through New York City, the canal, like the biblical river, seemed a gateway to a promised land of prosperity.

168.30   the oil of fools] Proverbially, flattery.

169.27–28   the divine Philippic of Cicero.] Juvenal gave this appellation to Cicero's *Second Phillipic* (44 B.C.E.), which faulted Marcus Antonius for, among many other things, exposing private letters to public scrutiny.

172.33   Mr. Clark's proposal] Kentucky congressman James Clarke had told Adams that he had heard that Pennsylvania representative Samuel D. Ingham had published a pamphlet accusing Adams of misconduct relating to his expense accounts as a diplomat in Europe, and urged him to reply in print. Adams, who was already aware of the pamphlet, informed Clark that it was instead focused on Adams's alleged monarchism and that he did not feel the need to respond.

174.9–10   a small printed pamphlet, by a Mr. Lewis Tappan] *Letter from a Gentleman in Boston to a Unitarian Clergyman of that City* (Boston, 1828).

174.38   the execution of the Tennessee Militia men] Six members of the 1st Regiment of West Tennessee Militia, then under Andrew Jackson's overall command, were court-martialed for desertion and executed in Mobile on February

21, 1815, the day before news of the signing of the Treaty of Ghent reached the Gulf Coast. The House Committee on Military Affairs was reviewing the records of the trials, searching for material that might embarrass Jackson.

175.27 Antient Pistol] Blustering soldier who appears in three of Shakespeare's plays: *2 Henry IV, Henry V*, and *The Merry Wives of Windsor*.

180.29 Willis Anderson] On August 30, 1827, a drunken Anderson had savagely beaten Alexandria night watchman Gerrard Arnold after his wife had told him that Arnold had manhandled her. Arnold succumbed to his injuries on September 9 and Anderson was convicted of manslaughter.

183.3 judge Brackenridge's letter] Henry Marie Brackenridge, federal judge for the western district of Florida, became the nation's first federal forester when Adams appointed him to be the superintendent of the newly established U.S. Naval Live Oak Area, near present-day Gulf Breeze, Florida.

183.6 Mr. Mercer] Congressman Charles Fenton Mercer of Virginia was also president of the Chesapeake and Ohio Canal Company.

186.19 *style ampoulé*] French: grandiose manner.

187.33–34 Senator from Kentucky] As he indicated in the margin of his diary, Adams was visited by Richard Mentor Johnson.

188.6 Southard's coming as Senator] Samuel Southard was not elected senator, but instead served as New Jersey's attorney general from 1829 to 1833.

188.32–33 an answer to the Boston federalists.] See Chronology for 1828.

190.11 "It is not in Man that walketh to direct his steps."] See note 45.15–16.

191.20 my manuscript upon the Brevet] Upon the death of U.S. Army commanding general Jacob Brown on February 24, 1828, Adams bypassed the next highest-ranking officers, Major Generals Winfield Scott and Edmund P. Gaines, who were rancorously advancing competing claims to seniority, and chose instead Alexander Macomb, the highest-ranking brigadier general on the army list, to fill the post. When Scott protested, citing the priority of his rank as brevet major general, Adams drafted "The Brevet, Observations on the claims to command of Brevet Major General Winfield Scott." A brevet rank was a quasi-official designation, conferred for honorary or temporary purposes in recognition of extraordinary service, and it remained unclear how it should factor into the ordering of the chain of command.

191.25 his Son Benjamin] Twenty-year-old Benjamin V. Crowninshield died five days later.

192.34–35 "As ever in my task masters eye."] Cf. John Milton, Sonnet 7: "On His Being Arrived to the Age of 23" (1631), l. 14.

193.33 Yet bate I not a jot of heart and hope] Cf. John Milton, Sonnet 22: "To Cyriack Skinner" (c. 1655), ll. 7–8.

194.30–31 his nephew . . . with his wife] Andrew Jackson Donelson was the nephew of Rachel Donelson Jackson. When his father died, the Jacksons took him and his two brothers in as wards. Donelson married his cousin, Emily Donelson, who served as hostess at the president's house in place of her deceased aunt with the aid of her own niece, Mary Ann Eastin.

195.9 Meridian Hill] Residence, built by John Porter, to which the Adamses relocated after leaving the Executive Mansion. A little more than a mile to the north of the White House, the site today is a park in the Columbia Heights section of Washington.

196.14–15 the Panama Instructions] In Adams's final message to Congress he made public the instructions Secretary of State Clay had prepared for the aborted U.S. delegation to the Panama Congress of 1826 (see note 125.33–34): "The motives for withholding them from general publication having ceased, justice to the Government from which they emanated and to the people for whose benefit it was instituted requires that they should be made known. With this view, and from the consideration that the subjects embraced by these instructions must probably engage hereafter the deliberations of our successors, I deem it proper to make this communication to both Houses of Congress."

CHAPTER X: 1829–1831

198.1 Dr. Reynolds] A science lecturer advocating the theories of John Cleves Symmes Jr. (see note 118.34–35), Jeremiah Reynolds had lobbied the Adams administration to organize an expedition to explore the South Seas and the southern polar region. When the House appropriated $50,000 toward such an expedition, Secretary of the Navy Southard hired Reynolds as a special naval agent to assist in the planning. But the Senate rejected the bill, and with little support in the new administration, Reynolds focused instead on mounting an expedition with private funding.

201.20–21 Pelham, or the Adventures of a Gentleman.] Novel (1828), originally published in two volumes, by English writer and politician Edward Bulwer-Lytton.

201.26–27 Vicar of Bray] A byword for political expediency and hypocrisy, from a popular eighteenth-century satirical song of the same name about a clergyman who retains his position by changing his principles.

202.6 Non licat cuivis adire Corinthum.] Latin translation of a Greek proverb meaning "Not everyone can go to Corinth," an allusion to the prohibitively expensive pleasures on offer in that prosperous city.

202.24 Dominie Sampson] Character in *Guy Mannering*, 1815 novel by Sir Walter Scott.

203.11 he hides it under a bushel.] Cf. Matthew 5:15.

203.14 Mr. Hamilton] James A. Hamilton, third son of Alexander Hamilton, was acting secretary of state, March 4–27, 1829.

204.3 the Porte] The government of the Ottoman Empire.

206.21 the Fable of the Wolf and the Dog.] The work of the seventeenth-century French fabulist Jean de La Fontaine.

206.35 the Fable of Simonides] Also by La Fontaine.

207.8–9 a Saturnian age of lead for poetry.] Cf. Alexander Pope, *The Dunciad*, Bk. I, l. 28.

208.12–13 My God! My God! why hast thou forsaken me?] Cf. Matthew 27:46.

209.9–10 The Law of my members wars with the Law of my heart.] Cf. Romans 7:23.

211.5–6 Nec lex est justior ulla.] Latin maxim: "Nor can there be a more just law [than that the artificers of death should perish by their own invention.]"

212.33 Thomas Morton's Book] *The New English Canaan*, 3 vols. (London, 1637).

213.5 Winthrop's Journal.] The journal of Massachusetts founder John Winthrop was published as *History of New England from 1630 to 1649*, James Savage ed., 2 vols. (Boston, 1826).

213.18–19 Letters of Madame du Deffand] There were multiple editions of the letters of French *salonnière* Marie Anne, Marquise du Deffand, to Voltaire and to Horace Walpole.

215.19 Waverly's.] Novel (1814) by Walter Scott.

216.24–25 Caps and Hats.] Referring to the principal political parties of eighteenth-century Sweden.

217.15 William Lee] Lee, a merchant and commercial agent, had been a Treasury Department auditor from 1817 until 1829, when he was removed from office by President Jackson.

217.17 Mr. Gallatin . . . at Baltimore] Albert Gallatin had returned to the United States after his last diplomatic post, as minister to Great Britain, 1826–27.

217.22 resigned his Office.] Gallatin had been secretary of the treasury under Presidents Jefferson and Madison.

218.39–219.1 a blue and a green faction] Referring to political factions in sixth-century Byzantium.

221.16 within the last six Months.] As both mayor of and U.S. attorney for New York City, 1801–3, Edward Livingston had been held liable for public funds embezzled during his administration. Only in 1826 was he able to repay the debt to the federal government, which with interest had amounted to $100,014.89.

221.19 Belknap's History] *The History of New Hampshire. By Jeremy Belknap, D.D. . . . To Which are Added Notes, Containing Various Corrections and Illustrations of the Text . . . By John Farmer, Corresponding Secretary of the N. H. Historical Society* (Dover, N.H., 1831).

221.31 Henry Lee] Lee, an amateur historian and member of the famous Virginia family, had written speeches for Andrew Jackson, who rewarded him with an appointment as U.S. consul in Algeria. But the Senate rejected his appointment. The "infamy" to which Adams refers was the notorious affair Lee conducted with his young sister-in-law (who was also his ward) while his wife was in mourning for the loss of their only child.

222.12–13 the detected correspondence between Timberlake and Eaton] Outgoing members of the Adams administration had discovered irregularities in the accounts of U.S. Navy purser John B. Timberlake and circulated anonymous letters suggesting that Timberlake and his friend John Eaton, formerly a U.S. senator from Tennessee and now Jackson's secretary of war, had conspired to defraud the government. Amos Kendall, fourth auditor in the Department of the Treasury, had been responsible for investigating the charges.

223.22–23 the Correspondence between him and Col'l Walker] In 1802, at the same time he publicized Jefferson's relationship with Sally Hemings, disgruntled newspaper editor James Callender also revealed that in the late 1760s Jefferson had several times attempted to seduce Elizabeth Moore Walker, the wife of his longtime friend John Walker. This revelation led John Walker to demand satisfaction from Jefferson, and to avoid a duel the embarrassed president was forced to acknowledge his actions and apologize to Walker in writing.

223.38 peine forte et dure] Latin legal phrase ("a hard and forceful sentence") often used to refer to pressing with stones to compel a plea.

224.38 Tun' contra Caesaris nutum?] From a letter of Cicero to Atticus (Bk. XIV, letter 10): "Are you going to oppose Caesar's will?"

225.18 incredulous Odi] From Horace, *Ars Poetica*, l. 188: "[For while upon such monstrous scenes we gaze,] / They shock our faith, our indignation raise." Translation from Philip Francis, *A Poetical Translation of the Works of Homer* (1742–46).

227.2 I was unable this morning] Adams complained in the previous day's entry that the "occasional pains which indicate an inflammation of the kidneys were this day extremely severe."

228.24–25 the Regent's Classics] Described in an 1828 advertisement for a new Regent's Classics edition of the tragedies of Seneca: "Under the denomination of 'Regent's Classics' the publishers of this collection [a consortium of London printers] have already brought forward nearly the whole body of Latin Authors, equal in typographic elegance and accuracy to the celebrated Elzevir Editions; and superior to them in the purity of the Text, corrected and amended as it has since been by the industry and sagacity of learned Critics, in different countries, and by the collation of Ancient Manuscripts."

229.19–20   Aio te, AEacida, Romanos vincere posse] Adams alludes to the story of an ancient oracle who made this famously ambiguous pronouncement, which may be translated either "I say, Aeacides, that you can defeat the Romans" or "I say, Aeacides, that the Romans can defeat you."

229.38–39   the Washington Hotel] Located at the corner of Broadway and Chambers Street, James Hamilton, proprietor.

230.3   the City Hotel.] Located at 113 Broadway.

230.4   Oliver Wolcott] Oliver Wolcott, Jr., had been secretary of the treasury under both George Washington and John Adams, 1795–1800, and governor of Connecticut, 1817–27.

231.35–36   the new Railway Church.] The First Parish Church (Unitarian) of Quincy, a granite structure dedicated on November 12, 1828.

232.29   the Act of Congress of April 1824] On April 30, 1824, Congress authorized the use of army engineers to survey lands for roads and canals that might serve a military function. The bill addressed President Monroe's constitutional scruples by enfolding internal improvements into provision for the national defense.

233.6   Synephebi] Fragmentary verse comedy by second-century B.C.E. Roman poet Statius Caecilius.

233.19   Sero arbores quae alteri seculo prosint] Repeating the phrase from *Synephebi*: He plants trees for the benefit of later generations.

237.9–11   "The heart knoweth . . . its joys"] Cf. Proverbs 14:10.

237.20   an old antagonist] Harrison Gray Otis, who in 1829, amid the controversy of the alleged disloyalty of New England Federalists during the Embargo and the War of 1812 (see note 243.18), published a pamphlet designed to "exhibit Mr. Adams as the author of an unfounded and calumnious charge."

237.30   the French Opera of Richard Coeur de Lion] *Opéra comique* (1784) by André Grétry.

238.24   chaff before the wind.] Cf. Psalm 35:5.

238.25–26   a Cherokee Indian is prosecuted] Corn Tassel (Utsi'dsata) was convicted of the murder of another Cherokee man, Sanders Ford, and executed by the state of Georgia on December 24, 1830, even though the crime was committed on Cherokee land.

240.13–14   The present English Ministry] The Whig government of Charles (Earl) Grey, in office 1830–34.

241.10–11   mais il n'y a que moi au monde qui a *toujours* raison] "But in all the world there is only me who is *always* right." Attributed to the Duchess de la Ferte, as spoken to her sister, Madame de Stael.

242.23 William Hobby] Hobby had accused an army paymaster of fraud during Adams's presidency, and now complained that the charges had not been properly attended to.

243.14 His Letter to Mazzei] Jefferson's April 24, 1796, letter to his friend, the Italian physician Philip Mazzei, in which he decried the rise of "an Anglican, monarchical and aristocratical party" in the United States, was published in a Paris newspaper on January 25, 1797, and in the New York *Minerva* on May 2, 1797, by which point Jefferson had become vice president. The publication soured Jefferson's relationships with Washington and others, and provided fodder for Federalist critics who charged that Jefferson and his followers were in the thrall of France.

243.18 his Letter to Giles] On December 25, 1825, Jefferson wrote a letter to former Virginia senator William Branch Giles relating details of a conversation he had had with Adams about the Embargo on March 15, 1808. Jefferson recalled that Adams had told him "that he had information of the most unquestionable certainty, that certain citizens of the Eastern States (I think he named Massachusetts particularly) were in negotiation with agents of the British government, the object of which was an agreement that the New England States should take no further part in the war then going on." Giles published the letter in the *Richmond Enquirer* in September 1827 hoping to foment discord among President Adams's supporters in New England. Adams was finally moved to reply in the *National Intelligencer* on October 21, 1828, pointing out, among other things, Jefferson's obvious confusion in conflating the 1808 Embargo debate with the War of 1812. Harrison Gray Otis reprinted and rebutted this letter in his 1829 pamphlet (see note 237.20).

245.18–19 the nomenclature of the antient Romans] The Roman naming convention, the *tria nomina*, involved a praenomen and nomen, which conform roughly to modern given and surnames, and a third identifier, the cognomen, which was often derived from a distinguishing personal characteristic (physical feature, occupation, accomplishment, etc.).

248.3 appointed with four others] Appointed on November 5, 1776, the committee to revise Virginia's legal code consisted of Jefferson, as chairman, Edmund Pendleton, George Wythe, George Mason (who resigned after a few months), and Thomas Ludwell Lee (who died in April 1778).

248.6 4 James I] That is, 1607, the year of Virginia's founding, and the fourth year of the reign of James I.

251.11 under the ribs of death] Cf. Milton, *Comus*, line 562.

252.15–16 the certain Lord . . . would himself have been a Soldier] Cf. *1 Henry IV*, I.iii.63–64.

252.24–26   Pends toi . . . n'y etois pas.] Hang yourself, brave Crillon, we fought, and you weren't there.

253.35–36   a London Bookseller] Piccadilly publisher John Stockdale, a friend of John Adams.

255.3   *fainéantise*] French: idleness.

255.20–21   every word that Mr. Kendall had said was true] Amos Kendall, the Treasury official responsible for auditing the agency created to carry out the colonization project, had written a damning report arguing that "a large portion of the expenditure at the Agency is not justified by the language or object of the act" establishing it.

256.34–35   a Poem of another character] Adams here begins work on a historical epic later published as *Dermot Mac Morrogh, or The Conquest of Ireland; An Historical Tale of the Twelfth Century. In Four Cantos* (1832).

257.25   Buchan] Scottish physician William Buchan, author of the popular practical guide, *Domestic Medicine* (1769).

257.27   mechans vers douze fois, douze cens] From an epigram by French poet Nicolas Boileau-Despréaux: "[Curse on the Wretch whose Rage to be a Wit / Tort'ring his Brain in Spite of Nature writ: / Whose heavy Strokes on *Reasons* Anvil thunder'd,] / Hammering out paltry Lines, twelve times twelve Hundred." Translation from *The Works of Mons'r Boileau Despréaux*, 2 vols. (London, 1711).

257.36   One short poem] "The Death of Children," published in the *National Intelligencer*, Vol. XI, July 25, 1811.

257.37–38   one translation] "The Thirteenth Satire of Juvenal," published in the inaugural issue of *The Port Folio*, January 3, 1801.

257.39   One Satirical song] "Horace, Book II, Ode 4. To Xanthia Phoceus. Imitated by Thomas Paine (Not the Boston Poet, but the sophist of Thetford,) and addressed to Thomas Jefferson," *The Port Folio*, No. 43, October 30, 1802.

258.4   the waters of Lethé] One of the five rivers of Hades, associated with oblivion.

258.26   Platina.] Platinum.

264.20   treading upon embers] Cf. note 84.10.

266.33–34   Mr. Whitney's . . . Mr. Potter's] Referring to Quincy's Congregational and Episcopal churches, the former ministered to by Peter Whitney, the latter by William P. Potter.

268.28–29   *my own, my native Land*] From *The Lay of the Last Minstrel*, 1805 narrative poem by Walter Scott.

269.19–20   unanimous save one] That one vote, by William Plumer Sr., an elector from New Hampshire, had been cast for Adams.

270.37   Non nobis domine sed nomini tuo sit gloria] Latin prayer of thanksgiving derived from Psalm 115:1: Not unto us, O Lord, but unto thy name be glory given.

CHAPTER XI: 1831–1835

275.26   flat, stale and unprofitable.] Cf. *Hamlet,* I.ii.133.

275.27–28   a double attack upon me this morning in the National Journal] The November 18, 1831, edition of the *National Journal* asserted that the anti-Clay behavior of former congressman John Bailey, Adams's longtime supporter and ertswhile clerk at the State Department, at the national convention of the Antimasonic Party had been orchestrated by Adams. It also mocked the editors of the *National Gazette* for suggesting that Adams, as a former president, could somehow remain above party as a congressman.

276.21   The child] Granddaughter Mary Louisa Adams.

276.27–29   namque Diespiter . . . volucremque currum.] "[For lo!] that awful heavenly Sire, / Who frequent cleaves the clouds with fire, / Parent of day, immortal Jove! / Late through the floating fields of air, / The face of heaven serene and fair, / His thundering steeds and winged chariot drove." Translation from Philip Francis, *The Odes, Epodes, and Carmen Seculare of Horace,* 4 vols. (1742).

276.31   Edward Everett's Address] *Address Delivered Before the American Institute of the City of New York, at Their Fourth Annual Fair, October 14, 1831* (1831).

277.8–9   Solomon . . . John the Evangelist] Solomon and the two Hirams are biblical characters who figure in allegories enacted during Masonic initiation ceremonies. The initiate portrays Hiram Abiff, the architect, or Grand Master, of Solomon's temple. Masons traditionally celebrate special seasonal feast days associated with John the Baptist (June 24) and John the Evangelist (December 27).

277.20   Eleusinian Mysteries.] Secret religious rites of ancient Greece, devoted to Demeter, goddess of the harvest, and her daughter Persephone, goddess of Spring.

280.25–26   Committee of the whole upon the State of the Union.] A parliamentary procedure by which the House of Representatives reconstituted itself as one large congressional committee, with lower thresholds for a quorum (100) and a forced recorded vote (25), and a streamlined process for debating amendments. The Committee of the Whole, as it was generally known, was often used as a device for expediting the passage of important bills.

281.8–9   laid upon the table] A parliamentary procedure to quash a bill without debate or a vote on its merits.

281.10 the Clerk] Matthew St. Clair Clarke was clerk of the House of Representatives from 1822 to 1833, and then again from 1841 to 1843.

283.13–17 Appleton . . . M'Kinnan] Anti-Jacksonian legislators all, save for newspaper editor Hezekiah Niles.

285.6 the remark of Gibbon] From volume II, chapter xxvi, of *The History of the Decline and Fall of the Roman Empire* (1781).

287.12–13 since I met them at Mr. Biddle's in Philadelphia] Adams first met Tocqueville and Beaumont at a dinner at Edward Everett's in Boston on October 1, 1831, after the duo had completed the first leg of their investigative tour of America, through New York, the Great Lakes, and Quebec, May–September 1831. Describing the dinner in his notebooks, Tocqueville found it remarkable that Adams "was received with all the politeness due an honored guest, but that was all. Most of the guests addressed him as 'Sir,' while a few used the honorific form 'Mr. President.'" He went on to observe that "Mr. Adams is a man of sixty-two who seems still quite vigorous in mind and body. He speaks French with ease and elegance. I was seated next to him, and we had a lengthy conversation." During that conversation, Tocqueville asked Adams "Do you regard slavery as a great blemish on the United States?" "Yes, certainly," Adams replied, "it is responsible for nearly all our present difficulties and fears about the future." Adams would see Tocqueville and Beaumont again in Philadelphia at the home of his friend Nicholas Biddle before they departed for the second leg of their travels, a large circuit through Pittsburgh, Memphis, New Orleans, and Norfolk, November 1831–January 1832. Translation by Arthur Goldhammer from Olivier Zunz, ed., *Alexis de Tocqueville and Gustave de Beaumont in America: Their Friendship and Their Travels* (University of Virginia Press, 2010), 242–43.

287.29 G. W. Erving] George Washington Erving had been U.S. minister at Madrid from 1814 to 1819.

288.18 Mr. Jenifer's Resolution] "Proposing an inquiry on the subject of removing the free people of color from the United States, and colonizing them in Africa, or elsewhere." (*Register of Debates*)

288.19 an amendment of Mr. Archer] William S. Archer of Virginia proposed that

a select committee be instructed to inquire into the expediency of recommending for adoption an amendment of the constitution of the United States, by which Congress shall have power to appropriate the revenue accruing or derivable from the proceeds of the sales of the public lands, in aid of the construction of such works of internal improvement as may be authorized, commenced, or patronized, by the States, respectively, within which the same are to be executed; and shall, in like manner, have power to appropriate the same fund of revenue in aid of the removal of such portions of the colored population of the States as they may respectively ask aid in removing, on such condition and to such place as may be mutually agreed on; for which purpose, Congress shall be authorized to acquire the territory it may consider the best adapted to the object, and to govern such territory in the manner in which the Territories of the United States are now governed, for such times as the occasion for which it shall have been obtained may require; after which, the said territory shall be established into a State, which shall be declared, or into several States, which shall be successively declared, independent of the United States, neither of which States shall, in any event, or at any time, be admitted into the Union of the United States.

289.26–27   the sear and yellow leaf.] Cf. *Macbeth*, V.iii.23.

292.38–39   the imprisonment of the Missionaries.] Samuel Worcester, a Congregational minister from Vermont, and Elizur Butler, a Connecticut physician, were two of eleven missionaries arrested by Georgia authorities in the summer of 1831 for living among the Cherokees "without license or permit" from the state. Nine of the missionaries soon left Georgia, but Worcester and Butler remained to face the four-year prison term. The convictions were overturned by the Supreme Court in *Worcester v. Georgia* (1832). Former attorney general William Wirt joined former congressman John Sergeant as counsel for the plaintiff in the case, which established the principle of tribal sovereignty within the United States.

294.2   the previous Question] A parliamentary procedure to close debate and call for a vote, better known today as cloture.

296.33   W. L. Stone] From November 1831 to April 1832, Adams had exchanged a series of letters on Masonry and anti-Masonry with New York journalist William Leete Stone. Stone published his portion of the correspondence in New York that year.

296.37   de fond en comble] French: from top to bottom; thoroughly.

297.20   Philip Doddridge.] The Virginia congressman died in Washington on November 19, 1832.

297.28   Thomas L. Thruston] Thomas Lee Thruston of Kentucky, son of D.C. circuit court judge Buckner Thruston, had been a clerk at the State Department during the Adams administration.

297.31   Theodore D. Weld] The future abolitionist, just twenty-nine in 1832, had been hired by reformers Lewis and Arthur Tappan to travel the country investigating schools and lecturing on behalf of the Society for Promoting Manual Labor in Literary Institutions.

297.33   Mr. Brooks] Massachusetts merchant Peter Chardon Brooks, son Charles's father-in-law.

297.35   Captain Gordon] William L. Gordon, captain of the U.S.S. *Ontario*, in between two several-year-long tours of duty in the Mediterranean.

298.9 Cary's Translation of Dante.] British translator Henry Francis Cary published a three-volume blank verse translation of *The Divine Comedy* entitled *The Vision; or, Hell, Purgatory, and Paradise, of Dante Alighieri* (London, 1814).

298.29 burning Ploughshares] Commonly used in medieval trials by fire.

299.10 the President's Proclamation] Issued that same day, declaring that "I consider, then, the power to annul a law of the United States, assumed by one State, *incompatible with the existence of the Union, contradicted expressly by the letter of the Constitution, unauthorized by its spirit, inconsistent with every principle on which it was founded, and destructive of the great object for which it was formed.*"

299.26 fellow Chaplain] Fr. Charles C. Pise had assumed the chaplaincy of the Senate on December 11, 1832.

302.12 private Bills] Measures that apply only to a particular person, group, or corporation without implication for the larger community.

306.31 Fort Independence] Newly reconstructed in 1833, on Castle Island in Boston Harbor.

307.6 Dr. Fisher] Harvard had recently received a $20,000 bequest from Beverly, Massachusetts, physician Joshua Fisher for the support of study in the natural sciences. The fund was eventually used to pay the annual salary of botanist Asa Gray.

307.13 Mr. Nuttall] English naturalist Thomas Nuttall had overseen the development of the Harvard Botanical Garden since 1823. He would leave the college in 1834 to join an expedition to the Oregon Country.

308.26 Alteri Seculo] See note 233.19.

309.11 He is gone to his account] Fellow American commissioner at Ghent Jonathan Russell died in Milton, Massachusetts, on February 17, 1832.

309.13 Bayard is gone] James Bayard, the only Federalist on the American commission, died in Wilmington, Delaware, on August 6, 1815.

309.39 Tremont-house] Posh, state-of-the-art Boston hotel located at the corner of Tremont and Beacon Streets; it was razed in 1895.

310.31–32 pour se faire valoir] French: to raise his profile.

313.2 ⟨shorthand symbols⟩] Adams developed his own shorthand to record both recurring features of the diaries, like meteorological observations, and thoughts of an especially personal nature, as here. The editors of the Adams Papers are still deciphering Adams's system.

314.19–20 Professor Dew's Review of the Debate] *Review of the Debate in the Virginia Legislature of 1831 and 1832* (1832) on the abolition of slavery, by William and Mary professor Thomas Roderick Dew.

315.8–9 objects to the term Bard as applied to Cicero.] As Adams had in an 1832 poem, entitled "Proem," he had sent to Lord for possible publication.

315.36 the fourth Book of Manilius] The *Astronomicon*, a poem in five books by first-century B.C.E. astrologer Marcus Manilius.

319.1 Hightstown] In central New Jersey, fifteen miles northeast of Trenton.

320.3 the fictitious signature of a writer] "Major Jack Downing" was a character created in 1830 by humorist Seba Smith, editor of the *Portland Courier*. The popular Downing letters soon appeared in newspapers around the country, and when Smith moved to Washington to cover the Jackson administration, Downing followed suit, bringing his folksy Yankee wisdom to the national stage.

322.16–17 the Memorial of Noah Fletcher] Davis had introduced a resolution to reinstate Noah Fletcher as assistant clerk of the House. In his memorial Fletcher protested that he had been dismissed "without any reasons assigned therefor, and . . . without any good cause."

323.7 par negotiis nec supra] From *The Annals of Tacitus*, Bk. VI, sect. 39: "[Not for any extraordinary talents, but because] he had a capacity for a level of business, and not above it." Translation from Craufurd T. Ramage, *Beautiful Thoughts from Latin Authors* (1864).

323.22 Egyptian Hieroglyphics] Rapid advances in Egyptology had followed the deciphering of the Rosetta Stone by French orientalist Jean-François Campollion in 1822.

324.29 M'Kinley's notice of yesterday] From the diary entry for February 5, 1834:

> In the House, the General Appropriation Bill was reported by [James K.] Polk, the Chairman of the Committee of Ways and Means, and then, till the expiration of the first hour, Bills at the third reading were taken up, and a number of them were passed — After the hour, the deposit question came up, and the Speaker [Andrew Stevenson] called up [Virginia congressman William] Archer, when [John] M'Kinley of Alabama, asked him to yield the floor to him for a moment as he had a notice to give to the house — Archer assented and M'Kinley said there had been debate enough upon this subject — That it was necessary to come to some decision, and he hoped immediately after Archer should finish his Speech, the House would take the question, and then he sat down — I rose to speak; the Speaker asked Archer if he yielded the floor — I told him it was merely to remark on M'Kinley's notice, and he gave me the floor — I asked what was the notice given by the member from Alabama? The Speaker answered that I had heard what he had said — I said I had heard him announce that he had a *notice* to give to the house; and then I heard him say, that immediately after Mr. Archer should finish his Speech, the House must take the question — Was that the Gentleman's *notice*? The Speaker laughed. M'Kinley made no reply, and I sat down.

326.9   bitter as gall] Cf. Proverbs 5:4.

327.25–27   "No! — let the candied tongue . . . follow fawning."] *Hamlet*, III.ii.54–56.

327.33   Mardis's Resolution] Submitted on March 18, 1834, by Alabama congressman Samuel Mardis, calling for a bill to require the secretary of the treasury to deposit public funds in state banks.

327.35   Wildes proposed amendment] From the diary entry for March 19, 1834:

> The first Resolution appended to the Report [of the Committee of Ways and Means] is, that the Bank of the United States ought not to be rechartered — [Richard Henry] Wilde of Georgia asked Polk whether he wished to speak upon the Report — Polk answered no. Wilde then moved to amend the first Resolution reported by the Committee, by adding thereto And that the reasons assigned by the Secretary of the Treasury for removing the public deposits from the Bank of the United States are unsatisfactory and insufficient.

330.23   Dowson's N. 1] Located on A Street on Capitol Hill, one of five townhouses operated as a boardinghouse by Alfred R. Dowson.

331.31   my manuscript] Of a speech Adams had been prevented from making on April 4 in opposition to the bill to transfer the public deposits to state banks.

335.20   the granddaughters of the Count de Rochambeau] The memorial from the Comtesse d'Ambrugeac and the Marchioness de la Gorée sought recognition for their late grandfather comparable to that which had been awarded to Lafayette. They also sought financial "support and assistance, in order to live in a manner conformable with their station."

336.27–31   Marshall's life . . . and Alden Bradford's History] The histories cited and referred to include John Marshall's five-volume *Life of George Washington* (Philadelphia, 1804–7); *The History of the Rise, Progress, and Establishment of the Independence of the United States: Including an Account of the Late War; and of the Thirteen Colonies, from Their Origin, to That Period*, 4 vols. (London, 1788), by William Gordon, a dissenting English clergyman who settled as a Congregational minister in Roxbury, Massachusetts, in 1772; *History of the Rise, Progress and Termination of the American Revolution*, 3 vols. (Boston, 1805), by Mercy Otis Warren, a close friend of Abigail and John Adams; *An Oration, in Celebration of Independence, delivered at Boston, July, 1819*, by Boston politician Samuel A. Welles; the third volume of Thomas Hutchinson's history of Massachusetts (see note 137.21), published posthumously in London in 1828; *The Life of James Otis, of Massachusetts: Containing also, Notices of some Contemporary Characters and Events from the Year 1760 to 1775* (Boston, 1823), by Boston civic leader William Tudor, Jr; and *History of Massachusetts, from July, 1775 . . . to the Year 1789* (Boston, 1825), by Massachusetts clergyman and politician Alden Bradford.

337.37–38   Titania . . . for Bottom] Cf. *A Midsummer Night's Dream*, III.i.

338.20   Edmund Charles Genet] See Chronology for 1793.

338.22   a serious Letter to my Son John] See Chronology for 1834.

338.38   not a Sparrow falls] Cf. Matthew 10:29.

339.31   Saurin] In the five-volume edition of *Sermons Translated from the Original French of the Late Rev. James Saurin, Pastor of the French Church at the Hague* published in London in 1800 by translator Robert Robinson, this sermon is the second in volume one.

341.13   Col'l Drayton] William Drayton had represented South Carolina in Congress from 1825 to 1833. In the wake of the nullification crisis he moved his family to Philadelphia in August 1833.

343.8–9   La Cretelle's History of France] Jean Charles Dominique de Lacretelle, *Histoire de France pendant le XVIIIe siècle*, 6 vols. (1808).

343.12   Mr. Plumer's conversation] Former New Hampshire congressman William Plumer Jr. had dined with Adams and nephew Thomas Boylston Adams at Quincy.

343.18   dissensions of a doit] Cf. *Coriolanus*, IV.i.21.

344.3–4   Sepulchre of Elisha.] Cf. 2 Kings 13:21.

CHAPTER XII: 1835–1839

351.12   my Resolution] The U.S. had for many years tried to secure reparations from France for depredations on American shipping during the Napoleonic wars. Finally, on July 4, 1831, a treaty (referred to at 351.27) was signed stipulating payment of 25 million francs in six annual installments. When the first payment came due, it was found that the requisite appropriation by the French Chamber of Deputies had never been made. Early in 1833, Jackson sent Edward Livingston, who had just resigned as secretary of state, to France to demand "prompt and complete fulfillment" of the treaty. The French government continued to delay, forcing Jackson to strike a more strident tone in his annual message on December 7, 1834, challenging Congress to adopt measures to preserve the national honor. (It was in the context of this Franco-American crisis that Adams delivered his eulogy for Lafayette on December 31.) The Senate's Committee on Foreign Relations rejected Jackson's call to action in its January 6, 1835, report, advising a wait-and-see policy. The House Committee on Foreign Affairs was slower to respond to Jackson's challenge, a dereliction that Adams attributed to Whig efforts to turn the crisis to partisan advantage. On February 27, 1835, the committee made a contradictory report that called on the president to break off further negotiation as dishonorable but deferring any measures to prepare for hostilities to the next Congress. Adams then introduced a resolution that called for the president to continue negotiations consistent with the national honor while forestalling "any legisla-

tive measure of a hostile character or tendency towards the French nation."
Adams's resolution afforded a face-saving formula for a weary Congress and
with some further modification in language it was adopted 212–0 on March 2.

351.14   the affair of the Chesapeak] See Chronology for 1807.

352.4–5   Be thou faithful unto death.] Cf. Revelation 2:10.

352.33–35   Swift's works . . . under the word Executive] There is no entry
for "Executive" in Johnson's *Dictionary*, but there is the following usage illustration under "Administration": "It may pass for a maxim in state, that the
administration cannot be placed in too few hands, nor the legislature in too
many. *Swift's Sentiments of a Church of England Man*." Adams was consulting
Walter Scott's nineteen-volume edition of Swift's works (1814).

353.20   Fanny] Adams's granddaughter Georgiana Frances Adams.

355.30   Montesquieu charges Harrington] In chapter six of *De L'Esprit des
Loix* (1748).

356.14   Mrs. Dunn's] Capitol Hill boardinghouse, located on D Street between Second and Third Streets.

356.27–28   Foy and Stewart] The credibility of these witnesses was cast in doubt
when it was revealed that Mordecai Foy worked occasional jobs at the Executive
Mansion as a blacksmith and that David Stewart owed Poindexter money.

357.23   Foot's Resolution] On December 29, 1829, Connecticut senator Samuel A. Foot introduced a resolution to limit the sale of federal lands in the
West, in part to retain an industrial labor force in the East.

358.16   the Rev'd Dr. Sprague] William Buell Sprague, minster of the Second
Presbyterian Church of Albany, was the author of numerous biographies of
religious leaders and an avid collector of autographs.

360.36   one of them occasionally insane] Henry Baldwin, associate justice
from 1830 to 1844, missed the entire 1833 term when he was hospitalized for
what was called "incurable lunacy."

363.14–15   the Roman Catholic Nunnery at Charlestown] Amid anti-Catholic
riots on August 11 and 12, 1834, a Protestant mob set fire to an Ursuline convent in Charlestown, Massachusetts, after rumors spread that a woman was
being kept against her will within its walls.

363.32–33   the Letters from Horace Walpole to Sir Horace Mann] Published
in a two-volume edition in New York in 1833.

367.39   Semper ego auditor tantum?] The opening line of the first satire of
Juvenal: "Shall I always be only a hearer?" Translation from *A New and Literal
Translation of Juvenal and Persius*, 2 vols. (1829), by Martin Madan.

368.6   John Howard Payne] New York playwright and outspoken opponent of Indian removal who angered Georgia authorities when he traveled to Cherokee country and spent several days at the home of Chief John Ross, conducting research to support his theory that the Indian nation was one of the lost tribes of Israel. Payne was arrested, beaten, and detained by the Georgia Guard, even though Ross's home was technically in Tennessee.

368.22–23   the Kinderhook school] Northern Democrats supporting Vice President Martin Van Buren (of Kinderhook, New York) to succeed Jackson as president.

369.27–28   an Englishman named Simonson] Adams has misremembered the name of James Smithson, with whose bequest he will be much occupied.

372.32   a pamphlet on Slavery] Called simply *Slavery*, a 167-page work by Unitarian minister William Ellery Channing.

374.18–21   But how he came . . . no one can tell] Smithson was indeed the illegitimate child of Hugh Percy (né Smithson), 1st duke of Northumberland. Himself unmarried and without children, Smithson bequeathed his estate to his nephew, Henry James Dickinson, son of half brother Henry Louis Dickinson, with the stipulation that he assume the ancestral name Hungerford. The will further stated that if Hungerford died without heirs, as happened on June 5, 1835, the estate was to pass to the U.S. government for the creation of what would become the Smithsonian Institution.

375.3   the Percy's and the Seymour's] Smithson's half brother, Lieutenant General Hugh Percy, served under William Howe in the early campaigns of the American War of Independence, participating in the battles of Lexington and Concord and Bunker Hill in 1775 and the battle of Long Island in 1776. He became the 2nd Duke of Northumberland in 1786. Smithson had required his nephew to adopt the name Hungerford because through it the family could claim a royal heritage, traceable through the Seymour line to the Tudor dynasty.

379.34   Holland's Life of Martin van Buren] *The Life and Political Opinions of Martin Van Buren, Vice President of the United States* (Hartford, 1835), by William M. Holland, a professor of ancient languages at Washington College (now Trinity College) in Hartford.

380.3–4   "l'ami de tout le monde"] French: "everyone's friend."

381.23   White electioneering Speech] Forester was speaking in support of fellow Tennessean Hugh L. White, U.S. senator and Whig candidate for president in the election of 1836.

383.30   which was in my own case] On July 11, 1832, his sixty-fifth birthday, Adams had asked to be excused from the vote on a motion of censure against William Stanbery of Ohio, submitting his reasons for doing so in writing for inclusion in the journal. His actions were protested by members concerned that a refusal to vote, if carried en bloc, could be used as a tactic by a minority to deny quorum on controversial measures.

387.21 the late James Madison] The former president had died on June 28, 1836.

388.9 alteri Seculo] See note 233.19.

389.2 Letter to Mazzei] See note 243.14.

390.28–29 Mr. Wirt's Life of Patrick Henry] *Sketches of the Life and Character of Patrick Henry* (1817) by former attorney general William Wirt.

391.7 Volney] French philosopher Constantine François de Chasseboef, Comte de Volney, a friend of Franklin and Jefferson, traveled to Spanish Louisiana in 1795 for what was described as a scientific expedition but which Federalists suspected was a covert mission to determine whether the territory was ripe for a French takeover. After some further ruffling of feathers with publications in Philadelphia, Volney left the United States in the spring of 1798 under threat of both the Alien and Sedition Acts.

393.15–16 the Empson and Dudley] Edmund Dudley and Richard Empson, privy councilors to Henry VII, were responsible for implementing the king's onerous tax regime on the nobility. After the king's death and the succession of Henry VIII, they were accused of corruption and profiteering and executed for treason.

394.18–19 a blue-light federalist of the Hartford Convention School] A derogatory term suggesting treasonous sympathy with Great Britain and arising from alleged instances during the War of 1812 when New England Federalists used blue lights to alert British ships that an American vessel was going to attempt to run their blockade. The Hartford Convention of December 1814–January 1815 was a meeting of New England Federalists convened to craft resolutions protesting the war and the Madison administration's handling of it; its resolutions reached Washington almost simultaneously with the news of the signing of the Treaty of Ghent and of Jackson's triumph at New Orleans, a coincidence that proved devastating to the political fortunes of the Federalist Party.

394.22 the Texian Imposture] In the spring of 1836 the newly independent Republic of Texas dispatched three commissioners, Stephen F. Austin, Branch Archer, and William Wharton, to Washington to seek a speedy annexation by the United States. Adams denounced the overture on the House floor, calling it criminal conspiracy between slaveholders and land speculators.

401.37 Matthias's Edition] A two-volume edition of the poetry, memoirs, and essays of Thomas Gray, issued in 1814 by British scholar Thomas J. Mathias.

406.27–28 "Youth at the prow, and pleasure at the helm"] Cf. line 74 of "The Bard" (1757) by Thomas Gray.

407.32 Jefferson's Manual] *A Manual of Parliamentary Practice for the Use of the Senate of the United States*, compiled by Vice President Thomas Jefferson and published in 1801.

407.38–408.1   the order of 18 January 1837] The latest iteration of the gag rule.

410.21   The Divorce, or Sub-treasury Bill] See Chronology for 1837.

411.6   Loco foco] A Democrat, from the popular name for a faction of the Democratic Party.

415.40   noli prosequi] *Nolle prosequi*, legal term declaring an abandonment by a plaintiff or prosecutor of all or part of a suit or action.

420.24   African Repository] *The African Repository and Colonial Journal*, monthly publication (1825–1919) of the American Colonization Society.

421.5   Phang and Snare.] Characters from *2 Henry IV*.

421.7   Mr. Charles Sumner] Fresh off a year of lecturing at Harvard Law School, the future senator from Massachusetts was preparing for a two-year European tour.

424.17–18   Donec eris felix . . . solus eris.] From Ovid, *Tristia*, I.ix.4–5: "Long as you prosper, num'rous friends you'll own, / If cloud o'ercast your hours, you'll stand alone." From an 1821 translation by Francis Arden.

426.14   The path of right is narrow] Cf. Matthew 7:13.

430.1   Fort Hill] Calhoun's plantation was eventually inherited by his son-in-law Thomas G. Clemson, who bequeathed the land and estate to the state of South Carolina to serve as the nucleus of the campus of the public university that bears his name.

430.15–16   the Orations against Ctesiphon . . . the second Philippic.] Landmarks of classical oratory by Greek statesmen Aeschines and Demosthenes.

430.25–26   Treaty of New Echota] Concluded December 29, 1835, in New Echota, Georgia, between representatives of the United States and a minority faction of Cherokees, this treaty provided legal justification for the Jackson administration's policy of Cherokee removal.

431.1   Quiz] A trick or practical joke.

433.7   he sent Onesimus back to his master Philemon] As recounted in Paul's letter to Philemon in the New Testament.

433.31   the decision of the Supreme Court] *Worcester v. Georgia* (1832). See note 292.38–39.

434.21–22   laudatur et alget.] From line 74 of the first satire of Juvenal: "[Probity] is praised and starves with cold." Translation by Madan (1829).

435.8   Schermerhorn's] Referring to John Freeman Schermerhorn, a Dutch Reformed missionary in western New York who in 1832 was appointed by Andrew Jackson to the commission charged with organizing the Cherokee removal.

435.24   a word spoken in Season?] Cf. Proverbs 15:23.

436.17–18   the late Philadelphia Mobs] On May 17, 1838, just three days after it opened, Pennsylvania Hall, the new meetinghouse of the Pennsylvania Anti-Slavery Society, was torched by a white supremacist mob. Adams had sent a letter to be read at the building's dedication ceremony on May 14: "I rejoice that, in the city of Philadelphia, the friends of free discussion have erected a Hall for its unrestrained exercise. My fervent wishes are, that Pennsylvania Hall may fulfill its destination, by demonstrative proof, that freedom of speech in the city of Penn shall no longer be an abstraction."

438.8   15th day, Texas.] By June, it was clear that the resolution to annex Texas, which had been referred (along with several resolutions from state legislatures in the North opposing it) to the Committee on Foreign Affairs in March, did not have sufficient support to pass the House. When, on June 22, the committee moved that the entire matter be laid on the table, a debatable motion, Adams took the opportunity to seize control of the House floor. He maintained his filibuster for sixteen days, railing against the gag rule and the "Texian imposture." During his speech on this penultimate day of the session, Adams read from previously unreleased 1830 correspondence between President Jackson and Arkansas territorial governor William Fulton regarding schemes by Sam Houston and others to separate Texas from Mexico, proof, as Adams saw it, of long-standing designs on the territory in the slaveholding South. By the time Congress reconvened in December, Texas had withdrawn its proposal to the United States for annexation, and the issue for the moment subsided.

438.31–32   Marlborough Hotel] Located at the corner of Washington and Franklin Streets, near the Old South Meeting House.

439.11   Mrs. Frothingham] Ann Gorham Brooks Frothingham was the sister of Abigail Brooks Adams and Charlotte Gray Brooks Everett, wife of Massachusetts governor Edward Everett.

439.25   born   .] Adams's grandson, the future historian, was born on February 16, 1838.

439.29   Legare's report] On June 13, 1838, South Carolina congressman Hugh Swinton Legaré presented a lengthy report of the Committee on Foreign Affairs on petitions from the New York Peace Society calling for international mediation of differences between the United States and Mexico.

441.9   the insult upon the sex] During the Texas debate, Maryland congressman Benjamin Chew Howard derided petitions from women:

> I think that these females could have sufficient field for the exercise of their influence in the discharge of their duties to their fathers, their husbands, or their children, cheering the domestic circle and shedding over it the mild radiance of the social virtues, instead of rushing into the fierce struggles of political life. I feel sorry at this departure from

their proper sphere, in which there is abundant room for the practice of the most extensive benevolence and philanthropy, because I consider it discreditable, not only to their own particular section of the country, but also to the national character, and thus giving me a right to express this opinion.

442.2–3   an English Orator and Poet] Richard Brinsley Sheridan.

443.9   Pearson] Adams had for several weeks been reading through *An Introduction to Practical Astronomy: Containing Descriptions of the Various Instruments*, 2 vols. (1829), by English clergyman and astronomer William Pearson.

446.39   mount Auburn.] Rural cemetery in Cambridge, Massachusetts, dedicated in 1831.

447.1   Maria Osborne Sargent, wife of Charles P. Curtis] Adams is mistaken: Maria Osborne Sargent Curtis was the wife of Boston merchant Thomas Buckminster Curtis.

CHAPTER XIII: 1839–1843

454.13   Parker's miniature.] Both Adams and his brother Thomas were painted in watercolor on ivory at The Hague in 1795 by a painter named Parker, possibly expatriate Englishman John Parker, known to have worked as a portraitist in the Netherlands in the 1790s.

454.20   Mais helas! il n'en est rien.] French: But alas! It is not so.

454.24   Dr. Channing's Letter] William Ellery Channing, *Remarks on the Slavery Question, in a Letter to Jonathan Phillips, Esq.* (Boston, 1839).

454.26   Junius] Pseudonym of a writer, possibly British pamphleteer Philip Francis, who penned a series of letters critical of the government of George III in London newspapers from January 1769 to January 1772. Popular in America, *The Letters of Junius* were issued in numerous editions throughout the late eighteenth and early nineteenth centuries. A similar observation was made by Edmund Burke in his *Reflections on the Revolution in France* (1790), where he observed that "the arguments of tyranny are as contemptible as its force is dreadful."

455.30   Common Council] Until 1909, Boston's government consisted of a mayor, an eight-member board of aldermen, and a common council comprising three representatives from each of the twenty-five wards in the city.

456.20   Maclaine's Mosheim] *An Ecclesiastical History, Antient and Modern, from the Birth of Christ, to the Beginning of the Present Century* (1764), a translation in five volumes by Archibald Maclaine, Presbyterian minister of the English church at The Hague, of *Institutiones Historiae Ecclesiasticae Antiquae et Recentioris* (1726) by German theologian Johann Lorenz von

Mosheim. Maclaine had been a friend of John Adams, and as president Adams was among the subscribers to a six-volume edition of the *Ecclesiastical History* published in Philadelphia in 1797.

456.22 Mr. Buxton's book] *The African Slave Trade and Its Remedy* (London, 1839) by British abolitionist and MP Thomas Fowell Buxton.

456.24–25 Theodore D. Weld's book] Abolitionist Theodore Dwight Weld's *American Slavery as It Is: Testimony of a Thousand Witnesses*, published by the American Anti-Slavery Society in New York in 1839, was a principal source and inspiration for Harriet Beecher Stowe's *Uncle Tom's Cabin*.

457.17–24 the Execution according to Indian Law . . . with their lives] Major Ridge (Nunnehidihi), his son John Ridge (Skah-tle-loh-skee), and nephew Elias Boudinot (Gallegina Uwati) were leaders of a faction of the Cherokee nation that favored acculturation with white society—both the younger Ridge and Boudinot had been educated at a missionary school in Connecticut and had married white women they met there—and were signatories to the Treaty of New Echota. The three removed to Indian Territory (Oklahoma) where, on June 22, 1839, they were assassinated by traditionalist supporters of Cherokee principal chief John Ross (Koo-wi-s-gu-wi).

458.32–33 the refusal of President to deliver up] In March 1799 an English sailor named Thomas Nash, wanted in England for mutiny and murder aboard H.M.S. *Hermione*, was seized in Charleston, South Carolina. Nash claimed he was an American citizen named Jonathan Robbins from Danbury, Connecticut, but President John Adams was unpersuaded and ordered him to be turned over to the British in accordance with Article 20 of Jay's Treaty. Although there was clear evidence that Nash was who the British claimed he was, Republicans in Congress proposed resolutions condemning the president for unjustly surrendering an American citizen to a foreign nation instead of remanding him over to the American courts for adjudication.

460.35–36 the 9th Article of the Treaty with Spain] "All Ships and merchandise of what nature soever which shall be rescued out of the hands of any Pirates or Robbers on the high seas shall be brought into some Port of either State and shall be delivered to the custody of the Officers of that Port in order to be taken care of and restored entire to the true proprietor as soon as due and sufficient proof shall be made concerning the property there of."

461.34 deo adjuvante] Latin: God willing.

463.25 the license Law] A measure to regulate the distribution and sale of alcoholic beverages, supported by an active temperance movement in Massachusetts.

466.4 the New-York Emancipator] The *Emancipator and Weekly Chronicle*, an abolitionist newspaper edited by Joshua Leavitt.

470.26 Mackenzie] Newspaper editor and former Toronto mayor William Lyon Mackenzie was a leader of the unsuccessful rebellion against British rule in Upper Canada (Ontario) in 1837. Fleeing to New York, he continued to publish his newspaper before being arrested and convicted of violating U.S. neutrality laws and was imprisoned for eighteen months.

472.31   Maundrell] *A Journey from Aleppo to Jerusalem, at Easter, A.D. 1697*, a travelogue by Englishman Henry Maundrell first published in 1703 and often reprinted with other contemporaneous accounts of the Near East.

474.12   my accident] Adams had suffered a bad fall in the House of Representatives two days earlier, on May 18, described by one of the body's junior clerks: "Mr. Adams was always the first man in the House, and the last man out of it; and, as I usually detained myself an hour or more after adjournment, in writing up my notes, I often came in contact with him. He was pleased to call at my desk very often, before he went home, and indulge in some incidental, unimportant conversation. On the day referred to, just as the sun was setting, and throwing his last rays through the murky hall, I looked up, and saw Mr. Adams approaching. He had almost reached my desk, and had uplifted his hand in friendly salutation, when he pitched headlong, some six or eight feet, and struck his head against the sharp corner of an iron rail that defended one of the entrance aisles leading to the circle within the bar, inflicting a heavy contusion on his forehead, and rendering him insensible." Adams dislocated his shoulder in the fall, as well. Eyewitness account from William Henry Seward's *Life and Public Services of John Quincy Adams, Sixth President of the United States* (1855).

475.20   like uncle Toby's armies in Flanders] Cf. Laurence Sterne, *The Life and Opinions of Tristram Shandy* (1759–67), Bk. III, chap. xi.

477.29   the theological school at Andover] The Andover Theological Seminary was founded in Andover, Massachusetts, in 1807 by orthodox Calvinists disturbed by Harvard's turn toward liberal religion.

478.1–2   Garrison and the Non-resistant abolitionists] Abolitionist William Lloyd Garrison organized the New England Non-Resistance Society, an offshoot of the American Peace Society, in September 1838. The group was opposed on principle to all forms of physical and legal retaliatory violence, from war and capital punishment to legal suits for redress of injuries.

478.2–3   Brownson and the Marat Democrats] Adams derisively likens New England Transcendentalist Orestes A. Brownson and his self-fashioned church, the radically egalitarian Society for Christian Union and Progress in Chelsea, Massachusetts, to Jean-Paul Marat and the extreme Jacobins of the French Revolution.

478.5–6   Pearce Cranch ex ephibis] Twenty-seven-year-old William Pearse Cranch, the youngest son of Adams's cousin and friend Judge William Cranch, was a Unitarian minister and an ardent Transcendentalist. The Latin phrase, *ex ephibis* (or *ephebis*, literally "from youth") here means "now grown."

481.5–6   "Flectere si nequeo superos, Acheronta movebo."] From Virgil,

Aeneid, VII.312: "If Heaven I can not bend, then Hell I will arouse!" Translation from H. Rushton Fairclough, *Virgil: Aeneid VII–XII, The Minor Poems* (London, 1918).

481.16–17 "flatteur dehonté, et calomniateur au besoin"] "Shameless flatterer and slanderer as needed." From Honoré-Gabriel de Riquetti, Comte de Mirabeau, *Histoire Secrète de la Cour de Berlin* (1789).

482.8–9 wrote upon my lecture] Adams was preparing what he elsewhere called his "Dissertation upon Faith," a popular lecture he would deliver at numerous venues in the early 1840s.

482.10 Brownson's defence] In July 1840 Orestes Brownson had published "The Laboring Classes," a review of Thomas Carlyle's *Chartism*, in the *Boston Quarterly Review*. The article, which espoused socialistic views, was quite controversial, especially in light of Brownson's avowed support for President Van Buren. The response led Brownson to issue a defense of the article in the October issue of the *Quarterly Review*.

485.3–4 quotation from St. Paul] Cf. 2 Timothy 4:7.

486.8 natale solum] Latin: native soil.

488.36 Mrs. Arguelles's] Pennsylvania Avenue boardinghouse operated by Elizabeth Arguelles.

491.14 Peters's Reports] *Cases Argued and Adjudged in the Supreme Court of the United States*, 17 vols. (1828–43), by Supreme Court reporter Richard Peters.

492.34 the case of the Antelope] On June 29, 1820, the crew of a U.S. revenue cutter boarded the *Antelope*, found drifting off the northern coast of Florida. On board the vessel were nearly three hundred Africans bound in chains, taken by an American ship captain named John Smith in a series of raids on Spanish and Portuguese vessels off the West African coast. Because slave trading was a federal crime, the ship was brought to Savannah, where its African captives were taken into U.S. custody for further adjudication. Representatives of the Spanish and Portuguese traders claimed ownership of the captives, while the United States filed to retain custody of the Africans with the intention of providing for their return passage to Africa. These actions resulted ultimately in a Supreme Court case in 1825, in which the Court found in favor of the foreign claimants, ruling that federal courts must recognize a nation's right to traffic in slaves if that nation's laws do not prohibit the trade.

493.5 Wheaton's Reports] *Reports of Cases Argued and Adjudged in the Supreme Court of the United States*, published annually from 1816 to 1827 by Supreme Court reporter Henry Wheaton.

493.30 Benton's pre-emption Bill] A temporary law granting squatters the right to buy land they had settled on before it was offered for public sale at auction.

494.13–14 the fraudulent Treaty] The Treaty of Buffalo Creek, concluded January 15, 1838, between the United States and members of the Six Nations of the Iroquois, providing for the sale of the tribes' remaining reservations in New York and their removal to the Kansas Territory. Pierce had been a signatory, but quickly repudiated it and on August 28, 1838, delivered an oration opposing Indian removal that was later published and widely circulated.

497.7 the 50th rule] "When a motion has been once made, and carried in the affirmative or negative, it shall be in order for any member of the majority to move for the reconsideration thereof on the same or succeeding day; and such motion shall take precedence of all other questions, except a motion to adjourn."

497.9–10 the 76th rule] "It shall be the duty of the Committee of Claims to take into consideration all such petitions, and matters or things touching claims and demands on the United States, as shall be presented, or shall or may come in question, and be referred to them by the House; and to report their opinion thereupon, together with such propositions for their relief therein as to them shall seem expedient.

497.30–31 second Mississippi Slavery case] *Groves v. Slaughter*, argued from February 12 to 19, 1841, in which Webster and Clay opposed Attorney General Gilpin and Mississippi senator Robert J. Walker.

499.14–15 the Virginia Convention] The Virginia Constitutional Convention of 1829–30.

501.3 tippecanoe clubs] Political clubs supporting William Henry Harrison, hero of the battle of Tippecanoe (1811).

502.36 never mentions hell to ears polite.] Cf. Alexander Pope, *Epistle to Burlington*, ll. 149–50.

507.5–10 the Governor of New-York . . . controversy with the executive authorities of Virginia.] In September 1839 a ship from Norfolk, Virginia, arrived in New York City; on board was a man escaping from slavery and three free black sailors who were assisting him. The fugitive was returned to Virginia pursuant to the Fugitive Slave Act (1793), statutory implement of the fugitive slave clause in Article IV, Section 2, of the Constitution, but New York governor William H. Seward refused to accede to Virginia's request that the free sailors be surrendered as well. In the ensuing controversy, Virginia's legislature passed retaliatory trade restrictions against New York and New York's passed a provision granting jury trials to fugitives.

509.21–22 One amendment] The Twelfth Amendment, ratified June 15, 1804, refined the process of electing the president and vice president, ensuring that there would be no repeat of the election of 1800, when the two Republican candidates, Thomas Jefferson and Aaron Burr, each received the same number of electoral votes for president.

510.33   the Speaker] Kentucky Whig John White was Speaker of the House in the Twenty-Seventh Congress, May 31, 1841–March 4, 1843.

513.22   the late Governor of North-Carolina] Edward Bishop Dudley was governor of North Carolina from December 31, 1836, to January 1, 1841.

516.3–7   "In very truth . . . for mine own part, so much."] Cf. 2 *Henry IV*, III.ii.222–27.

516.13–14   my Speech . . . on the M'Leod Resolution] In September 1841 Alexander McLeod, a Canadian, was arrested while on business in New York, and indicted for arson and murder. The charge stemmed from an incident several years earlier when, during the 1837 rebellion in Upper Canada, an American steamer that had been supplying arms and other material support to the rebels across the Niagara River was boarded by a band of sixty loyal Canadians under the command of British officers, torched, and sent over the falls. One American, Amos Durfee, was killed in the attack. McLeod later boasted of having been a member of the raiding party, and his arrest provoked an international crisis. Great Britain requested his immediate extradition on the grounds that if McLeod had participated in the attack, he had done so under orders, and was therefore not subject to criminal prosecution. New York refused to release McLeod, and though the Tyler administration sought to defuse the situation, the U.S. government was powerless to compel his release. The House of Representatives sided with New York, passing a resolution demanding of the president "whether any officer of the army, or the Attorney-General, had been directed to visit the State of New York for any purpose connected with the imprisonment or trial of Alexander McLeod; or whether, by any executive measures, the British government had been given to understand that McLeod would be released." It was in opposition to this resolution that Adams had risen to defend federal authority on September 4, in remarks that were soon published. McLeod was ultimately tried and acquitted in New York.

516.34   judge Greely] Adams has misheard or misremembered; the presiding judge was Philo Gridley.

518.28–29   The whig party . . . is splitting up] After the euphoria of Harrison's election, the unexpected advent of John Tyler to the presidency and his subsequent repudiation of Whig principles had left the party in disarray, even in its stronghold of Massachusetts.

518.38   ut olim] Latin: as in the past.

519.7   the Lady Elizabeth] Likely referring to President Tyler's daughter Elizabeth, then eighteen. In the autumn of 1841 there were rumors in the papers about Massachusetts Whig congressman Caleb Cushing courting "a Virginia belle who held a large number of slaves." Whether this was Elizabeth Tyler or not, Cushing's political courtship of President Tyler was real, resulting in his nomination to serve as secretary of the treasury, only to be three times rejected by the Whig majority in the Senate.

519.8   a curious show, but unsafe to stand upon] In his "Speech on American Taxation" (1774), Edmund Burke described the unlikely coalition that formed the new Chatham ministry as a "tessellated pavement without cement—here a bit of black stone and there a bit of white, patriots and courtiers, king's friends and republicans, Whigs and Tories, treacherous friends and open enemies," concluding "that it was, indeed, a very curious show, but utterly unsafe to touch and unsure to stand on."

522.17   by Tellers] That is, by a tallied vote.

524.23   the Secretary of the Treasury] Former congressman Walter Forward was secretary of the treasury from September 1841 to March 1843.

525.30   tricksy] Ornate.

527.3   Cilley duel] On February 24, 1838, Congressman Jonathan Cilley of Maine was killed in a duel by Representative William Graves of Kentucky. Henry Wise of Virginia and Wisconsin delegate George Jones were their seconds, and all three men were recommended for censure in the House. The House declined to follow through on the censures, but it did offer a bill to prohibit duels within the District of Columbia.

529.23   Moore's Love's of the Angels] 1822 poem by Irish poet Thomas Moore.

531.22   Io triumphe!] I triumph! From Horace, *Odes*, IV.ii.21.

533.35   Boulanger's] Restaurant on Pennsylvania Avenue at Sixth Street, operated by Joseph Boulanger, a former cook at the Executive Mansion.

534.37   the Creole case] In October 1841 the brig *Creole*, engaged in the coastal slave trade from Virginia to Louisiana, was redirected to the Bahamas after the 135 enslaved people on board revolted. The incident led to a diplomatic dispute between the Tyler administration and the British government, which refused extradition. Joshua Giddings's resolutions called for the federal government to cease "all attempts to exert our national influence in favor of the coastwise slave trade, or to place the nation in the attitude of maintaining a 'commerce in human beings,'" insofar as such actions "are subversive of the rights and injurious to the feelings of the free states, are unauthorized by the Constitution, and are prejudicial to our national character."

538.8   mesne process] A legal term referring to a writ issued at an intermediate stage of a legal proceeding.

539.32–33   indicted for Treason] Pearce had become embroiled in the short-lived Dorr Rebellion (1841–42), when insurgents led by Pearce's friend Thomas Wilson Dorr established a parallel government for Rhode Island based on a broader suffrage and other electoral reforms.

540.33–34   East-cheap . . . Tyburn.] Eastcheap, a street in central London, was the location of the Boar's Head Inn, fictional tavern where Falstaff held court in *Henry IV, Parts 1 and 2*. Tyburn was a village north of London (today in the vicinity of Paddington Station) where the city's criminals were executed until the late eighteenth century.

541.13 Captain Tyler's] The president carried this honorific by virtue of his command of a Virginia militia company during the War of 1812.

543.35 my Lecture upon Democracy] This lecture, which Adams would deliver at the Franklin Lyceum in Providence on November 25, was published as *The Social Compact: Exemplified in the Constitution of the Commonwealth of Massachusetts; with Remarks on the Theories of Divine Right of Hobbes and of Filmer, and the Counter Theories of Sidney, Locke, Montesquieu, and Rousseau* (Providence, R.I., 1842).

544.11 the commander in chief of the army] Winfield Scott was the U.S. Army's commanding general from 1841 to 1861.

547.9 General Jackson for declaring Martial Law] Early in December 1814, Andrew Jackson, recently arrived in New Orleans with intelligence that the British planned an assault on the city, established martial law, commandeering men and supplies as needed to erect defensive fortifications and jailing anyone who would dissent. "Those who are not for us," he threatened, "are against us and will be dealt with accordingly."

547.28 Moloch] Biblical name for a Canaanite deity associated with child sacrifice.

548.5 a Scapinade] A base intrigue in the manner of Scapin, or Scappino, a stock character from the commedia dell'arte.

548.30–31 my address at Braintree] *Address of John Quincy Adams, to his Constituents of the Twelfth Congressional District, at Braintree, September 17th, 1842* (Boston, 1842).

549.1–2 Sex horas somno] Edward Coke recommended six hours of sleep each night in *The First Part of the Institutes of the Lawes of England* (1628).

551.25–26 the great Massachusetts Latimer Petition] Resulting from the case of George Latimer, who escaped from slavery in Virginia to Boston in October 1842 and became the focus of popular resistance to the Fugitive Slave Act in the Bay State, more than fifty thousand of whose citizens signed a petition protesting "slave-catching" by Northern officials.

CHAPTER XIV: 1843–1848

553.7 the case of Edward Prigg] In *Prigg v. Pennsylvania* (1842) the Court ruled that the Fugitive Slave Act (1793), which provided for the return of individuals who escaped from slavery across state lines, precluded a Pennsylvania law prohibiting any black person from being taking out of the commonwealth into bondage.

553.29–30 I've lost a day . . . without his crown.] Cf. Edward Young,

Night Thoughts; or, The Complaint (1742), Night II, "On Time, Death, and Friendship," ll. 99–100.

554.38–555.3 The controversy . . . the second advent of Christ] Adams's survey of the swirl of current events includes the ongoing public dispute between Secretary of State Daniel Webster and Lewis Cass, recently returned from six years as U.S. minister to France. While at Paris Cass had been vocal in his opposition to the Quintuple Treaty (December 20, 1841), an agreement among Austria, France, Prussia, Russia, and Great Britain that declared the slave trade to be piracy and granted the mutual right of search to suppress it. For the Anglophobic Cass, this was a dangerous concession to Britain's naval might, and on his own initiative he vigorously lobbied the French government to withhold ratification. Cass likewise opposed the Webster-Ashburton Treaty (August 9, 1842), having staked his ground during its negotiation with the publication in Paris of *An Examination of the Question, Now in Discussion, Between the American and British Governments, Concerning the Right of Search*. Angered that the final treaty ignored the maritime issues that concerned him, Cass resigned his post and returned to the United States to continue his dispute with Webster through published letters in the newspapers. Adams also refers to the Great Comet of 1843, a particularly large comet with a long tail that was visible even in the daytime sky in February and March; to an unusually bright manifestation of the zodiacal light, a diffuse celestial glow visible in the night sky along the sun's ecliptic; and to the popular teachings of New York Baptist preacher William Miller, who had spurred a millennialist movement with his belief "that Jesus Christ will come again to this earth, cleanse, purify, and take possession of the same, with all the saints, sometime between March 21, 1843 and March 21, 1844."

555.5 the intelligencer] The *National Intelligencer* was Washington's dominant Whig newspaper.

555.21–22 Silas Deane . . . made a rumpus] Silas Deane had been dispatched by Congress in March 1776 to secure supplies in Europe to support the American cause and in 1778 he, Benjamin Franklin, and Arthur Lee negotiated commercial and military treaties with France. Soon after, he was accused of embezzling funds by Lee and was recalled by Congress (to be replaced by John Adams). Dissatisfied with his hearing before the Congress, Deane took to the newspapers, publishing in the December 5, 1778, edition of the *Pennsylvania Packet* "The Address of Silas Deane to the Free and Virtuous Citizens of America" attacking the Lee clan and defending his honor. The so-called Deane Affair was the young nation's first political scandal.

555.27 Mr. James Monroe was recalled] Monroe, minister to France from 1794 to 1796, had been recalled by President Washington because he was thought to have become overly supportive of the French Revolutionary cause and by extension that of the emerging Republican opposition at home. He returned to America in the spring of 1797 and the following December published *A View of the Conduct of the Executive, in the Foreign Affairs of the United States*, a five-hundred-page pamphlet defending his actions.

556.21 the Corinthian brass of Kinderhook.] Adams was not alone in his belief that Van Buren was likely to secure the Democratic nomination at the party's convention in Baltimore in May 1844.

556.23–24 Thomas ap Catesby Jones] On October 19, 1842, Jones, in command of the U.S. Pacific squadron, took possession of the capital of the Mexican territory of Alta California on the mistaken belief that war had begun between the U.S. and Mexico.

556.34 Waddy Thompson's diplomacy] Adams's former congressional foe was U.S. minister to Mexico from February 1842 to March 1844.

557.20 Washington Irving at Madrid] The celebrated author was U.S. minister to Spain from February 1842 to July 1846.

557.21 Mrs. Stewart] Delia Tudor Stewart, wife of U.S. admiral Charles Stewart, and daughter of family friends William and Delia Tudor.

557.32 David L. Child] Journalist, abolitionist, and husband of Lydia Maria Child.

558.8 the confederation of the New-England Colonies] Formed in 1643, a military alliance of the English colonies of Massachusetts Bay, Plymouth, Connecticut, and New Haven to coordinate policy toward the region's Indian tribes and the Dutch New Netherlands colony.

558.15–16 not in fancys maze . . . moraliz'd his song] Cf. Alexander Pope, *An Epistle to Dr. Arbuthnot* (1735), ll. 224–25.

560.11 the Charter] Issued by the English Crown to the Massachusetts Bay Company, a joint stock company, in 1629.

560.24 Bancroft tells his Story] George Bancroft, *History of the Colonization of the United States*, 3 vols. (1841).

560.29–30 The recent revolution in Rhode Island] See note 539.32–33.

561.35 The double representation of the Slave owners] Owing to the third clause of Article I, Section 2, of the Constitution, the so-called three-fifths clause, which apportioned representation "by adding to the whole Number of free Persons, including those bound to Service for a Term of Years, and excluding Indians not taxed, three fifths of all other Persons."

561.37–38 Semper ego auditor tantum?] See note 367.39.

562.20 the hounds of Acteon.] From Greek mythology, hunting dogs who devour their master after he is transformed into a deer.

563.7 I passed the day] As recorded in his diary. See page 26 of the companion to this volume, *John Quincy Adams: Diaries 1779–1821.*

563.25 a translation of Voltaire's philosophical dictionary] Adams made clear in his response to Joseph Emerson, a Congregational minister and educator from Connecticut, that he would have had little interest in translating Voltaire: "The truth is that Voltaire was a lively, sarcastical, disingenuous, prejudiced, fanatical disbeliever in Christianity, ready to assume the mask of religion, or to cast it away, just as it suited his interest or his humor; intent above all things upon making himself a name, and flattering himself that his easiest way to do it was by demolishing the Christian religion. I never thought his Philosophical Dictionary worth reading and I read his Bible only to despise it." Adams's letter was published in the *Connecticut Courant* and reprinted in newspapers around the country, including *Niles' Register*.

566.23 Gen'l Porter to Goat Island] Peter B. Porter of New York had led the state's militia in the War of 1812 and served as secretary of war during the last year of Adams's term. Goat Island is located in the Niagara River at the site of the falls.

567.13 Mount Auburn] See note 446.39.

568.7–8 female Seminary] The Utica Female Academy, incorporated 1837.

568.12 my mothers published Letters] From *Letters of Mrs. Adams, the Wife of John Adams. With an Introductory Memoir by Her Grandson, Charles Francis Adams*, 2 vols. (Boston, 1840).

568.25 the Bleecker house] Considered Utica's finest hotel.

569.7 water] To cool the wooden wheels of the train, before the heat from friction set them afire.

570.18–19 the tenth Article of the Ashburton Treaty] "It is agreed that the United States and Her Britannic Majesty shall, upon mutual requisitions by them, or their Ministers, Officers, or authorities, respectively made, deliver up to justice, all persons who, being charged with the crime of murder, or assault with intent to commit murder, or Piracy, or arson, or robbery, or Forgery, or the utterance of forged paper, committed within the jurisdiction of either, shall seek an asylum, or shall be found, within the territories of the other: Provided, that this shall only be done upon such evidence of criminality as, according to the laws of the place where the fugitive or person so charged, shall be found, would justify his apprehension and commitment for trial, if the crime or offense had there been committed: And the respective Judges and other Magistrates of the two Governments, shall have power, jurisdiction, and authority, upon complaint made under oath, to issue a warrant for the apprehension of the fugitive or person so charged, that he may be brought before such Judges or other Magistrates, respectively, to the end that the evidence of criminality may be heard and considered; and if, on such hearing, the evidence be deemed sufficient to sustain the charge it shall be the duty of the examining Judge or Magistrate, to certify the same to the proper Executive Authority, that a warrant may issue for the surrender of such fugitive. The expense of such apprehension and delivery shall be borne and defrayed by the Party who makes the requisition, and receives the fugitive."

574.21   tussis senilis] Commonly called "old man's cough," a pulmonary condition symptomatically like tuberculosis.

577.23   the Speaker] Virginia Democrat John Winston Jones was Speaker of the House from December 4, 1843, to March 4, 1845.

578.12   Appleton and Co.] D. Appleton & Company, New York publisher founded in 1831.

578.24   The Latimer petition] See note 551.25–26.

579.21   citadel rule] That is, the 25th Rule of the House of Representatives, governing the receipt of petitions, suppressing those related to slavery.

581.20   the sword of Orlando"] Also called Durendal or Durindana, the indestructible weapon of the legendary medieval knight Roland.

581.26   lethalis arundo.] The fatal shaft. From Virgil, *Aeneid*, IV.73.

581.29   the late Attorney General] Former South Carolina congressman Hugh Swinton Legaré was U.S. attorney general from September 13, 1841, to June 20, 1843, when he died in Boston, where he had traveled to attend the dedication of the Bunker Hill Monument.

582.16   I have named in the margin] "Adams, John Quincy; Ingersoll, Joseph Reed; Gilmer, Thomas W.; Davis, Garret; Burke, Edmund; Sample, Samuel C.; Morse, Freeman H.; Giddings, Joshua R.; Burt, Armistead."

586.25   Col'l. Gardiner of New-York] David Gardiner of East Hampton, New York, was the father of Julia Gardiner, President Tyler's fiancée. He was accompanied by the president's personal valet, an enslaved man named Armistead.

587.8   Justum et tenacem propositi virum] From Horace, *Odes*, III.iIi.1: The man who is just and resolute will not be moved.

595.22–23   the Astor house] New York's first luxury hotel, opened in 1836 at Broadway and Vesey Street.

599.2   United States Hotel] Four-story hotel located at the corner of Beach and Lincoln Streets, near the present site of Boston's South Station.

599.37   each holding up an ex-Senator] The Democratic Party had nominated former state senator Isaac H. Wright to challenge Adams; the Liberty Party, Appleton Howe. Adams would win convincingly with 57 percent of the vote.

600.4–5   the morning Chronicle] Edited by Joshua Leavitt, this was the daily edition of the *Emancipator* and organ of the Liberty Party in the election of 1844.

601.31   the name of Samuel Curtis] Curtis was the Whig candidate for the Massachusetts House of Representatives from the Quincy District. His name appeared immediately after Adams's on the party ticket, which Adams had copied into his diary.

603.33 Calhoun] The former vice president was secretary of state from April 1, 1844, to March 10, 1845.

606.6–7 "Why should I grieve, when grieving I must bear."] From Henry St. John, Viscount Bolingbroke, *Reflections upon Exile* (1716). Oft-quoted by John Adams.

608.36 Coleman's National Hotel] Large hotel at the corner of Pennsylvania Avenue and Sixth Street, Samuel S. Coleman, proprietor.

609.8 Carusi's hall] See note 94.35.

610.13 the Haverhill petition] See pp. 523 in this volume.

612.37–38 Victrix Causa deo placuit.] The victorious cause pleased the gods. From Lucan, *Pharsalia*, I.128.

613.26–27 As those we love decay . . . from the heart.] Opening lines of "On the Death of a Particular Friend," by Scottish poet James Thomson.

617.3 his Official Newspaper] The *Washington Union* (formerly the *Globe*), Thomas Ritchie, editor.

619.26–27 the Secretary of the Treasury] Former senator Robert J. Walker of Mississippi was secretary of the treasury from March 8, 1845, to March 5, 1849.

623.28–29 the new establishment of the Medical College] In 1847, the Harvard Medical School moved to North Grove Street in Boston, adjacent to the Bulfinch Building of the Massachusetts General Hospital.

624.22 she perished.] The steamship *Atlantic* foundered on the rocks off Fisher's Island in Block Island Sound on Thanksgiving Day 1846.

625.8 I wrote accordingly] As follows: "Mr. W. H. Emmons requests the acceptance by J. H. Meredith Esq. of two volumes of poems by the most pleasing English Poet of the present century — The Pleasures of Memory perhaps entitle him to a station among the druids of a former age, with the Bards of Avon and of Thames, and of Siloa's brook that flow'd Fast by the Oracle of God. John Quincy Adams."

626.17–20 Fair Lady . . . far between.] These lines to a female admirer are the last entry recorded in the diary. Adams suffered a cerebral hemorrhage the following day, dying two days later.

Index

Saint-Évremond, Charles de (French essayist), 306

St. Augustine, Fla., 7, 15

St. John, Gaius N. (Ohio politician), 572

St. Joseph River, 377

St. Louis, Mo., 66, 155

St. Petersburg, Russia, 165, 174, 181, 308, 340, 554

Salazar, José María (Colombian minister at Washington), 90

Salem, Mass., 310–11, 560

Sallust, 167

Saltonstall, Leverett (U.S. representative from Massachusetts), 479, 518

Sanchez, Bernabé (Cuban agent), 26, 28–30

Sandlake, N.Y., 407

Sanford, Nathan (U.S. senator from New York), 188

San Francisco, Alta California (Mexico), 556

Santa Anna, Antonio López de (Mexican president), 520, 576

Santa Fe, Mexico (now N.M.), 538–39

Sargent, Daniel (Boston merchant), 447

Sargent, Henry (American painter), 565

Sargent, Henry W. (horticulturalist), 565

Sargent, Mary Frazier (wife of Daniel Sargent/JQA's first love), 447

Sauks, 72

Saunders, Romulus M. (U.S. representative from North Carolina), 531, 584, 606

Saurin, Jacques: *Sermons*, 339

Savannah, Ga., 173, 176

Sawyer, William (U.S. representative from Ohio), 618

Schenectady, N.Y., 569

Schermerhorn, John F. (missionary), 435, 457

Schley, William (Georgia governor), 408–9

Scott, John (U.S. representative from Missouri), 88, 96

Scott, Thomas (biblical scholar), 101, 123

Scott, Walter, 202, 268, 297, 352, 625; *Waverley*, 215

Scott, Winfield, U.S. general, 18, 168, 191, 469, 521, 544, 586; presidential ambitions, 465, 556

Sealy, Mrs. (autograph seeker), 377

Sears, David (Massachusetts politician), 362–63

Seaton, William W. (newspaper publisher), 33, 256, 357, 401, 413, 442

Seaver, William (Quincy schoolmaster), 269

Secession, 444

Second Bank of the United States, 3, 10, 117, 164, 216, 229, 262, 274, 280, 298–99, 313, 322–24, 326–28, 331–33, 337, 393, 395, 406, 410, 444–45, 455

Sectionalism, 5, 8, 54, 56, 298

Sedgwick, Elizabeth Dwight (schoolmistress), 621

Seminoles, 70, 244, 253, 272, 291, 469–70, 496–97, 512, 536

Semple, James (U.S. senator from Illinois), 592

Semple, Matthew (abolitionist), 385–86

Senate, U.S. *See* Congress, U.S.

Senecas, 170, 192–93, 456–57, 493–94

Separation of powers, 352–56

Sergeant, John: U.S. representative from Pennsylvania, 19, 166, 484, 487–88, 491, 515; argues before U.S. Supreme Court, 259–60; and election of 1832, 301, 303; JQA visits in Philadelphia, 319

Sergeant, Margaretta Watmough (wife of John Sergeant), 484

Sergeant, Thomas (Pennsylvania jurist), 19

Sermons, 36, 85, 101, 112, 127, 132–33, 136, 152, 173, 181–82, 190, 202, 205–6, 208, 217, 225, 235–36, 261, 265, 289, 299, 326, 329, 339, 365, 373, 384, 399, 426, 432–35, 437, 468–69, 471–72, 476–78, 484–85, 502, 541, 563–64, 583, 591–92, 611–12

Sevier, Ambrose H. (U.S. senator from Arkansas), 592

Sewall, Samuel E. (Boston attorney), 542–43

Sewall, Thomas (Columbian College professor), 18, 215, 319

Seward, William H. (New York governor), 507, 567

This book is set in 10 point ITC Galliard, a face designed for digital composition by Matthew Carter and based on the sixteenth-century face Granjon. The paper is acid-free lightweight opaque that will not turn yellow or brittle with age. The binding is sewn, which allows the book to open easily and lie flat. The binding board is covered in Brillianta, a woven rayon cloth made by Van Heek–Scholco Textielfabrieken, Holland. Composition by Dedicated Book Services. Printing and binding by Edwards Brothers Malloy, Ann Arbor. Designed by Bruce Campbell.

THE LIBRARY OF AMERICA SERIES

The Library of America fosters appreciation of America's literary heritage by publishing, and keeping permanently in print, authoritative editions of America's best and most significant writing. An independent nonprofit organization, it was founded in 1979 with seed funding from the National Endowment for the Humanities and the Ford Foundation.

Monday 1. J

I.V. Monday | The new year began w
the course of the Seasons
bright Sun. a calm atmosphere, and all
Peace. The Presidents House was open as i
ternoon; and was crowded with visitors inr
found it necessary to assume a position in publi
forbids me from any public exhibition of par
feeling. Mr Clay whose public position, not pre
vant and escorted Mrs Ball of Tennessee, wife
also there. They afterwards came here, as di
of those who had been at the Presidents House.
visit spoken to Mr Van Buren; and the second
being surrounded by so many of his frien
the weather is very fine. No insignifican
the satirical reflection, implied in Clay's re

Donec eris felix, multos nun
Tempora si fuerint nubila, y
I snatched a quarter of an hour before noon
any visitors, just before reaching her hous
and Joseph L. Williams of Tennessee, and th
feeling of awkwardness at asking them th
visit Mrs Madison, I passed by there with a
have stayed and enquired if the were